ROMANTIC QUEST
AND MODERN QUERY

ROMANTIC QUEST
AND MODERN QUERY

Romantic Quest
and Modern Query

A HISTORY OF THE MODERN THEATRE

by TOM F. DRIVER

DELACORTE PRESS / NEW YORK

For K and S,
and P, who came
in the middle

CONTENTS

PREFACE

THIS BOOK is written from a certain perspective. It is intended as a history, but it is not encyclopedic, and in that respect as well as others it is not "objective" and had better not pretend to be.

We are now at a time when we can more or less readily perceive that the period of "modernity" is over. It will pass into history and be given, eventually, another name. This book may even help that to happen. I shall be sorry to see it go, but I have no wish to hold history back or to confine culture to a single variety of excellence.

The unsuspecting reader should not think, therefore, that in this book he will find a report on what is currently happening in the theater. If he wants to read about the contemporary theater rather than the modern, he must go elsewhere. However, if he wants a perspective on a century and a half of theatrical development antecedent to the contemporary, in the light of which our current stage will one day have to be judged, he might well follow me in the narrative I have to tell.

My choice of what to include, what to leave out, what to dwell on, and what to but mention in passing has been determined by the shape of my narrative and the motifs that are most germane to it. If the narrative proves, as I hope, to illuminate "the struggle of the modern" in the theater, and its meaning for modern culture, the selection will have been justified; but I certainly do not expect to escape the slings and arrows of those who will be outraged by my cursory treatment of certain figures I deem to be of minor importance in making modern theater what it has been or by my dwelling too long, as they will think, on figures whom I think best instruct us on the meaning of the modern theatrical adventure.

My historical thesis is that the modern theater can best be interpreted as a paradigm of the development of modern consciousness in Europe and America. It reflects political and social change only indirectly, but it clearly reveals, if we follow its purposes and its changes in style, the self-understanding of modern man, particularly the alienation he feels from nature, society, himself, and the past. I believe this thesis to be defensible, and I have tried to manage my exposition in such a way as to prevent its being taken in a simplistic manner; but the thesis has surely affected my choice of materials. Had it been otherwise, I should have had to compose an exhaustive (and exhausting) chronicle, which was not my intention.

When mentioning the titles of plays, I have thought it helpful to note in parentheses their dates of composition. To do this, however, is not always as simple as it sounds, sometimes because composition was spread over several years and sometimes because the sources of information are not consistent. The reader should therefore regard the dates given as generally, but not infallibly, reliable. Where the date of first performance is given instead of the date of composition, that fact is noted.

Assistance I have received while preparing this history has put me in debt to more persons than I can remember. I beg the indulgence of any who should be cited in the notes but have been overlooked. Particular thanks are due the Guggenheim Foundation, with whose help I began work on the manuscript. Also to Robert Corrigan, Richard Huett, Carolyn Heilbrun, Daniel Newman, and Anne, my wife, who gave me helpful criticism. I thank the officers of Union Theological Seminary for gifts both financial and spiritual.

TOM F. DRIVER

New York, 1968

INTRODUCTION

THE MODERN THEATER is distinguished from its antecedents by certain pervasive qualities and tendencies. Only by identifying these can one determine where, chronologically, the modern theater begins and what limitations of scope may be fairly established in order to give a succinct history of its development. This means that the author must say how he understands the term "modern" with reference to the theater. To do so is the purpose of this introduction.

There are, I believe, three principal characteristics of cultural thought that combine in the nineteenth and twentieth centuries to produce the "modern" mentality. They have, to be sure, many causes and corollaries, but short of attempting a complete cultural history one may see in these three characteristics the marks of the whole. The first may be called historicism; the second, a questing for reality, which turns after a time into a query about whether anything is real; and the third, a tendency to regard all experience ironically.

Men take it for granted today that in order to understand anything human (often to understand natural phenomena as well) they should search out its history—its genesis and the processes by which it has come to its present state. For modern man, historical investigation is not only *a* method, it is very nearly *the* method, an approach to reality that conditions all modern thought.

So pervasive has historicism become that we tend to forget it is itself a historical phenomenon. As a matter of fact, it revolutionized human thought only in the nineteenth century and then only in those places where European culture was dominant.

Although the theoretical foundations for a historicist view were laid as early as the first quarter of the eighteenth century in Italy, they did not produce any notable effect until the Romantic Movement appeared fifty years later in northern Europe. In his *Scienza Nuova*, published in 1725, Giambattista Vico (1688–1744), an elderly Neapolitan scholar of classical education, anticipated the principle of vitalism that biologists were soon afterwards to enunciate and that had far-reaching effect upon Shaftesbury, Rousseau, and other philosophers. The writing of history was, of course, ancient. There were also venerable "theories of history," explicit in Nicholas of Cusa and Augustine, implicit in Virgil, Thucydides, and the Deuteronomic writers of the Old Testament. All these, however, tended to see history as a realm of error into which man had "fallen." If the "salvation history" of the Bible, taken as a whole, implied something more positive, this was not made explicit before Cusanus and not broadly developed until after Vico.

It was Vico who conceived of the modern, as opposed to the classical, distinction between nature and history. The physical world—*il mondo della natura*—he said, has been created by God and can be properly understood only by Him. But *il mondo della nazioni* has been made by men, and they therefore enjoy knowledge of it. Though Vico called this the world of nations, its distinguishing characteristic is found in its being the product of human activity in history; it includes not only nations and their political fortunes but also the whole range of cultural productivity. This historical world, Vico maintained, is the one in which man is genuinely at home.

Vico's way of distinguishing between nature and history was radically different from that of his predecessors. In the first place, it exalted history by making it the bearer of human excellence and of knowledge. History was no longer mere deviation from static norms. In the second place, it dissolved the opposition between history and *human* nature. Nature was now equated with the physical world, and *human* nature moved over into the sphere of the historical. The concept of a static, ideal human nature was disavowed.

Upon the basis of this distinction, Vico came to a theory of historical cognition. Since man is native to history, he held, man is capable of re-evoking the past in the depth of his own consciousness. Given a certain amount of historical data to begin with, man is able, through his imagination, to overcome the gap that separates the past from the present.

Vico speculated upon the origins of civilization. Primitive men, in his view, had no faculties of reasoning, but they had exceptionally strong imaginations. They introduced magic religion, a "poetic" construct which became the basis of the family, of social institutions, and of agriculture. Only gradually did their poetic mentality give way to the more logical structures of reason.

Vico was not a romantic, but he invented concepts that German romanticists were to use, half a century later, as the basis of their revolt against the classicist tradition. These were the modern distinction between nature and history, the idea that the soul of the past can be re-evoked from the depths of consciousness, and the idea of the "folk genius." These concepts were indispensable to the romanticism that the *Sturm und Drang* writers of the 1770's began to spread over Europe.[1]

From the middle of the century, the ideas of Rousseau began to exert a strong influence. In 1749 Rousseau won a prize from the Academy of Dijon with an essay maintaining that the progress of the sciences and arts had contributed to the corruption, rather than the improvement, of mankind. This thesis, which Rousseau maintained and elaborated throughout his life, idealized the primitive past and lifted the life of feeling and intuition above that of the calculating reason. It contributed to the admiration for the "folk genius" that was so much a part of budding romanticism and provided ammunition for an attack upon rationalism. Scandalous to the authorities, liberating to many others, Rousseau's ideas did more than those of any previous philosopher to popularize the concept of the present as an outgrowth of the past, an idea later put to far different use by Hegel. Nostalgic as he was for the simple

1 A good discussion of this development is to be found in Erich Auerbach, *Figura: Scenes from the Drama of European Literature* (New York: Meridian, 1959).

life, Rousseau gave people to understand that they could exercise control over their destinies by comparing their present stage of civilization with those more simple and "natural" origins from which it had sprung. This teaching may be recognized as a secular version of the myth of the Fall, but it differed radically from the myth in emphasizing the historical continuity between the original paradise and the corrupt world that succeeded it. If history had brought about this result, Rousseau preached, it might also, through education of the young, bring about a return to the former, superior state. History, for better or worse, belongs to man and he to it.

Without Rousseau's *historical* critique of the effects of reason, it is doubtful that Immanuel Kant would have embarked upon his *logical* critique. Kant's *Critique of Pure Reason* (1781) provided an intellectual fermentation, almost infinitely variable, that has influenced modern thought in almost all respects. It has been particularly important in relation to the modern quest for reality and its gradual change into a query about whether any reality may be discovered, for Kant was the first modern thinker radically to challenge the assumption that human reason is grounded in reality. Adopting a deep epistemological skepticism, he drew a line between the phenomenal and the noumenal worlds, the world as it seems according to our perceptions and the world as it is "in itself." The former is only apparently real, and the latter cannot be known. Kant held that what we commonly take to be real is a system of appearances constructed by the forms of human imagination and the categories of the human mind. The mind acts on data filtered and channeled by the sensory organs. Man is thus, as it were, imprisoned by his own consciousness, by the very means at his disposal for making contact with reality.

In *The Critique of Judgment* (1790), Kant attempted in part to recover what he had previously given away. The agent of recovery he found in aesthetics—the experience of the sublime. Thus, the aesthetic intuition was made to compensate for the severe limitations of reason, and art became indispensable in the quest for reality.

It is the memory of romanticism that leads me to speak of a "quest" for reality. The legacy of romanticism that has been de-

cisive for the modern arts, certainly for theater, has been its rejection of the classicist spirit of coming to terms *with* reality and its
inclination toward a search *for* reality.

In all forms of romance, man goes upon a quest. He may seek
the Holy Grail, the Beautiful Woman, the Promised Land, his
soul's salvation, the ideal society, the true morality, or an unknown
goal. He may grope for the path of search. No matter; he is on a
quest. His task is not to strike a bargain or come to terms but to
find what is missing, if need be to create it. He does not imagine
that the reality he seeks is in the nature of a fixed order, an un-
changing truth somewhere awaiting him, but rather imagines
that it is a mystery, something unsearchable that must nevertheless
be searched. The hunt is therefore as important as the quarry,
perhaps more so. And the romanticist lives utterly in history—
that is, in his experience of change, his exposure to the passage
of all things through time.

To a spirit more inclined toward classicism, by contrast, reality
is *given,* one way or another. It is *there,* even if temporarily obscured, and wants recognition and a willingness to make whatever
adjustment is required. The real may be manifest to Reason. It
may have been disclosed by Revelation. It may be embodied in
custom and tradition. It may be inscribed in Law. Or there may be
a combination of these. At any rate, the primary human problem
is not to find reality but to come to terms with it. Drama is then
built upon the belief that man's *hubris,* sin, freedom, or blindness
gets in the way of his coming to terms with what *is.* Classical
tragedy shows the settlement that reality forces upon man, to his
destruction. Classical comedy shows the bargain man is finally
able to make with reality by the exercise of his wit or by his falling
providentially into line with the powers that be. Both these forms
have become suspect, if not impossible, for the modern theater.
They have been replaced, in the main, by a kind of tragicomedy
to be identified later, notably in the chapter on Chekhov.

The Romantic Movement of the late eighteenth and early nineteenth centuries was an early and conspicuous example of the
modern quest for reality and for meaning, but that quest has out-
lived the Romantic Movement, continuing to the present day. It
has been stimulated ever and again by the necessity modern man

feels to assert the validity of his interior life over against the stand-
ardizing and mechanizing effects of the industrial, and later the
technological, revolution. It has been fed also by warfare between
the natural sciences and the humanities and by modern political
revolutions waged in the name of freedom.

This modern quest, however, has carried within itself from the
start a tendency to be transformed into a query, to change from a
quest into a question. Putting a high value on subjectivity, it has
exhibited a reflexive tendency, turning toward itself in acute examination to ask whether even the quest has meaning and whether
all search for meaning is not futile. This leads to an intense self-
consciousness of modern thought, perhaps nowhere better expressed than in the late modern theater with its highly self-conscious techniques of theatricalism. Underlying this development
is a characteristically modern penchant for irony, particularly of
the type that Friedrich von Schlegel called romantic.

If we hold the modern historical consciousness in company with
the skepticism about knowledge such as Kant introduced in the
First Critique, we are in a position to appreciate the ground upon
which Schlegel stood when he developed the concept of "romantic
irony" in the period before his conversion to Roman Catholicism
(1808). Truth, he observed, changes as the subject moves from one
experience to another. The classical reaction to this had been to
assume that experience introduces error and must, by one means
or another, be discounted. Schlegel, imbued with the historical
consciousness of his German contemporaries, was of no mind to
repudiate experience in that manner. On the contrary, if there is
a contradiction between truth (supposedly immutable) and experience (which changes), then it is truth that will have to suffer.
Wisdom will depend on recognizing that truth is fickle.

The notion of truth as fickle is ironic; to prize experience for its
own sake is romantic; and the two combine as romantic irony. It
is not too much to say that the experience of truth as fickle or
"lying" became not only a motif but almost an obsession with
dramatists ranging from Kleist and Büchner through Ibsen, Shaw,
and Pirandello to Brecht, Beckett, and Ionesco.

Irony of some sort has been the stock in trade of dramatists in
all periods of history, if for no other reason than that the theater

employs masks. Theater is a place of contrived appearances, costumes, assumed identities. It is natural to capitalize on this fact by the use of plots and themes that depend on unmasking and the discovery of true identities. The irony of maskings could be said to be the perennial motif of drama.

In classical drama, irony is the result of information withheld. Perhaps the speaker disguises his true intent, offering an understatement or a wry comment that masks what he really means; such a figure the Greeks called an *eiron*. Perhaps the playwright withholds information from his characters that he gives to the audience. Oedipus does not know what the gods know, Teiresias knows, and we know—that Oedipus is the guilty man for whom Oedipus is looking. In time he will find out, and the irony will come home. A crass version of the same type of irony is often used in bedroom farces, when the husband does not know what the wife knows and we know—that the lover is hiding under the bed. The irony depends upon information that is lacking—that is, withheld from some but given to others.

Romantic irony, by contrast, depends upon there being too much information. That is, there is more information, knowledge, or insight than can be included in a single frame of reference. This, in turn, is the result of there being incompatible frames of reference to start with. Even the individual has more of these than he can harmonize. In this sense, he is not "one" but "many": he experiences self-alienation. Romantic irony stems from and expresses modern pluralism and self-alienation. Such modern irony has less to do with the contrast between the part and the whole than with the fact that the whole is unknowable while the parts overlap and contradict each other. It springs from an awareness that experience is too rich to be assimilated to a single point of view or even to any finite series of points of view taken together. Truth is always "beyond." Socratic irony is closer to this romantic, modern type than to the classical. That is why Kierkegaard was so enamored of it and used it even more intensively than Socrates himself.

The ironic element has, in the course of the development of modern drama, increased steadily, giving rise to new dramatic forms and creating new styles. In late modern drama, irony is so pervasive and so reflexive that it may be questioned whether the modern quest-turned-query has not reached a limit beyond which it cannot go.

I have characterized the modern spirit, then, as a combination of historicism, the quest for reality turning into query, and the pervasive use of romantic irony. These came together at the beginning of the nineteenth century, which indicates the time when the story of the modern theater's development may begin. It may also indicate the time when it should conclude, for there are signs that in the 1960's historicism began to lose its hold upon our contemporaries. If so, the story I here relate will give place to another that cannot yet be written.

1. THE ROMANTIC QUEST
AND THE MODERN QUERY:
GOETHE AND KLEIST

IN 1811 A YOUNG PRUSSIAN named Bernd Wilhelm Heinrich von Kleist, then in the thirty-fourth (and last) year of his life, wrote a play called *The Prince of Homburg*. Less famous than Kleist's comedy *Der zerbrochene Krug* (begun 1804; *The Broken Jug*), it is generally considered the most successful of the half-dozen plays he wrote during the ten years of his writing career. Kleist is best known as the author of *Die Marquise von O* (*The Marquise of O*), a short story that gives its title to a collection first published in English in 1933 and recently republished. He belonged to the generation that came to itself by coming through the French Revolution, entering fully into that spirit which we may call modern.

A decade before *The Prince of Homburg* was written, Johann Wolfgang Goethe finished Part I of *Faust*. Kleist's work was written between that date and the time that Goethe outlined Part II of his masterpiece. The two writers' careers touched at two points. At Weimar, Goethe produced *The Broken Jug* on the stage, a task he handled poorly because he cut that one-act play into several parts, spoiling its unity. At another time Kleist wrote to Goethe seeking support for a periodical called *Phöbus* that he had founded with Adam Müller. Goethe declined to help. He apparently had no understanding of the work of Kleist, whom he dismissed as a "hypochondriac," a true but insufficient judgment of the man.

For this Goethe is not to be severely blamed. Somewhat out of its time, certainly out of what then seemed the main current of literature, Kleist's work bore the marks of a modernity more obvious today than at the beginning of the nineteenth century. Both writers were German and both romanticists, yet they were separated by a spiritual gap. It is profitable to compare and contrast Goethe's *Faust*, Part I, the supreme achievement of premodern romanticism, with Kleist's *The Prince of Homburg*, since the change of taste and sensibility that began to appear early in the nineteenth century is fundamental to the subsequent history of drama.

We are concerned with a mutation in romanticism, the movement which had begun in Germany some forty years before *The Prince of Homburg* and which was changed by the French Revolution into something that was to prove eminently adaptable to the variety and pluralism of modern experience.

To think romantically is to think in terms of chiaroscuro: to see shadow as absence of light, to see light as the banishment or conquering of shadow, and never to see the one without thinking of the other. One way to characterize those forms of romanticism that now seem fairly remote from us in relation to those that partake of a more modern spirit is to speak of the way in which they combine the light and the dark. In the older romanticism the tones are less sharply contrasted than in the more modern. Both types are dependent on what Friedrich von Schlegel called "romantic irony," but the more modern intensifies the irony and tends to make it not merely a tonal quality of the work but its very substance. To emphasize contrast for its own sake, to push it to an extreme without breaking the unity of the over-all design, is to bring irony from a subordinate to a dominant position.

The opening scene of *Faust* discovers its protagonist among dusty, smoke-darkened books. It is night. Faust, who has long searched these books for enlightenment but has found only ignorance, is living in nocturnal despair.

> What though imagination spread her wings
> In early hope towards the things eternal,

Shrunk is her spacious realm in the diurnal
Defeat that loss and disappointment brings.[1]

As the night wears on, Faust takes from the shelf a phial containing a black-magic liquid, a "distillation of the deadly powers," that will enable him further to penetrate the darkness in search of an eventual light. He will not

blanch before the cavern black and fell . . .
But dare the narrow flaming pass of hell.

In the very moment when he raises to his lips the "chalice with dark opiate to dispense," dawn starts to break. We hear the sound of "bells and solemn choir" beginning the Easter hymn of this "morrow's awful imminence." Faust recognizes this music as "the angelic breaking of the darkened tomb." While he muses and the Resurrection hymn ascends, day gradually conquers night.

One might follow the imagery of light and dark through almost every page of *Faust*. The hymn of the three archangels in the "Prologue in Heaven" is a song of the "primal light" that alternates in the daily cycle with the "fearfulness of night profound." And in the last scene of Part I we hear Margareta answer Faust's "Now breaks the day" with her own "Day, yes, the day; the last dread day breaks in."

Darkness in *Faust* is felt as a deprivation of light, and the motivation of Faust is to overcome that deprivation, either by escaping upward into celestial light or by plunging downward so deep that he will reach the point where darkness is exhausted. The latter is the course he actually takes, and it sets him upon a quest. His very name has come to suggest to us a search for unattainable knowledge and power. He is driven by thirst for that which exceeds finite, human capacity:

I come at last to recognize my measure,
And know the sterile desert in my breast,
I have not raised myself one poor degree,
Nor stand I nearer to infinity.

(p. 91)

1 Translated by Philip Wayne (Baltimore: Penguin, 1949), p. 52. All quotations from *Faust* in this chapter are from this edition.

To get "nearer to infinity" he makes the bargain with Mephistopheles that is the mainspring of the plot. We should notice the romantic character of this bargain. It is manifest not only in Faust's motivation—the desire for infinity—but even more in the fact that it is a bargain made with a power that has but a quasi reality—with Satan, about whom there is always something unreal. He is defined by what he is *against,* not by what he stands *for.* Jesus called him the Father of Lies. Goethe portrays Mephisto as a demon of negative wit, scoffing at everything and in favor of nothing. He is the advocate of Nothingness, and such Being as he has is borrowed Being— illusion. In the conclusion of Part II we learn that it is actually impossible to make a bargain with Satan because he is ultimately without the power to keep his end of it. No bargain with him can be a bargain with reality, only one with unreality.

Faust himself, at the beginning, does not take the bargain seriously. The only thing he takes seriously is his own quest. The conditions Mephisto lays down are of little interest to him. When Mephisto says that he will serve Faust in this world if Faust will serve him on "the other side," Faust's reply is cavalier:

> The other side weighs little on my mind . . .
> From springs of earth my joys and pleasures start . . .
> The rest concerns me not.
>
> (p. 86)

So little does he think of the reality of what he is doing that Mephisto's insistence on a contract signed in blood seems to him petty and rather quaint. He acquiesces because it does not matter.

There is irony in this transaction. Faust thinks the bargain and its solemn contract a joke. It is Mephisto, the scoffer, who insists upon the seriousness of it. *We* know that later the tables will be turned: Faust will see the immensity of what he has done, and Mephisto will laugh. But there is a further irony: *Goethe* knows that in the final reckoning, ordained in Heaven, Faust will be proved right: the pact was *not* a pact with anything real, and it is therefore not ultimately binding. In the beginning Faust could not know this. He was right, but only wrongly right.

Although this irony is important for our appreciation of the dramatic poem, its stylistic treatment at Goethe's hands is mild. If one compares his *Faust* with Marlowe's, two centuries earlier, or with Dorothy Sayers' (*The Devil to Pay*), a century and a half later, he discovers that, however different in intention and merit, both works bring out the ironic potential of the material far more strongly than Goethe's. If it be thought that this is because Marlowe and Miss Sayers wrote the story in dramatic form whereas Goethe composed a quasi-dramatic poem, then one may mention Thomas Mann's *Dr. Faustus,* which, although it is a long, slowly developed novel, has a far sharper sense of irony than Goethe's poem. The difference is due not to the form but to the spirit.

In this connection, note also Goethe's handling of the "play within the play." His work opens, after the "Dedication," with a "Prelude in the Theatre." Here the director, the dramatist, and the actor speak about the play—its intention, its effect on the audience, and the manner of playing. This makes the rest of the work a "play within the play." The ironic potential of such a device is, however, not pursued in the balance of the text, which is written without further reference to the Prelude. Play acting, in short, is not a theme in *Faust.* Unlike Goethe, no modern author would have let such an opportunity pass. The Prelude shows that Goethe was aware of the opportunity, was aware, as one editor puts it, of "the threefold and often conflicting functions of good theater." [2] Yet the bulk of the text shows that Goethe did not wish to let this awareness determine his style.

The bargain Faust makes with something unreal is intended to achieve something unreal—infinity. Infinity is, by definition, outside what man can know and appropriate as real for him. This fact is the basis of such a modern play as Camus' *Caligula,* where it shows a certain antiromantic disposition in the author. It is also a theme in Ibsen's *The Master Builder* and in *Brand,* though Ibsen's attitude toward it is ambiguous. The longing for infinity is a longing to escape human reality rather than to accept it.

The motif of the quest in *Faust* is coupled with another characteristic of romanticism—namely, a sense of loss. We have already noted one of the earliest passages in which Faust speaks of it:

[2] Bayard Quincy Morgan, in the notes to his translation of *Faust* (New York: Liberal Arts Press, 1954), p. 117.

What though imagination spread her wings
In *early* hope toward the things eternal,
Shrunk is her spacious realm in the diurnal
Defeat that *loss* and *disappointment* brings.
(Emphasis added.)

The more Faust thinks about "things eternal" and about "early hope," the more he feels a W*eltschmerz* characterized by loss. When the angels sing of Easter morn, he recalls that

Time was . . . dear heaven's kiss
Would light upon me . . .
Then had the bells a sound of boding fulness . . .
(p. 56. Emphasis added.)

He remembers the departed "song of innocence, the joy of spring," and though he says he is again "earth's child," he does not mean it.

Faust is a story of what its protagonist loses and what he causes others to lose. Margareta sings at her spinning wheel:

My peace is gone,
My heart is sore,
It is gone forever
And evermore.
(pp. 150–151)

This when she had lost her heart to Faust. Later she will lose her virginity to him, then lose innocence of heart, become a murderess, and in the last scene of Part I feel herself lost body and soul. Her loss is Faust's perdition.

All romanticism indulges in nostalgia, whether it takes the sublime form of the Wordsworthian child "trailing clouds of glory" or the more acid form to be found in Bertolt Brecht's *Mahagonny*. Exile, estrangement, loss—terms that revolve around the myth of the Fall—are its perennial themes.

Kleist's *Prince of Homburg* is as romantic a work as *Faust,* and the reader who turns from the one to the other may not at first see how far he has turned. He reads a story of a gallant, hot-blooded soldier in love with a noble lady, to win whose hand he performs an act of daring on the field of battle and brings home trophies.

Instead of obtaining the lady, however, the hero is thrown into prison and sentenced to die for having disobeyed on the battlefield the orders of his commander. After many vicissitudes, he is reprieved and rewarded. Is this not simply a tale of gallantry in which the ideals of love and honor are finally vindicated?

On one level it is. Yet this work possesses another level, and there its modernity lies. The play has the form of a dream in which love and honor always triumph—that is, beyond romantic loss, the dream that compensates for the loss. And there is a dream within the dream.

In the opening scene the prince of Homburg is found lying on a garden seat at the castle of Fehrbellin. He is "half-waking, half sleeping . . . plaiting himself a wreath." [3] Count Hohenzollern, who watches, observes that the prince is "as dreamy / As a sleepwalker." Hohenzollern arranges a little pageant in which the elector of Brandenburg and his niece, the Princess Natalia, take part. The prince, in his sleepwalking state, participates in the charade. From the startled but not awakened prince, the elector takes the plaited wreath, winds his royal golden chain about it, and hands it to Natalia.

(*The* PRINCE, *with outstretched arms, follows after her.*)
PRINCE (*whispering*): Natalia! My love! My bride!
ELECTOR: Quickly, now! Away!
HOHENZOLLERN: What does the fool say?
COURTIER: What was that he whispered to her?
(*They all begin ascending the slope.*)
PRINCE: Frederick! My lord! My father!
HOHENZOLLERN: What devil's got into him?
ELECTOR (*still moving backwards*): Open the door for me!
PRINCE: Oh, my mother!
HOHENZOLLERN: Why, he's mad! Mad!
ELECTOR'S WIFE: Whom does he call mother?
PRINCE (*snatching at the wreath*): Oh, my dearest one! Why do you turn away from me? Natalia!
(*He seizes the Princess' glove.*)
HOHENZOLLERN: What was that?
COURTIER: The wreath?

[3] Quotations are from the translation by James Kirkup, in Eric Bentley, ed., *The Classic Theatre*, Vol. II (Garden City, N.Y.: Anchor Books, Doubleday, 1959).

NATALIA: No.

HOHENZOLLERN (*opening the door*): Quick, come in, sire! Let the whole
scene suddenly vanish from his sight!

ELECTOR: Back! Back into the darkness, Frederick, Prince of Homburg!
> Back into the dark and nothingness!
> If you will grace us with your presence,
> We shall meet again upon the field of battle.
> Victory cannot be won by dreams!

(*They all suddenly go inside. The door shuts with a great rattle of
chains. A silence.*) [4]

Hohenzollern then wakes the prince by sharply calling his name.
The prince falls as if shot by a bullet. He awakes in much
confusion, saying he hardly knows where he is, and begins to re-
count the "dream" that we have just seen with our own waking
eyes.

In the next scene, battle plans are drawn and orders given. Two
groups of people are on stage: the officers at their briefing on one
side, the ladies, including the princess, on the other. The prince is
in between. Battle plans are no reality for him, only the princess
and the question whether it is her glove he holds. He lets it fall to
the floor, and when it is returned to her their eyes meet. Two sentences about the glove pass between them, and she withdraws. The
prince, who has paid scant attention to his orders, wins the battle
next day heroically; but he attacks before he is supposed to, obey-
ing only the impulse of his heart. Expecting to be rewarded
for his victory, he is arrested and sentenced to die. Eventually,
however, he is reprieved.

In the final scene, in which the reprieve is announced, the dream
sequence is played out once more. Again the wreath bound with
the golden chain is given to Natalia as the astonished prince looks
on. This time, however, she brings it forward and puts it on his
head. Once more he falls unconscious. On awaking, he asks: "Tell
me, is this a dream?" To which the reply comes: "A dream: what
else?" And once again the men go off to battle.

The use of dreams is a standard literary device for raising questions about the reality of appearances. In *The Prince of Homburg*
Kleist has put a question mark over the whole romantic quest for

[4] Pp. 426–427. Quoted by permission.

love and honor. His query becomes more insistent the more we examine the play.

First, the characterization of the prince is highly ambiguous. The armies love him and are prepared to release him from prison by force if necessary. He has a heroic courage. Nobly ready to sacrifice himself to the "rules of war," he refuses to cringe at his sentence. Natalia loves him. In spite of all this, he does not impress us as a hero, for there is something quixotic about him. Looked at in one way, he is brave. Looked at in another, he is all panache. Early in Act II, when the battle is shaping up, Kleist inserts a bit of dialogue in which there is an oblique but clear reference to Don Quixote:

AN OFFICER: Is it true that he fell from his horse during the hours of darkness?
HOHENZOLLERN: I believe so, yes.
KOTTWITZ: He had a fall?
HOHENZOLLERN: Nothing serious! His horse shied at a windmill.

(pp. 442–443)

Second, and more important, the play has the form of tragicomedy. Its conflict is ostensibly the same as that in a tragedy of Corneille—love versus duty, or the promptings of the heart versus the requirements of one's office. Much of the dialogue is given to discussion of this problem. Yet whereas Corneille saw tragedy in such a conflict, Kleist sees tragicomedy. He is not sure that two irreconcilable claims (as in tragedy) are being made upon his hero, for he is not sure of the validity of either one. If the handling of the dream motif makes light of love and honor, the prince himself suggests that the elector's insistence upon obedience is a bit of play acting:

It seems my cousin Friedrich will play the part of Brutus . . .
And when he comes to me and tries to ape
Some antique Roman with a language
Dead as the ancient history in which his obstinacy lies embalmed,
I feel for him only pity and dismay!

(p. 461)

We are to remember this speech later, in Act V, when the elector calls for his uniform and wig and ceremoniously dons his regalia to meet the officers who have come to plead for the prince's life. Natalia urges the prince to save his own life by complying with the outward form of the ultimatum the elector has sent. At the end we are left to wonder if the whole plot has not hinged upon foolish insistence on outward form.

A distinguishing mark of tragicomedy is its concentration on form. The play becomes formal, and the form becomes playful. The principal sign of this playfulness is tragicomedy's improbable "reversals of the situation," of which *The Prince of Homburg* is full. The hero who is to be crowned with honor is heaped with shame; the prisoner led to the block is given his life and his lady's hand; the head of state who fell in battle turns up alive and free. So it goes. The writing delights in abrupt juxtapositions. For instance, Act I, Scene VIII, ends with the prince's exultant words:

> O great Caesar! Now I climb the ladder
> That will lead me to your star!

This is followed by the opening words of the following scene:

> Whoever it was that led the cavalry charges . . .
> Without awaiting my express command . . .
> He, I proclaim, is to be put to death!

(p. 457)

Furthermore, the entire central portion of the play, from the prince's arrest until his final deliverance, is made up of a dialectical argument about the justice of his sentence. Yes, the sentence was unjust, but mercy will set things right. The elector, in a nicely ironic move, agrees to pardon the prince if he will but write to him that an injustice was done. This turns the tables, for now the prince, instead of asking for his life, resolves to die in order to "glorify the sacred laws of war": this in turn forces upon the elector the question of mercy. In the last act Hohenzollern tries to convince the elector that he, the elector, was really the guilty one, since in the charade he deceived the prince and led him into confusion: "The whole thing was just a game; but to him / I later learnt, it meant much more." This argument is easily turned back on Hohenzollern himself, who discovered the dreaming prince and led the elector to him.

We are in a world of swift reversals, oversubtle reasonings, dreams, and happy endings. In short, we are in that kind of romance that is characterized by the miraculous and the extraordinary. "Indeed," says the elector in the first scene, "I thought we were living in a fairy-tale!" In prison the prince expects the elector to step down "like a god from the machine" and reprieve him at the last moment. After many a turn, that is what happens. The world of miraculous romance and the world of tragicomedy are very close together.

"The whole thing was just a game," but to the prince "it meant much more." The whole play is just a game, but it means much more. Beneath tragicomic form there is usually to be discerned a skepticism and a dissent. So it is in Euripides, in the Jacobeans (including the problem comedies of Shakespeare), and today in Ionesco and other "absurdists."

Beneath the mild exterior of *The Prince of Homburg* one may detect a query about reality that becomes ever stronger and more sweeping in the theater of modern times. Natalia, caught between her uncle, the sovereign, and the prince, her suitor, voices the protest most directly:

> The rules of war and of a soldier's life
> Must be obeyed, I know. How much more
> The rules of real, human love must be obeyed!
> The heart has its rules and reasons too.
>
> (p. 476)

Perhaps she does not know how revolutionary this doctrine is. She has never heard of Kierkegaard, perhaps not heard of Pascal, but she voices a sentiment that anticipates existentialism. Enough of this and all authority will tremble.

A few lines later Natalia describes how the prince longs to live. He has confessed to her in one of his many different moods that his one desire is to survive and that honor and dishonor are both alike to him. She calls this "A lamentable, a pitiable sight" and concludes, "Oh, how meaningless is human grandeur!" The play recovers from this cry of desperation and finishes on two feet, but we have heard the cry, and it rings in our ears at the last when we hear the army march away shouting, "Death to all the enemies of Brandenburg!"

Kleist has looked at love, courage, and discipline and has raised a query about their validity. His is a romantic play conceived throughout in irony; the modern spirit breathes softly but unmistakably through it.

2. ROMANTICISM OF
THE DREAM

WHEN AUGUST WILHELM VON SCHLEGEL (1767–1845) delivered in Vienna in 1808 the speeches later published as *Lectures on Dramatic Art and Literature,* he revealed himself to be one of the first critics to recognize the importance of social evolution for the understanding of art. Historical consciousness led him to perceive that the drama of the Greeks was different in kind from that of Shakespeare—different because each was the product of a historical culture having its own standards and sensibilities. Schlegel made historical relativity an ingredient of critical appreciation. Then, enunciating a criterion born of his own age and entirely characteristic of romanticism, he said that dramatic form is bad when it is "mechanical," good when it is "organic." "Organic," already a popular word, was destined to become a favorite of romantic theorists not only in literature but also in sociology, history, and other fields.

With respect to drama, the contrast between mechanical and organic meant two things. First, it meant that the structuring of dramatic action according to patterns of logical progression should give place to structures born of experience. Life, not logic, should govern the form. To give plays an organic form was to be faithful to the vagaries of experience. Second, and more specifically, the emphasis on organic form was a protest against the received tradition of dramatic theory and practice, and this was given force by a generalized protest against the cultural tradition as a whole.

German romanticism was, in no little part, a protest movement directed against the dominance of French neoclassicism. Schlegel's lectures on dramatic art and literature were delivered in Vienna because he happened to go there in the company of Mme. de Staël, then in exile, who was to carry German romanticism into France as soon as Napoleon's defeat permitted her to do so. The French had, since the Renaissance, made themselves custodians of the "classical rules" of dramaturgy. These were in fact mostly created by the Italian Renaissance but were thought to have the weight of antiquity behind them. What romanticism objected to was the static quality of "rules." If the way of writing drama must conform to changeless principles, historical experience is denied. Therefore, the classical tradition had to be challenged in the name of reality. This need was felt by men of letters to be as real as the political needs that led to the French Revolution. The results were, in their own way, as ambiguous. Yet it is possible to see the most important threads of the tangled skein.

At the turn of the century in 1800, three major forces were at work to produce three different kinds of dramatic writing. One was a reaction, swift but by no means total, against romanticism itself. It tended, especially in France, toward a reaffirmation of the classical rules, once more employed, as always, for the disclosure of moral truth. This reaction delayed the Romantic Movement's full-blown appearance in France. The other two forces were imbued with a lively historical consciousness, and their differences stemmed from an ambiguity in the term "history."

Historical consciousness regards experience in a positive light as the bearer of meaning. On the face of it, however, "history"usually suggests the past. It will do this the more wherever there is a strong sense of being separated from reality and wholeness. Then the concern for history will show itself as an interest in the long ago and far away, when, it is supposed, there were certain experiences of greatness, valor, and nobility that have been lost. The quest will be to recover a lost past. This attempt is likely to have particular appeal to the dramatist, because the stage seems to have the ability to bring the past bodily into the present by reenactment. So seductive is this possibility that it has probably brought more bad writers into the theater than any other single inducement. It has also ruined many a good talent.

To a more sophisticated mind, however, the term "history" does not necessarily imply what is past. History is continuous, and once the importance of it as existence and experience has been grasped, it can be recognized that the here and now is as "historical" as anything that occurred in the past.

Romanticism concerned with history as the lost past I call "romanticism of the dream," or "dream-romanticism." Choosing that name, I have in mind the same considerations as Stephen Spender when he speaks of a romantic penchant for "exploiting the historic past as contemporary dream, fortress and granary of stored impressions, which are accessible to a modern, just as he uses childhood for the same purpose." [1] Romanticism that is primarily concerned with the quality of present experience I call "romanticism of the here and now."

The distinction between these types is not absolute, inasmuch as a given writer may move from one to the other. But the distinction is useful because, in drama at least, romanticism of the dream has not usually survived the torments of modern experience. Most of its efforts have miscarried; and though it has not been extinguished and probably never will be, the plays written from within it almost invariably become passé a short time after their initial vogue. One of the reasons for this is that their authors are often tempted by the grandiose.

Romanticism of the here and now, by contrast, faces the challenge of imitating and interpreting present experience, and this has the result of building into it an almost inexhaustible potentiality for growth. It would be too simple to bring all these potentialities under the word "realism," which, as a style, is but a potentiality and not the *raison d'être* of this type of romanticism; yet realism was like a challenge to which romanticism of the here and now rose and which the other type, for the most part, avoided.

The rest of this chapter is devoted to romanticism of the dream, and the next to romanticism of the here and now.

[1] *The Struggle of the Modern* (Berkeley: University of California Press, 1963), p. 162.

The English Romantic poets of the first part of the nineteenth century are important in the history of drama only insofar as they show that romanticism of the dream can seduce even the best of talents. Wordsworth and Coleridge, who were fully mindful of the need for poetry to concern itself with present experience, set out to do the same in drama yet produced no such result. Wordsworth's *The Borderers* (1795–6), having no feeling of immediacy, is like a sluggish dream. Reading Coleridge's *The Fall of Robespierre* (1794), on which Robert Southey collaborated, one finds it almost impossible to believe that it was written about contemporary events. It makes of something that actually took place in the year of its composition a story as remote as that of the fall of Rome. The same turgid effect is engendered by *Remorse,* Coleridge's antiwar play of 1813. Lord Byron, who is perhaps the epitome of dream-romanticism, with its adulation of the heroic quester, did not put much reality into his *Manfred* of 1817, which leaves in its wake the impression of a literate escapism. Byron's *Marino Faliero* (1820) and *Sardanapalus* (1821) are best forgotten, as is the *Otho the Great* that Keats turned out in 1819.

Shelley's *Cenci* (1818) is of a different order of merit. Although it is anachronistically baroque, it is obviously the work of a genius. Shelley's flamboyant protest against the orthodoxies of his own age gave him a certain affinity with the Jacobean playwrights, visible in the subject matter of the *Cenci,* which deals with incest and revenge in Renaissance Italy. Shelley moved deliberately, like many Jacobean playwrights, to the frontier of what is tolerable and comprehensible in human experience, creating a play of cruelty and outrage. In 1935, therefore, when Antonin Artaud sought to launch in Paris a showcase for what he called the "Theater of Cruelty," he adapted Shelley's *Cenci* for the purpose, making it "one of the most astonishing spectacles ever mounted in France." [2] Other plays Artaud wished to perform in his "Theater of Cruelty" (he never got them on) were Tourneur's *Revenger's Tragedy,* Webster's *Duchess of Malfi* and *The White Devil* (all Jacobean), and Büchner's *Woyzeck* (1837). From Artaud there is a direct line

2 Sylvain Dhomme, *Le Mise en scène d'Antoine à Brecht* (Paris: Fernand Nathan, 1959), p. 273.

to Jean Genet, as from Genet back to the Jacobeans, and it was a sure instinct of Artaud that led him to lift the *Cenci* out of semi-obscurity, for it was a work born out of its time.

The English Romantic poets had an insufficient knowledge of the stage and its audience. They were also, unhappily, under the shadow of Shakespeare. It was a century before G. B. Shaw and T. S. Eliot stood up to say that, for the English dramatist, Shakespeare's influence was deadly and would have to be got out of the way.

In France romanticism of the dream fared somewhat better. The English Channel changed the meaning of Shakespeare's influence. On the British side he was a liability, a *non plus ultra* to block the path of the poetic dramatist. On the Continental side he brought liberty. A. W. von Schlegel's translation of Shakespeare, which began to appear in 1797, was probably the single most liberating work of the German romantic movement.[3] To this day, it is said, Germans have to remind themselves that Shakespeare is not one of the heroes of German letters.

In France, Shakespeare helped upset the formulas of classicism. His emissaries were Stendhal and Victor Hugo. In 1824 Stendhal wrote his essay *Racine et Shakespeare* in which he praised the freedom and naturalness of the Elizabethan above the classical formalism of France's greatest dramatist. Victor Hugo (1802–1885) wrote *Cromwell* in the same year that Stendhal wrote his famous essay, but he did not get it on the stage (it wasn't very good), and in truth he had not known very well what he was doing when he wrote it. In any case, he knew it was not a regular sort of tragedy. Then in 1827 he attended performances of Shakespeare brought to the Odéon from Covent Garden with a company headed by Charles Kemble and Miss Smithson. Hugo was not the only young man of Paris who attended those performances with astonished enthusiasm. The whole younger set was enthralled, among them Théophile Gautier, Hector Berlioz, and Alexandre Dumas, *père*. Berlioz was so moved that he married Miss Smithson.

The immediate result in Hugo's case was not a marriage but an essay, in which he made a proposal to *la littérature française:* She

---

[3] In the 1760's C. M. Wieland had already translated Shakespeare into German. His version was eclipsed by that of Schlegel.

should abandon classicism and elope to a new freedom with him and the writers of the future. He wrote:

> Behold, then, a new religion, a new society: upon this twofold foundation there must inevitably spring up a new poetry. Previously, . . . following therein the course pursued by ancient polytheism and philosophy, the purely epic muse of the ancients had studied nature in only a single aspect. . . . Christianity leads poetry to the truth. Like it, the modern muse will see things in a higher and broader light. It will realize that everything in creation is not humanely *beautiful,* that the ugly exists beside the beautiful, the unshapely beside the graceful, the grotesque on the reverse of the sublime, evil with good, darkness with light.[4]

What Hugo was after, obviously, was the freedom of a literary style to imitate the full range of experience (note the romantic casting of this in dialectical pairs of light and dark, good and evil) and to take on itself whatever expansiveness was necessary to accomplish this aim. That is why the romantic acting of the English players had excited him and his friends. The Shakespearean play sprawls. Moreover, if Othello is to murder Desdemona, no rule of decorum prevents Shakespeare from showing the crime on stage. (Charles Kemble, in his extravagance, stabbed Desdemona three or four times and smothered her, too.) The French already knew Shakespeare in print[5] and on stage in the acting of their own classical-minded performers, but it took the English company to show what the unleashing of romantic passion in the theater could be like. Hugo complained that in the classical style one was shown "only the elbows of the action."

In the name of the freedom that he proposed, Hugo preached a literary trinity, from which classical tragedy was conspicuously excluded. He said that poetry has three great periods corresponding to three literary forms, the ode, the epic, and the drama: "this threefold poetry flows from three great sources—the Bible, Homer, and Shakespeare." The greatest of these is Shakespeare: "The

---

4 Translated in Barrett H. Clark, ed., *European Theories of the Drama* (New York: Crown, 1947), p. 368.
5 Pierre Le Tourneur made a mediocre translation in 1776–1782, and François Guizot made a better one in the 1820's.

drama is complete poetry. The ode and epic contain it only in germ." [6]

The essay, printed in 1827 as the Preface to *Cromwell,* did not make that play any better, but it articulated what Hugo thought he was doing, and it set the stage, along with Stendhal's piece and Guizot's translations of Shakespeare, for the battle that French romanticists were by now only too ready to fight on behalf of their vigorous, ecstatic, and open-minded muse. There had already been skirmishes. In 1809, Népomucène Lemercier had disregarded the "unities" of time and place in his *Christophe Colombe,* touching off a reaction in the Napoleonic audience so violent that one spectator was killed.

French romantic tragedy may be said to have come in with Louis Philippe in 1830 and to have gone out a few years before his departure in 1848. The French were as volatile, and nearly as passionate, in their taste for drama as in their political choices. The first production of a Victor Hugo play, *Hernani* (1830), caused a riot. It is said that the line that sparked it was:

"Est-il minuit?—Minuit bientôt." [7]

To the modern ear, nothing could be less offensive. To the French ear of 1830, attuned to classical alexandrines, it was intolerably brusque. Moreover, as Maurice Valency notes, its rhythm is Shakespeare's (see, *Hamlet* I. iv. 3–4). Hugo's intention to offend was accurately perceived, and the critical battles raged.

Riding the wave of controversy, buoyed up by what was to be a short-lived vogue, Hugo wrote six more plays during the decade: *Le Roi s'amuse* (1832), *Ruy Blas* (1838), *Lucrèce Borgia* (1833), and *Hernani* were eventually made into opera, a transformation in which they had nothing to lose and everything to gain. *Marion Délorme* (1831) was a semirealistic story of a courtesan. *Marie Tudor* (1833), and *Angelo* (1835) completed the list.

In the production of romantic tragedy Hugo shared the limelight with Alexandre Dumas, *père* (1802–1870), whose *Henri III*

---

[6] Preface to *Cromwell,* in Clark, *op. cit.,* pp. 372 and 373.
[7] Maurice Valency, *The Flower and the Castle: An Introduction to Modern Drama* (New York: Macmillan, 1963), p. 61.

et sa cour had appeared two years before *Hernani*. During the
1830's he wrote half a dozen important dramas, of which one (*Antony*) was a melodrama with a contemporary setting. But, like
Hugo's, Dumas' efforts at realism were halfhearted because Dumas
was primarily concerned with what is distant, past, and grand. His
counterpart in England was the glamorously successful Bulwer-
Lytton (1893–1873), whose novelistic talents were brought successfully to the stage with *La Duchesse de la Vallière* (1836), *The
Lady of Lyons* (1838), and *Richelieu, or the Conspiracy* (1839).
In France, Hugo and Dumas were joined in their efforts by Alfred
de Vigny (1797–1863) and by Casimir Delavigne (1793–1843).

Romantic tragedy was destined to provoke a counterreaction in
a short time. By 1838, when Hugo was at the height of his powers
with *Ruy Blas,* the tide was already turning. The actress Rachel
began then to revive the classics, with much success. The resound-
ing failure of Hugo's *Les Burgaves* in 1843 marked the end of the
first period of romantic tragedy in France. A month later, the hit of
Paris was François Ponsard's *Lucrèce,* a neoclassical work.

It is difficult now to value in the French romantic tragedy of the
1830's and 1840's much more than the fight for an enlarged liberty
of dramatic convention. The extravagances of Hugo's plays, which
resulted from his having to wage literary battles and from his own
expansive nature, render them overly pompous for the modern
reader. Hugo's great contribution was his desire to unite the audience in a grandeur of passion, from which he rightly assumed that
the bourgeois audience had been severed. This reunion he
wished to accomplish through the excitation of feeling. Hugo's
achievement was to write scenes that, for a time at least, gave the
audience vivid experiences of wonder, astonishment, and vicarious
heroism. This is very nearly the most elemental retort that romanticism can give to rationalism. (Napoleon, with the impetus of the
Revolution behind him, had organized France down to its shoe
buttons, and middle-class commerce and the industrial revolution
were going even further to make the individual feel himself a functionary in the social machine.) All that Hugo missed was the realization that romanticism's ultimate retort to rationalism can only
be musical. That perception was left to Richard Wagner.

It is to Wagner that one must turn in order to see the dramatic culmination of dream-romanticism and the contribution it was destined to make to modern theater practice. For in Wagner the deepest concerns of the romantic tragedians were realized. There were three principal reasons for this.

First, Wagner was a composer, and one of such originality that he perceived, where others did not, the resources music could supply for that direct appeal to emotion that dream-romanticism intended.

Second, Wagner was possessed by a love of theater so radical that he was able to envision its complete reconstitution. Theater was for him the supreme art because it combined many arts into one. To his mind this meant that it promised to transcend the limitations of each particular art, fulfilling itself in a *Gesamtkunstwerk*. The idea is vague, but to this it owed its attraction, since it corresponded to that longing for an absolute beyond all specifics which lay at the heart of dream-romanticism.

Third, Wagner was a product of Germany at the time when a number of her intellectuals were beginning to explore primitive and other non-Christian cultures and to take, therefore, a very strong interest in mythology. The interest in mythology not only was historical and antiquarian but also reflected the tendency of historical consciousness to attempt to complete itself in mythological thought. Vico himself (see the Introduction) had asserted that the primitive past can be re-evoked from the depth of consciousness. For the romanticist it is all one whether we say that the study of history leads one back to prehistory and thus to myth or whether we say that one flees from the burdens of history to the refuge of transhistorical mythology. In either case the romanticist comes to see myth as a sort of organic root that has the power to orient and to nourish human experience, and Wagner offers a clear example of this process. He was aware that if one wanted to reunite modern man with the passion from which rationalism, industrialism, and commerce separate him, it was necessary to go beyond the merely adventuresome and the heroic and to return to the mythical, which is the more deeply human because it is superhuman.

Marvel, ye erudite critics, at the omnipotence of human minstrelsy, unfolded in the simple *mythos of the folk!* Things that all your

understanding can not so much as comprehend are there laid bare
to human feeling, with such a physically perfect surety as no other
means could bring to pass.[8]

It was while he was contemplating a work on Frederick Barba-
rossa (which he later abandoned in favor of one on Siegfried),
Wagner tells us, that he saw "Myth and History stand before me
with opposing claims . . .":

> My studies thus bore me through the legends of the Middle Ages
> right down to their foundation in the old Germanic *mythos;* . . . .
> What here I saw, was no longer the figure of conventional history
> . . . but the real naked man . . . the type of the true *human
> being.*[9]

Although Wagner spoke of myth and history as opposites, their
opposition was, for him, a dialectical one, not one of mutual contradiction. He came to myth by way of history, and it was precisely
in order to comprehend the meaning of the historical that he
plunged himself into the mythical.

> Had I chosen to comply with the imperative demands of history,
> then had my drama become an unsurveyable conglomerate of pic-
> tured incidents, entirely crowding out from view the real and only
> thing I wished to show; and thus, as artist, I should have met pre-
> cisely the same fate in my drama as did its hero: to wit, I should
> myself have been crushed by the weight of the very relations that
> I fain would master—that is, portray—without ever having brought
> my purpose to an understanding; just as Friedrich could not bring
> his will to carrying out. To attain my purpose, I should therefore
> have had to reduce this mass of relations by *free* construction, and
> should have fallen into a treatment that would have absolutely
> violated history. Yet I could not but see the contradiction involved
> herein; for it was the main characteristic of Friedrich, in my eyes,
> that he should be a *historical* hero. If, on the other hand, I wished
> to dabble in mythical construction, then, for its ultimate and high-
> est form, but quite beyond the modern poet's reach, I must go back
> to the unadulterated *mythos,* which up to now the folk alone has

[8] "A Communication to My Friends" (1851), in *Wagner on Music and Drama,* Albert
Goldman and Evert Sprinchorn, eds.; H. Ashton Ellis, trans. (New York: Dutton,
1964), pp. 262–263. Italics in original.
[9] *Ibid.,* p. 264.

hymned, and which I had already found in full perfection—in the "Siegfried." [10]

For Wagner, myth was the ultimate expression of human experience. "Experience is everything," he wrote.[11] The experience appealed to here is the product of event, memory, and emotion. Wagner's expressed aim was to bring "the drama's broader object to the cognizance of feeling." [12] To accomplish this it was necessary to create in the spectator a state of dreaming. The mind, he said, should be "placed in that dream-like state wherein it presently shall come to full clairvoyance, and thus perceive a new coherence in the world's phenomena." [13] The romantic quest for reality, rejecting what is given to "the waking eye of everyday," [14] seeks the clairvoyance of the dream.

The inevitable outcome of Wagner's dream-romanticism was the desire for an absolute beyond the dream. Re-entry into history proved impossible. Instead, Wagner's imagination traveled toward the cessation of dream in absolute sleep, which is death. After reading Schopenhauer, whom he called the greatest philosopher since Kant, Wagner declared that "the negation of the desire of life" is "the only salvation possible":

> If I think of the storm of my heart, the terrible tenacity with which, against my desire, it used to cling to the hope of life, and if even now I feel this hurricane within me, I have at least found a quietus which in wakeful nights helps me to sleep. This is the genuine, ardent longing for death, for absolute unconsciousness, total non-existence. Freedom from all dreams is our only final salvation.[15]

It was this dream-possessed, death-longing Wagner who carried the idea of "organic form" to its ultimate manifestation in theater, where it necessarily resulted in musical drama. It was Wagner who pressed toward a "total" employment of stage space, décor, and lighting for the purpose of establishing mood. Victor Hugo had pioneered in this, realizing that in the theater the romantic

10 *Ibid.*, p. 266.
11 *Ibid.*, p. 291.
12 *Ibid.*, p. 267.
13 *Ibid.*, p. 269.
14 *Ibid.*
15 Letter to Franz Liszt, Dec. 16, 1854; *ibid.*, p. 271.

dream requires it. Wagner made it a creed. He set the practice, though he did not invent it, of darkening the house lights, plunging the audience into obscurity so that its whole attention should be surrendered to the mood-creating stage. He dropped the orchestra into a pit, where it became the hidden source of an enveloping, primal sound. He got rid of box seats, from which spectators had looked across at each other for three hundred years, turning every chair toward the stage. Wagner conceived of the theater as a single, gigantic instrument whose every part would function in concert with the rest to transport an audience from the mundane to the mythical, from the partial to the absolute.

Doing all this as both poet and composer, Wagner took the theatrical expression of the romantic dream as far as it could go. His legacy has not, therefore, led to further development in kind, though there have been plenty of imitations and variations. All by himself, he invented, perfected, and exhausted the Wagnerian music drama, and he developed dream-romanticism so fully that all theatrical efforts in that direction after him have seemed lacking in strength. However, Wagner's general concept of theater has proved germinal. It has been employed for the achievement of quite un-Wagnerian ends, partly in realistic drama, partly in symbolist drama, and partly, because of the idea of "total theater," in twentieth-century departures as different as those of Bertolt Brecht and Paul Claudel.

It is Wagner's absolutism that today frequently dampens, where it does not extinguish, the fires of enthusiasm that once burned for him. The twentieth century has discovered that romantic absolutes, easily carried over into the political realm, result in orgies of human suffering. Myth does indeed feed history, sometimes with poison. The age has also discovered, as Wagner did, that love of the absolute eventuates in the love of death (*Tristan und Isolde*). All the same, it was Wagner's absolutism that enabled him to fulfill the aims of dream-romanticism, and it was while doing this that he spurred the revolution in theater techniques that has made the style and practice of theater what it is today. (See Chapter 5.)

A distinguishing mark of Wagnerian absolutism is its lack of irony. In Wagner there is no double vision. He never shows us, indeed he seems to withhold, the reverse side of the coin. There are those who see in his refusal to turn any subject around the mark of a charlatan. If that is what he was, we probably should add that he fooled himself as well. At any rate, he is open to the charge that can be brought against all dream-romantics: they neglect to speak about what we are to think when the dream is over. In this context we may note that irony is a means, however costly, for maintaining human vision. This is what "romanticism of the here and now" understood, and to its aims and strategies I now turn.

3. ROMANTICISM OF THE
HERE AND NOW

AFTER WAGNER, whose career spanned half a century, from 1833 to 1882, one has to return to the 1830's to take note of a more ironic kind of romanticism which dealt with the here and now. The first figure to notice, a loner in every way, stood somewhere between the two types.

Alfred de Musset (1810–1857) entered the literary life of Paris at eighteen years of age, when he published his *Contes d'Espagne et d'Italie,* a collection of rather Byronic poems. Ten years later he was passing into eclipse. Meanwhile, he produced some of the most exquisite distillations of romantic passion ever committed to paper.

His first play, *La Nuit vénétienne,* was a failure. It came at the end of the same year (1830) in which *Hernani* had raised such a storm, and Musset encountered a stubbornly hostile audience for which neither the play nor the performance was a match. Peter Meyer has recently described the opening at the Odéon (December 1, 1830):

> The first scene was played in comparative quiet, but booing started in the second and continued to drown out a great part of the play. The author was astonished, but continued to hope that all would be well with the scene between the Prince and Laurette. Mademoiselle Béranger, a beautiful young actress, exquisitely dressed in

white satin, leaned against the balcony trellis and looked out over the moonlit canal. Unfortunately, the scenery had just been painted and when she turned back to face the audience, her skirts were heavily barred with the green diamonds of the trellis. Pandemonium broke out and the management were forced to lower the curtain. On the following night the reception was much the same and Musset turned his back on the theatre, to devote himself to a life of pleasure.[1]

Musset did not again try to have his plays performed but published them for a reading audience. He wrote some twenty in all, of which thirteen appeared during the decade. *Andrea del Sarto* (1833) and *Lorenzaccio* (1834) are history plays drawn from Italian material. (Italy fascinated Musset, much as it had Shakespeare, as being a land of passion and intrigue—and also because of its traditions of stage comedy.) These two plays certainly display a romantic attraction to the long ago and far away, but they are by no means adulatory of their protagonists. *Lorenzaccio,* in particular, displays a sort of cool objectivity toward its introspective hero, even while it casts upon the audience the spell of a story of dark revenge. This combination of qualities gives the play a flavor much more modern than that of any of the dramas of Hugo or Dumas. It plunges as fully as possible into experience, all the while asking for the secrets of passion to reveal themselves. For this reason it avoids melodrama, from which Hugo and Dumas were never far removed.

Romance and irony received a very different treatment in Musset's *Fantasio* (1833). Fantasio, a man about town, is melancholic:

SPARK (*his friend*): You seem to me to be sick of the world.
FANTASIO: Ah, my dear fellow, to be sick of the world one must have tasted of it, traveled all over it.
SPARK: Well?
FANTASIO: Well, where can I go? Look at this old smoky town: there is no square, street, or alley I haven't roamed thirty times over; there are no stones that I haven't dragged my worn heels upon; no house of which I do not know what girl's or old woman's stupid head is to be seen eternally behind the windowpane; I cannot take a step without treading on my steps of yesterday. Still, dear friend, this town is

1 Introduction to Musset's *Seven Plays,* Peter Meyer, trans. (New York: Hill and Wang, 1962), p. xiii.

nothing compared to my mind. All its corners are to me a hundred times more familiar; all the streets, all the holes of my imagination are a hundred times more worn. I've roamed through it in a hundred times more ways, this dilapidated mind; I, its sole occupant! I've intoxicated myself in all its wineshops, I've wallowed there like a despotic king in a golden litter; I've trotted through it like a good merchant on a jaded mule; and now I dare enter only like a robber with a dark lantern in his hand.[2]

The court clown of the king of Bavaria has died, leaving the princess unhappy on the eve of her betrothal to the prince of Mantua. Fantasio decides, as a prank, to disguise himself as the dead clown, whose name was St. John. He hopes to cheer up the princess and to gain a mask for his own dispiritedness. Perhaps also he will escape his creditors. When the prince of Mantua arrives at court disguised as his own attendant, a plot of mistaken identities unfolds. Fantasio (alias St. John) humiliates the prince, a stupid ass, who departs in anger, calling off the match. The princess takes Fantasio to be the true prince. He, however, declares his identity and suggests that she pay off his debts in return for her having been helped to escape marriage to a stupid prince. On second thought, he has a better idea:

> If you think it worth 20,000 pounds to have been rid of the Prince of Mantua, give them to me and don't pay my debts. A gentleman without debts would not want to be seen anywhere. It has never occurred to me to be without debts.
>
> PRINCESS: Well, I'll give you the money. But take the keys to my garden. Whenever you are tired of being pursued by creditors, come and hide among the tulips where I found you this morning; be careful to have on your wig and your striped suit; don't ever appear before me without your twisted back and your silver bells, for that's the way I like you. You'll be my jester for as long as you wish, and then you'll go back to your affairs. Now you can go; the door stands open.
>
> (II.vii)

Fantasio, like other plays of Musset, has been said to combine "romantic grotesquerie *à la* Hugo" with an "un-romantic conclusion."[3] The so-called anti-romanticism of Musset (said to be in

2 Act I, Scene ii. Translated by Jacques Barzun. In Eric Bentley, ed., *The Modern Theatre,* Vol. II (Garden City, N.Y.: Anchor Books, Doubleday, 1955), p. 9.

3 John Gassner, *Masters of the Drama,* 3rd ed. (New York: Dover, 1954), p. 353.

sharp contrast with his lyric poetry) can be further highlighted by attention to his literary kinship with Pierre Marivaux, who in the eighteenth century had written light comedies in the Italian style. However, the plays of Musset are not really anti-romantic. Disillusioned with passion he may have been, but not with experience. Even in his most wry work, such as *Il faut qu'une porte soit ouverte ou fermée* (1845; "A Door Should Be Open or Shut"), the appeal to sanity is made not through reason or any belief in immutable reality but through experience. Romantic irony abounds in Musset, whether we think of the high sophistication of *Le Chandelier* (1835) or of his most personal play (reminiscent of his affair with George Sand), *On ne badine pas avec l'amour* (1834: *No Trifling with Love*).

For all Victor Hugo's adulation of Shakespeare, the short, unpretentious plays of Musset have a far more genuine Shakespearean quality than Hugo's. Musset understood, as Hugo perhaps did not, that Shakespeare is inimitable, but he also perceived that Shakespeare's rendering of experience in terms of a highly theatrical convention, employing the artifice of theater to convey the irony of life, may indeed be borrowed.

Not the least of the ironies of Musset is the fact that although his plays are, for the most part, truly theatrical jests, they have the reputation of being "closet drama," fit for readers only. As a matter of fact, they have been performed successfully on the French stage since 1847, when the Comédie Française mounted a happy production of *Un Caprice*. It is only outside France that Musset is thought to be too "literary" for the stage. *Barberine* (1835), with its plot frankly lifted from a subplot in *Cymbeline,* is a theatrical burlesque through which Musset's gentle cynicism is evident. If performed today on an open stage as a show piece for good actors, it would delight its audience, and so would any of the plays recently published in Peter Meyer's translation, *Seven Plays.*

When the Paris theater was experimenting with great verve in the 1920's and 1930's, Musset was frequently performed. Pierre Fresnay in 1928 was a memorable Perdican (in *On ne badine pas*) at the Comédie Française. Marguerite Jamois and Lucien Nat played in *Les Caprices de Marianne* under Gaston Baty's direction at the Théâtre Montparnasse in 1936. The same year, at the

Comédie, Baty directed Madeleine Renaud and Julien Bertheau in *Le Chandelier.*

These admired productions reinforce the point that Musset really does belong to the theater. In fact, it is his unusually theatrical use of theater that gives him his secure place in modern drama. Clear echoes of his theatrical playfulness are to be found in Christopher Fry, Michel de Ghelderode, and Eugène Ionesco. The imagination of Musset hit upon the *jeu de théâtre* as a poetic device for speaking of the allure and folly of human passion, and though his settings are usually in remote places at ill-defined times and are at most semi-realistic, he is almost always looking obliquely at himself and using himself as a model of human absurdity.

Beneath all this there lay a deep romantic wound. As he himself wrote, Musset pondered "a world worn out by Napoleon's wars . . . mourning for its lost illusions." [4] Sometimes, as in the famous speech by Perdican in *No Trifling with Love,* this poignant theme comes to the surface:

> The world is only a bottomless cesspool, where the most shapeless sea-beasts climb and writhe on mountains of slime. But there is in the world a thing holy and sublime—the union of two of these beings, imperfect and frightful as they are. One is often deceived in love, often wounded, often unhappy; but one lives, and on the brink of the grave one turns to look back and says: I have suffered often, sometimes I have been mistaken, but I have loved. It is I who have lived, and not a spurious being bred of my pride and my sorrow.[5]

The last sentences of this speech came from a letter George Sand wrote to Musset in May of 1834, a few weeks before the play was written. For Musset the theater was an indirect way, all the better if not too serious, to express the feelings of the wounded romantic heart.

In 1813, three years after the birth of Musset, there were born in Germany three persons of signal importance for the modern theater. One of these was Wagner. The others were Georg Büchner and Friedrich Hebbel.

[4] *Comedies by Alfred de Musset,* S. L. Gwynn, trans. (London: Walter Scott, n.d.), p. ix.
[5] Act II, in *Comedies.*

By 1837, before he had reached his twenty-fourth birthday, Büchner was dead. At twenty-one he had written a revolutionary pamphlet, *The Hessian Courtier,* that brought him into trouble with the authorities and forced him to flee his native Hesse. He went to Strassburg and later to Zurich, where he became a lecturer in comparative anatomy. At his death he left two major dramas, a short comedy, and two translations from Victor Hugo. A fourth play of his own, *Pietro Aretius,* he had destroyed.

Büchner's short comedy, *Leonce und Lena,* though a clever satire, has not been much remembered. But *Dantons Tod* (1835; *Danton's Death*) and *Woyzeck* (unfinished) are early, influential deposits of a style and quality that were to become increasingly influential.

The romantic spirit could not have been stronger than it was in Büchner, but neither could it have been directed toward ends more different from those of dream-romanticism. Instead of turning toward visions of pristine heroism and dream, Büchner's romanticism took the form of protest, sometimes savage, sometimes poignant, against the conditions of life. Büchner was a revolutionary in the days following Napoleon, when Europe was full of revolution that changed little. He was a socialist before Marx, a rebel in exile, but not a man with a program. His exile, more than political, more than geographic, was an exile of the spirit. One cannot read him without feeling that his protest was metaphysical, that he was haunted by a sense of cosmic alienation, unable to reconcile himself to finitude. In his plays he fastened upon events that were contemporary or very recent. He turned them, with great persuasiveness, into questions addressed to existence.

"The memory of Danton," wrote H. A. L. Fisher, "is red with violence." [6] He adds: "To Danton as to all statesmen in time of war terror was a necessary instrument of policy." [7] Büchner's Danton complains:

> The man on the Cross made it all comfortable for Himself, of course. He said: "It must needs be that offences come; but woe to that man by whom the offence cometh." They will, they must: al-

[6] *A History of Europe* (London: Collins, Fontana Library, 1960), Vol. II, p. 897.
[7] *Ibid.,* p. 898.

ways this must. Why should a hand be cursed which already bears
the curse of a must? Who put the must there, eh? Who is it inside
us doing the lying, whoring, stealing, and killing?

We're a lot of puppets, and the unknown powers have us on
strings. Ourselves, we're nothing! Just the swords that spirits fight
with—like a fairy story, you can't see the hands.[8]

The play tells of the death of this man of terror, who was also a
man of love and joy, at the hands of another man of terror, Robespierre. The play's contending forces, however, are not these two
personalities but rather those more ancient enemies, life and
death. The play includes a good deal of bawdry. Employed in a
manner reminiscent of Shakespeare, it brings onto the stage that
very force and abundance of life that death extinguishes. By its use
Büchner achieves a perspective quite different from that of dream-
romanticism, in which love and death are so often companions.
Büchner conjoins *sex* and death. Thereby he becomes the spokes-
man of a view more modern, more nearly Freudian as well as more
Dionysian, than dream-romanticism could entertain. He is the first
of the modern dramatists to engage in a ruthless stripping away of
post-Renaissance idealizations. He was thus a precursor of the
modern analytic age. We are shown, in the midst of a revolution
and among its most sophisticated champions, an elemental animosity between the old hag who is death and the young wench who is
life, and we are reminded that the latter turns into the former.
Robespierre, whose hand and heart are entirely death-dealing, has
nothing of bawdry about him. His is a deeper vulgarity. Danton,
though not a vulgarian, is a wencher. He is the funnel through
which life runs out to death. It is this that binds him to the common people. The glitter of his mind and the sympathies of his in-
stincts serve only to render his fate the more ironic and irrational.

Doubt about the meaning of life—whether it has any at all—pervades this work and colors its every line.

DANTON: The creation's spread too far, nothing's fallow any more,
everything's teeming. This is the suicide of oblivion—creation is the
fatal wound, we are the drops of blood, and it's now rotting in its
grave, the world.[9]

[8] Act II, Scene v. Translated by John Holmstrom. In Eric Bentley, ed., *The Modern
Theatre*, Vol. V (Garden City, N.Y.: Anchor Books, Doubleday, 1957), p. 111.
[9] Act III, Scene vii. *Ibid.*, p. 139.

Occasionally, the will to belief surges upward, fighting against an inevitable demise. Looking out the window of his cell, moved by the suffering of his comrades and his wife, Danton observes:

> Those stars are like glistening tears scattered about the night; there must be a terrible grief behind the eye that dropped them.[10]

A few moments later, however, Camille, another of the condemned, wakes up in fright from a nightmare, in which, he says,

> [The] sky came driving down upon us with all its light flashing, and I was struggling against these horrible stars. . . .[11]

The world in this play is a vast growth of systematic murder. Robespierre is its conscious agent, but it would go on without him.

In all modern drama there is hardly a more moving account of the twilight of faith than in the dialogue Büchner wrote for the end of the scene in which Danton and his friends are taken from prison to the guillotine. Philippeau, who is a believer, speaks:

> My friends, you don't have to get far above the earth to lose sight of all the confusion and glitter and see instead the few simple contours that God intended. We're deafened by the shrieking and yelling, but there is one ear that all this reaches only as a stream of harmonies.
>
> DANTON: But we're the unfortunate musicians performing on our unhappy bodies. Do you mean to say that the nasty bungling noises they produce are only to float up and die away as a voluptuous breath in these heavenly ears?
>
> HERAULT: Are we poor little suckling pigs for a lordly table, thrashed to death to make us tastier?
>
> DANTON: Are we children, put into the world to be roasted in the red-hot arms of Moloch, and tickled with beams of light to amuse the gods with our crowing?
>
> CAMILLE: And is the ether with its gold eyes a dish of golden carp, laid on the roaring dinner table of Olympus, with the gods always merry, and we poor fish dying, and the gods getting an eternity of cheap thrills out of the brilliance of our death agony?
>
> DANTON: The world is chaos. Nothingness is the world god yet to be born.

10 Act IV, Scene iii. *Ibid.*, p. 148.
11 *Ibid.*

(Enter the JAILER.)

JAILER: We can be going now, gentlemen; the carts are waiting outside.

PHILIPPEAU: Good night, my friends! So now we pull the great dark blanket over us, to put out our hearts and shut our eyes.

(The prisoners embrace each other.)

HERAULT *(taking* CAMILLE's *arm)*: Cheer up, Camille, we've got a lovely night for it. It's quite still, and look at the clouds—like a dying Olympus over France, with the shapes of the gods fading and sinking away.

(They go out.) [12]

Danton's Death is also remarkable for its form. Though the interest centers in Danton throughout, Büchner intended that his audience should see the Reign of Terror from many angles. The form he chose is therefore the antithesis of the classical, which would have limited his scope. He used exactly that technique that Piscator and Brecht were later to call Epic Theater, and he handled it in a manner they never surpassed. The play is strung together like a scenario. There are scenes in the drawing room, scenes on the street, scenes in the Committee of Public Safety, in the courtroom, in prison, in open fields, and on the Place de la Révolution. This epic freedom is equalled by Büchner's structural control. The order in which the scenes occur is not dictated by the plot, which has nothing in it except arrest, sham trial, and execution. The scenes are arranged so as to lift out, one by one, in accordance with a poetic sensibility, the various facets of the action, which is "to go to death." Consider, for example, the following sequence of six scenes:

III.ix. At the Revolutionary tribunal, Danton, deprived of the right of self-defense, denounces the Committee of Public Safety and draws cheers from the crowd.

III.x. In the street, a citizen denounces Danton and draws cries of "Down with the traitor!"

IV.i. In a scene of one speech six sentences long, Danton's wife sends him word she will die with him.

IV.ii. In the street, a president of the tribunal coolly explains that his own wife will be put to the guillotine.

12 Act IV, Scene v. *Ibid.*, pp. 154–155.

IV.iii. In prison, Danton and his friends talk, and even dream, of dying. They imagine the gods are dying, too, if not already dead.

IV.iv. The jailer and the carter, like gravediggers in *Hamlet,* discuss their trade.

And so on. The structure is experiential, since death cannot be comprehended but must be undergone.

Published when it was written, *Danton's Death* was not performed until 1902. It was, in large degree, the inspiration for Bertolt Brecht's first play, *Baal.* Chronologically, it stands near the beginning of modern drama. In spirit and technique, it belongs to the twentieth century.

Woyzeck is considered by some to be an even greater play. It is certainly more astringent, its irony deeper. Northrop Frye has proposed that ironic literature adopts a perspective in which the protagonist appears inferior to the reader (or spectator) in knowledge and power.[13] If the material is controlled in such a way that the protagonist-as-underdog retains one's sympathy while at the same time his limitations are emphasized, the result will be an ambivalence of judgment, and this will be manifest as a kind of irony. The more such a character is representative of something in *us* or something inherent in the human condition, while our insight remains superior to his, the deeper the irony will become. Of this definition of ironic literature *Woyzeck* might be considered the very model.

The story came from the newspapers. In 1824 at Leipzig a barber and soldier named Johann Christian Woyzeck was executed for murdering his mistress in a fit of jealousy. The case gave rise to a legal and medical controversy as to whether Woyzeck was insane. A Slav, the poor soldier Woyzeck was tormented by his Prussian superiors. The play describes his losing battle against their almost unconscious sadism and against psychological forces within himself that are unleashed by circumstances, forces he barely recognizes and cannot control. It is a study in futility, but its fascination arises from the discrepancy between the potential grandeur of the emo-

13 *The Anatomy of Criticism* (Princeton, N.J.: Princeton University Press, 1957), pp. 40 ff.

tions that move through Woyzeck and his incapacity to turn them toward any humanized ends. They become destructive. At the same time, the officers, whose intelligence is greater than his, display no humanity of feeling. Marie, who has betrayed Woyzeck, believing that all human affections are innocent, is slain by Woyzeck with his knife, an emblem of his enraged impotence. The following speech, with its implicit allusion to Othello, illustrates the irony of the style:

WOYZECK: The knife? Where's the knife? I left it here. It'll give me away. Nearer. Nearer yet. What place is this? What's that I hear? Something moving! No, it's quiet. Everything's quiet! What are you so white for, Marie? What's that red string around your neck? Who did your sins earn that necklace from? You were black with them, black! Did I bleach you white again? Why is your black hair hanging so wild? Didn't you braid your long braids today? Here's something! Cold and wet, and still. The knife! The knife! Got it? Get rid of it.[14]

Woyzeck, which Büchner left unfinished, is today best known in the operatic version, called *Wozzeck* (1925), composed by Alban Berg in a twentieth-century musical idiom of great power that is eminently suited to the ironic force of the text.

When Büchner died, Christian Friedrich Hebbel (1813–1863), who was the same age, had not yet written his first play. *Judith* was yet two or more years away.[15] Based on the apocryphal story of the woman who saved Israel by slaying the enemy captain Holofernes, this drama, like the bulk of Hebbel's work, suggests by its heroic theme and ancient setting that it should be classified with dream-romanticism. However, Hebbel owes his place in modern drama to a work of another sort: *Maria Magdalena,* his second important drama, written in 1843 or 1844 and performed in 1846. The perspective of this play is ironic in the same sense that *Woyzeck* is, and its irony increases with the passage of time, for it has to do with a domestic tragedy brought about by unenlightened adherence to a code of respectability that is unrealistic and inhumane. The major characters are destroyed by a system of values they are incapable of

14 Scene xxiv. Translated by Theodore Hoffman. In Eric Bentley, ed., *The Modern Theatre,* Vol. I (Garden City, N.Y.: Anchor Books, Doubleday, 1955), p. 31.
15 Sources give its date variously as 1839, 1840, and 1841.

transcending, though the play itself is written from a higher, more knowing, point of view.

Drawn from life, the story is that of a poor carpenter, Anton, whose daughter Klara is seduced by a scoundrel. To save the family honor, Klara's fiancé challenges the seducer to a duel, only to be fatally wounded. To save her father from disgrace, Klara drowns herself. Her dying fiancé reproaches himself and the others for having brought about her death by their pride. The father says simply, "I don't understand the world anymore," and the curtain descends.

Although the theme and certainly the title of *Maria Magdalena* are ironic, the style is not. Hebbel seemed ill at ease with the language of his working-class characters. German drama provided him with no models for conveying common speech (*Woyzeck* was probably unknown to him), and he seems to have lacked the ear to copy it from life. Never quite overcoming this hurdle, he was naturally unable to reach the further subtlety of imbuing the lines with the ironic quality inherent in his theme. Furthermore, he was not able, or did not think himself able, to count on the audience of the 1840's to take his story in an ironic sense. The code of honor according to which a "fallen" girl had absolutely to be avenged or to live forever in disgrace was, so it seemed, shared by the audience to such an extent that Hebbel felt himself required to attack it head on. *Maria Magdalena* thus turned out, in large part, to be a message play, a *pièce à thèse* based on classical rather than romantic irony. Yet Hebbel's intentions were divided. Half wanting to write a work of romantic irony, half wanting to shame the audience, he produced an aesthetic failure that nevertheless exercised an enormous influence on subsequent developments.

Maria Magdalena is usually honored as one of the first important attempts at realism. No doubt it deserves that credit, but today its realism does not seem very convincing. What survives is the irony, however confused. *Maria Magdalena* became a landmark in theater history because, in spite of its flaws, it was a bold search for reality within, not away from, everyday experience.

In his other work Hebbel tended to choose subjects long ago and far away—for instance, those of *Herod and Mariamne* (1850), *Gyges and His Ring* (1855), and a *Nibelungen* trilogy (1862, soon eclipsed by Wagner's *Ring*, which was in fact already written and was performed at Munich in 1865).

The key to Hebbel's strength lay in his Hegelian awareness that life is change and that the drama should reflect this and encourage it. "History," as Eric Bentley has said, "is his very mode of vision." [16] His weakness was that he never sufficiently shook himself loose from the notion that "history" means the past. These remarks are true *a fortiori* of Hebbel's contemporary, Otto Ludwig (1813–1865), though some consider Ludwig's dramatic theory to have been prophetic.[17]

Romanticism of the here and now took strong root in Russia. It was fed by a penchant for satire very much at home in that country.

The Romantic Movement came to Russia after the Napoleonic wars. Its height was thus later there than in Germany and ran from about 1825 to 1855, the dates of the reign of Nicholas I. What it replaced was not a Russian tradition of classicism, for there was none, but an imported French neoclassicism. Of Spain it has been said that the baroque never came to it because it had always been there. Something similar might be said of romanticism in Russia. The romantic spirit that came in about 1825 merely sent the Russians back to their own sources. Their native repository of folk legends and patriotic lore was large. They had also a strong national pride and a monarchy that controlled the theaters and loved to see itself reflected in the glories of the past. In V. Krinkovsky, Nicholas I found a dramatist who suited him well, and when he opened the Alexandrinski Theater in 1832, Krinkovsky's play *Pozharsky* was shown, all about how the monarchy in the seventeenth century was saved by a good prince. Another favorite was Nestor Kuholnik (1809–1868), who was not ashamed to write a play entitled *The Almighty's Hand the Fatherland Has Saved*. Still another was Nicholas Polevoy (1796–1846), critic and journalist who wrote *The Grandfather of the Russian Fleet*. His translation of *Hamlet* in 1837 initiated a period of romantic enthusiasm for Shakespeare.

Far and away the best among those who wrote for the Russian

16 *The Playwright as Thinker* (New York: Meridian, 1955), p. 28.
17 See Bentley, *The Playwright as Thinker*, pp. 26–27.

stage in the manner of dream-romanticism was the great Alexander Pushkin (1799–1837). He wrote (in 1830) a number of "romantic scenes" in verse, among them *Mozart and Salieri, The Stone Guest,* and *The Feast During the Plague.* These came five years after *Boris Godunov,* that dark story of guilt and national agony which is said to have been written under the influence of Shakespeare but which is thoroughly Russian in spirit and in its characterizations.

Romanticism of the dream actually produced little drama of merit in Russia. *Boris Godunov,* because of the censors, was not even performed until 1870 (at the Marinski Theater, in St. Petersburg), and that was only three years before Mussorgsky's operatic version pushed the original into the background. Russian dream-romanticism was rapidly diverted into opera and the novel, where it really belonged. It was romanticism of the here and now that was to lend distinction to the Russian stage.

This type of romanticism, as we have noticed, feeds on a heightened awareness of the present moment as historical reality. The new in history, especially if it appears problematic, stimulates it, and so does a sense of urgency regarding social change.

The young Russian generation that fought in Europe against Napoleon was liberalized by the experience. Many soldiers came home no longer patient with the "given reality" of Russian society. They were eager to strike out in quest of the new, both in the social sphere and in the realm of ideas. This spirit found ready marriage with a native Russian talent for satire, and out of this conjunction was born a vigorous, realistic, and revolutionary Russian comic theater.

One of its earliest monuments is *Gore ot Uma* (*Woe from Wit* or *It Is Folly to Be Wise*), by Alexander Griboyedov (1795–1829). Chatsky, the ill-fated hero of this satire, is an enthusiastic young nobleman returned to Moscow after three years abroad to find his girl Sophia infatuated with a spineless gentleman who believes that young people should not hold, let alone express, original opinions. As for the older generation, it has nothing but received ideas. One of Chatsky's main targets is a colonel who thinks all books ought to be burned. For his efforts to expose the hypocrisy of this society Chatsky is ostracized. He resumes his travels. Said Griboyedov: "In my comedy there are twenty-five fools to one reasonable man, and this man, of course, stands in conflict with the society surrounding him." [18] The censors naturally found this play objectionable. However, it was read widely in manuscript and found its way into print, its terse language going almost immediately into the common speech. It was allowed to be performed in 1831, ten years after Griboyedov started writing it, about eight after its completion; but by that date Griboyedov had already died—in Persia, where he was a Russian envoy and where a mob, incited by some unknown cause, killed him in 1829.

Behind *Woe from Wit* there lay many precedents in Russian stage satire, some of them by the famous Russian satirist Ivan Krylov (1768–1844), better known for his fables in verse. In the background also was Molière, particularly his *Le Misanthrope*. Yet Griboyedov does not stand at the end of the development of classical comedy but rather at the beginning of a development that was eventually to lead to Chekhov. His whole look is forward, and though the attitude of his comedy contains much common sense, it also pulses with that longing for a better society which Russian romanticism has fostered in all its better writers to the present day.

After Griboyedov, Gogol. *Revizor (The Inspector General)* was performed on May 1, 1836, at the Alexandrinski Theater with the emperor and his family present. It touched off such controversy in Moscow as can be compared only to the village squabbles in the play itself. Unable to stomach so much fuss, Gogol left Russia within six weeks and stayed abroad most of the time for twelve years. Between 1832 and 1837 he wrote five other plays: *The Gamblers, The Morning of a Business Man, The Servants' Hall, The Law Suit* (the last two are derived from an earlier effort, "The Decoration of Vladimir of the Third Category," 1832, which has not survived), and *The Marriage*. During this time he also published five volumes of short stories and essays, plus *Taras Bulba* (dream-romanticism of a Hollywood kind) and the nightmare story *The Nose*. He had a brief tenure as a spectacularly inept assistant professor of world history at the University of St. Petersburg:

[18] Quoted in Marc Slonim, *The Russian Theater from the Empire to the Soviets* (New York: Collier Books, 1962), p. 43.

[H]e used to appear with his cheek bandaged up so as to imply a swollen jaw hampering speech and dejectedly dealt out and distributed among his students little pictures of Roman ruins.[19]

"We spat at each other and parted company, I and the University," said Gogol.[20] *Dead Souls* (started in 1836, published in 1842) and *The Overcoat* (finished in 1841) were written abroad.

Many people know, even if they have never read or seen the play, the plot of *The Inspector General.* A young man (called Khlestakov), all his money lost at cards, is stranded at the inn of a small town. The local functionaries, expecting a visit from the inspector general, conclude on the instant that Khlestakov is he. Their self-delusion, for that is what it really is, delights the penniless Khlestakov, who uses it to provide himself with all necessary comforts, including wine, bribe money, and the mayor's daughter. Then he leaves town and, to the dismay of the inhabitants, the real inspector approaches.

"The play begins with a blinding flash of lightning," says Vladimir Nabokov, "and ends in a thunderclap. In fact it is wholly placed in the tense gap between the flash and the crash." [21] He is right, the miracle being that inside this "tense gap" we are treated to one of the most lively, boisterous, exuberant spectacles ever set down for the astonished delight of an audience. As Nabokov puts it:

> The whole world is one ozone-blue shiver and we are in the middle of it. . . . The characters are nightmare people in one of those dreams when you think you have waked up while all you have done is to enter the most dreadful (most dreadful in its sham reality) region of dreams. Gogol has a peculiar manner of letting "secondary" characters pop out at every turn of the play . . . to flaunt for a second their life-like existence. . . .[22]

Nabokov is at pains to declare that *The Inspector General* is not a piece of realism and not a social satire. Certainly that is not *all* it is, since it displays a pure joy of invention and a perfection of form

[19] Vladimir Nabokov, *Nikolai Gogol* (New York: New Directions, 1944), p. 157.
[20] *Ibid.*, p. 158.
[21] *Ibid.*, p. 42.
[22] *Ibid.*

and style that will doubtless render it immortal. Nevertheless it is disingenuous to deny that its mode is satire, as it was of Gogol himself to defend it by explaining it after the fact as an allegory, making the villagers representatives of the human passions and the genuine inspector the conscience of man. That it is only too real, allowing for comic convention, was proved by the fact that Russian society immediately felt itself indicted. Gogol would have been right if he had said that the real inspector stood for the conscience of Russia. Nabokov has most pithily described the circumstances in which the play was received:

> It is difficult to conjecture what pleased Nicholas I in *The Government Inspector.* . . . Given that the man had brains—at least the brains of a politician—it would rather detract from their quantity to suppose that he so much enjoyed the prospect of having his vassals thoroughly shaken up as to be blind to the dangers of having the man in the street join in the imperial mirth. In fact he is reported to have remarked after the first performance: "Everybody has got his due, I most of all"; and if this report is true (which it probably is not) it would seem that the evolutionary link between criticism of corruption under a certain government and criticism of the government itself must have been apparent to the Tsar's mind. We are left to assume that the permission to have the play staged was due to a sudden whim on the Tsar's part, just as the appearance of such a writer as Gogol was a most unexpected impulse on the part of whatever spirit may be held responsible for the development of Russian literature in the beginning of the Nineteenth Century. In signing this permission a despotic ruler was, curiously enough, injecting a most dangerous germ into the blood of Russian writers; . . . for Gogol's play was misinterpreted by the civic-minded as a social protest and engendered in the fifties and sixties a seething mass of literature denouncing corruption and other social defects and an orgy of literary criticism denying the title of writer to anyone who did not devote his novel or short story to the castigation of district police-officers and moujik-thrashing squires. And ten years later the Tsar had completely forgotten the play and had not the vaguest idea who Gogol was and what he had written.[23]

23 *Ibid.*, pp. 36–37.

Of irony in *The Inspector General* perhaps little need be said. It is not the kind born of religious or metaphysical doubt but instead is the kind (and this gives Nabokov his quarter) born of what we may call the mirror device, later to be pushed to extremes by Pirandello, Genet, and Beckett. As epigraph for the play, Gogol chose a Russian proverb that may be translated "Do not chafe at the looking glass if your mug is awry." The irony is that one doesn't know whether his face *is* awry unless he looks in the glass, and if the glass is of Gogol's making he then does not know whether to believe its reflection. Almost everyone enjoys *The Inspector General*, but starting with Gogol himself the strangest explanations of it have been given, all out of proportion to its apparent simplicity. It thus takes its place as the first, and perhaps the greatest, of the modern mirror plays designed to catch the spectator in a trap, which, ironically, he must help to devise. At the dawn of modern realism Gogol perceived that the question of what is real is an existential question, and he wrote with that insight a play so *deceptively* without guile that it is unsurpassed in its kind. Only an exceptionally lucid madman, which Gogol was, could have done it. In his genius he wrote a comedy that shows superbly well that romanticism of the here and now not only describes reality but also raises the question whether that reality is real.

We shall return later in the book to the growth of realism as a style. Its modern beginnings, as I have tried to show in this chapter, lay within a certain type of romanticism, the kind that refused to escape into the long-ago-and-far-away but instead concentrated on present experience, which it tended to interpret according to the spirit of romantic irony. There is a romantic current in all realism, even the type to be considered later that thinks of itself as anti-romantic. Where this romantic strain in realism is expressed as irony, the thrust is characteristically modern.

Before coming to realism properly so called, we must look at two lines of development that were highly important for it and indeed for other types of theatrical modernism that cannot be called realistic. The first of these is a line of development in popular theater that begins with entertainments called vaudeville and runs through to farce, passing meanwhile through a phenomenon called "the well-made play." The second is the revolution in the means and styles of putting plays onto the stage, which occupied all men of theater throughout the nineteenth century and continues without slack today.

4. THE WELL-MADE PLAY: FROM VAUDEVILLE TO FARCE

IN SPITE OF the egalitarianism that motivated the French Revolution, its cultural effect was the supremacy of the middle class. From this class came the major politicians of the Revolution. From it came Napoleon. To the middle class France owed the restitution of the monarchy in 1814, a compromise sanctioned by the Congress of Vienna and made tenable because it flattered the bourgeoisie to keep a monarch in the palace. Louis Bonaparte's *coup d'état* of 1848 was in turn accepted because it did nothing to counter and much to solidify the influential position of the middle class.

In no country in western Europe has a revolution *against* the middle class been successful. In these countries protest against the values and privileges of the dominant class has, for the most part, proceeded by peaceful means—by the gradual adoption of socialist and quasi-socialist measures and by the growth of a protest literature.

Were one to write in detail the history of popular drama in the nineteenth and twentieth centuries, it would turn out, for the reasons just stated, to reflect the history of middle-class taste. The overwhelming bulk of drama written, even more clearly the bulk of that performed, would show minor fluctuations in a basically consistent taste, essentially unchanged from Scribe's *La Petite Soeur* (1821) to the latest Broadway hits.

Around this mass, however, there has circulated a smaller body of drama conceived as contributing, in various modes, to a theater of protest. It is this satellite drama that draws most of the sympathetic attention of those concerned with the history of drama as art. It does so not only because many of the best critics—for example, Shaw—have been politically and ideologically prepared to *épater le bourgeois* but also because the genuine creativity of modernism cannot rest with the reality assumptions of a dominant class but must challenge them in the name of a consciousness open to historical change and looking toward understandings of reality yet to be born. The dynamic quality of modern drama, at once its vindication and its despair, arises from its ability to function as protest. Greatness is achieved when imaginative vision is combined with mastery of the resources of the stage. Yet a certain despair is inherent here, because the dramatist's protest requires him to attack that without which his work is impossible—the audience.

None of these problems concerned Eugène Scribe (1791–1861), at whom we must look in order to understand the popular bourgeois theater upon which the theater of protest feeds. Without Scribe, or whoever by any name would have done what he did, there would have been no Ibsen, no Shaw, no Pirandello, no Brecht.

Scribe came in as Napoleon went out—that is, when a pattern of life favorable to the bourgeoisie had been stamped upon France and when she could relax about it. The romanticism of Hugo, Stendhal, and Dumas was still a dozen or more years in the future and was destined to come and go while Scribe, unperturbed, manufactured hundreds of plays (estimates vary from 374 to 500), growing ever richer and more popular and dying a respected member of the Académie Française. The relation of his drama to modernism will concern us, but let us look first at his method.

He began as a writer of what were called *vaudevilles*. The word has had a long history, coming only at last to refer to that late-lamented English and American fare extinguished by television. In the fifteenth century the drinking songs and satirical ballads of Oliver Basselin of Normandy became popular under the name of his native village, Vau de Vire, later written *Vaudevire* and then corrupted to *vaudeville*. By the eighteenth century, French comedies often included interpolated songs and dances that were called vaudevilles, and the name was then taken over by light comedies usually composed in rhyming couplets. With the early Scribe, a vaudeville was a light, farcical entertainment including song and dance, aimed primarily at the gallery and hitting the rest of the house with scattered shot. Such were Scribe's *Une Nuit de la Garde Nationale* (1815; *A Night with the National Guard*) and *L'Ours et le pacha* (1820; *The Bear and the Pasha*). The latter had several *scènes de folie* in a seraglio.

While writing this sort of thing Scribe had ample opportunity to observe what best held an audience's attention and sent it home *bien content*. By the early 1820's he was ready to apply what he had learned, refined by careful analysis of his predecessors' plays, to the writing of "serious" drama. For forty years, often with a team of assistants and buying ideas when his own supply was low, he applied his principles to the production of comedies, tragedies (so-called), fantasies, historical plays, operas, and (most typically) plays of contemporary life. By sheer volume of production of an eminently marketable commodity he became the ruling figure of the French stage. When Wagner, at Königsberg about 1837, tried to break onto the operatic scene it was to Scribe that he sent the idea for a libretto, proposing that they collaborate. Scribe had already written librettos for Meyerbeer. The idea of a Wagner-Scribe collaboration is one of the funniest in history, but that is possibly not the reason why the famous Scribe left the proposal of the then unknown Richard Wagner unanswered.

Scribe fashioned what is known as *la pièce bien faite,* or "the well-made play." Although one of its virtues was that it was applicable to a wide range of subjects, periods, and even moods, its features are easily distinguishable.[1]

(1) The plot is based on a secret known to the audience and withheld from the major characters so as to be revealed to them in a climactic scene.

(2) The plot usually describes the culmination of a long story, most of which has happened before the start of the play. This "late

1 I have drawn the following points, with some modification, from the excellent summary by Stephen S. Stanton in his introduction to *Camille and Other Plays* (New York: Hill and Wang, 1957), pp. xii–xx.

point of attack" requires that the audience be informed of the antecedent material through dialogue or monologue that is called "exposition."

(3) Action and suspense grow more intense as the play proceeds, and this rise in intensity is arranged in a pattern achieved by the contrivance of entrances, exits, letters, revelations of identity, and other such devices.

(4) The hero (protagonist), in conflict with an adversary, experiences alternately good and bad turns in his fortune. This creates an emotional rhythm for the play.

(5) The lowest point of the hero's fortune is followed soon after by the highest. The latter occurs in a *scène à faire* ("obligatory scene") that characteristically hinges upon the disclosure of secrets.

(6) The plot, or part of it, is frequently knotted by a misunderstanding, a *quiproquo* (*quid pro quo*), in which a word or situation is understood in opposite ways by two or more characters.

(7) The dénouement (literally, the "untying," the resolution) is logical and hence clear. It is not supposed to have any "remainder" or unsolved quotient to puzzle the audience.

(8) The over-all action pattern of the play is reproduced on a small scale in each act. It is, in fact, the principle according to which each minor climax and scene is constructed.

It will be observed that the elements going into this mix are by no means unique to the well-made play and were certainly not invented by Scribe. Several of them, employed at least as early as Aeschylus, belong to the staples of playwriting.[2] But the recipe is Scribe's. It was worked out with such precision that his assistants could use it to produce a script as soon as they were given the basic idea. Sardou, upon whom the mantle of Scribe fell in the next generation, tells us that he trained himself by reading the first act of Scribe's plays and then plotting out the rest to see how close he might come to the original. He became very good at this exercise.

Anyone who wants to learn the Scribean technique can do so. It is one of the few matters in playwriting that can demonstrably be

[2] For a good short history of these elements in drama from the ancients to modern times, see Maurice Valency, *The Flower and the Castle: An Introduction to Modern Drama* (New York: Macmillan, 1963).

taught. As such it holds for the cultural historian only minor interest. More important than the technique itself is the spirit that brought it into being and that underlies its skillful employment.

The eight characteristics enumerated above may be called the formal characteristics of the well-made play. In addition to them one may note also a number that are substantial or thematic. They indicate the material of life upon which writers of this genre have tended to concentrate and the character of their perceptions about it. I mention four of these:

(1) The play is almost always topical, or at least appears to be, even when the setting is remote in time and space, and even when, on analysis, it turns out that time and place have little to do with the essence of the story and the characterizations. "Scribe," as Dumas noted, "was nothing if not up to date." [3] It was the same with Lindsay and Crouse in State of the Union (1945) and with Gore Vidal in The Best Man (1960). Each day's headlines may bring changes in the dialogue without any effect upon structure or characterization. Scribe's topicality was tailor-made to fit the taste of a middle class newly educated by the national system of schools and universities Napoleon had set up. Topical plays appealed to this audience's opinion of itself as well-informed. Universal education, which produces a large number of semi-educated persons who read mostly newspapers and magazines, has tended to provide a similar audience ever since. Plays catering to them therefore rapidly become dated as far as their details are concerned, though their structures are remarkably durable. Instead of reviving the old examples, however, theater managers produce new ones, because these best satisfy the criterion of topicality.

(2) The well-made play scrupulously avoids all metaphysical concerns and all suggestion of radical, as opposed to merely incidental, evil in society. (A villain, however, may be radically, unchangeably evil.) The reason for this avoidance is obvious. Metaphysics (in the realm of knowledge) and evil (in the realm of social morals) are imponderables. They cannot be reduced to logic, and when they are explored they lead to fundamental questionings of reality. That would obviously play havoc with the well-

---

[3] Quoted in Allardyce Nicoll, World Drama from Aeschylus to Anouilh (New York: Harcourt, Brace, n.d.), p. 490.

made structure. One therefore has to say that the well-made play is in substance anti-romantic. It is not its substance, however, that has contributed to the development of serious modern drama, except by way of reactions against it.

(3) Avoidance of metaphysics and radical social evil does not mean that the well-made play has to avoid religion—quite the opposite. As long as religious opinions and sentiments do not raise fundamental questions about the given order of things—a travesty of authentic religion, but never mind—it is admitted and even welcomed. Its usefulness is that it may be employed (whether "sincerely" or not is beside the point) to put a gloss upon the situation, lending it the guise of profundity. This is what is happening, for instance, when the courtesan Marguerite Gautier (*La Dame aux camélias*, Alexandre Dumas, *fils*, 1849) tells Armand that her death "is God's will." She says:

> Believe me, God sees more clearly than we do. . . . If ever you should love and marry some young and beautiful girl, as I hope you may one day, and if she should find the portrait and ask who it is, tell her that it is a friend who, if God permits, will never cease to pray for you and her.

The curtain line is, "Much will be forgiven you, for you loved much." [4] It has been said of Broadway that it has much religion but no faith.

(4) The well-made play almost invariably includes a difficulty between the sexes. In the nineteenth century this was usually a matter of social incompatibility between married or engaged persons, money, differing moral standards, the presence of a "third party" or a "fallen woman," and so on. In the twentieth century the problem often has a Freudian cast, as, for example, in the plays of William Inge or in *Tea and Sympathy* by Robert Anderson. It is *de rigueur* that the difficulty or misunderstanding between the sexes shall be capable of having a solution. When Strindberg (e.g., in *The Father*, 1887) drew a different picture, he struck at one of the foundations of the well-made play.

Other thematic characteristics of the well-made play—for in-

---

4 Quoted from the English version by Edith Reynolds and Nigel Playfair, in *Camille*, pp. 163, 164. Dumas took the first part of this play from life, but he finished it according to the example of Scribe.

stance, its preoccupation with money and social position—might be mentioned, but an exhaustive list would simply be a catalogue of middle-class values centering upon the family.

If we take the formal characteristics of the well-made play in conjunction with its thematic ones, we may perceive that the well-made play is a form of rhetoric. Rhetoric is defined as "the art of speaking well in prose, as distinguished from versification and elocution." A secondary meaning is "artificial elegance of language." What Scribe did was to elaborate a rhetoric of drama having to do not so much with the construction of prose as with the construction of plots and scenes. Prose was employed, but its excellence was not of primary concern. Consonant with traditional rhetoric, this theater rhetoric was a method for stirring the hearers. Scribe systematized the method. Its theory was enunciated in 1863 by Gustav Freytag in *Die Technik der Dramas*,[5] who thought he was describing the laws of drama for all time.

The substance of Scribean drama could not stand up to very much criticism. It was bound to be challenged, then discarded, by the modern spirit of irony. With the substance, the form had to be rejected or, as in the cases of Ibsen and Shaw, severely modified. However, Scribe's attention to form left a strong imprint on a goodly part of serious, ironic modern drama by providing for a resort to formalism.

It was apparent to everyone who cared to notice that the well-made play was a construction of artificial elegance. Its virtue was not that it was informative or challenging or the result of a high order of imagination but that it was playable—in other words, theatrical. Its *scène à faire* usually depended on a *coup de théâtre*. The well-made play was more unabashedly theatrical than the drama of any earlier period, save only those times when tragicomedy was in high fashion (notably, in the time of Euripides and that of the Jacobeans) and in some Restoration comedy. It therefore gave rise to theatricalism, which is deliberate thematic exploitation of the conventions of theater. From the standpoint of the mid-twentieth century it is quite as possible to see abstract theatri-

5 Translated from the sixth German edition by Elias J. MacEwan as *Freytag's Technique of the Drama* (Chicago: S. C. Griggs, 1895; reissued, New York: Benjamin Blom, 1968).

calism in a play by Scribe as it is to see abstract formalism in a nude by Ingres. In both cases it remained only for others at a later date to develop the formalistic tendency into a new sort of aesthetic experience, letting the "realistic" subject matter go by the board.

The contribution of Scribean theater to realism has, for this reason, not been nearly so important as its contribution to antirealism. The social reality in Scribe's plays was never very real, and except for superficial topicality it was never intended to be. The plays' *élan* was due not to their seriousness but to their playability, and their audiences did not rejoice in the *discovery* of any reality but in the *pretense* of it. It is in the affection for pretending that one must see the well-made play's connection with modernism. This is a sophisticated view of the matter, to be sure, but modern theater *is* highly sophisticated and is often characterized by its ability to distill an essence from an outmoded form. Ostensibly holding the mirror up to reality, Scribean drama actually fled from it into a world of pure fabrication. While we may not dignify this by calling it the modern quest for reality, we are obliged to see it as a rejection of the given. In no profound sense did this drama ever rise to challenge the presuppositions of its audience, but in almost every true sense its spirit was directed away from the actual world. It was bastard romanticism, and its natural child was Hollywood. Its legitimate offspring, perversely unacknowledged, is the theatricalism of the modern stage, exemplified in playwrights as different as Shaw and Ionesco.

Alexandre Dumas, *fils* (1824–1895), though not nearly as prolific as Scribe, rivaled him in popularity. It was his ambition to turn the Scribean technique toward serious ends, to make of the *pièce bien faite* a *pièce à thèse*. "The dramatic author who would know *man* like Balzac and the *theatre* like Scribe," he said, "would be the greatest dramatic author that ever existed." Dumas therefore took up the social problems of his day, mostly problems of values and social propriety, as he saw them. *Le Demi-monde* (1855)[6] pondered the "shadow society" of courtesans and their entry into the respectable life of Paris. *La Question d'argent* (1857; "The Money Question") dealt with capitalist finance. *Le Fils naturel* (1858;

6 The title is idiomatic and untranslatable. Literally "The Half-World," it has sometimes been rendered as *The Outer Edge of Society*.

"The Natural Son"), often called the first real thesis play, presented a picture of illegitimacy quite at odds with dramatic and literary cliché. *Une Visite de noces* (1871; "A Honeymoon Call") and *La Princesse Georges* (1871) both offered novel twists upon the marriage-triangle theme.

Dumas seems not to have realized that artistic form and content are inseparable. Balzac's *man*, even if Dumas had understood him, would be somebody else in Scribe's theater. What actually attracted Dumas in Scribe's play structure was its logic, which was indeed its primary feature and which was quite self-contained. In Dumas' work this logic had the effect of rendering the characters and situations abstract. He wrote his plays backward, planning first the dénouement and then constructing the forepart to lead to it. Nothing could be further from romanticism's ideal of "organic form." Thus, what finally carries is the artificiality, and although Dumas deserves some credit for having attempted a serious theater, the adjective, applied to his plays, makes us wince. Owing so much to Scribe, he never emerged from his shadow. *La Femme de Claude* (1873; "Claude's Wife"), in which Dumas attempted a symbolic work, is not impressive.

Émile Augier (1820–1889), who sometimes wrote with one eye fastened on Dumas, and who learned many tricks from Scribe, wrote only one work that is clearly of the well-made type: *Le Mariage d'Olympe* (1855; "Olympe's Marriage"). Most of his output was more original and will concern us later when we come to the growth of realism. Where originality like his was lacking, the marks of the well-made play predominated, as in François Poinsard, Paul Arène, Théodore Barrière, and Victor Séjour.

Scribean theater fanned out into other countries. In England it evoked from Bulwer-Lytton a play called *Money* (1840), one sign among others that the well-made play contained a hidden affinity with romanticism of the dream.[7] This was also shown by the work of Dion Boucicault (1820–1890), the Irish showman whose immensely popular, prolific output moved among plays of the Scribean type, melodrama, and a most naive kind of dream-romanticism. Less flamboyant, more narrowly Scribean, was T.W. (Tom) Robertson (1829–1871). Robertson's contribution to the growth of

[7] Another sign is that both types tend toward melodrama.

realism in English theater is often overrated. The realism he did advance had much more to do with stage décor and directing than with writing.

The Scribean inheritance came intact to Victorien Sardou (1831–1908), who carried it into the twentieth century and gave his name to an era of trivial theater that G. B. Shaw aptly christened "Sardoodledom." Sardou was industrious and single-minded, his one aim being to attract an audience and strengthen its attachment to respectable virtues. He was lucky to have good actors and a highly professional Paris theater to give his works the polish they needed—for instance, Sarah Bernhardt, for whom he conceived one vehicle after another. He was a force in the French theater throughout his career, which, like that of Scribe, survived unbroken while others' came and went. In 1891 he caused a tumult by attacking Robespierre in a play called *Thermidor*. Clemençeau had to take the matter to the Assembly, and on the second night, when Coquelin was on stage, the gallery interrupted the performance by blowing whistles. *Thermidor* will not excite anyone today, but such plays as *Les Pattes de mouche* (1860; published in English under the title *A Scrap of Paper*) may be read with amusement if one has time to squander. *La Tosca* (1887) was put to good use by Puccini, and *Madame sans-gêne* (1893; "Madam Devil-may-care"), once graced by Réjane, has recently served as a wide-screen vehicle for Sophia Loren.

Actually the style and spirit of Sardou tended toward farce. He himself realized this in what we are entitled to regard as his better moments. He revived the vaudeville. He also wrote farces on occasion, such as the risqué *Divorçons* (1880; *Let's Get a Divorce!*), which followed upon a law legalizing divorce in France.

Freer spirits turned more consistently to farce and with more abandon. Eugène Labiche (1815–1888), for one, wrote something like 150 entertainments between 1845 and 1875. The most famous of these is *Le Chapeau de paille d'Italie* (1851; *The Italian Straw Hat*), about the adventures of a poor fellow whose horse ate a lady's hat. It turns up ever and again on the modern stage, the product of that same Gallic clowning that has recently shown itself in *La Plume de ma tante* and in the stage version of *Irma la douce*. In *The Happiest of the Three* (1863) Labiche, acting on a suggestion of Francisque Sarcey,[8] turned the ever-present theme of adultery to farcical account, as also in *Célimare* (produced in 1863), written in collaboration with Delacour. In *Le Voyage de M. Perrichon* (1860; *M. Perrichon's Trip*) he took up Benjamin Franklin's dictum that people like those they help more than those they are helped by. *La Poudre aux yeux* (1861; *Dust in the Eyes*) makes fun of the masks people wear in society.

Sarcey was of the opinion that the farces of Labiche had very little in common with the well-made play. Perhaps he kept the genres too separated in his mind to recognize that the roots, and many of the techniques, are the same. As Marcel Achard later wrote of Georges Feydeau (1862–1921):

> [T]he events are linked together with the precision of a well-oiled machine. The *qui pro quo* precedes the imbroglio. Unexpected *coups de théâtre* superabound, follow one upon the other, and frequently become entangled . . . everything is regulated by an infallible geometry which marks the point of departure and traces the graph of the action.[9]

Farce has the advantage over the well-made play of making a more integral thematic use of its conventional contrivances. Labiche should be praised not, as he sometimes is, for injecting "a sense of purpose into the realm of farce" [10] but for realizing the farce in other people's sense of purpose.

Later in the century the farcical element in the well-made-play structure was emphasized by Georges Courteline (real name Georges Moineaux, 1860–1929) and Georges Feydeau. Of the two, Courteline is the more delicate (if that is the word) and the more specifically French in his dependence on nuances of the language and upon local customs, which he satirized neatly. No doubt this was what commended him to André Antoine, who produced his *Boubouroche* at the Théâtre Libre in 1893. Others of his plays,

8 Drama critic for *Le Temps* from 1867 to 1899. In 1863 he was critic for *L'Opinion nationale*. Sarcey, a champion of Scribe and Sardou, was a firm advocate of the well-made play.
9 Achard's essay on Feydeau, originally the introduction to Feydeau's *Théâtre complet* (Paris: Belier, 1948), is reprinted in Eric Bentley, ed., *Let's Get a Divorce! and Other Plays*, Mary Douglas Dirks, trans. (New York: Hill and Wang, 1958). The quotation is from p. 357.
10 Nicoll, *op. cit.*, p. 496.

such as *Les Boulingrins* (translated by Eric Bentley as *These Corn-fields*) were done at the Grand Guignol. His characters often had the unhappy but comic fate of running afoul of the courts, as in *Un Client serieux* (1897), or the military, as in *Lidoire* (1891). The law itself was the source of fun in *L'Article 330* and *Le Gen-darme sans pitié* (1899; *The Pitiless Policeman*).

Courteline said, "I have the ambition to be the man in France who has the most good sense." In Feydeau, however, the love of pure invention reigned, and although he was a keen observer of life, his observations were those of a dreamer who turned his re-ports into self-contained structures of comic energy. Achard quotes the description of him by Robert de Flers:

> [H]e was a poet: for who knew better than he the wealth of fantasy, as well as disenchantment, that hovers in the smoke-rings of a cigar? Through this gossamer cloud, he observed people, as it were, with an attentive absence of mind. He dreamed constantly. And, be-cause the stars seemed too far away, the moonlight too pale, and the ideal a bit weary, he dreamed of life—and that is why he seldom smiled.[11]

Feydeau himself said that he owed everything to his indolence. As a boy he was smitten with a love of the stage and wrote a play which so pleased his father that he was let off from doing his lessons that day.

> Instantly, I beheld the road to salvation. From that blessed day on, whenever I forgot to do my homework or to learn my lessons (believe me, this sometimes happened) I flung myself upon my notebook of plays, and my governess, nonplused, left me in peace. People are not sufficiently aware of the uses of dramaturgy.[12]

To this "indolence," and later perhaps to the many debts Feydeau ran up, we owe a large output of manic plays that send audiences into waves of ever-increasing laughter. *Champignol malgré lui* (produced in 1892; "Toad-Stool in Spite of Himself") ran for 1,000 performances, *Monsieur Chasse* ("Mister Run-for-it") rang up 927, starting the same year. Later came *L'Hôtel du Libre-Exchange* (1894; done on Broadway in 1957 as *Hotel Paradiso* with Bert

[11] Quoted in *Let's Get a Divorce!*, Bentley, ed., p. 354.
[12] *Ibid.*, p. 351.

Lahr), *Mais n'Te promène donc pas toute nue* ("Don't Walk Around All Naked Like That"), and many, many more. Best known in America is *Occupe-toi d'Amélie* (1908; "Keep an Eye on Amélie"), especially in the version by Noel Coward, *Look After Lulu,* which was a vehicle for Tammy Grimes in 1959.

In his last period Feydeau concentrated on the weak, stupid male married to the shrew. He thought of publishing several plays on this situation under the title "From Marriage to Divorce." Achard comments, "If the author had not made these ill-mated couples pass before fun-house mirrors that warp and magnify, they would be Strindberg characters." [13]

In farce the virtues of the well-made play, which are essentially theatrical, found their best popular expression, unless we consider the transformation they underwent at the hands of Ibsen and Shaw. Just because farce knew how to abandon itself to theatricalism it achieved a more penetrating view of society than did most of the "straight" plays of the time. Whereas the Scribean play was actually escapist under the guise of topical seriousness, French farce often turned out to be severely critical under the guise of escapism. The theatrical mirror inverts all functions.

The chief interest of the well-made play, then, lies in its theatricalism. Perceiving this, one is prepared to turn to the transformations in theater practice that have constituted one of the main preoccupations and greatest achievements of the modern theater.

13 *Ibid.,* p. 363.

5. THE REVOLUTION IN THEATRICAL MEANS

It is characteristic of theater reform that all serious effort is instinctively directed toward the *mise en scène*. —ADOLPHE APPIA

Si, au long de l'histoire, nous nous penchons sur les metamorphoses du théâtre, nous nous apercevons que, chaque fois, le théâtre tout entier est remis en question. . . . —SYLVAIN DHOMME

THE PLAYHOUSE MOST FAMILIAR TODAY—with its orchestra seats, balconies, proscenium arch, stage, wings, fly galleries, and artificial light—was an invention of the Italian Renaissance. From 1580, when Palladio began construction of the Teatro Olimpico in Vicenza, until the 1860's, the history of theater architecture and stage practice, though never without interest, contained no radical departures. Tradition reigned. It was by no means a static tradition. It allowed room for modification. Changes in taste could be reflected in varying styles of stage décor. Yet this tradition, passing from one generation to the next, determined the *ambiance* of the theatrical houses and formed the general conception of what a theater was supposed to be. Its architecture was essentially that of the Italian opera house, the lines of which were already foreshadowed in the Olimpico; the stage setting was arranged in the drop-and-wing manner (this in contrast to the Olimpico but still in harmony with Italian Renaissance painting); and the methods of acting and the actors' movements on stage were worked out by the company itself, sometimes headed by an actor-manager, with only such unity of conception as guidance by precedent afforded.

The modern theater is notable for having changed all that. Not in every particular, to be sure, and not so completely that we can speak of a disappearance of the tradition, yet more radically, more thoroughly, and with more conscious purpose than during three previous centuries. This change has profoundly altered the atmosphere of our theaters, the quality of experience one hopes to find there, even the very meaning of "theater."

We owe this change quite specifically to the modern spirit in drama characterized by the search for reality. The tradition of theater design and usage was a "given" which had to be alienated, set apart, in some manner rejected. This could happen only with the growth of historical consciousness.

Theatrical traditions die hard. The theater, being a social institution as well as an art, responds more slowly than most other arts to innovations in form. For this reason the growing historical consciousness of the late eighteenth and early nineteenth centuries was not reflected in theater practice until after it had made its appearance in other parts of culture and in a number of playwrights. Nevertheless, it finally came to those who staged plays as well as to those who wrote them, and when it did it put the entire conception of theater into question, calling for its reconstitution in such a way that it might become a serviceable instrument in the quest for a hitherto unperceived and perhaps unformed reality. A renewal of the theater began. By the end of the nineteenth century it had brought into being new modes of acting, new types of architecture, new concepts of setting and décor, and new methods of organizing and rehearsing the play, not to mention the profound effect it had upon playwriting itself; and this renewal is still going on today.

The first signs of change came, naturally enough, in a romantic concern with the past. They showed themselves in attempts to achieve authenticity in period costumes for historical plays. This concern, which is commonplace now, was then quite new. Although certain gestures had formerly been made in the direction of historical costuming, it had been thought sufficient if the costumes were merely different from contemporary clothing. What now began to happen was the application of historical research to the question of what an actor in a historical play should wear. On the surface of it, this was simply the theater manager's picking up a technique offered him by contemporary scholarship, but it also contained the germ of a more far-reaching principle—namely, that the theater might become flexible and transparent, yielding its immediate "presence" to whatever vision the playwright desired to arrange, and this not only with words but with the theater's entire physical apparatus.

Some of the early efforts at versimilitude betray a naïve sort of dream-romanticism. Here is how Charles Kean described his décor for *The Winter's Tale* at the Princess's Theatre in 1856:

> It is evident that when an attempt is made to combine truth with history, conflicting epochs cannot all be illustrated; and I have therefore thought it permissible to select a period which, while it accords with the spirit of the play, may be considered the most interesting, as well as the most instructive.
>
> The pivot on which the story revolves, is in fact the decision pronounced by the oracle of Delphi; and taking this incident as the corner stone of the whole fabric, I have adopted a period when Syracuse, according to Thucydides, had, from a mere Doric colony, increased in magnificence to a position in no way inferior to that of Athens herself, when at the summit of her political prosperity. An opportunity is thus afforded of reproducing a classical era, and placing before the eyes of the spectator, *tableaux vivants* of the private and public life of the ancient Greeks, at a time when the arts flourished to a perfection, the scattered vestiges of which still delight and instruct the world. . . .
>
> To connect the country known as "Bohemia" with an age so remote, would be impossible: I have therefore followed the suggestion of Sir Thomas Hammer, in his annotations on Shakespeare, by the substitution of Bithynia. The difference of name in no way affects the incidents or metre of the play, while it enables me to represent the costume of the inhabitants of Asia Minor at a corresponding period, associated so intimately with Greece, and acquiring additional interest from close proximity to the Homeric kingdom of Troy.[1]

Reminding us that in the fourth act Shakespeare brings on stage twelve rustics who "call themselves Satyrs," Kean explains,

> I have here ventured to introduce one of those festivals in honour of Bacchus, known under the title of "Dionysia," wherein similar

[1] Quoted in Allardyce Nicoll, *The Development of the Theatre,* 3rd ed. (London: Harrap, 1948), p. 193.

disguises were used, while the actors indulged in mad enthusiasm and extravagant merriment.

For the purpose of presenting with closer accuracy the domestic manners of the period, Leontes and his Queen Hermione, together with their Kingly guest, are first discovered towards the termination of a *Feast*. . . . As dancing and music invariably formed a portion of such entertainments, a representation of the celebrated *Pyrrhic Dance,* so popular throughout the principal states of Greece for its martial character, has been attempted.[2]

And so on. It is obvious that by 1856 the taste for "historical" settings had become modish. Four decades earlier it had hardly been thought of.[3] In 1823, J. R. Planché, playwright and antiquarian, designed for Charles Kemble at Covent Garden the first thoroughly "historical" production of Shakespeare, a *King John* in which the entire cast was dressed according to period. This innovation paid off handsomely at the box office. Planché later reported:

When the curtain rose and discovered King John dressed as his effigy appears in Worcester Cathedral, surrounded by his barons sheathed in mail, with cylindrical helmets and correct armorial shields, and his courtiers in the long tunics and mantles of the thirteenth century, there was a roar of approbation, accompanied by four distinct rounds of applause, so general and so hearty, that the actors were astonished; . . . a complete reformation of dramatic costume became from that moment inevitable upon the English stage.[4]

The importance that Victor Hugo, champion of dream-romanticism, attached to stage atmosphere has already been noted. In 1817, at London, gas lighting was introduced to the theater. The candlelight it replaced had been in use since late in the sixteenth century, when drama had first begun to occupy indoor thea-

2 *Ibid.*
3 At least not so far as costumes were concerned. There had been, to be sure, the so-called "illusionism" of P. J. de Loutherbourg, an Alsatian artist employed by Garrick in 1771 to decorate his plays at the Drury Lane. Loutherbourg got his effects with scene painting and did little with costume. In theater practice he is to be regarded as a pre-romantic, the precursor of a movement that took hold two generations after him.
4 Quoted in A. M. Nagler, *A Source Book in Theatrical History* (New York: Dover, 1959), p. 462.

ters. In 1846 an electric arc lamp was installed at the Paris Opera. By 1860 it was feasible to darken the auditorium during the performance, though this practice did not become widespread until later. Paul Fort (inaccurately) later claimed credit for this innovation, saying he introduced it at his Théâtre d'Art, founded in 1891. Antoine made the same claim for the Théâtre Libre, as did Lugné-Poe for L'Oeuvre. It is not known who actually started the practice, but it was certainly Wagner who first realized the great psychological difference this "plunge into darkness" made, and it was he who incorporated it fully into his concept of theater.

In addition to renewed costume design and exploitation of the possibilities inherent in artificial light, two other requirements had to be met before the stage could become a truly flexible instrument. The first of these was that drop-and-wing settings, which were essentially two-dimensional, had to be abandoned in a move toward some basically three-dimensional concept of the stage setting. The aim of this would be to place the actor within the set instead of leaving him to parade in front of a picture, for only thus could he be integrated fully into the instrumentality of the theater. The second requirement was that the actor had to be subordinated to the director. In fact, the director had to be invented and then gradually given the enormous power he holds today.

There is some evidence pointing to the use of a box set as early as 1794, but it is not conclusive. The first clear evidence points to 1832, when such a set was employed in London by the actress Mme. Vestris (Lucia Elizabeth Matthews, 1797–1856), who in the previous year had taken over the management of the Olympic. She was, incidentally, the first woman in history to be the lessee of a theater. In 1841 Mme. Vestris scored a success with the use of a box set for Boucicault's *London Assurance*. The side walls of rooms were built solidly from front to back so that the actors, instead of entering, as formerly, between side wings set parallel to the footlights, came in through doors set on hinges.

More than twenty years elapsed, however, before there appeared an embattled advocate of three-dimensional sets. He was Tom Robertson. From 1865 to 1871, at The Queen's Theatre in Tottenham Court Road, known as "the dust hole," Robertson, who was then writing popular plays in a somewhat realistic style, carried on a campaign for real doors on real hinges with knobs an actor could grasp. It is difficult to determine what he actually accomplished, but his doorknobs became famous.

Had Robertson lived longer (he died at forty-two), or had he argued his case more intelligently, he might have brought off a truly significant reform. In the event, it was left to Henry Irving definitely to establish the use of the box set on the English stage. In 1863 the family magazine *All the Year Round,* edited by Charles Dickens, carried a long protest against the drop-and-wing system still prevalent in England, contrasting it unfavorably with the Continental system of "raked flats" (arranged in the three-sided-box pattern and held up by braces) that Charles Fechter had instituted at the Lyceum, the theater Irving was to take in charge fifteen years later. In 1889, writing in *The Magazine of Art,* William Telbin, Jr., who was Irving's designer, showed that the system of painted wing pieces sliding in grooves was passé. Irving had gone over to the "new" method and carried London with him. By 1899, E. O. Sachs, in his *Modern Opera Houses and Theatres,* could say that "the brace is the method which has superseded the grooves."

The shift to a new ground plan for the set was accompanied by a demand for the use of more "practical" pieces *within* the set—solid objects of three dimensions instead of facsimiles painted on the scenery. Strindberg, in his foreword to *Miss Julie,* described the need:

> I have . . . kept to a single set, both in order to let the characters develop in their métier and to break away from over-decoration. When one has only one set, one may expect it to be realistic; but as a matter of fact nothing is harder than to get a stage room that looks something like a room, however easily the scene painter can produce flaming volcanoes and water-falls. Presumably the walls must be of canvas but it seems about time to dispense with painted shelves and cooking utensils. We are asked to accept so many stage conventions that we might at least be spared the pain of painted pots and pans.

No longer having to plead for a box set, Strindberg went further and asked for an asymmetrical one. He wanted the room to be shown at an angle and shown only in part, so that "our imagination is stirred into complementing our vision." He wanted the stage not only to convey the depth of a stereopticon picture but also to reveal itself as *space*. He knew that if the stage is regarded as usable space then it can be employed not only to increase the illusion of reality but also to assist the actor, to whom space for movement is as important as words for speaking.

Strindberg wrote the preface to *Miss Julie* in 1883 for the premier of the play at Antoine's Théâtre Libre in Paris. This was the veritable headquarters of naturalism, yet the conception of the stage as an enclosed three-dimensional space was to prove quite as important for anti-realism as for naturalistic and realistic drama.

Emphasis upon the actor as one who moves in a defined space had much to do with the rise of that figure of the modern theater called in America the director, in England the producer, and most accurately designated by the French as the *metteur en scène*. It was a heightened awareness, even a self-consciousness, about the theater as instrument and the stage (*scène*) as usable space that necessitated there being a person whose task it was to place the work upon or *into* the stage.

As long as the actor's use of the stage was determined by the old tradition, and as long as scene design remained within the bounds of a more or less conventional practice, the power of the modern director was not needed. Some member of the company, perhaps called the stage manager, could preserve order and get the play rehearsed. In the eighteenth century the so-called actor-manager came into being, and in the nineteenth he dominated most theaters. He was a star performer who gathered a company about him which he "managed," most often with the sole intent of giving support to his own performances. This system prevented chaos, encouraged training by apprenticeship, and had other virtues, but what it could not do was to integrate the leading performer himself into the theatrical instrument, for its purpose was the contrary— namely, to ensure that the theater would function as an extension of the star's individual capacities. The actor-manager invented many of the techniques the director proper would later use, and he set the precedent of there being a clear "authority figure"; but before the director as such could appear there had to be a new motivation, and that came with the concept of theater as *instrument* and its corollary that the actor is an extension of the theater's capacities, not the other way around.

Since the renewal of the theater emphasized the stage as three-dimensional space, the movement of the actor within that space became an aesthetic problem. If it was to be solved in a manner consistent with the notion of the theater as a single (though complex) instrument, the actor would have to be subordinated to another authority. It is no accident that this was first made clear to all Europe by a company that excluded star performers, was ruled by martial discipline, and was sponsored by a monarch, the Duke of Saxe-Meiningen, to whom the aesthetics of theater meant everything.

Thuringia in central Germany, with Meiningen as its capital, was no theatrical center such as Berlin, Paris, or London. Perhaps that was one of the reasons why Duke George II (1826–1914), when he took the troupe under supervision in 1866, determined to make it a company second to none, dedicating it to the talents of no actor-manager but to theatrical art as such. The repertory of his group contained few new plays, an indication that the emphasis was to fall heavily on the practice of theater rather than upon writing. The favored authors were Shakespeare and Schiller. In addition to the keen historical sense that artistic production of their works required there was the additional requirement of large casts. Thus were set the twin goals of authenticity in atmosphere and ensemble work in playing. The latter, especially in the frequent crowd scenes, required close attention to the movements of actors within the stage space, and it was for the management of this that the company became famous.

When the Meininger appeared in London in 1881, the critic of the *Athenaeum* compared their work with that of the English:

> There are few intelligent English playgoers . . . who would not be thankful for the chance of seeing constantly upon our boards representations such as German actors have now brought within our reach. . . .
>
> In the case of 'Julius Caesar' the most noteworthy features consisted of the arrangement of the tableaux and the disposition of the supernumeraries when, as in the case of the oration of Antony

over the body of Caesar, strong and growing emotion has to be expressed. From the picturesque standpoint these things were perfect. That they were wholly natural is less clear. . . .

A performance, however, of 'Twelfth Night' so picturesque and so faultless has not been seen upon the modern English stage. A chief reason why 'Twelfth Night' is rarely played in England is because there is no part prominent enough to suit the vanity of a star actor. The harmony and beauty which are the chief features in the performance of 'Twelfth Night' are impossible under the conditions ordinarily prevailing in England, and can never be obtained while the vanity of the individual is allowed to override the requirements of art.[5]

The Meininger toured Europe from 1874, when they had a great success in Berlin, until 1890, everywhere leaving a troubled wake of admiration and dissent. In 1888, the year after he founded the Théâtre Libre, Antoine saw the Meininger in Brussels. He was critical of many points, as we would expect the leader of theater reform in Paris to be, but he was also deeply impressed:

The Meiningen Company consists of some sixty-six artists of both sexes. All those who do not play a speaking part are required to appear nightly as supernumeraries in the play. If twenty players are cast for essential roles, the remaining fifty must, without exception, appear on the stage in ensemble scenes. In this manner, even those who are leading actors in their particular fields are each placed in charge of a group of supernumeraries whom they direct and supervise as long as the group is on stage. This obligation is so binding that when Hans von Bülow's wife, one of the leading actresses of the troupe, refused to meet it, saying she found it unworthy of her talents, she was dismissed, even though her husband was conductor for the Duke of Saxe-Weimar. The incident provoked such a quarrel that Bülow himself left the ducal court.

In this way the Meininger achieve ensemble scenes that are extraordinary lifelike.[6]

Antoine said that the Meininger's crowd scenes had "capitally perfected" the "mechanics of stage groupings." Indeed, he thought

---

[5] Quoted in Nagler, *op. cit.,* pp. 499–501.
[6] Letter to Francisque Sarcey, quoted in Nagler, *op. cit.,* p. 580.

some of it *too* mechanical, as had the English critics, and he came up with suggestions for improvement. The Duke of Saxe-Meiningen had said that it is "always an advantage to have an actor touch a piece of furniture or some other nearby object naturally. That enhances the impression of reality." [7] Antoine, of all people, complained that "they overdo the use of practicables, putting them everywhere." [8] He remarked favorably, however, on their lighting effects, which were electrical and included scenic projections.

The effects of the Meininger performances could be brought about only through iron discipline. To provide it the Duke employed a director named Kronek. Earlier in the same year that Antoine saw the troupe in Brussels it had visited Moscow, where the methods of Kronek were observed with fascination by the then young Stanislavski. Already concerned with the actor's internalization of his role, Stanislavski deplored the lack of attention Kronek paid to this matter, but he was mightily impressed by the director's supreme control, which he said "created a tremendous mood by itself and went down to the soul of the play." Here is his description, written years later, of how Kronek worked:

> Outside of the theatre Kronek's relations even with the third-rate actors of his company were simple and friendly. He even seemed to flaunt this simplicity of conduct. But as soon as a rehearsal began and Kronek mounted his usual place, he would be reborn. He sat in complete silence and waited for the hands of the clock to reach the time allotted for the beginning of the rehearsal. Then he would ring a large bell and declare in a quiet voice, *"Anfangen."* Everything quieted down. The rehearsal would begin at once and continue until he rang the bell again. Then he would make his remarks in a dispassionate voice, ring the bell again, repeat the fatal *"Anfangen,"* and the rehearsal would continue.
>
> And now there was an unexpected stop and confusion on the stage. The actors whispered, the stage managers ran about. Something seemed to have happened. One of the leading actors was late, and it was necessary to leave his scene out. One of the stage managers tells this to Kronek and waits for his orders near the prompter's box. Everybody is quiet. Kronek tires them out with a long pause. This pause seems to be endless, threatening. Kronek

7 John Gassner, *Form and Idea in Modern Theatre* (New York: Dryden, 1956), p. 20.
8 Quoted in Nagler, *op. cit.*, p. 582.

pauses, decides, while everybody stands as if awaiting sentence. At last he pronounces:

"While we are in Moscow the roles of the actor who is late will be played by actor Y, and as far as X is concerned, I will let him lead the mob actors in the rear. *Anfangen!*" [9]

The impressionable Stanislavski began to imitate Kronek's despotism and was in turn imitated by all the young directors of Moscow. He wrote,

> Only with time, as I began to understand the wrongness of the principle of the director's despotism, I valued that good which the Meiningen Players brought us, that is, their director's methods for showing the spiritual contents of the drama. . . . My gratitude to them is unbounded and will always live in my soul.[9a]

The drive to realize the full three-dimensionality of the stage had two aspects. Its aesthetic side would in a short time be developed in an austere, not to say abstract, way by designers such as Gordon Craig and Adolphe Appia and by directors such as Vsevolod Meierhold. Its ideological side, however, at least at first, was in accord with nineteenth-century positivism. As we speak of the actor's integration into the stage space, we may also speak of the integration of the character into his environment. These are two sides of the same coin. The latter has its roots in nineteenth-century Darwinism, sociology, and socialism, according to which the meaning of human character is found in its interaction with the physical, social, and economic environment. Obviously if such interaction is to be represented on the stage, the theatrical resources must be employed to create not only the appearance but also the atmosphere of the environment, the milieu. The person who saw this point earlier and more clearly than others was Émile Zola (1840–1902), and the one who did most to establish it in theater practice was André Antoine (1858–1943).

In 1873 Zola's *Thérèse Raquin*, adapted from his novel, was produced on the stage. The preface Zola then wrote for it, a sort of manifesto for naturalism in the theater, showed his theoretical in-

9 & 9a Konstantin Stanislavski, *My Life in Art*, J. J. Robbins, trans. (New York: Meridian, 1956), pp. 198–201.

tent. It also displayed Zola's temperament, at once romantic and quasi-scientific. Confessing that his play did not attain to the excellence he had hoped, Zola wrote:

> [I]f I were to criticize it, there would be only one thing I should not attack: the author's very obvious desire to bring the theater into closer relation with the great movement toward truth and experimental science which has since the last century been on the increase in every manifestation of the human intellect. The movement was started by the new methods of science; thence, Naturalism revolutionized criticism and history, in submitting man and his works to a system of precise analysis, taking into account all circumstances, environment, and "organic cases."
>
> In the theater, every innovation is a delicate matter. . . . But there comes a time when the public itself becomes an accomplice of the innovators; this is when, imbued with the new spirit, weary of the same stories repeated to it countless times, it feels an imperious desire for youth and originality.[10]

Zola expressed his conviction that "the experimental and scientific spirit of the century will enter the domain of drama." He said:

> We must look to the future, and the future will have to do with the human problem studied in the frame-work of reality. We must cast aside fables of every sort, and delve into the living drama of the two-fold life of the character and its environment, bereft of every nursery tale, historical trapping, and the usual conventional stupidities.

"The drama," he declared, "will either die, or become modern and realistic." [11]

What all this meant for the structure, style, and content of plays will concern us in the next chapter. At the moment we will trace its influence on theater practice. Zola, as critic and essayist even more than as dramatist, joined a battle in which he would not compromise. He would not dignify with the name of realism stage sets showing, in whatever degree of accuracy, Athens in glory or Rome in ruins. Romance of the dream he rejected absolutely. And

10 Translated in Barrett H. Clark, ed., *European Theories of the Drama* (New York: Crown, 1947), pp. 400–401.
11 *Ibid.*

he saw the Scribean skeleton under all the social padding in Dumas *fils*. He wanted to get rid of all posturing and show life as it grows *in situ*. In 1884 M. Becq de Fouquières, in the first modern French work treating seriously the problems of theater practice (*Essais d'une esthetique de la mise en scène*), wrote that the naturalist school "is entirely contained in the theory of the *milieux*." [12] As Zola put it: "Men submitted to facts and producing facts, that is the true theatre. . . ." [13] In 1886 the *Revue d'art dramatique* was founded. Its aim was to bring about a basic revision of theater practice. The following year Antoine founded the revolutionary Théâtre Libre.

Antoine was then an amateur. Earning his living as an employee of the gas company, he had been in charge of a little amateur group called Les Baulois, who put on Scribe, Labiche, and historical dramas. He founded the Théâtre Libre on pure enthusiasm and saw it fold, penniless, after seven years. Yet he himself rose to the top of the profession, passing from the Théâtre Libre to its successor, the Théâtre Antoine, and finally becoming director of the Odéon. He was his own teacher, and he changed the modern theater by insisting, as Brecht did later, that it should simply tell "the truth."

Finding that Les Baulois were hostile to new ideas and new scripts, Antoine broke with them to establish his own theater, also composed of amateurs. Working on a shoe-string budget for an audience, never large, composed of invited guests and a few subscribers, the Théâtre Libre mounted eight productions a year, most of which were given only two or three performances. A few moved briefly to larger Paris theaters. There were short tours abroad, on the last of which, in Rome in 1894, the company foundered for lack of funds.

The first offering took place on Wednesday, March 30, 1887, at the little rented theater on the Passage de l'Élysée des Beaux Arts (Place Pigalle). The card of invitation, marked *rigorously personal*, announced an evening of four short plays: *Jacques Damour*, the *pièce de résistance*, drawn from a story by Zola; two comedies;

---

[12] Quoted in Sylvain Dhomme, *La Mise en scène d'Antoine à Brecht* (Paris: Fernand Nathan, 1959), p. 33.
[13] *Ibid.*, p. 34.

and a drama in one act by Arthur Byl called *Un Préfet*—all in prose. In the audience were Daudet, Mallarmé, and the critic Jules Lemaître. Lemaître noted that "the stage was so narrow that it could be dressed only with elementary settings. And it was so close to us that scenic illusion was impossible." [14] Antoine played Jacques Damour, with "long silences." Sometimes he turned his back to the audience. "Make-up, clothing, bearing, gestures, expression, everything was true and seizing." [15] The press announced the arrival of a new theater, and thirty days later there was a second program: *En Famille* ("In the Family") by Oscar Méténier, an author who later became a mainstay of the Grand Guignol. Sarcey, Rodin, and Coquelin were present.

The works Antoine chose to present were remarkably varied for a man whose credo was "the truth" and whose reputation would have it that all his "truth" was naturalism. In the first months he chose plays by the poets Banville and Villiers de L'Isle Adam. Then in February he presented Leo Tolstoi's *The Power of Darkness*, hitherto thought by French opinion, including that of Augier, Dumas *fils*, and Sardou, to be unplayable. In June (1888) the theater was moved to the Boulevard de Strasbourg. Antoine visited Brussels, where he saw the Meininger, and London, where he saw Henry Irving. Returning, he proceeded to introduce to Paris the greatest living playwrights from abroad: Hauptmann, Strindberg, Ibsen, and Björnson. Also Turgenyev, who had died in 1883. He mounted dramas by Georges de Porto-Riche, Edmond de Goncourt, François de Curel, and Eugène Brieux, but also a farce (*Boubourouche*) by Courteline. After he established the Théâtre Antoine (1896–1906), his offerings included more Courteline, *Poil de Carotte* by Jules Renard (1900; "Carrot-Top"), *La Perisienne* (1885; "The Woman of Paris") by Henri Becque, and *Le Marché* by Henri Bernstein. Also Shakespeare: Antoine spent two years preparing *King Lear*, then went on to do *Julius Caesar*, each of which he presented uncut for the first time in France.

Antoine's desire to fill the stage with real objects picked up "on location," so to speak, has been exaggerated, though it is true that

14 Quoted in *Encyclopédie du théâtre contemporain*, Gilles Quéant, gen. ed., Vol. I (Paris: Les Publications de France, 1957), p. 33. My translation.
15 *Ibid.*

for a play called *Les Bouchers* ("The Butchers") in 1888 he insisted on hanging sides of real meat dripping blood, and true also that in another play he used a stream of running water that splashed on some of the audience. The "truth" he sought, however, was more subtle than the caricature these incidents invited, and he certainly did not settle for equating "truth" with "facts." He was concerned, like Stanislavski, with the actor's "unique experience of his character." He was haunted continually by the problem of finding the right balance among the many elements of production. He was particularly attentive to the movement of the actor within the stage space. He believed that the secret of life lay in its motion. His fame has come to rest upon his realistic stage settings, but he himself was far more concerned with the *actor* as the one who should reveal the depth of the stage. He understood "depth" in both its literal and its figurative senses. He wrote:

> There are two ways of staging plays, that which I have called "plastic" (settings, costumes, accessories, lighting), and that which I will call "interior," and which is an art still unknown among us. The latter will be, in effect, the art of revealing the most intimate depth of the work, whatever this work has of psychological or philosophical mystery, by the movements which the actor must accomplish; where to place him and how to move him *so that these movements may be revelations of the mysterious "depths" of the action quite as much as of the words. Truth is only a beginning.*[16]

To describe his activity Antoine picked up from Zola the word "experimental." It is a word that appears throughout the subsequent history of the theater with ever more frequent use. In the third number of the bulletin called *Théâtre Libre*, Antoine echoed Zola's assertion that "the experimental and scientific spirit of the century" would "win over" the theater and that it carried "the only renewal possible for our stage." [17] He wrote that he wanted to create *un lieu d'essai*[18] and *un simple laboratoire*

16 Quoted in Dhomme, *op. cit.*, p. 44. Italics in original.
17 Quoted in André Veinstein, *Du Théâtre Libre au Théâtre Louis Jouvet* (Paris: Billaudot, 1955), p. 22.
18 *Théâtre Libre*, 1889.

d'essai.[19] The word "experimental" was to become the battle cry of every little theater and every innovator from Antoine to the present. "Laboratories," "workshops," and "projects" were to proliferate as if theater were essentially a kind of applied science. In spite of the pseudo-scientific jargon the analogy perhaps expresses the modern theater's restless search for a "truth" that lurks, as Antoine said, in the "mysterious depths" of the dramatic action.

To "experiment" in the theater has usually meant to break with whatever is the reigning style and method, and in the 1890's breaks were made in many directions. There was a veritable eruption of that modern spirit that insists on rejecting the "given." In poetry and painting it produced new vocabularies, styles, and iconographies, and in theater it did the same. In the wake of Antoine's Paris "experiment" Otto Brahm established the Freie Bühne in Berlin in 1889. J. T. Grein founded the Independent Theatre Society in London in 1891. Similar "independent," "free," and "experimental" groups were formed elsewhere. In Paris the Théâtre Libre provoked an immediate and perhaps more radical reaction in two new anti-realist theaters.

Paul Fort's Théâtre d'Art was short-lived and too "literary" for its own good, but it marked the first recoil from Antoine's theatrical naturalism, and it came only three years after the Théâtre Libre. It was begun June 24, 1890, as the Théâtre Mixte and became the Théâtre d'Art the next year. Its founder was seventeen years of age. Paul Fort believed that the true end of Antoine's program would be a kind of poetry of the mundane, at best something on the order of Dostoievski. But as there was no French playwright of that merit, Antoine was reduced, as Fort saw it, to using the "subnaturalism" of Méténier, Alexis, and other slight talents. Fort himself would take another tack, aiming directly for the poetry of the spoken word. But he found no French playwright to suit that objective either. He wanted a French Shakespeare, or a contemporary Musset to write another *Lorenzaccio*. What he found was Maeterlinck, whose work he did present, but for the rest he had to turn to the Elizabethans, to Shelley's *Cenci*, and to poems never meant for the theater: *Le Soleil de minuit* ("The Midnight Sun")

19 *Ibid.*, 1890.

by Catulle Mendès, *Le Concile féerique* ("The Fairy Council")
by Jules Laforgue, and a whole list of works by Mallarmé, Ver-
laine, Rimbaud, Edgar Allan Poe, and La Fontaine. Fragments of
Paradise Lost were staged.

One of Antoine's significant moves had been to enlist contemporary visual artists in the service of his theater—Toulouse-Lautrec,
for instance—but he used them mainly to design programs. Paul
Fort asked them to design his décors. He got beautiful work from
Vuillard, Bonnard, Maurice Denis, and others. That was one of the
clearest signs that the theater was being conceived as part of the
general artistic revolution of the times, taking its cues not primarily from an autonomous theatrical tradition but from the contemporary cultural ferment. The Théâtre d'Art, dedicated to *la gloire
du verbe*, had the unexpected result of introducing into the
theater a new visual aspect. Everyone commented on the exquisite
harmony it achieved between décors and costumes.

In March 1892 the Théâtre d'Art came to an end, the victim of
its own preciousness. The same year seeds were sown for the foundation of a more durable anti-naturalist theater: Le Théâtre de
l'Oeuvre. Its guiding spirit was Aurélien Lugné, better known as
Lugné-Poe, who had learned most of what he knew about theater
from Antoine, for whom he had worked as actor and director from
1888 to 1890. He was, however, of very different temperament from
Antoine, being something of a dandy and given to daydreams. He
took up with a group of young painters including Vuillard, Bonnard, and Denis, whom he met through Paul Fort and who called
themselves "inspired prophets."

At Paul Fort's theater Lugné-Poe also discovered Maeterlinck's
L'Intruse (The Intruder). His head swam, he later said, between
naturalism and symbolism. Like Antoine, he wished to employ the
theater in a search for truth. Unlike him, he wanted to give poetic
symbols an important place in the search. "We want to make
known some works in which the idea alone dominates," he said. He
declared his interest in "new and unexplored thought." That being the case, it is no accident that he was drawn to Ibsen, in whom
"the idea" seemed all-important and whose plays were somewhere
between naturalism and symbolism. "I left things to Lugné-Poe
. . . hoping that he would turn toward Shakespeare," said Paul

Fort, "but he chose the Nordics. Good choice, besides." [20] Toward the end of 1892, when he was directing a group called Le Cercle des Escholiers, Lugné-Poe mounted a production of Ibsen's *Lady from the Sea*. Three months later (May 1893) he directed Maeterlinck's *Pelléas et Mélisande*. Its décor was unrealistic and evocative, the visual equivalent of Maeterlinck's literary style. With the artistic success of this production L'Oeuvre came into existence.

Two plays of Ibsen were done the first season: *Rosmersholm* and *An Enemy of the People*. The tendency of Lugné-Poe was to play Ibsen as much as possible in the manner of Maeterlinck. He pointed up every possible symbol in the text and encouraged his actors to speak in a sort of liturgical recitation. For this and because of his personal manner Jules Lemaître called him "a sleepwalking clergyman." It took a trio of real Nordics to wake him up. Two Danes and a Norwegian came to Paris to assist with *Rosmersholm, An Enemy of the People,* and then *The Master Builder*. They taught Lugné-Poe how to put the emphasis on characterization, action, and movement, toning down all poetic affectations and the overextended search for symbols. In 1894 Lugné-Poe met Ibsen, who said to him, "An author of passion ought to be played with passion." [21] Thereafter the manner of playing Ibsen at L'Oeuvre settled into what Lugné-Poe called "mitigated realism," and this worked admirably.

In 1896 L'Oeuvre produced the savagely antinaturalistic play of Alfred Jarry, *Ubu roi* ("King Ubu"). In one stroke this production vindicated Lugné-Poe's whole quarrel with naturalism and also, paradoxically, marked his break with symbolism. However antinaturalist it is, *Ubu roi* has about it none of the murkiness of symbolist poetry. It is theater through and through. Surprising as it may seem, this outrageous work led L'Oeuvre to a more simple and direct kind of playing. At the same time it established in a theatrical way that freedom from the literal which the best modern theater demands and which L'Oeuvre would put to exciting use in Claudel's *L'Annonce faite à Marie* ("The Tidings Brought to Mary"), in 1912. That production, with décors by Jean Variot, was a historic landmark in the French theater, remarkable for the

---

20 Quoted in *Encyclopédie du théâtre contemporain*, Vol. I, p. 24. My translation.
21 *Ibid.*, p. 54. My translation.

grandeur of its effect achieved by an imaginative simplicity of means. By 1912 however, Variot and Lugné-Poe had fallen under the influence of Appia, Craig, and Fuchs, to whom we shall come after taking note of Stanislavski's work in Russia.

When Antoine founded the Théâtre Libre in Paris, Konstantin Stanislavski (1863–1938), whose real name was Konstantin Sergeievich Alexeyev, was putting on amateur theatricals at his parental estate near Moscow, directing a group he had got together under the name of the Alexeyev Circle. This activity, which in 1887 had been going on about ten years, had all the earmarks of a dilettante enterprise sponsored by the vanity of a young businessman accustomed by his upper-middle-class family to patronizing the arts. That is all it would have amounted to if Stanislavski, as he was beginning to call himself, had not been possessed of a fever to renovate the several arts of the theater. Though he was not highly intellectual, he did have the intellectual's trait of trying to get to the very bottom of any problem he encountered, and he found the state of the theater problematic indeed. The more he learned about it through self-education, the acting of many roles, and much observation of professionals, the more it seemed to him that the theater was a bundle of dead habits that nobody bothered to examine. This was not true of really great talents one could sometimes see, such as Eleonora Duse and Tommaso Salvini (both Italian) and Fyodor Chaliapin. But no one seemed to know what could help persons of lesser talent to become creative. In short, the theatrical tradition was unreflective, and Stanislavski's task was to lay it open to critique. Rejecting the given for the sake of the new, his motto became, at least for a time, "All that can lead away from the Old is correct." [22]

At the end of 1888 Stanislavski moved his dramatic activity into Moscow, where he helped to found the Society of Art and Literature and took personal charge of its theatrical wing. Here he worked for ten years, managing his business affairs on the side (as he continued to do right up until the Soviet Revolution), mounting some 60 productions, and beginning to formulate his ideas on acting and directing. In the spring of '88 observations of the

[22] *My Life in Art*, p. 332.

Meininger troupe convinced him that unity of conception imposed by a strong directorial hand was indispensable, but even at that time he was already looking for another kind of unity as well— namely, that which an actor might be trained to bring to the integration of his role. The unity of the actor's person, it seemed to Stanislavski, ought to find an ideal meeting with the unity of the character he portrayed. If this could happen, it would relieve the actor of the necessity to piece out his performance from the traditional repertory of gestures and inflections. It was for this unity, regarding which the acting tradition seemed mute, that Stanislavski searched, and the famed "method" that he evolved was nothing other than the marks he laid out along his path of inquiry.

In 1896 Stanislavski became acquainted with Vladimir Nemirovich-Danchenko, dramatist, director, teacher, and critic, with whose work he had long been familiar but with whom he now for the first time began to associate. Stanislavski's description of him testifies to the ideal unity in theatrical art that both men sought:

> The theatre, which performs a cultural mission, demands of the persons engaged in it very much. To be the director of such an establishment one must be a talented expert in his own field, that is, understand art not only as a critic, but as an actor, a stage director, a producer, a literateur, an administrator. One must know the theatre not only theoretically, but practically. One must know the construction of the stage, the architecture of the theatre itself; one must know the psychology of the mob, understand the nature and the psychology of the actor, the conditions of his creative work and life; one must have a wide literary education, tact, sensitivity, breeding, restraint, mind, administrative abilities and much, much more. It is seldom that all these qualities are met with in one person. But they met in Vladimir Nemirovich-Danchenko.[23]

"In May or in June, 1897," Stanislavski wrote in his autobiography, "I received a note from Nemirovich-Danchenko, inviting me to a conference in the restaurant 'The Slavic Bazaar.'" [24] The meeting lasted from ten o'clock in the morning until three the

[23] *Ibid.*, p. 293.
[24] *Ibid.*, p. 294.

next, some seventeen hours of uninterrupted work, during which the foundations of the Moscow Art Theater were laid. Nemirovich-Danchenko was to have the veto over all literary matters, Stanislavski over those of artistic representation,

The theater opened a year and four months later on October 14, 1898, at the Hermitage Theater in Karetny Row. The opening production was *Tsar Fyodor*, a historical play by Alexis Tolstoi (1817–1875) written in 1868. Like all the "typical" plays of this theater's first eight years, according to Stanislavski, *Tsar Fyodor* continued the line of work done at the Society of Art and Literature, which means that it owed a great deal to the example of the Meininger. Stanislavski being still very much the autocratic director, the production made up in striking effect what it could not deliver in depth of interpretation. In view of the historical importance of the drive toward full three-dimensionality in the use of the stage, Stanislavski's description of the opening scene of *Tsar Fyodor* is worth quoting:

> The first scene was that of a feast in the home of Prince Shuisky to which he has invited his friends for the purpose of signing a demand that the Tsar divorce the Tsarina. The feasts of Boyars had old and outworn stencils on the stages of Russia. It was necessary to avoid these stencils at any and all costs. Therefore, true to my revolutionary principle, "the New at all costs," I placed this scene "on the roof" as the actors said. The left side of the stage was turned into a covered terrace with large wooden columns in the Russian style. It was separated from the footlights by a balustrade, which hid the lower halves of the bodies of the Boyars who sat and stood behind it. This gave a certain piquancy to the scene. The right half of the stage pictured the roofs of Moscow, the towers and the domes of the medieval city losing themselves in perspective. This gave a great deal of atmosphere and picturesqueness to the setting, and the terrace, which was only half as wide as the stage, did away with the employment of any great number of supernumeraries. If the feast had been shown on the whole stage, it would have looked but thin with the small number of extras we had at our disposal, due to our poverty.
>
> The covered terrace twisted backstage around a corner of the house and was lost in the wings. At the turning point there sat

many of the actors and supernumeraries, creating movement and gravitation from the stage to the wings, and giving an illusion of distance and free space to the whole scene.[25]

Another scene took place on a bridge:

> From the first wing on the left which pictured the highway, a log bridge was thrown to the last wing on the right where it descended to earth again. Under the bridge one saw a river, sailboats, rowboats. On the bridge was an endless procession of the most variegated figures dressed in the costumes of the ancient provinces of central Russia.[26]

Nothing here sounds revolutionary today, and to tell the truth the show provided only a momentary effectiveness at the time, yet the description shows that Stanislavski was experimenting with ways of setting the stage so as to achieve the greatest illusion of depth with the most economical of means and, more important, that he wanted to impart a sense of life overflowing the stage.

The second production, a week later, was *The Merchant of Venice*. (What Stanislavski's imagination did with the bridges of Venice he does not say.) The group's first real triumph came with its fourth production, on December 17, Chekhov's *The Sea Gull*. The Moscow Art Theater owed its good fortune with this play primarily to the insistence of Nemirovich-Danchenko, who had to persuade both the company and the author that *The Sea Gull*, which earlier had failed dismally in St. Petersburg, should be attempted once more, and by a group still feeling its way.

Nemirovich-Danchenko's instinct was absolutely right, but from the point of view of theater history it is significant that neither he nor Stanislavski understood Chekhov's play. Stanislavski confessed as much right from the start. He took on the role of the writer Trigorin partly at Chekhov's suggestion, but Chekhov's famous laconic remark to him upon seeing the play—"you need torn shoes and checkered trousers"—was in fact a condemnation of Stanislavski's entire interpretation of the part. Later Chekhov was to be furious at the director for his misinterpretation of *The Cherry Or-*

25 *Ibid.*, pp. 335–336.
26 *Ibid.*, p. 337.

chard as a tragedy, and he was constantly objecting to the realistic details—frogs, mosquitoes, crying babies—that Stanislavski insisted on adding to the script. As for Nemirovich-Danchenko, he saw in *The Sea Gull* only its depiction of contemporary Russian life, its deeper meaning having apparently escaped him.[27]

This misunderstanding, like Lugné-Poe's early misinterpretation of Ibsen, points to an important fact: the renovation of theater practice in the 1890's was by no means taking place simply as a response to the new playwrights. It had its own distinct motivation, and it followed a course that met the demands of the best new writing only at certain points. Without the Moscow Art Theater, Chekhov's *Sea Gull* would probably have remained long in oblivion, and he would probably have written neither *The Three Sisters* nor *The Cherry Orchard*. Without *The Sea Gull* the Moscow Art Theater would likely have folded during its first season. But this does not mean that the Moscow Art Theater was molded, even in its Chekhovian productions, to the mind of Chekhov. The ideal unity between dramatist and theater remained ideal, and the search for its realization has continued to be a prime motivation of the modern theater.

The Moscow Art Theater became famous for its realism. In the pursuit of the actual, Stanislavski and Nemirovich-Danchenko made extensive field trips to gather data. In preparation for the 1902 production of Shakespeare's *Julius Caesar,* for instance, they went to Rome, where they made faithful drawings of architectural monuments to reproduce in detail on the Moscow stage. "Of course," as Marc Slonim has said, "underneath all this attachment to realistic detail was the feeling of love, devotion, and romantic dedication." [28] Stanislavski denied that he and his colleagues ever intended to be naturalistic. "We never leaned towards such a principle," he said.

> Always . . . we sought for inner truth, . . . but as spiritual technique [*sic*] was only in its embryo stage among the actors of our company, we, because of necessity and helplessness, and

27 Ernest J. Simmons, *Chekhov* (Boston: Little, Brown, 1962), p. 429.
28 *Russian Theater from the Empire to the Soviets* (New York: Collier Books, 1962), p. 123.

against our desires, fell now and then into an outward and
coarse naturalism.[29]

Stanislavski's vocabulary, contrasting inner truth with outward
naturalism, is of the utmost importance. It shows that he perceived
the analogy that gave human meaning to the theater's drive toward
a fully three-dimensional stage. A three-dimensional *object* has a
center somewhere in its depth. A *play* conceived as three-dimensional has a center in which depth and unity coincide. And an
actor's *performance* either remains on the surface of character or
plumbs the depths, in which case it may acquire a unity congruent
with the depth center of the whole play. The search for unity and
the search for depth are the same. This is what Stanislavski perceived, and he made it his business to lay out a method the actor
might use in his search for the character's depth.

The method did not take shape until after 1906. The date marks
the end of what Stanislavski called the first period of the Moscow
Art Theater. In 1902 it had moved to the Kamergerski Theater,
having done in its first four years an *Antigone*, four plays of Ibsen
(*Hedda Gabler, An Enemy of the People, When We Dead
Awaken,* and *The Wild Duck*), three by Chekhov (*The Sea Gull,
Uncle Vanya, The Three Sisters*), some historical plays, some
Pushkin, and more. At the new location its repertory ranged from
the heavy realism of Leo Tolstoi's *Power of Darkness* and
Gorki's *The Lower Depths* to Maeterlinck's *The Blind, Interior,*
and *The Intruder. The Cherry Orchard,* Chekhov's last play, was
done, as well as his early play, *Ivanov.* Ibsen's *Pillars of Society,
Ghosts,* and *Brand* were put on. It was a repertory as varied as that
of L'Oeuvre in Paris and reminds us once more that realism and
anti-realism were not divided into mutually exclusive camps. Some
critics, writers, and literary partisans did try to draw a battle line,
but those who were engaged in theater renewal made no absolute
choice. "The fantastic on stage is an old passion of mine," said
Stanislavski,[30] who traveled to France to seek out Maeterlinck, ex-
perimented with stage sets of black velour against which the actors
moved in luminous costumes, and who established (in 1905) a stu-

[29] *My Life in Art,* pp. 330–331.
[30] *Ibid.,* p. 340.

dio, with Meierhold in charge, dedicated to the notion "that realism and local colour had lived their life and no longer interested the public. The time for the unreal on stage had arrived." [31] The search, always the search.

The Maeterlinck plays put on in 1902 failed. The experimental Studio went down in debt, having produced nothing to show the public. A tour through Poland and Germany met with a good reception in Berlin, but the Moscow Art Theater had reached a crisis. Wanting to assess the work that lay behind him, Stanislavski went on holiday to Finland in the summer of 1906. There the beginnings of his "system" took shape.

If one is to appreciate Stanislavski's excellence, a distinction must be made, as with all teachers, between the reality he aimed at and the manner he chose for reaching it. The latter in his case has tended to eclipse the former; his goal is valid at all times, while his particular path was determined by the historical situation that existed in theater practice when he began to work. There being at that time no systematized method for training actors, other than apprenticeship, he had to emphasize method, yet it is wrong to equate his "truth" with his method. There being a fossilized tradition among actors and, even in Stanislavski himself, a great tendency to rely on imitation, it became necessary to hail sincerity, truth, and real experience in contrast to "playing at living over," yet it is wrong to identify Stanislavski's "truth" with "real emotion." He spoke frequently of the "subconscious," yet the term had no clear psychological meaning for him, no more than its opposite, the "superconscious organic creativeness," which was pure expansive romanticism.

Reflection will show that Stanislavski's desire for method and his desire for sincerity are logically contradictory and become so in practice as well if they are not appropriated with a certain caution. An emotion found by a method, identified and cultivated for the purpose of enactment, is not at all the same as an emotion produced by an actual life situation. The emotion of an actor playing the scene of Hamlet confronting his mother can never be the *same* as the emotion of a man actually raving in his mother's chamber. The danger in the Stanislavski method, where it asks the actor to

[31] *Ibid.,* p. 433–434.

recall the feelings he has experienced in a situation analogous to that in the scene, is the danger of producing an "abstract" emotion hovering somewhere between life and art. It can appear like a cloud between the spectator and his perception of the scene being played. Knowledge of this danger would one day lead Brecht to reject the Stanislavski approach to acting, but Stanislavski himself was well aware of the problem.

What Stanislavski was really after was a dialectical movement generated between "sincerity" of emotion on the one hand and method on the other, which is the actor's equivalent of the dialectic between realism and theatricality in all stage presentations. This dialectic, to be generated in the actor, had the aim of all great acting, which was to pass beyond mere repetition, however convincing, into a creativity transcending technique and unpredictable in its effect. Thus, the goal of the method was not the *production* of emotion but the *control* and *release* of it under such conditions as might result in creativity.

The word "creative" resounds like a bell throughout Stanislavski's writings: in *My Life in Art,* in *An Actor Prepares,* and in the lecture notes called *The System and Methods of Creative Art.* The word is a touchstone of romantic thought, and the reverence Stanislavski had for it is the key to the actual content of his work.

"How can one force the emotions to leave their secret hiding places and take the initiative of creation into their hands?" [32] The basic answer Stanislavski gave to that question was that the actor must learn to *focus.* He must learn to concentrate all his energies and resources upon the situation in which the character he plays stands at a given moment. Such concentration is impossible as long as any part of the artist, even seemingly irrelevant parts, are not involved.

> That evening I discovered the greater value of concentration for the actor. Besides, I noticed at that performance that the concentration of the actor reacts not only on his sight and hearing, but on all the rest of his senses. It embraces his mind, his will, his emotions, his body, his memory and his imagination. The entire physical and spiritual nature of the actor must be concentrated on what is going on in the soul of the person he plays. I perceived

[32] *Ibid.,* p. 191.

that creativeness is first of all the complete concentration of the
entire nature of the actor.[33]

Those words describe a discovery made fairly late. Much earlier he
had been told by the famous actress Fedotova, "The first duty of an
actor is to learn to control his will," [34] a dictum he was repeating
years later: "That inner technique of which I preached and which
is necessary for the creation of the proper creative mood is based in
its most important parts on the process of will." [35] Along the way he
learned to call "on the help of restraint, on the *hiding of my emotions*." [36] "This created a fine state of mind and a feeling of well-
being in which I began to believe. Imagination had free play, details began to appear as of themselves. . . ." [37]

The method, then, had two purposes: first, to break down the
barriers between the different parts of the self, allowing and stimu-
lating all of the self to participate in the action at hand; second, to
focus those liberated forces in a precise way at the point where
creative flight begins. The aim of method is freedom.

From this it is clear that Stanislavski's repudiation of naturalism
was basic to him. Indeed, he cannot even be called an advocate of
realism unless the "real" is taken to include what results when the
artist passes beyond the given to create something that has never
existed before and that can exist only in art. This creativity begins
in the given—in life actually perceived and experienced and in the
specific conditions under which an actor works in the theater. It
understands the given with the greatest precision and the fullest
participation possible. But it does not content itself with the reproduction of the given. It rises toward a crystallization that is new
and that can never be defined in advance.

> While only actual reality exists, only practical truth which a man
> naturally cannot but believe, creativeness has not yet begun. Then
> the creative *if* appears, that is, the imagined truth which the actor
> can believe as sincerely and with greater enthusiasms than he be-

33 *Ibid.*, p. 465.
34 *Ibid.*, p. 82.
35 *Ibid.*, p. 527.
36 *Ibid.*, p. 186. Italics added.
37 *Ibid.*

lieves practical truth, just as the child believes in the existence of its doll and of all life in it and around it. From the moment of the appearance of *if* the actor passes from the plane of actual reality into the plane of another life, created and imagined by himself. Believing in this life, the actor can begin to create.[38]

Stanislavski's words point to an ironic dialectic between the real and the unreal that is basic to all artistic creativity. Its importance has always been known to disciplined writers, dancers, and musicians. Stanislavski brought it to the service of actors who had not the genius to perceive it unaided. He taught them to stress the real precisely in order that they might achieve the imaginative. Some of his vocabulary was unfortunate, leaving him open to misunderstanding. In time the Moscow Art Theater lapsed into a pedestrian realism that has been officially encouraged in the Soviet Union. Yet Stanislavski carried the renewal of the theater an important step beyond anyone else: he brought the criteria of three-dimensionality and unity into the aesthetics of the actor's work, showing the actor how to plumb for a depth too often ignored. He integrated the actor into the total instrumentality of the theater without reducing him to a puppet. At the heart of the theatrical enterprise, in the breast of the actor, he demanded and showed how to cultivate a living creativity.

It was a strange conjunction of luminaries when Stanislavski and Gordon Craig were brought together in 1911. The only thing they had in common, apart from the fact that both admired Isadora Duncan, was the desire to renovate the theater: their ways of doing it were miles apart. In Stanislavski's mind the actor was central; Gordon Craig "dreamed of a theatre without men and women, without actors." [39]

For five years and more Stanislavski had labored to tie his dreams of ideal acting to a practical working method; Gordon Craig did not much care whether his dreams of ideal stage design were practical or not, as long as they were "right." Stanislavski's reputation rested on bringing realistic details to the stage, Gordon Craig's on throwing them out. That Craig was invited to design a *Hamlet* for

[38] *Ibid.*, p. 466.
[39] *Ibid.*, p. 509.

the Moscow Art Theater is testimony to the catholicity of Stanislavski's interests, his willingness to try anything once.

Things began well enough. Craig, who had been recommended
to Stanislavski by Isadora Duncan, was commissioned to both design and direct the play. He understood the themes and imagery of
Hamlet superbly well, although in a quite unorthodox manner.
His interpretation made exciting listening, partly because it led
directly to the bold, abstract design he proposed. The Moscow Art
Theater had already done some far-out, unrealistic staging, not
only of Maeterlinck's *Blue Bird* but also of Andreyev's *Life of
Man. Hamlet,* however, was to be its first application of abstract
stage design to a classic; and with Craig's genius to count on, for
which a great deal of money was to be spent, expectations were
high.

Craig came to Moscow and charmed everyone, discussed the
whole project, and then withdrew to Florence to make sketches
and models. With these he returned after a year. He outlined the
whole interpretation of the play, scene by scene, character by character. Then he went back to Italy. "This moment," said Stanislavski, "saw the beginning of our tortures." [40]

The design called for the use of a series of exceedingly tall con-
vex screens that were to move apparently of themselves, shifting
before the eyes of the audience to produce ever new aspects under
special lighting. Craig said they must be made of some natural
material—stone, metal, or wood—because painted canvas or pa-
pier mâché was an abomination. But these gigantic screens turned
out to be impossibly heavy. Even if made of cork, they would have
weighed so much that to move them would have required rebuild-
ing the theater to install vast electrical shifts. After much casting
about, it was decided to use light wooden frames covered with
unpainted canvas. They would not give the right feeling of solidity and gloom, but at least they would be practical. Or so one
hoped. It turned out that these lofty structures would hardly stand
up. They had to be braced in makeshift ways, and to move them
required many stagehands, who could scarcely avoid being seen by
the audience. Spaces appeared between the screens, revealing
everything backstage. Stanislavski relates:

40 *Ibid.,* p. 519.

One hour before the first night performance, I was sitting in the auditorium and rehearsing the maneuvers of shifting the screens for the last time. The rehearsal ended. The scenery was put up for the first scene of the play and the stage hands were allowed to rest and drink tea before the beginning of the performance. The stage grew empty, the auditorium was as quiet as a grave. But suddenly one of the screens began to lean sideways more and more, then fell on the screen next to it, and the entire scenery fell to the floor like a house of cards. There was the crack of breaking wooden frames, the sound of ripping canvas, and then the formless mass of broken and torn screens all over the stage. The audience was already entering the theatre, when nervous work to rebuild the scene began behind the lowered curtain. In order to avoid a catastrophe during the performance itself, we were forced to deny ourselves the joy of shifting the screens in full view of the audience and to accept the help of the traditional theatrical curtain, which coarsely but loyally hid the hard work of the stage hands. And what oneness and unison the Craigian manner of shifting the screens would have given to the entire performance! [41]

As if this were not enough, when Craig had returned to Moscow he had not liked the work of the actors, and his criticisms had caused Stanislavski to doubt the usefulness of his whole acting method. Yet the production, lame as its creators thought it, ran for several hundred performances to become a controversial success and a landmark in the history of modern theater.

Gordon Craig (1872–1966) was the son of Ellen Terry. He had been an actor in Henry Irving's company, and it was no doubt Irving who first interested him in the matter of theatrical renewal. Craig has said, to the surprise of some, that he did not consider himself an innovator so much as a continuer of the work of Irving. Be that as it may, his ideas and designs, his theories of *mise en scène,* appeared quite revolutionary. After making his debut at thirteen in Irving's Lyceum Company and going on to distinguish himself in several Shakespearean roles, he quit acting when he was twenty-five. Four years earlier he began to direct, his first such task being Musset's *On ne badine pas avec l'amour.* Three years later he formed his own company to do *Romeo and Juliet* and *Hamlet.* He

41 *Ibid.,* pp. 521–522.

revived operas of Purcell and Handel. According to some, however, it was with Ellen Terry's production of Ibsen's *The Vikings,* in 1903, that he first succeeded in putting his theories into practice.

The reaction against stage naturalism, itself still quite new, was at this time breaking out in many places. In 1895 the Swiss theoretician Adolphe Appia (1863–1929) published *La mise en scène du drame Wagnérien* ("The Staging of Wagnerian Drama"), in which he tried to show that Wagner's operas called for a stylized décor rather than for the "realism" Wagner himself employed. (Appia's views have strongly influenced the productions at Bayreuth since World War II.) In 1899 Appia's second, more ambitious book appeared: *Die Musik und die Inscenierung (Music and the Art of the Theatre).* In 1902, Strindberg's *A Dream Play* was published. (It was produced in Stockholm five years later.) Also in 1902 Meierhold broke with Stanislavski to pursue his anti-realist bent. (He came back three years later to head the Studio on Povarskaya with Stanislavski's blessing.) In 1903, Max Reinhardt, who had become the inheritor and popularizer of the Meininger methods, turned to symbolism with Maeterlinck's *Pelléas et Mélisande* at the Neues Theater in Berlin. The same year, Apollinaire wrote *Les Mamelles de Tirésias (The Breasts of Tiresias),* to describe which he coined the term "surrealism." In 1905 Gordon Craig published his first influential essay, *The Art of the Theatre.*

Neither Craig nor Appia spent a great deal of time actually at work in the theater. Appia established himself in a villa near Geneva, the city of his birth,[42] and Craig edited a journal called *The Mask* at Florence from 1908 to 1929, afterward retiring to Genoa and later to Vence, where he died at the age of ninety-four.[43] Nonetheless, it is safe to say that these two men consolidated the renewal of the theater that had been going on for three-quarters of a century, raised it to a new level of development, and gave to modern theater practice the main features it now displays. Others were

[42] Appia made occasional sorties into directing: an *Astarté* drawn from Byron's *Manfred,* Paris, 1903; Gluck's *Orpheus* at Hellrau, 1912; the *Fêtes de Juin* at Geneva, 1914; *Tristan und Isolde,* conducted by Toscanini at La Scala, 1923; and *Das Rheingold* and *Die Walküre* at Basel, 1925.

[43] In addition to the productions of Craig mentioned above, other notable ones were Otway's *Venice Preserved,* Berlin, 1905; a *Rosmersholm* with Eleonora Duse, Berlin, 1906; and *The Pretenders* (Ibsen), Copenhagen, 1926.

more practical than they, but none dreamed as boldly or produced more provocative and influential designs.

Craig perceived before the turn of the century that the renewal of the theater, which seemed to contain so many contradictory features, was pointed toward a single conception: the theater is an instrument, which must be tuned in all its parts to produce a unity of experience. This conception belonged to realism as much as to anti-realism, to Stanislavski as much as his rebellious disciple Meierhold, to Antoine as well as to Paul Fort, to Strindberg's *Miss Julie* as well as to *A Dream Play*. To achieve excellence along any of these lines it was not sufficient merely to have actors—even the best actors—perform in front of an audience: it was necessary that *a style be imposed,* even if the style was removed as far as possible from "stylization." To do that required, ideally, that every aspect of the theatrical event, beginning with the architecture (later it would be said, beginning with the audience) should be created *ab initio* as parts of a single conception. Wagner had known that. But though he was the first to enunciate and try to effect such a radical proposal, he applied it only to his own works, of which he was author, composer, designer, *régisseur,* and chief publicity agent. Appia and Craig proposed to apply this concept to the theater *tout entier*. They proposed nothing less than going back to the beginning (the romantic wish for an "unfallen" theater, so to speak). That is the real source of the extreme simplification they reached in their designs. The search for the real would bring the theater to a radical self-purgation, a catharsis of its techniques; for the real is One, and only the single-minded reach it.

It is sometimes said that Appia and Craig restored to the theater a classical simplicity. Study of their sketches quickly reveals that their simplicity is of another order than the classical. The principle of classical simplicity is balance and order affirmed in the face of potential chaos. The principle of simplicity in Appia and Craig is abstraction, or "essentializing." Its opposite is not chaos but encrustation. It strives for a pristine purity. This comes across with great power in these men's sketches and is evident also in their theoretical writings, which take the reader on a quest for that which is elemental and simple in the rudimentary concept of theater. To achieve such simplicity requires a Promethean effort. Perhaps this was what led Jacques Rouché to speak of Craig's *simplicité grandiose*.

We may speak of the quest for the simple; yet in the theater, barnacled with old traditions and necessarily a collaborative enterprise, simplicity is not merely to be *sought;* it must also be *imposed*. The necessity for the imposition of style became clear at the end of the nineteenth century partly because of changes that romanticism brought about in playwriting and in the critical appreciation of plays of all times. Put briefly, these changes meant a diminution of the importance of plot. Meyer H. Abrams has pointed this up in his study of romantic imagination, *The Mirror and the Lamp*. He cites John Stuart Mill, for instance, as one for whom "plot becomes a kind of necessary evil." [44] Mill's opinion was that "the interest in plot and story 'merely as a story' characterizes rude stages of society, children, and the 'shallowest and emptiest' of civilized adults." [45] Mill was speaking of poetry, and he did not so much as mention drama among the arts he considered analogous to poetry in this respect, but he might justly have included it in his opinion.

The compensation that poetry can make for plot and argument by means of attention to diction must be made in drama partly by the same means but also, in even greater part, by resort to *theatrical* means. This is as true of a comparatively plotless naturalist work like Gorki's *Lower Depths* as it is of Maeterlinck's symbolist *Blue Bird*. In each the subordination of plot to other concerns requires the stage director's absolute mastery of the total resources of his métier, which is the theater itself and all within it. The same director may or may not be able to draw the most from two works so different in spirit, but the directorial function is the same in both instances and equally necessary. Bad direction can ruin these works, as it can ruin most significant plays in the modern repertory, whereas it can hardly do so with the well-made play (however much good direction may add), nor can it with plays in which the plot and the theme coincide. Romanticism made the total instrumentality of the theater an aesthetic necessity, and the

44 *The Mirror and the Lamp: Romantic Theory and the Critical Tradition* (New York: Oxford University Press, 1953), p. 24.
45 *Ibid.*

romantic genius of Wagner, Craig, and Appia brought it to fruition.

Appia went so far as to conclude that theater is essentially a quite different art from any in which narrative is important. He wrote,

> The novelist and the epic poet can evoke their heroes by means of description; their work is a story that is told, and the action is placed *in* the story, since it is not living [i.e., not enacted on a stage]. But the dramatic author is not merely telling a story; his living action is freed, stripped of all drapery. Every indication of specific place tends to bring it nearer to the novel or the epic, and to remove it further from dramatic art.[46]

These words might be read as the charter for the avant-garde plays of the twentieth century.

Finally we must note that Appia and Craig brought to a climax the long, groping struggle to achieve a truly three-dimensional stage. The hue and cry against scenery painted on flat canvas goes back at least to Tom Robertson, the origin of the box set lies in the previous generation, and the attempt to achieve an *illusion* of depth by scene-painting stems from the Italian Renaissance. Yet almost always the search for depth had been carried on in the name of realism. Appia and Craig (here the more credit belongs to Appia) showed that the true argument for the exploitation of three-dimensionality arises not from the need for realism but from the inherent nature of the theater and the stage, whether employed for the purposes of realism or for anything else. And they showed that this is so because of the nature of the actor. He is a three-dimensional, organic being whose expressive task (in contradistinction to that of a mere speaker of words) is accomplished by his movement in space. The primal manifestations of this are to be found in dance, out of which both Appia and Craig understood drama to have grown. The point led Craig, paradoxically—he was not above exaggerating grossly in order to be heard—to propose getting rid of actors and replacing them with "supermarionettes." Appia, always more architecturally concerned than Craig, bore

46 *The Work of Living Art,* H. D. Albright, trans. (Coral Gables, Fla.: University of Miami Press, 1960), pp. 43–44. First published in 1921.

down hard on the point in which they both believed: the actor's body and its expression of will in movement can be displayed to maximum advantage only if the stage is furnished with three-dimensional objects, in *opposition* to which the actor's body can reveal its solidity and its freedom. (The paradigm thus shifted from the dancer to the acrobat, whose ghost Appia and Craig saw behind the simplest gestures of the actor.) Hence they designed objects of great mass, such as those Craig envisioned for his Moscow *Hamlet*. Hence also came the platforms, pillars, inclined planes, and stairways of which Appia was so fond.

A Craig in some of his pronunciamentos or a Meierhold in his Moscow theater might all too literally turn the actor back into an acrobat or a marionette. To reap the benefits of the new insight, however, did not require pushing matters to extremes. The insight paid off by reminding the stage director that the primary asset of an actor in a theater is his *physical presence,* for the exploitation of which the theater, in the final analysis, exists. If to the actor's physical presence one could add the sort of spiritual presence Stanislavski sought, the acme would have been reached, provided that one further presence had also been taken into full account—that of the audience. The total instrumentality of the theater required that one arrange the maximum confrontation of audience and actor as present to each other. In this way the question of décor led to the question of architecture.

Confrontation between actor and audience was the particular concern of Georg Fuchs (1868–1949), founder, in 1907, of the Künstlertheater in Munich. The architecture of this theater attempted to illustrate the thesis of his book *Die Schaubühne der Zukunft* (1905; *The Stage of the Future*). This work, like his *Die Revolution des Theaters* (1909; *Revolution in the Theatre*), held that in order to be relevant to our civilization the theater must reject the picture-frame stage and the Italianate auditorium, with its hanging boxes and balconies. Fuchs proposed instead a sort of indoor amphitheater where, on a projecting stage, the action might be thrown forward into the midst of the assemblage. This plan became the basis for the vast Deutschestheater in Berlin and, with modifications, has influenced most of the so-called open stages of the modern theater.

The painters of the décor, said Fuchs, ought not to try to produce an *illusion* of depth. Their business is only with lines and planes. Depth belongs to the stage itself as part of the theater architecture and cannot be added by scenery. With this insight the line of development foreshadowed in the eighteenth century reached its culmination. The search for three-dimensionality, concentrated at first on the decorator's art, eventuates not in stereoptical illusion but in the discovery that depth is an inherent quality of the theater building, when it is conceived and designed as *a place for playing.* The steps in this process of discovery are these: (1) an attempt to achieve an illusion of depth pictorially by the art of painting on canvas; (2) rearrangement of the ground plan of the set so as to envelop the actor within the scene; (3) further integration of the actor into the scene by the introduction of ever more "practicable" objects, set pieces, and furnishings for him to touch; (4) realization that space is part of the actor's artistic métier and that his living movement shows itself in contrast to inanimate objects— properties, platforms, and other masses; and (5) release of the actor from the stage picture by taking the stage out of its frame and integrating it into the "playing place," to which the audience also belongs. In each of the five steps the constant factor is the push toward the conception of the theater as an integrated artistic instrument.

At the same time, the culmination of the search for the fully three-dimensional stage means that the wheel has come full circle. Modern theater practice touches hands with primitive theater, in which the décor tends to be symbolic, giving only the suggestion of place and mood, while it is the actor and the audience who use the theatrical space and give it its meaning.

This conception of theater art has been common to all the great modern directors, even ones as different in other respects as the opulent Max Reinhardt and the ascetic Jacques Copeau. More recently, it was basic to Artaud, and is the most important thing Peter Brook has learned from him. It remains fundamental to the very newest experiments in theater renewal, such as those of The Open Theater in New York and the Laboratory Theater of Jerzy Grotowski in Poland.

The modern theater's rediscovery of itself as *space* has been its single most important achievement. The irony is that while it was making this rediscovery the growth of technology was destroying the importance of space in the sensibility of the modern audience. The very greatness of the modern theater's achievement is sometimes felt as an embarrassment, an inheritance fought for and possessed but not really wanted. Of this we shall hear more, especially in the Epilogue.

6. THE SEARCH FOR
REALITY IN REALISM

Slowly, very slowly, has imitation come into its own,
and the stage learnt to hold a plain, unexaggerating,
undistorting mirror up to nature. —WILLIAM ARCHER

Revelatory art does not reproduce truth:
it opens the eyes . . . —PAUL KLEE

THE GROWTH OF "the modern" in drama has frequently been defined as the growth of realism. This view rests upon a strange interpretation of the facts, since the bulk of modern drama, popular or highbrow, has by no means been realistic in style. The question then arises why the growth of realism has seemed so important. The answer is that realism symbolizes, though it does not actualize, the latent intention of all modern drama, an intention I have already identified as a "quest for reality." Realism is the overt, literal expression of the modern impulse, and the equation of realism with modernism in drama is actually a synecdoche in which the most explicit example of the search for reality is made to stand for the whole.

In order that the true line of development be seen, it is necessary to recognize that real*ism,* as distinguished from the search for reality, is only one among several expressions of the modern in drama. It is neither the most fundamental nor the most important; it is only the one that seems (deceptively) easiest to define and identify.

When one gets down to it, realism turns out to be no easier to define than "the real." Realism, both as a style and as a theatrical movement, has led a precarious existence for the simple reason that the modern age has enjoyed no consensus in answer to the question "What is real?"

A simple view is William Archer's: realism is the undistorted imitation of nature, of course including human nature. Such a view very soon encounters a problem for which it contains no solution—namely, the aesthetic question about the status in reality of the *medium* of imitation, the art object (the play) itself. This question could be brushed aside as too philosophical for the theater if it did not contain another question no artist can long avoid: What is the relation between that which is imitated and the *means* whereby the imitation is made? If we say there is none, we place the work of art in a limbo and have difficulty showing that it does truly reflect what it is supposed to reflect; no judgment of its adequacy is possible. Furthermore, the artist must then be left to spend his time on the construction of a work having no definable, and hence no conceivably effective, relation to "the real," which had been his ostensible concern.

If, on the other hand, there is indeed a relation between art and that which it imitates, it follows that "imitation," in the sense of plain, undistorted reflection, is not a sufficient criterion for the judgment of art or a sufficient guide to the artist in his labors—for his task is then not to create a purely neutral transparency but to create a work which is "true" in aesthetic terms.

These formal considerations suggest why "realism" is hard to define and why it has not resulted in any large quantity of dramatic writing that may clearly be called "realistic." In the complete works of any major modern dramatist, the number of plays that we would readily agree to call realistic in the sense that they attempt to introduce little or no "distortion" is small. Some critics would hold that no such goal is possible for a playwright. Others would say it is possible and desirable but difficult to achieve. The fact is that no great playwright has held it as *the* goal of his art except for a brief period of time. That does not mean, however, that the aim of exact imitation of nature has had no beneficial effects upon playwriting.

Although the concern to reproduce, in the theater, life as it occurs outside has never been entirely lacking in playwrights, from the middle of the 1800's it began to occupy many with an intensity that was new. It will be sufficient to identify three roots from which this intense concern sprang. One of them was located within the theater itself, while the other two were nurtured by ideas belonging generally to the times.

Eugène Scribe may by no means be called the father of dramatic realism (his direct descendants remain pseudorealistic to this day), yet he may lay some claim to being, let us say, its uncle. One of the marks of the well-made play noted above was its penchant for topical subjects. Such subjects did not necessarily bring with them either the spirit or the style of realism, but they did provide a realistic veneer. The plays *seemed* to be about what was actually going on in the world, and at a superficial level they *were*. This is what attracted Alexandre Dumas, *fils*, to the work of Scribe. Dumas' intention was to employ the method for a more adequate interpretation of contemporary life. He failed to achieve his object only because he followed Scribe too closely. A more significant contribution was made by Émile Augier (1820–1889), who modified the techniques of Scribe and created a style nicely responsive to those problems of French society that occupied his attention.

In both Dumas *fils* and Augier the purchase made upon reality, the means by which they sought to surpass Scribe, was that of moral concern. That was both their strength and their limitation. For realism could not advance its claims very far as long as it was simply a question of replacing Scribe's superficial topicalities by a moral seriousness. What was needed was a new vision and, therefore, new techniques. Hence, the didactic element had to be dampened, which meant not that it had to be eliminated but that it had to be grounded in something less idealistic than moral fervor. This other grounding was to be provided by science, the rising prestige and authority of which was due to the positivistic spirit of the age.

In the background of that nineteenth-century thought which now began to influence French playwriting lay the thought of a man of the seventeenth century, René Descartes, and another of the eighteenth, Denis Diderot. Descartes' mathematical discoveries, so important for the growth of modern science, were perhaps remote from the playwrights, but Descartes' emphasis on analytical thought and upon the self-authenticating character of "clear and distinct ideas" was not, for it corresponded to the desire for disciplined objectivity which several litterateurs of the nineteenth century came to think necessary for the renewal of literature, among them Balzac and Flaubert. In the work of these writers, as in that of Zola soon after, one may see also the influence of Diderot. He had been the first important French literary critic to urge that the depiction of everyday occurrences and commonplace social types was a proper task for an author. He wrote in 1758,

> There is one method I have adopted of going about a work, a successful one to which I turn whenever habit or novelty obscures my judgment . . . and it is to seize the very thought of certain objects, transport them bodily from nature to my canvas, and examine them from a point where they are neither too far from me, nor too near.[1]

In the interest of objectivity Diderot advised the dramatist:

> [T]hink no more of the audience than it if had never existed. Imagine a huge wall across the front of the stage, separating you from the audience, and behave exactly as if the curtain had never risen.[2]

By the emphasis he laid upon objectivity Diderot sowed the seeds of realism, and in his own plays as well as in those of Beaumarchais the seeds began to sprout. It is hard to tell what they would have become without the powerful stimulus they received from positivism.

The early sketch of Auguste Comte's positivist philosophy appeared in 1822. From 1830 to 1842 his *Course of Positive Philosophy* was published, and by 1854 the *System of Positive Philosophy* was completed. The intent of the whole was to displace theology and metaphysics as legitimate inquiries into reality and to substitute for them a rigorous positive (i.e., empirical and scientific) method that should prevail in all the sciences. The integration and completion of the various disciplines was to become the work of sociology, which would thereby supplant theology as the queen of

---

[1] "On Dramatic Poetry," translated in Barrett H. Clark, ed., *European Theories of the Drama* (New York: Crown, 1947), p. 288.
[2] *Ibid.*, p. 299.

the sciences. In the study of literature, the spirit of positivism was soon manifest in Hippolyte Taine, who became famous in 1853 with his *Essay on the Fables of La Fontaine* and who in 1864 published his most important work, *The History of English Literature*. In Taine one may see a clear instance of the influence of historicist as well as positivist thought upon literary criticism. He held that the character of a given work of art is determined by three factors that he called race, milieu, and moment—that is, elements fixed by heredity, by physical and cultural environment, and by the particular point in history at which the work has been created. Taken together these may all be called "environment," and they summarized, especially for such a man as Zola, the environmental conception of human nature that was to be of capital importance for realist drama. But there was another important factor, too.

Gilbert Durand points out that Dostoievski, Balzac, and Zola belong to the "nocturnal regime" of the imagination by virtue of the fact that they seek out the humble and the degraded, seeing in it something of more worth than that which society customarily exalts.[3] In Zola and many of his playwriting contemporaries, the search for reality became a search *downward*, to find the great in the small, the high in the low, and light in dark. Such a search is thoroughly romantic, and in its extreme forms it results in an inverted spirituality not unlike the theology of Manichaeism.

There is perhaps no necessary connection between literary realism and theological Manichaeism, but in the late nineteenth century the former was touched by the latter to such an extent that to describe the "real" almost invariably meant to describe the dark underside of life. That tendency, which frequently aroused (as it still does) the uncomprehending ire of critics and audiences, was abetted by the social thought of the time insofar as it was informed by the ideas of Marx and other socialists. These thinkers were helping to shape a public awareness of the plight of the lower social classes and were insisting, as Marx put it, that the self-alienation of society is most clearly exposed in the burdens and conflicts of the proletariat. Such a view provided an additional reason for the

3 *Les Structures anthropologiques de L'imaginaire* (Grenoble: Presses Universitaires de France, 1960), p. 296.

dramatist to turn his attention *down* the social scale and to put upon the stage those laborers, peasants, derelicts, anonymous clerks, and petty officials who had previously been excluded from drama or else admitted there only as figures in comedy. They now became the bearers of the most serious truth.

The term "realism" is frequently associated with the term "naturalism." Discussion of the phenomena requires one to distinguish them. Today the more restrictive term is "naturalism." This was not true in 1881 when Zola, expressing his preference for "naturalism," said that this word enlarged the domain of observation in comparison with "realism," which restricted the literary horizon.[4] What Zola meant was that he wished to extend the literary domain in a particular direction—toward science, which had not been included in what at that time was known as "realism." He added that the choice of the word was not important because "naturalism" would end by having the meaning he and others would give it. That indeed occurred, with the result that "naturalism" became the more strict, "realism" the more general, term.

Zola wrote,

> Naturalist writers are those whose method of study holds as closely as possible to nature and humanity, at the same time permitting, let it be understood, the particular temperament of the observer to be free to manifest itself throughout his works however it seems good to him.[5]

This might fit the present-day meaning of "realism," but "naturalism" was held in more narrow bounds by the deference Zola paid to natural science. Naturalism, wrote Zola, is "the return to nature," the same turn the scientists made when "they began to study matter" and "phenomena" using the empirical method and proceeding by analysis. In literature also, he said, this means the return to nature, to "the exact anatomy" and the depiction of "that which is." [6] Thus, naturalism came to signify a style as free as possible of literary and theatrical conventions, focusing on the lower

---

[4] "Le Naturalisme au théâtre," in *Le Roman expérimental* (Paris: Charpentier, 1880), pp. 109–156. Reference here is to p. 147.
[5] Quoted in Lawson A. Carter, *Zola and the Theater* (New Haven and Paris: Yale University Press and Presses Universitaires de France, 1963), p. 68. My translation.
[6] Zola, "Le Naturalisme au théâtre," in *Le Roman expérimental*. p. 115.

classes or on the hidden underside of middle-class life, and frequently employing scientific theories for the interpretation of human behavior.

Yet since art demands, and Zola allowed, the play of the artist's temperament upon his material, naturalism proved an unstable formula. It tended to dissolve either into the less rigorous, less "scientific" thing called "realism" or else into symbolism, the latter because of the romantic element that naturalism carried within itself. "Romantic drama is a first step toward naturalistic drama," said Zola.[7] He called romanticism "the initial and troubled period of naturalism." [8] Yet although it produced a few great works, naturalism was destined never to emerge from its "troubled period."

In his youth Zola had been an out-and-out romantic. His literary aims were inspired by Hugo and Musset. His world view was highly religious. At the age of twenty he wrote to his friend Jean-Baptistin Baille:

> In our times of materialism . . . when the sciences . . . turn man proud and make him forget the supreme scientist, the poet has a sacred mission: at every time and place to show the soul to those who think only of the body, and God to those whose faith science has drawn away.[9]

Barely a year later Zola was declaring the superiority of science over contemporary poetry, and after five years he began to lay out the principles of what he would later call naturalism, sketching the ideas in a series of newspaper articles he wrote in 1865. He continued to develop these ideas in his first notes (1868) for the *Rougon-Macquart*. He was influenced in part by those painters, then new, later to be called Impressionists, whose work he thought instructive for literature; but in larger part he was influenced by the growing scientific spirit of the age. He began to think of the writer as a scientist.

The work of Taine seems to have led Zola toward the explicit attempt to use scientific laws and methods in writing literature. Though he found Taine too rigid, leaving too little place for the individual temperament of the author, Taine's triadic idea of race,

---

7 Quoted in Carter, *op. cit.*, p. 74. My translation.
8 *Le Roman expérimental*, p. 317. My translation.
9 Quoted in Carter, *op. cit.*, p. 6. My translation.

milieu, and moment helped push Zola toward a deterministic view of the characters in his novels and plays. He came to believe that it was possible to formulate laws of human conduct as rigorous as those set forth in the natural sciences, laws that would define the interplay of heredity, environment, and historical forces in the determination of human behavior. This expectation underlies the famous preface to *Thérèse Raquin* (1873), Zola's theater manifesto and his single most important contribution to modern drama. There Zola declared his "profound conviction . . . that the experimental and scientific spirit of the century will enter the domain of the drama, and that in it lies its only possible salvation." [10] He wrote:

> We must look to the future, and the future will have to do with the human problem studied in the framework of reality. We must cast aside fables of every sort, and delve into the living drama of the two-fold life of the character and its environment, bereft of every nursery tale, historical trapping, and the usual conventional stupidities.[11]

His own *Thérèse Raquin,* he said, lacked the usual details of intrigue. It had no "logic of facts" but instead "a logic of sensation and sentiment." It was "a purely human study." "The drama," he declared, "will either die, or become modern and realistic." [12] With these words Zola blew upon a clarion and offered to the theater in its search for reality a method that seemed to lend it the prestige of science.

Important as this treatise was, summing up as it did Zola's influential body of dramatic criticism, the plays Zola wrote were destined not to remain long on the boards. Some were dismal failures. Others, especially a number of adaptations he helped make from his novels, enjoyed great popular success only to fade away later. His first noteworthy play was *Madeleine,* written in 1865 but not produced until Antoine's Théâtre Libre took it up in 1889.[13]

Its story is that of a woman with a "past" who is happily married

[10] Translated in Clark, *op. cit.,* p. 401.
[11] *Ibid.*
[12] *Ibid.*
[13] In 1866 Zola turned this play into a novel, which appeared first under the title *La Honte* and later as *Madeleine Ferat.* When Zola became famous, several theaters asked for the script, but it seems to have been lost until Zola offered it to Antoine.

until her former lover comes on the scene. Hearing all, Madeleine's husband forgives her, but she cannot forgive herself. She desires a blessing from her mother-in-law, who stands for that respectability for which Madeleine longs. When an old, puritanical servant leads Madeleine to believe that such forgiveness has been denied, she commits suicide.

This plot is pure contrivance, but Zola did not think so. He believed it to be solidly based on science, because he had been impressed by the theory of a certain Dr. Prosper Lucas as interpreted by Jules Michelet in his study *L'Amour* (1859). According to this theory, a woman's first lover plants his hereditary traits in her, passing them on to all the children she may have, even those fathered by other men. Hence, a woman who has taken a lover is forever in bondage to her past. Zola extended this concept of a physical bondage to include a bondage in conscience. Thus, the play is about a "spiritual" bondage brought about through bondage to the past, expressed through the structures of the natural world. Though it would have horrified Zola to think so, his play is much closer to Manichaeism than to science.

In July 1873, Zola's *Thérèse Raquin,* which he had adapted from his novel of the same name, was offered to the public. The author had been challenged by the taunts of some critics that the "garbage" of the novel could find no place on the stage. He also desired to experiment with a dramatic construction that would, as he said, "omit the usual intrigue." The critics, overly severe, condemned the play to a short run of nine performances.

The plot of *Thérèse Raquin,* like that of *Madeleine,* culminates in suicide caused by memories of a guilty past. Thérèse and her lover, Laurent, murder her husband, M. Raquin. They then wait until any suspicion that might fall on them has passed. In the play's third act they come together on their wedding night. By this time old Mme. Raquin has discerned the truth, but she cannot speak out because she has been stricken with a partial paralysis. She attempts to spell out her message of indictment but cannot complete it. The scene is sheer melodrama. Zola moves boldly through it and then turns to an examination of the lovers' consciences. He arranges matters so that it is conscience, not exposure, that drives his protagonists to suicide. They die in their wedding chamber. Then the old lady recovers her speech and rings down the curtain with a frightful malediction pronounced upon the dead couple.

This grim morality play has been successfully revived from time to time.[14] Zola's disclaimer to the contrary, it is probably the play's intrigue and not its supposed inexorability that accounts for its appeal to audiences.

The year after the initial failure of *Thérèse Raquin* Zola reversed field and presented a satirical farce. It was called *Les Héritiers Rabourdin*. Performed in a poor theater by poor actors, it did not succeed, but it is doubtful that any actors could redeem this script, which was the result of a misguided effort by Zola to adapt Jonson's *Volpone* in the style of Molière.[15]

Zola's next play was no better. *Le Bouton de rose* (produced in 1878) employs the old plot of a woman's chastity put to the test in a stratagem devised by her own husband. Although the play passes muster as a diversion, the critics rightly expected more from Zola, and it closed after seven performances. In *Renée* Zola turned once more to a severe theme. He adapted the Greek story of Hippolytus and Phaedra in a manner different from the earlier treatments by Euripides, Seneca, and Racine.

With his *Renée* Zola wished to produce a naturalistic work that would be for the new drama what *Hernani* had been for romanticism some fifty years before. The script was written for Sarah Bernhardt, who promptly refused it. Three other managements, including that of the Théâtre Français, also turned it down. Finally produced at the Vaudeville in 1887, it closed after thirty-eight performances. Zola went beyond the classic and neoclassic versions of the story by allowing the stepmother and stepson to consummate their incestuous love, although for the sake of public taste he tried to soften this by maintaining that the boy's father had never consummated his own marriage to Renée and hence was not really her husband. The aim of the whole adaptation was to present a modern substitute for the Greek notion of fate, accounting for the disaster in positivist rather than metaphysical terms. Zola said that he would try to show "the double influence of heredity and environ-

[14] An adaptation by Thomas Job ran for nearly 100 performances in New York in 1945.

[15] There is, however, some evidence of successful performances in Holland and Germany. See Carter, *op. cit.*, p. 46.

ment." He also wanted to show that the stage, like the novel, could depict characters of mixed moral qualities who, being partly good and partly evil, would be nearer to reality than the usual figures in the popular theater.

It is unfortunate that Zola did not lavish upon *Renée,* or indeed upon any of his plays, the care needed to rid them of theatrical faults. He influenced the theater, in the last analysis, much more by his intentions than by his accomplishments. An advocate of naturalism and a foe of theatrical artifice, he wrote no play devoid of melodramatic intrigue and seems to have aspired, at least for a time, to excel in the tradition of Molière and Italianate comedy. A champion of science and an avowed enemy of religion, his conversion from religion to science was never complete. He recognized that science presented a certain spiritual danger. "Humanity, overcome by dizziness," he once wrote, ". . . is sliding over the steep slope of science; it has bitten the apple and wants to know everything." [16] Later Zola himself bit the apple; but he never swallowed it.

When Zola began his career about 1860, Émile Augier had already brought forth at least two of the most important works of nineteenth-century French realist drama. As a critic Zola recognized Augier's importance and never ceased to admire him, though he regretted that Augier depended too much on moral judgments and not enough on scientific observation for the grounding of his themes.

Le Gendre de M. Poirier (1854; *The Son-in-Law of M. Poirier*), Augier's first realistic prose drama, is also his masterpiece. Its construction owes something to French classicism, particularly in the symmetrical pairings of its characters; and the leading figure, M. Poirier, is a descendant of Molière's Georges Dandin and M. Jourdain. Nevertheless, Augier's play is solidly based on a social conflict of the Second Empire. M. Poirier is a merchant. Gaston de Presles is a marquis. They need each other, since the one has money without prestige, the other prestige without money. Their cooperation is made possible through the marquis' marriage to Poirier's daughter, Antoinette. The conflict of the play is the conflict between the values and standards of the two social classes, and it is in Antoi-

16 Quoted in Carter, *op. cit.,* p. 16. My translation.

nette herself that the crux and resolution of the conflict appear. Her husband recognizes at first no obligation to her beyond the mere act of raising her to the status of a marquise. He despises the greed and low taste of her father and is concerned only with "honor" and pleasure, pursued in his own world made up of aristocrats and women of easy virtue. Careless of his wife's feelings, he challenges to a duel his rival for the affections of a countess. Antoinette, who loves Gaston and can sympathize with his ideals, as her father cannot, tells Gaston that he can earn her forgiveness only by withdrawing from the duel and apologizing to the opponent. Caught between the incompatible ideals of family and "honor," Gaston at last concedes to his wife. As soon as he does so, she crosses to him, bestows a kiss, and pronounces the famous curtain line "Now, go and fight." It is a victory of principle accompanied by sympathetic insight into character, and it contains the essence of Augier's work. His plots are usually contrived to reinforce the political and domestic principles he advocates, but the scenes and lines are shaped so as to convey the true dramatist's sympathy with the most diverse types of character and points of view.

Augier wrote a number of social comedies castigating moral corruption and upholding the family. He also wrote a series of three political dramas attacking corruption in parliament and the press. *Les Effrontés* (1861; *The Impertinents*) was followed by *Le Fils de Giboyer* (1862; *Giboyer's Son*) and *Lions et renards* (performed 1869; *Lions and Foxes*). The second of these is probably his best play after *The Son-in-Law of M. Poirier*. The character Giboyer had been introduced in *The Impertinents,* where he appeared as the theater's first example of the bohemian journalist who sneers at society and writes anything for pay. In the sequel he has achieved success as a writer of political speeches. A younger man, Maximilien, is shocked to discover Giboyer's lack of intellectual integrity, but this jolt is superseded a few moments later by the revelation that Giboyer is his natural father. To combine filial sentiment with social criticism is typical of Augier, but the appeal of the mixture extends in drama far beyond him. It influenced the Norwegian Björnstjerne Björnson, especially in his play *The New System* (1879), and also the young Ibsen, and is retained in such recent American plays as *Death of a Salesman, Edward My Son,* and *Cat on a Hot Tin Roof.*

In *Le Mariage d'Olympe* (1855; "Olympe's Marriage") Augier countered Dumas' treatment of the courtesan in *La Dame aux camélias.* Augier referred scornfully to the popular theme of the salvation of the fallen woman whose soul was virgin "and other such-like metaphysical paradoxes." In *La Contagion* (1866; *Contagion*) he described the way corruption in the nobility infects the middle class. The last-act heroism of the protagonist Lagarde anticipates Ibsen's Dr. Stockman in *An Enemy of the People.*

In 1879, at the age of fifty-nine, Augier gave up playwriting because he felt that his aims would be better fulfilled by those to come after him. Within three years Henri Becque (1837–1899) introduced a social drama of greater severity than anything Augier had written: *Les Corbeaux* (1882; *The Vultures*). In this play Vigneron, the hard-working head of a family, dies, and his widow and three daughters are set upon by such "vultures" as Teissier, Vigneron's rapacious business partner. All are eager to get what they can of the inheritance. One daughter is forced to marry Teissier, whom she hates, solely in order to protect the family interests. The situation, in part reminiscent of Jonson's *Volpone,* is turned here into an acrid study of bourgeois greed. Unlike Zola, who in *Les Héritiers Rabourdin* had tried with poor judgment to treat such a situation in the style of classic comedy, Becque saw and realized its possibilities as mordant irony and social protest. His next play, *La Parisienne* (1885; *Woman of Paris*), was a bitter comedy. Its subject was marital infidelity, its conventions those of drawing-room comedy, which Becque employed in order to oppose the moral code they usually conveyed.

It was not in his techniques that Becque made an advance over his predecessors and most of his contemporaries. He did not adhere to naturalist theory and paid little attention to the technical problems presented by realism. He used monologues, asides, and long descriptive speeches that other playwrights considered archaic. His superiority lay in his attitude, the spirit he conveyed. He was quite ready to accept ordinary theatrical conventions, provided that he could employ them to irritate and mock the society they sprang from. He was therefore a Thersites, one of the chief of them among modern playwrights, though he wrote only two important plays. After the second he spent the remaining fourteen years of his life collecting material for a magnum opus about a financial scandal, a labor he did not finish. Perhaps he discovered that the documentation for scandal is infinite.

The "new wave" of realists in the 1880's and 1890's included many other figures. Among them were Georges de Porto-Riche (1849–1930), Jules Lemaître (1853–1914), Paul Hervieu (1857–1915), Henri Lavedan (1859–1940), Maurice Donnay (1859–1945), Eugène Brieux (1858–1932) and François de Curel (1854–1928). As Maurice Valency has said, "It is dispiriting to remember that barely a generation has passed since these names were chapter headings in the current surveys of contemporary drama." [17]

In 1914 George Bernard Shaw delivered a lecture at Oxford in which he compared Brieux with Sophocles and concluded that the superior playwright was the Frenchman. No doubt this opinion, like many others Shaw expressed, was calculated to shock. Even so, it is one of the Shavian utterances with which time has dealt most harshly. Shaw admired the reformer in Brieux, his courage in dramatizing such subjects as venereal disease and the greed of financiers, and his attacks upon the double standards of bourgeois "morality" that caused much needless suffering. It was the same courage Shaw had found in Ibsen. Brieux's fisticuffs, he wrote, "are not aimed heavenward: they fall on human noses for the good of human souls." [18] Be that as it may, the modern reader finds in Brieux plots laboriously contrived, characters molded to fit preachments, suicides thrown in to make the audience feel guilty, last-minute rescues, and didacticism abundant. On January 26, 1921, a London newspaper reviewed a revival of *Les Trois Filles de M. Dupont* (1897; *The Three Daughters of M. Dupont*) at the Garrick Theatre. By that time Brieux's work was already showing its age:

> This is the second time in three years that this essentially mediocre work has appeared in London, and all one can say is that only

[17] *The Flower and the Castle: An Introduction to Modern Drama* (New York: Macmillan, 1963), p. 115.
[18] Preface to *Three Plays by Brieux* (London: A. C. Fifield, 1917), p. xix.

the exceptionally fine acting excuses it. Much of the propaganda in the play—which is a plea for women's rights—is obsolete, and the remainder is valid in France, but has only a historical interest in this country. . . . Julie Dupont, the only married daughter of the three, finds it necessary in her most impassioned scenes with her husband to introduce big chunks of indigestible rhetoric about the woman question, and the other two daughters, one an old maid and the other a courtesan, point the moral of the play [so] obviously in their insistence on giving us all the reasons for their unhappiness, when the events have long ago made us familiar with them, that all they say has the tediousness of a familiar story inflicted upon us by one who has just heard it for the first time.[19]

The most important works of naturalism and realism came from Germany, Russia, and Scandinavia. The Scandinavian writers included, besides Ibsen and Strindberg, Björnstjerne Björnson (1832–1910), Grennar Heiberg (1857–1929), Jonas Lie (1833–1908), and Knut Hamsun (1859–1952). To the Russians we shall come later. In Germany there were Ludwig Anzengruber (1839–1889), Arno Holz (1863–1929), Johannes Schlaf (1862–1941), Max Halbe (1865–1944), Hermann Sudermann (1857–1928), Max Dreyer (1862–1946), and many others—all overshadowed by a single giant of many talents, Gerhart Hauptmann (1862–1946).

Hauptmann's career epitomized the destiny of naturalism. He wrote some twenty-five works for the stage in addition to numerous stories, novels, and epic poems. He began his artistic career as a sculptor after having studied science and philosophy at Jena. By 1885 he had decided to devote himself entirely to writing, and in 1889 the Freie Bühne in Berlin produced his first important play, *Vor Sonnenaufgang* ("Before Sunrise"). This work was exactly of the type the Freie Bühne hoped to encourage. Without a hero and virtually without a plot, it described the "disease" of alcoholism in a peasant family. Like Zola, Hauptmann based his work on a rigidly deterministic theory of heredity. He showed addiction to al-

---

[19] From a clipping that has found its way into my files but from a source I have not been able to identify. The transitoriness of the appeal of Shaw's latter-day Sophocles is underlined by the fact that a member of the cast of the 1921 revival interests us today more than does the author. She was Miss Edith Evans, whose performance, said another reviewer, "made me cry like a child." "Not for months have I been so deeply affected in a playhouse. The restraint, the conviction, the finish of the portrait of this yearning, self-sacrificing, ugly, ill-dressed spinster were almost perfect."

cohol as something passed down from one generation to the next along with moral depravity and defeatism. Audiences were offended, but the play secured Hauptmann's position as a writer.

He returned to the question of heredity in his next play, *Das Friedenfest* (1889; "The Feast of Reconciliation"), in which the inherited factor is a nervous disease. Two years after that he wrote a play called *Einsame Menschen* ("Lonely Men"), which, though written with Ibsen's *Rosmersholm* (1886) in mind, was less symbolic than it and more clinically psychological. Its hero, Johannes Vockerat, is a scientist twenty-eight years of age—Hauptmann's age when he wrote the play—whose parents are appalled by his advanced ideas and whose wife is incapable of understanding them. He finds a spiritual friendship with a young student named Anna Mahr. After she has been forced by his parents to leave their household, Johannes realizes the depth of his attraction to her and commits suicide in the little boat in which they had talked together of philosophy. The play may have owed something not only to *Rosmersholm* but also to Strindberg's stories called *Married*. Hauptmann dedicated the play to "those who have experienced it." Its title became a common phrase to describe the young generation of students who, alienated from the conservatism of their elders, considered themselves "einsame Menschen."

Hauptmann's next play was his masterpiece and one of the few enduring monuments of naturalist drama. *Die Weber* (*The Weavers*) was written in 1891–2. It was performed in 1893 at the Freie Bühne and in May of the same year at the Théâtre Libre in Paris, where it was one of Antoine's most successful productions. It depicts an uprising of peasant workers that occurred in 1844 in Hauptmann's native Silesia. The author dedicated this play, which was at first composed in pure Silesian dialect, to his father, from whom he had heard stories of his grandfather and great-grandfather, weavers like those depicted in the play. The work was inspired, however, by much more than these family recollections. Like *Before Sunrise*, it was Hauptmann's attempt to put into practice the theories of a group called Durch, which he, Arno Holz, and Johannes Schlaf had formed under the influence of a naturalistic pamphlet entitled *Die Revolution in Litteratur* written by Bleibtreu in 1886. *The Weavers* also gives evidence of direct influence from Tolstoi, whose play *The Power of Darkness* was written the same year as the Bleibtreu pamphlet.

In his research for *The Weavers* Hauptmann employed historical sources such as an economic study of the Silesian linen industry by Zimmerman that appeared in 1885. The weavers scratched out a bare subsistence by doing piecework at home. They brought their product to the company store, exchanging it for yarn, groceries, and hopefully some cash, though the money seldom appeared because the workers were almost always in debt to their employers. In the early part of the play Hauptmann describes this economic serfdom, and in the latter part he depicts the abortive revolution against it, the first victim of which is an old peasant who had refused to take any part in the uprising. The construction of the play, though it lacks the Brechtian "alienation effect," is close to what would be called "epic" today. Its many scenes in five acts are held together not by plot but by a common subject, which is the milieu of the linen industry and the social classes and character types it produces. Song plays a very important part in unifying the play, and so does humor, which Hauptmann found himself able to employ as a means of intensifying the naturalistic effect. He was never to write anything superior to this moving play, which has the ring of authenticity in almost every line.

Hauptmann's next two plays were comedies. *Kollege Crampton* ("Colleague Crampton"), about a drunken professor, was followed in 1893 by *Der Biberpelz* (*The Beaver Coat*). The latter, along with *The Weavers,* has been his most-performed play. It bears a striking similarity to *The Broken Jug* by Kleist, in which a judge who has to find out who broke a jug discovers he did it himself. In Hauptmann's play the "President of the Court" has to find out who stole a beaver coat and discovers it is his own washerwoman, whom he is wont to praise for her honesty. With this play Hauptmann became the first writer to caricature the monocled Prussian official, which he did with delightful and lasting effect. The teeming village life is also portrayed with rich comic dividend. If the play's plot looks back to Kleist's *The Broken Jug,* its satire of Prussian militarism anticipates Karl Zuchmayer's *Der Hauptmann von Köpenick* (*The Captain from Köpenick*, 1930).

Hauptmann was now at the height of his powers, but it was impossible for him to surpass the naturalistic achievement he had made with *The Weavers*. He felt that his artistic development depended on his being able to squeeze from naturalism some further kind of statement or awareness, and it was at this point that the religious and romantic component in his naturalism began to come to the surface. There was in his naturalism always, as in that of the theorist and dramatist Arno Holz, a pantheistic quality. The purely natural was attractive not merely because it was "scientific" but even more because it bore in its every detail "another" meaning; this notion derived from the belief that the natural, however mundane, was nevertheless the form of the divine. The search for the purely natural was thus at the same time a search for something else: a religious reality lying within the mysterious depths. Therefore, when he had mastered the naturalistic technique, Hauptmann was already on the road that would lead him to symbolism. The passage was made schematically in the strange play called *Hanneles Himmelfahrt* ("The Assumption of Hannele"), which he wrote the same year as *The Beaver Coat*, 1893. Hannele is a poor Silesian girl driven by her dismal circumstances to commit suicide. Her death is protracted, and in her fever she sees visions of heaven. These are mixed with scenes of her pitiable earthly surroundings. The spectator is not sure whether the visions are pure delusion or whether they represent the invisible, holy side of all sorrow and degradation.

In this half-naturalist, half-symbolist drama, Hauptmann leapt directly into the company of writers usually thought to be as far as conceivable from naturalism. Similarities with Maeterlinck and Hans Christian Andersen are obvious. There are clear anticipations of the folk lyricism of John Millington Synge.

The out-and-out symbolist works of Hauptmann no longer hold much interest for their own sake. They are important mainly as evidence that symbolism was the *terminus ad quem* of naturalism. In Hauptmann this is particularly clear, but it is true of all naturalist drama, which, wherever we look, is found restlessly moving between the real and the anti-real, desperately trying to unite the two sides of its vision.

Hannele was followed by *Die versunkene Glocke* (1896; "The Sunken Bell"), which tries to combine realism and symbolism somewhat in the manner of Ibsen's *Master Builder* (1892) and employs the same symbolic contrast between highlands and lowlands that is found in several Ibsen plays. *Fuhrmann Henschel* (*Drayman Henschel*), a naturalistic drama displaying once again some echoes of *Rosmersholm*, followed in 1898. With *Rose Bernd* in 1903 the period of Hauptmann's best work, which began in 1889, came to a close, although he continued to write until his death in 1946.[20]

It was not accidental that the greatest works of naturalism were created in eastern rather than in western Europe. In France, Zola tied naturalism so closely to science that he hobbled its artistic development, yet in doing so he showed himself very much a man of the West. In England naturalism never got a foothold. Instead, Shaw and others championed French and Scandinavian realism as a weapon of social reform. The farther east one looks in Europe the less important are the scientific and reformist motifs, while the more important become naturalism's poetic and romantic roots. Hauptmann, who surpassed Zola as a naturalist playwright, was also a symbolist. Austria's so-called naturalists, notably Schnitzler and Hofmannsthal, were in fact poets. As for Russia, one discovers there that naturalism might owe very little to theories of science and literature: it could develop even better from a religious tradi-

---

[20] Hauptmann's name was somewhat tarnished by his acceptance of the Hitler government. In *The Rise and Fall of The Third Reich* (New York: Simon and Schuster, 1960) William L. Shirer supplies the following vignette:

I shall never forget the scene at the close of the first night of his last play, *The Daughter of the Cathedral*, when Hauptmann, a venerable figure with his flowing white hair tumbling down over his black cape, strode out of the theater arm in arm with Dr. Goebbels and Johnst. He, like so many other eminent Germans, had made his peace with Hitler, and Goebbels, a shrewd man, had made much effective propaganda out of it, tirelessly reminding the German people and the outside world that Germany's greatest living playwright, a former Socialist and the champion of the common man, had not only remained in the Third Reich but had continued to write and have his plays produced.

How sincere or opportunistic or merely changeable this aging playwright was may be gathered from what happened after the war. The American authorities, believing that Hauptmann had served the Nazis too well, banned his plays from the theaters in their sector in West Berlin. Whereupon the Russians invited him to Berlin, welcomed him as a hero and staged a gala cycle of his plays in East Berlin. And on October 6, 1945, Hauptmann sent a message to the Communist-dominated "Kulturbund for the Democratic Revival of Germany" wishing it well and expressing the hope that it would succeed in bringing about a 'spiritual rebirth' of the German people. (p. 243)

tion that endowed the lowliest forms of life with infinite value.

The story of realism and naturalism in Russia continues right on from Gogol, Griboyedov, and others discussed in Chapter 3. Its next major figure was Ostrovski, but some note must also be taken of Ivan Turgenev (1818–1883), who stands rather outside the main line of development. He considered himself a western rather than an eastern European. His one long play, *A Month in the Country* (1850), is in some ways a work of modern realism and in some ways a throwback to classicism.

Turgenev was avowedly anti-romantic, which meant that he opposed what we have called dream-romanticism. For its chief exponent, Victor Hugo, he had no use whatever. He admired Flaubert and Balzac above all other French writers, but he was also taken with Musset, whose influence may be seen in Turgenev's two proverb comedies, *An Evening in Sorrento* (1852) and *Where It's Thin It Breaks*. Among the Russians he most honored Gogol and Tolstoi. His early plays were short comedies (*Penniless; The Parasite*, 1848; *The Bachelor*, 1849) filled with so much sharp and stinging observation of Russian types that they ran into continual trouble with the censors. *The Lunch with the Marshal of Nobility*, which shows a brother and sister disputing the inheritance left by their parents, anticipates the one-act "jokes" of Chekhov. In these works the realism stems from the native Russian comic tradition.

In *A Month in the Country*, however, a new element is present. Here the realism lies in subtle representation of psychological states and their gently modulated processes of growth and conflict. Seldom has anyone brought to the stage more successfully than Turgenev those materials and qualities that belong to the art of the novelist. Natalia Petrovna, a woman in her late twenties, is married to a rich landowner much older than herself. Courted by a neighbor, Rakitin, she accepts him not as a lover but as a friend, while her amorous feelings are stirred by the young Belyaev, her son's tutor. Belyaev, however, is interested in the seventeen-year-old Vera, who is Natalia's ward. We watch the growth of Natalia's jealousy. At the same time we observe Vera's budding sense of womanhood and her awareness that it is her right to determine her own destiny. The play's chief interest lies in the changing self-awareness of the two women, seen against the background of life on the estate. The subject is exquisitely handled. Eventually both Rakitin and Belyaev depart, leaving Natalia to face herself without prospect of any satisfying love.

The modern realism of this material, which was largely drawn from Turgenev's own experiences (on an estate in France rather than Russia, however) is balanced by a well-nigh classical appreciation of form. A subplot is suggested and deftly worked into the whole; each scene is skillfully rounded off in the French style; and the many cross-purposes that emerge in the final scenes are handled with rare ability. The work stands at mid-century, half looking back the long way to Molière and half looking forward to Chekhov.

Turgenev admired Gogol immensely and praised him at a time when it was politically rash to do so. It was, however, Alexander Ostrovski (1823–1886) on whom Gogol's mantle really fell. Although he did not possess Gogol's genius, he partly made up for it by prodigious industry. Learning his trade making translations from Shakespeare, Molière, Dumas, and others, he went on to write more than eighty plays, of which about fifty remain in the repertories of Russian theaters today, making him by all odds the favorite playwright in Soviet Russia. The Maly Theater in Moscow, in front of which a bronze statue of the playwright was erected in 1929, has been called "The House of Ostrovski," but his work is performed also in most other Russian theaters, including the Moscow Art.

The play of Ostrovski's that is closest to Gogol's work is *The Diary of a Scoundrel* (1868; also known as *Enough Stupidity in Every Wise Man*), which tells of a certain Glumov in whose eyes everyone else is stupid and dishonest. He sets out to advance himself by catering to others' dishonesty and is about to succeed when he makes the mistake of allowing his secret diary to be discovered, in which he has recorded what he really thinks of his associates. Like Khlestakov's letter in *The Inspector General*, this diary is read aloud, producing much consternation on the stage and much humor in the audience. When, after this, Glumov enters, he brazenly talks his adversaries down, telling them they have learned nothing they did not already know and that they should honor him more for his candor than they were prepared to do for his hypocrisy. By this outfaced approach he carries the day and makes Ostrovski's satire the more complete.

Though the situation in *The Diary* is in some parts reminiscent of *The Inspector General* (and of Griboyedov's *Woe from Wit*), Ostrovski's real affinity with Gogol lay in his persistent exposé of the spirit of autocracy, which he saw in business and in family life as well as in government. He was also like Gogol in perceiving that the true Russia was to be found among the anonymous members of the lower orders, "those obscure millions," Marc Slonim calls them, "who lived and toiled behind the splendid facade of a decaying nobility." [21] Such concern for the lower orders was, to be sure, partly born of a reformist attitude, which the imperial censors noticed; but even more it sprang from the native "Slavophilic" appreciation of the Russian "soul" as a quality rising from the soil of "Mother Russia." In this view the real Russia was to be found not in individuals and their particular ideas as much as in character types and basic attitudes. So subtly accurate was Ostrovski in his depiction of these types and attitudes that he won the love of Russian audiences at the expense of international fame. Only two or three of his plays are well known in other countries.

Romantic attachment to character types expressive of the Russian "soul" is matched in Ostrovski, as in Gogol, by a salutary penchant for satire. It is this combination of satire, "soul," and reform that makes Russian realism of the nineteenth century, of which Ostrovski is the best example prior to Chekhov, such a unique phenomenon.

Ostrovski's dramatic writing, which includes all his output except one book, extended from 1847 to 1885, the year before his death. His *oeuvre* is divided into works of prose realism (by far the larger division); historical plays in verse; plays about actors and the theater; and a few works drawn from folk tales, of which *The Snow Maiden* (1873) is best known. His masterpiece is considered to be either *The Diary of a Scoundrel* or *The Storm* (1860), the latter being his closest approach to naturalism. Its subject is one that pervades naturalism; suicide as the result of a lost struggle with conscience. The suicides in the plays of Zola, Hauptmann,

[21] *Russian Theater from the Empire to the Soviets* (New York: Collier Books, 1962), p. 77.

and Ostrovski, later in Tolstoi and Gorki, and to a lesser extent in Chekhov, Strindberg, and Ibsen, are suicides of those who have struggled with conscience at the depths of their being and have been defeated or exhausted by the ordeal. It is here, as clearly as anywhere, that one can see the "scientific" objectivity of naturalism open out into another dimension at once moral and ontological. A play of conscience without suicide is likely to be a "problem play," but the suicide of conscience bears a terror that reveals deep yearning for absolutes, however dark and threatening.

In *The Storm,* Ostrovski tells of a woman named Katerina whose husband, Tikhon, is under the thumb of a domineering father, one of those self-appointed autocrats called *samodurs* whose type Ostrovski portrayed often and well. Oppressed by her family situation, Katerina has a short affair with a handsome young man who has been similarly oppressed by his uncle. Katerina is afterward smitten with remorse. During a violent thunderstorm in which flashes of lightning illumine a scene of the Last Judgment painted on the walls of an old church (the effect is worthy of the filmmaker Ingmar Bergman), Katerina makes a public confession. This seals her doom, and after much torment she hurls herself from a cliff into the river Volga. The storm and the Judgment scene indicate that we have here another example of naturalism's affinity for symbolism.

In 1859 Ostrovski produced *The Ward,* sometimes called *The Protegée of the Mistress.* The same year Alexei Pisemski (1820–1881) brought out a play called *Bitter Destiny* (known also as *A Hard Lot*). Both plays were revolutionary in that their subject was the cruel treatment of serfs by the Russian landowners. Pisemski's was perhaps the more immediate in that it put on stage for the first time the life of the peasants (Ostrovski's play is set among the proprietors) and drew its protagonist from among them. Both works, by stirring public sentiment, contributed to the imperial decree two years later that emancipated Russia's serfs.

It has been said that *Bitter Destiny* was imitated by Leo Tolstoi (1828–1910) when he wrote *The Power of Darkness* in 1886, and some critics have held that Tolstoi's play did not surpass its alleged model. Both plays are set among peasants and show the passions that overwhelm them. In both a man kills a child and later gives himself up to justice. But Tolstoi's source was a story in the newspapers, and though *Bitter Destiny* is one of the best Russian plays prior to *The Power of Darkness,* it has neither the outer realism nor the inner depth of Tolstoi's naturalistic masterpiece.

Tolstoi's play describes a descent into moral darkness. Peter, the head of a peasant household, has become rich, and his second wife, Anisya, wants his money. In this greed she is encouraged by her friend Matrena, whose son, Nikita, works for Peter. Matrena schemes to have the money fall into Nikita's hands. Nikita, on his part, having recently seduced and then rejected an orphan girl, is looking for new adventures. A series of crimes begins. Anisya, with poison obtained from Matrena, murders her husband, Peter, and steals his money. She turns it over to Nikita, putting herself in his power, and he marries her. To his bed, however, he takes Anisya's teen-age stepdaughter, Akulina. She becomes pregnant, and the older women urge him to arrange a marriage for her, all the more because she is not very bright. However, her baby is born while the matchmakers are still at work. Matrena and Anisya, who are respectively the grandmother and stepmother of this infant (Anisya is also its stepgrandmother), decide that it must be killed. In the play's most gruesome and famous scene, they force the drunken Nikita to take the baby into the cellar and bury it.

NIKITA (*picking it up*): It's alive! Darling mother, it's moving! It's alive! What shall I do with it?
ANISYA (*switching the baby out of his hands and throwing it into the cellar*): Hurry up and strangle it and it won't be alive.

Nikita, half mad with drink, fear, and remorse, kills the baby. Matrena goes into the cellar and buries it.

NIKITA: Don't bury it; it's alive! There, it's wailing!
MATRENA: How could it wail? You squashed it into a pancake. You crushed its head.

The last act shows the wedding party for Akulina, whose marriage, with the aid of sufficient dowry, has at last been arranged. Nikita, overcome by guilt, almost decides to kill himself. Instead, however, he bursts into the party, kneels before the guests, and confesses each of his crimes. He asks forgiveness, "for Christ's sake." As the police take him in custody he says, "I did it all by myself. I planned it and I did it. Lead me wherever you want to. I shall say nothing more."

The Power of Darkness is notable for its sharp focus upon the details of Russian peasant life. But it is not simply realism that makes Tolstoi's play significant in modern drama. Rather, it is a certain spirituality that led Tolstoi to make supremely good use of a notion implicit in naturalism's preoccupation with the lower classes—namely, that the way to the real is the way *down*. The plunge Tolstoi asks us to make is not only into social deprivation, where the poor scramble like rats for the money of an old peasant, but also, and more importantly, into moral degradation, or evil. The play's progression (in moral terms, a *re*gression) is that of Nikita's deepening entanglement in a network of sin. As his father tells him, "Your wealth, y'see, has caught you in a net; in a net, you know." Thus, the milieu of the play is more than that of a certain stratum in society; it is a milieu of evil, in which human relationships are turned into bonds of murder, theft, and rape. What the spectator experiences is a descent into ever darker darkness, so oppressive that it comes to be felt as a power, a potency of sin, ensnaring the soul and killing it. Yet at the bottom of this pit there is salvation. The play contains four acts of descent and a fifth act of repentance. The light shines in darkness.

The spiritualized naturalism of Tolstoi recalls the Manichaean variety of Gnosticism, prevalent in Hellenistic times, in which evil was deliberately intensified for the sake of salvation. Orgies and other indulgences were cultivated so that the soul should be driven into a subjugation to the Evil One, from which it might at last be delivered in a climactic paroxysm. Only the appreciation of this motif makes the kneeling repentance of Nikita credible. To be believed, it must be seen as the last (and grandest) contortion of a soul ensnared by the *power* of darkness. The play's justification is its vision of grace achieved under the conditions of the greatest intensity of evil.[22]

---

[22] In addition to *The Power of Darkness*, Tolstoi wrote three or four other plays of note. His early pieces were of a didactic nature, adapted for the "people's" theater from his own stories. In 1891 he wrote *The Fruits of Enlightenment*, a comedy show-

The first performance of *The Power of Darkness* took place at the Théâtre Libre in Paris in 1888. Russian censors did not allow any performance in Russia until 1895. The play was then put on in St. Petersburg. For some reason it did not come to the stage of the Moscow Art Theater until 1902, but that turned out to be a memorable year, for within the space of a few months the Moscow Art Theater produced not only *The Power of Darkness* but also the first two plays by Maxim Gorki, including *The Lower Depths,* the only Russian play that might be considered the equal of *The Power of Darkness* in the naturalistic style.

As in Tolstoi's play, the motif in *The Lower Depths* that accounts for its greatness is the search for light in darkness. The setting is "a basement resembling a cave," part of a flophouse owned by one Kostiliov. It is inhabited by a group of derelicts who have lost all connection with the "upper" world and who drift in futility. There is a baron who professes to have rich relatives and associates. There is Klesch, a locksmith, whose wife lies dying behind a curtain. There is a drunken policeman, a shoemaker, a meat seller, and so on. The liveliest is Pepel, a thief, who gets himself entangled with the landlord's wife, Vassilisa, and her sister Natasha. When Pepel starts to make off with Natasha, Vassilisa pours boiling water over her sister's legs. There are two highly articulate characters: Luka, a pilgrim or vagabond-philosopher, who advocates belief in God or in anything else that will make life seem worth living; and Satin, who hymns the glories of man.

The play has no plot. Structurally it is held together by the arrival and departure of Luka and by Gorki's superb handling of the milieu, which seems to make every incident and detail "belong."

---

ing the nobility to be more superstitious than their ignorant servants. *The Root of All Evil* (1900) is a serious comedy about a drunken peasant, his wife, and a vagabond-philosopher who, as a type, anticipates Luka in Gorki's *Lower Depths. The Living Corpse* (1900), partly autobiographical, tells of a man who leaves his wife because he is a burden to her and his family. To release her he feigns suicide; later, his ruse discovered, he actually does kill himself. *The Light Shines in the Darkness* (unfinished) is even more strongly autobiographical and includes a good bit of self-satire and self-condemnation. *All Comes from Her* was also unfinished and has been seldom performed. Although *The Living Corpse* proved to be very popular, especially in Russia, Tolstoi wrote no play that rivals *The Power of Darkness,* his first serious dramatic effort.

In the lack of emphasis on plot, Chekhov's influence may be seen, but the method of characterization is not Chekhovian. It is far less subtle, yielding results more like line drawings than like Chekhov's pastels. There is a deliberate hardness about the method, and yet the play carries many romantic overtones. It is this combination that accounts for its appeal, though it is doubtful that Gorki himself realized this. He criticized the Moscow Art production for being too romantic, and in his later plays he turned to more consistent but less moving statements of a sociopolitical nature, becoming in time the very model of the "socialist realist" playwright. To one who reads *The Lower Depths*, however, it is clear that the Gorki who wrote it was haunted by two dreams. The one, expressed by Luka, is a dream of spiritual light (the name Luka means "light," and he is also called a "pilgrim") which would substitute faith, even illusory faith, for aimless pettiness and senseless violence. To the dying Anna, Luka avers that death is "Peace—nothing but peace! . . . like a mother to her little children. . . ." To the thief, Pepel, who asks if there is a God, Luka replies: "Whatever you believe in, exists." Later he tells Pepel: "He who seeks, will find. He who wants something badly, will find it."

The other dream, expressed by Satin, is that of the dignity of man. When others attack Luka as a charlatan who "beckoned them to go somewhere, but didn't show them the way," Satin defends him:

> The old man is not a charlatan. What is truth? Man—that is truth! He understood this. . . . He told you lies, but that was out of pity for you, damn and blast your guts! [23]

Later Satin offers his own creed:

> A man may believe or not believe—that's his own affair. Man's free—he pays for everything himself: for his belief, for his unbelief, for his love, for his intelligence—he pays for everything himself and that is why he's free! Man, that's the truth! What is man? It's not you or I or they—no, sir! It's you, I, they, Napoleon,

[23] Act IV. Quoted from *The Storm and Other Russian Plays*, translated and introduced by David Magarshack (New York: Hill and Wang, 1960).

Mahomet—all in one! (*Traces a man's figure in the air.*) Understand? It's tremendous. In this is the beginning and the end of everything. . . . Man! why, it's—magnificent! [24]

The play affirms unambiguously neither the visionary kindliness of Luka nor the extravagant humanism of Satin. Instead, it expresses the search for a reality dimly perceived and tentatively affirmed. It is a quest for glory in the midst of squalor, and the irony of its composition renders it at once modern and enduring.

This modernism Gorki forsook. Between *The Lower Depths* (1902) and the Revolution of 1917, he wrote ten other plays, none of which is memorable, all angry, all in quest of social reform but largely abandoning the quest for spiritual reality. Like Hauptmann and Tolstoi, Gorki wrote, early in his career, one great naturalist play. He then moved on to other kinds of writing, as if to prove the point that naturalism in the theater could not sustain itself long.

In western Europe no great work of naturalism emerged. In England the work of Henry Arthur Jones (1851–1929) and Sir Arthur Wing Pinero (1855–1934), extending from about 1885 to 1910 and once heralded as "the new realism," was touched neither by Zola's scientism nor by the religious longings of Hauptmann and the Russians. Its reformist spirit, actually not very deep, belonged to English pragmatism, tempered to some degree by the "social" plays of Ibsen. Although Pinero's *The Second Mrs. Tanqueray* (1893) and Jones's *Michael and His Lost Angel* (1896), to mention only two, were once admired as revolutionary works, they have lost most of whatever force they possessed. The same is true of the more impassioned and embattled plays of John Galsworthy (1867–1933), such as *Strife* (1909) and *Justice* (1910). The latter play is said to have brought about a reform in Britain's penal code, and its moral fervor is evident whenever the play is revived; but essentially these works failed to be engaged in what Stephen Spender has called "the struggle of the modern." [25] They were not concerned with extending the range of artistic sensibility to include new dimensions of reality beginning to be felt in their time. This was, to some extent, the concern of Harley Granville-Barker

24 *Ibid.*
25 *The Struggle of the Modern* (Berkeley: University of California Press, 1963).

(1877–1946) in plays such as *The Vorsey Inheritance* (1905), *Waste* (1907), and *The Madras House* (1910). His efforts, however, were too "literary" to affect the theater strongly, and his genius finally realized itself in directing and interpreting the plays of Shakespeare.

A good case could be made for the view that naturalism paid off in Britain better among the Irish than among the English. The Irish Literary Theatre, begun in 1899 and set up in the Abbey playhouse in 1904, had more than a little naturalism in its blood, especially in its foremost playwright of the early period, John Millington Synge (1871–1909). Yet since the Abbey Theatre and Synge himself were Irish, and were protégés of Yeats, such naturalism as they possessed was transmuted almost at birth into lyricism. We shall therefore return to them in a later chapter.

In the latter part of the nineteenth century the drama's search for reality led to realism, but it also led right out of it again. Imitation of the hidden underside of life (in poverty and in moral corruption) was symbolic of the general "search for reality," but by no means did it exhaust that search. It was no accident that the growth of dramatic realism took place at the very same time as did a new attempt to lure back to the theater the muse of poetry.

7. THE SEARCH FOR REALITY
IN POETRY AND IRONY

IN THE CHAPTER on theater practice (Chapter 5) I pointed out that advocates of a poetic theater, men such as Paul Fort and Lugné-Poe, followed directly on the heels of the naturalist innovator Antoine. Stanislavski presented himself as a devotee of Maeterlinck as well as of Gorki. The theater of the mid-twentieth century inherits not only a realist and naturalist drama that developed at the end of the nineteenth but also a revival of poetic drama that flourished at the same time. The history of drama since 1900 might plausibly be viewed as a lengthy, still uncompleted struggle to unite these separate tendencies.

In general, there have been two means of attempting such unity. One method has concentrated on language. It has assumed that drama is primarily a form of literature and must therefore find its excellence in the way that it employs words. In this view the problem of combining poetry with dramatic realism is the problem of finding a poetic line and diction flexible enough to imitate the thoughts, deeds, and passions of contemporary man. Another method, however, has located the problem not so much in language as in what may be called the theatrical image. In the stage settings, in the characters and situations, in the *mise en scène*—in short, in the way he employs the theater as an instrument—the playwright is to make his "poetic" utterance. The stage itself is to become his principal metaphor (an idea developed most fully by Pirandello, Beckett, and Genet) or at least to provide the material out of which the metaphors and symbols shall be generated.

The tendency of those attracted to the first method has been to write plays in verse, while that of those attracted to the second has been to write what T. S. Eliot called "the poetic play in prose." There are, however, numerous exceptions; the distinction to be kept in mind is not essentially that between verse and prose but that between verbal images and theatrical images. Even this distinction will not always hold; yet when it does not, we are likely to find ourselves confronted with a work approaching excellence, the playwright having transcended the categories that apply to less successful work. In this chapter I make a broad distinction between those playwrights who concentrated on the poetry of words and those who concentrated on the poetry of the theatrical image. The latter group will be found to have made the more intensive use of irony, because the idea of theatrical images introduces a note of deliberate self-consciousness into the playwright's style and subject matter, inducing a reflexive quality by nature ironic and closely attuned to "modern" consciousness.

Directing attention first to those who concentrated on language as the bearer of images, I call particular attention to Rostand, Claudel, Hofmannsthal, Yeats, and Synge. Of these, Claudel and Yeats will appear as the major figures, partly because they were the better poets and partly because they also had the liveliest appreciation of theatrical values. In such figures one can almost see theater struggling to be born again at the hand of poetic genius.

In the second part of the chapter I turn to certain playwrights who seem not to have become dramatists because they were poets but to have written plays because theatrical images crowded their heads. Their visions, as I have noted, tend to be highly ironic. In this group I discuss Jarry, Maeterlinck, Andreyev, Evreinov, Wilde, Schnitzler, and Wedekind. A mixed bag, indeed. The desire for a theatrical theater, stimulated by two generations of reform in techniques of acting and staging, and by a general cultural self-consciousness, found very diverse expression in all the countries of Europe.

In the late nineteenth century, when many persons, among
them some of the most articulate, were preaching the gospel of science, positivism, and clear and distinct ideas, it was only to be expected that other voices would raise a different cry. In France the
opposition to *Zolisme* turned once again to "romanticism of the
dream," to stories of the "long ago and far away" that appealed to
the eclectic taste of the *fin de siècle* public. The only surprising
thing was that this reaction should find a voice as vigorous as that
of Edmond Rostand in his *Cyrano de Bergerac* (1897).

Rostand (1868–1918) was by no means the only exponent of
dream-romanticism at the time. There were also Jean Richepin
(1849–1926) and his son Jacques Richepin (1880–1946), Catulle
Mendès (1843–1909), André Rivoire (1872–1930), and Edouard
Schuré (1841–1929). Schuré is sometimes mentioned, with Josephin
Péladan (1859–1918) and others, as one who revived classical
tragedy. At this period, however, there could be no question of a
genuinely classical spirit. When one notes among these writers the
very strong influence of Wagner, he may conclude that in spite of
their frequent use of stories from Greek plays they were romanticists of the dream.

From this group Rostand stands out by virtue of his charm. And
if we ask what qualities in *Cyrano,* his major play, render it charming, the answer is exuberance and self-mockery. Its setting, which is
the Paris of the well-born between 1640 and 1655, was deliberately
chosen as being that of a ceremonious and style-conscious society.
Cyrano, famed for his large nose but equally memorable, in Rostand's portrait of him, for his intelligent wit, is a self-dramatizer.
He casts himself, figuratively speaking, in the role of the sad clown,
displaying on the surface the utmost panache while underneath he
lives a life of loneliness and frustrated love.

The self-mockery of the character Cyrano extends to every part
of Rostand's play and accounts for all its tone. Instead of coming to
a dry or skeptical sort of irony, however, Rostand pushed forward
with an astonishing exuberance that lent to his jesting the air of
magnificence. This was possible for him because of his absolute
command over language. His final triumph, as he well knew, was
rhetorical. This was his excellence and also his limitation; in his

treatment of language there is small hint of a poet's search for reality. His play is thus a grandiloquent example of escapist dream-romanticism. Nevertheless, he wrote dialogue of such wit and verve that the stage success of *Cyrano* was virtually unprecedented.

Rostand's first produced play was *Les Romanesques* (1894; *The Romancers*), a long-forgotten parody of young love that has recently been revived as the basis of the Tom Jones–Harvey Schmidt musical, *The Fantasticks* (1960). In 1895 Rostand wrote *La Princesse Lointaine* ("Princess Faraway," published in English under the title *The Lady of Dreams*). In June of the same year George Bernard Shaw saw it performed by the French Company at Daly's Theatre in London. The most delightful part of his review[1] was devoted to a confession of ignorance of the French language, but this ignorance did not prevent Shaw from declaring the play "verbose." No one would expect the British champion of prose realism to admire the French dream-romancer, especially when the title role was acted by Sarah Bernhardt, a performer Shaw loved to lambaste; yet it is interesting to read what he wrote:

> The romance of chivalry has its good points; but it always dies of the Unwomanly Woman. And M. Rostand's Princess Far Away will die of Melissinde. A first act in which the men do nothing but describe their hysterical visions of a wonderful goddess-princess whom they have never seen is bad enough; but it is pardonable, because men do make fools of themselves about women, sometimes in an interesting and poetic fashion. But, when the woman appears and plays up to the height of their folly, intoning her speeches to an accompaniment of harps and horns, distributing lilies and languors to pilgrims, and roses and raptures to troubadours, always in the character which their ravings have ascribed to her, what can one feel except that an excellent opportunity for a good comedy is being thrown away? If Melissinde would only eat something, or speak in prose, or only swear in it, or do anything human —were it even smoking a cigaret—to bring these silly Argonauts to their senses for a moment, one could forgive her. But she remains an unredeemed humbug from one end of the play to the other. . . .[2]

[1] To be found in *Shaw's Dramatic Criticism (1895–98)*, selected by John F. Matthews (New York: Hill and Wang, 1959), pp. 86–94.
[2] *Ibid.*, pp. 86–87.

Shaw was right; Rostand did not always maintain the quality of self-mockery that endows *Cyrano* with its charm. The dreamy aspect of his romanticism too easily took over, and without an enjoyment of the author's lavish French little is left.

Matters did not improve with *La Samaritaine* (1897; *The Woman of Samaria*) or with *L'Aiglon* (1900; *The Eaglet*), in which Sarah Bernhardt played the son of Napoleon. Rostand was popular nonetheless, and the ten-year lapse between *L'Aiglon* and his next play was filled with expectation. *Chantecler* (1910) turned out to be an enormous spectacle of a quasi-symbolist nature. Nearly a ton of feathers were used in the costumes, in which the stars who made up the cast were dressed as chickens, owls, pheasants, and other birds. The play was intended to vaunt French nationalism and to dispel "all the shadows that threaten the genius of the French race." Though it attracted partisans, it was not a success. However, a revival staged in an even bolder expressionist manner in 1928 did succeed.

Paul Claudel (1868–1955), Catholic poet, French diplomat, and spiritual pilgrim, was utterly different from Rostand. Born the same year, they shared only their patriotism and their mastery of the French language. There is, to be sure, a sense in which Claudel's plays may be said to be examples of dream-romanticism. They are certainly romantic, in almost any sense of the word. In them, however, the quest for reality, virtually absent from Rostand, burns feverishly. Moreover, the reality sought is religious and metaphysical—religious in that the goal of the search is theophany, and metaphysical in that the search is preoccupied with the idea of the infinite.

Claudel's professional life was spent in the diplomatic service, which he entered in 1890. He held consular posts in Europe, the United States, and China. The Orient held for him a particular fascination, most obvious in his play *Partage de midi* (1905; *Break of Noon*), but clear also in the freedom that all his plays show from the constraints of European stage conventions. The years in which he was active as a diplomat (1890–1935) were also those of his major productivity as a dramatist. His first play, *L'Endormie* (*The Sleeper*), was written when he was fourteen. Four years later, in 1886, he underwent a stormy conversion to the Catholic faith, though he did not unite formally with the Church until Christmas 1890, when he took communion at Notre Dame. Meanwhile, in 1889, he had written the first version of his first major play, *Tête d'or* (*Head of Gold;* second version, 1894), which is also his only non-Christian work. The others are all predicated upon Christian mystical awareness, however troubled and however in search of certainty. In 1890 he wrote *La Ville* (*The City;* revised 1897), followed in 1892 by the first version of *L'Annonce faite à Marie* (*The Tidings Brought to Mary*) and in 1893 by *L'Échange* (*The Exchange*), which is set in America, where Claudel was living when he wrote it, and which, in its use of stock figures such as the multimillionaire who sings his praises to the dollar, shows Claudel's affinity with the many young artists of Europe who at that time and later entertained a comic-strip view of America. *Le Repos du septième jour* ("Rest on the Seventh Day"), a work highly experimental in form and dealing with an emperor's penance for his people, was written in 1896. There was then a break of some nine years before Claudel wrote *Partage de midi* (not produced until 1948). In 1909 came *L'Otage* (*The Hostage*), the first of a trilogy concerned with the restoration of the Bourbon house after Napoleon and, more important, with the fortunes of the Papal State. The others in this trilogy are *Le Pain dur* (1914; *Crusts*) and *Le Père humilié* (1916; *The Humiliation of the Father*). In 1910 Claudel reworked *La Jeune fille Violaine* for the second time (the first version of 1892 had been redone in 1898) and changed its title to *L'Annonce faite à Marie*. Many consider this medieval story of love and miracle to be his best play. Certainly it is his most "accessible" and popular. In 1914 he turned to farce with *Protée* ("Proteus"), in which Menelaus finds himself on a lonely island with Helen. Farce again is *L'Ours et la lune* (1917; "The Bear and the Moon"). *L'Homme et son desir* (1919; "Man and His Desire") is ballet-pantomime. Then in 1919 Claudel began five years of work on *Le Soulier de satin* (*The Satin Slipper*), his most magnificent dramatic conception. In 1927 he wrote *Le Livre de Christophe Colombe* (*The Book of Christopher Columbus*), the music for which was composed by Darius Milhaud. Another work conceived integrally with music was *Jeanne au bûcher* ("Joan at the Stake"), written in 1935 with Arthur Honegger as composer. Still another was *L'Histoire de Tobie et de Sara* (1942; *The Story of Tobias and Sara*), which was written for Stravinsky but finally composed by Dugend.

Throughout all this prodigious course of playwriting, which was accompanied by a large quantity of poems, articles, criticism, and correspondence, Claudel made virtually no concessions to popular taste. His choice of themes, his dramatic structures, and his expectations with regard to theater practice came out of the autonomy of his imagination; and while he kept thoroughly abreast of developments in the theater and was friend to a number of those who formed the avant-garde before World War I, he was part of no school or movement. The image one gets is of a lonely, busy giant.

This is not to say, however, that Claudel had little influence on twentieth-century drama. It is true that there is no list of playwrights who have followed in his train, but it is also true that he has done as much as any modern author to expand our ideas about what the theater can do, to show how it can be the instrument of a total vision, and to ally the actor's words with his gestures in a symbolic unity. In this sense Claudel was a precursor of the theater of Brecht and Piscator. He had begun to enlarge the modern concept of theater long before his famous collaboration with Jean-Louis Barrault began in 1943, the year Barrault staged *Le Soulier de satin* at the Comédie Française with Claudel working closely beside him. As early as 1914 Lugné-Poe had made theater history with a production of *L'Annonce faite à Marie* at L'Oeuvre, using hauntingly beautiful and beautifully simple designs by Jean Variot.

All this work of theatrical enlargement proceeded from a man who was, before everything else, a poet and whose plays must finally be judged by the way in which they employ the French language. Claudel is a very difficult writer to translate. In spite of the good translations, few in number, that Professor Wallace Fowlie has made, the best now available in English, Claudel remains an enigmatic figure in the English-speaking world, while the French audience, even the part that does not like him, recognizes instantly his force and beauty of utterance.

As a thinker Claudel appears to be something other than a modern. He was caught by the idea that the divine can be manifest only through the crucifixion of the mundane. His plays usually show the immolation of passion. Yet in his questing spirit Claudel was very much a modern, quite as dissatisfied with appearances as any Pirandello and equally attracted to the theater as that art which simultaneously masks and reveals. His difference from most other great moderns comes from his love of absolutes, which drove him, as it drove Wagner, in a Manichaean direction. His imagination moved toward a point where love, death, and beatific vision seemed to converge. His devotion to the absolute meant that he lacked the ironic quality that modern drama, in its principal development, was to find ever more important; but in his restless search for a reality behind the masks of experience he was modern indeed, a spiritual kinsman of Strindberg and O'Neill. Like them, and in spite of his Catholicism, he cannot be imagined until after Nietzsche.

Apart from Claudel, the two most important poetic dramatists of the period 1890–1914 were Hugo von Hofmannsthal (1874–1929) and William Butler Yeats (1865–1939). Gabriele D'Annunzio (1863–1938) was writing in the same period, but although between 1897 and 1909 he wrote ten celebrated plays, he is not to be considered a major figure. His flamboyant life, including his famous love affair with Eleonora Duse, eclipsed his plays, which were destined barely to outlive the style of *art nouveau* they so forcefully recall. By 1914 in England John Masefield (1878–1967), John Drinkwater (1882–1937), Lascelles Abercrombie (1881–1939), Eden Phillpotts (1862–1960), James E. Flecker (1884–1915), Laurence Binyon (1869–1943), and Gordon Bottomley (1874–1948) were all writing plays in verse. Binyon's cousin, Stephen Phillips (1868–1915), had initiated the post-Victorian attempt to restore poetry to the English stage (the plays of Tennyson, Browning, and other Victorians had not been stageworthy) with such works as *Herod, A Tragedy* (1900) and *Paolo and Francesca* (1901); but much greater work, of which Phillips seemed largely unaware, was already being done by Yeats in Ireland.

Yeats's approach to drama was utterly that of a poet whose exploration was inward. The lateral scope of drama, its extension over a wide range of human character and situation and over the history of drama in the West, did not interest him. Instead he cultivated a highly personal style and mined the folk material of Ireland. This led him eventually to the drama of the East, particularly to the Japanese Noh play, in which he discovered a form more suited to his purposes than anything in the Western tradition. In Yeats's plays imitation of life is subordinated to poetic imagination, narrative to the evocative power of symbol. In his theater the mask rules supreme, attended by two of its subsidiary forms—the dance and the poetic word.

Hofmannsthal, on the other hand, embraced the tradition, seeing himself as one called, like a priest, to preserve and reform its values. He was thus a "heavier" writer than Yeats, a man of Germanic seriousness (actually he was Viennese), and open to the charge of being pretentious. We think, when his name is mentioned, of his full-brass collaborators, Max Reinhardt and Richard Strauss, and of the noble grandeur of the presentations at Salzburg, where thousands came to be stirred by his adaptations of *Everyman* and of Pedro Calderón de la Barca's *Great Theater of the World*.

Hofmannsthal's early lyric dramas were concerned with the conflict between, on the one hand, the poet's aloofness from the human spectacle and, on the other, the necessity of his being deeply involved in experience. *Gestern* (1891; *Yesterday*), his first lyric play, enunciates such a theme; and *Der Tod des Tizian* (1892; *Titian's Death*) has a similar motif in the contrast between the beauty of "pure art" and the ugliness of reality. *Der Tor und der Tod* (1893; *The Fool and Death*) depicts the Fool as a dilettante, a mere actor, who, in the hour of his death, recognizes that he has really lived no life at all.

These plays, and some half dozen others written in the 1890's, were short. Hofmannsthal wrote his first full-length play, *Das Bergwerk zu Falun* (*The Mine at Falun*) in 1899. He then turned directly to the dramatic tradition and began a series of adaptations: Sophocles' *Elektra* (1903), Thomas Otway's *Venice Preserved* (1905), and *Oedipus and the Sphinx* (1906), which deals with events preceding those in Sophocles' play. There followed a comedy, *Cristinas Heimreise* (1908; *Cristina's Journey Home*). In 1909 Richard Strauss turned Hofmannsthal's *Elektra* into an opera. This led to their collaboration the next year on *Ariadne auf Naxos*. At this time Hofmannsthal also translated *Oedipus Rex* for a production by Max Reinhardt. *Jedermann* followed in 1911, the same year as *Der Rosenkavalier*. The rest of Hofmannsthal's major work for the theater came after World War I. *Die Frau ohne Schatten* (1919; *The Woman Without a Shadow;* libretto for the opera by Strauss): *Der Schwierige* (1921; *The Unmanageable,* a comedy); two adaptations from Calderón de la Barca—*Das grosse salzburger Welttheater* (1922; *The Salzburg Great Theater of the World*) and *Der Turm* (1925, revised 1927; *The Tower*), adapted from *La vida es sueño (Life Is a Dream)*; and two other librettos for Strauss—*Das aegyptische Helena* (1928; *The Egyptian Helen*) and *Arabella* (published posthumously in 1933).

Even more than Claudel, Hofmannsthal is likely to impress us today as a throwback to premodern romanticism. His career seems almost Faustian, so exalted was its aim, so serious its sense of mission. Irony is almost entirely absent from his work, while the romantic sense of loss, of the world's betrayal of the ideal, is very strong. Hofmannsthal's theater shows the persistence into our century of a heady romanticism, of a kind that more "modern" writers have found it their business to protest against and to deflate.

Yeats was different. Equally romantic, and devoted to "a correlation between the highest in literature and the highest in national life," [3] Yeats wooed rather than bulldozed his culture. His works for the theater are fragile. Yet, since they respect the tentative, evanescent nature of human self-knowledge, their fragility becomes a strength. "Whatever we lose in mass and in power," he once wrote, "we should recover in elegance and subtlety." [4]

Yeats's dramatic writing began in 1892 and continued until shortly before his death in 1939. The *Collected Plays*,[5] a hefty volume, includes twenty-six works, which range in length from the sixty-page, three-act *Unicorn from the Stars* (1908) to short one-acts of no more than twelve pages, such as *Calvary* (1920) and *Purgatory* (1939). The style also varies from the naturalism of *The Countess Cathleen* (1892) to the almost pure symbolism of *The Resurrection* (1931). There are two translations from Sopho-

---

[3] Quoted in Ronald Peacock, *The Poet in the Theatre* (New York: Hill and Wang, 1960), p. 117.
[4] *Ibid.,* p. 119.
[5] New York: Macmillan, 1934; London: Macmillan, 1952.

cles. This *oeuvre,* so delicate in its parts, yet adding up to a sum and quality of such large proportions, was wrought integrally with Yeats's development as a poet; Yeats the poet and Yeats the playwright can hardly be distinguished, certainly not separated. He was one of those inspired playwrights to whom the distinction between poetry of words and poetry of theatrical images will scarcely apply.

He formed the Irish Literary Theatre with Lady Gregory, Edward Martyn, and George Moore in 1899. In 1904 this became the Abbey Theatre, under which name it achieved renown as one of the world's major centers of theater renewal, along with the Moscow Art Theater (founded less than a year earlier) and J. T. Grein's Independent Theatre Society in London, the Freie Bühne in Berlin, and the Théâtre Libre in Paris, all of which were formed about a decade before.

Ronald Peacock has justly written,

> In Yeats three things work together which in creative writers had for a long time been antagonistic: spiritual, dramatic, and poetic values. . . . His plays, therefore, which have so distinct an originality that they might seem to call for a judgment only on their intrinsic value, have in fact a wider historical significance as well. For the continuity of drama and its connection with the mainstream of poetic writing his work is much more important than that of either Synge or the "realists." [6]

One reason for this achievement lay in Yeats's willingness to trust *both* the poetic and the dramatic image. He would subordinate an image neither to "characterization" nor to theme. Instead, he seemed to let these emerge from the disciplined flow of the images. This was bold, and it was something the theater sorely needed. No other modern poetic dramatist writing in English has been so daring. Eliot, for instance, wrote plays in which the images seem always derived from themes. Yeats's reward is to be the only modern whose work keeps alive the genuine possibility of a poetic theater in the English language.

In him also the search for reality was much in evidence. He rejected the scientism of his age: it gave answers much too clear, too inhibiting to the spirit. For Yeats a non-mysterious reality could

6 *Op. cit.,* p. 125.

hardly be real. In Paris he met Sar Paladan, Strindberg's teacher of magic and the occult. This meeting, plus, we may think, a certain Irish credulousness, made Yeats a believer in spirits, migratory souls, demons, the psychic influence of the moon, and much else that seems obscurantist. His interest in these matters was, however, utterly sincere, and he used them not to answer the question what is real but to aid his search. He became learned in occult Neoplatonism, which supported his quest and gave it shape.

The search was reflected in Yeats's use of language. Under the influence of Douglas Hyde and other scholars, he came to desire a resurrection of Gaelic, but he never committed himself to the exclusive use of this language. Instead, he brought its resources to bear upon his use of English, to broaden it, make it deeper, and render it more flexible. In this way he stretched the mind of the listener and sent him on a search for dimensions of the psyche normally unattended. It was Yeats's Irish English that finally broke Shakespeare's power over English poetic drama.

> I call before the eyes a roof
> With cross-beams darkened by smoke;
> A fisher's net hangs from a beam,
> A long oar lies against the wall.
> I call up a poor fisher's house;
> A man lies dead or swooning,
> That amorous man,
> That amorous, violent man, renowned Cuchulain,
> Queen Emer at his side.[7]
>
> (THE ONLY JEALOUSY OF EMER, 1919)

The English-speaking stage has seldom known a poetic idiom as direct, yet at the same time as evocative, as this. By the simplicity and suppleness of his voice, whether in verse or in prose, which he frequently intermixed, Yeats was able to bring into his theater an unseen yet powerful world of spirit.

WISE MAN: And wither shall I go when I am dead?
ANGEL: You have denied there is a Purgatory,
   Therefore that gate is closed; you have denied
   There is a Heaven, and so that gate is closed.

[7] *Collected Plays* (New York: Macmillan, 1934), p. 185.

WISE MAN: Where then? For I have said there is no Hell.
ANGEL: Hell is the place of those who have denied;
    They find there what they planted and what dug,
    A Lake of Spaces, and a Wood of Nothing,
    And wander there and drift, and never cease
    Wailing for substance.[8]

                             (*The Hour-Glass,* 1914)

Yeats's poetic theater, however, is by no means purely verbal. In fact, its words, taken alone, are not highly dramatic. They require to be spoken in the simple, imagistic settings and with the music and dancing for which Yeats conceived them. For instance, the following is what he suggested for *The Cat and the Moon,* a short playlet written in 1926:

> The scene is any bare place before a wall against which stands a patterned screen, or hangs a patterned curtain suggesting Saint Colman's Well. Three Musicians are sitting close to the wall, with zither, drum, and flute. Their faces are made up to resemble masks.[9]

One notes that the stage setting is as simple as the poetic line. A pure doctrine of theatrical economy is here at work, and it must not be forgotten that Yeats was strongly influenced by Japanese Noh drama as well as by French symbolism and was more successful than any other playwright in bringing the quality of these sources to fine expression in the Western theater. His elaborate theory of masks, too intricate for recapitulation here, showed a profound understanding of theatrical imagination in its bearing upon human personality.

Of the writers associated with Yeats in the renaissance of Irish drama, Lady Gregory (Isabella Augusta Persse, 1852–1932) and John Millington Synge (1871–1909) eclipsed Yeats in popularity. Lady Gregory's work is not of deep interest; Synge's is.

Although Synge wrote in prose, he was a poet. He pursued not the poetry of the theatrical image but the poetry of the word, and it is hard to remember that the words are not in verse.

He went to Trinity College in Dublin and then to Germany to

---

[8] *Ibid.,* pp. 201–202.
[9] *Ibid.*

study music. By 1894 he had arrived in Paris, settled on the Left Bank, and set himself to become a literary critic. He left Paris in 1896 to tour Italy and again in 1898 to visit the Aran Islands. The next year, in Paris, Irish letters caught up with him in the person of Yeats. "Go west," said Yeats in effect, meaning to the west of Ireland, and Synge once more went off to the Aran Islands, arriving there in a canvas canoe.

Much is said about Synge's having copied the natural speech of the Irish. He said so himself:

> In writing *The Playboy of the Western World,* as in my other plays, I have used one or two words only that I have not heard among the country people of Ireland, or spoken in my own nursery before I could read the newspapers. . . . When I was writing *The Shadow of the Glen,* some years ago, I got more aid than any learning could have given me from a chink in the floor of the old Wicklow house where I was staying, that let me hear what was being said by the servant girls in the kitchen.[10]

This is no doubt true enough, but what Synge fails to mention and most commentators fail to emphasize is that the playwright's ear is as important as the natives' speech, which of course is why Synge and not Ireland, not Lady Gregory, "A.E.," or Yeats is the author of his plays. Though Synge can have carried little with him in the canoe he paddled toward the islands, he did possess an ear trained among the musicians of Germany and the symbolist poets of Paris. It is a mistake to regard the Irish theater as a miracle that sprang unwatered from virgin soil, as if it had nothing to do with that "search for reality" that was changing the look of painting, the sound of music, the cadence of poetry, and the shape of drama everywhere in Europe. Synge was very consciously reacting, like Yeats himself, against the new realism in European and English drama. That meant particularly the new Ibsenism which Shaw and William Archer were pushing in London with Jones, Pinero, and (soon) Galsworthy as minor advocates. But Synge was also trying to avoid what he regarded as an overcivilized development in literature that provided richness "only in sonnets, or prose poems, or in one or two elaborate books." "One has, on one side, Mallarmé and

10 Preface to *The Playboy of the Western World,* in *The Complete Works of John M. Synge* (New York: Random House, 1935), p. 3.

Huysmans producing this literature; and, on the other, Ibsen and Zola dealing with the reality of life in joyless and pallid words." [11]

All this means that Synge's playwriting was oriented, however negatively, to English and European drama and would not have come about without the ferment that was already manifest in the work of Zola, Ibsen, Antoine, Grein, and others in theater, plus the symbolists in poetry. The latter were as important to Synge as to Yeats, although in a different way. They gave Yeats some of his technique, vocabulary, and images; they taught Synge to discern the imaginative vitality in colloquial idiom. Without the symbolists we would have no *Riders to the Sea* and probably not the virtues of Synge's other plays as well.

During much of 1902 Synge was in London working on his first plays. *The Shadow of the Glen* was produced in Dublin in October of 1903 by the Irish Literary Theatre. It was followed the next year by another one-act play, *Riders to the Sea,* which was performed in the newly acquired Abbey Playhouse. This play is so exquisite, so actable, and of such evocative power that one may call it perfect within its own carefully defined limitations. The subject is death by drowning. The action is simply to receive the harbingers of death and to mourn the passing of man. Existence is but a protrusion from the sea, to which all life returns, rising and falling like a wave. The play's language is at once plain and symbolic, and its beauty lies in its rhythm.

> I've had a husband, and a husband's father, and six sons in this house—six fine men, though it was a hard birth I had with every one of them and they coming to the world—and some of them were found and some of them were not found, but they're gone now, the lot of them. . . . There were Stephen, and Shawn, were lost in the great wind, and found after in the Bay of Gregory of the Golden Mouth, and carried up the two of them on one plank, and in by that door. . . .
>
> There was Sheamus and his father, and his own father again, were lost in a dark night, and not a stick or sign was seen of them when the sun went up. There was Patch after was drowned out of a curagh that turned over. I was sitting here with Bartley, and he a baby, lying on my two knees, and I seen two women, and

11 *Ibid.*

three women, and four women coming in, and they crossing themselves, and not saying a word. I looked out then, and there were
men coming after them, and they holding a thing in the half of a
red sail, and water dripping out of it—it was a dry day, Nora—and
leaving a track to the door.[12]

The Well of the Saints came in 1905, *The Playboy of the Western World* in 1906. *The Tinker's Wedding* was published in 1909,
the year in which Synge, at the age of thirty-eight, underwent an
operation for cancer and died. *Deirdre of the Sorrows,* unfinished,
was published in 1910.

Broadly speaking, all of these are plays dealing with the people
and their ways, and they were intended to celebrate Irish life by
combining, as Synge said, reality and joy. The Irish public, however, was not overjoyed. It felt itself attacked and rose to battle.
The rowdy premier of *The Playboy,* January 26, 1907, became a
vivid moment in the history of the modern theater, a Gaelic incident comparable to the Paris premier of Hugo's *Hernani* long before. John Gassner has described it:

> The audience which had already had an encounter with Synge
> about *The Shadow of the Glen* became increasingly resentful as
> they heard the oaths multiplying and saw Irish vestals fluttering
> around a professed parricide with unconcealed admiration. Pan-
> demonium broke loose, the audience stamped, booed, swore in
> Gaelic, sang "God Save Ireland" and shouted with unconscious
> self-criticism that "what would be tolerated in America will not
> be allowed here." The bedlam continued on successive nights,
> until on the fifth night police were placed in the Abbey to main-
> tain order. But the presence of the "Saxon myrmidons" struck
> patriots as only another example of unparalleled treason to Eire
> by those "degraded Yahoos," Yeats and his co-directors. The latter
> also took the unkind precaution of padding the floor with felt to
> absorb the stamping, and this combination of law and upholstery
> at last enabled the actors to make themselves heard.[13]

As a matter of fact, Christy Mahon, the "playboy," was a parri-
cide only in intention. He did no more than wound the old man,
who later appears and takes his son in hand. But the villagers in the

[12] *Riders to the Sea,* in *Complete Works,* pp. 93–94.
[13] *Masters of the Drama,* 3rd ed. (New York: Dover, 1954), p. 558.

play, deceived by Christy's "gallows story" and swept off their feet by his dash, had been had. The Dublin public felt the same. Their reaction to Synge and the whole Abbey Theatre (duplicated by that of the American Irish when the group visited the United States in 1911) was essentially comic—and Syngean comedy at that. It left in its wake feelings of indignation and shame.

Perhaps it was because he had been so loudly booed that Synge was, in other quarters, praised too highly. Some hailed him as the greatest writer of English dialogue since Shakespeare. Ronald Peacock rightly suggests that "we might venture now, without losing our admiration for the rarity of his achievement, to see that his star does shine so very brightly because there were so few others in the sky: and to see, too, that it is a luminary wholly attached to a nineteenth not a twentieth-century orbit." [14]

The swing from the nineteenth- to the twentieth-century orbit was to be made not by those who concentrated on the poetry of words but by those who would also develop a poetry of the theatrical image. It was through leaving the latter essentially untouched that Synge remained "wholly attached" to the nineteenth-century orbit, whereas Yeats, though certainly a word-poet, was equally aware of the symbolic power of the stage and therefore has had more to do with the development of the modern than any of his contemporary poet-dramatists of the English language.

Two kinds of development led toward what I have called the poetry of the theatrical image. One of these was symbolism, which was best employed by Yeats, though it was most conspicuous in the plays of Maeterlinck. The other was theatricalism, which emphasized an immediate encounter between the audience and the performance, abjuring illusion and seeking an intense awareness of the theatrical moment.

In 1896 a raucous, insulting, and notorious kind of theatricalism burst upon Paris. On the evening of December 10 a distinguished audience had made its way to the Théâtre Nouveau, where Lugné-Poe's Théâtre de l'Oeuvre was installed. The play to be performed was *Ubu roi* (*King Ubu*), the first work of a 23-year-old Frenchman named Alfred Jarry (1873–1907). The curtain parted, and the actor Firmin Gémier came forward. He was dressed as a fat, ugly "King," an absurd glob of humanity whose very appearance

14 *Op. cit.*, p. 106.

was insulting. After looking disgustedly over the audience, he hurled toward it the play's opening word, *Merdre!* (The common word is *merde.* Jarry's impudent form of it has been nicely rendered as "Shittre!")

Such an obscenity had never before been uttered on the French stage. The audience retaliated with catcalls, boos, and a general commotion. Some spectators left immediately. Others, like the critic Sarcey, stayed for a time and then gave up. Those who remained to the end were intensely divided.

Ubu roi had gone through several versions and one private performance (1888) before its public premier. It was begun when Jarry was a student at the *lycée* in Rennes, where he and his fellows had written marionette scenes in parody of one of their teachers, whose name was Hébert and whom they had dubbed Père Hébé. In the final version we have Ubu, a captain in the Polish army. He has once been king of Aragon, and the play ends with the suggestion that he may one day be king of France. His fortunes, however, are rather up and down. Egged on by his wife (a parody of Macbeth and his Lady here), he kills King Wenceslas and becomes king of Poland. He slaughters the royal family. He then proceeds to kill everyone who has any money, which he confiscates, just as Caligula later does in Albert Camus' play, but without the philosophical rationale. Whereas Caligula reasons that "all things are possible," Ubu says simply, "I will do whatever I please." Furthermore, he is manic and comic. He sets out to fight the czar of Russia. He gets routed in battle. He flees. Finally, he sets sail for France.

Ubu—ugly, dirty, and fat—was a projection of Jarry's infantile urges and adolescent rebellion. The latter was directed not only against society but also against the world and life. Jarry continued to write of Ubu in several later works, including *Ubu cocu* (1897 or 1898; "Cuckold Ubu") and *Ubu enchaîné* (published 1900; "Ubu Bound"), but by the time he was thirty-four, Jarry had drunk himself to death. Before Freud had begun to publish his works on psychoanalysis, Jarry had put the id directly on stage. In his life he demonstrated that the id unbound searches for death.

The historic importance of *Ubu roi*, however, lies not in its antisocial and proto-Freudian content but in its theatricality. It was performed on a virtually bare stage. When a prison door was to be unlocked, an actor stood with his arm outstretched while another put a key into his hand, turned it as in a lock, moved the arm while simulating the noise of a creaking hinge, and went "through." Jarry wrote to Lugné-Poe what manner of staging he wanted (and got):

> Mask for the principal character, Ubu; . . . A cardboard horse's head which he would hang round his neck, as they did on the medieval English stage, . . . One single stage-set or, better still, a plain backdrop, . . . A formally dressed individual would walk on stage, just as he does in puppet shows, and hang up a placard indicating where the next scene takes place. (By the way, I am absolutely convinced that a descriptive placard has far more "suggestive" power than any stage scenery. No scenery, no array of walkers-on could really evoke "the Polish Army marching across the Ukraine.") . . . The abolition of crowds . . . just a single soldier in the army parade scene, and just one in the scuffle when Ubu says "What a slaughter, what a mob, etc. . . ." [15]

The word for Ubu and the theatricalism he spawned in the modern theater is "direct." Not the direct imitation of life—imitation cannot, in any case, be direct—but the direct expression of the imaginative life and the direct, anti-illusory, confrontation between the work and the audience. It was in the 1890's that a similar directness came into painting, which then began to turn from the painting of *scenes* to the painting of *paintings*. This means that such work is not controlled by explicit reference to external reality but is aimed directly at the passions and intellect of the viewer. In painting this mode is called abstract, though it is actually concrete and is so referred to by the French. In drama it is called theatricalism. It might as well be called the method of positive theater, because it is characterized by its emphasis on the positive (i.e., "given") presence of the performance and its images.

Jarry's theater, though it might be said to have symbols in it, is not symbolist. "Symbolism" has been defined as the attempt to achieve in poetry the effects of music, making use of clustered images and metaphors. Nothing could have been further from

15 Translated by Simon Watson Taylor in *Selected Works of Alfred Jarry*, edited by Roger Shattuck and Simon Watson Taylor (New York: Grove Press, 1965), pp. 67–68. The letter is dated 8 January 1896.

Jarry's intention, and it is therefore on a different terrain that one encounters the outstanding "symbolist" of the theater, the Belgian playwright, Maurice Maeterlinck (1862–1949).

Maeterlinck wrote his first play, *La Princesse Maleine* (*The Princess Maleine*) in 1889, a year after *Ubu roi* was privately performed, two years after Antoine founded the Théâtre Libre, and a year before Paul Fort launched the Théâtre d'Art (at first known as Théâtre Mixte). In the season of 1890–1, Paul Fort introduced Maeterlinck to the stage with a production of *L'Intruse* (*The Intruder*), written, as was *Les Aveugles* (*The Blind*), in 1890. *Les Sept Princesses* (*The Seven Princesses*) came in 1891. The following year Maeterlinck wrote one of his greatest plays, *Pelléas et Mélisande*. It was put on stage by Lugné-Poe on May 17, 1893, and led directly to the establishment of his Théâtre de l'Oeuvre, which was rising from the ashes of the short-lived Théâtre d'Art, subscriptions to the new theater being sold the very day after *Pelléas et Mélisande* was given its remarkable performance. Among the purchasers were Zola, Sardou, and Pierre and Marie Curie.

One of Maeterlinck's admirers was Octave Mirbeau (1850–1917), novelist, critic, and playwright, who devoted a long article to the Pelléas performance. The company had created, he wrote, "around the characters an ornamental framework rather than concerning themselves, as in the normal method, with imitations of real dwellings and true forests." Furthermore, the color scheme of the décor was notable. It was

> graduated in heavy tones, in deep blue, mauve, orange, moss green, moon-green, the green of water, connected by violet tints and grey-blues, to the costumes of the actors, culminating in that of Mélisande, which was the lightest in tone.[16]

This simplification of the décor, its transformation from literal statement to a more "abstract" and immediate communication of atmosphere and feeling, was invited by the script that Maeterlinck had written, which was unspecific about the time and place of the action and was an attempt to place the spectator in rapport with what Maeterlinck later called "one of the strange moments of a

---

16 Quoted in *Encyclopédie du théâtre contemporain*, Gilles Quéant, gen. ed. Vol. I (Paris: Les Publications de France, 1957), p. 50. My translation.

higher life that flit unperceived through my dreariest hours." [17]

That Maeterlinck's nonliteral, symbolist attempt should be at once realizable in Lugné-Poe's production indicates, first, that the poet's imagination was indeed theatrical (even if it might also be said not to be highly *dramatic*) and, second, that the French theater itself was at that moment ready to receive such an imagination and to collaborate with it. The play and its production marked an important step toward what was later called "pure theater," and it was, by the same token, half way toward achieving Walter Pater's norm for all art, "the condition of music." Its closeness to music was accurately perceived by Claude Debussy when, nine years later (1902), he turned the play into an opera, creating one of the major works of the modern musical theater, the most significant achievement in that domain between Wagner and Alban Berg's *Wozzeck* of 1920. After *Pelléas* and before World War I, Maeterlinck wrote a dozen other plays, of which the most famous is *L'Oiseau bleu* (1908; *The Blue Bird*) and the best *Monna Vanna* (1902). Ten more were written between 1918 and 1940, but Maeterlinck's quiet visions seemed somehow out of place or even irrelevant after the catastrophe of 1914–1918. These visions, except in respect of their free use of the stage, did not belong to the future.

Maeterlinck wrote:

> I have grown to believe that an old man, seated in his armchair, waiting patiently, with his lamp beside him; giving unconscious ear to all the eternal laws that reign about his house, interpreting, without comprehending, the silence of doors and windows and the quivering voice of the light, submitting with bent head to the presence of his soul and his destiny . . . I have grown to believe that he, motionless as he is, does yet live in reality a deeper, more human, and more universal life than the lover who strangles his mistress, the captain who conquers in battle, or "the husband who avenges his honor." [18]

The stage picture Maeterlinck drew in these words is static. He used the adjective himself and based his dramatic theory upon it.

The theatrical importance of this famous illustration lies not in the fact that the image is static but that it is an *image*. To protect the image from being dissolved into mere activity, from being turned in the theater into a mere copying of motion, Maeterlinck rendered it static. The stage and what appeared thereon should not divert the spectator with incidents but rather generate an activity in the mind and soul. This would occur when the stage put copying at a minimum and *signification* at a maximum. Rendering the image static and surrounding it with an aura of the indefinite were strategies for the achievement of this end. Theatrical symbolism was a means of driving the dramatic action into the interior of the spectator (see Maeterlinck's play *Intérieur*, 1894). Chekhov would show that it was possible to do this even better by rendering the symbols less obvious and more natural, by diffusing them, as it were, throughout the spectrum of an ordinary scene. But Maeterlinck rightly perceived that the stage is by nature symbolic. What he did not perceive was that its tendency to symbolize, once recognized, must be curbed and disciplined.

After their production of Chekhov's *The Cherry Orchard* in 1904, the Moscow Art Theater turned next to Maeterlinck, mounting *The Blind* and *Interior* on October 2. In September 1908 they created the first performance anywhere of *The Blue Bird*. That summer Stanislavski had traveled all the way to Normandy to visit Maeterlinck at his country estate and confer with him about the script. He wanted to "soften some of the scenes" so that the play would not "strike the spectator as being of the theatre theatrical." [19]

Stanislavski's attraction to Maeterlinck is explained by the fact that Stanislavski, for all his celebrated realism, knew as well as Maeterlinck that the life of the theater lies in its *signification,* the end to which all else is means. He had taught himself the art of standing still on the stage, had learned that he expressed the inner life most when outwardly he did the least. His method for teaching acting focused on a certain still-point from which creativity springs. Like the Belgian symbolist, though by more diverse means, he sought to use the theatrical instrument so that its best moments became images poetic in nature. Hence, Stanislavski en-

[19] *My Life in Art,* J. J. Robbins, trans. (New York: Meridian, 1956), p. 498.

couraged not only Maeterlinck but also such Russian theatrical poets as Andreyev and Evreinov. The Moscow Art Theater had a symbolist period from 1904 to 1911.

Leonid Andreyev (1871–1919) was the most acclaimed Russian playwright (he also wrote short stories and novels) active in the years immediately before the Great War. In 1907 his symbolic morality play, *The Life of Man,* was produced both by Stanislavski at the Moscow Art and by Vsevolod Meierhold at the Kommissarzhevskaya Theater. The Stanislavski production used backcloths of black velour, while the actors' costumes were of luminous materials. When the play began the only thing visible was a burning candle at the left of the stage. The figure named Somebody in Grey called to the audience: "You who come here, you who are sentenced to death, behold the life of man." The life shown was one of greed and unhappiness, in wealth as in poverty. At the end of the play the candle was blown out.

At the Moscow Art Theater in 1909 Nemirovich-Danchenko directed Andreyev's *Anathema,* which contrasts the spirit of negation with kindness and faith, the latter qualities symbolized by a lowly Jew named David Leiser. In *Black Masks* (1908) a man fights a duel with his own double. The Maskers in this play are nameless powers that invade the human soul. *King Hunger* shows its title figure presiding over the masses while the wealthy dance away their time.

In some of his plays, such as *The Days of Our Life* (1908), *Anfisa* (1909), and *The Waltz of the Dogs* (1914), Andreyev employed a more or less realistic convention, although he found ways to add symbolist elements even to these. In *He Who Gets Slapped* (1915), his best-known play outside Russia, he combined realism, symbolism, and theatricalism by telling the story of a clown in a circus. "He," the clown, is an intellectual who hides his loneliness and his meditative life behind the role of a patsy.

The Revolution put an end to Andreyev's contributions to the Russian stage. In addition to the plays mentioned above, he had written five others, a total of thirteen in a span of eight years. His work was not truly profound, but it played an important part in the theater's search for poetic images, and that is why it has always interested "experimental" theaters in the West.

Nikolai Evreinov (1879–1953) was even more theatrical than Andreyev. He was a director, an actor, a theoretician, a musician, and a producer as well as a writer, and his conviction was that theater represents a basic play urge in man that is not to be judged primarily on aesthetic grounds. Men are always acting, always playing roles, and there is no important break between art and life. Whereas a naturalist might conclude that if there is no break between art and life the theater should imitate life, Evreinov drew the opposite conclusion: life should be theatricalized. Thus, Evreinov's plays are mostly about playing. *The Fourth Wall* (1915), a two-act comedy, ridicules a naturalistic director who is trying to stage *Faust* and whose efforts to achieve the perfectly natural on stage lead him finally to build a "fourth wall" right across the front of the set. The audience is left to glimpse Faust through a window, but the actor, who wants to be seen, commits suicide. *The Theatre of the Soul* (1912) has clear anticipations of Pirandello and Ionesco. A professor explains that the self is made up of many "I" 's. To each of them the world looks different, and society makes a different response to each. The idea is unsettling, but one can see that with two characters on stage the doubling and crossing of their various selves has comic possibilities. Evreinov developed these, and the play turned out to be both frightening and funny. In 1919, having written numerous short plays, Evreinov wrote *The Chief Thing*, one of his most successful works. Its hero is called Paraclete. Naturally he is a theatrical director. Having formed a company of actors, he sends them not onto a stage but into the world, where they are to play their various roles. They enter a boardinghouse and change the unhappy destinies of its occupants, adding a new dimension to paltry lives and saving some from suicide and crime.

Evreinov was the boldest of the Russian theatrical imagists. In St. Petersburg he organized two seasons of what he called Ancient Theater (1907–8 and 1911–12) in which, with the lavish help of many artists, he mounted examples of medieval, early Renaissance, and Spanish Golden Age plays. His work was contemporaneous with the early experiments of the directors Meierhold and Alexander Tairov (1885–1950), who, in reaction to Russian realism, were developing anti-realist techniques. It was the period when Evgeny Vakhtangov was modifying the approach of Stanislavski to encourage a greater scope of expressive behavior on stage, even grotesquerie and buffoonery. It was the period when Sergei Diaghilev, through his journal *The World of Art* (begun 1898), was encouraging new styles in painting, bringing the new painters into the theater, and founding in Paris his Russian Ballet (1909). Evreinov established a theater of "smaller forms" called The Crooked Mirror, which from 1908 to 1918 enchanted Russians with its comic sketches, parodies, and variety shows. For it he wrote a series of "monodramas" on his favorite theme, the "theatricalization of life."

Beyond the developments already mentioned in this chapter, which have to do with various attempts to render the modern theater poetic, we must notice still another marked tendency the theater displayed in the years before World War I—exploitation of the possibilities of irony. This may be illustrated in the work of three otherwise disparate writers: Oscar Wilde, Arthur Schnitzler, and Frank Wedekind.

Irony is an inevitable concomitant of theatricalism. It is possible, however, to approach irony not only by way of theatricalism but also by way of a more literary ironic tone and view, and it is this we consider now.

The contributions made by Oscar Wilde (1854–1900) to the repertoire of drama may be quickly summarized. His playwriting began in 1883 with a soon-forgotten melodrama called *Vera, or the Nihilists*. In 1891 he wrote a verse play, also soon forgotten, *The Duchess of Padua*. He proved in these two works that he was no innovator in form. In 1892 he wrote in French a play for Sarah Bernhardt. This was the celebrated *Salomé*. Considered decadent —which, if true, is its outstanding merit—this long one-act play was banned by the lord chamberlain in England until 1905. It was first performed (without Sarah Bernhardt) at L'Oeuvre in Paris in 1896, the same daring year as *Ubu roi*. In 1905 Richard Strauss composed the opera based on it. After *Salomé*, Wilde turned (the same year, 1892) to comedies. *Lady Windemere's Fan* was followed by *A Woman of No Importance* (1893). On January 3, 1895, *An Ideal Husband* was performed, and five weeks later *The Importance of Being Earnest*, which turned out to be both his best and his last play. Court trials, scandal, Reading Gaol, and exile filled the remaining five years of that unhappy man's life.

Theatricalism, as I said, leads to irony. It is also true that irony leads to theatricalism. If Oscar Wilde had been able to capitalize on this fact, he would have revolutionized the drama in England. As it was, he let his ironic wit romp within forms already archaic by the time he used them. The inherent drive of his style toward theatricalism was clearly seen by Shaw. Reviewing *An Ideal Husband* in 1895, Shaw wrote:

> In a certain sense Mr. Wilde is to me our only thorough playwright. He plays with everything: with wit, with philosophy, with drama, with actors and audience, with the whole theatre. . . . It is useless to describe a play which has no thesis: which is, in the purest integrity, a play and nothing less.[20]

Shaw always discerned the right things. *An Ideal Husband*, which some thought a thesis play since it dealt with corruption in the Cabinet, was correctly seen by Shaw to have no thesis and to be pure play, on which account he lauded it. But Shaw quickly tired of works without any thesis, and what he might indulge in Wilde in January he was by no means still ready to condone, and in a purer form, in February. He saw immediately that *The Importance of Being Earnest* was farcical, and on that account he lambasted it.

From the historical point of view, all Wilde's works and particularly his best, *The Importance of Being Earnest*, are difficult to describe. This play is perfect in its kind. The difficulty is to know the importance of that *kind* for the development of modern theater. And what kind is it?

The play is of the genre of drawing-room comedy, which Shaw and Wilde, picking up from Congreve and Sheridan, both brought to such a pitch of perfection in the 1890's that all subsequent work in it (even that by Somerset Maugham, Noel Coward, S. N. Behrman, Philip Barry, and T. S. Eliot) has seemed a trifle pale. Wilde's play differs from the rest in being also a kind of farce. It hovers between farce and comedy of manners, the lines belonging more to the latter vein, the absurd plot wholly to the former. This

[20] *Shaw's Dramatic Criticism (1895–98)*, pp. 4–5.

is a delightful brew, and also an ironic one: viewed according to its plot, the play is utterly trivial, while if it is understood through its lines, it is a devastating commentary on English society. The comment, moreover, is invariably set forth in paradoxes and oxymorons that seem to become more apt the more they defy common sense. No one has ever combined frivolity and seriousness better than Wilde and we should, as Eric Bentley has pointed out, show ourselves insensitive if we dismissed him for the slightness and delicateness of his accomplishment.[21]

There is, however, a certain negative point to be made, at least in the context of our story about irony and modernism, and even if Wilde's audience need not bother. It is this. The Wildean irony is not, and was never intended to be, an instrument used in the search for reality. Its bifocalism was required not because Wilde perceived a rift in the world but because of the pleasure the two angles of vision created. This pleasure was the instrument of a certain seriousness, yes—but not of any sense of *discovery*. Wilde's irony therefore has subtlety of wit but not of imaginative perception. It is classical irony, not the romantic kind that Schlegel identified. That this is a fault cannot be said, but that it places Wilde outside the main stream of modernism is undeniable.

Matters stand different with Arthur Schnitzler (1862–1931). Like Wilde he was interested in the behavior of *fin de siècle* society, especially relations between the sexes, the "double standard," the question of fidelity, and the matter of keeping up appearances. These topics might appear very much the same in Vienna as in London. Unlike Wilde, however, Schnitzler regarded these matters as inherently ironic. He was not content simply to speak ironically about them: he viewed them as ironic in themselves. Thus, his comedies contain tragic elements, and his tragedies are close to being comedies. To him the soul is a "vast domain" full of contrasting and contradictory impulses. In society, man is a role-player, an actor who cannot know the full meaning of the role he plays. The playwright, whom Schnitzler sometimes compared to a puppet master, is himself a puppet in God-knows-what performance. The conscious life goes on in some unclear relation to an obscure unconscious. Thus, the tone of Schnitzler's work is skepti-

[21] *The Playwright as Thinker*, 1st ed. (New York: Reynal & Hitchcock, 1946), p. 172.

cal. Some hold it to be cynical, yet Schnitzler is seldom the complete victim of his skepticism, never the nihilistic attacker of everything à la Jarry. In fact, he is less cynical than Wilde, which is one reason that he could probe deeper. A moral ironist must affirm with an intensity equal to his denial, as Schnitzler did. The ironic force thus generated pushed him to the frontiers of dramatic form as he knew it and led him to write highly original plays.

Anatol (1893), an early work, and one of the most famous, may serve as illustration. Its "hero," the title character, is a philanderer in search of constancy. Yet the constancy that part of his soul desires, another part consistently destroys. He is first seen in a high state of agitation over a girl, Cora, whom he suspects of being unfaithful to him. His friend Max suggests that Anatol hypnotize the girl (Schnitzler had studied medicine and when *Anatol* was written had only recently given up medical practice) and ask her his question outright. But as soon as she is hypnotized, Anatol refuses to ask the question. He prefers the ambiguity of his doubt to the certainty of knowledge, and he settles for her affirmation, while hypnotized, that she loves him. After she has awakened, Max reflects that women can lie even while hypnotized, but at least they are happy.

Anatol tires of Cora and on Christmas Eve goes shopping for a present for another girl. Along the way he meets still another, named Gabrielle, who offers to help him select the gift. When Anatol has described how his girl has made him a gift of her whole life "for the present," Gabrielle selects flowers and says to send them with the message that they were chosen by one who might love as well but hasn't the courage.

Deciding to leave Vienna, Anatol hands to Max for safekeeping a bundle of letters and other mementos of his past affairs. Among them is an envelope containing "dust," the remains of a flower that was once sent him by Bianca, a circus acrobat he knew for two hours but who had vowed to remember him always. Max knows Bianca and is expecting her at any moment. When she arrives, she does not remember Anatol at all.

There are several other episodes. In one, Anatol and his mistress Annie agree to part when they are no longer in love, rather than be unfaithful. But Anatol does not keep the promise. Later he decides to break off the affair, only to be surprised by Annie, who jumps the gun and announces that she is in love with another man. Anatol retaliates by telling her of his unfaithfulness. She confesses she has deceived him also.

At last Anatol decides to get married. On the eve of his wedding he goes out for a last fling and brings back to his apartment a former love named Ilone. She asks him to spend the next day with her, and Anatol has to confess that he is getting married. She leaves the apartment with the prediction that she will one day be back again. No doubt. And others, too.

The thematic irony of such a play is obvious enough. So also is the ironic character of Anatol, who is so ambiguously presented that some commentators hold him to be the object of Schnitzler's ridicule while others regard his philosophy of living for momentary happiness to be Schnitzler's own. The truth is that Anatol pursues two conflicting values—the immediate and the constant—and his character is destroyed by their perpetual antagonism.

The conflict between the momentary and the enduring is, moreover, reflected in the form of the play, and it is this which renders the work of particular interest. It is actually not one play but a series of seven one-act plays. Each of them captures, in an exquisitely self-contained way, a moment in the life of Anatol. The question is, What is their unity? When put together, do they suggest a beginning, middle, and end? Hardly. And yet they do have some sort of completeness, both more and less of it than any of the seven would have alone. Here lies the "sense" of the work. It teases the spectator with something akin to the ancient philosophical dilemma of the one and the many and suggests that this problem is reflected in the question of the integrity of an individual's life. The "moments" in a life are clear enough. Taken together, they suggest a unity in the whole of it. Or do they? Do they perhaps shatter or preclude the possibility of such unity? This is the question the episodic—or, rather, beadlike—structure of *Anatol* raises. Its answer is left by Schnitzler in ironic suspension. *Within* each episode there are many other ironies, most of them clustering about the relation between man and woman with its dialectic of fidelity-infidelity.

Reigen (1896–7; *Hands Around,* often known by its French title, *La Ronde*) is a still drier statement of a similar irony. Its ten episodes or "dialogues" link ten characters in a daisy chain of love-making. In the first, we see a whore with a soldier. In the second, the soldier seduces a parlor maid. In the third, the maid gives herself to a "young gentleman." In the fourth, he has a rendezvous with a "young wife." And so on. In the last scene we are back to the whore again. The circular pattern of this work, plus the fact that each episode is a variation on a single theme, gives unity. But this unity is so obvious and so purely formal that it negates itself. The spectator is left with three possibilities: either the scheme is too formal for the material, in which case the substance (human sexuality) is mocked; or the formal pattern fits the substance, in which case the substance is nil; or, finally, the substance is so rich that *no* pattern will fit it, in which case the circular form mocks itself. Schnitzler gives the spectator no means of choosing between these interpretations. He leaves the matter in ironic suspension.

Schnitzler's playwriting career may be said to have begun in 1891 with his first full-length play, *Das Märchen* (*The Fairy-Tale*). It was followed by *Anatol,* then by *Liebelei* (1895; *Light o' Love*). This, his most popular work in his native Austria, is the story of a girl who kills herself after she learns that her lover has died in a duel fought for another woman and that she, therefore, had been only a toy to him. *Freiwild* (1896; *Free Game*) attacked the custom of dueling and the custom of treating young actresses as "free game." Then came *Reigen*. In the thirty-four years between that work and his death in 1931, Schnitzler wrote more than twenty-five other plays, but his major contribution had already been made.

With Schnitzler's shorter-lived German contemporary, Frank Wedekind (1864–1918), dramatic form moved even further in the direction of irony. For this reason Wedekind was a forerunner of expressionism, of Brecht, and of the "absurdist" playwrights. At the same time he harked back to the very beginning of the modern period, to Georg Büchner. In his German predecessor, whose work was just coming to be recognized for its power and "modernity," Wedekind found a method of construction and an intensity of utterance highly congenial to him. He borrowed without hesitation and was, as happens with men of talent, the richer and no less original for his borrowing.

Wedekind attacked the naturalists head on. An early comedy, *Die junge Welt* (1890), satirizes them. Yet Wedekind was not one to substitute the symbolic (à la Maeterlinck) or the cartoon-like (à la Jarry) for the natural. On the contrary, his gift lay in letting his imagination play *upon* the natural. He disliked natural*ism* but not nature, which he squeezed, pressed, and distended until it took a highly expressive form in his work. He did not have Hauptmann's strain of mystical pantheism. Instead he had an artistic ambivalence toward his material, loving it and attacking it, destroying in order to create. He was a moralist, but this did not mean he had a program for society or that he dramatized moral problems as such. It meant he searched in nature itself, and in human nature, for a sense of what ought to be. This search was passionate and like a wrestling match. Wedekind's irony is not detached. Life did not amuse him very much. If Wilde's irony is that of play, Wedekind's is that of deep involvement, of work and pain.

Frühlings Erwachen (1890–91; *Spring's Awakening*) is about puberty. It shows two boys and a girl awakening to desire while still in school. They are thwarted by bourgeois repressiveness and dull education. The girl dies at the hands of a quack doctor, one boy is put into a reformatory, and the other commits suicide.

The play is sometimes described simply as an attack on middle-class morality and a plea for enlightened sex education. When last performed in New York (1963), it was dismissed by the reviewer for the most influential newspaper on the grounds that our degree of enlightenment today has rendered its message obsolete. But the play has much more in it, and the attack on bourgeois child-rearing was never its principal focus.

Spring's Awakening was the first modern drama to focus upon the subject of sex. Love and the amorous and social relations between the sexes had, of course, always been represented on the stage. In some ancient and Renaissance drama (e.g., Euripides' *Hippolytus* and *The Bacchae* and Machiavelli's *Mandragola*) sex had been the subject. Some of the lighter French comedy, and certainly French farce, had dealt with it according to the fashion. But the "serious" modern drama had to find its way to this subject again. It did so in the 1890's at the same time that Freud did so in psychology, yet before he was widely published. Schnitzler, the doctor-turned-playwright, friend of Freud, writing at the same time as Wedekind, was certainly interested in the subject; but he treated it by way of comment upon society and upon personality. Wedekind brought it forward in its own right and focused upon it as a source of power, joy, and destructiveness. In *Spring's Awakening,* sex education and the attitudes of middle-class parents are ancillary to the main theme, which is the ambiguity of the sexual drive itself. If this is not seen, one's interpretation of the play becomes sentimental, and one fails to appreciate the depth of the irony.

The construction of *Spring's Awakening* is episodic, but there are various kinds of episodic playwriting, and Wedekind's is less like that of Schnitzler and more like that of Büchner. Each scene, relatively autonomous and not leading necessarily to the next, nevertheless reflects an aspect of the central theme and action. The whole forms a mosaic of rather large stones. The subtlety lies in the contents of each scene and in the unexpressed relation between the scenes.

Three scenes in Act II may be mentioned as illustrative of the technique. In Scene ii, Mrs. Bergmann converses with her fourteen-year-old daughter, Wendla, who wants to be told "how it all comes about." The answer finally given is that "one must love the man— to whom one is married—love him as only a husband can be loved. One must love him, Wendla, as you at your age are incapable of loving. . . . Now you know."

WENDLA (*getting up*): God in Heaven!
MRS. BERGMANN: Now you know what trials lie before you!
WENDLA: —And that's all?
MRS. BERGMANN: So help me God! [22]

Scene iii is a monologue. The schoolboy Hänschen Rilow "bolts the door behind him and lifts the lid." He takes from his shirt a reproduction of Palma Vecchio's "Venus."

[22] Quotations are from the English version by Eric Bentley, in Eric Bentley, ed., *The Modern Theatre,* Vol. VI (Garden City, N.Y.: Anchor Books, Doubleday, 1960).

Hast thou prayed tonight, Desdemona? You don't seem to be at your prayers, fair one—contemplatively awaiting whoever might be coming—as in the sweet moment of dawning bliss when I saw you in Jonathan Schlesinger's shop window. . . . It was you or I; and the victory is mine.

He recalls "the dear departed with whom I have fought the same battle here"—six pictures of nudes, and now a "seventh wife-murder." He thinks of the others there may be in the future. He kisses "the blooming body, the budding, child's breast, the sweetly rounded—the cruel [because pressed together] knees . . .":

> It is the cause, it is the cause, my soul.
> Let me not name it to you chaste stars!
> It is the cause!—

> (*The picture falls into the depths. He closes the lid.*)

Scene iv, which follows, takes place in a hayloft. Wendla Bergmann climbs up the ladder to Melchior, lying in the hay. The scene is very short—thirteen lines.

WENDLA: People love each other—if they kiss—don't, don't—
MELCHIOR: There is no such thing as love! That's a fact.—It's all just selfishness and self-seeking.—I love you as little as you love me.—

She becomes pregnant.

Melchior is sentenced to the reformatory, from which he later escapes. Moritz, a lad whose sexual awakening has not succeeded in liberating him from extreme introversion, commits suicide. In the play's last scene, Melchior comes to the cemetery where Wendla is buried. There he meets the shade of Moritz with "his head under his arm," who explains that to the dead all things are visible. "We look through the actor's mask and watch the poet putting his mask on in the dark. . . . We observe lovers and see that they blush before each other, sensing that they are deceived deceivers." The two boys are joined by The Man in the Mask. Moritz is trying to get Melchior to join him among the dead. The Man in the Mask sides with the living. Morality, imagination, life, and death are discussed. The Man in the Mask at last draws Melchior with him, departing from the grave of the dead.

MORITZ (*alone*): — . . . I shall lie on my back again, warm myself with the putrefaction, and smile . . .

Wedekind called this play "a tragedy of childhood." But it is no tragedy. It is a study of the pathos of spring, wrought with a pervasive irony. The peril implicit in the stirrings of life has seldom been described so vividly on the stage. The society and the young adolescents are partly foolish and partly the victims of an irreconcilable conflict between humanity and nature. Wedekind saw and communicated the irony without despair.

In almost all of Wedekind's work, an ironic view of life determines the dramatic form. Thus, this chapter on poetry and irony may conclude with him, though we shall subsequently have to return to more recent, and in some ways even more astringent, voices of irony (Chapter 14). Here I have tried to show that many of the major playwrights near the turn of the century and after were feeling their way toward a kind of drama that would transcend common distinctions between poetry and prose. They would do this by making the language employed subordinate to a prior aesthetic reality that I have called, for lack of a better term, theatrical imagery. The drive to achieve this is as evident in Claudel and Yeats as in Andreyev and Wedekind, though they come at it, we may think, from different sides.

The drive toward a theatrical theater aims also toward an ever more ironic one. How profoundly this is true will be made evident when we discuss later phases of the modern theater. There we shall see that the "theatrical theater" of irony is an expression of modern philosophical doubt. Simultaneously it is an affirmation of courage.

The four truly outstanding playwrights of the turn of the century—Ibsen, Chekhov, Strindberg, and Shaw—have so far been largely excluded from our narrative. They display their greatness most clearly in their refusal to be subordinated to a discussion of any particular type of playwriting or any single line of development. They deserve their reputations as giants of the modern theater because their work fulfilled many tendencies and climaxed many achievements that went before them. They added what was given by their genius, and in them the growth of a whole period found its culmination.

To culminate one movement or period is to launch another. Thus, in writing about Ibsen, Chekhov, Strindberg, and Shaw I hope to describe the massive and manifold hinge upon which the modern drama turned from the nineteenth to the twentieth century.

8. HENRIK IBSEN
(1828–1906)

IN IBSEN OF NORWAY many of the most important lines of development in nineteenth-century European drama came together. Using threads spun by others, he wove the richest, most varied tapestry of any playwright of his age, yet he was not very well educated (his formal schooling ended when he was about fifteen), and he seems not even to have read a great deal—perhaps more than he let on but not as much as would be expected of a man who became the most famous literary figure of his time. One is inclined to say that Ibsen had no right to gather into his life's work so much of what had gone before him, no earned ability to put to its highest use the dramatic experimentation of his predecessors. He had no more right to do this than did Shakespeare in the Elizabethan age; but history does not work by rights, and it is hardly possible to account for Ibsen's having become the giant that he was and is.

Many people do not like Ibsen's plays, and very few can honestly say that they love them. Loving and liking Ibsen are beside the point: respect is what he wanted and gained. It is the nobility of his work, its grandeur, its scope, and its authentic report of a restless moral nature that commands attention and compels tribute.

In Ibsen the search for technique and the search for truth go hand in hand. They are not, however, identical. One does not have the impression that for Ibsen the form *is* the truth or the truth the form, the way one has it with Chekhov or Strindberg; and this is the reason why few people swoon over Ibsen as artist, however much they admire his technical and moral achievements.

He did say that his search was for the right form. Early in his life he subscribed to the literary theory of Johan Ludvig Heiberg that the important thing in art is not *what* but *how*. And in his later years Ibsen did try, it seems, to make the search for form and the search for truth into the same search; but for most of his life they were two separate concerns that he held together by sheer force of will.

We are confronted, in the phenomenon that goes by the name of Henrik Ibsen, not with the natural flowering of a talent, as in the case of Chekhov, or with the outpouring of a temperament both wild and lyric, as in the case of Strindberg, but with a moral will conjoined to a poetic mentality. This conjunction produced in Ibsen a well-nigh prophetic desire to scourge and revivify his people. It also made him desire intently to become a great and respected man. The latter desire was fulfilled, and the former, although its result could not be so radical as to satisfy a prophet, was nevertheless accomplished in high degree. The historic result of Ibsen's work is, in fact, even more evident in the realm of morals than in that of poetry and drama. More than any other single figure, he deserves to be called the father of the new morality, a phrase used in his own time and again recently to denote that type of moral concern which does not counsel conformity to precept but instead councils fulfillment of the self through uncompromising exercise of responsible freedom.

Ibsen in his own day was so much admired as a champion of the new morality and of social reform that there has been a recent tendency to try to correct the record by regarding him primarily as a poet. M. C. Bradbrook, for instance, writes:

> To see Ibsen merely as the precursor of Shaw and Brieux when he was also the precursor of Strindberg and Tchekov is to retain at this late date the false perspective of his contemporary critics and admirers.[1]

[1] *Ibsen, the Norwegian* (London: Chatto & Windus, 1948), p. 2.

There can be no doubt, however, that Ibsen's contemporaries saw in him what was really there and that their understanding of him as a moralist was in no way false to Ibsen's own intentions and achievements. Indeed, it was just the moralist in him that for a long time put off the foremost Scandinavian critic of the time, Georg Brandes (1842–1927), who was in a good position to understand Ibsen's poetic powers but who also feared that "an unpropitious destiny" seemed to have allotted Ibsen "the task of serving as the representative of polemical poetry." [2] The comment was made after Ibsen had finished *Brand* and was reiterated after Brandes read *Peer Gynt*. The works of the middle period, which were to follow, cannot justly be said to be less polemical, though they mark an advance in insight and craft. Even in the late work, where the drama and the poetry are best united, Ibsen comes across as a striver after the Absolute, a moralist chastened but neither defeated nor deflected from his task.

There is no way to praise Ibsen as poet without admiring his moral indignation. This is what Brandes came eventually to see. One may err in finding only the propagandist in Ibsen. One may err in judging him only by the realistic plays of the middle period, for which he has become most famous, and by seeing these as "problem" plays. Yet even when one has adjusted his sights and looked at the whole of Ibsen's life and work, he will find that the element of poetic acceptance in Ibsen is everywhere overshadowed by the factor of moral judgment. Ibsen had a Calvinist conscience without Calvin's respect for law. He had a Lutheran intensity without Luther's belief in Grace. He was caught up in the romantic quest for the Absolute, which he turned sharply inward toward the will and the conscience of the solitary individual. He took Kierkegaard's question, How does one become a Christian?, and turned it into the more general yet more desperate question, How does one become a man? The question how to become what one is supposed to become is the moral question par excellence, and there is no work of Ibsen's that does not concentrate upon it and explore its inner dramatic tensions.

2 *Henrik Ibsen*, authorized translation by Jesse Muir, revised by William Archer (New York: Benjamin Blom, 1964), p. 22.

Like the modern drama in general, the drama of Ibsen has its roots in an early romanticism that by hindsight may appear flighty, dreamy, and perhaps irrelevant to modern experience. His earliest writing dates from the time when he was apprenticed to an apothecary in the little town of Grimstad on the southern coast of Norway. He had been born at Skien, not far away, the eldest of five children (an infant born before him had died) in the family of a prominent merchant. When he was eight years old the family business failed, and when he was sixteen he began to fend for himself, moving to Grimstad, where he hoped that his work for an apothecary would keep food in his mouth and lead to university studies in medicine. Instead, owing entirely to his rich inner nature, it led to the beginning of a literary career. He wrote a few poems, some of which were published in newspapers. In 1849, when he had been at Grimstad five years, he wrote his first full-length play. Called *Catiline,* it was written in Danish iambic pentameter and dealt with the conspiracy against Cicero in 63 B.C. It is the only Norwegian literary work that reflects the February Revolution of 1848.[3] Ibsen and his friends Christopher Due and Ole Schulerud thought that the play would create a stir in Norwegian literary and dramatic circles, and when they found that no publisher would risk it, they arranged to publish it themselves. Due made a clean copy, and Schulerud took it to the capital, Christiania (now Oslo), in 1850, where it was published on April 12.

Two weeks later Ibsen came to the city himself. He intended to prepare for his entrance to the university and to continue his writing. After some study he passed the matriculation exams with conditionals in Greek and mathematics; but that was as far as his university career proceeded. He turned instead to journalism.

Ibsen had brought with him to Christiania the manuscript of another play. Written just before *Catiline* in the fall of 1849, it was a one-act piece called *The Normans.* Although *Catiline* had not made any sort of stir, Ibsen persevered in his devotion to historical plays that served the cause of romantic nationalism. In the late spring of 1850 he revised *The Normans,* changed its name to *The Warrior's Barrow,* and offered it to the Christiania Theater, which

---

3 Halvdan Koht, *The Life of Ibsen,* 2 vols., Ruth L. McMahon and Hanna A. Larsen, trans. (New York: Norton, 1931), Vol. I, p. 50.

put it on the stage the next fall without much success. During 1850 Ibsen began another play, which he called *The Grouse of Justedal.* Also an exercise in romantic nationalism, with themes drawn from Norwegian folk legends, it turned out to be so dull that Ibsen left it unfinished.

Ibsen's development at this time, and later, cannot be understood without reference to the political and cultural situation of Norway. Politically, the country was more or less subject to Sweden. It had been severed from Denmark in 1814 as part of the European settlement after the Napoleonic Wars and had tried to establish itself as a constitutional monarchy. However, the Swedes forced it to accept their king, although a separate constitution and parliament (the Storting) were allowed. Throughout the nineteenth century Norwegian nationalism ran high, and Ibsen was one of its foremost advocates, his zeal exceeded only by that of his friend and literary rival, Björnstjerne Björnson (1832–1910), to cite whose name, said Georg Brandes, "is like hoisting the Norwegian flag." [4] Norway did not succeed in restoring its own king to its ancient throne until 1905.

Culturally, Norway was under the hegemony of Denmark. Since Denmark was the southernmost country of Scandinavia, European thought tended to reach Norway through the mediation of Danish publishers and critics, and there were many in Norway who believed that "culture" was synonymous with Danish ways. This was particularly true in the theater. For instance, Ibsen himself wrote *The Warrior's Barrow* mostly under the influence of the Danish poet and dramatist Adam Oehlenschläger (1779–1850). The principal theater in Christiania employed a company of Danish actors and made up its fare mostly from Danish works and popular European successes. No native theater worth speaking of existed. The Danish critic Brandes wrote in 1867:

> The first requisite for the awakening of our sister-country's powers
> was that the flood of culture should flow so far north that from
> Denmark it could spread with fertilising power over Norway; the
> next that, on the separation of Norway from Denmark, and her
> consequent attainment of independence and political freedom,
> this same flood should retreat, leaving behind it its fertilising de-

4 *Op. cit.,* p. 131.

posit. The poetical growth which then shot up has attained its most delicate and beautiful development in the story, in Björnson's peasant-novels, but its highest significance in the serious historical play.[5]

In the early 1850's Ibsen had not yet written a significant historical play, but he had begun to practice for it, and he had begun to make himself slightly known in the major city of his country by having a play performed at the theater and by writing, though mostly under a pseudonym, for several newspapers, in which he published a certain amount of poetry, some reviews of the theater, reports on the transactions of the Storting, and occasional essays. He lived in respectable poverty.

It was Ole Bull, the famous violinist and fierce nationalist, who brought Ibsen into closer contact with the theater. In 1851 Bull came to Christiania to get money from the Storting for the national theater he had founded the previous year in Bergen. He did not get the money but he got Ibsen, and the two traveled to Bergen together in October. Ibsen signed a contract "to assist the theater as a dramatic author."

The new playwright in residence, as he would be called today, found himself with no play in his head (a condition not unknown in such circumstances), so after writing a few prologues for special celebrations at the theater he took a travel grant and went off to study theaters in Denmark and Germany, with the promise that when he returned he would act as stage manager and instructor. He left on the trip in the spring (1852) and returned in July. Because his money ran out he did not visit Berlin and Hamburg as planned, but he did meet the eminent critic Heiberg in Copenhagen (much disappointed that Heiberg talked mainly of food), and he visited Dresden, where the most important thing he did was to read a new book called *Das moderne Drama,* by Hermann Hettner.

This work began to open Ibsen's eyes to the possibilities that lay in the historical play, for it was Hettner's thesis that the dramatist's interest in historical material should lie not primarily on the factual plane, not in the recapitulation of some past moment, but in the moral and psychological reality of what had happened. The

[5] *Ibid.,* pp. 7–8.

thesis is not strange today, but it represented a turn in romantic thinking that has been very important for modern culture: that the importance of history is not in its facts but in their moral interpretation. Hettner was advocating what Shakespeare had done instinctively, and he was in line with what Hebbel was then doing in his historical plays and what Büchner and Kleist had done earlier. The thesis made it possible for Ibsen to connect his interest in the historical play with the moral and psychological tensions of his own inner life. In short, it enabled him to existentialize history.

During the trip to Copenhagen and Dresden, Ibsen wrote a comedy called "St. John's Night," based on Scandinavian folk songs. Performed on January 2, 1853, at the third anniversary celebration of the Bergen National Theater, it was such a failure that Ibsen refused ever to let it be printed. At the anniversary two years later he was ready with a better play. *Lady Inger of Östraat,* written in 1854, is a historical tragedy concerned with Norway's unsuccessful attempt to preserve its freedom in the sixteenth century. It was Ibsen's first play in prose and thus the first anticipation of his later belief that prose is the only form of speech truly compatible with drama. At the time, however, Ibsen's outright rejection of verse was a good fourteen years away.

Equally as interesting as Ibsen's use of prose in *Lady Inger* was his recourse to the devices of Eugène Scribe. Ibsen was learning his craft in part by the imitation of popular European plays. Had he not done so, he would probably not have achieved the excellence of play structure to which he came in his middle period. *Lady Inger* shows particular indebtedness to Scribe's *Les Contes de la reine de Navarre* (1850, performed at the Bergen theater in 1854) and to his *Le Verre d'eau* (1840).

The Bergen theater, although it was founded to promote a national Norwegian drama, had to fill out its program with foreign plays. Therefore it put on many French "boulevard plays," which seem to have been as popular in Norway as everywhere else. Both in Bergen and in Christiania, Ibsen had full opportunity to see such plays and to assist in their production. It was from them that he learned, gradually, the sort of suspense that holds an audience and how the relation between different character types can set a plot going and keep it moving to the end. Ibsen was never a slave to this kind of writing, and the instances in his work of specific imitation, as in *Lady Inger,* are few; but one should not take the attitude that it was somehow beneath Ibsen or dangerous for him to learn from the Scribean example. Without it he could not have developed from a writer of festival poems and romantic folk dramas into a writer of plays outstanding for their forceful compactness. The superb technique of *A Doll's House* and *Ghosts,* in which every element is locked into every other and in which the suspense is largely generated by the gradual exhumation of a buried past, is unthinkable without the maturation of a talent that had early learned some valuable lessons from the sort of theater that holds an audience by plot and intrigue alone. This is the importance that must be attached to Ibsen's ten years of work as a theater man, five in Bergen and five succeeding them in Christiania.

From being playwright in residence at Bergen he went on to become the stage manager, but he was never much good at such work. He was too timid to tell his actors what to do, made no innovations in the manner in which the plays were set and played, and was by turns diligent and negligent in the amount of time he expended on his theatrical duties. The theater he directed later in Christiania failed. He preferred to give his plays to the "establishment" theater there, rather than to the one under his own management, to which he gave a good bit less than the whole of his attention. Ibsen simply did not have the temperament to be effective in the management of a company. He was too much the individualist, unable to teach and barely able to get along with other people, whom he was not above blaming for his own failures.

Ibsen stands rather outside that line of development I have traced in Chapter 5, so important to most modern drama, in which the stage itself is conceived as an expressive instrument and its resources are explored as intensively as a poet may explore the possibilities of language. That was foreign to Ibsen. One reason, perhaps, is that there were in Scandinavia at the beginning of his career no theater men of genius from whom he could learn. Yet he seems never to have tried to learn such things abroad. He was not interested in theater people, and the performances of his plays did not much matter to him beyond what they represented of public acceptance and honor. He thought much more of the reading public. If his imagination had not been inherently dramatic, if he had not had a mind so dialectical that the dramatic form suited its expression better than any other, he would no doubt have written novels instead of plays.

Lady Inger, in spite of its use of popular techniques, did not please the audience. For his first success Ibsen had to wait upon his third play performed at Bergen, which was *The Feast at Solhaug,* written in 1855 and performed on January 2, 1856. Ibsen later wrote:

> The performance closed with numerous curtain calls for the author and actors. Later in the evening the orchestra, accompanied by a large crowd, gave a serenade outside my windows. I almost believe that I let myself be carried away into making a sort of speech; at least I know that I felt extremely happy.[6]

For Ibsen, this comment is effusive.

The play was based on ancient ballads, with its plot indebted to *Une Chaîne* (1841), a comedy by Scribe. There were also several similarities to a play called *Svend Dyring's House* (1837), by the Danish poet Henrik Hertz, although Ibsen, always jealous of his originality, pointed out that *Svend Dyring's House* owed more to *Kätchen von Heilbronn* (1810), by Kleist, than his own play owed to *Svend Dyring.*[7] The remark tells us that Ibsen had read Kleist, whose ironic approach to romantic material anticipates similar tendencies in Ibsen. From Hertz, according to Brandes, Ibsen learned "to fashion a metre akin to that of the heroic ballads . . . with a dramatic value not inferior to that of the iambic pentameter." [8] *The Feast at Solhaug* is also written partly in prose, and it succeeded in fusing the two effectively.

For his next work Ibsen turned again to the old ballads, and his method of handling them was even closer to Hertz's than before. *Olaf Liljekrans,* written during 1856, was performed on January 2, 1857, the people of Bergen crowding to the theater because of the popularity of *The Feast at Solhaug* the year before; but it flopped. The following fall one Olaf Skavlan wrote a parody of the ballad

6 Koht, *op. cit.,* Vol. I, p. 114.
7 Brandes, *op. cit.,* p. 89.
8 *Ibid.,* p. 88.

style, *The Feast at Mare Hill,* which put an end to national romantic drama in Norway.

Ibsen, however, was to write two more Scandinavian historical plays. In 1857, the year in which he moved to Christiania to become artistic director of the newly reorganized Norwegian Theater there, he wrote *The Vikings at Helgeland,* based not upon the old ballads but upon the Viking sagas and, like them, cast in prose. After several vicissitudes, it was presented at the Christiania Theater in April 1861.

Meanwhile, in 1858, Ibsen had married Susannah Thoresen of Bergen. This faithful woman remained Ibsen's wife until his death, traveled with him, made a home for him during the long years of his self-imposed exile, and bore him a son; but not much else is known of her. She was ever in the shadow of her husband, that internationally known champion of the dignity and independence of women.

Ibsen's last Norwegian historical play, by far the best of them all, is *The Pretenders,* written during the summer of 1863. Like *The Vikings,* it is in prose. By that time Ibsen had come to feel that prose was more suitable for historical subjects, while poetry was better for plays of contemporary life. During this period, Björnson was also experimenting with the prose historical play, and that may have influenced Ibsen, although the styles of the two writers were as different as their personalities, Björnson being quite extroverted and Ibsen the opposite.

The Pretenders is the most popular of all Norwegian historical plays, and only the knowledge it presupposes of Norwegian history keeps it from having an international popularity. The Meiningen players, however, were quite successful with it in 1875, as was Max Reinhardt at the Neues Theater in Berlin in 1904. On the surface, the work is a plea for Norwegian national consciousness, since it tells the story of King Hakon IV (ruled 1217–1263), the greatest monarch of medieval Norway, who won the throne from his rival, Earl Skule, because, according to Ibsen, he possessed "the kingly thought"—the idea that all the Norwegians, divided like the Greeks into separate, warring peoples, should be one. Hakon is contrasted with Skule, who has many of the virtues Hakon lacks, especially a warrior's bravery, but who has not the "right" to the throne because he is not endowed with the kingly thought. Brandes happily compared the two characters to Aladdin and Nureddin, the one blessed by fortune, the other fated only to rival him.[9]

The relation of Hakon and Skule, in the way that Ibsen has developed it, gives the play a second theme more important than the first. This has to do with a character's becoming what his destiny requires him to be, which means that he must first identify the destiny that is his and then learn to hold it fast by faith. After Hakon perceives that he will become the king because it is his right to do so, he is beset by doubts as to whether this right is unmistakably his. However, his confidence returns to sustain him. It is otherwise with Skule when he for a time gains the throne. Like the rich young ruler who went away sorrowful from his interview with Jesus, Skule puts a question to the skald, Jatgeir.

KING SKULE: What gift do I need to become a king?
JATGEIR: Not the gift of doubt; else would you not question so.
KING SKULE: What gift do I need?
JATGEIR: My lord, you *are* a king.
KING SKULE: Have *you* at all times full faith that you are a *skald?* [10]

In this passage we come directly upon Ibsen. The question Skule addresses to the seer is the one that Ibsen addressed to himself. The tension between what one *knows* of himself and what he is willing to *believe* of himself tormented Ibsen until his career as a writer was well launched, and even after; and it plagues almost all the major characters of Ibsen's plays. In *The Pretenders* Ibsen is not sure whether he is Hakon or Skule, whether he has the right and destiny to be an artist or whether he is only a pretender to the name.

Ibsen's belief that God or nature gives each individual a destiny is not far removed from the Protestant conception of Providence, from which it is derived. Not for nothing had Ibsen come from a Protestant family of extreme piety. He rejected its dogma but kept, partly under the influence of Kierkegaard, much of its ethic. Ibsen is almost unique among the major figures of modern drama in

9 *Ibid.*, pp. 13 ff.
10 Act IV. Translated by William Archer in *The Works of Henrik Ibsen* (New York: Willey Book Co., 1911), Vol. I, p. 310.

being an intensely Protestant writer. Only Shaw may be compared with him in this respect. In his secular yet not unmystical way, Ibsen went his family one better by proving in his work that his "call" was as genuine as that of any religious believer, that he took it more seriously than church people theirs, and by urging in play after play that a man can fulfill himself only by obedience to the destiny that is laid out for him and that requires total sacrifice.

In *The Pretenders* the vocation of Hakon is inseparable from the destiny of his nation. Later Ibsen severed the individual from society, as he himself was severed from Norway to become its gadfly from afar; but he never forsook the prophetic thought that one must give himself totally to that which is required of him. The clearest and most insistent enunciation of this thought is found in *Brand*, which was Ibsen's next play. Meanwhile, however, he had already begun to seal his fate by writing a comedy that was, as he later said, "a forerunner" to *Brand*, "in that I described there the conflict that prevails in our social conditions between reality and the claims of idealism in everything that concerns love and marriage." [11] He had begun *Love's Comedy* in 1858 and finished it in 1862. Then he had written *The Pretenders*, in which the greatness of Norway was extolled. But *Love's Comedy* had already, in Ibsen's own mind, closed the gates of compromise between the individual's high calling and the nation's ordinary ways.

The career of the Ibsen whom everybody knows began with *Love's Comedy*, though the plays that most people read begin with *Brand*. In *Love's Comedy* Ibsen turned from dramatizing the heritage and calling of a nation to the dramatization of how the individual's calling sets him at odds with his people. The motif was not absolutely new in Ibsen. It had furnished the substance of a good bit of his poetry and had been important in his very first play, *Catiline*, in which we witness a rebellion through the eyes of a rebel. The words of Catiline that open the play express the very thought that possessed Ibsen in his maturity:

> I must! I must! A voice deep in my soul
> Urges me on,—and I will heed its call.[12]

[11] Letter to Edmund Gosse, April 30, 1872. *The Oxford Ibsen*, James Walter McFarlane, ed., Vol. II (New York: Oxford University Press, 1962).
[12] Translated by Anders Orbeck. In *Early Plays by Henrik Ibsen* (New York: Oxford University Press, 1921), p. 9.

The romantic tone is obvious; also the moral seriousness. For a time, Ibsen put his romantic moral seriousness at the service of national consciousness. By the time he was thirty he saw that this would not work. Morality did not really belong to a people but to persons. The most one might look for was, to use a more recent phrase, "moral man in immoral society."

Years after *Love's Comedy* was published Ibsen wrote that it had "roused a violent storm of exasperation in Norway." [13] He said,

> People mixed my own personal affairs in with the discussion, and my general reputation suffered greatly. The only person who approved of my book at the time was my wife. She is just the sort of character I need—illogical, but with a strong poetic instinct, generous in thought with an almost violent hatred of anything petty. None of my countrymen understood anything of this, and I had no inclination to confess myself to the crowd. So then I was outlawed; they were all against me.[14]

In the Preface to the 1867 (Copenhagen) edition of the play, he wrote that in Norway it had "evoked a storm of ill-will, more violent and more wide-spread than most books. . . ." [15]

There is exaggeration in these comments. They more nearly describe what Ibsen liked to believe than what actually took place. It is true that the few reviews the published play got were highly critical, but Ibsen neglected to say that the play's verse was generally praised, and he overlooked the defense that Paul Botten-Hansen published in *Illustreret nyhedsblad*. It is true that the play's unflattering portrait of the clergy, in the person of Pastor Straamand (i.e., Strawman), provoked the anger of the government's Ecclesiastical Department, which took revenge by vetoing Ibsen's request to the Storting for an author's stipend; but it is also true that his friends, led by Björnson, came to the rescue with money of their own, and that eventually the stipend was granted. Perhaps it was the reaction of the Ecclesiastical Department that Ibsen was thinking about when he said he was "outlawed," but how could he have expected to be treated nicely by the establishment? As he himself wrote, "When, in my comedy, I cracked the

13 Letter to Edmund Gosse, April 30, 1872.
14 Letter to Peter Hansen, October 28, 1870.
15 *Oxford Ibsen*, p. 359.

whip as best I could over love and marriage, it was only right and proper that the majority should shout up on behalf of love and marriage." [16] Surely the play was controversial, but if not, it would have been a failure. Neither the Christiania Theater nor the theater in Trondheim, to whom he also offered it, would put it on when it was new. Ten years later, however, when Ibsen's reputation had grown, the play had its premier at the Christiania Theater (November 24, 1873) and was a popular success. Bergen saw it in 1879, happily and without sensation.

Though there was anger and deep concern in Ibsen when he wrote *Love's Comedy,* one who reads it now is struck by the absence of stridency and the subordination of its anger to a general tone of light satire and detached comedy. Ibsen had, after all, begun it the year he got married; so unless he was going to reveal a violent antipathy to his new estate, he would have to portray the hazards of marriage in an amused rather than an angry voice, and that is what he did. The play has been called Ibsen's *Love's Labors Lost,* and the comparison is a good one, especially as regards the multifaceted irony that plays all around the subject of love and as regards the character Falk, whose befuddlement by love, covered over with delightful rhetoric, reminds one of Shakespeare's Berowne. The play satirizes conventional engagements and marriages and conventional religion, but it also satirizes Falk's idealism, so that at the end of the play one is no more sure than at the end of *Brand* how far the author would have one identify with the protagonist's ideal. In both plays, after showing the conflict between the ideal and the real, Ibsen steps back, in this case into a bemused reflection on the human "comedy," as if he were already far from the scene. His spiritual exile had begun.

The plot of *Love's Comedy* is simple. A young poet named Falk (i.e., falcon) is in love with Svanhild, the daughter of his landlady, Mrs. Halm. His roommate, Lind, a theological student, becomes engaged to the other daughter, Anna. Styver, a clerk in a government office, is engaged to a girl called Miss Skaere. Mrs. Halm's villa is visited by Pastor Straamand with his wife and eight of their twelve children. Another visitor is Guldstad, a middle-aged businessman. There are also various students, guests, relatives, and

16 Preface to the second edition.

engaged couples. Thus, Falk's love for Svanhild must be declared in a veritable nest of old loves, new loves, and marriages. But the love that Falk dreams of is not like the others. Its purpose is not to begin a family, to shelter his bride, or even to perpetuate love but only to inspire him to poetry. On this basis he woos Svanhild, inviting her to regard him as a falcon and to set him soaring. The first act is climaxed by her reply to him, a marvelous speech that reveals her unusual character while exposing Falk to gentle mockery. Clearly she loves him, but she is not to let him settle the issues of life with rhetoric:

> You used an image that helped me to see
> just what your 'flight in freedom' really means.
> You likened yourself to a falcon, who
> must beat against the wind to reach the heights;
> I was the breeze that was to bear you up . . .
> and without me you couldn't rise at all.
> How pitiable! How utterly puny . . .
> yes, laughable, as you yourself admitted!
> And yet your simile bore fruit; for I
> saw in my mind another, different emblem,
> not like yours, impotently lame and false.
> I saw you as a kite, not as a falcon,
> a paper kite, fashioned of poetry,
> which in itself is and remains a trifle
> while the important feature is the string.
> The body was of paper obligations
> payable, some day, in poetic gold;
> the wings were sheaves of flapping epigrams
> that painlessly belaboured the thin air;
> and the long tail was a newfangled satire
> designed to lash the errors of our days,
> which managed to produce a feeble whisper
> of venial peccadilloes, nothing more.
> And in this guise you lay before me, crying
> 'Send me aloft wherever the wind takes me!
> 'Let me soar upwards with my little rhymes;
> 'though your mamma should scold you, don't forsake me!' [17]

She drives him to a more serious concern with life:

[17] Translated by Jens Arup. In *The Oxford Ibsen*, pp. 135–136.

> Writing a poem down on paper is
> something belonging within study walls,
> while only living deeds belong to life,
> and only they bear upwards to the heights;
> but you must choose between them as you will.[18]

The Ibsenesque motif of the play is thus revealed as choice. Lind chooses to give up his call to missionary work in America in order to provide for his wife-to-be. Pastor Straamand long ago chose the life of family and pastoral responsibility over the romantic love of his youth. (Incidentally, he makes a brilliant defense of his choice when taunted by Falk.) At the climax of the plot, Svanhild is forced to choose between Falk and Guldstad, the one offering her a free life "on the heights" devoted to noble deeds, the other offering her security and companionship in the "autumn" of life. She chooses Guldstad. The love between her and Falk, she knows, cannot endure in marriage. It can survive only as a memory, for the springtime will pass. Falk accepts this verdict and the reasons for it—in fact, shares in the decision. He departs with a group of students in a boat, headed for a life of adventure. As the curtain falls, we hear them singing:

> And what if I've run my poor vessel aground?
> Still, putting to sea was delightful! [19]

It is said that Ibsen modeled Svanhild on his bride, Susannah Thoresen. Clearly there is a good bit of Ibsen in Falk, who is torn between devoting himself to words and to action. Falk achieves Ibsen's dubious solution of the problem by trying to equate action with writing, although he clearly sees that they are not the same.

Yet, unlike Falk, Ibsen married his Svanhild, thus compromising the picture he held of himself as the dedicated idealist. He was further compromised by having a personality that could not, like Björnson, combine social action and creative writing. He extolled deeds, but he was too impractical to carry them out except on paper. He was that unhappiest of dreamers, the one who dreams of adventures and wakes up at his desk. He was a romantic turned by Kierkegaard and by the inner tendencies of romanticism itself into

18 *Ibid.*, p. 136.
19 *Ibid.*, p. 202.

an existentialist. But he was not brave and could not do what he urged. Neither could he achieve Kierkegaard's "religious stage," in which the despair of the ethical man is overcome by a leap of faith.

Because these inner tensions marred Ibsen's picture of himself, it was necessary that the picture be restored by a bold stroke. Therefore, he exiled himself from Norway.

Certainly Ibsen did not fully know what he was doing when he set out for Copenhagen on April 5, 1864. When he got there, however, history provided him with the occasion he needed to crystallize his emotions and set his course. To say that Ibsen "needed" what history now gave him is not to minimize the importance of the Danish war with Germany or the genuineness of Ibsen's moral reaction to it. Perhaps every writer needs history, and needs in it exactly that which is morally outrageous. But writers, like other people, react to events in various ways, and Ibsen's reaction was thoroughly characteristic of his own temperament. He determined to stay away from his homeland and to devote himself to his art and to the moral failures of man.

In April 1864 Denmark was fighting a desperate battle against German troops. Bismarck's soldiers had entered the territory of Schleswig in February and were now focusing their attack upon the Danes massed at Dybböl. Earlier there had been much talk of Scandinavian unity, and both Sweden and Norway had promised to come to the aid of Denmark if she were attacked. Those promises now turned out to be empty. The Swedish foreign ministry had hoped to forestall the German attack by words, and when the issue was joined it refused to redeem its words by deeds. For Ibsen the whole moral problem of man was demonstrated in such behavior. He had been a Norwegian nationalist and simultaneously an advocate of Scandinavian unity; now, with Denmark left in the lurch to defend itself alone, a hopeless task, there was no honor in past promises of Scandinavian unity and none in Norway. That the Germans would probably have won anyway against the combined forces of the three countries did not make any difference. The size of the armies involved and the chances of success were beside the point. The only things that mattered were courage and faithfulness, or rather the lack of them.

On April 18, while Ibsen was still in Copenhagen, Dybböl fell.

His biographer says that the battle "seemed to lacerate his very being." [20] Soon afterward Ibsen began traveling south. He passed through Berlin in time to see the Danish cannon that had been captured at Dybböl paraded through the streets while the people spat into them in vulgar triumph. Ibsen's letters describing the sight are full of outrage and sorrow. He combined in his mind the injury done to the Danes and the injuries, partly real, partly fancied, done to himself. He kept going south. He stopped for a time in Vienna and then proceeded to Rome. It was his first visit below the Alps, and it opened his eyes to a richness of culture he had never known in the northern land of his birth.

Except for *Emperor and Galilean* and parts of *Peer Gynt*, all of Ibsen's succeeding plays are set in Norway, but he did not return there for any great length of time for twenty-seven years. From 1864 he spent the rest of his life in rented rooms, mostly in Italy, part of the time also in Germany, finally, in old age, back in Oslo. He wrote at regular hours, methodically, like a self-employed clerk. He read little and brooded much. He became the most famous of Norwegians and perhaps the most famous literary figure of Europe. He was vain and was jealous of his originality, his reputation, his honors from foreign governments, and his fees. He was shy, conservative in dress and behavior, and possessed of few friends because he thought that friendships cost too much in time and thought. He did not keep up with his family in Skien, and his thoughts about them, except his sister Hedvig, as reflected in a few letters, are cold. Although it is reported that his conversation could at times be brilliant and stirring, there is no way to make Ibsen an attractive figure, and one should not try. He had too much anger and resentment. He was bitten too deeply by conscience and made too hard by the conviction that in his struggles he was utterly alone. Almost everything he wrote was intended to show how far society and the individual are from what they ought to be. Such a thought is not profound. Ibsen's profundity lies not in his big thoughts but in his moral seriousness and in the astuteness of many of his observations of detail. A romantic moralist to the end of his days, he leaves one with the feeling that if striving could attain to the Absolute he would have reached it. He recognized that it could

[20] Koht, *op. cit.*, Vol. I, p. 232.

not, and he therefore concluded that the important thing was not the achievement but the pursuit of the goal. Ibsen's life seems to have contained little more grace than that of Brand. Even the gracefulness of construction in a few of the plays comes across as a moral achievement and not a gift. Like all romantics he made creativity one of his constant themes, but the dark morality of his conscience served to obscure divine creation and to blot out its inherent goodness. Thus, there is a dualism in Ibsen that leads to his preoccupation with what one of his commentators has called "the destructive power of genius." [21] This dualism, according to which the greatest light produces the greatest darkness, became ever more evident in his late work and fills every line of his last play, *When We Dead Awaken*.

Ibsen's spontaneous creativity, to the extent that he had it, comes out in his depiction of character. In this regard, both in quantity and quality, he surpasses almost every other dramatist except Shakespeare. To bring a character vividly and fully to life through dialogue that can be spoken on a stage is enough for a dramatist; but if, as Ibsen did, he masters and even perfects the craft of play construction, the result will be of an astonishing grandeur. Ibsen may not, like Shakespeare and Chekhov, teach us to love life, but he shares some of the capacity of the ancient Greeks to make us respect it and to do the best with it that we can. Focusing upon Norway, he shows a rugged landscape lit by the terrifying thought of a morality that is absolute in its demand.

After April 1864, Ibsen's biography ceases to be of more than casual interest. As M. C. Bradbrook has said (with justifiable overstatement), "there is nothing to record." [22] After this his life seems to have taken place entirely inside his head, and while it is possible to read of his movements from Rome, to Ischia, to Frascati, to Dresden, to Munich, and so on, there is nothing in this chronicle to throw great light upon the works that he was all the while producing. The quintessence of Ibsenism is not what Shaw said it was but the romantic quest turned inward.

The plays that Ibsen wrote in his exile are to be divided into two

21 Bradbrook, *op. cit.*, p. 2.
22 *Ibid.*, p. 15.

groups. The first include the great, rambling, powerful, visionary works: *Brand* (1866), *Peer Gynt* (1867), and *Emperor and Galilean* (1873), plus the comedy *The League of Youth* (1869). The second is made up of the plays belonging to his so-called middle period, the realistic dramas that are thought of by the public whenever the name Ibsen is mentioned: *Pillars of Society* (1877), *A Doll's House* (1879), *Ghosts* (1881), *An Enemy of the People* (1882), *The Wild Duck* (1884), *Rosmersholm* (1886), *The Lady from the Sea* (1888), and *Hedda Gabler* (1890). The third group was written during the first nine years after Ibsen's return to Norway in 1891: *The Master Builder* (1892), *Little Eyolf* (1894), *John Gabriel Borkman* (1896), and *When We Dead Awaken* (1899). These four plays pass quite beyond realism, extending the direction already set in the later part of the middle period, and they reveal how much a romantic poet Ibsen had always been, even when he posed as a "photographer." In 1900 he became very ill. He died in Oslo on May 23, 1906, and was given a state funeral.

A history of the modern theater has to take account of Ibsen's masterworks and assess them as a whole but must not attempt to add to the flood of critical commentary that each of the plays has brought forth. How is this to be done? The important thing is to see the line of development, which is necessary in order to recognize the shape and balance of Ibsen's *oeuvre* and to understand how it epitomizes the course of nineteenth-century drama as a whole.

The beginnings, as we have seen, were in poetic romantic drama of national striving. In *Love's Comedy* the striving becomes located in the individual, who is thus set at odds with society. This enormous subject Ibsen at first presented in comic perspective. In Italy, however, he returned to it with almost deadly seriousness, producing in *Brand* his most indignant work and his greatest expression of the Kierkegaardian motif that occupied much of his thought in the early part of his career. *Brand* has the distinction of being a work of great poetry that stands exactly on the border between romantic striving and existentialist self-examination. It shows how the one turns into the other, producing an attitude that is almost equally blended of the love of life and hatred for it. The reader can feel the ambivalence if he observes his reactions to the character of Brand. At one moment one has nothing but admiration for the man's courage, his uncompromising vision, and the force of his nature, compellingly associated with the mountainous grandeur of Norway. At the next moment one is terrified by the cold lack of compassion in the figure and the presentiment of his destruction, which, although it actually is accomplished by an avalanche, proceeds psychologically from within Brand. "Purity of heart," Kierkegaard had said, "is to will one thing." Brand has such purity. What Kierkegaard did not add but Ibsen shows is that such purity is incompatible with life.

The figure of Brand was partly modeled on a preacher named B. A. Lammers who came to Skien shortly after Ibsen had left for Grimstad. Lammers brought to the town a reformist program he had gotten, or thought he had, from reading Kierkegaard. Lammers' insistence upon a pure religion and absolute individual commitment to its demands led him out of the state church. In Skien he organized a free church that two of Ibsen's family joined. By such excess of zeal Ibsen was instinctively repulsed. He rebuffed the efforts his family made to convert him to their new convictions. At the same time he was something of a Lammers himself, for he was a moral reformist constitutionally opposed to compromise. In making Brand a clergyman he did not intend to restrict the meaning of his play to the religious sphere. Brand might equally have been an artist or a politician, he said, for the demands of the ethical are just as severe upon them, the opportunities for compromise just as prevalent and dangerous.

In Kierkegaard's existential philosophy, tension is generated by the incommensurability between the infinite and the finite. Kierkegaard's attack upon Christendom was motivated by his observation that people get around this incommensurability, even in their religious life, by pretending that it does not exist. Hegel tried to overcome it systematically in his philosophy, and the man in the street overcame it by paying it no attention. But it was there, nonetheless, in the heart of Christianity, which pinned man's eternal happiness upon a finite historical figure—Jesus of Nazareth. No logic could make this plausible, and no striving could overcome its inherent contradiction. It could be dealt with only by an inward appropriation. Thus, Kierkegaard advocated the proposition that "truth is subjectivity," meaning that man's relation to the infinite is a matter of inward appropriation and is not capable of objective proof. Reflection upon the gap between the infinite and the finite leads man to the point where he must either fall into despair or make a leap of faith.

In Ibsen's vocabulary, with its romantic coloration, Kierkegaard's gap between the infinite and the finite becomes the gap between the ideal and the real. Furthermore, Ibsen does not allow that despair may be overcome by a leap of faith: he shows only the difference between the man who strives after the ideal with his whole being and those who avoid such arduousness by accommodating themselves to "the way things are." This means that the Ibsenesque man, represented in his clearest form by Brand, corresponds exactly to Kierkegaard's ethical man. And he is driven to despair, which is why Brand's death is spiritually, if not literally, a suicide. The rejection of the aesthetic in favor of the ethical is one of the qualities in Ibsen that Shaw was later to appropriate. Like Ibsen, Shaw entertained no possibility of moving beyond the ethical to the religious. Unlike Ibsen, Shaw did not portray the ethical as leading to despair.[23]

The demonic side of Brand's drive toward the Absolute, which Ibsen must have recognized in himself, is represented in the play by Gerd. It is she who lures Brand to the Ice Church. Pursuit of the Ice Church, which is pursuit of the ideal devoid of human substance, but which Brand identifies with the fulfillment of his own nature, can end only in death.

The voice Brand hears as the snow and ice come rushing upon him at the end of the play utters two words that, in the context, are highly enigmatic: *Deus caritatis*. Are they a judgment upon Brand, who has devoted his life and all its energies to a God who is without caritas? Are they supportive words, meant to indicate that the austerity of God, which Brand has represented, is really a form of His love? Are they ironic in the sense that they say what God is supposed to say, while in fact He may not exist or may be, like the avalanche and Brand himself, a force to which love is quite irrelevant? If we take the words as a judgment pronounced upon Brand,

---

23 On Ibsen's awareness of the difference between the aesthetic and the ethical, see especially his poem *On the Fells* (1860).

the play is weakened in structure. However, if we take them in some other way, or leave them out of account entirely, the play becomes a highly ambivalent account of the destructive power of genius. Brand's genius, however, is not that of intelligence or of artistic imagination but of ethical purity.

Brand made Ibsen internationally famous and gave him a vast reading public. All his works thereafter were published in large editions, reprinted many times. When *Brand* was finished, Ibsen turned immediately to *Peer Gynt*, which he completed within the year and in which his writing of verse reached its highest degree of variety and felicitous expression.

Peer Gynt is made of the same existential romanticism as *Brand*, but the cloth has been turned to its other side, so to speak. The motif of love, treated negatively in *Brand* until (perhaps) the very last words, is here made integral to the story. Whereas Brand is the man of action par excellence, Peer Gynt is the man of inaction, a hollow drifter who expects variety of experience to give him substance. His story is a mockery of the romantic quest, for Peer Gynt travels the earth in search of he knows not what and finds nothing. His "search" is really a tourist voyage, from which he can get no spiritual return because he brings to it no investment of self. Thus, his climactic encounter is not with a Gerd, who would be the demonic part of himself (though he met demons in every quarter), but with the Button Molder, who is the symbol of his lack of substance. Empty, Peer cannot be judged. He can, however, be redeemed. That is, he can be endowed with substance by love. The love that his faithful sweetheart, Solveig, bears for him rescues him from nothingness, and the comedy ends with the reprieve of its anti-hero.

Although the love motif of *Peer Gynt* is in danger of appearing sentimental, it should not be rescued from sentiment by holding that Ibsen meant it ironically. Solveig's love for Peer is emblematic of the romantic conviction that love in its ideal form, which is the longing for reunion with that to which one essentially belongs, is creative by nature and is a protection against destructive forces. This conviction is ontological in character. *Peer Gynt,* from first to last, is a play about Ibsen's view of the essential nature of human life. It is not, as some of its first interpreters thought, an allegory about Norway. It is the intellectual companion piece of *Brand*.

Peer Gynt was a revolutionary play with respect to dramatic form and theatrical quality. It must be considered a forerunner of the epic style, which had already been entered upon by Büchner and which was later to be developed and theoretically justified by Piscator and Brecht. Spreading his drama out in episodic fashion and holding it together in story rather than in strictly dramatic form, Ibsen had the instinctive good sense to give it a very great number of superbly theatrical moments—that is, moments when every theatrical resource is martialed to create a precise focus of audience concentration. *Peer Gynt* has more scenes of unforgettable vividness than any other of Ibsen's works. The images of Peer's behavior at the wedding party, his encounter with the trolls and with the Great Boyg, his driving the imaginary horses on the foot of the deathbed of his mother, his incarceration in the lunatic asylum at Cairo (a scene not surpassed by any avant-garde playwright to this day), and his meeting with the Button Molder—these cannot be eliminated from the mind once it has envisioned them. Although *Peer Gynt* is unique in Ibsen's work and cannot therefore be easily compared with his other plays, it strikes one as an achievement which he did not surpass.

After *Peer Gynt* there had to be a turning. As it happened, it was the most radical of Ibsen's life, more radical than the later shift that came after *Hedda Gabler*. He had exhausted the possibilities of the poetic play. There might be verse yet to be written for the stage, and he could write it if he wanted to, but it could not be more expressive than what he had already done. Moreover, he had brought the poetry of language into the closest sort of rapport with the symbolic possibilities of the theater. He had made not only the words but also the stage his poetic vehicle. Therefore he had to do what every artist does when he has used up a certain form and style: return to ordinary life and start out again.

These thoughts were surely in Ibsen's mind when he finished *Peer Gynt,* though they are not the reason that he gave for turning his back upon poetic drama, and indeed upon the writing of all poetry. What he did, which was completely characteristic of his temperament though at odds with his philosophy, was to put the burden of his choice onto someone else. He, who was so independent that he could not bear much company and who worked alone if ever a writer did, found reasons external to himself for what he would surely have done anyway from inner motivation. The eminent Danish critic Clemens Petersen had written a negative review of *Peer Gynt,* saying, among other things, that "neither *Brand* nor *Peer Gynt* is true poetry." Ibsen replied in anger to Björnson, whom he wrongly held to be somehow responsible for what Petersen had said. "My book *is* poetry," he wrote, "and if it is not, it shall be. The conception of poetry shall in our land, in Norway, come to adapt itself to the book." It was a justifiable and not-far-from-true defense. Then Ibsen turned around and said he would have nothing more to do with poetry at all. "If I am not a poet," he wrote in the same letter, "I have nothing to lose. I shall try my luck as a photographer." The comment, thrown out hotly onto the page, reveals that he had already been thinking about a change of direction. His succeeding sentences provide a fine specimen of the Ibsen rhetoric of ire. "My contemporaries up there I shall portray, individually, person by person, as I have done with the language agitators [i.e., those who had opposed Ibsen's efforts to achieve a common spelling in the Scandinavian languages]; I shall not spare the child in its mother's womb, not the thought or mood behind the word, in any soul that deserves the honor of being included." [24]

Thus the great modern rupture with poetic drama was made. Prose drama was certainly not at the time unknown, as some plays of Björnson and of Ibsen himself make evident, not to mention what had gone on in Germany and France; but the pre-eminent place of poetic drama in the tradition had never been challenged head on. Ibsen threw down the gauntlet—not really because of what Petersen said about *Peer Gynt* but because the master builder knew that he had a steeple to climb. He turned soon to *The League of Youth,* a comedy rich in its evocations of Norwegian small-town life. After that he dove into history, to come up with one of his largest though not most successful works, *Emperor and Galilean.* It was the last play about the long ago that he was to write.

In the story of the conflict between the apostate emperor Julian and the Christian religion, Ibsen found two of his great concerns

24 Koht, *op. cit.,* Vol. II, p. 49.

combined—rebellion against orthodoxy, and the meaning of Christianity in relation to the natural drives and longings of man. The will to harmonize conflicting tendencies entered into every page of *Emperor and Galilean,* and thus the play took on a Hegelian form. Julian's paganism is antithesis to Christianity's thesis, and the conclusion of the play points toward a "third kingdom," in which the two will be united in synthesis. The division of history into three great epochs is a familiar one in the history of Western thought, going back at least as far as Joachim of Floris (twelfth century) and reappearing in the nineteenth century in the writings of Comte and Marx. Ibsen's use of the scheme is not original enough to generate much enthusiasm, and he does not depict the anticipated "third kingdom" with sufficient clarity to make it more than a vague hope. But perhaps the main trouble with *Emperor and Galilean* is that Ibsen was trying to work upon too vast a canvas with historical materials that, although he studied them diligently, were not deeply implanted in his imagination. The play is divided into two parts, and in the second especially Ibsen did not succeed in fulfilling the conditions that his mentor, Hermann Hettner, had laid down for the historical play—namely, that it should find its substance in moral and psychological reality more than in reconstruction of past occurrences. Though Ibsen understood fully the point of this wise advice and tried to follow it, he was never able, except perhaps in *The Pretenders,* to make historical materials work well for him. On the contrary, his genius lay in getting a high yield from contemporary situations and in revealing the mythical and symbolic content which they carried beneath their surface. After *Emperor and Galilean* Ibsen was ready to embark upon the kind of material for which all his earlier writing now began to appear as preparation.

Pillars of Society came first, after a hiatus of four years. Then, at intervals of two years, *A Doll's House* and *Ghosts,* and, one year later, *An Enemy of the People.* Then, at regular two-year intervals again, *The Wild Duck, Rosmersholm, The Lady from the Sea,* and *Hedda Gabler.* The history of modern drama contains nothing else like this sustained productiveness of one sure work after another. Ibsen had reached his high plateau (by no means a monotonous land), and while he was on it he made the most of his powers. In

The League of Youth, Emperor and Galilean, and *Pillars of Society* Ibsen mastered the techniques of prose dramatic writing, and in the remaining works of his middle period he employed what he had learned in the service of ever more astute representations of the substance with which he was concerned.

Pillars of Society, A Doll's House, Ghosts, and *An Enemy of the People* may be regarded as moral studies in which Ibsen was concerned with fairly specific rights and wrongs. Of these four, the first and last stand close to melodrama because the issues they take up are without great complication. If Ibsen were not so good at characterization and the depiction of local detail, the stridency and self-righteousness of these works would ruin them. *An Enemy of the People* is perhaps the low point on the high plateau because it came so directly out of Ibsen's smarting reaction to the storm created by *Ghosts.* It is the work of an angry middle-aged man. On the other hand, its immediate predecessor, *Ghosts,* is the greatest work of the four, and this is because in addition to presenting a superb characterization, that of Mrs. Alving, and to having a classically constructed plot, it treats a moral issue of utmost complexity.

The moral questions raised in *Ghosts* are of such a nature that anger is an insufficient response to them. Ibsen was not angry but analytic when he wrote it, and when the public became angry at the play and its author it revealed the inadequacy of its understanding of the social roots of individual suffering. As in Greek tragedy, a net of past evil closes in upon Mrs. Alving, to her horror. Unlike what occurs in Greek tragedy, however, she is not crushed by Nemesis. That fate is given to her son, Oswald, who has inherited syphilitic disease from his father. Mrs. Alving is left to suffer the revenges of Nemesis vicariously, more fully conscious of what is happening to her son than he is himself. And she is forced into the immensely painful choice of whether to end his suffering by poisoning him or to hold back and experience with and through him a protracted agony. The final curtain falls at the moment when this choice is about to be made. In the past, for the sake of respectability and in the vain hope of sparing both herself and her husband, Mrs. Alving had made choices which later events proved to be unenlightened and destructive. Her life is a series of wrong choices for which she is only partly to blame, her ignorance of the right being partly the result of society's hypocritical blurring of moral issues and partly the result of her own state of semi-liberalization. At the final curtain she is presented with yet another choice, although the irony is that it is now too late for either possibility before her to end the evils that have descended. This final choice is like a ghost of those former ones, hideous and unproductive. The play is full of ghosts of the past, which deform the present and render it impotent.

Compared with *A Doll's House*, therefore, *Ghosts* is a more relentless play. Nora of *A Doll's House* is also haunted by past decisions, ones whose consequences she did not foresee. It is indicative of the tone of the play, however, that its dying character, Dr. Rank, is a subordinate one, whereas the death of Oswald is central to *Ghosts*. Nora's story is that of an awakening, the girl turning into a woman, her doll's house of a home recognized for what it is and at last forsaken. In *A Doll's House* it is not too late, though it is almost too late, as the melodramatic device of the foreclosed loan and the Scribean device of the dreadful letter in the mailbox testify. However, enlightenment comes in time, yielding the superb discussion scene in the last act that Shaw admired so much, and enabling Nora to make her exit with the great door reverberating behind her.

Ibsen's moral studies of fairly clear right and wrong reached their acme in *Ghosts*. His control of play structure in what we may call the classical mode—where the structure is easily identifiable and where the parts fit logically together—also reached its highest point in that play. It is important to see that this particular pinnacle was reached just a bit later than midway in Ibsen's career and that the plays which contribute directly to it make up only a small fraction of his total dramatic writing. Ibsen wrote twenty-five plays in all. Of these, *Ghosts* is the sixteenth. He wrote plays for almost fifty years. *Ghosts* was written in the thirtieth year after his first play, *Catiline*, and when he had still two decades of writing ahead of him. Of the total number of his plays, the four moral studies climaxed by *Ghosts* represent less than one-sixth. The plays of the middle period number eight, less than one-third of Ibsen's total dramatic writing. Ibsen's work is greater in number and kind than the popular image of him conveys.

With *The Wild Duck* Ibsen began to enlarge and deepen the nature of his moral concern. This could no longer be summed up in the pursuit of the ideal, as in his early writing. It was no longer focused upon specific rights and wrongs, as in the four moral studies that began his middle period. That focus had perhaps been destroyed by the outburst, *An Enemy of the People*. In *The Wild Duck* he began to oppose all that is doctrinaire, all systems of thought and prejudgments of value that tend to destroy the living power in man. To this end he employed with consummate skill his ability to evoke the particularities of Norwegian life, its individuals, its social tendencies, and its landscape. The attitude of social revolt, which had been paramount in him from *Love's Comedy* to *An Enemy of the People,* came now to an end, though it could still flash out in certain passages, and something like the old romantic search for reality took its place. Indignation gave way to questioning. Still concerned with morality, Ibsen became increasingly interested in its relation to the actual. He tried to ponder its connection with those forces pushing toward life and toward death which contend in man to produce his varied destinies and common fate.

In *Rosmersholm* the mythical power of Norwegian folklore provides the color and depth for a story of fateful love between two exceptionally intelligent people. Here as so often, Ibsen showed his capacity for drawing female characters with even greater strength and credibility than his male characters. Rosmer, the apostate priest, is finely drawn, but even more remarkable is the way in which Ibsen gains one's fascination with and admiration for Rebecca, the murderess who goes finally with Rosmer to suicide. The dark moralities and psychological inevitabilities of this play are unsurpassed in modern drama.

In *The Lady from the Sea* the waters play as important a role as do the mountains and the isolated manor house in *Rosmersholm.* Again, Ibsen created an outstanding role for an actress in the leading female part. Yet it was in *Hedda Gabler* that he wrote his greatest feminine part, because of all the women in his plays Hedda is the one he employs least in the service of an idea. He understood in his imagination exactly who she was and what she did, but he did not understand the mystery of her behavior. Thus, he recorded her in a spirit closer to comedy than to tragedy, though closest of

all to what has since been called the absurd. Often concerned with
the destructive power of genius, Ibsen here took up the destructive
power of non-genius. Hedda is a woman of intelligence, but she has
no developed powers. She is bored, most of all with herself, and far
from being a creator who destroys in order to create, she is a barren
person who destroys when she is in the presence of creativity. Such
behavior, however typical it may be of certain human beings, is
preposterous. Ibsen's highlighting of its absurdity is intensified by
showing the utter lack of comprehension in the characters surrounding Hedda, particularly her husband, Tessman, and her
would-be lover, Judge Brack. The ending of the play, though
Hedda's suicide is carefully prepared for, is deliberately anti-cli-
mactic.

As Ibsen's first great turning, the one from poetry to prose, had
occurred after his creation of the anti-hero, Peer Gynt, so his second
one, toward romantic symbolism, occurred after his creation of the
anti-heroine, Hedda Gabler. The play was finished in 1890, when
Ibsen was sixty-two. The following year he returned to Norway.
The reasons he gave for ending his long exile (broken by only one
visit, in 1885) had mostly to do with looking after publishers, fees,
copyrights, and such things; but one is entitled to suppose that
Ibsen intended to die in his homeland and that he knew his long
period of revolt against it was over. He could at last face the fact
that it was not Norway that bothered him but life itself. He came
home to struggle with existence.

The four plays that Ibsen wrote in Norway in the 1890's are
saturated with death-romanticism. In every one of them, life creates guilt and spawns a desire for death. Death comes like the
breaking of a great wave to destroy the very life that reached upward to it. The four plays are like four such waves beating upon
the shore of the aging Ibsen's life. Outwardly he retained the daily
routine, yet he was ever more deeply withdrawn into himself.

The best of these four plays is the first, *The Master Builder*, with
its awkward, unrealistic, yet compelling story of the famous archi-
tect challenged by a young girl, and by memories of his early
dreams, to climb the steeple of the church he has created, from
which great height he plummets to his death. This play combines
romantic striving, existential individualism, longing for death as

the Absolute, and deep insight of a psychoanalytic nature. It preceded the publication of Freud's *Interpretation of Dreams* by eight years. *Little Eyolf*, which followed, has considerably less power, although, in the Rat Wife, Ibsen created a good example of those encounter-figures, such as the Button Molder in *Peer Gynt* and the Stranger in *The Lady from the Sea*, whom he handled with extraordinary talent.

John Gabriel Borkman* and *When We Dead Awaken* are closely related in theme. The leading character in each play has sold his soul (his life, as Ibsen puts it) for a great prize, and each discovers too late that life itself is the prize to be sought. Borkman, the embezzler, had risked all for gold, which he calls his kingdom, while, in the other play, Rubek had, as Irene reminds him, put art ahead of flesh and blood. In one sense the action of both plays is retributive—death to those who sold life away and who perceive their mistake only in time to suffer in full awareness. Yet in another sense the plays are less rational than that and more psychologically penetrating, for both Borkman and Rubek long with most of their being for the death that comes to them. Their recognition of their failure to love life brings not repentance but anguish and a renewed longing that only death can fulfill.

Badly flawed in its construction, *John Gabriel Borkman* is a realistic play, near to melodrama in some parts, that tries to embody a poetic vision of life and death. *When We Dead Awaken* is symbolic and visionary throughout. In fact, it is not really a play but a pseudo-dramatic poem. Ibsen subtitled it "A Dramatic Epilogue." He said, however, that he did not intend it to be his last play. Calling it an epilogue, he meant only that it was the end of the group of plays that he thought had begun with *A Doll's House*. "If I write anything more," he said, "it will be in quite another context; perhaps, too, in another form." [25] Ibsen thought that this work marked the end of his realistic period. Actually, that had ended with *Hedda Gabler*. If the reason for the break cannot be found in the dynamics of Ibsen's own inner development—I think it can—then one may note the possible influence of Strindberg, whose portrait Ibsen kept on his wall at this time and whose sym-

[25] See Michael Meyer's introduction to the play in *When We Dead Awaken and Three Other Plays* (Garden City, N.Y.: Anchor Books, Doubleday, 1960), p. 306.

bolic drama *To Damascus* Ibsen had read in 1898, the year before he wrote *When We Dead Awaken.*[26]

The play has had its fervent admirers as well as its detractors. Although some very astute critics have been among the former, including Shaw, James Joyce, and recently Robert Brustein, it is difficult to share their enthusiasm.[27] The work has never been successful on the stage, and it is difficult to see how it could be. In this play Ibsen not only outran the limitations of dramatic form; he also outran his own powers as a poet. He attempted to express a vision of death as resurrection—a freeing of the self from its imprisonment in flesh—in the most concrete terms. This is indeed a genuine poetic task, but Ibsen was not able to bring it off. Furthermore, the resources of the stage, although he taxed them to the limit with mountain-side settings and a climactic avalanche, were not used expressively. Because Ibsen's own artistry is not firm in the writing of the play, one has difficulty crediting Rubek's talk about the artist in himself. Yet if Rubek's artistic powers have not been real, then the tension in him between art and human love is false or beside the point. Nothing is harder for an artist to communicate directly in writing than that quality which makes him an artist. It is clear that in *When We Dead Awaken* Ibsen wanted bravely and without reticence to expose this aspect of himself and to assess its worth in human terms. Clear also is his dreadful hope that in death he would find the justification for his life, which he knew to be marred by a coldness of heart that had led, enabled, or perhaps forced him to sacrifice his own happiness and others' for the sake of his writing. Yet although these poignant matters are indicated in *When We Dead Awaken,* they are not credible in the form they there received. Reaching so high, Ibsen's powers of characterization failed him. The play communicates a painful feeling of spiritual turbulence and exhausted powers. It indulges itself in tired clichés of death-romanticism—death is the ultimate union of lovers and the ultimate meaning of existence. Owing to this throbbing concern for the ultimate, which the play affirms without

---

26 *Ibid.* Randolph Goodman has suggested a strong influence of Strindberg's life and writings upon *Hedda Gabler.* See Goodman's "Playwatching with a Third Eye," in *The Columbia University Forum,* Vol. X, No. 1 (Spring 1967), pp. 18–22.

27 See especially Brustein's *The Theatre of Revolt* (Boston: Little, Brown, 1964), pp. 78–83.

irony, Ibsen's last work is far less "modern" than most of what he had done from *Love's Comedy* onward.

Solitary by choice, Ibsen remains a solitary figure in the development of modern drama. Yet in that solitude he sums up, more than any other single dramatist, the history of the nineteenth-century theater. This in spite of the fact that he read little of the work of others and insisted that he was not influenced by anybody. It is no discredit to Ibsen if he absorbed more than he liked to think. It was his destiny as a dramatist to combine the romantic quest with techniques of construction learned from Scribe and the ancients and to carry these to a level of strength and passion they have achieved nowhere else in modern times. He also absorbed naturalism without becoming a naturalist. He turned poetic drama into prose without letting it become prosaic, and he showed that the way to poetic drama in the modern period must lead through prose. He was not a great prose stylist, yet he often made ordinary-sounding prose as expressive as much poetry. He did this by making it utterly dramatic.

In spite of his achievements and the adulation he has received ever since the 1860's, Ibsen has not exercised a very clear influence upon modern drama. Such influence as he has had, mediated mostly through Shaw, was not in line with his own intentions and has been a misinterpretation of what he was doing. It is the French well-made play and not its Ibsenesque transmutation that is the real father of the hundreds of "problem plays" that have filled so many theaters in the twentieth century. Ibsen cannot be said to have changed modern drama nearly as much as Strindberg and Chekhov did. Perhaps the reason for this lies in Ibsen's pervasive moralism, which was present in all his work, not only in those I have called the "moral studies." We admire a moralist, but we generally find another way to go. The irony is that Ibsen would have thought this to be right. He believed, as has recently been said, that the greatest good was for the individual to be "freely and strongly himself." [28] The modern theater could not be freely and strongly itself if it followed in Ibsen's way.

Perhaps it is the mark of the greatest figures that they do not fit

<hr />

[28] Carolyn Heilbrun, "The Woman as Hero," in *The Texas Quarterly*, Vol. VIII, No. 4 (Winter 1965), pp. 132–141.

well into the stream of history, at least not the history that comes immediately after them, but instead cast longer and less distinct shadows. We are still, more than half a century after his death, too close to Ibsen to know what he will eventually mean as a contributor to the history of drama. All we know is that if we look backward we can hardly see past him, so much of what is there did he absorb into himself; and if we look forward we expect that we shall encounter him again.

9. AUGUST STRINDBERG
(1849–1912)

NONE BUT A PSYCHOLOGIST, an intrepid one at that, can make sense of the life of August Strindberg. Hallucination and reality, science and religion, history and fairy tale, sanity and madness, whole galaxies of contradictory ideas swirled in his head. "The confused and complex current of inspiration, which runs through his works from his youth onwards," says one of his interpreters, "defies temporal division." [1]

With Strindberg the important thing is not, as it was with Ibsen, to see how he matured and passed through early, middle, and late periods. Rather, it is to try to approach him in mid-career, see what he was up to then, assess its value for us, and work out to his other creations as best we can. In this chapter, therefore, I start with Strindberg round about his fortieth year, near the end of the first of his three stormy marriages and at a time when one of his most famous and praiseworthy plays, *The Father*, was recently completed. Circling from there I deal with his naturalist period, which was ended by an emotional and spiritual crisis in 1894–1896. Afterward, I come to the major history plays, anticipated by some of Strindberg's earliest work, and then to the religious plays and

[1] Brita M. E. Mortensen, in Brita M. E. Mortensen and Brian W. Downs, *Strindberg, An Introduction to His Life and Work* (Cambridge: Cambridge University Press, 1949), p. 116.

193

the Chamber Plays. From the lonely man's last days in Stockholm I circle back to his birth in the same city, as a means of transition to the chapter's concluding remarks upon the nature of Strindberg's dramatic art and its importance for the modern theater. What I want to communicate, among other things, is that although there are definable periods in Strindberg's career he was a man who defied time. In almost any of his works one may find the whole of the man revealed, so deeply do they have their source in his embattled consciousness.

We pick up the skein in the years 1888–1889. At this time Chekhov, totally unknown to Strindberg, was writing early work such as *The Bear, A Wedding,* and *The Wood Demon.* Ibsen, not at all unknown to Strindberg, who scornfully referred to him as "the famous Norwegian blue-stocking," was finishing *The Lady from the Sea* and beginning *Hedda Gabler,* in which Strindberg's influence is clearly to be discerned. In the winter of 1889 *A Doll's House* was performed for the first time in London. The Théâtre Libre in Paris, founded in 1887, was having its first great success with Tolstoi's *Power of Darkness,* which Augier, Sardou, and Dumas *fils* had all declared unplayable. The Meiningen players were opening the eyes of Stanislavski in Moscow and of Antoine in Brussels. Gounod's *Romeo and Juliet* was having its première at the Opéra, while the Opéra-Comique offered Lalo's *Le Roi D'Ys.* The Moulin-Rouge opened its doors, Renan published his *History of the People of Israel,* Zola published *The Earth,* Bergson his *Essai sur les données immédiates de la conscience.* Van Gogh painted "Portrait of the Artist" and "The Windmills," and the Eiffel tower was put up for the Paris exposition.

In 1888 Strindberg wrote to Nietzsche. The letter was sent from Holte, Denmark, where Strindberg had gone to consult the doctors at a nerve clinic in hopes of getting a certificate of sanity, for he believed that his wife and relatives were trying to have him committed. The doctors refused to cooperate unless he stayed in the clinic some weeks for observation. This he refused to do, fearing that once in he would not get out.

Nietzsche, who had heard about Strindberg from Georg Brandes in Copenhagen, had written Strindberg and sent two of his books. Strindberg replied: "Dear Sir: Without doubt you have given mankind the deepest book [*Thus Spake Zarathustra*] that it possesses, and what is more, you have had the courage and perhaps the urge, to spit these splendid sayings in the very face of the rabble. I thank you for that!" [2] The fact that Strindberg had not read *Zarathustra* at this time, and never did read it, did not deter him from expressing his admiration for it.[3] "I close all my letters to friends: "Read Nietzsche! That is my *Carthago est dilenda* [sic]!" [4] But to Nietzsche's appeal for help in getting his work translated, Strindberg replied in the following manner:

> In any case, your greatness from the moment you are known and understood will also be lowered, when the sweet rabble grow familiar with you and greet you as one of themselves. It is better for you to preserve the noble seclusion while we, the other ten thousand higher ones, put forth on a secret pilgrimage to your shrine, there to gather according to the heart's desire. Let us protect the esoteric doctrine, preserve it pure and unimpaired and not permit it to become common property except through devoted disciples—in whose name I sign myself,
>
> AUGUST STRINDBERG [5]

The correspondence between the two egoists, both fighting against madness, the philosopher unsuccessfully, as it soon appeared, is full of mutual flattery. Apparently Strindberg sent to Nietzsche, on the heels of the letter quoted above, a copy of his play *The Father,* which had been completed the year before (1887); and he must have sent him also a copy of a letter about the play he had received from Zola, for in his next letter Nietzsche mentions them both:

> I read your tragedy twice over with deep emotion; it has astonished me beyond all measure, to come to know a work in which my own conception of love—with war as its means and the deathly hate of the sexes as its fundamental law—is expressed in such a splendid fashion. But this work is really destined to be presented by M. Antoine in Paris at the Théâtre Libre! Simply demand this of

2 V. J. McGill, *August Strindberg* (New York: Brentano's Publishers, 1930), p. 287.
3 Mortensen and Downs, *op. cit.*, p. 41.
4 McGill, *op. cit.*, p. 287.
5 *Ibid.*, p. 288.

Zola. At the moment he prizes it very highly when he attracts attention to himself.[6]

The letter was written in November. *The Father* had already been published, with a preface by Zola, and had been acted at the Casino Theater in Copenhagen twelve months before. Strindberg had written the play in Bavaria, where he had also written, about the same time, his second novel, *The People of Hemsö,* and had begun *Le Plaidoyer d'un fou* ("The Confession of a Fool"), the fifth of his autobiographical volumes. (The first four volumes were all composed in 1886.) In the midst of work on *Le Plaidoyer* Strindberg removed his family from the shores of Lake Constance and went to Copenhagen to see *The Father* performed. He said when he watched it in rehearsal that he did not know whether he was seeing a drama on stage or his very life.

A month after the Copenhagen performance, Zola wrote to Strindberg:

> Your play interests me very much. The philosophical idea is very daring, and the characters are boldly drawn. You have traced the doubt of paternity with a powerful and disquieting effect. Finally, your Laura is the true woman in the unconsciousness and the mystery of her qualities and faults. She will remain buried in my memory. In all, you have written a very curious and interesting work, in which there are, especially at the end, some very beautiful things. To be frank, however, the recourse to analysis there troubles me a little. You know that I am not much for abstraction. I like my characters to have a complete social setting, that we may elbow them and feel that they are soaked in our air. And your captain who has not even a name, your other characters who are almost creatures of reason, do not give me the complete sense of life which I require. But the question between you and me here is really one of race. (Sic!) Such as it is, I repeat, your piece is one of the few dramatic works which has moved me profoundly. Believe me your devoted and sympathetic colleague,
>
> ÉMILE ZOLA[7]

As a matter of fact, Strindberg had written in *The Father* a better example of dramatic naturalism than Zola was ever to

[6] *Ibid.,* pp. 288–289.
[7] *Ibid.,* pp. 298–299.

achieve, but he had also done things in the play that Zola did not include in his naturalist program. He had achieved a very deep psychological penetration, and he had brought forward into a thoroughly contemporary setting some important characteristics of Aeschylus' Agamemnon and Shakespeare's Lear, two great tragic heroes who do battle with women. The overpowering sense of inevitability in *The Father,* in which the male is destroyed by the female, depends more on its presentation of a psychological archetype than upon social forces, although the rendering of the social setting and the character types to be found in it are highly authentic.

The Father was based on two of Strindberg's preoccupations closely associated in his mind. One was his love, hatred, and fear of women. The other was Ibsen.

In *The Confession of a Fool,* written, as noted above, at about the same time as *The Father,* Strindberg gives a gruesome account of his marriage to the Baroness Wrangel, Siri von Essen, who divorced the baron in order to marry Strindberg in 1877 and also (Strindberg was never sure which was the real motive) to pursue a career on the stage. After ten years the marriage had become impossible. The story is told that when the family traveled from Bavaria to Denmark, Strindberg made his wife eat separately from him in the dining rooms. Asked by an acquaintance who the lady was to whom Strindberg had nodded, Strindberg replied: "She was once my wife, now she is my mistress." [8] In 1891 the marriage ended in divorce.

For all its horror generated by Strindberg's doubts about his wife's fidelity, her possible Lesbianism, her desire to poison him, the parentage of their children, and much else, *The Confession of a Fool* is a book of rich, black humor. Its comedy is based on the unhappy fact that Strindberg adored his wife and fell in love with her repeatedly while at the same time he thought she was destroying him with malice aforethought. He was perfectly aware how ridiculous a figure this made him. The book is full of self-ridicule and Strindberg's suspicion that he might be mad.

The Father contains similar motifs, played without humor. The Captain (Strindberg) is destroyed by his wife, Laura (Siri),

[8] Mortensen and Downs, *op. cit.,* p. 43.

through the doubts she instills in him about whether he is the father of their daughter Bertha. One cannot tell whether this torture actually proceeds from the wife-mother or whether it is self-inflicted, owing to some wish for death in the Captain's personality. Even if it is the latter, however, it proceeds from life—or from what Strindberg often called the "powers"—and of life the proper symbol is Woman. Thus, Woman is responsible for the entire story. She brought the Captain (i.e., Strindberg; i.e., mankind) into existence at birth and is now helping him out of it again, once his usefulness to her is past. At the end of the play the *coup de grâce* is delivered by the Nurse, who entices the Captain into a strait jacket so that he can be led off to an asylum. At that point the Nurse replaces the wife as eternal Woman, representative of birth and death.

Strindberg was very proud of the effect his play had on the audience. He wrote to Nietzsche (with how much truth it is impossible to know) that at the Copenhagen theater "an old lady fell dead during the performance . . . , another woman fainted and when the strait-jacket was produced on the stage, three-quarters of the audience rose like one man and ran from the theatre bellowing like mad bulls!" [9]

While the dominant mood of the conclusion of the play is pity (with terror, too, I think) for the vanquished male in the toils of the trapper, it also contains a clear warning to men that they must try to avoid a similar fate. "Omphale! Omphale!" the Captain shouts to Laura. "You cunning woman, lover of peace and contriver of disarmament. Wake, Hercules, before they take away your club!" [10]

This warning to all men was also, in Strindberg's mind, something of an answer to Ibsen, especially the Ibsen he thought he saw in *A Doll's House*, which had been published some eight years earlier. "In the old days," says the Captain, "the smith forged the soldier's coat, now it is made by the needle-woman." [11]

Ibsen had intended *A Doll's House* to be not a defense of woman against the tyranny of the male but a defense of the individual

9 McGill, *op. cit.*, pp. 292–293.
10 *Six Plays of Strindberg*, Elizabeth Sprigge, trans. (Garden City, N.Y.: Anchor Books, Doubleday, 1956), p. 56.
11 *Ibid.*

against the tyranny of social conformity. Strindberg might have hailed it if he had been of a mind to view it in that light, which means if he had not grown envious of Ibsen after once having come under the strong influence of *Brand*. Strindberg also desperately needed some champion of women's rights whom he could treat as a scapegoat. Ibsen, who had all Europe at his feet, was cast in this role.

Strindberg did not, of course, do "the famous Norwegian blue-stocking" any harm by his attacks, but he hit the bull's-eye none-theless and in a strange way, for Ibsen happened to admire Strind-berg's plays above all others written by his contemporaries, and Strindberg, as noted in the previous chapter, eventually got his portrait hung on Ibsen's study wall. "I can't write a line unless that portrait is there," said Ibsen. "He will be greater than I." [12] It was Ibsen who described Strindberg best. "The man fascinates me," he said, "because he is so subtly, so delicately mad." [13]

Strindberg thought that the character of Hedda Gabler had been suggested to Ibsen by Laura in *The Father* and by Tekla in *Creditors* (1889). He also thought that the suspicions aroused in Hjalmar Ekdal in *The Wild Duck* about whether Hedvig is his own daughter were meant to refer to Strindberg's case, and he be-lieved that Ibsen had been bribed by Strindberg's enemies to write the play, which he called a "scurrilous pamphlet." [14]

Although *A Doll's House* is certainly not about feminism or "the woman question," there is no doubt that it owes part of its fame and some of its substance to the fact that it was contempora-neous with movements then springing up in many countries on behalf of the rights of women. It is not an accident that what Caro-lyn Heilbrun has called "the woman as hero" became a literary phenomenon when women began to ask for the vote and to seek careers outside the home.[15] Strindberg knew this, and he viewed the entire phenomenon with the greatest hostility. But his hostility was certainly mixed with attraction, for three times he married women who sought public careers. His first wife, Siri von Essen,

12 G. A. Campbell, *Strindberg* (London: Duckworth, 1933), p. 56.
13 Robert Brustein, *The Theatre of Revolt* (Boston: Little, Brown, 1964), p. 88.
14 Campbell, *op. cit.*, pp. 74, 80.
15 "The Woman as Hero," in *The Texas Quarterly*, Vol. VIII, No. 4 (Winter 1965), pp. 132–141.

aspired to be an actress. His third, Harriet Bosse, to whom he was married from 1901 to 1904, really could act. His second, Frida Uhl, whom he married in 1893 and divorced the following year, was a journalist. Quite contrary to all the evidence, Strindberg supposed in every case that he was getting the ideal mother whom he sought. In his old age he became more or less engaged to still another actress, Fanny Falkner, but she, wise at nineteen years of age, drew back in time.

The Father was Strindberg's most direct dramatic retort to Ibsen. It even includes a reference to Ghosts: the Doctor makes a speech expressing his sympathy for the much maligned Captain Alving, whom, he complains, Ibsen did not even permit to appear in the play to defend himself![16] Yet Strindberg did not allow his tilting at Ibsen to deflect him from his main antagonist, who was simply Woman. The Father has established itself, along with Tolstoi's "Kreutzer Sonata," from which it is separated by only two years, as one of the most powerful statements in all literature of the war between the sexes.

In spite of the misgivings he expressed, Zola admired The Father sufficiently to ask Strindberg for another play, and so in 1888 he wrote Miss Julie, which has become by far the most often performed of his plays. As it turned out, it was the first of his plays to be done by the Théâtre Libre, but they did not get around to it until January 1893. For the occasion Strindberg wrote the famous preface, already cited in Chapter 5.[17] It is one of the prime documents in the history of modern stage realism, giving as it does such a damning description of what most theater practice, even at that late date, was like and calling for the introduction of methods to enable the theater more accurately and naturally to represent life upon the stage. Strindberg wrote it specifically to encourage the then revolutionary aesthetic of the Théâtre Libre.

In 1894, shortly before its existence ended, the Théâtre Libre produced The Father. This play had already been done in 1890 by the Freie Bühne in Berlin, which went on to Miss Julie in 1892 and four other Strindberg plays, including Creditors, in 1893. It

16 Robert Brustein, op. cit., p. 89, points out that Strindberg neglects to add that before the end of Ghosts "Captain Alving's blackened memory has been partially whitewashed again."
17 See above, p. 63.

was in the winter of 1892–3 that Strindberg met the adventurous spirits behind this theater, Otto Brahm and Paul Schlenther. Incidentally, *The Father* was censored in Berlin although it had passed freely in Copenhagen, while with *Miss Julie* the situation was reversed, censors at all times and places being notoriously unpredictable.

Strindberg's connections with the theater world were sporadic, hectic, and subject to all the vicissitudes of which the rest of his life was full. When he went up to Copenhagen in 1887 to see *The Father* performed, he stayed on for about a year and a half and there conceived the idea of founding a Scandinavian experimental theater modeled, as he announced in the press, on the French Théâtre Libre. Some plays he had already written and those he planned to write would form the repertory, and the leading actress would be his wife, Siri von Essen, who unfortunately appears to have had no great endowment of talent. On March 9, 1889, the Experimental Theater opened at the Dagmar Theater in Copenhagen. The triple bill included *The Stronger, Creditors,* and *Pariah*. Because of the censor, *Miss Julie* could not be performed publicly. Therefore on March 14 and 15 it was put on privately at the Students Association of the University, with Siri von Essen as Julie. After three performances in Copenhagen and one in Malmö, Sweden, the Experimental Theater came to an inglorious end, partly because the press was more or less hostile toward the dangerous figure it considered Strindberg to be and partly because the author could not get along with his wife. In April he left for Stockholm without her.[18]

Strindberg wrote his first play about modern life (save for a youthful work, *The Freethinker*) in 1886. It bore the title *The Camp-Followers*. In 1887, with the collaboration of Axel Lundegärd, he revised it and changed its name to *The Comrades*. Then came *The Father* and *Miss Julie*. In 1889 for the Experimental Theater he wrote the one-act tour de force, often performed, called *The Stronger*, which has a cast of two women, only one of whom speaks. *Creditors, Pariah,* and *Simoon* were also written for that theater. Later the same year he adapted for the stage his novel *The*

18 Børge Gedsø Madsen, *Strindberg's Naturalistic Theatre: Its Relation to French Naturalism* (Seattle: University of Washington Press, 1962), pp. 113–115.

People of Hemsö, which is about the inhabitants of the skerries off the coast near Stockholm. In 1892 he wrote six naturalist one-act plays, of which the strongest and best known is *The Bond* (known also as *The Link*). A dramatization of a divorce proceeding in which the bond between the two parties is their child, it reflects Strindberg's own divorce and his anguish over the loss of his three children. The other plays in this group are *Debit and Credit, The First Warning, Facing Death, Motherly Love,* and *Playing with Fire.* Also in 1892 he wrote the sorrowful fairy-tale play *The Keys of Heaven,* which, like *The Bond,* reflects the loss of his children.

Thus, from 1886 to 1892, when he wrote his most famous plays, one may think of Strindberg's dramatic work as centering upon the style of naturalism and the motif of the war between the sexes. Strindberg's connections with Zola, Antoine, and Brahm and his efforts to form a theater of his own show him as a participant in the international renewal of the theater taking place at the time. He had caught the startled, not fully comprehending, yet sympathetic eye of Georg Brandes, who was, as has been noted above, the foremost Scandinavian critic of the time. Strindberg's correspondence with Nietzsche reveals him to be, if not a philosopher, yet a champion of the most daring intellectual thought of the day, entertaining dreams of a higher culture and holding that what society takes for insanity may be a superior kind of intelligence that can hope for no acceptance in the average mind.[19] Yet the plays he wrote at this time, his most famous works, are dominated by fear.

Just when Strindberg was achieving an international reputation as a writer of naturalistic plays he began to tire of naturalism and of the theater in general. Furthermore, he entered into the worst emotional disturbance of his life, the so-called Inferno Crisis, named after Strindberg's own account, *Inferno,* published in 1897. For the details of the playwright's suffering at this period, the reader should turn to that book or to the vivid recapitulation by Elizabeth Sprigge.[20] As in a vortex, there now swirled Strindberg's fear of demons, hatred and terror of women, passion for true sci-

19 His correspondence with Nietzsche was brought to an end with receipt of the following letter: "Herr Strindberg: —Eheu! No more! Divorçons! The Crucified One." Thereafter Nietzsche disappeared into the asylum at Jena. See McGill, *op. cit.,* p. 294.
20 *The Strange Life of August Strindberg* (New York: Macmillan, 1949), pp. 154–169.

ence mixed with occult, desire to uncover the one true secret source of all matter, pursuit of alchemy, and theosophy, and much more. Totally obsessed, in the span of two months Strindberg passed from being the lionized author of the unquestioned triumph *The Father* (Paris première, December 18, 1894) to a state of abject poverty in the Latin Quarter, crazed with his scientific experiments, his hands burnt from trying to use his fireplace as a smelting furnace, his clothes so shabby he could not enter even a modest restaurant, his bitterness so deep that he refused help from all his friends. Now twice divorced, he was bereft of family. He suffered hallucinations and practiced black magic. His torments continued for the better part of two years and abated only when he came to believe that they were trials laid on him by God for the purification of his soul.

For five years (1892–1897) Strindberg wrote nothing for the stage. When he returned to it he wrote a long (eventually a three-part), highly symbolic play, *To Damascus* (Parts I and II were written in 1897–8), the expression of his newly found religious faith and the peace that had come temporarily upon him.

In 1898, Strindberg wrote *There Are Crimes and Crimes,* which is semi-naturalistic, and *Advent,* a religious play that anticipates both in title and theme his later and better-known work of piety, *Easter* (1900). Then in 1899 Strindberg embarked upon a period of furious productivity, the mere catalogue of which challenges one's belief. Largely under the influence of Shakespeare, he conceived the idea of writing a series of plays that would show the sweep of Swedish history and the hand of Providence in it from the late thirteenth century to the latter part of the eighteenth.[21] Strindberg here shows, although to the discerning it was already clear, that his many sharp attacks upon his fellow countrymen and their cultural inadequacies were based, like his hatred of women, on a love too great rather than too small.

Strindberg's writing of history plays had begun, unsurprisingly, in the first year that he wrote any plays at all, in 1869, when he was twenty. It was then he composed, according to the acceptable models of the time, a five-act tragedy called *Hermione.* It was a

21 Walter Johnson, *Strindberg and the Historical Drama* (Seattle: University of Washington Press, 1963), pp. 13–14.

revision of an earlier play of the same year entitled *Hellas in De-cline* and dealt with the conquest of Athens by Philip of Macedon. The following year he wrote a play about Sweden's King Erik XIV, which he destroyed. (Much later he wrote another on the same subject.) He also wrote then a tragedy, *Blotsven,* which he also tore up, but in 1871 he rewrote it in unrhymed verse in one act and called it *The Outlaw.* This play, which owes much to Ibsen's early work and to Björnson and Oehlenschläger, has an Icelandic subject. Its story of the shift from paganism to Christianity as seen in one particular family anticipates the more recent play by Christopher Fry, *Thor, with Angels.* Also in 1871, Strindberg planned his first important historical play, *Master Olof,* which is about Sweden's transition in the sixteenth century from Catholicism to Protestantism. He finished it in five acts of prose in 1872 and rewrote it several times thereafter, notably in a poetic version of 1876. Of his early history plays, *Master Olof* is the only one that became part of the cycle Strindberg conceived at the end of the century. In 1880 he wrote a play with a medieval Swedish setting, *The Secret of the Guild,* as a vehicle for Siri von Essen, and another, *Ritter Bengt's Wife,* in 1882.

Such, then, was Strindberg's experience with the historical play when, shortly after the "Inferno Crisis," he began to work on his great Swedish cycle. In 1899 he put on paper *The Saga of the Folkungs, Gustavus Vasa, Erik XIV,* and the first part of *Gustavus Adolphus.* A spirit more methodical, working less under a great spiritual pressure, might have taken four or five years to pen as much. In 1900 Strindberg wrote *Easter* and the short *Caspar's Shrove Tuesday.* He finished *Gustavus Adolphus* in 1901 and the same year wrote *Engelbrekt* and *Charles XII.* We might think that enough, but that year he also found time to write both parts of *Dance of Death*—an excruciating exposé of married bitterness that came right on the heels of his marriage to Harriet Bosse (for in this year he got married also, his third try)—and he wrote *Midsummer* and began *The Crown Bride.* The marriage started to go bad a month after it was contracted. Knowing this, and looking at the enormous and varied materials Strindberg wrote at this time, one can fairly guess at the turbulence of his spirit. In addition to writing six history plays, he was delving back into naturalism for *Dance of Death,* indulging in pious preachment in *Easter,* tossing off trifles like *Caspar's Shrove Tuesday* and *Midsummer,* and writing the first of his Chamber Plays. *The Crown Bride* was shortly joined by *Swan-White* and *A Dream Play,* all published in 1902.

He returned to history plays in 1903 with *Queen Christina* and *Gustavus III.* By this time he had conceived still another vast cycle, not confined to Sweden but interpreting the history of the world! So in 1903 he devoted himself also to a play about Moses (*Through Wilderness to Promised Land*), one about Socrates (*Hellas*), another on the Christ (*The Lamb and the Wild Beast*), and, finally, one about Martin Luther (*The Nightingale of Wittenberg*). Not surprisingly, only one of these, the last, was finished. As soon as it was, he wrote Part III of *To Damascus* (1904). He was to write ten more plays before he died, of which three would be Swedish history plays: *The Last Night* and *The Regent* (1908) and *The Earl of Bjälbo* (1909).

It is a popular misconception that Strindberg's history plays are early work, from which he passed into the more mature and modern naturalism, which in turn finally gave way to avant-garde expressionism.[22] The tendency of naturalism to turn into symbolism and in some cases, including Strindberg's, into expressionism is unmistakable; but the history play, as such, cannot be fitted into this sequence. The stuff of history, especially when the author is conscious of belonging to a national, religious, or world history that unites him with other men, is a challenge to a dramatist's powers that seems to be of a different order from those presented by the social and psychological realities of his own time. This challenge Strindberg felt more strongly in his later years than he did earlier. It is as if he wanted his abilities as a writer, so frequently used to mount attacks upon his countrymen and to expose the torments of his own miserable life, used somehow in the formation of a national historical consciousness, the like of which he thought no nation had known since the age of Elizabeth. He failed, of course, to attain anything remotely comparable to Shakespeare's universality, yet his history plays did win an immediate popularity in Sweden, which they have kept. That their audience outside Sweden is se-

---

[22] Such an opinion is to be found, for instance, in Martin Esslin, *The Theatre of the Absurd* (Garden City, N.Y.: Anchor Books, Doubleday, 1961), p. 252.

verely limited is mainly due to the fact that Sweden's role in modern world history has been peripheral.

The years of Strindberg's restless wanderings to and fro between Stockholm, Berlin, Copenhagen, Bavaria, Paris, Brussels, and Switzerland came to an end with the Inferno Crisis. He spent some time in Lund to benefit from, if not actually to enjoy, the quiet of the place, and then he returned to the capital city. After his third wife left him in 1903, he lived alone in Stockholm for the rest of his life.

His seclusion in those years was entirely of his own making. He had no bell on the door of his apartment, and visitors who came to it were advised by a sign to make their inquiries on the floor below. Above him the Falkner family lived. They tended to many of his needs (when they cooked for him, they were rewarded with his chronic suspicion that all cooks were poisoners—compare the rapacious cook in *The Ghost Sonata* and the mother who starves her children in *The Pelican*), and their daughter Fanny came every morning to help with secretarial tasks, to bring news of the people Strindberg avoided, and to fall in love with him. Strindberg got her a job as a member of the Intimate Theater.

This theater was founded in 1907 on the Norra Bantogret in Stockholm in a house that seated 161 persons and had a very low ceiling and a long, thrust stage. On November 26, 1907, it opened with the premier of Strindberg's play *The Pelican*. The actor-manager was August Falck, who had already taken *Miss Julie* and *Pariah* on tours through the provinces. The money was raised by him and Strindberg, and the theater turned out, though this was not the original intention, to be one in which only the works of Strindberg were presented. Thus, in his latter days, and mostly by luck, Strindberg achieved something that any playwright might dream of—a theater devoted entirely to his own plays, encouraging him to write for its particular requirements, allowing him to take as much or as little interest in the staging as he desired, and giving some of his works well over a hundred performances.

Strindberg directed one of the plays there himself. This was *Swan-White*, the second most popular of the theater's offerings, performed 152 times. It was outstripped only by *Easter*, which had

182 performances.[23] Although Strindberg did not spend a great deal of time at the Intimate Theater, he took an active interest, especially in the stage settings. His *Open Letters to the Intimate Theater* contain, in addition to essays on plays by Shakespeare, a number of significant notes on acting and décor. He was an advocate of the most simple means and desired to get as many effects as possible by the use of lights playing upon a stage hung with black velvet. (In this, his experiments remind one of those Stanislavski carried on about the same time in Moscow.) His love of the simplified, almost bare stage was more in line with future developments than Strindberg probably imagined.

In addition to his counsel and his financial support, Strindberg also gave the Intimate Theater new plays. When these were published, at the end of 1907, he called them Chamber Plays, by analogy with chamber music. The collection included *The Pelican, The Storm, After the Fire,* and *The Ghost Sonata.* There was a fifth Chamber Play, *The Black Glove* (1909), which the Intimate Theater did not produce, and an Arabian Nights entertainment, *Abu Casem's Slippers* (1908), which Strindberg sold to a touring company. His last dramatic work, *The Great Highway* (1909) is more nearly a poem than a play.

During this period, in his secluded apartment, Strindberg wrote a daily newspaper column. He also experienced the last of his several religious conversions. He repented of his earlier agnosticism, his experiments in alchemy, and his blasphemies and said that he was going to go through his works and strike out all the offensive passages. For a time August Falck was afraid he might actually do it. Strindberg, who had so frequently attacked Christianity, began now to champion the state church and to declare that it ought to have control over all governmental appointments. He read the Bible intensively, calling it "the only truth," and died holding it to his breast. He also championed the labor movement, which responded by celebrating his sixtieth birthday (January 22, 1909) with a torchlight procession past his windows while in another part of town three theaters offered festive performances of his plays.

23 Downs, *op. cit.,* p. 79. The role of Eleonora had been first acted by Harriet Bosse at the Royal Theater in 1901.

The celebration of his sixty-third birthday was an even bigger affair, having the full cooperation of the press and government. About four months after it was over, Strindberg succumbed to abdominal cancer.

He was the last of the three great Scandinavians who scourged the modern conscience and helped to shape the modern self-understanding. The others were Kierkegaard and Ibsen. Of the three, the profoundest and most influential, even in the theater, was Kierkegaard, without whom neither Strindberg nor Ibsen would have been the same. Owing to the strength of his emphasis upon romantic interiority and the problem of communication, Kierkegaard's influence upon twentieth-century theater has been enormous.

Like Kierkegaard, Strindberg was born of a union between his father and a servant woman. He interpreted his parentage as a stigma never to be removed and called one volume of his autobiography *Son of a Bondservant,* identifying his mother with Hagar and himself with Ishmael.

Strindberg's mother had borne his father three illegitimate children before the tardy man married her, which he did two years before Johan August was born. She had come to the house of her future husband, who was a steamship agent, as housekeeper and mistress. She lived with him nineteen years, bore him twelve children, of whom seven survived infancy, and died when August was thirteen years old. Even before her death, while she was ill, her husband acquired a new housekeeper, and as soon as possible after he was widowed he married his second servant like the first. The family lived in squalid poverty. The young Strindberg felt unloved by both of his father's wives and was frequently whipped by his grandmother, who saw to it that more whipping was administered by the boy's father at the end of the day. Hatred and fear of the father, unrequited love for the mother, and anxieties of poverty seem to be the only too obvious roots of Strindberg's later marital, financial, and spiritual troubles. But the sources of his inventiveness, his radical daring, his talents as a writer, his prodigious energy, and the particular jumble of ideas that made up his "thinking" remain mysterious. The psychic scars that he bore were the scars of an age as well as those of an individual.

Religion was always in him, even during the periods of atheism. An unreligious man does not get hauled into court, as Strindberg did in 1884, for having described the Eucharist as an "impudent fraud." It is easy to see his religion as a search for the good father and as an attempt to keep at bay the wild forces that raged within, but unless one takes such factors categorically as the explanation of all religion, they do not explain Strindberg's spiritual pilgrimage. As the art of plays like *The Father, Miss Julie,* and *Dance of Death* cannot be reduced to the psychological morbidity they display, so Strindberg's persistent belief in Providence and the role it played in his life cannot be reduced to the traumas of childhood. In short, a reductionist approach, whether to Strindberg's religion or to his aesthetic accomplishments, is too easy. A better lead is Robert Brustein's suggestion that all of Strindberg's efforts, like his experiments in alchemy, have to do with the transmutation of base material into higher.[24]

"To me falls the task," wrote Strindberg, "of bridging the gap between naturalism and supra-naturalism by proclaiming that the latter is only a development of the former." [25] The sentence shows his acute awareness of what was required of the drama in his age and of his role as one who bore within him the seeds of the drama's future development. Naturalism was necessary to that development because it represented a chastening of the romantic imagination. It was like a funnel through which the romantic imagination was forced to flow. The constriction deepened the appreciation of character, the relation of character to environment, and the dynamics of human psychology. Naturalism forced the playwright to consider more seriously than at any time since the start of the nineteenth century the limitations and possibilities of stagecraft, because it forced him to conceive of the décor as a representation of the character's environment. From this it was only one step to the conception of the *stage* as the *actor's* environment, which is the underlying principle of expressionism. The knowledge and appreciation of the theatrical medium which naturalism gave to the writer made possible the less constricted uses of the stage that came about when naturalism began to expand into symbolism, expres-

24 Brustein, *op. cit.,* p. 87.
25 Quoted in Madsen, *op. cit.,* p. 158.

sionism, and other post-realistic styles of the twentieth century.

The general pattern of romanticism's constriction into realism and naturalism and its subsequent expansion again into more expressive forms is to be seen throughout European literature from about 1880 to 1910. It can be observed even in Zola, not to mention playwrights more creative than he, and also in the development of the novel, although there the process took longer. Ibsen's plays show this pattern clearly, but the paradigm of it is the dramaturgy of Strindberg. It fell to Strindberg to be painfully exposed to the major influences of his age and to absorb them into his own fiery subjectivity, whence they emerged in works of art stamped with the imprint of tormented genius.

Whereas Ibsen, the principled individualist, liked to cover his tracks and pretend to have been influenced by nobody, Strindberg told everything and left the clearest indications of the forces that worked upon him. In his religious life he was first under the spell of the piety of his family, which he later cast off. His first play, *The Freethinker* (1869), was indebted partly to Ibsen's *Brand,* partly to Kierkegaard (both directly and through *Brand*), and partly to Theodore Parker (of all people), the Unitarian divine from Massachusetts whom Strindberg read in Swedish translation and whose disciple for a time he became. Later, owing to Darwin and the French positivists, Strindberg became a thumping atheist and attacked Christianity from all sides. Then, as noted, he became a devotée of Nietzsche. He took up the study of various natural sciences, including chemistry, botany, biology, and geology, and was by no means inept in these subjects. Then his interest in orthodox science gave way to an interest in alchemy, to which he devoted endless hours of experimentation. He also took up the study of psychology, especially the work of H. Bernheim, Théodule Ribot, and Charles Letourneau. He studied hypnotism and practiced it on several persons including his wife Frida Uhl, but he was even more interested in the power of suggestion that one mind has over another in waking life, as can be seen in such plays as *The Father, Miss Julie, Creditors,* and *The Ghost Sonata.* After the Inferno Crisis he came under the strong influence of Swedenborg, of whom he first learned from reading Balzac's *Seraphita* but of whom he was taught more by Frida Uhl's mother, who also nearly converted him to Catholicism. Swedenborg gave him a way of interpreting by a positive light the hellish nature of his personal experiences. Strindberg's mind ranged so widely and with such erratic enthusiasms that one never knows when reading him to what influential figure he will next point. In his answers to questions put to him in 1897 by George Bröckner, he declared that one of the two historical figures he considered most important was Bernard of Clairvaux! (The other was Henry IV of France.)[26]

The influences upon Strindberg in the field of drama were no less varied and distinct. Shakespeare was the most important for his later history plays, as were Björnson and Ibsen for the earlier; but he also owed something to Hugo. When he entered upon his naturalist period, he absorbed Zola, the Goncourt brothers, Maupassant, Huysmans, Alphonse Daudet, Henri Becque, and Dumas *fils*, as well as lesser figures like Oscar Méténier and Henri Lavedan.[27] Later he found himself able to appreciate and laud the symbolist theater of Maeterlinck, whose imprint upon his Chamber Plays is unmistakable. In the realm of theater practice, he learned from Antoine and Brahm and later from Max Reinhardt. Gordon Craig's ideas, however, he resisted, because they seemed to him to give too much over to stage design at the expense of the actor and the spoken word.[28] Finally, he received some influence from the theater of the Far East, with which he became acquainted through his studies in philology.

As these influences poured into Strindberg, there to mix with his subjective genius in such a way as to make him one of the true culminators of nineteenth-century drama, so the influence proceeding from him has been great. He has been second only to Chekhov in his influence on twentieth-century drama. The wave of nineteenth-century realism came to a climax in his naturalistic plays of tormented family life. Then it broke, creating his free,

26 Elizabeth Sprigge, *Strange Life*, p. 232.
27 Madsen, *op. cit.*, p. 12.
28 Sprigge, *Strange Life*, p. 215. Craig came to Stockholm about 1908 but did not meet Strindberg. However, when Bernard Shaw came, Strindberg took him to see *Miss Julie* at The Intimate Theater and introduced him to the company. This was after Shaw had first proposed to call on Strindberg at two o'clock on a certain day, to which Strindberg had replied, "at two o'clock I shall be unwell." (Sprigge, p. 214.)

highly subjective form called expressionism. Both types have exercised strong influence upon the major dramatists after him.

In America, for instance, Strindberg's influence has been more pronounced than that of any other playwright. Without his example, Eugene O'Neill would probably not have developed in such a way as to become the first American playwright of international importance.[29] Strindberg's influence upon Tennessee Williams is no less strong than that upon O'Neill, and perhaps even easier to see. The line from *Miss Julie* to *A Streetcar Named Desire* is direct. Just as important, throughout Williams' work, is the Strindbergian quality of combining naturalism with a strong subjective bias, of the work's being colored by what Strindberg called the "soul" of the writer, and of this subjectivism's finally breaking the bounds of realism to express itself directly in semipoetic form, as in Strindberg's *Dream Play* and Williams' *Camino Real*. Strindberg's shadow falls strongly upon Edward Albee's *Who's Afraid of Virginia Woolf?*, which is a transformation of Strindberg's *Dance of Death* into the "pop" mode and "camp" style of the 1960's.

In Europe, Strindberg's influence has come mostly through his expressionism, which opened the way for the German expressionism of the 1920's, although the social concerns of the latter were quite un-Strindbergian. Even more important has been the influence of Strindberg's expressionism upon the so-called absurdist theater since World War II.

Mention of this last development may serve as a reminder of what has been Strindberg's most important contribution to modern theater—namely, the more or less direct representation, by theatrical means, of irrational elements in human psychology. Probably Strindberg could not have found the way to do this if his own emotions had not erupted with such volcanic force. However, the important thing was not the eruption itself but the means that Strindberg found to turn its irrational content into theatrical form.

29 I read "practically all the classics and of course all the moderns," said O'Neill, "Ibsen and Strindberg, especially Strindberg." (McGill, *op. cit.*, p. 10.) It was no empty gesture when O'Neill, in accepting the Nobel prize, paid homage to Strindberg as Sweden's greatest writer. It was only ironic, as O'Neill indicated, that the Swedish academy had never seen fit to honor the prophet in its own country.

Strindberg was not alone in this accomplishment. Büchner and Kleist had preceded him. Jarry was his contemporary, as was Maeterlinck with his gentler mysteries. We have also to think of Tolstoi and Hauptmann. Yet none of these stands as Strindberg does like a giant on the threshold of modern sensibility, able to be considered along with Freud as one who cast the materials of the irrational unconscious into such form as would change the modern understanding of human nature.

Part of this accomplishment Strindberg owes to the skeletal simplicity with which he rendered the situations in his naturalist plays. In *The Father* and *Miss Julie* the pattern of male-female antagonism is so clear and is uttered with such primitive candor that we plunge at once beneath the surface of life, delving right through the social environment, which is by no means slighted, and through the level of rational plausibility to the heart of a fear and a hatred that are generated in the irrational depths of the self. By the time he came to write *Dance of Death*, Strindberg was able to suggest this irrational cauldron through the use of quite ordinary dialogue that both hides and reveals the wild forces behind it. We may note, by way of example, the opening lines of the play, an exchange between the Captain and his wife in their dwelling in the military fortress by the sea:

CAPTAIN: Won't you play something for me?

ALICE (*indifferently, but not snappishly*): What am I to play?

CAPTAIN: Whatever suits you.

ALICE: You don't like my repertory.

CAPTAIN: Nor you mine.

ALICE (*evasively*): Do you want the doors to stay open?

CAPTAIN: If you wish it.

ALICE: Let them be, then. (*Pause.*) Why don't you smoke?

CAPTAIN: Strong tobacco is beginning not to agree with me.

ALICE (*in an almost friendly tone*): Get weaker tobacco then. It is your only pleasure, as you call it.

CAPTAIN: Pleasure—what is that?

ALICE: Don't ask me. I know it as little as you—Don't you want your whisky yet?

CAPTAIN: I'll wait a little. What have you for supper?

ALICE: How do I know? Ask Christine.

CAPTAIN: The mackerel ought to be in season soon—now the Fall is here.

ALICE: Yes, it is Fall!

CAPTAIN: Within and without. But leaving aside the cold that comes with the Fall, both within and without, a little broiled mackerel, with a slice of lemon and a glass of white Burgundy, wouldn't be so very bad.

ALICE: Now you grow eloquent.

CAPTAIN: Have we any Burgundy left in the wine-cellar?

ALICE: So far as I know, we have had no wine-cellar these last five years—.[30]

We have here a pastiche of the opening of a well-made play, two characters passing the time of day and filling the audience in on the circumstances of the house. But the tone is something else. No communication worthy of the name takes place on the rational level of this conversation. Every word points elsewhere—to some recess of consciousness, some primitive order of being, where, as we may already guess, communication means attack. Before the end of the play, we will see attack and counterattack played over and over again, like a ritual ordained in darkness, until at last the Captain, deprived of the power of speech by an apoplectic stroke, minutes away from his death, rouses his failing muscles and spits upon the face of his lifelong partner.

All this is latent in the opening scene, where the hidden violence is carried in the very banality of the dialogue. The scene might almost have been written by Ionesco; it reminds one of the inanities of the opening conversation between Mr. and Mrs. Smith in *The Bald Soprano,* which hide and yet anticipate the verbal explosions to occur later in the play.

In *The Ghost Sonata* Strindberg developed a technique of representing the irrational through juxtaposition of poetic images and elimination of rational plot. He used the same technique in *A Dream Play,* but there the presence of obvious imagery, such as the growing and burning castle with its phallic meaning and the imported Eastern symbolism, weakens the effect. *The Ghost Sonata* is stronger because its effect depends upon the juxtaposition of unin-

[30] Strindberg, *Plays,* translated by Edwin Björkman (New York: Scribner's, 1912), p. 148.

terpreted images brought together by a mysterious mutual gravity.

The transition that Strindberg made from the naturalist plays of sexual warfare, which reached their climax in *Dance of Death,* to the Chamber Plays, with their irrational and mystical qualities, shows that even in the former work Strindberg's psychological concerns were also religious. That is why Nietzsche appealed to him, for Nietzsche, like Schopenhauer, interpreted the Will as an ontological principle. Thus, Strindberg was enabled to see that his own struggle against destructive forces both within and outside him had a universal as well as a particular significance. His subjectivity was his truth. This was the Kierkegaardian insight from which his life would not let him escape, and the strength of his expressionist plays is the proof of its validity. It was through his passionate subjectivity that Strindberg became the influential modern that he is.

Evert Sprinchorn has said that Strindberg is Prometheus, "tortured into revealing his secrets by having his liver eaten out by one of Zeus's vultures." [31] Strindberg himself said that he was Jacob wrestling with the angel of God. [32] What is certain is that he had experience of the demonic, in Paul Tillich's sense of this word as referring to "the structures of destruction." [33] It is equally certain that Strindberg was able to turn his encounter with the demonic into the communicable structures of art rather than simply being destroyed by it. Toward the end of his life he achieved a kindliness and a peace that testify to the authenticity of his spiritual wrestling.

The modernity of Strindberg has to do with the confluence in him of the psychological and the spiritual under the sign of a dreadful rending of the soul and the promise of its reconstitution. It is characteristic of the modern temper that it believes that its journey into the underworld (the underground, as Dostoievski called it) of irrational and disorienting subjectivity is not pure loss but instead the prerequisite of a new and fuller realization of humanity. None of the four great dramatists who stood at the threshold of twentieth-century drama—Ibsen, Strindberg, Chekhov, and

[31] Introduction to *Miss Julie,* E. M. Sprinchorn, trans. (San Francisco: Chandler Publishing Co., 1961), p. vii.
[32] Sprigge, *Strange Life,* p. 172.
[33] Cancerous cells, which are a form of death-giving life, are the best illustration of Tillich's concept of the demonic. Strindberg died of cancer.

Shaw—understood this better than Strindberg, and of none save him can it be said that his dramatic work as a whole exemplifies its meaning. Strindberg is the contemporary and the patron of all those in the theater who engage knowingly in "the struggle of the modern." More than any other dramatist he bore that struggle within himself, exposed to all its bitter lashing against knowledge, certainty, and faith, yet enduring in the belief that the struggle would prove eventually to contain its positive meaning if only the record of it were set down truthfully and without evasion, however chaotic it be.

One can say of Strindberg that he bore the sufferings of an age. The age was that latter part of the nineteenth century which looked into the heart of darkness and saw there all the demons that have since paraded more fully in the light. The Inferno through which Strindberg passed was not only his own. It was also that of a culture, and he was right to think that his madness contained knowledge too intense for the majority. He gave the modern drama its most excruciating visions of hell. For that reason he also gave it its only adequate basis for speaking of hope.

10. ANTON CHEKHOV
(1860–1904)

IT IS THE MEASURE of Chekhov's standing as a dramatic artist that the first and most important things to be said about him, even from the point of view of the historian, can be said only in the language of dramatic criticism. The quantity of writing that Chekhov did for the stage is minuscule compared to that of Ibsen, Strindberg, or Shaw, not to mention many less celebrated playwrights of his time. The quality of his writing can be matched by some of the plays of his three great contemporaries. Chekhov's importance lies neither in the quantity of his playwriting nor in its sheer excellence but in the combination of its originality and depth.

Starting from the most ordinary and widely popular theatrical forms of his day, Chekhov went on to achieve a kind of playwriting utterly new in the history of drama and of the greatest importance for the theater that has come after him. In order to appreciate this fact it is necessary to consider the formal principle of his plays and its relation to the dramatic tradition of the West.

The Chekhovian break with "the Aristotelian tradition" in drama is more radical than any other in modern times—more radical, for instance, than the later one made by Bertolt Brecht, even though Brecht was more self-conscious about his program and set forth his ideas more systematically. Yet perhaps it is misleading to speak of a Chekhovian "break" with Aristotelianism, for it is only in the light of Aristotle's thought that Chekhov's achievement can be understood, and the principal categories of Aristotle's dramatic theory remain the most helpful in interpreting the Chekhovian play. What we have to deal with is a transformation of the Aristotelian understanding, a transformation that is none the less radical for remaining within the traditional terms of discussion. The quality of radical transformation from within, avoiding the overt clash of supposedly opposite principles and yet achieving the most far-reaching changes, is entirely typical of Chekhov, who did not like to pose as a reformer and did not enjoy creating antagonists, but who was nevertheless a mighty foe of all that stood in the way of the renewal of life and letters.

David Magarshack has described Chekhov's development as one which moved from plays of "direct action" to plays of "indirect action." [1] The terminology is helpful, but it does not take one to the heart of the matter. It is true, as he insists, that Chekhov is badly misunderstood wherever it is supposed that his plays contain no action. They are not static, they have a wealth of incident, they include their fair share of shootings, suicides, marriages, deaths, and other "dramatic" occurrences. They are, like all good plays, imitations of action. Magarshack is right to insist upon this and to hold that in Chekhov there occurs a shift in the *kind* of action portrayed, together with a corresponding change in the *manner* of imitation. Yet to call this a shift from direct action to indirect is not the most accurate way to describe it. In order to be more precise, it is necessary to examine the concept of action.

The best modern discussion of the Aristotelian concept of action is Francis Fergusson's *The Idea of a Theater*.[2] Fergusson relies partly on previous analyses in Kenneth Burke's *A Grammar of Motives* and *Philosophy of Literary Form*. Fergusson has also written a further explication in his introduction to Aristotle's *Poetics*.[3] The categories developed in these sources pertaining to Aristotle's idea of "action" provide the most useful tool for understanding Chekhov.

---

[1] *Chekhov the Dramatist* (New York: Hill and Wang, 1960).
[2] Garden City, N.Y.: Anchor Books, Doubleday, 1953.
[3] New York: Hill and Wang, 1961.

The basic scheme to be kept in mind is the so-called tragic rhythm of action, which Burke divides into three "moments" called *purpose, passion,* and *perception.* The tragic hero initiates the tragic action by attempting to fulfill a certain purpose. His behavior is intentional and is directed toward a goal that he takes to be achievable—for instance, Orestes' intention to restore justice by avenging the murder of Agamemnon or Oedipus' intention to rid Thebes of its plague by discovering and punishing the killer of Laius.

The hero's purposeful action does not, however, lead directly to the intended conclusion. Instead, it leads to the second phase of the tragic action, which is a suffering (a passion, in the root meaning of that word). Orestes, having committed the act of vengeance, is pursued by Furies and driven half mad. Oedipus, having begun the search for the unknown killer, endures the hostility of Creon, Jocasta, and Tiresias and endures also the terrible suspicion that the quarry he seeks may be himself.

The second phase of the action, the endurance of suffering, leads finally to the third phase, which is the achievement of perception. Out of the suffering, partly because of the nature of impassioned experience and partly owing to the arrangement of the plot, there comes a deeper knowledge of reality than was at first possessed. This perception, which Aristotle thought was most dramatically achieved in a scene of "recognition," constitutes the moral and spiritual fulfillment of the tragic pattern.

When Aristotle spoke of tragedy's imitating an action "that is serious, complete, and of a certain magnitude," he was referring to the entire tragic pattern in something like the above-mentioned three sequential modes. That was what he meant by completeness. Burke calls the pattern a rhythm because it occurs not only once in the over-all structure of a tragedy but also many times over in smaller scale in the individual scenes and confrontations.

It is perhaps obvious that the Aristotelian pattern of action, to the extent that the above description fits it, is in basic harmony with certain fundamental premises concerning human nature and historical reality that have persisted in Western culture from antiquity until recent times. With some oversimplification, one might say that these premises persisted until the period of romanticism and the rise of that modern form of historical consciousness to which I referred in the introduction to this book.

The tragic pattern consorts quite well, for instance, with that interpretation of the life of Christ which has formed the core of traditional Christian belief: the purposeful mission of Jesus led to his passion, which was followed by "recognition" or perception of the truth.[4] This way of interpreting the Gospel story, which is surely not the only way possible, was perhaps natural in a culture that had already found the Aristotelian concept of action to be consonant with its view of human nature and history. The basic assumption, in both Christian and non-Christian thought, was that man is a rational being who embarks upon certain courses of action with deliberate intentionality, only to have his aims confounded by aspects of reality of which, in his finitude, he was ignorant. Yet in the long run, it was believed, there is a certain benefit, both individual and cultural, to be derived from the suffering that rational man must endure. History is thus understood to be a combination of factors, partly rational and partly beyond reason, which in the end "add up" to a unity. However mysterious and unjust particular historical events may be, history is not without its seriousness, its completeness, and its magnitude.

The dramatic literature of Europe has, for the most part and in a variety of styles, rather consistently imitated throughout its long development some such notion of historical reality as that just sketched. The notion of the rational, though flawed and partially ignorant, hero has persisted. The drive toward "unity of action," sometimes insisted upon through very rigid rules, sometimes sought by more intuitive means, has been of utmost importance to writers, critics, and audiences. The influence of the medieval theater, formally so unlike the classical theater, did not cancel out this drive, although it occasioned, especially in Shakespeare, important changes in style and convention. Sometimes the pattern was debased, as in melodrama, or trivialized, as in the popular drama of intrigue. But it persisted nonetheless.

4 The resurrection of Jesus is, of course, nontragic. Rather, it is tragic-comic, in a sense quite different from the tragicomedy of Chekhov, to which I shall come later. But the basic pattern of tragedy is undisturbed by the Gospels' kind of tragicomedy. This is why the idea of a Christian tragedy, to which there are many objections, has remained tantalizing throughout Christian history.

Romanticism bore within itself motives and presuppositions that were to eventuate in Chekhov's transformation of the tragic pattern in a more profound way than it had ever been changed before. The most significant factor was the weight romanticism gave to subjectivity, to the feelings, the sensibilities, and their relation to the "truth" of any situation. Almost equally important was the new type of historical consciousness that accompanied romanticism, according to which it is useless to seek any typical pattern in history. Historical reality ceased to be the re-enactment, in however varied a number of forms, of a single pattern and became instead a "process" characterized by the emergence of the new and presenting to the observer at any given moment a unique texture and configuration of experience.

This kind of understanding could not be accommodated in drama through adherence to Aristotelian "completeness" and "magnitude," not even as these had been modified by Shakespeare and by romantic playwrights influenced by him. The Aristotelian pattern could be abandoned in one way by Strindberg's expressionism or Maeterlinck's symbolism, but these both had the liability of falling into that extreme sort of subjectivism which cut itself off from historical reality, whereas the more genuine romantic insight was that there is an intimate connection between subjectivity and history, or, to put it differently, between human sensibility and social reality. What was required was a way of being subjective and objective at the same time, a way of seeing the subjective as that which makes the objective real (that is, not merely a scientific construct) and the objective as that in which the subjective is received and fulfilled. This way of looking at life could find its way to the stage only if the drama could develop some new method of construction so that its fundamental meaning would spring not from the traditional pattern of action but from the expression of a sensibility, using techniques that actors could employ in front of an audience. The finding of the way to do this was the work of Anton Chekhov.

As a participant in the literary movement broadly called realism, and also by personal temperament, Chekhov was the enemy of what he called "subjectivism" in writing. "Subjectivity is an awful thing," he wrote to his brother Alexander, "even for the reason that it betrays the poor writer hand over fist." He insisted in the same letter that subjective writing "is not inborn in one; it is acquired" and that it "is as easy to give up that self-acquired subjectivity as to drink a glass of water." But what this means is that the writer should avoid the temptation to set down only that which is pleasing to himself and which is therefore an indulgence. And the reason that this indulgence must be forgone is that there is a higher duty. One's obligation is to explore the full texture of the scene that is being described. "One needs only to be a bit more honest," he wrote, "to throw oneself absolutely overboard, not to push oneself as the hero of one's novel, to deny oneself for even half an hour." [5] It is clear from other parts of this letter, as well as from Chekhov's practice as an author, that the subjectivity he wanted to eliminate is that which puts the writer ahead of his material. Chekhov was far from being opposed to that subjectivity which is part of the scene and in fact gives it its claim to be considered "real."

"Life consists in action," said Aristotle, "and its end is a mode of action, not a quality." The person who encounters Chekhov's plays for the first time is likely to think that they are indeed imitations of qualities, not action. It is their tone, their music, or their poetry, as it is called, that strikes him more forcefully than anything else. He is immediately aware that a certain texture of life is being presented, and he may be little aware of anything else.

Although this understanding of Chekhov's plays is naïve, it is the point from which the right start must be made in judging what Chekhov did to the art of drama. He subordinated the pattern of action to the texture of the scene. The only error is to think that *no* pattern of action remains, a point to which I shall return very shortly.

From the point of view of the actors and the director we can say that Chekhov's technique is such as to make ensemble playing an absolute necessity.[6] Ensemble work of a very high order is required in Chekhov because the nuances of the relationships between the characters and between each of them and the environ-

---

5 S. S. Koteliansky and Philip Tomlinson, trans. and eds., *The Life and Letters of Anton Tchekhov* (London: Cassell, 1925), p. 55.
6 Witness the utter failure of *The Sea Gull* in its first performance and its subsequent success at the Moscow Art Theater.

ment take precedence over the "story." The proof of this is to be had even when one is reading the plays in an armchair. It is possible to take great pleasure from the isolated scene or act, quite apart from the position it occupies in the whole play and with a minimum of curiosity about how it will all "turn out." The meaning of this simple fact is that the primary object being imitated is not a pattern of action but the texture of certain selected moments in life. The reason this is meaningful as well as pleasurable is that, in accordance with late romantic thought, life itself is considered not as action so much as process, movement, and change.

We may now attempt to see exactly what Chekhov did with the Aristotelian pattern. It had, we recall, three sequential modes—purposeful action, consequent endurance of suffering, and eventual gain of new perception. A drama moved from the first to the third by way of the second, and its unity came from the equal importance of the three. Chekhov's innovation was to bring the second mode to the fore and to dampen the other two. The main body of the play centers upon the "passion" of the characters—that is to say, upon their process of undergoing experience.

Because all Chekhov's art consists of the balance he maintains between the elements he introduces, it is important in judging his treatment of the tragic rhythm of action to see what a delicate balance he holds. It is not the case that his plays have *only* to do with the texture and quality of experience. The situations he describes are indeed the result of purposive action undertaken by one or more of his leading characters, and the experience that such action causes all to suffer does lead to an increased measure of perception. The tragic rhythm is still there.[7] But it has been put, as it were, into another shape. It has been given a new balance, in which the mode of passion or of experience undergone is paramount, while purpose and perception are correspondingly minor presences. They partly define and flavor the situation, but they do not determine it, and they do not give it its meaning. The meaning is in the experience itself and in the "truth" of its representation. This is the great romantic achievement of Chekhov, whose search for real-

---

7 Eric Bentley has insisted on this point, emphasizing Chekhov's villains and the actions they stir up. See *The Life of the Drama* (New York: Atheneum, 1964), pp. 54–55. The only question—and it is crucial—is where the accent falls.

ity was the search for the texture of a certain kind of life which he knew at first hand in rural Russia and which he brought to the stage with such penetrating insight into its experienced quality that it became of universal modern significance.

Chekhov's characters are not entirely passive drifters on the stream of life. They could hardly be called characters if that were the case. Yet their purposiveness is not strong. It does not dominate their behavior, does not flow into vigorous action, and therefore does not define them or what happens to them except in a minimal way. In this regard, they are the shadows of tragic heroes. What they initiate they do not complete, not even to the extent of their finite abilities and knowledge. Hence, what they experience is the result not of action carried out but of action begun and left unfinished. They prefer to experience their experience rather than simply to see it as part of a pattern.

It follows that the perceptions the characters gain are mere shadows of those stabbing insights that come to tragic heroes. Awareness begins to dawn at the end of Chekhov's plays but never fully breaks. Therefore what the characters express at those times is not truth but half-truth; and from this, together with our knowledge that the half-truth is entirely as much as can come to these persons under the circumstances, comes the great and unsentimental poignance of the endings of the plays. The speech of Sonya that closes *Uncle Vanya* (1896), in which she speaks of the comfort of work in this life and rest in the hereafter, is admirable because we see it expresses the highest insight of which she is capable while at the same time we know that it is inadequate as a statement of the human situation.

Chekhov's "truth" is therefore complex. On one level it is the experience itself as it is undergone by the characters in their situation, and on this level it is to be respected. Yet on another level it is *our* experience of *their* experience, which is a different thing, since, at least for this moment, we are spectators, not participants, although in "real life" we may be very like those we now see on the stage. The combination of these two levels of "truth" constitutes the "truth" of the experienced play, which obviously is nothing like the sort of truth that can be enunciated in propositional form or made the subject of scientific investigation. It can be got at only by aesthetic means. And the art to which it is most congenial is that of theater, the theater being that art which most depends upon the mixture of participation and observation. Chekhov is a master of ironic movement from one perspective to another, and he redoubles his irony by allowing his characters themselves to engage in such a movement. Many of them are extremely conscious of watching themselves in their moments of subjective passion.

Uncle Vanya provides a good example of Chekhov's treatment of purposive action. Each of the main characters has certain desires and dreams of acting upon them, but none does so with vigor. Sonya, in love with Astrov, desires to communicate her feelings to him, but she cannot bring herself to speak directly and therefore asks her stepmother Yelena to serve as go-between. Nothing comes of this mission except a set of exquisite disappointments. In the meeting between Yelena and Astrov it becomes apparent that Astrov is interested only in Yelena. She returns his interest merely in passing, and he accepts this circumstance with a kiss. At the moment of their embrace they are discovered by Uncle Vanya, who also desires Yelena and is informed in this way that his feeling will not be returned.

The situation is love at cross purposes, and one remembers that *Uncle Vanya* is Chekhov's rewriting of his earlier play, *The Wood Demon,* an apprentice work full of the intrigue and counterintrigue of popular drama. Yet whereas *The Wood Demon* had ended happily with its various sets of lovers paired off as in ordinary comedy, Chekhov's revision brings no lovers together but resigns all, as Eric Bentley has pointed out, to reflection upon what might have been.[8] The reason for this decline into a mood of not-quite-stoic resignation is that the initial efforts toward action were undertaken only tentatively in the first place. That is true of Astrov's twilight kind of ardor for Yelena, of Uncle Vanya's similar desire, and of Sonya's longing for Astrov, muffled by her shyness and her inability to believe in her own qualities and capabilities.

Much the same sort of tentativeness belongs to the principal action of the plot, which springs from the Professor's intention to sell the family estate. Although the estate belongs to Sonya, who has inherited it from her mother, the Professor's first wife, and al-

8 Eric Bentley, *In Search of Theater* (New York: Vintage, 1954), pp. 322–343.

though it has been kept intact through the management of Uncle Vanya, the retired Professor has conceived the idea of selling it in order to provide for his old age and to relieve Vanya and Sonya of their labors in keeping it up. The scheme is not without its merits for all concerned, and the pedant has obviously given it due thought before he calls the family together to announce his proposal. Nevertheless, he is irresolute. The moment that he perceives that Uncle Vanya is shocked and objects to the idea almost before hearing it, the Professor begins to change his mind. His purposive act, therefore, amounts to no more than a proposal, from which he begins to back away as soon as its consequences start to emerge.

The scene culminates in the play's climax, or rather its anticlimax, since the circumstances described and the lack of strong resolve that produces them cannot eventuate in anything we might properly call a climax. This anticlimax reveals much about the Chekhovian method and its technical corollaries. Uncle Vanya leaves the stage in great agitation. He decides, instantaneously and without any deliberation, to shoot the Professor, whom he has heretofore admired and slaved for but whom he now begins to suspect is devoid of nobility. To reassure Vanya and to make peace with him, the Professor follows him offstage. We hear a shot. The Professor runs back on stage pursued by Uncle Vanya, who now fires point blank at a range of about five feet—and misses. He throws the gun down and subsides into outraged, self-pitying impotence. Everyone is shocked, but no one thinks of calling the police, since the incident is exactly that—an incident. Upon everyone's gooselike chatter, as the Nurse calls it, the act curtain descends.

The scene is terribly funny, even while it is sad and expresses deep human frustration. It is a paradigm of the Chekhovian treatment of the tragic rhythm of action. Vanya's intention to shoot the Professor is half-baked. It has a certain goal and leads to an incident, but it is conceived without serious thought and produces an abortive gesture. It engenders in Uncle Vanya only a dim awareness, a kind of resignation to the impotence of his situation and character, without its being of a thorough kind that could be called insight. The experience of the incident therefore serves as no bridge between purpose and perception. Rather, minimal purpose and perception serve only to frame the incident, which exists for its own flavor, its particular combination of the tragic and the comic, and also its suggestion of the absurdity of life as it actually occurs in the less-than-dramatic circumstances in which most people find themselves.

Much debate has gone on about whether Chekhov was a writer of comedy or of tragedy. He believed that the interpretation of his plays by Stanislavski tended too much toward the tragic and was too lugubrious. When he was writing *The Cherry Orchard* he said he "thought [he would] call it a comedy," indicating a felt ambivalence about it. The fact is that Chekhov's major plays, from *Uncle Vanya* on, are tragicomedy. In them we find a blend of the comic and the tragic, which is the consequence of the transformation of the tragic pattern in such a way as to bring the mode of passion to the fore. Within the suffering of experience as such, the comic and the tragic are both present. The savoring of them in their mixture, and the knowledge that both belong to the fabric of life, inextricably twined, is the principal quality of the Chekhovian play. What Chekhov discovered was that the way to produce this effect was not to obliterate the Aristotelian tragic action but to change its emphasis so that the purposive action and the perception of the truth became subordinate to the experience that lies between them.

Tragicomedy has a long history. Some of the plays of Euripides are best described by this term, and in the Renaissance there was a genre of plays, very popular, that went by the name. Yet tragicomedy before Chekhov was quite different from the tragicomedy that he devised. The older kind was most pithily described by John Fletcher in 1608 in his preface to *The Faithful Shepherdess:*

> Tragi-comedy is not so called in respect to mirth and killing but in respect that it wants deaths, which is enough to make it no tragedy, while it brings some near, which is enough to make it no comedy.

The idea of tragicomedy John Fletcher had in mind, the idea that informed tragicomedy until the time of Chekhov, depended upon a "reversal of the situation." The action undertaken by one or more of the characters led toward misfortune—that is, toward the possibility of tragedy—but through the intervention of some out-side power or some lucky happening, or through the revelation of some essential piece of information, the course of the action was changed, so that the plot ended with some kind of reprieve rather than destruction. In this sense, tragicomedy was a potential tragedy that turned, somewhere along the way, into a comedy.

Fletcher pointed out that tragicomedy, as he understood it, did not depend upon "mirth and killing"—that is, the mixture of the laughable and the terrible. Such mixing might occur, as for in-stance in the humorous parts of *Hamlet* or *Macbeth;* but this possi-bility was not, for Fletcher and his contemporaries, the basis of tragicomedy.

In Chekhov, however, it was precisely this possibility which be-came realized in tragicomedy. It is the mixture of the laughable and the lamentable that characterizes modern tragicomedy. This possibility can be realized only when the tragic pattern of action (which is the basis of classical comedy as well as tragedy) is changed in the way I have described above. Then the multi-toned and "impure" character of experience is revealed, and the stage becomes the place where its mixture of qualities can be made evi-dent.

Behind this Chekhovian development in drama lies the pica-resque novel in fiction and also the kind of short story that Che-khov himself was master of, which depended for its effect upon an ironic blend of sensations. The faithful presentation of this mix-ture, together with fidelity to behavior, custom, and environmen-tal setting, was what Chekhov meant by "realism." With regard to the dramatic tradition it was utterly revolutionary, and the fact that he was able to realize its consequences, or at least many of them, in masterpieces of dramatic subtlety is what accounts for Chekhov's supreme importance in the history of modern drama.

It is necessary to point also to the irony in Chekhov's plays. I have suggested that the intensification of irony is one of the most important features in the development of modern drama. To this development Chekhov's contribution could hardly be exaggerated. His irony is neither mordant nor cynical. It is not even underlined, and therefore it is possible to be only slightly conscious of it.

Nevertheless, it is highly significant in all his more important plays.

The ironic double perspective of Chekhov resides in the fact that the audience takes a different view of matters from that taken by the characters. It is one thing to be Sonya or Treplev or Gaev in their respective situations. It is quite another thing to be their observer in the audience. Moreover, the difference is not simply that between actual involvement and vicarious participation. The difference is between two different levels of insight, according to which the audience, although it is induced to participate in the characters' dilemmas and frustrations, nevertheless possesses, or feels itself to possess, a greater awareness of what is going on and what is lacking than do the characters themselves. The same might be said of one of Zola's pieces of naturalism, and this indicates the kinship between Chekhov and naturalism. However, in Zola the effect is not trenchantly ironic as it is in Chekhov, and that is because in Zola the two perspectives have so little to do with each other. Zola's observation of his characters, mainly because of the pseudo-scientific method he employed, is utterly unlike his characters' insight. In Chekhov the two perspectives, although distinct, are intimately related. This fine association of two separate points of view is what produces the true pitch of Chekhov's irony, which is always strong and never blatant. Chekhov's irony is romantic in its subtle gradations of tone and modern in its intellectual avoidance of confusion and sentimentality.

Eric Bentley, who is one of the critics most acutely aware of Chekhov as a writer of tragicomedy, has suggested that "what Chekhov is after" in *Uncle Vanya* "is not reversal but recognition . . . in Aristotle's sense, 'the change from ignorance to knowledge,' but with a Chekhovian application." [9] He explains the Chekhovian application as follows:

> In the Greeks, in much French drama, and in Ibsen, recognition means the discovery of a secret which reveals that things are not what all these years they have seemed to be. In *Uncle Vanya*, recognition means that what all these years seemed to be so, though

[9] *In Search of Theater*, p. 326.

one hesitated to believe it, really is so and will remain so. This is
Vanya's discovery and gradually (in the course of the ensuing last
act) that of the others.[10]

Professor Bentley is on exactly the right track here, but surely his
observation has to be qualified. Though Uncle Vanya and the
others do become aware that what might have been has passed
them by, such awareness is more full on the part of the audience
than on the part of the characters in the play. This is what accounts
for the effect of Sonya's concluding speech. As I noted above, there
is a difference between her capacity for insight and ours, the privileged spectators, even if this difference lasts only as long as we are
in the theater. And it is just this difference which casts upon the
tragicomedy the gentle yet pervasive Chekhovian irony.

The double perspective is also what made it possible for Chekhov to speak of his plays, at times, as lessons offered to his countrymen about how they ought to live. He was not consistent in this,
and his critics have not agreed on how much moral intent they
ought to see in the plays. Now and then, however, Chekhov said
that his plays were to show his fellow Russians how mean and
comic were their lives. "It is shameful to live like that," he said.
But he knew—or rather felt, for the attitude seems to have been
innate—that an author should not moralize at the expense of ceas-
ing to sympathize with his characters. Therefore, he made the spectator identify with what he saw on stage, while he also made him
perceive, better than the characters, the futility that comes from
preferring the sensations of living to the life of action.

In his *Ethics* Aristotle gave an analysis of the concept of action
that throws some light on his use of the term in the *Poetics* and also
upon Chekhov's drama. His general term for action is *energeia*,
which he says is of three different kinds: *praxis*, the doing of something with an end (*telos*) in view; *poiesis*, the making of something; and *theoria*, the grasping of a thought or concept by the
mind. Each of these is a form of action, the first in the realm of
historical occurrences, the second in the realm of aesthetics, and the
third in the realm of purely mental work.

When Aristotle speaks of the "action" of a tragedy in the *Poet-*

10 *Ibid.*

ics, the term he uses is *praxis.* It should now be clear that Chekhov, while he did not entirely eliminate it from his later plays, reduced *praxis* to an almost minimal level. So also he reduced the element of *theoria* far below the level at which it occurs in tragedy, again not eliminating it. What actually happens is that the action of *theoria,* the grasping of insight, is increased in the audience in the measure that it is decreased in the characters. It is transferred from the one place to the other. It is this which gives the spectator at the Chekhov play such an important sense of being a collaborator in the realization of the work. A fortiori, the actor is Chekhov's collaborator in a way that surpasses the actor's contribution to previous plays. The transference of the action of *theoria,* which we may also call the act of interpretation, from the character to the actor and also, in a second movement, from the stage to the audience was one of Chekhov's most radical innovations in dramatic writing, and it has been of the utmost importance for the subsequent development of the drama.

Is there anything to be said about Aristotle's third term, *poiesis?* Although it was part of the tradition, from the Greeks on, that the playwright is a poet whose act is to fashion the object that is his play, it was not until Chekhov that the theater discovered in how radical a way this idea might be taken. It was Chekhov who taught the theater (and the critics) that a play is to be conceived as a work of art made up of elements so carefully chosen and brought into such harmony with one another that they create a "world" or a "reality" that is unavailable except to the imagination and incommunicable except through the medium of the particular structure that is the play.

I do not mean, of course, that no such thoughts about plays had ever been thought before. I do mean that such thoughts could not be taken as seriously with regard to drama as they were with regard to poetry as long as the Aristotelian pattern dominated one's notion of how a play should be written; for that pattern implied that a play is basically an "imitation" of a reality outside the play. It was Chekhov, a realist, who finally broke the dominance of that pattern and freed the playwright to consider his work of art as a structure that could be, more than had ever been thought before, a self-contained entity. The realist who did this was also, of course, the inheritor of romantic ideas about aesthetics and imagination. He lived at a time when painting, poetry, and sculpture were also cutting themselves free of "copying" in order to follow more exclusively their own internal requirements. Chekhov belonged, realist that he was, to that late nineteenth-century development which turned the romantic quest inward upon itself, and he turned the drama inward upon *itself* as no playwright had ever done before.

Perhaps Chekhov would not have done this if the external reality he was writing about—the Russian landed class in the "twilight" of the empire—had not already turned inward toward reflection and sensation, away from vigorous historical action. Thus some of the ingredient of the art he created was already in the life of the time. Yet such was Chekhov's creativity as an artist that he was not merely content to describe the phenomenon of inwardness by a method of direct imitation. Internality, reflection, and the savoring of sensation became part of his method as well as his subject. That is the real reason why he had to modify the Aristotelian pattern so greatly in his later plays, as he did not do in the earlier ones, and that is why when we approach the Chekhovian play we find analogies from other forms of art coming strongly to mind: we speak of the "music" of his plays, their "poetry," their rhythm, harmony, and dancelike motion, and their effect upon us that is so similar to that of certain kinds of painting. All this in spite of the fact that his plays are utterly of the theater and employ that medium superbly.

In Chekhov, gently and without fanfare, almost without consciousness of what is happening, the modern dramatist becomes the *poietes* who fashions a work of art that is its own justification for being. Only by the invention of a modern kind of tragicomedy could this happen, for only in the mixture of the laughable and the sorrowful could there be that blend of supposed opposites that would correspond to the audience's flux of sensations in life, and, thus, only in that way could the play achieve a sufficiently meaningful interiority of its own. In Chekhov there is an affinity, yet also a tension (exactly as in all great art), between the internality of the spectator and the internality of the work. Chekhov eschewed always that kind of subjectivism which made the work nothing but the expression of the artist's (and the spectator's) internal feelings, and those who followed him best avoided that kind of thing too. For Chekhov, the world is still "out there" and to be taken seriously. But what is "out there" in each case is something that is also "in" the artist and the spectator—namely a fabric, a texture, a blend of qualities, a richness of immediacy that cannot be forced into the patterns of traditional form. That which is immediate requires its own form, which only the artist can bring into being. When he does so he turns inward—toward his own internality, that of the spectator, and that of the work he is fashioning. What he then produces is something that testifies to the intimate, the indissoluble unity of the subjective and the objective.

If there is anything we may learn from Chekhov's plays it is that life is one and that the respect we owe to the unity and integrity of the work of art is of a piece with the respect we owe to the unity of life.

In August of 1883, when he was in the twenty-fourth year of his life and had been studying medicine for four years, Anton Chekhov wrote a letter in which he described the difficult circumstances under which he was forced to write. The letter was addressed to N. A. Lakin, editor of a magazine called *Oskolki* ("Fragments"), a humorous publication to which Chekhov was contributing in order to earn a bit of money:

> I write in most hideous circumstances. Before me is my non-literary work mercilessly whipping my conscience; in the next room howls the child of a relation who has come to stay with us; in the other room my father is reading aloud to mother "The Flaming Angel" . . . someone has wound up the music-box and I can hear "Fair Hélène." I long to run away to the country, but it is 1 o'clock in the morning. It is hard to imagine a setting more abominable for a writing man. My bed is occupied by a visitor who comes up to me every now and then and starts a talk on medicine. . . . I have the misfortune to be a medical man, and there is no one who does not consider it necessary to chat with me on medicine, or, when bored by medicine, to talk about literature. . . .
>
> The baby howls!! I give my word of honour never to have children. . . .[11]

[11] Translated in Koteliansky and Tomlinson, *op. cit.*, pp. 65–66.

The household in which Chekhov was living was one which included his parents, brothers, and sisters, plus various hangers-on. The young medical student was its mainstay and virtually the head of the family, since his father had never really found himself after moving to Moscow and had to rely on his one responsible son, the two older ones being of very little help. In the second year of medical studies Chekhov had begun to write from sheer financial necessity. He had a gift for writing rapidly, which was fortunate because the pay was so low that it took many words to produce the barest income.

The family was up from the south and up from slavery. Chekhov was born, on January 17, 1860, in the city of Taganrog on the Sea of Azov, the northeast part of the Black Sea. There his father ran a grocery store until 1876, when his business failed owing to the railroads' having by-passed the port and depressed its economy. Anton Chekhov's father had begun life as a serf. Anton's grandfather had saved money and bought his family's freedom in 1841, then moved south from the Vozonezh province to become employed on the estates of Count Platov, not far from Taganrog.

When the grocery shop failed, Anton Chekhov's family moved to Moscow. Two of his brothers had already gone there to study, Alexander to the University and Nicolai to the School of Painting. Anton stayed behind, alone, to finish his course at the grammar school in Taganrog, but when he completed it in 1879 and was admitted to the university for studies in medicine, he also came to Moscow. The duties he then assumed were of three kinds. First, there was his medical career. Second, responsibility for the care of his family, who looked to him not only for money but also for practical wisdom and kindliness. Third, his writing, which at first was nothing more than a source of bread money but which shortly came to be his first obligation, for it dawned on him within a few years that he had a considerable artistic talent, and he believed that a talent imposed responsibility.

In March 1886 Chekhov received a letter from the then famous writer D. V. Grigorivich congratulating him on some of his stories. Chekhov's reply marks the beginning of his serious thought about himself as a writer:

If I have a gift which I ought to respect, then I confess before the purity of your heart that I have not respected it till now. I felt that I had it, but I had grown accustomed to consider it insignificant. . . . All those near to me have always regarded my writing with condescension, and persistently advised me, in a friendly way, not to give up real work for scribbling. . . . I am a doctor and am steeped ear-deep in my medicine, so that the saying about catching two hares has troubled no man's peace of mind more than mine. . . .

Up till now I have taken my literary work extremely light, carelessly, casually. I don't remember a single story at which I worked for more than a day, and "The Sportsman," which you liked, I wrote in a bathing-shed! As reporters write their notes on fires, so I wrote my stories: mechanically, half-consciously, without caring a bit about the reader or myself. . . .

And now, unexpected and undreamed of, comes your letter. Forgive the comparison; it had the effect on me of a governor-general's order to leave the city within twenty-four hours! . . . that is, I suddenly felt the imperative need to hurry, to make haste in getting out of the place where I was stuck. . . .

All my hope is for the future. I am only twenty-six. Perhaps I shall succeed in doing something, although time runs swiftly.[12]

Not long before, Chekhov had also received the attention of A. S. Souvorin, editor and publisher of *Novoye vremya* ("The New Times"), the largest and most popular daily paper of Russia, published in St. Petersburg. Souvorin asked him to become a contributor to the paper, and that enabled Chekhov to get "out of the place where I was stuck." His friendship with Souvorin, which was highly beneficial, owing to the publisher's influential position and his interest in the theater, lasted until the time of the Dreyfus case in France, when Souvorin's defense of the French army and his attack upon Dreyfus proved more than Chekhov could tolerate.

From 1886 onward, Chekhov's prominence as a writer grew. He had received no notice for his first book, *Stories of Melpomena*, published in 1884, but there were many reviews of his second, *Motley Stories*, which came out in 1885. Three years later the nation's foremost literary journal, *Severny vestnik*, published "The

12 *Ibid.*, pp. 71–73.

Steppe," after which Chekhov appeared frequently in its pages. He was awarded the Pushkin Prize by the Imperial Academy of Sciences in 1888. He had by that time contributed over four hundred stories, novels, sketches, *feuilletons,* and law reports to fourteen different publications. Many of these were published under pseudonyms, but after he began to write for Souvorin's paper he used his own name. He received his medical degree in 1884 and began his medical practice, gradually giving it up for literature. Also in 1884 he suffered his first hemorrhage of the lungs, a sign of the disease that was to bring him to death at the age of forty-four.

Chekhov began to write plays while he was in grammar school, according to his brother Michael, who says that in the seventh form Anton wrote a serious drama called "Fatherless," later destroyed, and a vaudeville called *Not For Nothing Did the Chicken Sing.*[13] From his Taganrog student days there came also a farce, the first of many, *A Clean-shaved Secretary with a Pistol.*

About 1920, when the Chekhov family papers came to the Central State Literary Archives in Moscow, there was discovered the manuscript of a long play now called *Platonov,* which seems to have been written around 1881. It was neither published nor performed in Chekhov's lifetime but is recognized today as the beginning of Chekhov's development as an important dramatist. Like most of the stories that he was writing at the time, it is humorous. Nevertheless, it is by no means a farce. Its central character, who anticipates the neurotic Ivanov whom Chekhov was to create a few years later, is a half-humorous, half-tragic eccentric, and the play has a few other features of the tragicomic genre that Chekhov was eventually to make into a new form of drama.

In 1884 Chekhov wrote two one-act plays, *On the High Road* and *The Swan Song,* but it was not until 1887 that his public career as a dramatist can be said really to have begun. In the fall of that year F. A. Korsh, who ran an important theater in Moscow, asked him to write a full-length, four-act play. The invitation excited Chekhov enormously, and he wrote *Ivanov* in ten days' time. When it was produced at Korsh's on November 19 the reaction was mixed, but there was enough excitement to correspond with the author's mood and to elate him still further. He was called on stage

13 *Ibid.,* p. 29.

after the second act and again at the end, when the house was filled with an uproar made of boos, hisses, bravos, and much applause. Impressed as he was with the lively response, Chekhov nevertheless doubted whether the audience had understood his play, which he intended to be an unmasking of the type portrayed in the central character, "the intellectual," as Ernest J. Simmons puts it, "who dreams pleasantly about his past accomplishments but quails before the abuses of the present, then experiences a vague sense of guilt over them, and ends with unstrung nerves among the 'shattered' and 'misunderstood' people of society." [14] The play was done in St. Petersburg shortly after the Moscow première and received an even better reception. It was not published until 1889.

By that time Chekhov was already at work on his next full-length play, *The Wood Demon,* having written between times the one-act farce *The Bear* (1888). He had at first proposed to write *The Wood Demon* in collaboration with Souvorin, but this did not pan out, so he wrote it by himself during most of 1889. Frequently discouraged, he started a completely new draft in September, which he submitted the following month for consideration by theaters in both St. Petersburg and Moscow. Both rejected it, and the actor A. P. Lenski in Moscow wrote him:

> Write tales. You refer too scornfully to the stage and to dramatic form. You esteem them too little to write a play. This form is more difficult than that of fiction, and—forgive me—you are too spoiled by success in order, so to speak, to start fundamentally to study dramatic form from the beginning and to love it.[15]

On the heels of this communication came one from Nemirovich-Danchenko, Chekhov's friend who was later to form the Moscow Art Theater with Stanislavski: "Lenski is right, you ignore too many of the demands of the stage, but I've not observed scorn for them, rather simply a lack of knowledge of them." [16]

What is clear in retrospect is that the established playwriting conventions of the time did not permit Chekhov to do what he wanted to do with the dramatic medium. Therefore, the more he followed the conventions the worse matters got, except, of course,

14 *Chekhov: A Biography* (Boston: Little, Brown, 1962), p. 138.
15 *Ibid.,* pp. 197–198.
16 *Ibid.,* pp. 197–198.

in the vaudevilles and farces, for which he had a natural facility. He was ready to throw *The Wood Demon* away when the actor N. N. Solovtsov, another friend, read the play and said it was just what was wanted by the new Abramov Theater in Moscow. Chekhov sat down immediately to revise it once more and continued to work on it through the rehearsal period. Yet when it opened on December 27, 1889, it was condemned by almost all the critics. Chekhov refused ever to let it be published, although there were several requests.

The Wood Demon, as later rewritten, became one of Chekhov's greatest artistic successes, and the reason has entirely to do with the persistence of the author and his relentless search for the form that could embody the new conception of dramatic art toward which he was groping. The changes that he eventually made in *The Wood Demon*, which he transformed into *Uncle Vanya*, have been well described by David Magarshack (in *Chekhov the Dramatist*) and even better by Eric Bentley (in *In Search of Theater*). The melodramatic effects, the conventional happy ending with its pairing off of lovers, the attitudinizing over the idealism of the character called the Wood Demon (Astrov in the later play), all disappeared, and in their place came Chekhov's first great modern tragicomedy. There was no one to teach him how to do it. Perhaps only failure drove him onward—that is, failure to achieve his aims in drama, for in fiction he was then eminently successful—plus the spur of the statement that he could not or would not learn the techniques of the stage.

There is some debate as to when Chekhov rewrote *The Wood Demon* as *Uncle Vanya*. The date usually given is 1896. However, some evidence points to the possibility that he completed the revision in March and April of 1890, that is, very soon after the performance of *The Wood Demon*.[17] In any case, the revised work was not produced until 1898, when it was, according to Chekhov, "a great success" in the provinces. That was the same year that *The Sea Gull* was produced at The Moscow Art Theater, and the following year *Uncle Vanya* was done there.

To go back to the latter 1880's, we may note that while he was

17 *Ibid.*, p. 200, n. 4.

working on *The Wood Demon* in 1889, Chekhov wrote also his famous one-act farce *The Proposal*. The following year he wrote another, *A Tragedian Against His Will*. It was in 1890 also that he made his celebrated trip to the island of Sakhalin, which lies off the coast of Siberia, north of Japan. His decision to make such a long and hazardous trip to a place he had scarcely ever spoken of mystified his family and his friends. All his reasons for going can hardly be known, but the ostensible one was to write a lengthy nonfictional report on conditions in the penal colony there, to which he said thousands of prisoners had been exiled and on which the government was spending millions. To Souvorin he wrote that his only regret was that "it is I who am going there and not someone else who knows more about the business and would be more capable of arousing public interest." [18] He left Moscow on April 21, 1890, by rail, but as the trans-Siberian railway had not yet been built, he was forced to cover thousands of miles in horse-drawn carriages. His health was not good; he coughed a great deal and occasionally spat blood but endured the weeks of jolting over primitive roadways with patience and fairly good spirits. The last several thousand miles of the journey were covered by boat on the Amur River. In July he arrived at his destination and set about systematically interviewing the colonists by the hundreds, as if he were a researcher in the social sciences. He made the return trip mostly by sea, visiting Singapore, India, Ceylon, and the Suez Canal. This was in lieu of his first plan to come back by way of the United States, which he finally decided would be too expensive and too dull. He got off the boat in Odessa and returned to Moscow by train, reaching there on December 8 after a journey of eight months. A set of impressions, *Across Siberia*, was published in 1890; another, *Runaways in Sakhalin*, in 1891; and his major report, *Sakhalin Island*, in 1893. These did not cause any sensation, but they did initiate other investigations of the island and led to certain reforms in administration and living conditions. "I'm glad that this rough convict's garment hangs in my literary wardrobe," Chekhov wrote to Souvorin. "Let it hang there!" [19]

18 March 9, 1890. *Ibid.*, p. 212.
19 January 2, 1894. *Ibid.*, p. 305.

Meanwhile, stories and short plays continued, as always, to flow from his pen, and in 1895 there came a new major play, *The Sea Gull.*

The story of this play's initial failure, which had a traumatic effect upon Chekhov, and its subsequent triumph is well known. He finished writing the play in November of 1895. Unlike his work on the previous long plays, in which he had been groping without any sure sense of direction for the dramatic style that was to be uniquely his, in *The Sea Gull* he felt his power surely. Of course there was a good bit of rewriting as he worked, yet so clearly did he now see the solution to the structural problems that had plagued him earlier that he was able to turn more of his attention to the specific problems of language. He filled the play with a variety of tones appropriate to the various characters, worked freely and naturally with literary allusions, of which the most important are to Shakespeare's *Hamlet,* and employed the symbolism of the sea gull so deftly that its richness was apparent to him. He rightly held greater expectations for this play than for any he had attempted before.

It was produced at the Alexandrinski Theater in St. Petersburg on October 17, 1896, with Chekhov in the audience, at least for the first part, for he waited out the last part in one of the dressing rooms. By the time the curtain went up he was already full of foreboding. He knew that he had written a highly unconventional play, "something strange," as he called it. Though it ended with Treplev's suicide, it bore the label of comedy. It began forte and ended pianissimo, as he said, and was thus deliberately anticlimactic. It was what he wanted, or pretty close to it, but how could the audience be expected to understand, especially when some who had read it, including Nemirovich-Danchenko, had registered a number of criticisms? Besides, the rehearsals had been insufficient. The actors, some of whom were very gifted and whom Chekhov admired, particularly Vera Kommissarzhevski, did not understand the play and had barely had time to learn their lines. As if this were not enough, the play was to form but half of a double bill, it being common then in Russia for two full-length plays to be put on the same night. As for the audience, it had not come to see

Chekhov at all but a popular comic actress who did not appear until the second play.

"The play came a cropper and fell with a crash," said Chekhov in a note to his brother Michael the next day. "Throughout the theater was a strained feeling of perplexity and disgrace. The actors played abominably, stupidly. The moral is: I must not write plays." [20] He had gone for a long walk when he left the Alexandrinski, and on his return to Souvorin's house, where he was staying, he refused even to see his beloved sister Masha. "If I live to be seven hundred," he said to Souvorin, "I'll not give another play to the theater. In this field I'm a failure." [21] And the next day, about to leave town, he wrote to his host: *"Never* again shall I write plays nor have them staged." [22] He departed forthwith for his country house at Melikhovo, south of Moscow.

Though Chekhov thought *The Sea Gull* dead and his career as a dramatist with it, its merits were certain to be discovered sooner or later. Later rather than sooner it would have been except for Nemirovich-Danchenko. Some eighteen months after *The Sea Gull's* failure in St. Petersburg, this gentleman laid plans with Stanislavski for the joint venture that was to become the Moscow Art Theater. Danchenko, in spite of the criticisms he had offered when he first saw the script, held a secret admiration for Chekhov's play. As it was his prerogative to select the repertory of the new theater, which was to open in the fall of 1898, he wrote Chekhov in May asking for permission to include *The Sea Gull* in the first season's offerings. Naturally he met with refusal. The very idea filled Chekhov with pain. However, a new letter was sent off, and this time Chekhov gave in, mainly out of friendship.

The first play put on by the new theater, Alexis Tolstoi's *Tsar Fyodor,* was a success, but it was followed by no less than five failures. A sixth would have been more than the new venture could stand. One can therefore imagine the anxiety with which the company drew near to *The Sea Gull.* Rehearsals of it had begun in the summer, when the entire season's repertory was prepared, and al-

20 Translated in Koteliansky and Tomlinson, *op. cit.,* p. 235.
21 Quoted in Simmons, *op. cit.,* p. 370.
22 Translated in Koteliansky and Tomlinson, *op. cit.,* p. 235.

though the actors came increasingly to like the play as they worked on it over an extended time, Stanislavski said that he could not understand it. He continued to maintain this attitude through all the preparations, on which he nevertheless worked diligently.

When the performance took place on December 17, Chekhov was in Yalta. His chronic tuberculosis had become worse the last year, and he had been advised by his doctors to live in the south. Therefore he had sold his house at Melikhovo and gone to live at Yalta, where he eventually built a dacha. In the early part of September, when he was still in Moscow, he had seen rehearsals of the play and been pleased. He knew of the success of *Tsar Fyodor* but seems not to have been aware of the failures that had dogged the company since. So, although he was naturally anxious over the play on account of its previous failure, he did not know how much was riding on it in addition to his own reputation as a playwright.

Stanislavski has described the play's opening from the perspective of the company:

> The production was necessary to us because of the material circumstances of the life of our Theatre. Business was in a bad way. The administration hurried our labors. And suddenly Anton Pavlovich fell ill in Yalta with a new attack of tuberculosis. His spiritual condition was such that if "The Seagull" should fail as it did at its first production in Petrograd, the great poet would not be able to weather the blow. His sister Maria Pavlovna warned us of this with tears in her eyes, when, on the eve of the performance, she begged us to postpone it. You can judge of the condition in which we actors played on the first night before a small but chosen audience. There were only six hundred rubles in the box office. When we were on the stage there was an inner whisper in our hearts:
>
> "You must play well, you must play better than well; you must create not only success, but triumph, for know that if you do not, the man and writer you love will die, killed by your hands."
>
> These inner whisperings did not aid our creative inspiration. The boards were becoming the floor of a gallows, and we actors the executioners.
>
> I do not remember how we played. The first act was over. There was a gravelike silence. Knipper [Olga Knipper, who was playing Arkadina; she was shortly to become Chekhov's wife] fainted on

the stage. All of us could hardly keep our feet. In the throes of despair we began moving to our dressing rooms. Suddenly there was a roar in the auditorium, and a shriek of joy or fright on the stage. The curtain was lifted, fell, was lifted again, showing the whole auditorium our amazed and astounded immovability. It fell again, it rose; it fell, it rose, and we could not even gather sense enough to bow. Then there were congratulations and embraces like those of Easter night, and ovations to Lilina [Stanislavski's wife], who played Masha, and who had broken the ice with her last words which tore themselves from her heart, moans washed with tears. This it was that had held the audience mute for a time before it began to roar and thunder in mad ovation.[23]

In Yalta, Anton Pavlovich, as they called him, received a telegram announcing "success colossal" and saying "we are mad with joy." It was followed by another from Nemirovich-Danchenko: "With wonderful unanimity all newspapers acclaim success of *The Sea Gull* as brilliant, tumultuous, enormous. Reviews of play rapturous. For our theater success of *The Sea Gull* surpasses success of *Fyodor*." In his reply Chekhov said, "I grieve that I'm not with you." [24]

He saw the play on May 1, at a special performance put on at his insistence in the rented Nikitski Theater, with about ten people in the audience besides himself. The season was over, the sets and costumes had been stored, and the play had to be re-rehearsed; but Chekhov, who had come up to Moscow, begged to see the play dearest to him, and they did not refuse. Stanislavski says the performance was "middling." When it was over the actor-director, who had played Trigorin, breathless to know what the author thought of his interpretation, received the famous cryptic comment which he came later to think was brilliant but which at the time puzzled and disappointed him. "Wonderful!" said Chekhov. "Listen, it was wonderful! Only you need torn shoes and checkered trousers."

The playwright knew, first and foremost, the quality he was after, and knew that he wanted it not only for its immediate effect but because it belonged to the total fabric of his play. The torn

23 *My Life in Art*, J. J. Robbins, trans. (New York: Meridian, 1956), pp. 355–356.
24 Translated in Simmons, *op. cit.*, p. 451.

shoes of Trigorin belonged somehow to the fragile heart of Nina and the exhaustion of life in Treplev.

One reason the Moscow Art players put on the special performance for Chekhov, even though they knew they could not do their best under the circumstances, was that they wanted permission to do *Uncle Vanya*. To their chagrin, Chekhov had given the play in February to the Maly Theater. It is hard to know why he did so, except perhaps that he was flattered at the request from the oldest and most prestigious theater in Russia. However, it turned out that the Maly's literary committee did not like the play. There were certain changes they wanted, particularly in that anticlimactic third act, in which Uncle Vanya tries to shoot the Professor. Their objections seem to have been both aesthetic and social. Since some of the committee were distinguished professors, it is possible their vanity was threatened. "It is impossible to think," Stanislavski records their report as saying, "that an enlightened, cultured man like Uncle Vanya could shoot on the stage at a person with a diploma. . . ." [25] Chekhov is said to have broken out "into prolonged and happy laughter when he quoted the above sentence, which later became historical." [26]

The Moscow Art now pressed for the play, giving the special *Sea Gull* performance to humor the author, and *Uncle Vanya* became theirs. It was performed the following October 26 (1899), with Olga Knipper as Yelena and Stanislavski as Astrov. The first-night audience seemed to like it, but the reviews were not enthusiastic. However, as the players warmed up to it in succeeding performances and as the audiences began more fully to understand Chekhov's method and point of view, it became more and more popular and took its place in the permanent repertory along with *The Sea Gull*.

Chekhov now began to feel an intimate kinship with the Moscow Art. It had rescued his playwriting from the grave. It was led by Nemirovich-Danchenko, an old and much admired friend. Even Stanislavski, whose acting Chekhov did not much like, seemed to be getting better. And Chekhov was more and more attached to one of the company's leading actresses, Olga Knipper. He

25 *My Life in Art,* p. 360.
26 *Ibid.,* p. 361.

wrote to Nemirovich-Danchenko, who had confided that he was growing tired of the burdens of the theater:

> Oh, don't get weary, don't grow cold! The Art Theater will supply the best pages of the book that will one day be written about the contemporary Russian theater. This theater should be your pride, and it is the only theater I love, although I have not been in it once. If I lived in Moscow, I would try to get on the staff, if only in the capacity of a janitor, so that I could help out a little and, if possible, keep you from growing cold to this dear institution.[27]

During the late summer and early fall of 1900, Chekhov wrote for his now beloved theater a new play, *The Three Sisters*. Rehearsals began immediately, while Chekhov, who had been in Moscow for the first cast reading, went off to Nice for his health and revised extensively, finishing this task in December. The play was performed on January 31, 1901, Olga Knipper playing Masha. Its success was only moderate. It was several years before the public and most critics came to recognize in it the profound effectiveness that Nemirovich-Danchenko and Gorki noticed at once.

Chekhov married Olga Knipper on May 25, 1901, in Moscow. The circumstances could hardly have been more "Chekhovian." He told his friend, the actor Vishnevski, to invite the couple's friends and relatives to a large dinner. While this gathering waited for their host and hostess, Chekhov and Olga quietly got married in a church, after which they went to Olga's mother's house and thence to the station to leave town. Vishnevski and the others received a telegram saying what had happened. The honeymoon was "enjoyed" at a sanatorium in Ufa Province, where Chekhov took treatment for his health.

The Cherry Orchard was begun in the spring two years later. In September 1903, Chekhov wrote to Stanislavski's wife, the actress Lilina: "Not a drama but a comedy has emerged from me, in places even a farce." A few days later he wrote to Olga (owing to his health and her work, they were apart much of the time): "The last act will be merry, and indeed the whole play will be merry and giddy." [28] The script was finished in October. Both Stanislavski and

27 November 19, 1899. Translated in Simmons, *op. cit.*, p. 487.
28 September 21, 1903. *Ibid., op. cit.*, p. 604.

Nemirovich-Danchenko were ecstatic when they read it, but the former's interpretation revived an old difference between him and Chekhov. The actor-director persistently saw more tragedy in Chekhov's works than did the author. They had grown angry with each other during rehearsals of *The Three Sisters* on just this point, and now Stanislavski said of *The Cherry Orchard:* "This is not a comedy or a farce, as you wrote, it is a tragedy whatever the solution you may have found for the better life in the last act." [29] Stanislavski's endemic "realism," his emotional response to what he called the all-important "mood" in Chekhov's plays, and his general sobriety of temperament made him always a little blind to the subtle shadings of Chekhov's dramatic art and to their structural novelties, which issue in what Eric Bentley has called "the half-tone." When Chekhov said that the whole play would be merry and giddy, he did overstate the matter, but he was nearer the mark than Stanislavski's insistence upon tragedy.

The play was performed for the first time on January 17, 1904, as part of a celebration arranged for Chekhov's forty-fourth birthday. He was in Moscow but stayed away from the theater fearing the sort of public homage he detested, the flatteries and pomp which he had frequently satirized in his fiction and short plays. However, he was prevailed upon to appear at the end of the third act, when he was brought on stage, roundly applauded and cheered, and forced to listen to a long set of speeches. The performance by the actors was not very good, owing to inadequate preparation, and this was pointed out next day in the press. Nevertheless, *The Cherry Orchard* became the most successful of Chekhov's plays.

The success occurred in spite of Chekhov's conviction that the directors of the Moscow Art had misinterpreted his intentions. "Nemirovich-Danchenko and Stanislavsky see in my play something entirely different from what I have written," he said to Olga in a letter the following April, "and I'm willing to stake my word on it that neither of them has once read my play through attentively." [30]

In the spring Chekhov began to sketch out in his mind a new

29 *Ibid.,* p. 606.
30 *Ibid.,* p. 617.

play, but it was never to be written. On Friday, July 1, with his wife and doctor at his side, Chekhov died at Badenweiler in Germany, where he had gone for a cure. Olga described his death in this way:

> In the night he woke, and, for the first time in his life, asked for a doctor. . . . Two Russian students, brothers, were staying at the hotel. I asked one of them to fetch the doctor, and myself began chopping ice to put over Anton's heart.
>
> The doctor arrived and ordered champagne for Anton, who sat up and said significantly to the doctor in German (he knew very little German), *"Ich sterbe."* Then he took the glass, turned his face to me, smiled his wonderful smile, and said, "I have not drunk champagne for a long time." He drank the glass to the bottom, lay down peacefully on his left side, and presently was silent for ever. . . .[31]

Silent he was and is only in a manner of speaking. One thinks of the silences that occur in his plays and knows that they speak as much as words. One thinks of the small number of his plays and knows how quickly the talent that produced them was extinguished. Yet what was there spoken has not and will not cease to be heard. I do not mean only that his plays will continue to be performed and loved. I mean also that in them, more than in any other modern, the theater of this age finds its source and inspiration. For it was he, more than any other, who found the way to overcome the tragic dominance that had held sway over the art of drama for millennia, even in plays that were merely serious or lightly comic rather than tragic. Chekhov changed the latent ritual underlying the Western conception of drama.

He therefore gave this art a new beginning, and if it sometimes seems that this beginning came too late, when the theater had already ceased to be a very important part of society, nevertheless it is Chekhov who even now gives one the hope that the theater may still, in some new way, show itself adequate to the transformations that modern life is undergoing. It was Chekhov who prepared the way for Pirandello and Giraudoux and Brecht and Beckett and Ionesco. There is even Shaw's debt in *Heartbreak House*. These

31 Translated in Koteliansky and Tomlinson, *op. cit.*, p. 304.

are writers of very disparate kinds, and it is not to be held that Chekhov actually *accounts for* them; but it would be true to say that each of them owes to Chekhov a great deal of the freedom in which he moves and a great deal of the insight that the drama may be most relevant to experience when it does not move within the *ambiance* of tragedy but goes instead toward the greater ironic possibilities in tragicomedy.

It was a friend of Maxim Gorki's who judged Chekhov's talent best when he said that he was *heretically talented.* The heresy, which I have described as the modification of an ancient dramatic pattern, has proved to be of a liberating and revelatory kind.

When he forwarded the comment to Chekhov, Gorki expressed what every lover of theater must feel in Chekhov's presence: "So you don't want to write for the theater?! You must, by God! Forgive me that I write so boldly, but truly I feel terribly fine and merry and I love you." [32]

[32] Translated in Simmons, *op. cit.,* p. 452.

11. GEORGE BERNARD SHAW
(1856–1950)

ON THE SURFACE, Shaw was not a romantic at all. He considered himself part of "the anti-romantic movement in literature and art," [1] and he said that his works should be judged by the utilitarian standard of how much good they accomplished in society. Taken in that way, their romanticism is negligible and Shaw was the anti-romantic prophet and reformer he advertised himself to be.

The truth is a little different. Rhetorician and reformer he was. Certainly he eschewed every expression of sentimentality and was as devoid of nostalgia as a man can be. Yet it is only by seeing the romantic beneath the reformer, the musician beneath the orator, that one may discern Shaw's position in the modern theater and how it was that he became one of those in whom the nineteenth-century drama reached its culmination.

George Bernard Shaw, born in Dublin of a nominally Protestant family and formally educated only to his fourteenth year, came to London at the age of twenty in 1876. At that time Henry Irving was in his heyday at the Lyceum Theatre. His vastly popular production of *The Bells,* a melodrama, had had its première five years before; and his Shakespearean productions, such as the famous

[1] Letter to Archibald Henderson, quoted in Henderson's *George Bernard Shaw: Man of the Century* (New York: Appleton-Century-Crofts, 1956), p. xxiii.

Hamlet of 1874, were in full swing, while, at the Sadler's Wells, Irving had a Shakespearean rival in Samuel Phelps. Gilbert and Sullivan were hard at work (*Broken Hearts* had been written in 1875), and Dion Boucicault was churning out with characteristic ease his melodramatic adventures. The French were sending their best artists regularly to perform in London, among them Rachel in her revivals of French tragedies. Salvini and Ristori came to London from Italy. Ibsen, as yet scarcely known in England, was at the beginning of his middle period, writing *Pillars of Society*.

For the first nine of his London years Shaw earned almost nothing. He was supported by his mother, who had preceded him to London, and to a lesser extent by his father, a sufferer from alcoholism who remained in Dublin. During this time Shaw wrote five novels. In 1882 a lecture by Henry George led him to read Karl Marx and to become a socialist. In 1883 he became one of the first members of the Fabian Society. Rejecting the Marxist doctrine of the necessity of class warfare, the Fabians planned a gradual transformation of capitalist society into socialist. Shaw contributed to and edited the group's most famous publication, the *Fabian Essays*, in 1889.

By 1888 Shaw had found a job as music critic for the *Star*. Two years later he switched to the *World*, where he continued to write music criticism until 1894. Then, in 1895, he became drama critic for the *Saturday Review*. Although this marked the beginning of his sustained impact on the British theater, Shaw had become known as an interpreter of drama four years earlier, when he published *The Quintessence of Ibsenism* (1891).

The book, which had grown out of a paper Shaw had delivered for the Fabian Society in July 1890, came to birth just when Ibsen was becoming widely known in England. In 1884 Henry Arthur Jones and Henry Herman had presented their English adaptation of *A Doll's House* under the title *Breaking a Butterfly*. This effort badly misrepresented Ibsen, but it got his name before the English public. *The Pillars of Society and Other Plays* (*Ghosts, An Enemy of Society*), with an introduction by Havelock Ellis, was published in London in 1886. The William Archer five-volume edition of Ibsen, *Ibsen's Prose Dramas*, began to be published in 1890. By the time Shaw's little book appeared, J. T. Grein's Independent Theatre had opened with a production of *Ghosts*, Florence Farr had put on *Rosmersholm* at the Vaudeville Theatre, and Marion Lea and Elizabeth Robins had produced *Hedda Gabler*. A great deal of Ibsen controversy was in the air, and Shaw undertook, with characteristic lack of modesty, to explain what it was all about. The next year he wrote a socialist discussion play of his own, *Widower's Houses*, which was performed by the Independent Theatre Society. This did not reach a wide audience, so it was as a champion of Ibsen and as a play reviewer that Shaw first established himself, as far as the public was concerned, in relation to the theater.

Shaw's is the liveliest body of dramatic criticism in the English language, but it can hardly be said to be the most fair. Fairness, which is an admirable quality in a judge, is by no means the most important virtue for a lion tamer; and as a critic Shaw was much more like a lion tamer than a judge. He did not care whether history, looking back, would regard him as a man who handed down sagacious opinions. The important thing was to keep the beasts at bay, with each assigned a stool of proper height and himself holding command in the center of the ring, all the while putting on a lively performance. This breath-taking act was staged, if not for the glory of God, then certainly for the glory of man in his evolution toward freedom and wisdom, which was perhaps the same thing. Thus, it was necessary to crack the whip at Sarah Bernhardt every time she growled and to praise the grace of Eleonora Duse whenever she moved. One had to knock down Edmond Rostand for his verbal excesses and to lift up Eugène Brieux for his frank treatment of social problems. Shakespeare, though he could not be banished, had to be exposed as a magnificent irrelevance, while Ibsen was heralded as the savior next to Shaw.

The audacity of the performance was, and is, superb. The marvel of it is not that Shaw's lashing rhetoric caused him sometimes to utter judgments that were quite wrong but that in spite of it he was so often right. The lion-taming act that was Shaw's criticism had as one of its aims to show the reader what the theater could and ought to be, and this purpose was followed so well that even today the reader of that criticism finds himself not only delighted by its verve but also instructed as by a master teacher.

On March 30, 1895, reviewing the performance of *Rosmersholm* that Lugné-Poe's Théâtre de l'Oeuvre brought to London, the impish critic Shaw noted that Pastor Rosmer's library had been furnished with a volume of Shaw's plays:

> That he should have provided himself with a volume of my own dramatic works I thought right and natural enough, though when he took that particular volume down and opened it, I began to speculate rather uneasily on the chances of his presently becoming so absorbed as to forget all about his part.[2]

Shaw's comment not only reveals his tendency to talk about himself in his reviews (he sometimes did this in his plays, too); it also causes one to wonder what Shavian volume it was that Pastor Rosmer could possibly have had on his shelf in 1895. By that date Shaw had written four plays: *Widower's Houses* (1892), *The Philanderer* (1893), *Mrs. Warren's Profession* (1894), and *Arms and the Man* (1894). No "volume of dramatic works," however, was published until 1898, when Shaw, eager to reach the large public that the stage performances of his plays had not yet brought him, published in two volumes *Plays: Pleasant and Unpleasant*. The "unpleasant" ones were the first three mentioned above, while the "pleasant" ones included *Arms and the Man, Candida* (1895), *The Man of Destiny* (1895, a one-act play about Napoleon), and *You Never Can Tell* (1896). In 1895 the only Shaw play in print was *Widower's Houses,* which had been published by Henry & Co. as the first number of the Independent Theatre Series of Plays, edited by J. T. Grein. As this hardly amounts to a "volume of dramatic works," we may assume that Shaw was stretching the facts, partly for journalistic effect and partly because he was already dreaming of things to come. Or perhaps Lugné-Poe had gotten up a mock volume to flatter the author-critic he knew would be in his audience.

Grein had gotten *Widower's Houses* by asking Shaw to write something for his Independent Theatre. Agreeable, Shaw had turned to an unfinished play that he and William Archer had begun in 1885. Archer had supplied a scenario based on a plot he found in one of Augier's plays, and Shaw had written two acts.

[2] *Shaw's Dramatic Criticism (1895–98)* selected by John F. Matthews (New York: Hill and Wang, 1959), p. 35.

They gave it up as a bad job, but when Grein made his request Shaw added a third act, and the play was put on before an audience made up of applauders and booers. Shaw later said that he had distorted Archer's original plan for a romantic "well-made play" by turning it into a "grotesque realistic exposure of slum landlordism, municipal jobbery, and the pecuniary and matrimonial ties between them and the pleasant people with 'independent' incomes who imagine that such sordid matters do not touch their own lives." [3] Thriving on controversy, Grein asked Shaw for a second play and was handed, the following year, a script called *The Philanderer.* This proved impossible to cast because Charles Wyndham, who was wanted for the lead, refused to act in it. Shaw's next play, *Mrs. Warren's Profession,* was denied a license by the lord chamberlain, since it argued that prostitution was an inevitable result of capitalism. The ban on it was not lifted until 1924, though the Stage Society put on "private" performances in 1902. Its first commercial showing came when Arnold Daly produced it in New York in 1904, where a large public clamored to see it and where the police arrested every member of the cast. Brought to trial, the actors were acquitted.

Shaw's "unpleasant" plays represented their author's attempt to be realistic in a sort of documentary sense. Their didactic aim was to call for the establishment of a good society by showing the badness of the present one. The revolutionary posture and the realistic method were not, however, congenial with Shaw's temperament. They were too negative. He could not confine himself to exposing the bad, for what he was interested in was that good and positive force for change which he understood as basic to the human condition. It was his awareness not only of the desirability of change but, even more, of its inevitability and goodness that marked Shaw's genius. This positive emphasis upon change linked him with philosophers as disparate as Nietzsche, Bergson, and Whitehead. He was the disciple of no philosopher, but he shared with several the conviction that all things are in process and that life cannot be adequately defined by reference to eternal verities, fixed orders of truth (whether in philosophy or science), or stable patterns in society. These, he thought, are all relativized by a progressive force

3 Preface to *Nine Plays* (New York: Dodd, Mead, 1935), p. xii.

of life which carries men and institutions forward, some to fruition and some to wreckage, as on the current of an undammable stream.

For this reason the Shavian view of life is comic. The notion that history tends toward progressive fulfillment belongs to a comic rather than a tragic sense. The picture of man as the product of a force more powerful, more intelligent, more extravagant, and more benign than he is comic. To see this force assert itself most strongly in the mating instinct is again comic. And if to all this is added the Shavian wit, there results an atmosphere so pervasively and incorrigibly comic that to find its equal one has to go back to Molière.

The question of Shaw's antecedents is somewhat confusing. On the one hand, it has been argued that his playwriting evolved in large measure out of the popular theater of the late nineteenth century. On the other hand, Shaw denied this and said that he was really a throwback to Scheherazade. By this he meant that, unlike Pinero, Jones, Wilde, and some others fashionable in London just before him, he had avoided the well-made-play techniques of Scribe, so heavily dependent on intrigue, and had returned to the good old art of telling tales. "I threw off Paris," he recollected in his later years, "and went back to Shakespeare, to the Bible, to Bunyan, Walter Scott, Dickens, and Dumas *père,* Mozart and Verdi, in whom I had been soaked from my childhood." [4]

Actually, these alternatives are not as mutually exclusive as Shaw made out. If it is impossible to fit any of his plays, especially those after *Mrs. Warren's Profession,* into a Scribean pattern, it is equally impossible to imagine the bulk of Shaw's plays up until *Heartbreak House* as having been conceived without the prior existence of the *pièce à thèse.* If nothing else, the *pièce à thèse* taught Shaw that the theater could and should be used as a forum of ideas. But beyond that it taught him to integrate ideas, plot, and characters. Even if he did not like the word "plot" very much, he did quite a lot of plotting. But he knew something his immediate predecessors did not, or could not use if they did: that the plot, the characters, *and* the ideas are all functions of something more basic

[4] "My Way with a Play," in *The Observer* (London), September 29, 1946. Quoted in E. J. West, ed., *Shaw on Theatre* (London: MacGibbon & Kee, 1958), p. 268.

than themselves, to which for the moment we may give the name *élan*, picking the term up from Bergson's phrase *élan vital*.

Shaw's shift from the "unpleasant" plays to the "pleasant" was no mere catering to public taste. It was an attempt to appeal to a basic level of response in his audience, less rational than anything the *pièce à thèse* tended to get at, closer to the springs of a positive and future-oriented life force. Shaw wrote:

> The "pleasant" plays deal with life at large, with human nature as it presents itself through all economic and social phases. 'Arms and the Man' is the comedy of youthful romance and disillusion, 'Candida' is the poetry of the Wife and Mother—the Virgin Mother in the true sense and so on and so forth. . . . I am rather flattered than otherwise at the preference of my friends for those plays of mine which have no purpose except the purpose of all poets and dramatists as against those which are exposures of the bad side of our social system.[5]

The quotation describes Shaw's relation to the plays exactly. If they have to do with "economic and social phases," nevertheless the accent falls on human nature and the archetypal forms through which poets have taught us to recognize it—the soldier and the lady, the wife-mistress-mother, and so on. When Shaw says he has no purpose with these except that of all poets and dramatists he is, of course, entering a strategic disclaimer. His choice of subjects and genres may have been conventional; his *purpose* was to express his understanding of the life force *through* the conventions. He wished to sell the idea that human beings should take hold of their own future, since otherwise it will take hold of them. The entertainment consisted of showing man how life outwits him through a kind of sublime benevolence. A secularized Providence was celebrated, a jovial Providence that plays Shavian jokes on the audience in order to do it good. "Telling the truth," Shaw said, "is the greatest joke in the world." [6] When he said he wanted people to

---

[5] Letter, June 10, 1896, from *Advice to a Young Critic*, pp. 49–50. Quoted in Martin Meisel, *Shaw and the Nineteenth-Century Theater* (Princeton, N.J.: Princeton University Press, 1963), pp. 134–135.
[6] Henderson, *op. cit.*, p. xxxii.

prefer his "pleasant" to his "unpleasant" plays, he was joking—
that is, telling the truth.

Shaw could hardly have come to this sense of his theatrical purpose had it not been for his deep involvement in the thought, the
drama, and the opera of the nineteenth century. The notion of
history as the product of organic development oriented toward
progressive fulfillment was thoroughly of that age. It is also the
part of Shaw from which the twentieth century has become most
removed. But our concern at the moment is the debt he owed to
nineteenth-century dramatic conventions, which has been well
documented by Martin Meisel.[7]

The well-made play, the melodrama, the romantic comedy, and
the farce were familiar to Shaw not only because they dominated
the Irish theater during his early life in Dublin and the London
theater toward which he migrated as a young man but also because
they were the stock in trade of the operatic theater, which was
Shaw's first love. He never hesitated to flail any and all idio-
cies of thought he might find in popular forms of theater, but he
did not attack the forms themselves—at least not directly, for he
wanted to use them, and you cannot use a form you have destroyed.
He was only too well aware that in the hands of an Ibsen or a
Brieux, to cite two unequal talents he admired, the well-made play
could be turned to an exposition of the most useful ideas. In other
words, the well-made play was a serviceable vehicle, and Shaw had
two reasons for liking vehicles. For one thing, he was a propagandist—or, if you like, a rhetorician—and thus had to have a well-
oiled vehicle at his disposal. For another, he believed that the life
force employs events and circumstances for its own purposes,
which means that he who exploits the vehicle available to him is
doing exactly what nature does and may therefore regard himself
as engaged in a most proper activity.

Thus, when Shaw went to the popular theater for his inspiration
he was, with perfect justification, having it both ways. He was ap-
pealing to what was ordinary and unsophisticated in his audience
while at the same time he was putting the audience in touch with
that force of life which was moving mankind toward its sublime

7 *Op. cit.*

destiny. That is why, underneath the Shavian rhetoric, we may descry the utterly romantic notion of the primitive sublime.

Not that the rhetoric is only veneer. The rhetoric carries the wit, and the wit is dialectical, and Shaw without his dialectical wit is not Shaw at all. It is because the wit is dialectical that it serves to flavor Shaw's romanticism rather than to obliterate it.

Dialectic is an imitation of process. It plays one point of view off against another in such a way that a new level of insight is achieved. This in turn is challenged by an opposing or ironic slant. A new level emerges, on which new oppositions appear, and so on. Such a dialectic employs logic, but logicality, at least in the Aristotelian sense, is not its *raison d'être*. By the same token, consistency is not its principal obligation. Shaw was famous for his lack of consistency. The arguments the characters in his plays carry on are those he carried on privately with himself, which is why he was so good at stating all sides of a question. But, having stated them, he was not in the least interested in balancing the result in order to achieve a fair-minded, well-rounded conclusion. The value of the argument lay not in its conclusion but in its process. Any conclusion would be tentative and partial; it would represent only a certain stage in the development of things. To get stuck at that stage was to be entrapped by what Shaw disparagingly called "the ideal," which was dead, whereas life was in argument itself, wherein one can experience movement and strength. This is why one returns to a Shaw play and takes pleasure from it even if he is quite familiar with its plot and its ideas, and no matter how much he may disagree with those ideas; over and above its rational content, the dialectic of the argument expresses the vitality of life, and this is what endows Shaw's best works with durability.

Shaw perceived that the dialectic of the mind is just as much an expression and instrument of the life force as are courtship and marriage. Like them, it serves a general purpose transcending its particular manifestations. So in a Shaw play "thinking" is just as exciting and just as comic as making love. The dialectic of the mind belonged to the romantic in Shaw just as much as did his infatuation with opera. When he called himself anti-romantic, that meant simply that he opposed what was gushy, sentimental, postured, and nostalgic—in short, flabby or escapist romanticism. As for genuine anti-romanticism in Shaw, the most that can be said is that he preached the wisdom of coming to terms with reality, which is a classicist principle; but then it has immediately to be added that the reality he had in mind was ever-changing, ever on the way toward new stages of being. Toward any particular established order, political or intellectual, he was habitually iconoclastic. Face him with an assumed reality and he would immediately show that it was passing away. Reality stayed never the same; therefore the true accommodation to be made was accommodation to change.

Candida, the best and most popular of the "pleasant" plays, is a work of Dionysian spirit. In some ways it may be regarded as Shaw's *Doll's House.* Like Ibsen's play it addresses itself to the estate of marriage in a respectable household where the husband regards himself as the upholder of solid values, the benevolent head of his family, and the source of its strength. Both plays show that the strength actually belongs to the wife and that her supposed dependence on her husband is but the mark of a relation that is the opposite of what it seems. Like Ibsen's play, *Candida* reaches its climax when this state of affairs is brought into the open, forcing a decision about the future of the marriage. And as in Ibsen, the climax includes not only the decision but also the reasons for it.

In *The Quintessence of Ibsenism* Shaw had called particular attention to what he called "the technical novelty" in Ibsen's plays:

> Formerly you had in what was called a well made play an exposition in the first act, a situation in the second, and unravelling in the third. Now you have exposition, situation, and discussion; and the discussion is the test of the playwright. . . . The discussion conquered Europe in Ibsen's *Doll's House;* and now the serious playwright recognizes in the discussion not only the main test of his highest powers, but also the real centre of his play's interest.[8]

The "discussion scene" of *A Doll's House* takes place when Nora sits down with Torvald to examine their marriage and during their discussion realizes and discloses why she has decided to leave him. In *Candida* there occurs the famous "auction scene" in which

8 New York: Hill and Wang, 1957, p. 171.

the heroine asks Morell and Marchbanks to bid for her. It ends with the line "I give myself to the weaker of the two." As soon as it dawns on Morell, the husband, that she means him and not Marchbanks, the teen-age poet, Candida says, "Let us sit and talk comfortably over it like three friends," and the play concludes with two pages of "discussion." The technicality of a "discussion" scene is more or less superfluous in a Shaw play, since almost all the scenes are discussions anyway, but the fact that he arranged the ending of *Candida* in this way shows that he had his interpretation of Ibsen's play very much in mind when he wrote his own.

Even if *Candida* is Shaw's *Doll's House*, it is nevertheless much more a Shavian than an Ibsenesque play, and the differences all point in the direction of Shaw's comic romanticism. It is a work much closer to popular theater than *A Doll's House* is. It is a comedy about a domestic triangle, in which a marital crisis is precipitated by the attentions a wife receives from a poetic admirer. Similar situations were to be found in Tom Taylor's *Still Waters Run Deep* (1855) and *Victims* (1857) and in Sardou's *Divorçons* (1880) and *Nos Intimes!* (1861).[9] In such a triangle it is easy to picture the prosaic, unimaginative qualities of the husband in contrast with the exciting unconventionality of the poet-lover. Unlike Candida's, Nora's choice was not between two men but between two definitions of herself—Torvald's and the one she was beginning to find through her own experience. Of course, Candida's choice between Morell and Marchbanks implies also a decision about her personal identity, but Candida lacks the quality of lonely self-realization that is Nora's chief attribute. This means that Nora is more heroic. Her heroism is dramatized by her departure from the house, going out alone and slamming the great door behind her. Candida makes instead a conventional choice: she remains with her husband, and it is Marchbanks who goes out alone. She is unconventional not in *what* she does but in her *reasons* for doing it. Moreover, the reasons are unconventional only in the context of what is expected in a domestic comedy, not in the context of real life. Candida is more articulate and, of course, more candid than most women; otherwise, she is not very different from them. Behind her, as we are not allowed to forget, stands Shaw;

9 See Meisel, *op. cit.*, pp. 226–233.

and what Shaw is interested in with regard to her choice is that it is the choice of a *function*. This overshadows, for him, the question of identity. It is not really a question of who Candida shall be but of what she will do. The play celebrates the triumph of social function over individual posturing. Morell, the social liberal who can do nothing without his wife but who, with her help, is socially useful, is chosen over the poet Marchbanks, whose poetry is mostly pose and who would not know what to do with Candida if he got her.

The Dionysian spirit of *Candida,* although its unlikely habitation is that of an Edwardian parsonage, is quite unmistakable. The play is predicated upon the Dionysian assumption that the female is superior to the male. Let the man make the speeches; it is the woman who gives him life, and the speeches do their job only if they bring society into line with her life-giving urges. Olympian and chthonic deities, though any mention of them in the play would be out of place, are hovering in the wings. Give the Olympians your sympathy and the revenge the earth gods take would land you in tragedy or in some such Strindbergian vision of horror as *The Father.* Give the chthonic deities, who are mostly feminine and whom Dionysus serves, the upper hand and you are in comic celebration of life. Marchbanks knows this. He is perhaps Dionysus in disguise, the handsome, dreamy ephebos who has no real place in the world of men and who therefore assumes that the woman belongs to him. But it is precisely *because* Marchbanks knows the score that Candida has only a temporary use for him. Her real business is with her "Olympian" husband, the liberal social activist who must be convinced of his dependence on woman if he and his good ideas are to be saved from tragic waste. So Marchbanks, like a Euripidean Dionysus, is sent packing. He will turn up in another household, and then another, always the same age and always with the same function. It is his destiny as one of the minor gods to be a catalyst in the male-female relation, hated by the man and employed, with kind thanks, by the woman.

All this would be comic if Shaw left it at that, but perhaps comic only by definition and not necessarily funny. In order to deepen the comic effect and to render the situation mockingly humorous, Shaw twisted the usual understanding of the feminine. What he highlighted in Candida was neither her sexuality nor her fertility. He refused to define the feminine primarily in terms of an organic relation to the male or to the child. Rather, he suggested that the truly feminine quality is to live by one's wit. Candida is one in a long line of Shavian heroines who win out over men not so much by their physical charms or their matriarchal dominance as by their cleverness, their agility, and their skill at changing the signals.

To live by one's wit; what, in this view, is the opposite of that? It is, in part, to be dull and to manage things by sheer force. But even more it is to live by position, to expect deference from others because of what one *is* rather than to accomplish a task through what one *does*. The "Womanly Woman," whom Shaw unmasked in *The Quintessence of Ibsenism,* was the woman who defined herself by reference to a "duty" she presumably owed to men rather than to herself. She was called "womanly" if she deferred to her husband, but in Shaw's eyes the price of this was her humanity. Her counterpart, no more human, whom Shaw attacked elsewhere, was the "Unwomanly Woman." She expected deference from men simply because she was a female. Shaw attacked her because she was purely the invention of certain men who, being prone to the masculine conceit that *their* superiority lay in *their* very being, could conceive of the exalted woman only as one who received tribute because she was *another* sort of being. Shaw determined to cast such humbug aside by insisting on the priority of function over being. The Unwomanly Woman was all wrong because she subordinated feminine wit to an illusory feminine "being." If women applauded such a "being," it was because, existing in virtual slavery, they found it profitable to encourage the illusion.

The opposition between feminine wit and masculine position reflects and points to a more basic opposition that is fundamental to the structure of *Candida* and to all of Shaw's best work. I have already called this the opposition between function and being, but it would be equally correct, and more useful in the discussion of Shaw's aesthetic, to call it an opposition between dynamics and form. In form, *Candida* is a quite predictable play. What saves it is the comic vitality that springs from beneath its surface. This vitality eventually destroys the play as far as any credence in its realism is concerned. The play becomes a preposterous invention, a masquerade for a set of bouncy ideas, a tinseled ritual to celebrate wit and feminine irony. Each of its characters is a caricature, and at times its rhythm accelerates to a frenzy quite out of keeping with the well-managed household Shaw so carefully establishes at the beginning. Far from ruining the play, this destruction of its realism both saves it as entertainment and shows us what it is all about: a Dionysian impudence which exposes all form as mere foil to vitality, husk around a germinating kernel, something expendable by Nature, that great and intelligent expender.

The many plays Shaw wrote after the "Pleasant and Unpleasant" series, and before World War I, may be grouped in four categories. The first is melodrama, which was one of those dramatic genres so popular and so full of stereotypes that it lent itself easily to the Shavian opposition between form and dynamics. Of this sort are *The Devil's Disciple* (1897), *Captain Brassbound's Conversion* (1899), and *The Admirable Bashville* (1901) and also the one-act plays *The Shewing-up of Blanco Posnet* (1909) and *The Glimpse of Reality*, subtitled "A Tragedietta" (1909). In all of these Shaw drew very close to the line that separates melodrama from farce. *Blanco Posnet* is called "A Sermon in Crude Melodrama," *Brassbound* is called "An Adventure," and *The Admirable Bashville*, which is a blank-verse adaptation of Shaw's 1882 novel, *Cashel Byron's Profession*, has the subtitle "Constancy Unrewarded." *The Devil's Disciple*, with its swaggering, loquacious, and uncommonly heroic protagonist, Dick Dudgeon, is simply called "A Melodrama in Three Acts"; but its peppery dialogue, its impudent hero, and its buoyant plot, in which the British Army almost hangs the wrong man with no complaint from him ("Hang away and have done with it!") and in which, as it turns out, no hangings take place at all, makes it a melodrama thoroughly comic in spirit.

Man and Superman (1903) and *Pygmalion* (1913) may be classed, along with *Candida* and *Arms and the Man,* as romantic comedy, and they are among Shaw's best plays. The principal motifs of *Man and Superman* are the same as those already mentioned in *Candida*. The difference is that *Man and Superman* is, in every sense of the word, an expansive play. The cast is large, and the scenes reach from London to Granada, not to mention the dream sequence of the third act known as "Don Juan in Hell," which conveys both a cavernous and a starry vastness. This scope is not required by the plot, which could just as well be set within the confines of a drawing room. By moving about, however, Shaw added comic literalness to the cliché proposition that the female pursues the male: he showed her tracking him over a continent and following him through hell to heaven. Most of all, however, the scope gave Shaw opportunity to include numerous variations on his single theme and to generate among his characters an apparently endless flow of talk. This talk becomes the carrier wave for the "ideas," and it is in the "ideas," quite as much as in any of the characters, that the play shows its dynamic quality.

Three aspects of the comic are particularly to be noticed in *Man and Superman*. The first is the irony, present in the play's title and assumed throughout its length, according to which the male, who fancies himself a superior creature, is shown as a mere foil to that which surpasses him. He is surpassed by the female, who is superior to him because she knows how to use her "weakness" to advantage; and he is surpassed by the "superman" of the future, that more intelligent and more humane creature yet to be born of the human race.

Shaw's "superman" owes only his name to Nietzsche. He is in fact simply a way of referring to that future good society and that improved human intelligence that Shaw intended, as an ally of nature and history, to help bring about. Shaw used the ancient fertility motif of comedy, the familiar theatrical ritual of courtship and marriage, as a pretext for a new proclamation. The future, he declared, belongs to the Kingdom of Man—born of Woman. Like every wise prophet, he appealed to the past. He told his audience: this future apotheosis of the *really* superior man—i.e., superior to himself—is what your comic celebrations and conventions are all about and have been from the beginning. He reinforced his argument by bringing in no less a witness than Mozart and by employing the oft-told story of Don Juan according to a new interpretation. What that interpretation was can be most readily perceived by contrasting Shaw's Don Juan with Kierkegaard's, though the latter's treatment (in *Either/Or*, 1843) was, as far as I can find out, unknown to Shaw. We are dealing with two independent, contrasting romantic uses of Don Juan, both starting from Mozart.

To Kierkegaard, Don Juan is the "aesthetic" man who wants to savor all experience. The impossibility of fulfilling such a desire pushes him into despair. He might overcome it by moving from the "aesthetic" to the "ethical" plane of existence, where purpose rather than experience would become his organizing principle; but since he refuses this movement he plunges ever deeper into anxiety and dread.

Shaw's Don Juan, by contrast, is the "ethical" man par excellence, and Shaw's "aesthetic" man is the Devil. Thus, Hell is a most pleasant place for any who, like the Commander, do not mind an aimless, though otherwise full, existence. To Shaw's Don Juan such an eternity is horrible. He demands action and self-realization, the program of the ethical man: "To be in Hell is to drift, to be in Heaven is to steer." Hence, after an hour of dialectical conversation in which this insight is finally achieved, he departs. Anna follows him to heaven, where, apparently, the inhabitants do marry and are given in marriage.

Into Shaw's comedy of the sexes a Puritan ethic of work and self-improvement has been stuffed. A dialectician no less than Kierkegaard, Shaw displayed not the slightest hint of Kierkegaard's awareness that even the ethical life issues in despair. In Kierkegaard's view, despair is the natural lot of man and requires, if it is to be overcome, a leap of faith. To Shaw, despair is the result of faulty intelligence, and the leap required is into the future. The spirit is Dionysian and the comedy, for all its ideational flight, is earth comedy.

Another comic motif to be noted in *Man and Superman* is the conflict between the generations. Terence, Plautus, Shakespeare, and Molière, to mention only those and no more, had all built comedy around a conflict between the young, who want to get married and establish a life on their own terms, and the old, who want no marriages except those that perpetuate the *status quo*. In Shaw's play, Ann Whitefield and John Tanner, along with Violet Robinson, Hector Malone the younger, and Octavius Robinson, represent the ambitions of the young, while the inflexibility of the older generation is manifest in Roebuck Ramsden, Hector Malone the elder, and Mrs. Whitefield. The older generation is also very much present in the will left by Ann Whitefield's deceased father. Ann's pursuit of Tanner is not only the female's chase of the male; it is also the pursuit of ways and means to outwit or mollify the older generation; and part of the comedy of Tanner's position is that as a young revolutionary he must support Ann's program of rebellion against authority even while he fears the result it will have in making him her victim. As usual, Shaw twists the convention he is using. He makes Roebuck Ramsden, the old fogey, a model of nineteenth-century liberalism, whose "progressive" views do not in the slightest prevent his being an obstacle in the way of the young. Shaw also arranges the dead Mr. Whitefield's will so that Ann is made the ward of John Tanner, whom she intends to marry. Thus the two are yoked together by a device that also keeps them apart. And when Hector Malone (Senior) tries to split Violet Robinson away from his son, he argues loudly *against* the *status quo,* although that is what he is really trying to preserve.

In short, Shaw uses the comic war between the old and the young as a way of pitting against each other two types of liberalism —the one worked out according to the "best principles" of Darwinian and Spencerian evolutionism, the other not violently but nevertheless deeply revolutionary, radical in spirit and bearing no regard for even the more liberal forms of respectability. The world we are shown is thus, through and through, a world of change. There is no possibility that things might remain as they are. Any real battle between the eternal and the temporal, the fixed and the moving, is ruled out from the start. The only question is whether change shall be slowed down by being made to conform to the good manners of the elderly or whether it shall be given its head in accordance with the freedom envisioned by the young. Shaw has great fun showing that the Roebuck Ramsdens of this world are absurd because they are materialists who try, in the name of progress, to hold back the spiritual clock. He also delights in showing that such persons are overcome by young iconoclasts who are propelled by a momentum not of their own making and quite beyond their own comprehension.

The third aspect of the comic to be remarked upon in *Man and Superman* is Shaw's use of the classical figure known as the *eiron*.

In Greek comedy the *eiron* is a self-deprecator. He employs a strategy of self-effacement to protect himself from the blows of fate, the caprice of the gods, and the chastisements of authority. He tries to lie low, to adopt a protective coloring, to speak the truth indirectly if at all, and by various other means to conceal his true feelings and identity. In this way he may escape the notice of those who could do him harm, or at least may prevent their destroying his real self. The strategy of the *eiron* is the strategy of the underdog and has to do with cunning and trickery as means of survival and even victory. He is vividly and simply depicted in the person of Eliza Doolittle's father in *Pygmalion* and more subtly in Eliza herself.

The counterpart of the *eiron* is the *alazon,* a boaster who thinks of himself more highly than he ought to think. In tragedy his pride has considerable foundation in actual virtues, yet he incurs the notice of the jealous gods and becomes the tragic victim. In comedy his pride has no adequate foundation, and he becomes the butt of jokes, many of them engineered by the cunning of the *eiron.* In *Pygmalion* he is Professor Higgins. The relation of the *eiron* to reality and to the *alazon* has given us the word "ironic." It is a relation in which appearances are deceiving and in which truths are spoken indirectly. This conception is the basis of Shavian irony.

Shaw's irony is pervasive in the sense that it is present in all his writing and is one of the main components of his style. But it is not pervasive in the sense of belonging to his view of reality itself, for in Shaw's eyes the world does not forever withhold its meaning, is not ultimately mysterious, and is certainly not "absurd." Unlike many moderns Shaw turned to irony not because it expressed his philosophy but because it was useful as a strategy. He himself was the *eiron,* doing battle continuously with every *alazon* who came his way. If he talked a great deal and called attention to himself, it was always from behind the mask of a buffoon and was accompanied by a good bit of sand thrown in his opponents' eyes. The *eirons* in the plays are projections of Shaw himself, and at the same time they are agents of the life force, which on its own part treats man ironically, biding its time and acting in unlikely ways, the better to pursue its evolutionary and creative task.

In *Man and Superman* the principal *eiron* is Ann Whitefield.

Her appearance is demure; the picture of herself that she paints by word and gesture is that of obedience and dependence; to her elders she defers; before all men she is pliant and respectful; she gives the air of one who has no control over anything and who waits for decisions to be made around her. In short, she is a woman to be watched. Shaw has allowed her a sign of her true nature by giving her to wear in the first scene a giant feather boa. This piece of cuddly apparel is in truth the mark of one who swallows victims whole. Given the chance, Ann Whitefield will compromise anybody in order to gain her way. Apparently pliant to men, she actually envelops them. She is pliant only to the life instinct within her, which is the source of her power. She is the *eiron* to Roebuck Ramsden's *alazon,* and to John Tanner's, and she will outlive them in the future as she outwits them in the present. Having fainted in Tanner's arms, she backs him into a corner by telling everyone that he has proposed. This victory in her pocket, she is perfectly happy for him to "go on talking." He has all the great words and she has all the secrets. *Man and Superman* is a comedy of the sexes in which sexiness has no part. It is not needed, the feminine *eiron* being endowed with superior strategies.

One may now perceive why the theater was so apt an instrument for Shaw's purposes. The theater, as all right-minded people know, is a harlot. In her house painted pleasures are sold, and she lives by her enticements. But what if her gaudy advertisements are modified and she is converted from merely playing the seductress to an actual feminine function? Her masks will then become devices of an ironic strategy, and men who come to her for pleasure will be led on to their genuine humanity. For the strategic ironist the theater is the instrument of instruments, the art of disguise perfectly suited to his purpose. No wonder Shaw wrote play after play with an energy that would astound us if we did not know the pleasure this artifice gave him in the depths of his purposeful existence. And no wonder Shaw fell in love ever and again with actresses. It was their vocation to remind him of *his* vocation. When they failed or refused this high calling, he excoriated them. "You have reached the stage," he wrote to Florence Farr, "of the Idiotically Beautiful. There remain the stages of the Intelligently Beautiful and finally of the Powerfully Beautiful; and until you have attained the last you will never be able to compel me to recognize the substance of that soul of which I was shown a brief image by Nature for her own purposes." [10]

A third group of Shaw's plays can be thought of as discussion plays or, better, talk pieces. Of course, all Shaw's plays include a great deal of talk, and none of those in this group is a "discussion play" in that technical sense Shaw described in *The Quintessence of Ibsenism*. Nevertheless, *Major Barbara* (1905), *The Doctor's Dilemma* (1906), and *Heartbreak House* (begun in 1913, finished in 1919) are plays that exist almost wholly in their "speeches" rather than in plot, character, or spectacle. The last three elements exist in them only to provide a framework for the talk. The same is true of *John Bull's Other Island* (1904), *Getting Married* (1908), *Misalliance* (1910), *Fanny's First Play* (1911), and the one-act play *Overruled* (1912).

It is not possible here to discuss any of these plays in detail, which would be necessary in order to show the excellence that the first three of them, at least, possess; but it should at any rate be said that in them Shaw mastered what is perhaps the most difficult feat a dramatist can perform—creating dialogue that is thoroughly dramatic in its own right, even apart from its revelation of character or its advancement of plot. Shaw is one of the few dramatists of our era (perhaps Brecht is another) who has written plays to which the phrase "drama of ideas" literally applies. There is a difference between the drama *with* ideas and the drama *of* ideas. Shaw's talk pieces are the latter. The drama in them consists of the dialectical conflict among the ideas themselves, and the course of the arguments is plotted with just as much clarity, precision, rhythm, climax, and dénouement as the plot of any romance or intrigue. For this reason the plays retain their interest even when the pure content of the ideas is familiar or is made obsolete by social change. What one continues to respond to is the play of mind, the vigor and the agility of the dialectic. Shaw demonstrates not merely that drama is thoughtful but that thought is dramatic. The mind functions by overcoming opposition within itself, just as a play functions by overcoming oppositions built into it from the first. This

---

[10] August 20, 1891. In Clifford Box, ed., *Florence Farr, Bernard Shaw, W. B. Yeats: Letters* (New York: Dodd, Mead, 1942), p. 8.

recognition of the inherently dramatic character of thought is again comic, on the principle Samuel Johnson had in mind when he said that life is a comedy to him who thinks, a tragedy to him who feels. Not that tragedy is unthinking, but the subordination of experience to a scheme of mental oppositions is the operation of a comic mind. Thus, the worlds Shaw conjures up in his talk pieces are artificial worlds in which no fully sentient being could live, because Shaw's abstracting and comic mind has deliberately removed from the characters their existential quality.

Even so, the talk pieces pertain not only to thinking but also to feeling. They correspond to a side of human nature that is at once intellectual and musical. The Shavian drama of ideas is Shavian opera. It includes duets, trios, quartets and sextets. It is not lifelike, but there is life in it. It makes a direct appeal to mind, but it also makes one to spirit, for it points to a kind of sublime absolute in which mind and spirit are one and from which base matter is passing away.

In 1898, the year after he had written *The Devil's Disciple* and the same year he published *Plays: Pleasant and Unpleasant,* Shaw decided to write a drama for the heroic actor Forbes Robertson and for the actress Mrs. Patrick Campbell. *Caesar and Cleopatra* was the result.[11] "*Caesar and Cleopatra,*" said Shaw on the occasion of the play's opening at the Savoy Theatre in London (1907), "is an attempt of mine to pay an installment on the debt that all dramatists owe to the art of heroic acting." He added, paying compliment to the actor and to himself at the same time, that he wrote it for Robertson "because he is the classic actor of our day, and had a right to require such a service from me." [12] Shaw further explained that the heroes of older dramas had ceased to be believable and that his treatment of Caesar had been determined by the desire to

[11] Mrs. Campbell gave the play its "Copyright Performance" in Newcastle in 1899, but because of her falling out with Robertson she did not appear in it thereafter. Students performed the play in Chicago in 1901. Its first commercial production took place in Berlin in 1906 with Albert Steinröck in the lead. Robertson, with Gertrude Elliott as Cleopatra, played it first in New York in 1906. This production, which Shaw had helped Robertson direct, was then brought to Leeds in September 1907 and to London in November.

[12] *Play Pictorial,* No. 62 (October 1907). Quoted in Raymond Mander and Joe Mitchenson, *Theatrical Companion to Shaw* (London: Rockliff, 1954), p. 63.

make him "credible," because he was "a very modern man indeed." Unfortunately, Shaw let it be known, the critics in America (where the play had already been performed by Robertson) had not understood this. They had found the historically accurate parts of the play fantastic but had accepted Shaw's modern topical allusions as "grave Roman history."

It is a bit difficult to see why Shaw was not pleased with the reactions he attributed to the American reviewers. Ignorant of historical fact they may have been, but if Shaw's intention was to show that Caesar was in fact "a very modern man," and if the critics accepted the play's modernisms without challenge, then he must have succeeded in his aim. The critics found the modernisms more credible as history than the parts that were "dramatized Mommsen or transcribed Plutarch." The truth probably is that Shaw *was* pleased and chose an upside-down way of saying so, the better to play a joke on history and the audience at the same time —and to have the last word, which, since he was playing schoolmaster to an age, was very important.

The schoolmaster's lessons now took the form of historical extravaganza. *Caesar and Cleopatra* was the first of a large group of his plays, some on historical subjects and some not, best described as extravagant entertainments. Three such works belong to the period before World War I: *Caesar and Cleopatra, Androcles and the Lion* (1912), and the short "Thumbnail Sketch of Russian Court Life in the XVIII Century (Whom Glory Still Adores), *Great Catherine*" (1913). In Shaw's later life the extravaganza appealed to him so much that he made it the bulk of his work after 1918. *Saint Joan* (1923) is the best among these, the best of Shaw, one of the true monuments of the modern theater, and to it we return later. Yet the extravaganzas also include *Too True to Be Good* (1931), which is Shavian horseplay about politics, and the "Metabiological Pentateuch," *Back to Methuselah* (1918–1920), written in five parts (the first set before the Fall, in the Garden of Eden, and the last "in the year A.D. 31920") and rightly said by Jacques Barzun to be Shaw's "longest and worst play." [13]

Like romantic comedy and melodrama, the extravaganza was a

13 "G. B. S. in Twilight," in *Kenyon Review*, Vol. V (Summer 1943), p. 343.

popular kind of theatrical entertainment that Shaw took over for his own purposes. German postwar expressionism influenced Shaw's later use of it. Ill-defined and of a sprawling structure, it did not lend itself particularly well to the Shavian dialectic between dynamics and form. Shaw's penchant for it revealed his basic impatience with strict form, his eagerness to move beyond it in the name of spiritual vitality. In this his romantic progressivism was clearly manifest, though it sometimes ran away with him and became merely a naïve exuberance. Only in *Saint Joan* and perhaps in *Caesar and Cleopatra* did he make this kind of writing into a major work of art.

When the guns of August 1914 began to shoot, Shaw's *Pygmalion* had finished a run of 118 performances at His Majesty's Theatre, where Herbert Tree played Higgins to Mrs. Patrick Campbell's Eliza. Shaw had started to write a new play called *Heartbreak House,* a partly Chekhovian, partly allegorical picture of Europe on the eve of war, on which he was to work off and on for six years, until 1919. When it was performed in London in October of 1921, it was his first major play to be seen there in seven years. Except for a few short skits, Shaw was absent from the London stage all during the war, and after it he was not the same.

The position of Shaw in the changed climate after World War I has been well described by Julian B. Kaye in his perceptive book *Bernard Shaw and the Nineteenth-Century Tradition,* in which he holds that Shaw should be regarded as "the last of the Victorian men of letters" in spite of the fact that he lived and was active until the mid-point of the twentieth century:

> In 1914, Shaw was fifty-eight. It is no denial of his extraordinary abilities to say that his mind at that time had already been completely formed and that his future experience would not change his *Weltanschauung*. At this point the war brought about a complete change in the *Zeitgeist* of the modern world. (Indeed the early years of the twentieth century may well be called, in accordance with the terminology of Halévy's *Histoire du peuple anglais au XIXᵉ siècle,* the epilogue to the nineteenth century.) Shaw was unable to acclimate himself to the catastrophic atmosphere of our era; furthermore, he was unable to understand that the fundamen-

tal problem of the twentieth century is the survival of Western civilization itself rather than the establishment of a more efficient and equitable economy.[14]

One should observe, I think, that the survival of Western civilization and the establishment of a more efficient and equitable economy are probably not two separate issues but two sides of the same. Without the latter, the former is surely put in doubt. People of the 1970's are becoming aware of this again, the crisis of the two world wars having become history by now while social injustice very clearly persists and the threat to Western civilization is by no means past.

Even so, the point is that Shaw's philosophy and temperament were such that he did not share the apocalyptic sense of doom, of cultural disintegration and spiritual chaos that most of the Western world did experience in the aftermath of the Great War. He came closest to it in *Heartbreak House*, his semi-Chekhovian play (written with Chekhov in mind) that is a very poignant and perceptive testimony to the sense of a catastrophic ending brought on by the advent of the war. Even there, however, he did not capture the desperate sense of loss and the urgency of a new cultural synthesis that marked more "modern" art of the time and was soon to be epitomized by T. S. Eliot's *The Waste Land*.

Given who he was and what he thought, Shaw apparently could not believe that the wellsprings of culture might have become poisoned or—the more radical belief to which many came—that life is a horrible joke in which man's efforts to realize the divinity within himself is, as Sartre was one day to say, "a useless passion." Shaw's passion for taking hold of the ship and steering it (see his Don Juan and also Captain Shotover in *Heartbreak House*), so admirable in most contexts, may in others become a liability, particularly when one is insufficiently prepared to notice the demonic nature of certain political situations. This is the way one can best understand Shaw's professed admiration in the 1930's for those mighty steerers of ships of state, Stalin, Mussolini, and Hitler, each devoted to programs, however different, that bore the name of "socialism." I do not suggest that Shaw was taken in by

14 Norman, Okla.: University of Oklahoma Press, 1958, p. viii.

labels, but it is interesting that he had no use for Franco. In him he immediately spotted the aristocratic and reactionary element. The others were radical. They aimed to construct "new" societies officially based on egalitarianism. That their radicalism might be evil rather than good Shaw did not for a long time perceive, he who did not think in terms of good and evil but in the quite different terms of perfection and imperfection. He remained a believer in progress while the world was experiencing a moral retrogression at least as bad as, if not worse than, any previous one in its history. Shaw's belief in progress was impervious to "setbacks," for it was never empirically grounded. It was a tenet of faith, being, as I have said, a secularized version of Providence. The path of secularization had led through Blake, Hegel, Goethe, René Strauss, Henry George, Marx, Schopenhauer, Nietzsche, and Bergson.

Shaw's popularity as a playwright and pundit increased throughout his lifetime, all the while that he became a figure quite cut off from the spirit of the age. Whether that paradoxical state of affairs was good or bad for his playwriting is hard to say. Most of his plays after 1918 are poor. Among them are to be found *Back to Methuselah* (1918–1920), *The Apple Cart* (1929), *Too True to Be Good* (1931), *On the Rocks* and *Village Wooing* (1933), *The Simpleton of the Unexpected Isles* (1934), *The Millionairess* (1936), *Geneva* (1938), *In Good King Charles's Golden Days* (1939), *Bouyant Billions* (1947), and *Why She Would Not* (1949).

The list is impressive, the more so for a man aged sixty-four to ninety-three, but it does not bespeak a talent in its maturity. Yet in the early part of this same period are to be found *Heartbreak House* and *Saint Joan*. They belong in the same grouping because they could not have been written in prewar times, yet they are unlike the rest because of their mastery and depth. The greater one is *Saint Joan*, of which, since it is one of the glories of the modern theater, I must give some account.

Earlier I called *Saint Joan* an extravaganza, which may seem an inappropriate name for a work many have considered to be a great modern tragedy. "Extravaganza," however, is closer than "tragedy" to Shaw's own description, "a chronicle play," and there is no doubt that when speaking of *Saint Joan* we must find some way to refer, as "tragedy" does not, to the wide expanses upon which the play manages in six scenes and an epilogue to open. The play is extravagant (i.e., lavish) in its thought, its language, its pageantry, its appeal to religious and heroic emotions, and in the scope it gives to acting talent. It manages to be a pageant and a drama both at once. It is a history play second only to the best of Shakespeare's, and in respect of its originality in historical thinking it is superior to them. Only a mind genuinely magnanimous could have conceived it, and only a very rich dramatic talent could have composed it.

The play has a very clear rising and falling action, supplemented by an epilogue. There are two climaxes, one at the end of the third scene when Joan's forces are at full tide and another in Scene vi when she withdraws the recantation the court has got from her by trickery and faces the stake. The first is a climax of rising expectations; the second, of self-awareness in the heroine. With respect to strict form, therefore, and excluding the Epilogue, we have an Aristotelian tragedy: the movement through purpose, passion, and perception (the triad discussed in the foregoing chapter) is clear and convincing. Joan undertakes to unite France and rid it of the English. At the moment when this purpose, at once nationalistic and religious, is apparently assured, antithetical forces rush in from every side, causing the heroine to fall into a period of suffering focused ultimately in her trial, conviction, and martyrdom. The "flaw" in her that brings this about will occupy us shortly, for its nature is integral to Shaw's concept of history and his reason for writing the play. At the moment of her most intense suffering, which is when she learns that in spite of her recantation she is to be imprisoned for life, Joan comes to her clearest perception of reality: she must not recant and may not submit to imprisonment, for that would be, while living, to forsake life. It is better, while dying, to live.

JOAN (*rising in consternation and terrible anger*): Perpetual imprisonment! Am I not then to be set free?

LADVENU (*mildly shocked*): Set free, child, after such wickedness as yours! What are you dreaming of?

JOAN: Give me that writing. (*She rushes to the table; snatches up the paper; and tears it into fragments.*) Light your fire: do you think I

dread it as much as the life of a rat in a hole? . . . You promised
me my life; but you lied (*indignant exclamations*). You think that
life is nothing but not being stone dead. It is not the bread and
water I fear: I can live on bread: when have I asked for more? It is
no hardship to drink water if the water be clean. Bread has no sorrow
for me, and water no affliction. But to shut me from the light of the
sky and the sight of the fields and flowers; to chain my feet so that
I can never again ride with the soldiers nor climb the hills; to make
me breathe foul damp darkness, and keep from me everything that
brings me back to the love of God when your wickedness and foolish-
ness tempt me to hate Him: all this is worse than the furnace in the
Bible that was heated seven times. I could do without my warhorse;
I could drag about in a skirt; I could let the banners and the trum-
pets and the knights and soldiers pass me and leave me behind as
they leave the other women, if only I could still hear the wind in the
trees, the larks in the sunshine, the young lambs crying through the
healthy frost, and the blessed blessed church bells that send my angel
voices floating to me on the wind. But without these things I cannot
live; and by your wanting to take them away from me, or from any
human creature, I know that your counsel is of the devil, and that
mine is of God. His ways are not your ways. He wills that I go
through the fire to His bosom; for I am His child, and you are not
fit that I should live among you. That is my last word to you.
   (*The soldiers seize her.*)[15]

After this, Joan is excommunicated and abandoned to "the secular arm" to be burned. What is the "flaw" that has led her to this
fate?

When we ask this question about a Sophoclean or Shakespearean
tragic hero, we expect to find, in answer, some moral fault such as
pride, anger, scrupulous hesitation, or the like, which, though
blended with the hero's virtues, is at variance with Divine Will or
the orderly structure of the cosmos. Hence, however evocative of
pity and fear, the nemesis of high tragedy is the instrument of *diké*,
or justice. Obviously that is not the case for Joan. Her condemnation is an injustice. Therefore her "flaw" is not a fault but a virtue.
The name of it is genius. Nevertheless, like the high tragic hero,

15 Quoted from the edition published by Penguin Books (Harmondsworth, Eng.,
1967), pp. 137–138.

Joan brings about her own destruction. It is in the nature of genius to do so. The reason takes us to the heart of Shaw's interpretation of history.

The function of genius is to raise mankind from one stage of evolution to another. (I speak, of course, of a moral and spiritual evolution, not of that materialistic, purely biological Darwinian theory Shaw always opposed.) To do his work, the genius is born, as it were, out of due time. He is the embodiment of that which the life force intends to make of all mankind, the natural child of life's true vitality and purpose. His relation to history is therefore dialectical: he represents what history is in its genuine aim and purpose, but he stands athwart what history actually is at the present moment, its existing stage of development and insight. The genius understands the present better than it understands itself, because he sees it through the eyes of its future. One can also express this by saying that the genius views history according to its potential rather than its actuality, he interprets it as a dynamic breaking through existing form. He is, as a consequence, a threat to the *status quo,* whose representatives destroy him. Joan is destroyed by the Church and the feudal lords because she is, as Shaw depicts her, the avatar of Protestantism and nationalism, and the French king she has raised up, Charles Dauphin, is neither strong enough nor yet willing to save her. She brings destruction upon herself through her inability to compromise.

In this perspective, with its rather Hegelian overtones, history is always out of phase with itself. Partly it thrusts forward to the new and higher stage, partly it pulls back into the familiar. The result is a clash, some aspect of which almost every scene of Shaw's every play describes, which accounts for his pervasively dialectical style. But in *Saint Joan,* at least, there is no emergent synthesis. To rule it out is the function of the Epilogue. It is set in 1456, a quarter century after Joan's death, but because it includes an emissary from the year 1920, the year of Joan's canonization, it takes place as if in the present. Although nationalism and Protestantism have meanwhile come into their own and although Joan has become a cultural heroine and a saint, her offer to return to life is met with dismay. Not even now, when her particular battles have been won, is she welcome in the world, where the *status quo* has ever to defend itself against incursions of the future-oriented spirit of life. "O God that madest this beautiful earth," the lovely Joan implores at the play's conclusion, "when will it be ready to receive Thy saints? How long, O Lord, how long?"

When . . . ready . . . how long? The key words here as throughout are *time* words, and the tragedy, if that should be the term, is of preparations and resistances. But perhaps the term is comedy.

In spite of the play's tragic pattern, which, if insisted upon, must lead one to consider the Epilogue a superfluous addendum of poignancy, one should perceive the preponderance of the comic in the play. The whole work is informed by a vision of history that is essentially comic. Of course, affairs turn out badly, and the Epilogue makes it clear they would so again if the saint or her equivalent returned. But that very hint of repetition (a bit more than a hint, in fact) is itself a comic flair. A proper tragic hero is unique. He must, at least, be considered so within the convention of the play. Joan is anything but unique. She is merely the fifteenth-century representative of her type. There were others before (Socrates, Jesus, and Caesar are Shaw's usual examples), and there will be more hereafter.

Shaw is at pains, for instance, to show that there is nothing all that special about Joan's hearing "voices." What they instruct her to do is plain common sense. To be sure (this is part of the joke), common sense is not all that common. Yet it is the native property of mankind, and no special revelation is required to account for it.

The same goes for Joan's mission. If she were a proper tragic heroine, whether religious or secular, it would have to be maintained that her mission was, in principle, given to her and no one else. "O cursed spite that I [not Horatio, not Laertes] was born to set it right." Joan, however, insists that what she is doing could be done by anybody if only they would. God's business, she tells the dauphin, is every man's business. In their failure to do what it is obvious they ought to do, and what Joan does, except in her brief moment of recantation, without blinking an eye, all the characters in the play reveal themselves as comic figures. Much of Shaw's art resides in depicting their comic natures with deft variety and gradation. The gamut is run from the satirized chauvinism of the English chaplain de Stogumber through the bafflement and startled admiration of Robert de Baudricourt, the irrelevance and petulance of Charles Dauphin, the worldly hypocrisy of the bishop of Beauvais, the ponderous practicality of the earl of Warwick, and so on. Even the Inquisitor, whose role might be imagined to cause fear and who is never *laughable,* is seen through Shaw's eyes of detachment. He is so precisely *located* in his historical function that he cannot become a figure of terror.

In fact, Shaw puts into the Inquisitor's mouth, as he does with all the characters, a better and more convincing rationale for his function than the historical records provide. This is necessary in order to maintain the dialectical presentation, and so well is it done that few spectators have ever listened to the Inquisitor's long speech early in Scene vi without being astonished by its brilliance.

There are two more points to make about the play's comic character. The first has to do with Shavian anachronisms. Here is a well-known example. Cauchon, bishop of Beauvais, is talking of Joan with the earl of Warwick, and the time is almost a century before Luther:

CAUCHON: . . . I see now that what is in your mind is not that this girl has never once mentioned the Church, and thinks only of God and herself, but that she has never once mentioned the peerage, and thinks only of the king and herself.

WARWICK: Quite so. These two ideas of hers are the same idea at bottom. It goes deep, my lord. It is the protest of the individual soul against the interference of priest or peer between the private man and his God. I should call it Protestantism if I had to find a name for it.

The anachronistic "Protestantism" brings to the audience a smile, if not a laugh. But the point goes much deeper than if Shaw were simply making a schoolboy's joke. Beyond the specific anachron*isms,* the play is written with an anachronistic *quality,* which flavors every scene, every strong encounter between the personages, every characterization, and determines gradually the stance one shall take with respect to the entire action. It is Shaw's principal device for achieving the wide scope of the play, to which I referred earlier. I can describe this best by use of a cinematic image. Though its structure is more tight than most historical plays, which tend to be very episodic, this play manages to avoid what I may call a historical close-up. (Think, for instance, how different in style, pace, and scope it is from Carl Dreyer's film *Joan of Arc*, made in the same decade.) It is as if Shaw had pulled his camera back to a point (it is the point he occupies habitually) where we can see not only the events of 1431 and thereabout but also the movement of history between then and now, as well as much of what came before. In short, the play is full of allusions, far too many to count, to the historical knowledge we already possess, and this it interprets at every step in light of that spiritual (and historical) avatar whom Shaw takes Joan to have been. She is at once a figure *in* history, a figure out of phase with her own time, and one who makes visible the dialectical process *of* history. She is an object lesson whose example convicts men of meanness, but she is also a consolation and a hope. For in spite of her death, Joan lives. As the conclusion of the Epilogue leaves her in possession of the stage (albeit with nothing else on it), so she is also left in possession of her epoch in history; and as a genius of the life force, she represents that which cannot ultimately fail.

We have been led, thus, to the final point regarding the play's comic character—its affirmation in historical terms (as Joan's final speech before the Epilogue affirms it in personal terms) of the goodness of life. This point and the previous one are two aspects of the same thing. The play's scope is a function of Shaw's posture of detachment from the action (which does not preclude many kinds of involvement) expressed through the anachronistic quality of the style. This detachment, in turn, is a function of Shaw's basic affirmation of the creative goodness of life.

Tragedy requires a vision informed by the belief that the world is so split between powers of good and powers of evil that man cannot succeed in his noblest endeavors. The more he succeeds the more will he fail, and he must therefore prove his heroic or moral (i.e., individual) superiority over a morally inferior cosmos. Christianity tends, obviously, to dissipate such a vision, but its Western (Roman) orthodox form does not obliterate it, because the Fall is taken so seriously that the moral nature of the world is rendered at least ambiguous if not, as in certain heretical doctrines, given over to dualism. Hegel tried to show that the divisions manifest in tragedy can be understood as aspects of historical dialectic, thesis and antithesis clashing in the tragic agon at any particular time in history, but not the result of any ultimate dualism and tending, in the long course of history, toward a synthesizing unity. Thus, tragedy is the result of man's historical finitude, a condition that history itself will ultimately overcome by the process of ever more perfect realization of its own Idea.

Shaw, more than any other modern playwright, realized that the Hegelian view transmutes tragedy into a species of comedy. It does so, not by negating tragedy, but by fulfilling it. This is implicit in the philosophical detachment, or transcendence, of Hegel's perspective. Introduced to that, one may either reject it as knowing too much, the way Kierkegaard did in his preference for the paradoxical state of finitude, or he may push it forward, as Shaw did, to its basic, though qualified, affirmation of historical process. Dialectical divisions then serve to retain a certain tragic element in the picture and (no small benefit) to provide a springboard for wit (Shavian wit is never casual, it has too much dialectical force behind it), while the ultimate affirmation of the whole finds expression in comic distance.

The marvel of *Saint Joan,* through and beyond its extraordinary theatrical vividness, is the way it blends and caresses these several elements so that each shines in a well-nigh pure aesthetic light. A production can go wrong by stressing either the tragic or the comic so much that the irony of their combination is lost. But one can also go wrong by failing to see that this irony is of a classical type, based on a knowledge transcendent to experience, rather than of that more characteristically modern type that despairs of such knowledge and thus makes irony the master rather than the servant of a world view.

Shaw's virtue was that, in spite of his empiricism, he did not draw his opinions from experience. He got them from his agile theoretical intelligence and from his faith—there is no other word —in the eventual perfection of man. His limitation was the corollary of that: he was often so insensitive to experience that he could not let it teach him its own delicate mysteries. In this respect, he was the opposite of Chekhov.

Shaw was one of the culminators of nineteenth-century drama. Of the four who belong to this group—Shaw, Chekhov, Strindberg, and Ibsen—it is Shaw who brings us to the end of that age which died at the beginning of the Great War. Shaw lived until 1950. His work in the thirty-six years from 1914 to the end of his life was by no means negligible, seeing that it included not only *Heartbreak House* but also *Saint Joan*. Shaw was not equipped, however, to take account of that great rending of the spirit which occurred when Europe's age of liberty, revolution, and progress ended in a paroxysm of self-slaughter. In his attempt to cope with the new and disheartening situation, Shaw often seemed to be flailing at the wind. His personality, always vigorous, came to appear more important than his creations. The realities he could mould into dramatic shape seemed to have fled. He was more subject to the destructive character of time than his own philosophy or his longevity and wit would lead one to suppose.

There are ironies that Shaw, the ironist, was not able to perceive. One of them is that the reality of evil, which he so consistently explained away, should have blatantly asserted itself in the new age he worked so hard to bring in.

Drama has traditionally represented evil by two means—through the depiction of characters who are villains or at least flawed by some villainous trait and through the representation of fate as malevolent. Being a comic writer, Shaw pictured fate as unfateful. He turned it into a destiny of benevolent purpose. As for villains, it was part of Shaw's twisting of dramatic conventions to show that the villains were no more villainous than the good guys. Conceiving all character as function, he had no room for the notion that a character might *be* good or evil. This upset conventional opinions and in that respect was liberating and useful, but it entailed an unfortunate corollary. It meant that the human condition could no longer be understood as participation in a struggle between good and evil. The concept of evil disappeared, and the dramatic dualism of man's moral ambivalence was turned into a mighty spectacle of the progressive realization of the good.

One of the ironies of the history of thought in the twentieth century is that the relativizing of absolutes, so characteristic of the nineteenth century, has proceeded apace, while at the same time the reality of evil as a surd force acting in and upon man has become more and more evident. As this has happened, Shaw has had more and more to be regarded as a nineteenth rather than a twentieth-century figure.

Those who have helped more than Shaw to fashion the drama of the twentieth century have been men of the European continent who did not take many cues from him and whose methods were born of an agony that was alien to him. We must say that while Shaw's roots were deeply embedded in the modern drama as it evolved in the nineteenth century, his own flowering was something unique, something it has been almost impossible for others to learn directly from. More than any other major modern playwright, Shaw transcends the theater. More than any other, he seems to exhaust, all by himself, the particular kind of playwriting he devised. He took the comic aspect of nineteenth-century romanticism absolutely as far as it could go without its turning bitter. But there were deeper ironies than his, steeped in bitterness, and with their darker spirit the new age was unfortunately to find a closer and sadder communion.

12. THE AMERICAN THEATER

SHORTLY BEFORE World War I there began a number of artistic movements that, taken together, initiated what is now popularly known as "modern" art. These movements came into their own during the war's aftermath. Cubist painting began around 1910. Stravinsky's *Sacre du printemps* (*Rite of Spring*) moved its first audience to raucous demonstration in 1913. His *L'Histoire du soldat* had its première in 1918. Joyce's *Ulysses,* begun in 1914, was published in 1922, the same year as Eliot's *The Waste Land.* The first Dada publication came out in 1917, and André Breton issued the *Surrealist Manifesto* in 1924.

The period of "classic modern," as it is now sometimes called, lasted through World War II and *its* aftermath, while since the late 1950's we have witnessed a groping after a new direction, the merits of which cannot yet be determined.

The American theater, insofar as it enters into the development of Western theater generally, is coextensive with the "classic modern" period. For this reason I shall use the account of its flourishing as a means to transfer attention from the essentially nineteenth-century purview that has occupied us so far to the twentieth-century developments that will be our concern henceforth. Such a strategy should not be taken to imply that the American theater embodies the aesthetic norm by which other theater in this period is to be judged. On the contrary, the American theater in most respects dimly mirrors the European theater, of which it has always been an extension. Thus, the perspective on the American theater adopted here will perhaps not become entirely clear or seem fully justified until, in later chapters, the narrative of the European development is completed.

There is one respect, however, in which American theater is particularly instructive for the understanding of all theater in the past fifty years, and that is its exposure to the forces of change brought into modern society by technology. In my opinion these forces have been extremely hard on the theater. They dissolve its public into a mass audience, which then deserts the theater in favor of mass media, mass sporting events, and such technological "entertainments" as the automobile. These forces splinter the theater public into fragments holding specialized points of view, making it ever more difficult for the playwright to address an audience as if it were truly representative of *respublica*. The theater becomes private, the affair of various coteries, and thus loses its traditional *raison d'être*. (I shall say more on this subject in the Epilogue.)

Certain creations of technology, especially rapid transportation, the motion picture, and electronic communication, also tend to destroy the aesthetic basis of theater, which lies in the appreciation of finite space. In societies in which everyone is on the move, theater is felt as anachronistic because it fixes the audience and the players in a certain place and a certain time. It has not the spatial fluidity of the screen, the microphone, and the tape recorder. When Artaud, as we shall see in Chapter 14, called for a theater that would be a "poetry of space," he was displaying simultaneously a sure feeling for theater and a culturally reactionary posture.

The American theater has been particularly exposed to the cultural forces induced by technology not only because America is perhaps the country in which modern technology is most advanced but also because American theater is at the mercy of the box office, having had only once, through the Federal Theater Project, and with unhappy results, any sizable support from the state. In America, more than elsewhere, theater is a business. It therefore feels acutely the tension between artistic aspiration and popular taste. The story of the American theater is that of an attempt, not entirely successful, to create an indigenous art for a mass audience that is highly materialistic and is experiencing an astonishingly rapid growth in material power and technical knowledge. It is no accident that the international importance of American theater followed the growth of American military and economic power.

American drama came to be taken seriously in Europe only with Eugene O'Neill (1888–1953). Before him, Clyde Fitch was the only American playwright who gained much notice there, and he did not recommend himself to those concerned with an artistic and forward-looking theater. A number of American actors and actresses had been received favorably in England and on the Continent—for instance, Edwin Booth in the late 1850's, Joe Jefferson in the mid-'60's, and John Drew, Ada Rehan, James Lewis, and G. H. Gilbert in the '80's—but on the whole, American drama was ignored on the other side of the Atlantic until O'Neill was noticed there in the 1920's. In 1923 Gaston Baty successfully produced *The Emperor Jones* at the Odéon, three years after the play's première in New York. In 1926 Alexander Tairov in Moscow did *The Hairy Ape* and *Desire Under the Elms.* Georges and Ludmilla Pitoëff mounted *The Hairy Ape* in settings of radical design in Paris in 1929. The same year Armand Salacrou wrote a long article on the American theater in the journal *Correspondance,* published by the Atelier of Charles Dullin. Tracing the history of the American theater from 1767, Salacrou gave climactic importance to the Provincetown Players and the work of O'Neill. His article is one of only three on American drama that appeared in the voluminous publications of the avant-garde theaters of Paris from the Théâtre Libre to the Théâtre Louis Jouvet.[1]

By the turn of the century the divisive feelings occasioned by the American Civil War had been more or less overcome. The settlement of the American continent was symbolically completed with the admission of Arizona to the Union as the forty-eighth state in 1912. The consolidation of industry on a nation-wide scale occurred before World War I, as the antitrust acts of 1890 and 1914 make clear. Of most importance for the theater was the great wave of urbanization that took place at this time. New York City com-

---

[1] *Correspondance,* No. 11 (Dec. 1929), p. 21. See André Veinstein, *Du Théâtre Libre au Théâtre Louis Jouvet* (Paris: Éditions Billaudot, 1955), p. 235.

bined its five boroughs into one metropolitan government in 1898 and built its first subway in 1904. In this period the American theater took on the aspect it has worn until very recently, with New York City considered the theatrical capital of a "benighted" hinterland.

Considered in relation to the development of modern drama as a whole, the American theater prior to World War I was not significant. Throughout the nineteenth century there was a great deal of activity, but aside from the reputations of certain actors little that is memorable remains. A few works can be seen, in retrospect, to have foreshadowed the growth of realism that was to come. There was, for instance, *The Poor of New York*, produced in 1857 by the ubiquitous Dion Boucicault. This work, adapted from a French model entitled *Les Pauvres de Paris*, was the first of a large number of plays that have depicted the slum life of the city, including Edward Sheldon's *Salvation Nell* (1908), Elmer Rice's *Street Scene* (1929), Sidney Kingsley's *Dead End* (1935), and the musical *West Side Story* (1957). Similarly, it was Boucicault's *The Octoroon* (1859) that introduced the racial question to the American stage.

Students of the growth of realism also cite Steele MacKaye's *Hazel Kirke* (1880), a drama without a villain and a kind of American third cousin to Friedrich Hebbel's *Maria Magdalena* (1844). They note the stage representations of the Irish-American community written and produced by Edward Harrigan in the 1870's and 1880's, which moved William Dean Howells to say that the now-forgotten Harrigan was "part of the great tendency toward the faithful representation of life which is now animating fiction." [2]

Let note also be taken of Bronson Howard's popular romance, *Shenandoah* (1888), which brought the Civil War onto the stage by means of a tale about lovers separated by the conflict. More interesting now is James A. Herne's *Margaret Fleming*, an Ibsenesque piece, attacking the double standard in marital fidelity, which Herne and his wife staged in a small hall in Boston in 1891,

[2] *Harper's Magazine*, July 1886. Quoted in Barnard Hewitt, *Theatre U.S.A., 1668 to 1957* (New York: McGraw-Hill, 1959), pp. 248–249. I am indebted to Professor Hewitt's richly documented book for much information in this chapter.

the same year that J. T. Grein founded his Independent Theatre in London. There was to be no successful theater on this model in America until the Provincetown Players began operation in 1916, but Herne made a try. Unable to secure a suitably intimate theater, Herne took over a lecture hall and staged his play before black velvet hangings.

The story of *Margaret Fleming* is that of a wife who leaves her adulterous husband, meets him again after some years, almost forgives him, but insists that they part once more, agreeing to be friends but knowing that they cannot respect each other as man and wife. The play was popular among a few avant-garde enthusiasts, but it had no other success. Audiences and critics who a year or two later were to object to Ibsen's *Ghosts* as "sewerage" were not likely to be warm toward an American imitator of the Norwegian "crank," as Ibsen was frequently called.

Perhaps the best talent among American playwrights of the pre-World War times belonged to William Vaughn Moody (1869–1910). Moody's *The Great Divide,* presented by Henry Miller and Margaret Anglin in 1906, and *The Faith Healer* (1910) were the best examples of American realism up to their time. The most prolific talent was that of Clyde Fitch (1865–1909). Though he died when he was forty-four, he had written more than forty plays, plus several translations and adaptations. It was in Fitch's *Captain Jinks of the Horse Marines* (1901) that Ethel Barrymore became a star.

In the first two decades of the new century, American theater attempted to describe the highly industrialized and commercial society that was then taking shape in the nation. For instance, Edward Sheldon, after having scored a notable success with *Salvation Nell,* in which Minnie Maddern Fiske displayed a new, naturalistic style of acting, went on to focus upon interracial tension in *The Nigger* (1909) and upon machine politics in *The Boss* (1911). Sheldon remained a significant theatrical figure right through the '20's and '30's by collaborating with Sidney Howard and others.

Contemporaneously with the theater's increased drive toward realism and social concern there occurred an important change in the way the theater was managed; and while this came about partly because of the demands of realistic staging, it also tended to compromise all efforts to treat the theater as an art. The change I speak of was the shift of power in the theater from the actor-manager to the producer. It had been happening gradually in the last quarter of the nineteenth century. Now, owing to a few very strong personalities like Charles Frohman, Augustin Daly, and David Belasco, it became a *fait accompli*. In 1895–6 Frohman combined interests with Sam Nixon, Fred Zimmerman, Al Hayman, Marc Klaw, and Abraham Erlanger to form what was called The Syndicate, a theatrical empire based upon the ownership of theaters and the mounting of plays to fill them. This powerful trust was later succeeded by that of the Shuberts. The Syndicate was fought by certain producer-directors, such as Belasco, and by playwrights, such as James A. Herne, but its power was secure. Its holdings were vast. Between 1900 and 1910 Frohman alone owned theaters in New York and London worth over five million dollars, paid salaries to over ten thousand employees in the amount of thirty-five million dollars a year, and spent half a million a year in advertising.[3] At this time "the road" was built up for the export of New York's theatrical fare to the rest of the country. Plays had, of course, long toured the length and breadth of the land, but not as a mere adjunct of the New York theater. With The Syndicate, New York became the theatrical capital of the whole nation, as it also at this time became the nation's financial capital.

No sooner had this structure been formed than the theater began to face the most serious competition in all its history, the motion picture. It was the destiny of the movies to take over the function of providing romance and spectacle for the man in the street— that is, to appropriate exactly the function The Syndicate had been formed to fulfill. *The Great Train Robbery* was made in 1903, which was the same year that Victor Herbert's *Babes in Toyland* was produced on the stage. Griffith's film *Birth of a Nation* came in 1915, *Intolerance* in 1916. By 1918 the movies had cut deeply into the theater's business, and in 1923, the year John Barrymore went to Hollywood, the movies began to hire away the great stage performers. The first commercial talking picture, *The Jazz Singer,* was released in 1927, which led to a vast Hollywood

<hr/>

3 Hewitt, *op. cit.,* p. 257.

importation of playwrights, who were given tickets on luxury rail-road trains and shipped west. The American theater began to become obsolete in the very decade in which it came out of the shadows into an international light.

In this period of ferment there were certain important contacts between American theater and the more creative parts of the European. The Abbey Theatre visited New York in November 1911, creating a stormy protest.[4] The following January, Max Reinhardt brought his first work to this country, a production called *Sumurun,* which was an Arabian Nights story mounted with designs by Ernst Stern. Thus, within three months New York saw one of the best examples of European realism and also the more poetic staging that was beginning to take its place.

In early 1915, owing to the fortunes of war, Harley Granville-Barker, one of the most literate and sensitive directors whom the English have produced in modern times, found himself in New York to stage a series of plays at Wallack's Theatre. His offerings were an adroit mixture of the old and the new: *Androcles and the Lion, The Man Who Married a Dumb Wife* (by Anatole France), *Midsummer Night's Dream,* and *The Doctor's Dilemma.* Walter Prichard Eaton described the innovations the director made:

> The first thing he did on taking possession of Wallack's Theatre was to build the stage out over the orchestra pit and the first two rows of seats, with entrances made through the former stage boxes. At the front of this almost Shakespearean platform stage were neither footlights nor rail. People in the front row of seats could literally touch the feet of the actors when they came to the edge. The next thing he did was to install arc lamps for illumination, combined with white spots from the balconies. Thus all the light comes from overhead, and is as nearly pure white as possible. The next thing he did was to build a small revolving stage twenty feet back of the proscenium opening, for use in "Androcles and the Lion." [5]

4 A riot broke out at the first New York performance of *The Playboy of the Western World.* (See above, p. 139, for a description of a similar fracas in Dublin.) In the main, however, the visit of the Abbey was well received, and it gave the American theater some players and playwrights to emulate.
5 From *Plays and Players* (Cincinnati: Stewart & Kidd, 1916). Quoted in Hewitt, *op. cit.,* p. 317.

For *The Man Who Married a Dumb Wife* Granville-Barker chose a young, virtually unknown American designer named Robert Edmond Jones, who later became the greatest of America's theater artists and was the man who, more than any other, brought the European renewal of theater practice to the American stage.

In addition to Granville-Barker the war brought another and even greater director to the United States. On November 27, 1917, Jacques Copeau and the Compagnie du Vieux Colombier opened the first of two seasons at the old Garrick Theatre, which was rebuilt and decorated to Copeau's specifications. At this point the theatrical renewal in America touches one of the most important theater movements in Europe, at which we must take a brief look.

Copeau was of a generation born into theatrical modernism. The year of his birth, 1879, was the year in which Zola's *L'Assommoir* had its première in Paris and Ibsen's *A Doll's House* in Copenhagen. Having grown up in the theater atmosphere created by Antoine and Lugné-Poe, he came to maturity thinking that a second wave of theater reformation was needed. He assimilated the contributions of Appia, Craig, Fuchs, Stanislavski, and Meierhold. In method and theory he was less doctrinaire than any of these, prepared to learn what he could from each; but in his passion to reform the theater from the ground up without compromise he was the most doctrinaire of all—or, to be more exact, the most ascetic. In his formative days he moved among men of letters. He wrote drama criticism for the journals *L'Ermitage, Grande revue,* and *La Nouvelle Revue française.* For the last one he wrote the manifesto of the theater he founded: "Un Essai de renovation dramatique: le Théâtre du Vieux Colombier." [6] Other founders of his theater also associated with *La Nouvelle Revue* included Gaston Gallimard, Jean Schlumberger, and André Gide.

Le Théâtre du Vieux Colombier, located in semi-obscurity at 21, rue du Vieux-Colombier, on the left bank, opened on October 15, 1913, with a bill comprising Molière's *L'Amour médecin* and Heywood's *A Woman Killed with Kindness.* In eight months the group mounted fifteen plays, most of them revivals but including also plays by Jean Schlumberger, Henri Ghéon, and Paul Claudel. In May there was an absolute triumph with *Twelfth Night,* which

[6] *La Nouvelle Revue française,* Sept. 1, 1913.

displayed for the first time in France the full verve and poetry of Shakespearean comedy. This production was as important to the renewal of French theater practice in the twentieth century as the visit of the English Shakespearean actors had been to the Parisian Romantics in 1827. It demonstrated that the simplicity, freedom, and fluidity of the new staging served better than other means the imaginative qualities in great dramatic writing. The Vieux Colombier, as done over by Copeau, had a simple, open stage with no front curtain. Its design, integral with that of the small auditorium, was strong, yet its greatest virtue was that it complemented the work of the actor, displaying his talents to the full.

Twelfth Night ended the first season of the Vieux Colombier, and before the next could begin war had broken out. Most of the company went into service. In 1915 Copeau went to Florence to see Gordon Craig, returning by way of Switzerland to visit Adolphe Appia. In January 1917 he was sent to give lectures in the United States at the behest of Georges Clemenceau, who made in this way a gesture of friendship toward the country he hoped to bring as an ally into the war. Later in the year Copeau's actors were released from military duty. They assembled in New York and put on two seasons of French plays. In spite of the performances' being in the French language, they drew healthy audiences and stirred much comment.

Religious fervor, which eventually led Copeau to abandon the theater, had not yet taken hold of him when he was in New York. At that time the theater itself was his religion. He was the most dedicated exponent of simplified staging and ensemble acting then working anywhere. He combined a purity of intention with diligent pursuit of an adequate technique for releasing the poetic power of a script. His two seasons' work in New York were crucial to his own development, which otherwise the war would have completely blocked, and they offered New York such an example of theater art as it could not have seen in any other way.

Meanwhile, Americans were beginning to renovate their own theater through efforts that originated outside of show business. Early in the 1900's George Pierce Baker began his 47 Workshop, an informal course in playwriting that he taught at Harvard until 1924 and later at Yale. This workshop gained considerable interest abroad among those interested in the new theater. Writers who studied with Professor Baker included Eugene O'Neill, S. N. Behrman, Sidney Howard, George Abbott, Philip Barry, Paul Osborn, George Sklar, and Albert Maltz.

In 1915 there was founded what would be called today an off-Broadway group, known as the Washington Square Players. It lasted until 1918, after which it was reorganized and turned into the Theater Guild. The year 1915 also saw the founding on Cape Cod of the Provincetown Players, led by George Cram Cook, Susan Glaspell, Robert Edmond Jones, and others. When these summer visitors to the Cape returned to New York, they converted a stable on Macdougal Street into the Provincetown Theater. There they grouped a number of very energetic talents around them, including some members of the Washington Square Players, and gave America its nearest equivalent to the Théâtre Libre of Paris. Their great discovery was a member of their own group, a man who had attached himself to them from the first, Eugene O'Neill.

O'Neill had published a small volume of plays called *Thirst* in 1914. The Provincetown Players put on his *Bound East for Cardiff* in the summer of 1916. Several of his one-act sea plays, including *The Long Voyage Home,* were put on at Macdougal Street thereafter. The short plays suited the limited resources of the small theater and its small company. But in 1920 the Provincetown Players rented the Morosco Theater uptown and put on the full-length *Beyond the Horizon,* which catapulted them and O'Neill into fame and won him a Pulitzer prize. "The performance of Eugene G. O'Neill's tragedy 'Beyond the Horizon' at the Morosco Theater," wrote Ludwig Lewisohn in *The Nation,* "establishes America's kinship with the stage of the modern world." [7] It was a judgment that time has not corrected.

Many critics have disliked O'Neill intensely. Others have tried to like him and failed. Even his champions have admitted that he lacked much sense of how to use the English language. Yet from 1920 to the present O'Neill has towered over all other American playwrights by virtue of his forcefulness, his variety, his thematic grandeur, and his near-tragic view of man. In spite of his Nobel

[7] Hewitt, *op. cit.,* p. 332.

prize, he is by no means a great literary figure, but as a considerable talent of the theater his position is secure.

American playwriting in the 1920's was prodigious. "In the ten years from 1920 to 1930," Barnard Hewitt writes, "as many talented playwrights appeared as in the preceding 170-odd years of American drama." [8] It was as if floodgates had been opened. O'Neill was not only the most talented of the lot, he was also the most prolific. During the decade 1920–1929 he wrote and had produced in New York nineteen plays. Fourteen of these were "full-length" plays, and some were a good deal longer than what is usually meant by that term. Of the total, no fewer than eight have remained highly significant for one reason or another. These are *Beyond the Horizon, The Emperor Jones* (1920), *Anna Christie* (1921), *The Hairy Ape* (1922), *All God's Chillun Got Wings* (1924), *Desire Under the Elms* (1924), *The Great God Brown* (1926), and *Strange Interlude* (1928).

Every play in that list is marked by O'Neill's peculiar way of combining naturalism and expressionism. *Beyond the Horizon, Anna Christie, All God's Chillun Got Wings,* and *Desire Under the Elms* are more easily classed as naturalistic works, the others as expressionistic, but it was O'Neill's pleasure to mix the forms. In this regard he was the child of both Wedekind and Strindberg, neither of whom he could match in artistry but both of whom he surpassed in the daring with which he tackled the perennial mysteries of life. Such ambition, or recklessness, is thought by some to have been his principal weakness, since it sometimes resulted in sophomoric philosophizing. What keeps this criticism from demolishing O'Neill is the ceaseless search for the apt dramatic form in which he engaged, plus the fact that his concern with man's fate was thoroughly grounded in his own tragic life.

In the second half of the decade O'Neill became more and more interested in the quest for a religious meaning in life. *Desire Under the Elms,* one of O'Neill's most tautly constructed works, does not show this quest directly but contains it just under the surface. The fate that controls the Cabot family has about it a mystery that is almost personal and requires a sort of Calvinist respect.

8 *Ibid.,* p. 381.

In *The Great God Brown* the use of masks and of pairs of complementary characters is designed to show the mystery of human personality, which O'Neill understood to be divided against itself because it is separated from its creative ground. Thus, he introduced the prostitute Sybil as the embodiment of the Earth Mother to whom man yearns to return. The Freudian implications of this figure were not as important to O'Neill as its more ancient, and partly Eastern, religious meaning. Many of the same concerns were present in the larger and then more fashionable play *Strange Interlude*. In *Lazarus Laughed,* which was begun in 1926 and performed in 1928 at the Pasadena Playhouse in California (it has never been done commercially in New York), O'Neill tried to express the religious impulse in positive, nontragic terms. The message that the resurrected Lazarus brings from the other side of the grave in this outlandish play is that "there is only laughter." The work is a kind of long stage poem laden with expressionistic devices. It fails partly for want of an adequate technique but also because O'Neill had no genuine feeling for the sublime, which he could well suggest only in the negative instances of man's separation from it.

When the unsuccessful *Dynamo* was produced in 1929, O'Neill stated plainly that he was engaged in a religious quest. He informed his audience that the play was the first of a planned trilogy "that will dig at the roots of the sickness of today as I feel it—the death of an old God and the failure of science and materialism to give any satisfying new one for the surviving primitive religious instinct to find a meaning for life in." [9] No major playwright of the twentieth century has devoted himself so fully to the romantic quest as O'Neill. He did it so consistently and with such extravagance that he seems almost an anachronism in this age. By temperament he possessed little of that irony which marks the best of twentieth-century drama and gives it a sharp cutting edge, but he was forced into a certain amount of it by the times in which he lived and by the dramatic forms which he imitated. Gradually, however, his quest turned into the modern query, and this drove him to more and more introspection during the 1930's and 1940's,

9 Quoted in Barrett H. Clark and George Freedley, eds., *A History of Modern Drama* (New York: Appleton-Century-Crofts, 1947), p. 690.

while most American drama was turning outward toward social concern.

In the mounting of his plays O'Neill had the collaboration of the best talent in the American theater. *The Emperor Jones*, produced at the Macdougal Street theater by the Provincetown Players, was directed by George Cram Cook and brilliantly designed by Cleon Throckmorton. *Anna Christie* was directed by Arthur Hopkins, who had directed Alla Nazimova in three of Ibsen's plays in 1918 and Gorki's *Lower Depths* in 1919. *Anna Christie* was designed by Robert Edmond Jones, as was *Desire Under the Elms*, and Jones directed *The Great God Brown*. In 1928 the Theater Guild, in an astonishing burst of energy, produced *Marco Millions* and *Strange Interlude* two weeks apart, the former designed by Lee Simonson, the latter by Jo Mielziner. It was a time of creative formation in American stagecraft as well as in playwriting.

Of the playwrights other than O'Neill who contributed to the flood of new writing that poured onto the stage in the '20's, one has to say that they had enormous energy and enthusiasm, that they were more talented than anyone had a right to expect given the previous history of the American theater, and that they were determined to create a national, living theater of which the country could be proud. At the same time it is necessary to observe that they had a penchant for the ephemeral; they wrote good plays that have for the most part gone with the wind.

This being so, it is not surprising that their greatest accomplishments were in the field of comedy. The glory of the '20's, apart from O'Neill, lies in the comic inventions of George S. Kaufman and Marc Connelly (*Dulcy*, 1920; *Beggar on Horseback*, 1924), S. N. Behrman (*The Second Man*, 1927), Philip Barry (*Holiday*, 1929, and four others before it), and George Kelly (*The Show-off*, 1924). A due appreciation of this comic talent remains to be written. That lies outside the scope of the present study, but whenever it is done it will show that in the comedy of the '20's and '30's the American stage reached its highest point of urbanity.

In 1923, three years after *The Emperor Jones* and one year after *The Hairy Ape*, Elmer Rice brought forth the most purely expressionistic play and perhaps the best example of the genre done in

America, *The Adding Machine*. The first part of this work, which describes the obsolescence of the individual, Mr. Zero, in the age of technology, is full of bitter irony and is excellent. The latter part, in which Mr. Zero returns from a most unsatisfying Paradise and capitulates to the system, is much less strong. At the end of the decade, Rice turned to naturalism in *Street Scene* (1929). Its picture of New York slum life, with its implicit call for the renovation of society, is drawn with great realism, but the play lives today only in the operatic version later made by Kurt Weill.

In the fall of 1924, Maxwell Anderson and Laurence Stallings created something of a landmark in American drama by drawing in *What Price Glory?* the first realistic picture of war the American stage had seen. In the same year came Sidney Howard's *They Knew What They Wanted;* two years later Howard wrote, in *The Silver Cord,* one of the first American melodramas based upon Freudian ideas, a genre that has occupied the American theater ever since.

John Howard Lawson, the Marxist playwright and theoretician of the art of drama, produced a socially concerned example of expressionism in 1923 in *Roger Bloomer,* following it two years later with *Processional*. These, among Lawson's best works, were important precursors of the left-wing theater of the next decade. The '20's also saw a number of plays dealing in various ways with the Negro in American society, including O'Neill's *All God's Chillun Got Wings* (1924). Others were DuBose Heyward's *Porgy* (1927), Paul Green's *In Abraham's Bosom* (1926), and the highly successful *Green Pastures* (1930), which Marc Connelly based upon Roark Bradford's stories, *Ol' Man Adam and His Chillun.*

The work of the decade was a mélange of Marx, Freud, folk material, expressionism, and realism. Except for important parts of the work of O'Neill, there was a virtual absence of internality in the plays of the period. That is, the aspect of life that has come to be called existential was hardly present at all, probably because American thought had not yet absorbed enough European philosophy to be able to deal with it and because of a conscious effort to avoid everything that smacked of romanticism. Irony was kept at a minimum. Lively as it was, the American theater was more sensitive to the stylistic innovations of European theater than to the profound content the styles had been invented to convey, a limitation that has endured in American theater to the present. Even the highly literate and perceptive Stark Young, one of the best of all American drama critics, found himself saying in 1923, on the occasion of the visit of the Moscow Art Theater to New York, that "Chekhov differs only in depth and technical perfection, not in kind, from Clyde Fitch." Young held that in Chekhov the Moscow players did not bring with them a drama that was "in any sense new." [10] Chekhov's radical newness went unnoticed while the American theater produced in great quantity playwriting that missed the new by trying for it too hard. Apart from comedy, and apart from O'Neill, the real achievements of the time lay in the work of stage designers like Robert Edmond Jones, Lee Simonson, Norman Bel Geddes, and Jo Mielziner. Beginnings were also made in the genre that was to become the most vital part of all American theater—the musical. Somewhere between the old and the new musical lay Rudolf Friml's *Rose Marie* of 1924. Three years later the first really modern example of the genre was produced: *Show Boat,* written by Edna Ferber and Oscar Hammerstein II, set to music by Jerome Kern, and designed by Joseph Urban. Urban proved in this work that the décor of a musical could be expressive as well as spectacular.

It was in this decade also that America experienced its first severe case of what Robert Brustein has recently called "repertory fever." In 1926 Eva Le Gallienne founded the Civic Repertory at the Fourteenth Street theater. It opened with *The Three Sisters* and played for six seasons, presenting thirty-four plays, including works by Ibsen, Chekhov, Benavente, Schnitzler, and Giraudoux. Repertory in this country has always been difficult, for it is purely a transplant. The great democracy of the New World has no tradition of patronage of the theater by the crown, out of which the important repertory theaters of Europe have grown. Neither the existence of university theaters nor the patronage of philanthropists and foundations, not even the work of stalwarts like Miss Le Gallienne, has been able to make up for this lack.

10 In Hewitt, *op. cit.,* p. 350.

The financial disaster that came at the end of the 1920's hit the theater hard. Although the theater did not collapse, it became the "invalid" it has since remained, and there came into it a note of desperation about its future. The building of new theaters in New York virtually stopped. Discerning persons became aware that there would never again be a mass audience for live theater, partly because it had become too expensive an art and partly because such an audience belonged henceforth to the movie house. To less-discerning persons the dream of a new popular theater remained, compromising all their efforts for integrity. The conflict between fascism on the one hand and democracy and socialism on the other promoted in many the ideal of a popular theater expressive of the aspirations of the working class. In no significant sense did a working-class audience for theater develop in this country—the movies became ever more popular, and there was no strong class consciousness anyway—yet it did happen that the theater audience of the '30's was the most engaged of any during this century. This audience had the clear notion that what was being done by playwrights, actors, and directors was being done for it and with the intention to promote responsive action. The universal testimony of those who worked in and observed the theater of that time is that going to the theater then produced an excitement far above any it has afforded more recently.

The theater devoted itself to social reform not only in the work of many playwrights but also in the formation of numerous institutions. The mainstay of the theater remained, of course, the commercial enterprise called Broadway, dominated by the Shubert family and catering to the same middle-class audience it depends upon today. Nevertheless, on the fringes of this commercial establishment there were organized a number of groups devoted to various kinds of politically leftward theater. The League of Workers' Theaters, organized in 1932, and the New Theater League, which succeeded it from 1935 to 1941, were communist. They came out of earlier amateur organizations such as the Worker's Laboratory Theater, the Proletbühne, and the Theater Collective. The Theater Union (1933–1937) and the Labor Stage (1936–1940), the latter sponsored by the International Ladies' Garment Workers'

Union, belonged to the period of the United Front. The Group Theater (1931–1941), organized by three employees of the Theater Guild—Harold Clurman, Cheryl Crawford, and Lee Strasberg—has been frequently accused of communist control. Although two of its most famous associates, Clifford Odets and Elia Kazan, admitted in 1952 that they had been members of the Communist Party, communists did not achieve direction over the Group Theater as they certainly had intended to do.[11]

The Federal Theater Project (1935–1939), being a creation of Congress, was of course not set up to bring about social reform, yet many of its productions had a lively social relevance. It was accused of communist sympathies and was killed by Congress partly for that reason, though Professor Himelstein says the real reason was that the theater "as such was hated by Puritans in Congress." [12]

Out of the Federal Theater grew the Mercury (1937–1941), in circumstances narrated below. Finally, there was the Playwrights' Company, liberal rather than "left-wing," organized in 1938 by Maxwell Anderson, S. N. Behrman, Sidney Howard, Elmer Rice, and Robert E. Sherwood for the purpose of producing their own plays. It was a sort of protest from within the establishment, not far removed from the commercial theater as such; but since its members were all men of liberal social concern, its offerings tended to be plays that hit upon public issues.

The American theater of the 1930's produced few plays that want resurrection today, but it brought to prominence a number of luminaries—Lillian Hellman, Sidney Kingsley, Elia Kazan, Harold Clurman, Cheryl Crawford, Robert Lewis, Lee Strasberg—who have dominated the "serious" American theater ever since, and it provided a number of theatrical "moments" that have become legend. Among them is January 6, 1935. At the Civic Repertory Theater on Fourteenth Street an evening was organized by the New Theater League and staged by the Group Theater. The bill included *Waiting for Lefty,* a one-act play by an unknown, Clifford Odets. Harold Clurman has described what went on:

11 The story of communist attempts to dominate the American theater in the 1930's has been told by Morgan Y. Himelstein in *Drama Was a Weapon* (New Brunswick, N.J.: Rutgers University Press, 1963).
12 *Ibid.,* p. 110.

The evening had opened with a mildly amusing one-act play by Paul Green. The audience, though attracted by the guest appearance of a good part of the Group company, had no idea of what was to follow.

The first scene of *Lefty* had not played two minutes when a shock of delighted recognition struck the audience like a tidal wave. Deep laughter, hot assent, a kind of joyous fervor seemed to sweep the audience toward the stage. The actors no longer performed; they were being carried along as if by an exultancy of communication such as I had never witnessed before. Audience and actors had become one. Line after line brought applause, whistles, bravos, and heartfelt shouts of kinship.

. . . When the audience at the end of the play responded to the militant question from the stage: "Well, what's the answer?" with a spontaneous roar of "Strike!" it was something more than a tribute to the play's effectiveness, more even than a testimony of the audience's hunger for constructive social action. It was the birth cry of the thirties . . . .

The audience, I say, was delirious. It stormed the stage, which I persuaded the stunned author to mount. People went from the theatre dazed and happy . . . .[13]

The leading agitator on stage was Elia Kazan. The direction was by Sanford Meisner and Clifford Odets. The play was performed for several Sunday evenings on Fourteenth Street, and in March it moved uptown under the Group's aegis. By June it had been performed in fifty American cities.

Another evening: June 15, 1937. Outside the Maxine Elliott Theater some 600 people waited to be admitted to the première of a new opera written by Marc Blitzstein and rehearsed by John Houseman and Orson Welles for Federal Theater Project 891. The opera, as the audience might have learned by rumor, was a kind of musical agitprop (a short didactic form the communists had introduced to this country through the Proletbühne) and "living newspaper" (an outgrowth of the agitprop developed by the Federal Theater as a way of dramatizing current events and issues). *The Cradle Will Rock,* as Blitzstein's opera was called, told in episodic form the story of workers and educators morally com-

---

[13] *The Fervent Years* (New York: Hill and Wang, 1957), pp. 138–139.

promised by the steel industry. The workers strike, and when they march on the courthouse their leader sings:

> There's a storm that's going to last until
> The final wind blows . . . And when the wind blows . . .
> The cradle will rock!

While the audience waited to go into the theater, it was announced that authorities of the Works Progress Administration (WPA) in Washington had, in effect, canceled the show by banning all Federal Theater openings until July.

> Orson Welles and John Houseman decided to open the show without government blessing. While Houseman was on the telephone trying to rent another theater, Welles was outside holding the audience. In an impromptu speech he told them to be patient, and he introduced Will Geer, one of the cast, to entertain them with two of the show's songs. When Houseman succeeded in renting the Venice Theatre, Seventh Avenue and Fifty-ninth Street, Welles invited the crowd to journey the twenty blocks north to see the opera that was banned. The young producers left behind the sets, the costumes, and the orchestra. Rather than face the charge of having prevented Federal Theatre employees from returning to private industry, WPA authorities granted the actors leave of absence.
>
> At this point Actors' Equity refused to allow the actors to appear on the stage because of certain union regulations. But Welles and Houseman successfully evaded this ban on a *stage* production by having the cast perform from the front row of the orchestra, from the aisles, and from the boxes. On the stage Marc Blitzstein sat in the spotlight against a blue backdrop and played the accompaniment on a "tinny piano." Orson Welles stood near him and explained the stage action as the actors sang.[14]

Thus began the Mercury Theater, led by Houseman and Welles. It went on to present Shakespeare's *Julius Caesar* in Nazi dress, Thomas Dekker's *The Shoemakers' Holiday,* Shaw's *Heartbreak House,* and the first American performance of Büchner's *Danton's Death.*[15]

[14] Himelstein, *op. cit.,* pp. 114–115.
[15] The last-named failed, as it did also in 1965 when it was revived at the Repertory Theater of Lincoln Center; in neither case did the American director understand that the genius of the play lies in the existential and ironic self-examination of Danton.

Throughout the '30's, from Paul Green's *The House of Connelly* (1931, the first Group Theater presentation) through Odets' *Awake and Sing* (presented in 1935 after *Lefty* but written earlier) and his *Golden Boy* (1937), and on to Anderson's *Key Largo* (1939) and Hellman's *The Little Foxes* (1939), the American drama was treated to a feast of competence. If one is tempted to condescend to this work now that times have changed and tastes are more jaded, he should remember that the more recent American theater has not for even one season manifested a sustained competence to match that of almost every season in the decade before World War II. In the twilight of its popularity, the American theater then possessed an authority and confidence it has not regained.

Yet from the historical point of view the work of that time led nowhere. It was good, often very good, without being great, but it contained virtually no seeds that were to germinate during and after the war. The reason for this is that the theater of the '30's in America, in spite of the feeling of newness that accompanied it, was in fact the last stand of Scribean drama. It did not all fit the Scribean pattern, strictly conceived, to be sure, but it was nevertheless of the ethos of the well-made play—entertainingly serious, topical, educational, often solid in technique, cleverly or at least carefully plotted, and incorrigibly middlebrow. It was often Marxist without being committed to Marxism, even when written by communists. It was often Freudian without Freud's tragic understanding of human destiny. It was frequently melodramatic, garnished with political or psychological themes, and when it avoided melodrama it seldom escaped pathos. It became rapidly dated, lacking that deep sense of the human predicament which saves great dramatic writing from the erosion of time. That it dug in where it was gave it strength; its weakness was that it did not dig deep. Even works then hailed as masterpieces, like Maxwell Anderson's *Winterset* (1935), now seem archaic. But the prolific Ander-

---

Instead, both times it was presented as a didactic history play showing the evils of a dictator's use of violence, thus pushing Robespierre to the center of the play, where he does not belong. The fate of this work in the American theater shows only too clearly how far that theater is from the ironic existentialism that has marked the best modern drama. It also shows how superficial has been most of our theater's understanding of the "relevance" of drama to public life.

son is the least of the playwrights who were then thought great, because he mistook pretentiousness for profundity.

In the '30's as in the '20's, the theater's genius for the ephemeral paid off better in comedy than in "serious" drama. One of Kaufman and Hart is worth half a dozen of Odets, evidencing the sharper vision and the greater awareness of finitude. In 1930 George S. Kaufman, who had been busy all through the '20's in collaborations with Marc Connelly, Edna Ferber, Alexander Woollcott, and others, teamed with Moss Hart, his junior by fifteen years, for the first of their many joint efforts, *Once in a Lifetime*. The story of how this came about has been vividly and mockingly told by Hart in his autobiography, *Act One*.[16] There followed, in addition to three more or less serious plays, *You Can't Take It with You* (1936, very successfully revived in 1965 by the APA-Phoenix Repertory), *The Man Who Came to Dinner* (1939), and *George Washington Slept Here* (1940).

The wit of S. N. Behrman's comedies was more sophisticated than that of Kaufman and Hart, though Kaufman was one of the great conversational wits of all times. Behrman sometimes let social preachment get in the way of his fun, thus blurring, paradoxically, his best social insight; but he was right on the mark in *Brief Moment* (1931), *Biography* (1932), and *No Time for Comedy* (1939). So also Philip Barry was at his best in high comedy such as *The Philadelphia Story* (1939) and less convincing in such ponderous allegories as *Hotel Universe* (1930) and *Here Come the Clowns* (1939).

As with comedy, so with the American musical: it embodied more of the times and was more mature than it seemed. Of *The Band Wagon* (1931), by Kaufman, Howard Dietz, and Arthur Schwartz, a musical in which the Astaires danced, Brooks Atkinson rightly said it would make it "difficult for the old-time musical show to hold up its head." [17] *Of Thee I Sing* (1931), on which Mr. Kaufman also collaborated, along with the Gershwin brothers and Morris Ryskind, is the best of all satires of American politics. In 1935 came *Porgy and Bess*, which DuBose Heyward adapted from his novel and play, assisted by Ira Gershwin, with George Gersh-

16 New York: Random House, 1959.
17 Quoted in Hewitt, *op. cit.*, p. 384.

win writing the music. At the end of the decade, in 1940, came the best of the musicals by Richard Rodgers and Lorenz Hart, *Pal Joey,* notable not only for its score but also for its unglossed picture of low life in the city and for its anti-heroic protagonist, whom Gene Kelly played with gusto.

Thornton Wilder's *Our Town* and William Saroyan's first two plays belong to the end of the '30's, but they are discussed in a later chapter.

Meanwhile, as if in another country, O'Neill marched his solitary way. He removed himself from the *ambiance* of the theater, withdrew from New York saying no man should write for the theater unless he is a thousand miles away, and cultivated that internal depth his contemporaries seemed to lack.

Mourning Becomes Electra was produced by the Theater Guild in 1931. Designed by Robert Edmond Jones, directed by Philip Moeller, and starring Alla Nazimova as Christine and Alice Brady as Lavinia, the performance lasted five hours, with an hour's intermission for dinner. As is well known, the work is an adaptation of Aeschylus' *Oresteia* and, like its model, consists of three plays. The locale is changed to the mansion of a New England family in the time following the Civil War, and the motivations are accounted for in Freudian terms. O'Neill intended that the story's fatality should spring from psychological sources, leaving theology and ontology aside. Although justly famous, the work is not one of O'Neill's best. It suffers from a certain obviousness of concept, and its language is limp. O'Neill was to achieve a greater sense of fatality and better psychological motivation of his characters in later, more personal works. One may criticize *Mourning Becomes Electra,* however, only while paying tribute to its ambition. It is the nearest American equivalent to such large European works as Ibsen's *Emperor and Galilean* and Hauptmann's tetralogy on the house of Atreus.

O'Neill followed *Mourning Becomes Electra* with a play that could hardly have been more different. *Ah, Wilderness!,* unique in O'Neill's career, is a sentimental comedy. Permeated with warmth and written from a bemused point of view, it contemplates a boy's first love, his comic encounter with the town prostitute, and finally his engagement to the girl next door. Watching all this, the parents decide that "the end of love is better than the beginning." All this was a far cry from *Welded* (1924), for instance, in which O'Neill had depicted marriage with an almost Strindbergian horror, and it was far also from the tortured views of family life that O'Neill was to write thereafter.

For a brief time, however—in the three years that followed *Mourning Becomes Electra*—O'Neill seemed determined to find a positive philosophy of life. Having offered a paean to American domesticity in *Ah, Wilderness!*, he next brought out a play in which the leading character, tormented by a split personality, finds wholeness in a return to the Catholic faith. This was *Days Without End*, produced in 1934 and a quick failure. O'Neill himself had a split attitude toward Christian faith: he wanted it, but it was not in him. His deepest beliefs were Manichaean. The only kind of salvation he was able to accept had to be found in despair and under the weight of inevitable corruption. He was a romantic "a little in love with death," as he would later say in *Long Day's Journey into Night*, though the love was in fact more than a little.

After *Days Without End*, O'Neill was silent for twelve years. No new play of his reached the stage until after World War II. He was writing most of the time, but that work he did not wish to show. About 1935 he started to compose a cycle of nine plays under the title *A Tale of Possessors Self-dispossessed*. This was to be a spiritual history of America from Colonial times to the present, showing through characters mostly fictional the deadening effect that possessions have upon those who possess them. The American people, he said in 1946, "are the greatest example of 'For what shall it profit a man if he shall gain the whole world and lose his own soul?' We had so much and could have gone either way. . . ."[18]

Drafts of the first two plays in the cycle were written in the '30's and later destroyed. Between 1935 and 1939 he wrote the third, *A Touch of the Poet*. During the same period and until 1941 he made three drafts and further notes for the fourth, *More Stately Mansions*. Meanwhile in 1939 he put the cycle temporarily aside to write *The Iceman Cometh*. Like *Anna Christie*, it is set in a bar and rooming house on the Lower West Side modeled on a place

[18] Quoted in John Gassner, ed., *O'Neill, A Collection of Critical Essays* (Englewood Cliffs, N.J.: Prentice-Hall, 1964), p. 167.

called "Jimmy-the-Priest's," where O'Neill had lived in 1909. But it is a very different work from *Anna Christie*. It is a prime example of naturalism turned into symbolism, and in this respect it is frequently and aptly compared with Gorki's *Lower Depths*.

Because it is a forbidding work whose characters are mostly alcoholics, *The Iceman Cometh* has often been defended on the grounds of its realism. Such defense is beside the point. O'Neill used the conventions of naturalistic theater in order to express the antithesis he saw between idealism and the wish for death. Life, O'Neill insisted, is tolerable only when accompanied by idealizing illusions. These are the "pipe dreams" of the play's alcoholic characters, and alcohol is, in the play, a symbolic elixir of life. To remove it and the illusions it fosters is to confront death. Only a few of mankind have sufficient courage for this and they only, perhaps, when they are driven to it. The play makes it clear, however, that O'Neill admires those few who are stoic enough to be "converted to death." [19]

A Touch of the Poet incorporates some of the same ideas as *Iceman*, particularly in its treatment of the central character, Major Cornelius Melody. They appear again in the autobiographical *Long Day's Journey into Night*, which O'Neill wrote in 1940. Taken together with *Iceman*, this play represents the highest achievement of O'Neill. Its description of life as a descending arc that begins in love and hope and passes through suffering into hatred, despair, and death, told through the passage of a single day in the life of O'Neill's family and into which are woven recollections of the past, is of a deeply moving simplicity. Nothing in American drama surpasses it.

O'Neill wrote the short monologue play *Hughie* in 1941. Two years later he wrote *A Moon for the Misbegotten*, based on his memories of his brother and saturated, like the other late works, with a romantic attachment to death.

All of this late work O'Neill kept to himself. Only in 1946 did he let one of the plays, *The Iceman Cometh*, reach the stage. The rest he kept hidden, some to be destroyed when he died, the

19 For a more detailed exposition of this thematic material, its effect on the play's style, and its similar occurrence in *A Touch of the Poet* and *Long Day's Journey into Night*, see my essay "On the Late Plays of Eugene O'Neill," in Gassner, ed., *O'Neill*, pp. 110–123.

rest to be withheld for twenty-five years. In secret and without overt reference to the social and political crises through which the nation was going, he produced the best dramatic writing of which the American theater can boast.

When the smoke and atomic dust of World War II had cleared away, O'Neill permitted *The Iceman Cometh* to be shown. Produced by the Theater Guild, it had no great success, largely because the director (Eddie Dowling) failed to understand the elements of the play that lie beyond naturalism. O'Neill's orchestral treatment of motifs therefore emerged as merely repetitious speeches. But the failure was due even more to the audience's unfamiliarity with modern literature of despair and with existentialist thought. Thus, although O'Neill had held his play back for seven years, it was still ahead of its time in America. The situation had changed ten years later when José Quintero directed the play at the Circle in the Square. This off-Broadway production in the spring of 1956 was one of the best-conceived and most rewarding events in the American theater since World War II.

A Long Day's Journey into Night had received its première at the Royal Dramatic Theater in Stockholm in early 1955, according to the wishes of the playwright's widow, Carlotta Monterey O'Neill. With the success of *Iceman* she entrusted to Quintero the direction of *Journey*, which he opened on Broadway in the fall of 1956 with Frederic March and Florence Eldridge in the leads. The following May there was a Broadway production of *A Moon for the Misbegotten*, which the Theater Guild had been unable to cast properly when it attempted to mount this play in 1947, closing it after the tryout in Columbus, Ohio. In 1958 *A Touch of the Poet* was performed, first in Stockholm and later, under Harold Clurman's direction, in New York. *More Stately Mansions*, unfinished by the author but adapted by Karl Ragnar Gierow, was seen in Stockholm in 1962, and in 1967 it was produced in America with Ingrid Bergman, Arthur Hill, and Colleen Dewhurst, under Quintero's direction.

These productions, plus numerous revivals of other plays off Broadway, meant that O'Neill was almost as much produced in the late '50's and in the '60's as he had been in the '20's. No other American playwright has received as much attention both here and abroad or as large an audience over the span of two generations as has O'Neill. Though many consider him a playwright *manqué,* he has a staying power that is extraordinary.

Apart from O'Neill, the American theater in the '40's and '50's now appears as having shown great promise that went largely unfulfilled. The period was dominated by the reputations of Arthur Miller and Tennessee Williams, with William Inge somewhere in the running. There are hundreds of respectable plays for the chronicler to record. The historian, however, whose task is different from that of the chronicler, finds in this period little that warrants sustained attention.

Moreover, the American theater in this time lacked the excitement it knew in the '30's, when the theater, good or bad, was a place in which the public confronted public issues and when going to the theater had something to do with participating in the life of the times. All that has disappeared. The theater has suffered the same fate as the church. For some, though not for many who influence public opinion, attendance has remained fashionable. For others it has become a kind of duty, as if a cultic practice had to be maintained for its own sake and perhaps for the sake of an anticipated reformation. For most it has become irrelevant, an activity ever more remote from the age. There is some hope that the so-called regional, civic, or resident theaters recently come into being in Minneapolis, San Francisco, Dallas, Houston, Providence, Washington, and elsewhere may change the situation. At present the balance of theatrical weight, measured in the number of productions mounted and the number of actors employed, has shifted from New York to the rest of the country considered as a whole. Still, the blight that affects the New York theater is one to which other theaters in America cannot be immune, since on the one hand it has to do with the lack of good writing and on the other it is a function of modern urban life. As urbanization spreads it will hamper the theater across the land as it has already done in New York.

Speculation about the future is not in itself a historical task. I shall return to it only in the final chapter. For the present, it is necessary to give some account of why the American theater after World War II is, in retrospect, so disappointing.

The period of highest hope began in 1945 with Tennessee Williams' *The Glass Menagerie* and lasted until about 1950, the year following Arthur Miller's *Death of a Salesman*. Williams' play, the most Chekhovian of his works (he later turned more Strindbergian, though without being able to match the wild Swede's power), combined theatrical inventiveness with poignant and authentic expression of its characters' frustrated lives. The former quality was not always well controlled—for instance, the picture of the absent father that lights up whenever he is mentioned was a mistake—but it did show a capacity to extend realism toward a semi-poetic use of the stage; and it was employed, for the most part, in ways that increased one's sense of the human substance so touchingly present in the play's lines.

In 1945 there also appeared a promising play by another new author, Arthur Laurents. *Home of the Brave* was no doubt pat in many ways, but its story of ethnic prejudice in a society that had just fought a war against racial bigotry included many genuine touches. The following year Garson Kanin's *Born Yesterday*, the most delightful comedy of the postwar years, suggested that socially relevant comedy was not dead.

Williams followed *The Glass Menagerie* with *A Streetcar Named Desire* in 1947. It went immediately into popular lore, its ill-met and diametrically opposed characters Stanley Kowalski and Blanche DuBois becoming as well known as Othello and Desdemona. The production, designed by Jo Mielziner and directed by Elia Kazan, taken together with Williams' prose that kept turning into a kind of poetry and with the haunting music of Paul Bowles, ushered in a period of "poetic realism" in the theater, of which Kazan was the leading exponent and practitioner. It seemed that all the elements of modern theater—the Chekhovian focus upon the quality of experience, the Strindbergian occupation with sexual violence and with expressionistic methods, the poetic revival in drama, the anti-illusionism of the Continental theater, Pirandello's interest in illusion and reality, and whatnot—were finding their synthesis in an American talent. Moreover, Williams' locales and his characters were completely American, and he made of them vehicles of expression for his fears about the decadence of modern society, its violent animosity toward things tender, sensitive, and human. *A Streetcar Named Desire* was thus a high point of international as well as of American theater in the postwar period.

Later it became clear that Williams' attitude toward violence was highly ambivalent, that he partly adored it and tended to make it the primary characteristic of nature, men, and God, and that as a result his pleas for what is tender and loving could only rarely escape sentimentality. This ambivalence was already present in *A Streetcar Named Desire*. Later it became more obvious, and since it was something unresolved in Williams, it led to his becoming ever more shrill. He tended to lose what had at first been his greatest asset—the ability to speak in carefully nuanced tones.

A Streetcar Named Desire opened in the same year as the first of the widely noticed plays of Arthur Miller. He had attracted some attention in 1944 with *The Man Who Had All the Luck*, but it was only with *All My Sons* (1947) that he became prominent. This was a play that had all the social relevance one might have dreamed of in the theater's most liberal period. It was tightly knit, with characters clearly delineated; it was timely, and it hit hard. If Strindberg and Chekhov stood behind Williams, Ibsen was to be seen looking over Miller's shoulder. But only a part of Ibsen—the part that did the moral studies, and in fact only a part of that part, just as much as could be got into the well-made play. Nevertheless, a talent and a conscience were emphatically present in Miller.

The next round belonged to Williams, who in 1948 offered *Summer and Smoke*. Here in Alice Winemuller was the neurotic Strindbergian woman again, once more keenly observed and sympathetically drawn by Williams from Southern life. (Williams' depiction of Southern characters has always been more accurate than most of his critics have dreamed.) The play has not the powerful shocks of *A Streetcar Named Desire*, but it is more delicate and its psychological reality more convincing. Four years after its Broadway production it was better done, to much acclaim, off Broadway at the Circle in the Square.

Mister Roberts, the comedy of naval life in wartime, adapted by Thomas Heggen and Joshua Logan from Heggen's novel, also appeared in 1948. As writing there was nothing distinguished about it, but the direction by Joshua Logan attracted much attention. Here was one more proof that the skills of the theater arts had been thoroughly learned and would, in cooperation with the work of the new generation of playwrights, lead to a great era of theatrical excellence. But the directing of the two brightest hopes, Logan and Kazan, soon became mannered, their effects promptly cliché. This was especially true of Logan. Both men, like most other American directors, shied away from the classics, not only because they found few actors likely to distinguish themselves in such works but also because their directing techniques were unsuited to material not drawn from contemporary life. Logan and Kazan were masters of pseudo-realism, they were not interpreters of the insights of great dramatic writers. Furthermore, they differed from such European directors as Peter Brook and Roger Blin in that they did not persevere in a kind of "pure" theatricalism of the type I shall discuss later. They hovered, as it were, between literary and theatrical values, and it is this ambivalence in their work that leads one to speak of their directorial style as "pseudo-realistic," whether one is thinking of Logan's treatment of Inge's realistic play *Picnic* or Kazan's handling of Archibald MacLeish's poetic and expressionistic *J.B.*

Kazan was the director of *Death of a Salesman,* which came to the stage in 1949. Working again with Mielziner, he created from Miller's script one of the most impressive mood pieces that has ever been seen on the American stage. There were very strong performances from Lee J. Cobb as Willy Loman, Mildred Dunnock as Linda, and Arthur Kennedy as Biff. As with *Streetcar,* the situation and characters of *Death of a Salesman* became universally known.

Much of the frustration and disappointment that many persons have experienced with regard to recent American theater has been connected with the fact that this play by Arthur Miller has failed to stand up to reflection. By a quirk of history, it has had to bear more weight than is just. It seemed the best that the postwar generation of widely acclaimed playwrights could do, and it has proved not good enough. Experimental in structure, quite outside the tradition of the well-made play, serious in intent, skilled in its characterization, it nevertheless palls under close scrutiny. Its merit is all on the surface. When that, which is essentially mood, has been absorbed, there is little more to receive.

A few critics, notably John Gassner, perceived this at the time and were spared the disappointment of others. The trouble with the play is that it has the mood and tone of profundity but lacks the substance. It asks to be taken as if it had something to tell us of our society and a type of man it produces, but it provides no insights. Neither does it provide the material out of which they might be gained. As Gassner wrote, "Mr. Miller's insights are all expected ones; they are observations rather than discoveries." [20]

The most serious flaw in the play is that its thematic content is confused. In part Miller seems to blame Willy Loman for his dishonesty and lack of will, portraying these qualities as leading to his decline and suicide. Yet Miller also suggests that the values of white-collar society are to blame: they rob Willy of the opportunity for self-fulfillment and drive Biff to escape from such society altogether. It is not possible to hold both interpretations at once. They are not the result of an ironic view but of an indecision in Miller's mind.

The play is also flawed by sententiousness. This is most notable in Linda's famous speech about how attention must be paid to Willy Loman "because he is a man" and in the Epilogue, in which Biff sums up the errors of his father: "He never knew who he was." At these and several other moments, the playwright stands very much in the way of his characters. In truth, Willy Loman does not deserve as much attention as he has received, because he exists in a limbo somewhere between being an individual and being a type and is convincing as neither. His popularity has been due to the audience's willingness, in times of economic abundance, to indulge its feeling that "something" is wrong. Had Miller been more of an Ibsen, he would have convicted that audience of possessing a sickly conscience. But Miller's later work has made it clear that his own conscience is not robust. Gassner was right when he said that *Death of a Salesman* "is one of the triumphs of the mundane American stage." [21]

20 *The Theatre in Our Times* (New York: Crown, 1954), p. 367.
21 *Ibid.*

After 1949 disenchantment began to set in. William Inge made his debut in 1950 with *Come Back, Little Sheba*. His work began in sentiment and quickly declined into foolish propaganda for the healing qualities of domestic love.

Williams has continued to labor with admirable diligence. In this he is exceptional among contemporary American playwrights. He not only writes much, he also revises his failures and tries them out again, refusing to blame the audience or the critics when his work is not acceptable to them. At the same time he experiments. In *The Rose Tattoo* (1952) he wrote a comedy of an earthy, passionate kind. In *Camino Real* (1953) he turned to extravagant, symbolic expressionism and proclaimed that for the innocent of heart there is a way out of the hell of modern decadence. The theme was juvenile, but the script afforded director Elia Kazan the opportunity to create a theatrical tour de force. In *Cat on a Hot Tin Roof* (1955), a play with two poor acts and one that is excellent, Williams constructed, in the second-act encounter between Brick and Big Daddy, one of the finest confrontation scenes in American drama. In *Orpheus Descending* (1957), *Suddenly Last Summer* (1958), and *Sweet Bird of Youth* (1959) he explored, though with too much indulgence, the violence that men, nature, and perhaps God inflict upon beauty. That was also his theme in *The Night of the Iguana* (1961), which, for all its faults, was better than its immediate predecessors because of the gentleness Williams communicated to its central part, easing off from the stridency that overtook him in that period. *The Milk Train Doesn't Stop Here Anymore* (1962) was an unmitigated disaster in both versions in which Williams brought it to Broadway, as was *Period of Adjustment* (1960), which was Williams' attempt to write a comedy about marriage, a subject he obviously regarded with something near horror. In *Gnädige Fraulein*, one of two plays presented under the general title *Slapstick Tragedy* (1965), he was more avant-garde. The quick demise of this production was unjustified.

Arthur Miller's work has been of steadily lessening vigor since *Death of a Salesman*. It is true that both *The Crucible* (1952) and *A View from the Bridge* (1955), after doing poorly on Broadway, were revived for lengthy runs off Broadway, but it is also true that the issues in both these plays are sensationally overdrawn and the characters too neatly divided into the good and the bad. Miller was not represented by a new play between 1955 and 1963, though he wrote a screenplay, *The Misfits* (1960), for his wife, Marilyn Monroe. A character based on her is prominent in *After the Fall*, Miller's play that opened the Repertory Theater of Lincoln Center's first season in 1963. Much of this work consists of monologues delivered by its protagonist, who is a stand-in for the author. With more candor than many people desired, in this autobiographical work Miller revealed himself in his political and marital history as a weak figure, unwise in his public actions and barely able to love in his private life. The moral content of the play, which centers upon the inevitable wrongs that persons inflict upon each other, is sound, but the intellectual content is shallow. For the Repertory Theater's next season Miller wrote *Incident at Vichy*, a series of dialogues among victims of Nazi terror. It proved to be without strength. In *The Price* (1968), Miller returned to the situation of a family haunted by choices its members have made in the past, in which he sees America's relation to its own immediate past. The play is without dramatic distinction, its one interest being that here for the first time Miller showed himself capable of creating a genuinely comic character, though even that one, a Jewish furniture dealer, is a stock figure.

In addition to the intellectual limitation that Miller's works display, they have had the further embarrassment of being written in anachronistic style. About 1956, when the work of Beckett and Ionesco began to be known in this country, expectations of critics and students with regard to dramatic form were transformed radically. Of course, the commercial theater did not much change, and newspaper criticisms, which had become a kind of consumers' report, were for the most part hostile to the avant-garde; but this only meant that there was a severe rift between the devotees of theater art and the institution of theater business. Miller was caught in between.

There was, and remains, little in the American theater since World War II that devotees of theater art could find to praise. An exception was Marjorie Barkentin's stage version of the Cyclops sequence from James Joyce's *Ulysses*. Called *Ulysses in Nighttown*

(1958), it opened off Broadway under the direction of Burgess Meredith and had the enormous benefit of Zero Mostel's performance as Leopold Bloom. It rightly achieved an outstanding measure of prestige, since the imaginative staging was entirely worthy of the material from which the play was made.

The following year The Living Theater was discovered. Directed by Julian Beck and his wife, Judith Malina, it had been in operation for several years, first on the Upper West Side and then in a second-floor location on Fourteenth Street, before it became widely known with its 1959 production of *The Connection,* by Jack Gelber. Later in the year it staged *Many Loves,* a curious and formerly neglected set of three short plays by William Carlos Williams. Its repertory also included works by Pirandello and Brecht, Ezra Pound's adaptation of Sophocles' *Women of Trachis,* and several plays by formerly unknown authors, of whom Gelber became the most renowned.

The Living Theater was perhaps too arty, or too anti-art, which in this case came to the same thing. Its actors were unknown and mostly untrained. Its methods were makeshift, partly out of necessity and partly from necessity rationalized into a virtue. The directors liked to pretend that theater is entirely anti-illusionist, but this meant that their audience had to be as much a part of the show as the actors. That, of course, was simply illusion of another sort, and the spectator at The Living Theater found himself as convention-bound and illusion-ridden as ever he was at the most "realistic" play. The distinction between pretending-to-be-involved and exercising-the-imagination was not frequently maintained at The Living Theater. Nevertheless, it was a theater very much alive and kicking until the Internal Revenue Service tried to kill it in 1963 for nonpayment of taxes. It then went into exile in Europe, where it underwent a transformation of technique and intention. Peripatetic, tribal, cultic, and professedly anarchistic, "le Living," as the French called it, developed a number of productions (they are hardly to be called plays) in repertory, the most celebrated being *Frankenstein, Mysteries and Smaller Pieces, Antigone,* and *Paradise Now.* These were brought to America when the Becks and their troupe made a sensational return in 1968. By that time The

Living Theater was no longer "modern." It had become an avatar of "the new theater," a recent shift in style and content that is post-modern and lies outside the scope of this book.

The Connection, by Jack Gelber, was The Living Theater's most famous production before its European sojourn. It attracted the unstinted praise of the avant-garde, who had so little else to applaud in the American theater. *The Connection* is an enactment of a situation in which a number of heroin addicts gather in sombody's "pad," where they wait for and finally get a "fix" brought by a savior figure in white, named Cowboy. The greatest virtue of this nonplay is its documentary quality, which is enhanced by the device of having much of the action photographed, as it proceeds, by a reporter with a camera and portable lights. Its weakness is in its attempt to convince the audience that it, too, is hooked—if not on heroin then on God, hope, or something. The parallel is forced. The play would have been a better example of avant-garde theater if it had contained less message.

After Gelber, Edward Albee. By 1960 changed expectations about what theater should be had reached the point where it was necessary to have a popular American playwright of "the absurd." It was in this context that Edward Albee became a culture hero almost immediately after the first American performance of a short play, *The Zoo Story,* in 1960. *The American Dream* followed in 1961, and in the next year Albee moved onto Broadway with the sensational success *Who's Afraid of Virginia Woolf?* The same year Arthur Kopit's *Oh Dad, Poor Dad, Mama's Hung You in the Closet and I'm Feeling So Sad* was produced by the Phoenix Theater. Kopit's play was brighter, less ponderous, but undoubtedly more juvenile than any of Albee's. He provided Albee with only a temporary rival for public favor. The patent inadequacies of Albee's subsequent plays—*The Ballad of the Sad Café* (1963, adapted from a story by Carson McCullers), *Tiny Alice* (1964), *Malcolm* (1965, adapted from a novel by James Purdy), and *A Delicate Balance* (1966)—have not so far impaired his fame.

Albee's work is open to a number of severe criticisms, of which two are most important here. First, his work is extremely derivative, showing the mixed and undigested influence of Beckett,

Strindberg, Ionesco, Pirandello, Tennessee Williams, T. S. Eliot, and others. Second, his mixture is a brew that seems calculated, consciously or unconsciously, to cater to a debased popular taste. The substance of his work, considered with reference to either its always-moral content or its form, or both together, is no greater than that of Scribe's, and Scribe's skill, although he wrote in a very different style, was considerably greater. Albee achieved a popular and critical success out of all proportion to his substance and skill. This was simply because public taste had swung so far from the "dramatic" toward the "theatrical" that it required a celebrity figure on whom to pin its expectations in that regard. This shift in sensibility, to which we shall return later, is more important than Albee himself. He is an apt one to symbolize it, however, because he does display an extraordinary flair for a heightened theatricalism. If this flair were accompanied by a suit-able candor of expression and a disciplined ability to organize ma-terial, he would be what the public holds him to be—the crown of the theater's development in the 1960's.

The American musical's progress since World War II deserves brief comment. Rodgers and Hammerstein's *Oklahoma!* (1943), adapted from Lynn Riggs's *Green Grow the Lilacs* (1931), is frequently and justly cited as having achieved an integration be-tween story, lyrics, music, and dancing that had previously been unknown in the popular musical theater of America. Most impor-tant was the employment of dance in a modern idiom to express American character and atmosphere. This was the work of Agnes De Mille, the choreographer.

In spite of their having attempted a few off-beat musicals after *Oklahoma!,* it was not Rodgers and Hammerstein who were to realize the potentialities they helped generate in 1943. Weill's *Street Scene* (1947), his *Lost in the Stars* (1949), and Blitzstein's *Regina* (1949) were all musically superior to Rodgers' work in this period, though perhaps not better than what he had done be-fore the war in collaboration with Lorenz Hart. The baroque effectiveness of Gian-Carlo Menotti's operas for Broadway, impres-sive on first hearing, turned out to lead to a dead end. Cole Porter's *Kiss Me, Kate* (1948) was a very bright inspiration, but it was based on a Shakespearean play, *The Taming of the Shrew,* and thus did not go in the most important direction the musical was taking, which was toward the expression of American motifs, characters, and atmosphere.

In 1950 Abe Burrows, Joe Swerling, and Frank Loesser collaborated on *Guys and Dolls,* drawing their material from one of Damon Runyon's stories of Broadway low life. It succeeded in doing what the musical must do in order to achieve immortality—disarming the highbrows. The urbane directing of George S. Kaufman had no little to do with this accomplishment, but all the components, including the choreography of Michael Kidd, were in harmony, and in the "Fugue for Tin Horns" and other inspired songs Loesser brought the genuinely popular and the genuinely inventive together. His doing so, plus work by others in the same direction, prepared the way for the remarkable enthusiasm which greeted the revival of the Brecht-Weill *Threepenny Opera* in 1953 at the Theatre De Lys in Greenwich Village. Adapted by Marc Blitzstein, it ran for more than six years, luckily endowed with the presence of Weill's widow, Lotte Lenya, who repeated her original performance as Jenny, first given in Berlin in 1928.

The two important musicals of 1956, *My Fair Lady* and *Candide,* were both drawn from non-American literary sources. The former, with music by Frederick Lowe, made the longest run of any musical in Broadway history, while the latter, with a score by Leonard Bernstein, perished in a short time, leaving a small but devoted group of mourners. The historical importance of *My Fair Lady* rests on the fact that it was a thoroughly literate musical, in spite of the fact that Alan Jay Lerner's adaptation of Shaw's *Pygmalion* took much of the bite out of the original. *Candide* was even more literate. Perhaps, however, it had too many collaborators. The book, drawn from Voltaire, was by Lillian Hellman, the lyrics by Richard Wilbur, Dorothy Parker, John Latouche, and Leonard Bernstein. As directed by Tyrone Guthrie, it became too busy for its own good, and its episodic diversity did not help. Nevertheless, because of its score and its many excellent lyrics, it is probably the most admirable failure among American musicals.

The following year (1957) Bernstein provided the score for an even more notable musical, *West Side Story,* which, although adapted from *Romeo and Juliet,* was utterly expressive of American locale and of twentieth-century experience. The book was the work of Arthur Laurents and Jerome Robbins, the latter known before only as a choreographer, and the lyrics were by Stephen Sondheim. Robbins also directed and choreographed the show, and it was hard to tell where one of these functions stopped and the other began, since his entire conception was choreographic. The inspiration welled from his rich feeling for the gestural life of teen-age slum dwellers. The spoken dialogue was weak, and the lack of experienced actors in the cast did nothing to hide this fact; but the weight of the piece was fortunately carried by the music and dancing.

Few American works of the time can be remembered with such pleasure as this one, and for a reason that has not been much noticed. In this musical play the American theater caught better than in any of its other work the irony that belongs to the best modern theater. The fundamental conception of *West Side Story* is bitterly ironic. Shakespeare's play is a tragedy that brings youth into conflict with adult authority, forcing the young lovers to pay the price (death) that is required for the restitution of social order in Verona. In *West Side Story* adult authority does not exist. The few adults who appear, such as the social worker, the police, and Doc, the druggist, are ineffectual. Hence, they are satirized by the young. It follows that the catastrophe, occasioned by gang warfare, occurs amid social anarchy. The play's bitter revelation is that there is more "order" in the improvised life of the young than in public institutions. This ironic reversal of the Shakespearean framework of the story, which is given clearest utterance in the song "Gee, Officer Krupke!" is the principal source of the show's power, the merit of the music and the dancing being that they express the ironic conception of the whole. *West Side Story* is the high point thus far reached by the American musical, and for significant force it has probably been exceeded in recent American drama only by *A Streetcar Named Desire*, *The Iceman Cometh*, and *Long Day's Journey into Night*.

The longest run of any musical in America has been achieved by *The Fantasticks*, which Tom Jones and Harvey Schmidt adapted from Edmond Rostand's *Les Romanesques*. It has little of the trenchancy of *West Side Story* or of *The Threepenny Opera*, but it is worth noting that in its own way it is saturated with ironic self-mockery and that its attitude toward the romance of young love is heavily laced with satire. This is true of the lyrics, the treatment of the plot, the music, and the staging. Add to this a certain amount of farce and a moderate tendency to cuteness and the reason for its popularity is clear.

In spite of several bright moments, the American theater after World War II failed to shift the center of interest in the development of modern theater from the eastern to the western side of the Atlantic. The American film in the same period lost the world importance it formerly had, though it must be observed that the American theater has at no time influenced the European in a manner comparable to the way Hollywood influenced European movie makers until the 1950's. American work in modern dance, poetry, and music has also been of seminal importance abroad, and this is even truer of American painting since World War II. It is necessary to ask why the American theater has not quite fulfilled the promise it seemed to offer after each of the two world wars.

As mentioned earlier, American theater suffers, when compared to the British and European, from the lack of a tradition of crown-sponsored theater such as most European countries knew from the Renaissance until the advent of democratic governments. In varying degrees and under various arrangements, the tradition of royal sponsorship was then continued through parliamentary support. In the United States there has never grown up a feeling for theater as a social ritual protected, at least in principle, by the highest authorities and expressive of national solidarity. In this country, theater has had to develop itself from the grass roots, which is, from a psychological and sociological point of view, a virtual impossibility. The feeling for theater as a social ritual is disappearing throughout the modern world wherever industrialism and technological society have spread. Since the feeling was never deeply rooted in America, it has been more vulnerable here than elsewhere to competition from movies and television, which are the technological media for the telling of stories. That American films were almost purely conceived as a mass product for technological society rather than as an art growing out of the traditions of Western civilization meant that they, in their turn, suffered acutely when technology brought television into being.

The matter can be put in a perhaps simpler way by saying that the theater in America has had no tradition to protect it from being judged by its ability to earn money. Thus, the advent of mass culture has embarrassed it acutely. The concept of an elite, valued as such, is as vital to theater as the concept of a priesthood and a few faithful souls is to the church. American playwriting has been hampered and compromised by the lack of any such ideal in this country. The very suggestion that this is a problem is likely to sound reactionary. If it does, the only defense is that the theater is at once the most iconoclastic and the most traditional of all arts. It merits these adjectives not simply because certain dramatists have been iconoclasts and others traditionalists but because the tension between the two tendencies is inherent in drama itself.

American drama in the twentieth century has also been impoverished by the fact that romantic irony has never been as strong here as in Europe. Insofar as our intellectuals have cultivated awareness of the inner self, they have mostly done so under the tutelage of psychoanalysis, and that in a neo-Freudian form. This is a form of introspection that does not contribute very much to an ironic world view, being too rationalistic and too much oriented toward therapy. The tragic part of Freud's understanding of human nature has been mostly discarded in America. Here, owing to the national history, there is little sense of man's being born to catastrophe. Perhaps for that reason, but at least consonant with it, American philosophy has had no strong tradition of ontological speculation. Thus, it is not surprising that American drama is notable for its lack of ontological depth. The patterns of narrative and of stage action that it arranges seldom seem to symbolize a quest for reality. The distinction between what is illusory and what is real, which has been the continuing interest of European drama from the time of Aeschylus, is not at home on the American stage except in meretricious forms. O'Neill aside, the best American theater has come where deep substance is not asked for or appears only indirectly—that is, in comedy, in certain works of social protest, and in the musical.

There is no important American tragicomedy. Albee's travesties are the nearest thing to it, and that is not very near. Aside from early Tennessee Williams and a few scattered plays, American drama has shown an almost complete inability to learn from Chekhov. That is perhaps the most revealing thing that can be said about it. It is a theater so dedicated to the ephemeral that it cannot even learn to imitate the quality of passing experience, cannot probe the "now" of passing time. Snapshots, but not internal analysis. Perhaps a profound American drama cannot come without a longer shadow of suffering than this people has yet endured. Art is bought at a very high price.

13. LYRIC AND MYTH: THE PERSISTENCE OF THE ROMANTIC DREAM

THE "QUEST FOR REALITY" as it has been followed in the modern theater offers two major divergent paths. One is the pursuit of experience as it presents itself in contemporary psychological, social, political, and aesthetic forms. The playwright asks, first of all, what is going on? But his principal question is always, What is the connection between the experiencing self and that which it experiences? This path Ibsen, Strindberg, and Chekhov took in their more "modern" works.

The other major path, which concerns us in this chapter, turns toward the past and toward folk materials. Those who take it seem to feel that reality is to be discovered in what has happened to man in the past, or in what is held for true in the storehouse of ancient belief. Those who take this path do not often think of themselves as being on a quest for reality, since they suppose it already to be given in a certain heritage. It has only to be communicated to the audience so that men may see how the ignored or forgotten reality conditions their lives and may thus be moved to come to terms with it. Yet the modern audience is not prepared to accept either history or any body of belief as normative. It will accept them only as varieties of human experience. If a playwright prefers these over immediate experience, he reveals himself as a nostalgic who perpetuates in the twentieth century that "romanticism of the dream" we have already noticed in the nineteenth.

It is no accident that much, though not all, of this kind of drama in the twentieth century has been written in verse. The reason has been that the nostalgia of content spills over into a nostalgia of form, producing the stubborn belief that the best drama has been and will be verse drama. One might trace the fortunes of poetic drama in modern times, showing its decline when Ibsen turned to prose after *Peer Gynt,* the triumph of prose on the English stage in the work of Shaw, the return of poetry in the plays of Yeats, Eliot, and Fry, and the revival of poetic drama on the Continent. He would then show how this revival turned out to be artificial and how the better writers of stage prose proved to be more imaginative, as well as consistently more modern, than the advocates of verse.

I shall not tell that story, for to do so would require lengthy attention to the techniques of dramatic verse. The important historical point in any case is simply this: The writing of verse drama has remained, in modern times, a stubbornly technical matter. Dealing with modern verse drama, one can hardly get *beyond* technical considerations, which means that these particular technical problems do not contain great cultural importance for this age. With other technical problems it is different. The function of the director, the method of an actor's work, the construction of a play without a plot, the relation of stage dialogue to speech heard in the street, the nature of theatrical symbols—all these are of enormous interest *as* technical problems *because* they are more than technical. They are ways of entry into the meaning of theatrical art in our time. This has not proved to be the case with the technicalities of verse, as is shown by the fact that even T. S. Eliot's remarkable success in handling the technical problems has made little difference to our understanding of what modern theater is all about.

The matter can be put differently by noting that there are some modern plays that can be praised *in spite of* their being in verse, almost none to be praised *because* of it. There may come a day when the values of society have changed sufficiently to make such a judgment obsolete, but at present the tendencies are still in a different direction. They point ever more strongly toward what Eliot called "the poetic play in prose," which he rejected out of hand but which proved to be more fruitful than the poetic play in verse, which he favored.

Of those who have followed the quest for reality into the past, the most important have been a certain number of religious dramatists. We must think here of those who have had an identifiable and more or less positive relation to a specific religious tradition, and in the nature of the case this has meant playwrights of Christian persuasion, or at any rate writers of plays to be interpreted in Christian terms. Far and away the most important of these is Michel de Ghelderode (1898–1962), a Belgian, but in order to appreciate the nature of his accomplishment it is necessary first to look at a few others, especially Ernst Barlach (1870–1938), Paul Claudel (1868–1955), Henri Ghéon (1875–1944), André Obey (b. 1892), Charles Williams (1886–1945), Christopher Fry (b. 1907), and T. S. Eliot (1888–1965).

Barlach was a sculptor and graphic artist who brought to the theater the same sort of vision he employed in his other arts. His *Der tote Tag* (1912; "Day of Death") was one of the earliest expressionist dramas in Germany. Gradually his plays gave up all traces of realism and became free expressions of the religious search for purity and salvation, all the while being saturated with an acute awareness of sin, which belonged to the north-German Protestant mysticism that shaped Barlach's faith. His most important play is *Die Sündflut* (1924; "The Flood"), an awesome account of the purging and reshaping of creation by God, as drawn from the story of Noah. Also notable are *Der Findling* (1922; "The Foundling"), in which the pope, Death, and the Devil are treated as Punch and Judy figures, and *Der blaue Boll* (1926; *The Blue Boll*), which is about the religious search for a transformed life. Barlach's plays are perhaps a bit heavy to deserve the highest praise, but they do deserve to be better known than they presently are outside Germany.

Claudel's work has already been mentioned, but he must figure again in the present discussion. The first play of his so-called papal trilogy, which fastens upon the possibility of a return of political power to the Vatican, was performed in 1914; the other two, *Le Pain dur* (*Crusts*) and *Le Père humilié* (*The Humiliation of the Father*), though finished by 1916, were not put on until 1949 and

1953, respectively. Their performances belong to a period in which a revival of religious, poetic drama seemed to many to point toward the future. The most outstanding event of this time in the French theater was Jean-Louis Barrault's production in 1943 of *Le Soulier de satin* (*The Satin Slipper*), which Claudel had written between 1919 and 1924.

The production took place in German-occupied Paris. The play was of such length that at least three evenings would have been required for a complete performance, and at first Claudel insisted that it be put on in full. Later he consented to an abridgment made by Barrault that played for four and three-quarter hours. The cast included Marie Bell, Madeleine Renaud, and Barrault himself. The music was by Arthur Honegger, the design by Lucien Coutaud. Working together with Barrault and Claudel, these men devised a production that astonished and captivated the audience, an offering bolder and more daring in its use of the total resources of the theater than anything formerly seen on the French stage.

Barrault has said that when he worked on *Le Soulier de satin*, and later (1949) on *Partage de midi* (*Break of Noon*), he had the feeling that he was creating classics on the stage, as if he had been in on the creation of a tragedy of Racine in the seventeenth century.[1] It may be that posterity will vindicate him in that opinion, but it is barely possible now to think that Claudel's theater, for all its grandeur, is destined for immortality. The demands it makes upon production, especially in such works as *Le Soulier de satin* and *Le Livre de Christophe Colombe* (1927) are excessive; but in addition to this, Claudel's nostalgia for epochs of faith and his dualistic kind of Christian doctrine remove him from the major tendencies of modern thought. *Le Soulier de satin,* which is set in Spain at the end of the fifteenth century but is cosmic in its scope, is, like most of Claudel's work, a story of passion unfulfilled. This story becomes the vehicle of a theme similar to St. Paul's utterance in the Epistle to the Galatians: "The flesh lusts against the spirit, and the spirit against the flesh." Also in *Partage de midi* the love of a man and a woman for each other is played off against the love of the soul for God, and Claudel suggests that it is by descent into the

[1] *Reflections on the Theatre,* Barbara Wall, trans. (London: Rockliff, 1951), p. 178.

miseries of human passion that one may finally be delivered from the flesh and attain communion with the Most High.

There is no doubt that this doctrine, which borders on the heretical as far as Catholic teaching is concerned, was an outgrowth of Claudel's own experience. Nevertheless, it was not that experience itself or the experience of men in general that he wished to communicate but the doctrine he had formulated out of it. Beneath the experience of love he discerned the truth of God, and in quest of the latter he took his audience, proceeding according to the formula that the lower love, when pursued to its end, would turn one toward the higher. In Claudel's mind the theater of the East and the *autosacramental* of Catholic Spain provided the inspiration through which the modern theater might recover its destiny and purpose. It is precisely this appeal to an age of faith and a sacramental theater that renders Claudel's dramas inaccessible to most persons, especially to those who are not in a position to savor the pungency of his use of the French language. In Claudel the infinite is so real that the finite can gain reality only by becoming a ladder (which, paradoxically, one *descends*) to the infinite. Experience becomes the way to the real, but inasmuch as it does so, it loses intrinsic interest, which is why Claudel's theatricality lies always under the suspicion of being fake.

In this respect Claudel's theater exemplifies the difficulty plaguing all religious drama in the twentieth century, the radical disjunction between the symbol and the reality symbolized. Religious theater has been under the terrible handicap of having to devote its attention to mere signs, because it has held that lived reality and ultimate reality are deeply estranged. Only through an ironic style could the two be brought together, but most religious playwrights have not wanted to risk the possibly corrosive effects of such a style. The nearest they have wanted to come, for the most part, has been to write gentle comedy, usually allegorical. In France the two who did this best were Henri Ghéon and André Obey. Ghéon (whose real name was Henri Vanglon) was a friend of Jacques Copeau, who produced Ghéon's *Le Pauvre sous l'escalier* ("The Poor Man Under the Staircase") at the Vieux Colombier in 1921. In 1925 Ghéon founded a troupe called Les Compagnons de Notre-Dame, which played in cathedrals and rented halls. The most famous production of any of his plays occurred in England in 1926, when Sir Barry Jackson directed *L'Histoire du jeune Bernard de Menthon* (*The Marvelous History of Saint Bernard*) at Malvern. Among amateurs Ghéon's most popular play has been *Le Noel sur la place* (1935; *Christmas in the Marketplace*), which presents the story of Jesus' birth as a play within a play done by gypsies in a public square. Almost all his plays, many of them quite artless, proceed by way of distancing the religious material—either thrusting it into the past or locating it among naïve and quaint characters or turning to whimsy and fable. These strategies all pushed him in the direction of "theatrical theater," anti-illusionism, and epic construction, but he had not the skill to make full use of the ironic possibilities in such theater.

Obey is remembered primarily for *Noah* (1931). Many of his plays are not on religious themes. These include *Le Viol de Lucrèce* (1931; *The Rape of Lucrece*), which was translated and adapted by Thornton Wilder; *La Bataille de la Marne* (also 1931; "The Battle of the Marne"); *Vénus et Adonis* (1933), and *Oedipe* (1948; "Oedipus"); and an adaptation of Reginald Rose's *Twelve Angry Men* (1958). But he did write other religious plays, such as *Lazare* (1951; "Lazarus"), and a Christmas entertainment, *Les Trois Coups de minuit* (1958; *Three Strokes at Midnight*).

Noah was written for a company grown from the ashes of Jacques Copeau's enterprise after Copeau, full of religious fervor, had withdrawn from Paris to Burgundy. One of his disciples and collaborators, Michel Saint-Denis, returned to Paris in 1931, took over the Vieux Colombier, redesigned it with the help of André Barsacq, and founded there La Compagnie des Quinze, which created a repertory mostly of works written by Obey.[2] *Noah*, one of the more remarkable plays of the twentieth century, is at once ultrasophisticated and primitive. Its appeal to pre-industrial society

2 Saint-Denis later founded the London Theater Studio, which, through one of its students, George Devine, led to the English Stage Company of recent years. In the late '50's Saint-Denis was called to consult with the Juilliard School of Music about the founding of its professional theater school at the Lincoln Center for the Performing Arts in New York. These activities, plus his work with Tyrone Guthrie and Laurence Olivier at the Old Vic and his Dramatic Center of the East at Strasbourg, have enabled Saint-Denis to exert a significant influence upon recent theater art.

and folk consciousness puts one in mind of Connelly's *Green Pastures* and Wilder's *Our Town,* but its art surpasses both of those works, not least for the reason that it puts upon the actors more full and joyous responsibilities. Actors of the right personalities may perform *Green Pastures* or *Our Town* well, but to do *Noah* well requires that the actor conceal his personality and express himself through highly disciplined techniques of voice control and bodily movement. The acting required descends from the *commedia dell'arte* and is thoroughly presentational in character.

Francis Fergusson writes:

> [The appeal of *Noah*] is to the full poetic or histrionic sensibility rather than to the mind. But to make this "poetic realism" acceptable on the modern stage, Obey adopts the rather coy attitude of the teller of fairy tales. . . . Obey places his [scene] in a timeless countrified realm, the French equivalent of Grandma Moses' modern-primitive paintings of idyllic farm scenes.[3]

This judgment is exact. If one is content to take *Noah* as an extraordinarily skilled example of the art of theatrical make-believe, anti-illusionist but of strong appeal to the histrionic imagination, it affords enormous pleasure and along with it the therapeutic experience of putting the adult for a time in the freshened world of the child. Moreover, it does the latter without sentimentality, unlike Maeterlinck's *Blue Bird,* for instance. But the play can hardly be taken "only" as art, for the substance of the myth it recreates is the absolute sovereignty, omnipotence, and graciousness of God; and this substance is at war with the very principle of make-believe. It would be possible to approach this dichotomy head-on through a bold irony, but Obey glances at it only sidewise. The delight of the play does partly lie in its irony, the tongue-in-cheek quality it displays throughout, such as letting Noah converse with God by telephone; but irony never gets to the center of the play's utterance. Therefore, for all its merits, *Noah* fails to take its religious content seriously.

In Scotland, James Bridie (1888–1951) pursued a course similar to that of Ghéon and Obey, though without their theatrical sophis-

3 *The Idea of a Theater* (Garden City, N.Y.: Anchor Books, Doubleday, 1953), p. 217.

tication. Like them, he gained acceptance for the Biblical material by making it humorous, choosing the more outlandish stories and treating them almost in cartoon fashion. The intention was anything but impious. In fact, it was homiletic. But one looks here in vain for anything that could be called an utterance of the Word or anything like Karl Barth's admonition to read with the Bible in one hand and the newspaper in the other.

Charles Williams is another matter. This employee of the Oxford University Press, sometime lecturer at Oxford University, and friend of Eliot, C. S. Lewis, and J. R. R. Tolkien, was a poet, critic, student of the occult, maverick historian of theology, writer of allegorical novels, and a mystic. His theology was based upon his appreciation of romantic love, of which he found the foremost example in Dante but which did not exclude the romanticism of the nineteenth century. When he was asked to write a play for the Canterbury Festival in 1936 he came forth with an exceedingly complicated stage poem called *Cranmer of Canterbury*, in which an ambivalent attitude is maintained toward the figure of the Skeleton, who symbolizes Death, Cranmer's tempter, and also his guardian angel. The play is one of the more significant religious dramas of the century, because of its taut use of language and its intricate processes of thought; but unfortunately it is conceived with very little sense of the stage. Even more complicated is *Seed of Adam* (1936), but in *The House by the Stable* (1939) and *Grab and Grace* (1941) Williams wrote two eminently actable and charming comic allegories. The first, as its name indicates, is a Christmas play, but the action and the principal interest center upon an Everyman figure in a contest at dice with Satan, who is called Hell. The birth of the Child is treated as off-stage counterpoint to Man's hazard of soul, a device that works theologically as well as theatrically. *Grab and Grace,* the sequel, is even better. Its convention is that of drawing-room comedy, though the convention is stretched very far by consistent allegorization and by comedy bordering on farce. There is a comic agon between Charity and Self-Respect, two females, that degenerates into hair pulling, and there is a happy invention by which Grace is represented as a frisky boy. The play is hilarious without being cute.

Christopher Fry's Biblical plays are *The Firstborn* (1940–1946) and *A Sleep of Prisoners* (1951), but most of his other work is also religious in nature, including *A Phoenix Too Frequent* (1946), *Thor, With Angels* (1948), *The Lady's Not For Burning* (1948), *Venus Observed* (1950), *The Dark Is Light Enough* (1949), and *Curtmantle* (1960). The last-named takes its place with Eliot's *Murder in the Cathedral*, Anouilh's *Becket ou L'Honneur de Dieu*, and Tennyson's *Becket* as one of four modern works on the struggle between Henry II and Thomas à Becket.

Christopher Fry is very nearly the most flamboyant rhetorician who has written for the English stage since Shaw. (Only John Osborne might be said to surpass him in this respect.) Fry's dialogues and set speeches bubble with exploded meanings, and he has displayed an uncommonly good sense of how to make situations fit words so that the ear is prepared for the sort of verbal effervescence it is to receive. However, it has also to be said that Fry has very little dramatic sense. That is, he does not know how to join an issue through the instrumentality of plot and accumulating action, which is why one thinks of him more as a rhetorician than as a dramatist. This fault is partly overcome by his sticking mainly to comedy, but only partly, for in its fundaments comedy is no less dependent on the imitation of action than is tragedy. From the religious point of view, therefore, Fry ends up by making religion seem finally a mere arrangement of words, a sort of victory over suffering and ambiguity achieved by semantic skill. This result is particularly at odds with Christian faith, which holds that such victory is achieved within the realm of historical action. Fry has expounded a kind of faith that rests upon the illumination of the soul rather than upon divine action in history. Whatever might be said about that position theologically, it is of no help to the dramatist, who is not privileged to separate enlightenment from the imitation of action. For this reason the only work of Fry's that is deeply satisfying is the short play *A Phoenix Too Frequent*, which is written with classic simplicity and wit.

Graham Greene's *The Living Room* (1952) and *The Potting Shed* (1957) contain no suggestion of either poetry or comedy. Greene's strategy for dealing with the disjunction between the religious symbol and what it symbolizes has been to intensify the incommensurability between natural experience and revealed truth.

Into the middle of an Ibsenesque realism he has plopped Catholic supernaturalism and an almost magical faith in the sacraments. The latter he represents with no little theatrical force by depicting priests who are in some way misshapen. In *The Power and the Glory*, Greene's novel that has been adapted for the stage, the priest is an alcoholic who has forsaken his vow of celibacy. In *The Living Room* he is a cripple in a wheelchair, retired from his duties. In *The Potting Shed* he has lost his faith and taken up the bottle. Greene holds to the doctrine that the ordination of a priest is an irreversible act: however derelict the priest be, he possesses sacerdotal power. By stressing the incongruity between the priest's life and his office, Greene capitalizes upon the gap between experience and divine reality. In *The Potting Shed* this is further emphasized by centering the plot upon a miracle, the resurrection of a dead person.

It is to Greene's credit that he has seen that no amount or kind of human experience as such would be a sufficient predicate for faith, and that he therefore has based his plays upon rude confrontations between the natural and the supernatural. But for this he paid a double price. First, he mocks his chosen convention of realism without intending to, since the style of realism simply will not accommodate a reality that is sacramental or an event that is miraculous. Second, his "realistic" theater turns highly baroque. Its effect lies precisely in the shock of the supernatural being introduced into the natural, and although such a shock can usually be effective at the moment it occurs, it must lack the power to stand up to reflection.

On the English stage, the foremost talent devoted to religious theater in this century has been that of T. S. Eliot. His reputation as a poet and critic had already been made when in 1933 he was persuaded by E. Martin Browne to write a play for the diocese of London. This turned out to be *The Rock*, which was interesting in the way it employed certain conventions of the music hall for religious purposes. Its full script, however, was of little literary merit, and Eliot allowed only the choruses to be preserved. He was next asked to write the festival play for Canterbury, to which he responded by composing *Murder in the Cathedral* (1935), which has proved to be his finest play. Eliot himself was dissatisfied with it as a work for the theater, not so much because it failed to hold the stage, which was certainly not the case, but because he felt that its medieval setting and its sainted hero separated it from the modern audience. Therefore he turned in his succeeding plays to contemporary settings, with people, as he said, "like ourselves, living in houses and apartments like ours, and using telephones and motor cars and radio sets."[4] *The Family Reunion* (1939) is set in a manor house in the Midlands. *The Cocktail Party* (1949), *The Confidential Clerk* (1953), and *The Elder Statesman* (1958) are set in fashionable London.

Eliot went about his playwriting with a threefold intention. He determined to write plays about ordinary people, plays in which verse was spoken, and plays that would communicate religious ideas in nonreligious language. Technically he succeeded in all three respects, but that is to say that he failed, for a merely technical success in these matters is a failure to show that the technicalities are important. Eliot had chosen a task at which the more he succeeded the more he was bound to fail. None of the four plays he wrote after *Murder in the Cathedral* comes near that work in power or in "relevance," in spite of its technical weaknesses as a drama and its remoteness from the ostensible concerns of modern secular man.

Aiming to write about "people like ourselves," Eliot chose the wrong people—namely, rich people living in manor houses or in chic apartments in Mayfair. That this class was to become incapable of bearing the meaning of modern experience was not apparent, perhaps, in 1937 when *The Family Reunion* was written or even in 1949, the time of *The Cocktail Party*. Nevertheless, it soon became obvious when the theater of England was radically changed by young playwrights who wrote of upstarts from the slums, the mill towns, and the red brick universities, people entirely alienated from the values and traditions of proper English society. Eliot's "realism" was nothing other than the convention of drawing-room comedy, inherited by him from Sheridan, Wilde, Shaw, Noel Coward, and dozens of lesser writers. The convention was becoming exhausted just at the moment when Eliot took it up, and for the reason that it was thoroughly bourgeois and had to lose

4 *Poetry and Drama* (Cambridge, Mass.: Harvard University Press, 1951), p. 31.

its force when the attacks on the bourgeoisie, which had been going on more than a century, finally found their way into the assumptions of a whole generation. If this generation cared little for religion, it cared less for polite society.

With respect to the communication of religious ideas in nonreligious language, Eliot again proved that it could more or less be done, but at the sacrifice of clarity. Into the convention of drawing-room comedy he imported his own adaptations of the plots of pre-Christian plays by Aeschylus, Sophocles, and Euripides. There was a pleasant ingenuity in the way this was done. Eliot then made these adapted plots function as allegories of Christian theological motifs—the search for the true father, the finding of a vocation, the expiation of inherited sin, and so forth. Yet in every case, Eliot stopped at the point where his audience might have wished him to begin. That is, he succeeded in *introducing* the themes and in threading them through the plot toward a final narrative resolution, but he did not communicate much to the audience of his own thought or feeling about the theological matters brought up. As his essays on his own plays show, the reason was his obsession with the problem of *how* to communicate with his audience and his comparative neglect of *what* it was that needed communicating. Hence, there is no marriage of form and content in Eliot's modern-dress plays, but only a contrived relation.

With respect to the use of verse in the modern-dress play, Eliot's technical success was the most pronounced. Like Yeats, he got completely out of the shadow of Shakespeare by finding a viable alternative to the iambic pentameter line. Unlike Yeats, he discovered a poetic analogue for the rhythms of modern speech. This accomplishment may turn out in future to have been of no little importance. However, it has not yet proved to be of much use, because the modern theater has gone in quite another direction in its pursuit of poetic quality. Verse, as such, is not required for this pursuit. Instead, the theatrical image and the free flow of scenes according to imaginative sequences other than narrative have been made the bearer of poetic expression. This has resulted in what Eliot called "the poetic play in prose," which he identified with Maeterlinck and from which he deliberately turned away.

The possibilities of the poetic play in prose have turned out to be vastly more varied than Eliot thought. They are by no means confined to the static style of Maeterlinck but range from the ballad-inspired lyricism of Brecht to the ritualism of Genet. Compared with these, and with Beckett, Ionesco, and Pirandello, even with certain passages in the far-from-brilliant John Osborne, Eliot seems to have confined himself to the prosaic play in verse. As he said himself, much of the verse he wrote for the stage was of such a kind that it might equally well have been written in prose, the genuine poetry being reserved for moments of heightened emotion. This strategy reflected a terrible misunderstanding of why poetry is needed, if at all, in the theater. Moreover, drawing-room comedy is not in the least a poetic convention. Stylized it may be but not poetic, as Wilde, Shaw, and Coward, three of its best writers, knew. Eliot's verse could not but seem unnaturally grafted onto such a convention.

The result of these matters is that the main thing Eliot accomplished was to show that the gap between modern experience and religious thought is even greater than it might otherwise have appeared. For all his liveliness and skill, and for all the comic humor that bubbles in his plays, Eliot's Catholicism, traditionalism, and royalism come over in the theater as anachronistic and nostalgic, convicting him of that very romanticism against which he had once pitched himself in battle under the tutelage of Ezra Pound and T. E. Hulme. To be a classicist in a romantic age is to long for what is not and thus to be a romantic all the same. This was not what Eliot seemed to be in the '20's, when he wrote *The Waste Land,* one of the prime documents of modernism, and *Sweeney Agonistes,* the comic fragment that has in it more of modern drama than any of his plays; but it is what history made him appear in his later years, and it has become all the more obvious in the time since 1955, or thereabouts, when modernism came to an end and was replaced by a popular culture more antibourgeois than any that had existed before.

We may best see Eliot's mistake in rejecting the poetic play in prose by turning now to the work of Michel de Ghelderode. Ghelderode's plays, taken as a whole, are the most authentic and dramatically viable body of religious drama of modern times. A few of his plays, such as *Barabbas* (1928) and *Pantagleize* (1929), will bear comparison with the very best plays of this century, and his *oeuvre* is not unworthy to be mentioned alongside that of Pedro Calderón de la Barca or the religious plays of Lope de Vega. What makes Ghelderode's deeply religious theater so remarkable today is that it can be, and often is, considered as an important part of the avant-garde theater of the mid-twentieth century.

Martin Esslin, in *The Theatre of the Absurd,* distinguishes the work of Ghelderode and certain others such as Audiberti and Schehadé from the theater of the absurd by referring to the former as the "poetic avant-garde." Noting that there is a good bit of overlap between the two groups, he distinguishes them by saying that "the 'poetic avant-garde' relies to a far greater extent on consciously 'poetic' speech; it aspires to plays that are in effect poems, images composed of a rich web of verbal associations." [5] This, of course, describes "the poetic play in prose" that Eliot identified. Yet it would be a mistake to suppose that the theater of Ghelderode is primarily verbal, for if ever there was a master of the employment of the resources of the stage able to make poetry "emerge from the concrete and objectified images of the stage itself," [6] it was Ghelderode. His control of the theater medium, analogous to the painter's control of mass, line, and color yet without making the stage a mere animated painting, was superb. If Ghelderode was a "literary" playwright, as in part he was, it must not be forgotten that he was profoundly inspired by the Flemish painters and also by Flemish traditions of popular, lowbrow theater, including puppetry. The circus clown is as important an influence upon *Pantagleize* as upon Beckett's *Waiting for Godot,* and both plays are full of the memory of Charlie Chaplin.

Son of a curator of rare books, Ghelderode grew up, he said, with the smell of the library in his nostrils. He married, had no children, and lived most of his life as a semi-recluse. His head was full of visions, and he tended to see the world as a fantastic place, a sort of mixture of the qualities to be found in Spanish and Flemish painters—El Greco, Velasquez, Hieronymus Bosch, the Breughels,

5 Garden City, N.Y.: Anchor Books, Doubleday, 1961, p. xxi.
6 *Ibid.*

and the modern Fleming, Emil Nolde. In this visionary quality, native to Ghelderode's personality and deeply conditioned by a particular cultural tradition, is to be found the reason why Ghelderode was able, better than any other modern, to create a convincing religious theater. The gap between modern experience and religious symbolism did not exist for him. To be sure, he was visited with many religious doubts, was anticlerical, and held a perhaps heretical personal theology. His plays reflect not a "simple" faith but a tortured one, which makes it possible for him to be appreciated perhaps better by the secular than the pious. But Ghelderode bypassed entirely the question how one might communicate religious visions to secularized society. He had none of the evangelical impetus that proved a handicap to Eliot. Instead, his position was entirely "confessional," as religious language puts it, or "expressive," as one says of artists. It is the force of the expressive energies pouring from him and creating, by their own necessity, the forms required for their utterance that leads one to call his theater "authentic." Ghelderode was concerned totally with an artist's quest for reality. To be sure, he was highly nostalgic: most of his plays are not about "modern life" at all. But what made his nostalgia respectable and saved it from weakening his art was that he lived in it thoroughly. He did not try pathetically to "go home again." He was already there and knew that it was as full of contradictions and unexplained shadows as any other place.

Thus, Ghelderode did not have the problem that Eliot posed to himself, that of how to bring poetry and life together. They were already one, and the problem was how to unravel that mystery or, better, how to embody it in theatrical form. Ghelderode told his interviewer,

> When I was quite a child, I was sensitive to public demonstrations —processions, parades, fairs, strikes, popular disturbances—to all open-air entertainments, funerals as well, triumphal entries, liturgical pomps, carnivals, masked balls. Equally, I conceded a great deal of importance to furniture, to clothes, to decoration, to the world of things that are believed to be dead. I was struck by everything that ordinarily doesn't surprise other children: dummies in shop windows, electric signs, statues in gardens, the enigmatic

Hermes in the old park, the gesticulations of the trees, all that was color or movement—or seemed to contain mystery.[7]

Such a way of looking at things leaves no room for anything that could be called "ordinary life." Ghelderode's childlike wonder seems to have remained with him all his life, and he made the closest association between the poetic imagination and the sense of the supernatural:

> Take note then, that a being endowed with any poetic sense is sensitive to the supernatural. . . .
> That some people never perceive the encompassing supernatural proves nothing. Let us say that they are impervious to everything, to poetry, to music, to light, to love, to the cries of the world, to the chorus of the dead, to the phosphorescence of the living, to metamorphosis, to anamorphosis.
> Only the brute can deny that we are surrounded by the supernatural. . . .
> You can perceive it, unexpectedly come across its messages in the humblest things, the most everyday things. I have an angel on my shoulder and a devil in my pocket! In order to reassure you, I don't say that everything breathes the supernatural; but could you dissociate it from art without great damage? [8]

Out of such a vision Ghelderode wrote, first for the puppet theater, then for the popular religious theater of Belgium, and later in isolation, more than a score of plays, every one of which is excellent reading and most of which are of superb theatricality. Of these the following deserve mention: *Le Cavalier bizarre* (1920; *The Strange Rider*), in which Death comes to a home for the aged; *La Mort du docteur Faust* (1926; *The Death of Doctor Faust*); *Christophe Colomb* (1928), containing lively satire of the New World; *Escurial* (1928), one of the most haunting of modern plays, set in a decaying palace in Spain and showing a king and his jester exchanging roles; *Barabbas* (1928), which views the Crucifixion as if from the jails and gutters of Jerusalem; *Les Femmes au tombeau* (1928; *The Women at the Tomb*), in which we are shown the bitchiness of all the women whom Jesus encountered in the Gospels

---

7 "The Ostend Interviews," in Michel de Ghelderode, *Seven Plays*, George Hauger, trans., 2 vols. (New York: Hill and Wang, 1964), Vol. I, p. 15.
8 *Ibid.*, p. 13.

but which ends with a clear focus upon the agony of Mary, his mother; *Pantagleize* (1929), a clowning, fantastic story of a political revolution, a work in which Ghelderode is closest to the "absurd" theater; and *Fastes d'enfer* (1929; *Chronicles of Hell*), in which a deceased bishop is unable to pass into the next world because, being evil, he has gagged on the Host in his mouth. *Sire Halewyn* (1934; *Lord Halewyn*) is quite Maeterlinckian.

In Ghelderode religious theater in the twentieth century reached its highest point. Beside work of this imaginative force, popular and semi-religious plays, such as Archibald MacLeish's *J.B.* (1958), a version of the Job story, stand convicted of mere playing with holy things, and the didactic religious theater of Eliot is shown to have had a failure of nerve. The only modern religious dramatists who measure up to Ghelderode are Paul Claudel and perhaps Ernst Barlach.

Barlach's expressionism was bolder and more uncompromising than that of the American expressionist Thornton Wilder (b. 1897), whose *Our Town* (1938) is a remarkable piece of work. It possesses a serenity, a sureness of touch, and a theatrical inventiveness that ensure it a permanent place in the repertory of world theater. Its bare stage stripped to the walls, its use of the stage manager as narrator and commentator, and its employment of the fewest of props, plus its village locale, combine to make it a representation of the "theater of the world." But whereas the seventeenth-century Christian Calderón wrote of "the great theater of the world," Wilder's world is a little theater. The play's appeal to the emotions lies precisely in its dwelling upon the smallest, most commonplace details of unpretentious life, affirming that they have their place in the benevolent eye of God.

Considered purely as theater craftsmanship, the use of the idea of theater as metaphor, and the lyric affirmation of life in pre-industrial society, *Our Town* is unimpeachable. Yet it requires also to be considered with respect to its religious content or, to put it another way, as an example of the theater of ideas, for it is by no means a species of "pure" art (if that exists) standing above ideas, nor is it a simple entertainment that can afford to have its ideas dismissed. One has therefore to ask whether Wilder's sentiment for small-town life and his complacent understanding of human existence is sufficient, and the answer is no. Two specific objections must be made to his thought.

First, Wilder's unhistorical view of man is contrived. The drive toward eternity is characteristic of most religions, and it is possible to suppose that historical time is irrelevant to what should concern man most. However, it is not possible to pretend that in Western civilization the idea of history has not been profoundly important in the shaping of human consciousness. Thus, either Wilder's American setting must be inappropriate, or he should have taken its relation to history more seriously—that is, to show some awareness of the historical gap that separates Grovers Corners from the more highly industrialized society that has grown up around it. Neither Claudel's preoccupation with eternity nor Ghelderode's visionary supernaturalism is open, as Wilder's theater is, to the charge that time has been abolished. In those writers temporality is deplored, but it is also taken seriously as an endemic part of the human condition. Wilder pretends otherwise, and it is this pretense that also robs *The Skin of Our Teeth* (1942) of its claim to seriousness. Purporting to show man in his evolution from prehistorical time to the present, this expressionist play is based upon the conceit that the hazards of human life are everywhere and at all times the same. An identical notion underlies *The Long Christmas Dinner* (1931), a one-act play in which several generations enter, grow old, and die during the course of a single meal, showing that the more things change the more they remain the same, an essentially precious and undramatic conception.

Second, Wilder's theater includes no evil. To be sure, there are temptations and near-failures—in *The Skin of Our Teeth* a would-be villain nearly shoots the main character; but all such troubles are shown to melt away in the great totality of being. Inability to handle the moral problem of evil is also a fault of Shaw's theater,[9] but Shaw largely overcame this fault through a vigorous dialectic of ideas and a thoroughgoing interpretation of history, both of which are lacking in Wilder.

Wilder's most satisfying plays are his least ambitious: *The Matchmaker* (1954), a farce; and *The Happy Journey to Trenton and Camden* (1931), a vignette of a family on a Sunday drive in

[9] See above, Chapter 11.

an automobile. *The Alcestiad* (1955, revised 1957) has never achieved satisfactory form, and the three short plays in *Plays for Bleecker Street* (1962) are marred by coyness. Wilder is one of the more erudite playwrights in the modern theater, but his plays, unlike his novels, have a quality of studied naïveté that seems unseasoned by maturing experience.

Like the religious dramatists, those playwrights who turned to folklore and to lyric extolment of the people tended to shy away from the fuller uses of irony and paid the price of failing to come to grips with the complexities of modern experience. That does not mean they always wrote bad plays; but such work exists in backwater, little moved by the main currents of the modern theater. In this group we must put S. Ansky (1863–1920), James M. Barrie (1860–1937), Sean O'Casey (1884–1964), Paul Vincent Carroll (b. 1900), Denis Johnston (b. 1901), Federico García Lorca (1899–1936), and William Saroyan (b. 1908). The major dramatic talents here are O'Casey and Lorca.

Ansky's famous play, *The Dybbuk* (1914), is based on Hassidic beliefs and ought perhaps to be considered as religious drama. However, its force comes from its folk consciousness rather than its religious thought. It was first produced in Yiddish in 1920 in Vilna, the capital of Lithuania, and two years later it received its famous production in Moscow under the direction of Vachtangov, who was then working with Stanislavski and was permitted by his master to assist a group of Jewish actors in the establishment of a Hebrew-speaking theater. At that time Hebrew was not the spoken language of any people, save for its use in Jewish worship, and the idea of creating a Hebrew theater was extremely bold. The production, an international success, launched the Habimah Theater, today the national theater of Israel. *The Dybbuk* is a very moving play about the exorcism of a demon that possesses a young bride. It has been kept in the repertory of Habimah continuously since 1922, Vachtangov's production faithfully adhered to—perhaps too slavishly, since after many years it has become rigid and archaic. The play itself, however, remains full of vitality, as other productions show, but Paddy Chayefsky's *The Tenth Man* (1959) used the plot of *The Dybbuk* in a shamefully trivial way.

O'Casey's work has enjoyed immense notoriety and also, among certain members of his audience, a following that borders on discipleship. In addition, O'Casey's was a personality so winsome that one is tempted to give him more than his due as a playwright. In some ways he came close to the basic concerns of modern drama, particularly in his feeling for the tragicomic aspects of experience, which he embodied first in dramas treating of the Irish Rebellion and later in free-form plays extolling the goodness of man and showing his hilarious and pitiful sojourn in life.

O'Casey's plays, however, have never quite escaped Irish provincialism. This, plus their melodramatic effects and, in the later works, heavy doses of O'Casey's idiosyncratic temperament, keep them in the second drawer. *The Shadow of a Gunman* (1922) and *The Plough and the Stars* (1926), both serious plays about the Irish troubles, are particularly flawed by melodramatic excesses. More human, ever ingratiating, is *Juno and the Paycock* (1924), with its sharply edged, benevolently satiric character portraits. *The Silver Tassie* (1928) an antiwar satire done partly in expressionist manner, has become quite dated. Of the later plays, *Purple Dust* (1940) is the most stageworthy, although its humor is excessively broad.

If O'Casey, who became a communist, left Ireland for the south of England, and achieved an important international reputation, is yet touched by provincialism, the other Irish, save only Yeats, have felt its limiting effect even more. Paul Vincent Carroll's *The Wise Have Not Spoken* (1934), *Shadow and Substance* (1934), and *The White Steed* (1939) have been widely done but are not of major import. The same is to be said of Denis Johnston's *The Old Lady Says "No!"* (1929), *The Moon in the Yellow River* (1931), which contains some lovely comedy, and *The Golden Cuckoo* (1938).

The whimsy that James Barrie poured forth in great amounts from Scotland, beginning with *The Admirable Crichton* (1902) and going on through *Peter Pan* (1904), *What Every Woman Knows* (1908), *Dear Brutus* (1917), *The Old Lady Shows Her Medals* (1917), and *The Boy David* (1936), not to mention fourteen other plays, was always designed for a special taste. With the passage of time it seems to retreat ever further into its own cuteness. One wonders whether the same fate will overtake William Saroyan, whose Armenian-American verve and good spirits have issued in plays that once flashed brightly but do not make one long for their revival. Both his best plays were written in 1939: *My Heart's in the Highlands* and *The Time of Your Life*. Saroyan's romantic attachment to the nobodies of this world was displayed again in *The Beautiful People* (1941) and became antiwar propaganda in the short *Hello Out There* (1942). His attempt at theatrical symbolism in *The Cave Dwellers* (1957) seemed labored. The argument over Saroyan has usually been about his sentimentality, which some like and others deplore. What matters is that he has consistently, in his sixteen-or-so plays, devoted himself to lyric expression of the goodness of little people, and this rapture has prevented him from developing the irony that shows forth in patches in his work, particularly in *The Time of Your Life*.

Lorca's dramatic accomplishment was considerable, and because he achieved it through the lyric expression of folk materials, his position in modern drama is unique. In this respect he may be compared only with Yeats. He employed verse so well that in his better plays one accepts it without reserve, grateful for the marriage the playwright has achieved between the narrative and the poetic imagery in which it is set forth.

His earliest play was *El maleficio de la mariposa* (1920; *The Butterfly's Evil Spell*), but the first to become well known throughout the world was *La zapatera prodigiosa* (1930; *The Shoemaker's Prodigious Wife*), a farce done in *commedia dell'arte* style about a shrewish wife and how she never changes. There are traces of the *commedia dell'arte* also in *Así que pasen cinco años* (1931; *If Five Years Pass*), to which is added symbolism of a kind that only Lorca seemed able to get away with, such as the appearance of an ace of hearts struck through with an arrow to underscore the pathos of the death of a young girl. Such symbolism is found also in *Bodas de sangre* (1933; *Blood Wedding*), in which one of the speaking characters is the moon. This poetic conceit does not work unless the acting reaches the level of lyric rapture that is in the lines. However, the story of *Blood Wedding* is sure fire, a tale of conflict between passion and society. An Andalusian bride, wed to the husband of her family's choice, is abducted by her childhood lover. The runaways know that their stolen love can end only in death, and the play shows how this happens.

In dramatizing the affinity between passion and death Lorca excelled, not only because this theme has a deeply romantic psychological appeal but also because Lorca was able to show it embodied in Spanish mores and character. Lorca seems utterly Spanish in his use of language, choice of symbols, and in the communication of Spanish pride and fatalism. His plays have the brilliance of surface and darkness of substance that belong to flamenco music. *Yerma* (1934), "a tragic poem," is a stronger work than *Blood Wedding*. It is the story of a marriage that ends in murder because the wife's passion is too great to tolerate her husband's lack of love. Frustrated love is also the theme of *Doña Rosita la soltera* (1935; *Dona Rosita the Spinster*).

Lorca's greatest work is *La casa de Bernarda Alba* (1936; *The House of Bernarda Alba*), which takes place in the house of a widow who has five daughters. The mystique of virginity hangs over this play even more than over Shakespeare's *Measure for Measure* and without any of the latter play's suggestion of forgiving grace. By Spanish custom, the eldest of the daughters should be the first to marry, but in Lorca's play the youngest is in love with the fiancé of the eldest and does not restrain herself from making tryst with him. Bernarda Alba shoots him, and the youngest daughter hangs herself. The mother then stifles the emotions attendant on such a catastrophe and announces proudly that her daughter died a virgin. There are few works in which emotions are as frighteningly confined by social custom and austere morality as in this play, which deserves to be considered among the finest achievements of the modern stage. Lorca's own passions of a political nature led to his death. He was executed in 1936, soon after the beginning of the Spanish Civil War, because of his support of the Republican government.

Most good drama is rooted in the manners, customs, and attitudes of particular societies. Ibsen and Chekhov are the foremost modern examples of this, Lorca is another; even Genet, the anti-realist, writes of the mores of prison society and the underworld. It makes much difference, however, whether the dramatist fastens his attention upon the people simply because they are people or whether he finds in them the conflicts and contradictions that belong to existence as such. To do the former is to remain in provincialism, however great the dramatic talent may be. To do the latter is to renew and expand dramatic art. Robert Lowell's *The Old Glory* (1964), based on stories of American history by Melville and Hawthorne, is a recent instance of the way in which a people's heritage may be employed to create vigorous theater of universal import, and for this reason it has raised new hopes for the American theater. Writing about Colonial and Revolutionary America, Lowell captured certain "ironies of American history."

We must now turn to playwrights who have been in the main stream of the development of modern drama by virtue of their several abilities to dramatize ironies of existence. They took the other major path mentioned at the beginning of this chapter, going not to the folk and not to the past for inspiration but to the manifold of contemporary experience.

14. IRONY AND THE DESTRUCTIVE FULFILLMENT OF THEATER

TWENTIETH-CENTURY DRAMA has been notable for the variety of its styles, motifs, and intentions. Yet its principal growth has been toward an ever more pervasive irony, by which is meant the maintenance of an attitude of affirmation and negation toward whatever is in the field of vision and the accompaniment of this attitude by acute self-awareness. The ironist is not always sure that what he sees is real, but he is sure that he sees it. He knows that the reality he seeks lies neither in the subject nor in the object alone but in the interchange between them.

We have followed the growth of irony in modern drama almost from the start of this narrative, but now we will see it with greater intensity and in such a way that its cultural meaning will become clearer. Here two figures of the modern theater will have for us a particular importance—Antonin Artaud and Samuel Beckett. It is not so much their influence, however widespread, that gives them prominence here as the fact that each epitomizes, in quite different ways, the most important tendencies and aims of the modern theater.

The modern age has been shaped by several types of thought that bear deeply ironic connotations. We may point, in physics, to the theory of relativity; in psychology, to the split between the

conscious and the unconscious; in sociology, to the theory of ideological motivations. The phenomenological analysis of subjectivity
carried out by existentialist philosophy also generates very ironic
understandings. Most important has been the modern historical
consciousness, which renders all absolutes relative.

In these several branches of modern thought one may discern a
common element: philosophical skepticism about the adequacy of
the human mind to know and embrace reality. Descartes, and later
Kant, cast their shadows here. The so-called subject-object split
that Descartes introduced into modern consciousness has never
been overcome. With Kant, although it took another form, the
problem was renewed. Hegel attempted to overcome it with a theory of history as the progressive and dialectical self-realization of
the Ideal, but the principal cultural result of his labor has been
what we have called the modern historical consciousness, wherein
all human experience is relativized and, contrary to Hegel's intention, divorced from all real connection with solid truth. The Hegelian synthesis rapidly broke into two parts. One, calling itself
objective, focused upon scientific method. It has dealt with the
natural rather than the historical world; and its successes, both
theoretical and practical, have been so great that they have intimi-
dated all those aspects of man and culture which they have not
successfully absorbed. The other, by various names, has sought to
preserve the values of subjectivity. It has dealt with the historical
and cultural world. In philosophy its dominant voice has come to
be called existentialism.

There are thus two principal splits in modern consciousness, one
between the knowing subject and all the objects of its knowing, the
other between the "objective" sciences and the "subjective"
humanities. These two schisms are obviously related, and their coexistence is such that they amplify each other. Certain individuals,
lucidly aware of the modern situation, find its internal tensions
almost too great to bear.

This situation is the one that modern drama has had, willy-nilly,
to cope with. Where it has done so consciously and courageously it
has contributed that which has been most significant in the development of the modern theater, and where it has done something

else it has been of less historical moment. This is the criterion I have been using and shall continue to use in tracing the course of the modern theater.

As we go forward, it will be well to keep in mind certain motifs that help relate the theater's development to the underlying crises of modern culture. One of these is irony, which is the stylistic resort a split consciousness must come to in its attempt to speak of a reality from which it feels itself cut off. Another is the transmutation of the romantic quest *for* reality into the modern query *about* reality. The search *for* turns into the question *whether*. Could we know the real even if we came to it? And is there anything, after all, that deserves the name "reality"?

A third such motif is that of alienation. The estrangement of the self from the world, from society, and from itself is a prominent result of the aforementioned factors and has been a preoccupation of modern analyses of man from Hegel, Marx, and Feuerbach to Freud, Sartre, and Marcuse. We shall see it expressed in the theater by the representation of consciousness as a prison from which it is almost impossible to escape.

Finally, we shall encounter the motif of "theatrical positivism," a term that will require elucidation as we proceed. In brief, it refers to the theater's strategy of regarding itself as its one, sure, positive reality. As Wallace Stevens wrote that "poetry is the subject of the poem," so the theater has tended to affirm that its own subject is theater. It has thus embraced its own alienation, in a perhaps desperate effort to absorb the world into its own mode of being.

In recent years the dramatic forms one may expect to find in the theater have changed more radically than in any other period. The twentieth century has provided two major sources for the change, one German, the other French. Both may be called expressionism, though only the German, frequently directed toward social protest, usually bears this name. The French variety, oriented more toward psychological liberation, is usually called surrealism. Both names came into drama criticism from the fine arts.

The innovations of Strindberg and Wedekind were important influences upon the shape and spirit of expressionism, and it was from those writers that the expressionism of Eugene O'Neill in

America was derived. The influence of Chekhov was less direct but has proved to be even more profound.

It is significant that the first German expressionist play, the short *Mörder, Hoffnung der Frauen* (1907; *Murder, the Women's Hope*), was written by a painter, Oskar Kokoschka (b. 1886), for the expressionists clearly intended to abandon the "dramatic" way of structuring plays and to replace it with something closer to other arts. I have already described the indebtedness of Michel de Ghelderode to Flemish and Spanish painting. More recently Eugène Ionesco has dwelt upon the importance of modern painting as a source of instruction for the playwright. However, it is probably most helpful to recognize in expressionist plays a type of structure that is musical. Thematic material replaces plot as the principle of unity, and themes in counterpoint are frequently employed.

At the same time, expressionists were aware of useful precedents for their work within the dramatic tradition provided one looked away from classical influences toward romantic ones, particularly to Shakespeare with his multiscene and multiplot construction, and then to the *Sturm und Drang* period, especially Goethe's *Faust* and the radical work of Büchner that came after it. There was also the less bookish tradition of "theatrical theater" represented by the circus, the puppet show, street players, and cabaret. Important, too, was the medieval Christian theater, which had not hesitated to put God, man, and the Devil on stage and in bold strokes to portray the whole history of man from Creation to Last Judgment.

These influences had all been making themselves felt throughout the nineteenth century; now they jelled in combination with nihilist tendencies in philosophy and the appearance of the unconscious as a subject of study by psychology. There seemed to be not only artistic precedents but also strong promptings in the rest of culture to reconstitute dramatic form.

Although Kokoschka's play of 1907 was the first German expressionist play, the movement is often said to have begun with *Der Bettler* (1911; *The Beggar*) by Reinhard Sorge (1892–1916), in which the author attempted to create for the stage something simi-

lar to the interior monologue of the modern novel.[1] The movement did not last long. Already, by 1919, in *Drums in the Night,*
Bertolt Brecht was satirizing the style and moving beyond it.
Meanwhile a large number of writers had given to the movement
an intensity that made it one of the more important "moments" of
twentieth-century theater. Among these were Paul Kornfeld (1889
–1942), George Kaiser (1878–1945), Franz Werfel (1890–1945),
Walter Hasenclever (1890–1940), Carl Sternheim (1878–1942),
Ernst Toller (1893–1939), and Ernst Barlach (1870–1938). Imbued with the spirit of German radicalism around the time of
World War I, the work of these men seemed a few years ago to
have become outdated. In the apocalypticism of the atomic age,
however, and in light of the absurdist theater that followed World
War II, it has again become "contemporary."

The ironies that expressionists dwelt upon and that led them to
some of their outlandish constructions were several. The most important was a strong sense of the contrast between the surface of
experience and its depth. Insofar as drama is an imitation of life,
the dramatist is required to show his audience how things appear
in everyday life. But if these appearances seem important only because one's gaze lacks penetration, and if the genuine motivations
of men proceed from irrational depths that are antisocial, then the
dramatist must also imitate the depth. The resultant bifocalism is
ironic, and it was precisely this that led the expressionists to invent
a kind of drama that was neither naturalistic nor, in any familiar
sense, poetic, although it was a blend of both. Naturalism contributed sharp descriptions of behavior, which were rendered in almost cartoonish style. It also contributed frankness of language and
a penchant for focusing upon the ordinary man rather than upon
heroic or princely figures. Poetic drama contributed a restless
search for trans-rational images, unexpected symbols, and freedom
from the conventions of workaday prose. The tension between the
surface and the depth also led the expressionists to oscillate between moments of startling originality and others merely banal.

Walter H. Sokel has pointed out another persistent irony in ex-

[1] See Walter H. Sokel, ed., *Anthology of German Expressionist Drama* (Garden City,
N.Y.: Anchor Books, Doubleday, 1963), p. xv.

pressionist plays.[2] On the one hand, expressionism frequently employed a romantic protagonist endowed with a "mission" to regenerate and redeem the world. On the other hand, expressionism parodied this mission in an "acid and macabre presentation of a meaningless, insanely materialistic world."[3] A similar ambivalence is to be noticed in the expressionists' attitude toward religion. Anti-theism was usually part of their general stance. Yet some among them, like Barlach, could write deeply religious plays. Others, like Sorge and Werfel, did so part of the time. All, even when most anti-theistic, displayed a noticeable spiritual sensitivity. They deserve to be understood as belonging to that important modern phenomenon, the religious protest against religion. That is why their contemporary and compatriot, Paul Tillich, made so much of them in his theological analysis of culture, *The Religious Situation*, which he wrote in 1926.[4]

Tillich perceived that the expressionists had broken with the spiritual and ideological assumptions of bourgeois society and that the most important sign of this break was their style. Bourgeois society, together with its values, was attacked not only with ideas but, even more importantly, with a style that was an affront to rational presuppositions. This change in style, which implied change in dramatic form, was rightly discerned by Tillich to be motivated by a new kind of spirituality. Though Tillich did not say it, the hallmark of the new spirituality was its feeling for irony. That is to say, all certainties were suspended, and this led not to despair but to an ambivalent engagement with life and its mysteries.

The French variety of expressionism, usually called surrealism, was anticipated by Alfred Jarry, whose work has been discussed above. French expressionism was less titanic than the German, less given to thoughts of reforming mankind, but it relied equally on dreamlike images and sequences and is also to be understood as the elaboration of techniques designed to break the reigning style of bourgeois culture in the name of subjective power. There was a

2 *Ibid.*, pp. xxii ff.
3 *Ibid.*, p. xxiii.
4 *Die religiöse Lage der Gegenwart* (Berlin: Ulstein, 1926). Translated by H. Richard Niebuhr as *The Religious Situation* (New York: Holt, 1932; Meridian, 1956).

good bit of communication and sharing of aims between the German expressionists, the French surrealists, the futurists in Italy, and the constructivists in Russia.

We must note in France, as in Germany, a strong tendency to shape drama according to principles already established in other arts. For instance, the first surrealist drama was *Les Mamelles de Tirésias* (*The Breasts of Tiresias*), from the subtitle of which the very term "surrealism" was taken. Its author, Guillaume Apollinaire (1880–1918), is even better known for his contributions to avant-garde poetry and painting than for his contributions to the theater. His play, performed in 1917 but written perhaps as early as 1903, tells the fantastic story of a wife who changes her sex. Not to be outdone, the husband changes also—and gives birth to thousands of children. By no traditional standard is this play a drama. It may be a farce. If so, it is farce with its substance drawn from dreams in which impossible metamorphoses occur. It obviously has more to do with surrealist painting and poetry than with what audiences, even today, expect to find in the theater. The most famous of the French surrealists, Jean Cocteau (1889–1963), came to the writing of plays by way of ballet, in which he had collaborated with and learned from Stravinsky, Milhaud, Satie, Dufy, Leger, and other innovators in music and painting.

In the wake of World War I, the theater seemed to enter upon a period of veritable contortionism in its attempt to keep pace with other arts. It was, of course, inevitable that the theater should be deeply affected by other arts and the cultural tides to which they were responding. However, in its self-conscious zeal not to be left behind, the theater revealed an anxiety about its position in modern culture that has plagued it throughout the twentieth century. In its outspoken desire to be as "relevant" as other arts, the theater confessed that its position as an art central to culture had more or less been lost. All important modern plays are touched by this sense of loss—some beneficially, since they sound a poignant note among their ironies, and some adversely, since they betray a frantic tone.

Of Cocteau's considerable number of plays, those of most note are *Les Mariés de la Tour Eiffel* (1921; *The Eiffel Tower Wedding Party*), a mad and joyful carnival; *Orphée* (1926; *Orpheus*);

and *La Machine infernale* (1934; *The Infernal Machine*), which is a modern, highly Freudian adaptation of the Oedipus story. Of this play Francis Fergusson rightly says: "Modern life, with its disabused clarity, its small shrewdnesses, occupies the foreground, while the different reality of the mythic pattern is in the surrounding darkness." [5] Fergusson notes that the strategy is similar to that used by Joyce in *Ulysses,* and this helps one to understand the quality of Cocteau's irony, which rests upon the incongruous overlay of the drably familiar on the exaltedly mythical. Like Joyce, Cocteau does not ask his audience to choose which of these levels is the more real. He affirms them both and sees each ironically refracted through the other.

Jules Romains (b. 1885) and Fernand Cromelynck (b. 1885) both employed surrealistic elements in less radical ways than Apollinaire or Cocteau. Romains' *Knock; Ou Le Triomphe de la Médecine* (1923; *Doctor Knock*), about a country doctor who turns his practice into a giant industry, was an international success following its première by Louis Jouvet at the Comédie des Champs-Élysées. Cromelynck's most popular play was *Le Cocu magnifique* (1920; *The Magnificent Cuckold*).

The surrealist movement provided Antonin Artaud (1896–1948) with his entrance into French culture. In 1923 Jacques Rivière, editor of *La Nouvelle Revue française,* found the young and unknown Artaud's poems too lacking in grace for inclusion in that magazine. This started a lengthy and illuminating correspondence between the two men, in which Artaud wrote anxiously of his slender hold upon reality:

> I suffer from a frightful malady of the spirit. My thought takes leave of me step by step. It goes from the simple fact of the thought right on to the exterior fact of materialization into words. Words, forms of phrases, interior directions of thought, simple reactions of the spirit, I am in constant pursuit of my intellectual being. So, when *I am able to seize upon a form,* however imperfect it be, I fix it, in the fear of losing all my thought. I am underneath myself, I know it, I suffer from it, but I affirm it in fear so as not to die all at once.[6]

[5] *The Idea of a Theater* (Garden City, N.Y.: Anchor Books, Doubleday, 1953), p. 210.
[6] Letter from Artaud to Jacques Rivière, June 5, 1923. In *Oeuvres complètes,* Vol. I Paris: Gallimard, 1956), p. 20. My translation.

This paragraph announces, though even its author did not know it at the time, the essence of Artaud's approach to the theater and the reasons for its increasing importance in this age. We shall come back to it. The year after this correspondence began, André Breton published the *Surrealist Manifesto,* and in 1925 Artaud, who had become known to Max Jacob and Breton and other surrealists and had got some of his own poems published under the title *Tric-trac du ciel,* was made editor of the third number of *La Révolution surréaliste.*

Meanwhile, Artaud had begun work as an actor. He had come to Paris in 1920 at the age of twenty-four and had played a part for Lugné-Poe, then became, for a short time, a member of the Atelier of Charles Dullin, playing twelve roles in works by Calderón, Molière, Pirandello, Cocteau, and others. He also acted in films, including early work by Abel Gance and René Clair. In 1926 he did the role of the monk Massieu in Carl Dreyer's *The Passion of Joan of Arc,* through which his lean face has become familiar to thousands of film buffs. Altogether, by 1935, when he quit the screen, Artaud had made some twenty films, among which figure Brecht's *Threepenny Opera,* made by Pabst in 1930, Fritz Lang's *Liliom,* and Abel Gance's *Lucrèce Borgia,* in 1935, in which Artaud played Savonarola.

In 1927 Artaud founded with Roger Vitrac (1899–1952) the Théâtre Alfred Jarry, which gave performances at the Comédie des Champs-Élysées. Before financial troubles closed in, four sets of plays were done, including Artaud's *Ventre brulé ou la Mère folle (Burnt-out Womb, or The Mad Mother),* Vitrac's *Les Mystères de l'amour (The Mysteries of Love)* and his more important play, *Victor ou les Enfants au pouvoir (Victor, or the Children in Power).*

Vitrac's work is rather on the border line between surrealist theater, from which Artaud was now pulling strongly away, and the type of theater later created by Ionesco. The title of *Victor* is a mocking allusion to a 1797 play by Guilbert de Pixerécourt, *Victor ou L'Enfant de la forêt,* which has the historical distinction of being one of the first works ever to be designated a "melodrama." Vitrac's play shows a household terrorized by a precocious nine-year-old boy, played by an adult actor in short pants. In the first act everything is seen through the eyes of the child. In the second, all is seen from the perspective of the grown-ups. The comedy is rich, its satire falling upon bourgeois manners, the French language, French patriotism, and marriage. Pixerécourt's play, conceived as an opera, had ended up as a straight play with musical accompaniment—hence, a "melodrama." Vitrac's piece employs only a trombone, used now and again to announce that a certain female character has broken wind. The play frighteningly avers that the battle between children and parents is irreconcilable and that the children are bound to win at the expense of parental sanity. It was successfully revived in 1963 by Jean Anouilh, who directed it himself as an act of loyalty to his deceased and neglected friend Vitrac.

But let us return to Artaud: His career, if that is the word for it, became increasingly quixotic after the failure of the Alfred Jarry Theater. He met Jouvet and tried with little success to interest him in his ideas. He witnessed the Balinese Theater at the Colonial Exposition in 1932 and found in it the realization of much that he had dreamed of in theater. He became ever more interested in myth and ritual. In 1935 he announced the foundation of the Theater of Cruelty, which opened and closed with a production of *Cenci* adapted by Artaud from the works of Stendhal and Shelley. Thereafter he went to Mexico (1936) to give lectures on the theater but most of all to study Indian rituals and the cultic use of drugs. Artaud had been a user of drugs since his early days in Paris, perhaps partly to ease the pain, both physical and mental, in which he lived most of the time. Eventually (1945) he published a book on the Mexican Indians, *Au Pays des Tarahumaras* (*In the Land of the Tarahumaras*).

Returning to France, Artaud was nearly mad. He traveled to Ireland where, as he later wrote to Jean-Louis Barrault, "I came back to [God] at Dublin in September 1937, where I made confession and had communion after twenty years of estrangement from his worship and several years of atheism and blasphemy, with which all my writings are constellated." [7] Artaud, however, was soon expelled from Ireland, evidently because he was given to fits of violence. He came back to France and spent the next nine years,

[7] Quoted in Claude Mauriac, *L'Alittérature contemporaine* (Paris: Albin Michel, 1958), pp. 43–44.

including the whole period of the war, in asylums for the insane.

Part of the time Artaud manifested symptoms of paranoia. His doctors were particularly disturbed by his preoccupations with voodoo magic and alchemy. (Strindberg, too, had been obsessed by alchemy. Note also the appeal for an alchemical theater in Artaud's *The Theater and Its Double.*) From time to time he had hallucinations, and he was often certain that destructive forces were attacking his mind and his body. He was given repeated treatments of electric shock, which caused unspeakable suffering for one who held desperately to his thought lest it "take leave" of him "step by step."

Artaud was released from captivity in 1946 and took up residence in a rest home in Ivry. He continued to write prodigiously, as he had done all along. Much of his writing is obscene. The obscenity was partly due to his suffering and hatred of society, but more importantly it reflects his interest in the bodily equivalent or incarnation of thought, a motif to which we shall soon pay more attention. *The Theater and Its Double,* his most influential work, written from 1930 to 1933, when its various parts appeared in *La Nouvelle Revue française,* was published as a whole in 1938. His other most important writings not yet mentioned include *L'Art et la mort* (1929; "Art and Death"), *Héliogabale ou l'anarchiste couronné* (1934;"Heliogabalus, or the Anarchist Crowned"), *Les Nouvelles Révélations de l'être* (1937; "The New Revelations of Being"), and *Van Gogh, le suicidé de la société* (1947; "Van Gogh, the Suicide of Society"). But there was much more, including a vast correspondence, poems, short plays, and many notes on film and theater. His collected works run to nine volumes.

On January 13, 1947, Artaud gave a "lecture" at the Vieux Colombier. His friends and followers from the Parisian theater were present, also some enemies; and he upset them all by a performance that mixed lucidity with confusion, calm with frenzy, imagination with hallucination. This solo performance was, Georges Charbonnier has said, the only time when the Theater of Cruelty has ever really existed—"that day when Antonin Artaud gave his own body as the spectacle."[8] A year later, Artaud's play, *Pour En Finir Avec Le Jugement de Dieu (To End God's Judg-*

[8] *Essai sur Antonin Artaud* (Paris: Éditions Pierre Seghers, 1959), p. 197.

ment), commissioned by the French Radio Service, was denied broadcast, in spite of support for it by Raymond Queneau, Roger Vitrac, Louis Jouvet, Jean-Louis Barrault, and others.

On March 4, 1948, Artaud died at Ivry. He had been right about the destructive forces attacking his body, even as his mind had certainly been long under siege. He succumbed in the night, seated at the foot of his bed, to a cancer of the colon.

In many ways, Artaud must appear a minor figure in the modern theater. He wrote no plays that can appeal to a wide audience. He had no success as a director. He founded no school and developed no technique for the realization of his ideas. The English translation of *The Theater and Its Double* did not appear until 1958. Most of his writings are obscure, and the number of directors who have learned much from him is small, though they include three of the best at present: Roger Blin in France, Peter Brook in England, and Jerzy Grotowski in Poland. What, then, is the significance of Artaud in the development of the modern theater?

The answer lies in this: if one understands what the theater was in Artaud's mind, in his imagination, then he understands that which the modern theater has been straining to become, for better or worse, ever since World War I and even before. He understands why the avant-garde theater took the tack that it did after World War II and why the signal works of twentieth-century theater have been such superb representations of modern consciousness while being at the same time so alienated from society and thus from their own audiences. For in Artaud the theater is at once the glory and the despair of man. We must now attempt to understand this, and the task is made no easier by the fact that a purely Artaudian theater cannot exist, so invertedly "mystical" are its precepts, and most of the time we will be concerned with things that will probably seem unrelated to the theater. Yet this is to be expected, perhaps, of a man who thought that the existing theater had lost all knowledge of what the theater really is.

The motifs of Artaud's writing are religious. With respect to Christianity, as well as other religions, he was never neutral. Blasphemous most of the time, uttering cries of hatred against Jesus Christ and his Church, at other times adoring, he never departed from the religious imagination or the shadows cast upon his spirit by his early religious upbringing in Marseilles. Thus, he assumed the role of priest and prophet, however accursed, which explains the nature of his relation to the actual theater, which heard itself truly accused and described by him and hardly knew what to do about it.

Let us read him on the subject of Christianity, at one of those moments, the most frequent for him, when he was in wrath against it:

Rodez, 7 September 1945

My dear Henri Parisot,

  I wrote you at least three weeks ago a couple of letters instructing you to publish the *Journey to the Land of the Tarahumaras,* but appending to it a letter replacing the *Supplement to the Journey,* in which I was fool enough to say I had accepted conversion to Jesus Christ, while in very fact Christ is that which I have always most of all abominated, and this conversion was merely the result of a frightful spell which had made me forget my very nature and had made me swallow, at Rodez, under the guise of Communion, a frightful number of wafers destined to preserve me for as long as possible, and if possible for all eternity, in a being that is not my own. This being consists of ascending into the sky as a spirit instead of descending deeper and deeper as a body into hell, that is into sexuality, soul of all that lives. While that which is Christ carries the being away into the empyrean of clouds and gasses where since the beginning of time it has been dissolving. . . . Like Jesus Christ there is supposed also to be one who never would descend to earth because man was too small for him; and so he stayed in the abysses of infinities, like some so-called immanence of God who indefatigably and like some Buddha in his self-contemplation awaits the day that BEING will be sufficiently perfect for Him to descend into it and slip inside it, which is the infamous scheming of a slothful and cowardly rotter who would never have wanted to suffer the Being, the Being in its wholeness, but to make it suffer by proxy for another, in order subsequently to exorcise this wretched other, and relegate it to hell. . . . I want you to understand that it was not Jesus Christ I went looking for among Tarahumara, but myself, me, Antonin Artaud, born September 4, 1896 at Marseille, 4 rue du Jardin des Plantes, out of a uterus I had nothing to do with and which I have never had a thing to do with even previously, for this is no way to be born, to be copulated and masturbated for nine months by the membrane, the yawning membrane which toothlessly devours, as the UPANISHADS say, and I know that I was born otherwise, born of my own works and not of a mother, but the MOTHER tried to get me and you have seen how that turned out in my life. I was born only in my own labor-pangs and if only you could do the same for yourself, dear Henri Parisot. . . . And Jesus Christ is this thing born of a mother who also tried to get me for himself, and that long before the beginnings of time and the universe, and I went to heights of Mexico only to rid myself of Jesus Christ, just as I plan on going some day to Tibet in order to flush god and his Holy Ghost out of me.[9]

This passage shows, in the very force of its negativity, that the principal religious motif in Artaud's thought is incarnation, even though he declared that such a doctrine was a lie. He could not get around it because his insistence on the body as the *source* of all thought was, at the same time, an insistence that the body is a *spiritual* state. This is not the familiar doctrine that the spirit is the flower of natural existence but rather a belief that the bodily state is spiritual from its inception, provided one attends fully enough to its actual, immediate pressure. The difficulties Artaud had in enunciating and holding to such a view are to be compared only to the difficulties of the Church Fathers in formulating the simultaneous humanity and divinity of Christ, and it was just for this reason that Artaud both hated and loved the Christ figure, though his alienation was so great that he could not love anything long at a time.

Charbonnier, who has written of Artaud with extraordinary perception,[10] says that his entire project consisted of the attempt to live his own body—a body, one should remember, that was ill throughout his life following a childhood attack of meningitis, in physical pain more often than not, and eventually dead of cancer. The drive of this pained man toward the concrete was so severe that Artaud divided the body itself into parts he considered more and less concrete. The parts of the body which were most corporeal and toward which all tended were bone, or rather the marrow of

9 Translated by David Rattray. In *Antonin Artaud Anthology*, Jack Hirschman, ed., 2nd ed., rev. (San Francisco: City Lights, 1965), pp. 82–83.
10 *Op. cit.*

bone, and blood, while the bodily organs were less corporeal and were hated. A schizophrenic view, to be sure, but let us pursue it.

In the realm of the aesthetic, the pursuit of the corporeal will tend to manifest itself as a preoccupation with form, while the right or fully adequate form will prove itself to be forever elusive, beyond one's grasp. An example of this tendency may be seen in Artaud's letter to Jacques Rivière previously cited. "Words, forms of phrases, . . . I am in constant pursuit of my intellectual being. So, when *I am able to seize upon a form,* however imperfect it be, I fix it, in the fear of losing all my thought." The emphasis is Artaud's. We may think, as Rivière did upon receiving the letter, that here is nothing but a young author saying that he has to search for the right turn of phrase; but as Artaud's life showed, there was something more in it than that.

Artaud believed that his thought, which he tended to regard in itself as a *thing,* was identical with its incarnation, which meant its form, and apart from that it would cease entirely to exist. Thus, the form must be fixed, however imperfect. It must be held as concrete and cannot, in fact, be improved. For we are not dealing here with any theory of correspondence whereby the form or phrase will be valued according to its approximation to some transcendent ideal. Instead, the phrase will be valued precisely as that particular which it is. When Rivière said that Artaud's lines were infelicitous, Artaud, who knew this, did not care to learn to improve them but felt that his whole intellectual being was threatened, since it existed precisely *in* those lines, however "rough" or "imperfect."

Every writer may have something of this feeling, but most writers will discipline it by reason, by the desire for intelligibility or at least expressive adequacy. For Artaud that was not the game. He might be more or less satisfied with a given expression, but the measure of it was not lucidity, not even that "aptness" that "difficult" modern poets strive for. Instead, it was corporeal density. "Density," in the sense of bodily firmness, not intellectual burden, was a favorite word of Artaud.

The paradoxical drive to incarnate that which has no existence (or even subsistence) if it is *not* embodied, this drive of the spirit downward into specific, concrete, and finite form, is, it can be seen, an ultimate predication of a positive theatricalism. All theater is masking, to be sure. But what if the mask is not the sign or symbol of something anterior to itself but rather the very actuality of a spiritual state that has no other existence but in that mask? The mask is not the *occasion* of the manifestation, as when one says that only by reading *Hamlet* can you know what Shakespeare meant by *Hamlet;* it is the *reality* of the manifestation, as in the case of a person, whose mask (*persona*) is the *same* as himself. The personality is the form of the soul, but the soul is nothing other than the personality, which in the last analysis is the body. What has to be realized, therefore, is the body, which is no longer the vehicle of the soul. If anything, this relation is reversed. The soul, the spirit, the intellect, the realm of aesthetics and ideas—all this, if we must speak of it at all, is the vehicle of the body, in whose service it should properly exist.

Now, the theater is a body. The theater arises from itself and goes toward itself and has no essential relation to anything that is not part of its own self-generation and self-realization. The theater is the body in its ultimate function and is the ultimate spiritual state. It is its own positive datum and is fulfilled in the degree that it is concrete.

By this approach, we have pushed *drama* away. (It will be readmitted later as a practical necessity, but on limited terms.) A drama is an ideal construction, noted down in certain script words by a playwright and waiting for a stage production more or less adequately to realize the ideal that exists *in potentio* in the script. It is ideal in two senses. First, it exists *as* an ideal, to be approximated. It endures in imagination. Second, it is made of words, and words are the vehicles of ideas. Thus, Artaud's radical project of a truly corporeal theater requires in the first instance the substitution of theatrical for dramatic values. The playwright is the enemy, and it is necessary to attack his principal commodity—words.

The reader of *The Theater and Its Double* finds himself taken little by little into a region of theater from which words have disappeared. Artaud said he would "abolish the word." The place of words would be taken by gestures, sounds, lights, costumes—all that is physically real and holds the spectator in unmediated rapport with itself. "Things do not move me except as they affect my flesh and coincide with it at the exact point where they stir it, and not beyond that point. Nothing moves me or interests me except what addresses itself *directly* to my body." [11]

Most important of all is space. The theater, Artaud insisted, is a certain filling of space with body and gesture. Nowhere does his sure aesthetic sense show better than here, and if one feels that his prescriptions make of theater something closer to dance than to drama, that is the right conclusion. The "poetry of space" he sought was found by him more nearly reached in Balinese theater, which looks to Westerners like dance, and in the rituals of Mexican Indians, than anywhere else. I do not know that he ever saw Martha Graham, but if he had it is likely that her poetry of bodily space that seems to proceed from the marrow of the bone would have excited him. He would have been bothered only by her tendency toward consistent, therefore ideational, symbols, such as the red cord.

Yet if the word is "abolished" from Artaud's theater, it can be readmitted in a certain way. If Artaud "abolished" the word, he did not, as has been frequently observed, deny himself the privilege of using words, in his theater as in his poetry. The word may be present in Artaudian theater provided it comes there not as the expression of an idea but as a "body." Its *physical* presence is allowed, even insisted upon. The word is a sound. It has a certain density, a certain weight. It is not a sign, or if it is, it is such only secondarily. It is a *thing,* and it enters and leaves the stage in the same way that an actor enters and leaves in his body, a gesture begins and ends, a property is on or off, a costume is worn or not. The theater has no inherent need of the word, but it may use it if it consents to be a bodily substance.

By the same token, the theater has no need of plays, of dramas, but it may use them if they are seen as the point of departure rather than the final cause of the presentation. This is director's theater with a vengeance, though it has to be added that the director's job is cut out for him—to achieve a poetry of corporeal space. This cannot be done if the play is paramount, and Artaud made himself very clear when he said that Shakespeare was the cause of the downfall of the Western theater. This remark shows the big difference between Artaud and Copeau, whose programs at some

11 "Fragments of a Journey in Hell," in *Artaud Anthology*, p. 43.

points overlap. Copeau, as we saw earlier (Chapter 5), found in Shakespeare the very inspiration for a renewal of the theater's capacity to employ the actor and his space poetically. Artaud understood well this quality in Shakespeare and the Elizabethan theater in general, but he saw also that in Shakespeare the nonverbal poetry *assists* the words, which are supreme. Thus, Shakespeare is an inspiration (however inimitable) to playwrights and an enemy of theater as such. Artaud preferred the Jacobeans because of their heightened theatricalism and their introduction of antisocial themes such as incest. Inferior as poets and dramatists, they were superior in respect of the body and the theater positive.

Artaud's treatment of the word in the theater has been followed, ironically, even more by playwrights than by directors. We come closer to Artaudian theater in the early plays of Ionesco, and certainly in Genet, than in most productions advertised as "theater of cruelty." In those playwrights the word is ancillary to the theatrical reality, and if it be allowed temporarily to take its own lead, it always confounds itself and subsequently returns to its genuine status as a property of the stage. The verbal explosion of sense into sound near the end of Ionesco's *Bald Soprano* is a clear instance of this. That passage is wrongly interpreted if it is taken to portray the degeneration of sense into nonsense or of verbal communication into nothingness. On the contrary, it is the transmutation of more or less rational speech into a pure, and hence subrational, theatrical substance. The word becomes incarnate as sound and fury, but instead of signifying nothing it signifies the body.

"There is," said Artaud, "a certain thing above all human activity: it is the example of this monotonous crucifixion, this crucifixion wherein the soul is forever being lost." [12]

It belongs to Artaud's religious imagination, as well as to his tormented psyche, that he carried the motif of incarnation forward to that of crucifixion—needless to say, crucifixion without a resurrection. This is the "logic," such as it is, by which we pass from the theater positive to the theater of cruelty.

By theater of cruelty, Artaud did not mean that the theater will select for depiction certain acts and these will be cruel ones. To

12 *Artaud Anthology*, p. 45.

think so is to take him in a bastard way and promulgate a theater no better than the terrors of television. He meant instead that the theater will depict acts, and only acts, and these will all manifest themselves as species of cruelty. "An act is a cruelty." By the same token, a thought, which is an act of the body-mind, is also a cruelty, and the more we recognize thought as act, the more we will perceive its cruelty. "The real pain," he said, "is to feel thought shifting inside you." [13] And then:

> I don't mean a thought lengthwise, a thought having the time-dimension of thoughts; I mean one thought, a thought by itself, but a thought FROM INSIDE; but I don't mean a thought by Pascal, a philosopher's thought; I mean a twisted fixation, a sclerosis of a specific state. Catch that! [14]

At least two reasons are to be discerned for Artaud's insistence that every act is a cruelty. The first is theological, a denial of the benevolence of the Christian God. Artaud believed most of the time that we are born into a world controlled by destructive agencies, wicked forces or deities against whom we have no hope of prevailing. The Christ is to be hated not because he succumbed to the cruelty of the world but because that destiny is represented to the faithful as a victory. That transports it at once into the gassy heavens and denies the flesh.

Beyond this, however, there is another reason for holding that every act is a cruelty: it is cruel in the sense that there is nothing to *redeem* it, in other words, to *humanize* it—neither an intentional cause nor a final cause nor any place it might have in a divine or human story. An act is a surd, and a surd is cruel because it has no meaning. The notion is similar to that of Genet when he (later) held that the only beautiful (that is, true) act is unmotivated, the *acte gratuit*. For Genet there is no contradiction in calling such an act beautiful and also cruel, nor did Artaud see any such contradiction. Artaud maintained, however, that such cruel beauty and truth belongs to every act, once it is seen for what it is.

"Cruelty" here does not mean, then, only those acts society and

13 *Ibid.*, p. 36.
14 *Ibid.*, p. 37.

conscience ordinarily label cruel. It applies not only to murder and torture but also to kissing, eating, and every other kind of deed.

The body, which suffers cruelty, also inflicts cruelty, since its nature is to be both passive and active. The theater, being a body, lies under the passive necessity to be sensitive to the cruelties of the world. And insofar as it is active, the theater-body is a house of acts where cruelty is renewed in quintessential form. Quintessential, because only in the theater can the really "pure" act occur. The theater breaks our habits of expectation by means of which we try to "redeem" the cruelties of the world when we cast them into dramatic patterns—that is, fictions of moral justification. The theater in its purity is not dramatic. It is the place where the actual reality of the world appears. The theater positive is the actual world. It is the world come fully into its own.

But when we say "world" here, we must be clear what that means. It is not society but nature. The whole function of theater is to expose the abyss that yawns between society and nature. Society is dramatic: it sees human behavior under the aspect of ideas, continuities, and plots. Nature is theatrical: it is a series of acts (not actions), unconnected, and present to consciousness unmediated by reason. To bring this difference forward, the theater goes by a strong inclination toward certain acts that are clearly antisocial. These are crimes, especially murder, and sexual license; but strongest of all is incest, for this act above all others makes clear the inherent clash between nature and society, as is evident in the fact that in society incest is taboo.[15] Thus, one can see why even the popular theater is attracted to social scandal and why much is permitted in the theater that is not tolerated in society. Social custodians try always to see that crime is punished in dramas, but men of the theater try to get around this and are scornful of "poetic justice" in all its forms.

The point in all this has to do not only with the obvious instances of theatrical depiction of crimes and sex but also with the theater's pervasively antisocial posture whenever it has not been made socially subservient and thus begun to die.

We are now led to still another motif in Artaud's thought, one

[15] For this insight I am again indebted to Georges Charbonnier, *op. cit.*, pp. 158–162.

that is also partly religious but that he shares with modern culture and with the modern theater in general. I refer to the motif of alienation.

The theater positive is *le théâtre aliéné*. Anti-dramatic theater is anti-social theater. Artaud asked for a theater of gesture, of bodily reality. He added that it should be a source of plague and contagion. But contrary to what is often supposed, he did not ask for a theater of ritual or ceremony. Rituals and ceremonies are social, not of nature. From such the theater must sever itself, even if, on the way to something else, it will find much to learn from such highly social products as Balinese theater and Mexican Indian ritual.

Anti-dramatic theater is popularly called anti-realistic. In spite of all we have just said about such theater's being of the reality of nature, there is a sense in which the term "antirealistic" is justified, and in more than a superficial way. That such theater will not and does not "copy life"—i.e., social reality—is obvious. With surrealism it could be argued that a subconscious reality was depicted and, further, that the aim of doing so was to change social reality. There could be a surrealist revolution. Indeed, if we think of modern commercial design and also much of modern intellectual life we can see that such a revolution did in fact take place. Surrealism was anti-establishment but not anti-social and, as its very name reminds us, not anti-realistic in any but a conventional sense of the real.

Of Artaud's theater, however, and with recent theater more or less consonant with his, one is obliged to say that it is deeply anti-realistic, and this because, unlike surrealism, it attempts a deliberately metaphysical theater on the basis of an impossible metaphysics.

"I regret ever uttering the word [metaphysics]," said Artaud, and with good reason. Nevertheless, he uttered it again and again and could not have done without it, for he was in search of a reality that neither social convention nor ordinary physics could give him. The reality he sought was beyond what the bodily senses could discern; beyond logic also. I have called it a surd reality—in other words, an absolute. "With me," said Artaud, "it is the absolute or nothing." This is the cry of a complete romanticist (which the best, though tempted, have avoided), and it is the cry of a modern consciousness deeply alienated from the only reality man can know —namely, that which is mediated through the senses, through reason, and through society.

Artaud suffered acutely from the knowledge that he was stuck with himself and his own thought: "At each stage of my thinking machine there are gaps, traps. . . ." [16] "This God has disposed of me to the point of absurdity. He has kept me alive in a void of negative and furious renunciations of myself." [17] "I resolutely abominate all reality." [18] On the one hand, a pursuit of the real furiously into blood, marrow, bone. On the other hand, a spiritual pursuit aiming at a metaphysical truth in the absence of reason. As one of the Fragments has it, speaking of a system that was never constructed: "To confront the metaphysical system I made for myself as a consequence of the void I carry within me." [19]

Although Artaud did not like the word, he lived and thought always in a dialectic, though perhaps a dialectic *manqué*. A man cut off from reality, living for a spiritual absolute while devoted utterly to the concrete, all his thinking, and especially that concerned with the theater, was characterized by a dialectical movement between the obscene and the sublime. "Plato, you make us shit." The line and the whole passage from which it is taken is a brilliant piece of invective—brilliant just because the Platonic ideal and the corporeal negation of it are so firmly interconnected in Artaud's mind.[20] The idea of the one creates the idea of the other, and the two oscillate in never-ending pulses. The Artaudian dialectic therefore leads to deeper and deeper alienation. His drive toward the absolute body was not the cause of the alienation but a symptom of it, for the truth is that Artaud was the captive of his consciousness and could no more get out of it than he could cease writing, which he did only on the day he died.

From the historical point of view, Artaud was slightly ahead of his time. Owing to his particular psychological make-up and his acute sensitivity to purely theatrical values, he intuited what the whole program of theater renewal in his time was actually about,

16 *Artaud Anthology*, p. 37.
17 *Ibid.*, p. 57.
18 *Ibid.*, p. 60.
19 *Ibid.*, p. 41.
20 "Shit to the Spirit," *Artaud Anthology*, pp. 106–112.

more than did such contemporaries of his as Copeau, Saint Denis, Dullin, Pitoëff, Jouvet, and Barrault, who were more practical and more accomplished as theater artists. In the main, Artaud's proposals for theater could not be appropriated until the mid-1950's— that is, until the "modern" period, strictly speaking, had drawn to a close. For the modern, from Ibsen until Beckett, was concerned to rescue the cultural tradition by embracing its manifold contradictions. It remained social, in Artaud's sense. More recently, the tradition has come under attack. It has seemed as if the aim is to abolish the cultural tradition, especially that of the West, by subjecting it to an ironic treatment of withering force. At such a time Artaud's theatrical declaration of war upon reason and society can be and has been of considerable influence.

The late modern theater, however, would have gone in an Artaudian direction even if Artaud had never existed. His distinction is that of a visionary, not of a man of action. The point is that his vision was so accurate that through it we can see the very core upon which the late modern theater has been wound. It has two principal elements, which are two aspects of the same substance: the conception of theater as its own positive datum (which I call the theater positive), and that of theater as a mirror of human consciousness imprisoned within itself. These are, as it were, the physical and mental sides of the modern theater's alienation from society and from itself. They might lead us to write off the modern theater as a suicide if we did not remember, as Artaud pointed out in writing of Van Gogh, that some suicides are actually created by society. The late modern theater has become, through preparations going back a century and a half, an extraordinary representation of the alienated psyche of modern man. If this alienation is in future to be overcome, it will not be by any agency of the theater but by changes that will take place outside.

That core of the late modern theater that Artaud helps us to see will become now the reference by means of which we shall find our way selectively through the late modern theater and its dramatists. From other points of view that would be unfair; it is necessary, however, to our keeping our focus upon what has been the most important line of development of the modern theater, a line projected from the beginning of this study. The aim is to see where our theater has recently come and why. That some writers and practitioners went in a different direction is perhaps, from an ideally catholic point of view, nothing against them. It means only that they have maintained values and techniques that must appear idiosyncratic in light of the theater's modern preoccupations.

This said, we may turn briefly to the three major French dramatists who rose to prominence following the surrealist movement—Giraudoux, Anouilh, and Montherlant. Like all major figures, they resist being typed, since their works synthesize numerous tendencies, and this is especially the case with Jean Anouilh (b. 1910), who has written more than thirty plays in a wide variety of styles. Yet Anouilh constantly expresses a deeply ironic view of human behavior. This irony is based on a conception potentially tragic: that human love, morality, and friendship are inevitably destroyed by social and psychological forces. From this tragic insight, Anouilh fashions bitter comedies, gruesome farces, unheroic history plays, and ambiguous adaptations of classical tragedies. His extraordinary skill is applied to tragicomedy, the predominant "serious" form of theater in this century.

Anouilh's irony is most easily perceived in his adaptation of *Antigone* (1942). The situation and plot are Sophocles', but the actors are put into modern dress, and the language is colloquial, albeit with moments of high rhetoric. Written and performed in German-occupied France, the play's production was allowed by the resident powers because Anouilh's Creon makes a case for absolute obedience to the state that is rational, lucid, and unimpeachable. Nevertheless, one's emotions are with the rebellious Antigone. Through the irony of this double view, Anouilh was able to extol the Resistance while seeming to defend the *status quo*. At the same time the plot lent itself to Anouilh's tragic theme of the destruction of innocence. His Antigone is a romantic idealist who is inevitably beaten down by Creon's political realism.

The corruption and destruction of innocence occurs ever and again in such Anouilh plays as *L'Hermine* (1931; *The Ermine*), *Jézabel* (1932), *Le Voyageur sans baggage* (1936; *Traveller Without Luggage*), *Eurydice* (1941; *Legend of Lovers*), *Le Bal des voleurs* (1932; *Thieves' Carnival*), *Le Rendezvous de Senlis*

(1937; *Dinner with the Family*), *Léocadia* (1939; *Time Remembered*), *L'Invitation au château* (1947; *Ring 'Round the Moon*), and *La Répétition ou L'Amour puni* (1950; *The Rehearsal*).

The wistful irony of *Colombe* (1950; *Mademoiselle Colombe*) is typical. At the conclusion of this bitter love story, in which Colombe is corrupted by the cynical morals of theater people, the play's prologue is repeated. It is a love song that the audience must now accept as prelude to disillusionment and betrayal.

The plays listed above belong to what Anouilh calls his "pièces noires," "pièces roses," and "pièces brillantes." More bitter and more deeply tragicomic are his "pièces grinçantes," the best known of which is *La Valse des toréadors* (1951; "The Waltz of the Toreadors"). This grotesque comedy of excellent construction tells of a retired general who fancies himself a great lover yet is tyrannized by his bedridden wife. The scene in which she excoriates him while standing upright in the center of their marriage bed is unforgettable. Strong as this play is, it is perhaps excelled by *Pauvre Bitos, ou Le Dîner de têtes* (1956; *Poor Bitos*), which is about a Resistance fighter who secretly thinks of himself as an incorruptible Robespierre. To show him that they are aware of his vanity, his friends appear at dinner wearing the masks of well-known figures of the French Revolution. With his secret fantasy exposed, Bitos is reduced to impotent self-pity. The spectator's attitude toward him is a controlled blend of scorn and sympathy.

The well-known *L'Alouette* (1953; *The Lark*), which exists in two English versions (one by Christopher Fry and another by Lillian Hellman), recounts the story of Joan of Arc and, strangely enough, is not conceived in an ironic mode. Thus, it differs sharply from Shaw's *Saint Joan* (1923). Perhaps it was to avoid following Shaw's precedent that Anouilh steered clear of irony in this particular case. In Shaw's great play the sympathies lie clearly with Joan, as they do also in *The Lark;* but Shaw's treatment of Joan's religious inspiration is highly ironic, and the tension between the vision of the heroine and the selfishness of society is more ironic still. This is one of the reasons why Shaw's play, unlike Anouilh's, is among the major works of the century. Another is that Shaw had a very firm grasp on the historical materials. Anouilh's treatment of historical fact often seems slipshod, as if he could not be bothered to finish his research, a fault that is most serious in *Becket ou L'Honneur de Dieu* (1959; *Becket*).

Whether he succeeds or fails, Anouilh is almost always audacious. In *Becket* he did not shrink from the attempt to dramatize Becket's conversion, which he handled successfully by rhetorical tour de force. Audacious also is *La Petite Molière* (1959; *Little Molière*). Adapted from Anouilh's film version of the same materials, it dares to employ on the stage a cinematic principle of construction. Most such attempts fail for lack of respect for the theatrical medium, but in this case Anouilh turned the inherent liability into a virtue. In *La Grotte* (1961; *The Cavern*) he put himself on the stage to explain that "the play we are going to perform tonight is one I've never succeeded in writing." As the play unfolds he makes it look as if this is really the case, though in fact he is only teasing the audience, the better to surprise it with an unusually well constructed climax.

Anouilh's combination of theatrical skill and mordant irony is consistently impressive. His only shortcoming as an artist is that his personal temperament is stamped so strongly on all his works that it tends to obscure their universal significance. To put it differently, he frequently leaves the impression of being arbitrary.

An idiosyncratic temperament was also the liability of Jean Giraudoux (1882–1944), although there is no doubt that Giraudoux was a brilliant writer whose works many hold in high regard. His first work for the stage, *Siegfried et le limousin* (1928; *Siegfried and the Dragon*), was an adaptation of his novel *Siegfried*. It was followed by *Amphitryon 38* (1929). The lightly ironic tone of this play stemmed from Giraudoux's consciousness that he was writing no less than the thirty-eighth version of the ancient story, whose subject, after all, is nothing but a marital squabble on Olympus. The piece is full of Giraudoux's bemused view of the human condition, and, like all his plays, it is untouched by bitterness. The irony is more trenchant in *Judith* (1931). Unlike the Biblical heroine, Giraudoux's Judith is in love with Holofernes, whom she kills not for patriotic reasons but out of love-hatred, to become a national heroine against her will. In *Intermezzo* (1933; *The Enchanted*) Giraudoux turned to fantasy, mixing the real and the fantastic in a blend all his own to show the hidden mystery and beauty of life, especially when visited by love. In *La Guerre de Troie n'aura pas lieu* (1935; *The Trojan War Will Not Take Place*, called *Tiger at the Gates* in Fry's adaptation), *in Électre* (1937), and in *Sodom et Gomorrhe* (1943), Giraudoux returned to Greek and Biblical tales. The play about the Trojan War is woven of subtle ironies based on the insight that war is inevitable in spite of every rational and emotional objection to it. Both sides agree that the war should not occur, but it happens anyway.

Giraudoux's most famous play is *La Folle de Chaillot* (1945; *The Madwoman of Chaillot*), in which the blend of fantasy and reality, young love and economic greed is especially skillful. The rococo cast of characters, their nonconformist behavior, and the play's satiric and fanciful climax provide vivid, enduring images. Nevertheless, it cannot be denied that the essence of the play, the notion that man is innately good, is sentimental. It does not square with the evil that Giraudoux describes in other plays and even in this one. In *Pour Lucrèce* (1953; *Duel of Angels*), a very skillfully constructed play, Giraudoux wrote of a conflict between sensuality and chastity. The latter comes to a tragic end through a plot of devilish ingenuity, but Giraudoux's sympathies are carefully balanced. His aim is to show that neither the Fair nor the Dark Angel —neither purity nor sensual indulgence—embodies the spontaneity of genuine love. Like most of Giraudoux's plays, this one is a wry condemnation of the ways of the world, even while these are accepted as permanent. That they are judged in the light of an almost mystical ideal of love shows Giraudoux's persistent romanticism, to which he gave a flavor all his own.

The plays of Giraudoux and Anouilh are almost always touched, sometimes heavily, more often lightly, with a self-conscious theatricalism. They are conceived as games to be played, and they therefore give actors much opportunity to display their skills. However, both authors are much more "literary" than is allowed in the theater positive, toward which they point but at which they do not quite arrive.

The world of Henry de Montherlant (b. 1896) is a darker one. Montherlant's severity, his strictness of style, his concern with heroism, and his penchant for the plays in historical dress all suggest that he should be considered as belonging among the nostalgic romantics of this century mentioned in the previous chapter. One quality alone precludes that, and it is decisive in his work—a tone suggesting that the hero is a very special figure who cannot be held up as an ideal because he cannot be imitated and may not even exist. Montherlant employs the theater as if it were an instrument of magical power for the invocation of stories and actions that exist quite apart from the real world, dwelling only in the theater of the mind. This he manages to convey in a dramatic style that is vigorously realistic, though it is also heavy and ornate. In the tension between a strict, realistic style and a sense of the ideality of all theatrical representation, the irony of Montherlant resides. It is compounded by a strategy he frequently employs of setting up two possible motives for the hero's actions and then showing that neither of these motives is the real one, which is to be discovered only in the deep recesses of irrationality and instinct. Thus, in *La Reine morte* (1942; *Queen After Death*) King Ferrante has at least two plausible motives for having arranged the murder of his son's wife. The marriage had been morganatic, and the king might have acted for practical reasons of state, or he may have desired for more personal reasons to preserve the purity of the royal line, or both motives may have coincided. The play moves toward the discovery of the true motive, which at last is found in the king's unconscious desire for evil. Analogous treatments of motives are to be found in *Fils de personne* (1943; *No Man's Son*), *Malatesta* (1942), *Le Maître de Santiago* (1947; *The Master of Santiago*), *Port Royal* (1954), and other plays. Montherlant's dramas are mostly of a Spanish baroque character. The combination of this quality with a twentieth-century concern for unconscious motivations gives his plays a subsurface irony and a highly formal theatricality.

Except in a few notable instances, the fullness of the modern protest against the theatrical, religious, and philosophical traditions of the West was not, as I have said, expressed until quite recent times. Büchner's work is a signal example of the protest's breaking through after the upheaval of the French Revolution. Throughout the nineteenth and early twentieth centuries the spirit of protest occasionally cast up such radical works as the plays of Strindberg, the diatribes of Jarry, the outbursts of the expressionists. However, it required World War II and the threat of atomic annihilation to bring the protest to the point where it could change the very notion of theatrical form.

Philosophically, the protest was embodied in existentialism, the most influential form of which, after Kierkegaard, was that worked out by Jean-Paul Sartre (b. 1905) during and after World War II. In his famous dictum that "existence precedes essence," Sartre stated in its most succinct form the philosophical meaning of the modern search for reality. That is, he affirmed philosophically that human existence is not a departure from a given norm or ideal reality but is instead the process by which man brings into being the values and goals that he professes. Accordingly, the search for reality is not a search for what has been lost or has always awaited discovery but rather a search for what proceeds from the self in its free encounter with the world and with other selves. From this it follows that what is beyond the self has no meaning in itself (*en-soi*), and from this in turn emerges the now familiar modern notion of "the absurd." Here one can see very clearly the turning of the romantic quest into the modern query. Doubt about meaning ceases to be doubt about whether the right discoveries have been made and becomes doubt about the self. It becomes doubt about whether life affords any possible meanings at all.

Sartre did not, of course, invent this way of thinking. It had its philosophical precedents, partly in Kierkegaard, partly in Nietzsche, partly in the early writings of Martin Heidegger; and it had antecedents in much nineteenth-century literary romanticism. What Sartre did was to enunciate the thought at great length, with involved chains of dialectical reasoning, and to force it into the consciousness of an entire generation.

Beginning in the 1920's, a quite different type of philosophy enunciated the modern query in another way. Logical positivism, succeeded by the so-called analytic philosophy, of which Ludwig Wittgenstein was the principal mentor, rejected metaphysics as a verbally "meaningless" study and pushed in the direction of showing that both logic and language are "games." The result of this line of thought was to imprison human consciousness in its several game forms and to cast radical doubt upon the possibility of the discovery of any truth extrinsic to the mind. That this philosophy was closely identified with scientific method made no difference in this regard, for the scientists themselves, notwithstanding the great strides their researches were making, were more and more wary of equating their discoveries with "truth." They were content to employ theories and working hypotheses, these always subject to modification or abandonment in new situations, while "the meaning of meaning" became an acute philosophical problem with no satisfactory solution. One had the positivity of language, the observable, apparently consistent behavior of the physical world, and the self confronted with choices, but no over-all structure to bind these three together, no ontology for any of them, and nothing at all of a transcendent order.

What is important to note in all this is the radical positivism that runs through it. Positivism began as an attempt to sheer off from the observable world all overtones of spiritual, metaphysical, and other inherently symbolic meaning. In this sense it was "scientific" and helped clear the way for ever more experimental research. But it did not stop there. It went on to regard human language and culture in the sole light of their positive "givenness." Out of this arose the tendency to regard such phenomena as "games," for it is in the nature of games to be self-enclosed and to require no other justification than that they exist in such and such a form and seem thereby to give pleasure. In the Sartrean form of existentialism, even the self is regarded in a positivist light. It is "given"—in Heidegger's formula, it is "thrown" into existence —and it generates of itself all structures of meaning. But even "meaning" may at last reveal itself to be nothing more than an arrangement of words, as Sartre has strongly indicated by calling his autobiographical volume *Les Mots* (*The Words*).

Given such an impetus from modern philosophy, given the tendency of modern drama to move toward ever more overt theatricalism, and given certain barbarities of twentieth-century history (Dachau, Hiroshima) that seem past comprehension, the theater has evolved a positivism of its own, not in the form of a doctrine but of method and style. The theater has found it natural to regard the theatrical performance as a game with rules set down in the script, to concentrate upon theater *as theater,* as *act* rather than the imitation of action. The more self-conscious it has become, owing to the increase of knowledge about the history of theatrical styles and forms, the more this feature has been accentuated.

The tendency to conceive of theater as theater positive can be seen to have increased throughout the nineteenth century, as has been noted frequently in the earlier parts of this study. With expressionism and the major playwrights between the two world wars, the tendency increased still more. After World War II, and partly under guidance from Artaud, it became a veritable program that generated a new set of canons for judging the playwright's success. One may say that World War II dealt the deathblow to the aesthetics of theatrical illusion.

Ironically, Sartre himself did not much lean toward positive theatricalism when he composed his plays. On the contrary, he was so inclined to employ the boulevard theater of Paris as an instrument of communication that he wrote plays of ideas only mildly experimental in form. His first play, *Les Mouches* (1941; *The Flies*), a version of Aeschylus' *Oresteia,* is his most radical in form. In *Huis-Clos* (1944; *No Exit*) he turned to the drawing-room play. To be sure, he rendered it symbolic, turning his script into a series of interlocking ironies produced by his characters' refusal of existential freedom. Sartre's drawing room is hell, a prison of bad faith. But when all is said and done, the interest of *No Exit* resides in its philosophical content more than in its form and style. The phenomenon of human freedom, set forth in the negative instance of its failure, interested Sartre much more than did the phenomenon of the theater itself. The same is true of his other plays, including *Morts sans sépulture* (1946; *The Victors*), *La Putain respectueuse* (1946; *The Respectful Prostitute*), *Les Mains sales* (1948; *Dirty Hands*), *Le Diable et le bon dieu* (1951; *The Devil and the Good Lord*), and *Les Séquestrés D'Altona* (1959; *The Condemned of Altona*). All these plays are examples of symbolic realism. Closer to Ibsen than to Chekhov or Strindberg, they do not hesitate to use the bourgeois theater in order to attack bourgeois conceptions. Much the same is to be said, a fortiori, of the plays of the religious existentialist Gabriel Marcel (b. 1887).

The picture changes slightly with Albert Camus (1913–1960). Like Sartre, Camus adhered to a strict style employed for the communication of ideas previously worked out in nontheatrical writing. Yet Camus had a stronger sense than Sartre of man's being a rational creature in an "absurd" universe, and this gave his plays a somewhat more radical tone.

Camus' first play, *Caligula* (1943), is a work of much originality. The emperor, in love with his deceased sister and desirous of a perfect happiness no man can attain, decides there is nothing to prevent his issuing whatever decrees he likes and so decides to rule Rome according to a capricious will. He institutes a reign of terror, the atrociousness of which is seen not only in the murders and confiscations he orders but even more in his deliberate blasphemy and unreason. The plot, in which Caligula is finally brought down, turns upon the innate human integrity of a few of the senators, principally Cherea, who embodies Camus' sense of the necessity to resist barbarism, even if there is no rational reason to do so. *Caligula* is clearly a morality play, but in many scenes, such as Caligula's shattering of his mirror image, and later the contrived banality of the Venus–Virgin Mary litany, Camus achieved a very forceful theatricalism that extended the play's range of feeling beyond what the moral theme itself required. Although Camus opposed Caligula, it was Caligula who gave the play its theatrical stamp.

In his later plays Camus was never again as much an innovator as in *Caligula*, written when he was twenty. *Le Malentendu* (1944; *The Misunderstanding*) has a bizarre plot in which a mother kills her son, not knowing who he is; but the style of the play is straight realism. *L'état de siège* (1948; *State of Siege*), set in Spain and based on the same theme as Camus' novel *The Plague*, and *Les Justes* (1950; *The Just Assassins*), a study of the morality of assassination, employ a formal, rhythmic type of prose dialogue and show a keen sense of dramatic values but open no new directions for theatrical style.

Perhaps it is best to think of Sartre and Camus, along with the French playwrights mentioned earlier in this chapter, as belonging to the spirit of the World War II period, when, after all, their principal ideas were formed. Alternatively, they may be considered as forming a bridge to the newer type of playwriting that was to come; but if they form such a bridge it is more because of their intellectual thought than because of their uses of the theater.

Right on their heels, however, and partly building upon their thought, came playwrights quickly identified as forming an avant-garde. They still bear the label today, more than twenty years after the first of them, Jacques Audiberti (b. 1899), wrote his first play, *Quoat-Quoat* (1946). They have also been called "the Paris School," or simply "the new playwrights." Since the appearance of Martin Esslin's book *The Theatre of the Absurd* in 1961 they have been most generally known as the "absurdist" playwrights. Esslin included twenty writers in the first edition of his study, of whom the most notable are Samuel Beckett, Arthur Adamov, Eugène Ionesco, Jean Genet, Jean Tardieu, Fernando Arrabal, Max Frisch, Günter Grass, Robert Pinget, Harold Pinter, N. F. Simpson, Edward Albee, Jack Gelber, and Arthur Kopit. This list includes quite disparate talents whose perspectives vary considerably. The Americans mentioned, the last three, do not exactly belong to the grouping. Esslin deliberately excluded from the "theater of the absurd" certain dramatists who might be thought to belong to it, notably Michel de Ghelderode (discussed in the previous chapter), Jacques Audiberti, Georges Neveux, Georges Schehadé, and Jean Vauthier. Ghelderode, to be sure, was of a different generation. Esslin confessed that it was difficult to distinguish between the "poetic avant-garde" he held these playwrights to represent and "the theater of the absurd." In historical perspective the important point is that all of those cited broke with the bourgeois forms of theater and constructed plays distinguished by their theatrical positivity. That is, the medium of expression became, in Esslin's words, "the concrete and objectified images of the stage itself." [21]

What we have now to consider, therefore, is the way in which the theater of the 1950's, tended to draw its content from its own form. This is what is meant by its theatrical positivity and what is meant also by its employment of irony as its very substance. What has occurred is a shift from thinking of drama as the imitation of

[21] *The Theatre of the Absurd* (Garden City, N.Y.: Anchor Books, Doubleday, 1961), p. xxi.

action or of life to thinking of it as the imitation of theater and of consciousness. When theater imitates theater the result is an intensification of the *sense* of theater, an ironic reduplication of the theatrical idea.

Eugène Ionesco has written,

> Since Picasso, painting has been trying to free itself from all that is not painting; literature, anecdotes, history, photography. Since Picasso, therefore, painters have been trying to rediscover the fundamental schemas of painting, pure forms, color used as color. And here it is not a question of aestheticism or of what today is called, somewhat incorrectly, formalism, but rather of reality expressed pictorially, *in a language as revealing as that of words or sounds.* If we thought at first that there was a certain disintegration of pictorial language, we have discovered since that basically it was a question of an asepsis, a purification, the rejection of a parasitic language. Similarly, it is after having disarticulated theatrical elements, after having rejected false theatre language, that we must try as painters have done, to rearticulate them, purified and reduced to their essence.
>
> The theatre can only be theatre. . . .[22]

Ionesco went on to say that the theater has tried for too long to be "ideology, allegory, politics, lectures, essays or literature." He stated that it is just as wrong to conceive of theater as any of these as it would be "to claim that music should be archaeology, or painting, physics and mathematics." [23]

There is, of course, much in painting since Picasso that cannot be considered as "pure forms, color used as color." In the 1960's "anecdotes, history, and photography" came back into painting with a vengeance and re-entered the theater as well. Nevertheless, Ionesco's statement isolates that which was indispensable to the late modern theater in its search for autonomy—namely, positive concentration on its own techniques, divorced from rational "meaning." Ionesco wrote:

> To push the theatre beyond that intermediate zone which is neither theatre nor literature is to restore it to its proper frame,

[22] "Discovering the Theatre" (1958). Translated by Leonard C. Pronko. In Robert W. Corrigan, ed., *Theatre in the Twentieth Century* (New York: Grove, 1963), p. 91.
[23] *Ibid.*

to its natural limits. It was necessary not to hide the strings, but to make them even more visible, deliberately evident, to go all the way in the grotesque, in caricature, beyond the pale irony of witty drawing room comedies. Not drawing room comedies, but farce, an extreme burlesque exaggeration. Humor, yes, but with the methods of burlesque. A hard comedy, without finesse, excessive. No dramatic comedies either. But a return to the intolerable. Push everything to a state of paroxysm, there where the sources of tragedy lie. Create a theatre of violence: violently comic, violently dramatic.

Avoid psychology, or rather give it a metaphysical dimension. Theatre is an extreme exaggeration of feelings, an exaggeration which disjoints the real. It is also the dislocation and disarticulation of language.[24]

The emphases Ionesco desired had not been found by him in the theater he saw in the fashionable houses. He did discover them, however, in Punch and Judy shows, to which he had been taken as a child. These did not pretend to imitation of life but instead created, by strictly theatrical means, elemental confrontations that belonged, so Ionesco thought, purely to the world of imagination. He conceived the idea of breaking the tyranny of words in the "literary" theater. He would restore to the theater its visual and primitive qualities. He would exalt the importance of things (stage properties) and of what he called the "moving architecture of scenic images." [25]

It was while groping for such conceptions as these that Ionesco composed his own early plays, La Cantatrice chauve (1950; The Bald Soprano), La Leçon (1951; The Lesson), Les Chaises (1951; The Chairs), Victimes du devoir (1953; Victims of Duty), Jacques, ou La Soumission (1953; Jack, or the Submission), and Amédée, ou Comment s'en débarrasser (1954; Amédée, or How to Get Rid of It). In all these works the world of things is utterly intractable, and to such a world human language, gestures, and motivations are assimilated. Words multiply, like the chairs and their invisible occupants in The Chairs and like the furniture of Le Nouveau locataire (1957; The New Tenant). Logic is pursued

24 Ibid., p. 85.
25 Ibid., p. 88.

relentlessly for a time, then exploded as if it were a breakable physical object. In *The Bald Soprano* the proposition that if a doorbell rings it is because someone has rung it is examined at great length and finally abandoned as a useless conception. It is as though David Hume's critique of "the law of causality" were being demonstrated in a laboratory of the insane. All relationships, whether of logic, grammar, custom, or marriage, are treated as a series of theatrical games whose rules may be changed at will. The treatment is relentless, every game being driven to its conclusion in a pure energy devoid of logic. Ionesco's work seems related to the early thought of Ludwig Wittgenstein much as that of Molière was to the thought of Descartes. Ionesco reduces "game" theory, as Molière reduced formal logic, *ad absurdum*.

At the same time, and for the same reasons, Ionesco broke down the distinction between tragedy and comedy. He wrote:

> It seems to me that the comical is tragic, and the tragedy of man, derisory. For the modern critical spirit nothing can be taken entirely seriously, nor entirely lightly. I have tried in *Victims of Duty* to drown the comic in the tragic; in *The Chairs*, the tragic in the comic, or if you wish, to oppose the comic to the tragic in order to join them in a new theatrical synthesis. But it is not a true synthesis, for these two elements do not mix completely with each other, they coexist, they repulse one another constantly, each setting the other into relief; they criticize each other, mutually deny each other, constituting through this opposition a dynamic balance, a tension.[26]

One may observe in such language the ancient idea of the "coincidence of opposites," pointing here to no vision of ultimate unity but to a rude dynamic of existence. It is precisely this feeling for the mutual attraction and repulsion of opposed qualities that enables irony to become the substance of Ionesco's theater and that turns it away from the classical ideals of comedy and tragedy toward a modern tragicomic mixture that is serious, *in*complete, and of a questionable magnitude.

Nothing could show Ionesco's sure understanding of modernism better than his appreciation of a critical spirit that hovers between

26 *Ibid.*, pp. 86–87.

seriousness and lightness, finding the one in the other, and therefore manifesting itself in theatrical irony. Ionesco realized that if
the protest against bourgeois theater is made purely in the name of
subjective feeling it does not go beyond the dream-romanticism of
the nineteenth and twentieth centuries. What it must do, through
its subjectivity, is to challenge the metaphysical (or rather, as he
says, the anti-metaphysical) assumptions of the society. This is the
source of Ionesco's persistent concern with logical structures and
the taken-for-granted plausibilty of human relations. He makes the
normal world appear highly problematic and then shows that the
affective response we shall make to this revelation is both positive and negative, a dynamic compound of hilarity and metaphysical sadness. Ionesco is not the proponent of any metaphysical asser-
tions. Instead, he simply guides our perceptions of the mundane
toward a level of metaphysical questioning. To be aware of a metaphysical dimension of existence, precisely because one is aware of
the arbitrariness of existence, and yet be unable to make confident
metaphysical affirmations—this is for Ionesco not a situation of
pathos but one of tragicomedy. It is the ironic suspension of man
between two worlds, the one arbitrary, the other not clearly real.
This metaphysical expectancy, as one perhaps may call it, is
achieved by Ionesco on the basis of a theatrical positivism; and if it
is philosophically questionable, that is because it has been arrived
at not by philosophical means but sheerly by imaginative exploitation of theatrical images and conventions. Ionesco's theater is not
in the service of any philosophical position, or of any psychology,
sociology, or politics. It communicates philosophical awareness
through a purely theatrical imagination.

This is not to say that Ionesco, when he composes a play, has no
ideas in his head. In *Victims of Duty,* for instance, it is clear that
the idea of duty is present throughout and that Ionesco began to
write the play with such an idea in mind. What matters, however,
is how the idea is handled. It is not subjected to rational analysis,
upon the basis of which the play is thereafter constructed. Nor has
a plot been conceived to demonstrate this or that aspect of the idea
of duty. Rather, the analysis of the idea is carried through by
means of a series of scenes, situations, speeches, and events that are
generated, the one out of the other, according to a "logic" of the-

atrical imagination rather than rational deduction. Yet the principle of organization employed may not be characterized as one of pure feeling. The structure of the play does not correspond merely to a pattern of emotions. The assumption is that although the theatrical imagination is compounded of reason and emotion it transcends them both and has a validity in its own right. It is a way of apprehending, or at least seeking, reality that does not admit the a priori hegemony of either thought or feeling but insists upon its own legitimacy. Whether the result can be called "cognitive" remains an open question, but the question is also open for symbolic logic and science, as well as for all forms of intuition.

Thus, the general proposition is that the theatrical imagination is not subservient to any other form of mental activity. It is a positive datum of consciousness, beyond which no other form of thought can go. Perhaps it points to a reality (or to what is here the same, an absence of reality) beyond itself that it cannot encompass, but in this respect it is like all other kinds of human thought. It is this sense of being halted at the brim of consciousness (very different from being at the center of a breakdown of consciousness) that gives Ionesco's theater, at its best, the claim to enduring greatness in spite of its often deliberately trivial appearance.

All the so-called absurdist playwrights of recent times have operated on the basis of conceptions that Ionesco has articulated better than anyone else. They do not all succeed in maintaining the balance of qualities that Ionesco calls for. Sometimes, as in the work of Jean Tardieu, grotesquerie takes over. Sometimes, as in the plays of N. F. Simpson, what emerges is harmless farce, zany expeditions into the hilarity of the irrational. Sometimes, as in much of the work of Harold Pinter, the eerie is cultivated for its own sake and then combined with vague suggestions of moral wisdom. In Ionesco's own work the didactic element sometimes takes over, as in *Tueur sans gages* (1959; *The Killer*), and *Rhinocéros* (1960), which demonstrate the bad political consequences of conformism. However, in *Le Roi se meurt* (1962; *The King Dies*) and in *Le Piéton de l'air* (1962; *The Airborne Pedestrian*) he recovered the balance exactly, with sure effect.

At its best, absurdist theater leads one to the edge of consciousness and invites him to peer into the darkness beyond. Then it pulls back into the ambiguous givenness of the human situation, which is shown to be strictly analogous to the ambiguity of the theatrical situation with its curious blend of the real and the unreal, the rational and the irrational, the tragic and the comic, the spontaneous and the determined. If one can speak of reality here, it resides in the ironic ambiguity of all qualities, "facts," and possibilities. Says Ionesco,

> Light makes shadow deeper, shade accentuates the light. Personally, I have never understood the distinctions that are made between the comic and the tragic. Since the comic is the intuition of the absurd, it seems to me more hopeless than the tragic. The comic offers no escape. I say: hopeless; but in reality it either falls this side of despair or hope, or it goes beyond it.[27]

Goes beyond it to where? There is no conceivable answer, just as there is no conceivable way to rid oneself of the intuition of the "beyond." To be on "this side" and to be "beyond" are complementary notions, the one unthinkable without the other. They are aspects of a single state of consciousness, which exists as a "given," without location in the world. Likewise the magic of theater is given, no longer as a temple or a market place or a forum, but as a pure contrivance without essential relation to the world or to society. The stage is simply a pool of light, like consciousness itself, in the midst of unintelligible surroundings. Artaud, at once darker and more lucid than Ionesco, put it best: "I can neither live nor die, nor am I capable of not wishing to die or live. And all mankind resembles me." [28]

The popular understanding of such theater as pessimistic is beside the point. As Ionesco indicates, modern tragicomedy does not lie on the same plane with either despair or hope. Though he does not say it, the reason is that the historical dimension of human existence has here been set aside. Despair and hope have to do with man's progress through time. Modern tragicomedy knows of no such progress, is aware of no end, good or bad, to any development. Rather, it tends to suggest eternal repetition, as in *The Bald Soprano* and *The Lesson*, which end exactly as they began. One of

27 *Ibid.*, p. 86.
28 *Artaud Anthology*, p. 58.

the marks of modern tragicomedy is a profound dislocation in time, as if it were impossible to tell one day from another.[29] By the same token it becomes difficult for the characters to know their identity, to recognize each other, and to be sure that any place is not also some other place. This dislocation is primarily not philosophical or psychological but aesthetic. Theatrical time and theatrical space are by nature discontinuous with "historical" time and space. They are abstractions created by the conventions of the art, and when they are fastened upon intently they cease to "locate" man with respect to the world at large. At most they may suggest that the world at large cannot be "located" either but is simply a datum of consciousness.

Whether all this is pessimistic or optimistic cannot be determined from within the art form itself. Hope or despair becomes pertinent only as the spectator departs from the theater and re-enters, as it were, the world of history and action, which presumably he must do. At that point he will be confronted with a decision, which is to ascertain whether, in his own judgment, the experience of the dislocated consciousness that he has had while watching the play is constructive or destructive with regard to his future actions.

The ethical importance of this theater, in other words, is strictly dependent on aesthetic "purity." It requires one's temporary removal from and subsequent re-entry into the realm of work, decision, and human history. Of course, it is possible to absolutize the aesthetic and thus to suppose that no "real" possibilities exist for man except those that art contains. Yet it may be suggested that this would be to give the work of art an ontological bearing it had not claimed for itself. It would be to regard it as imitation of life (which theater was long considered to be) rather than as imitation of consciousness. A more consistent view would be to regard the purely theatrical theater, which is the purely aesthetic theater, as pointing to the possibility of ethical decision without containing

[29] This dislocation is a corollary of the theater positive's tyranny over language. It is only by means of the word that memory and anticipation can enter actively into human existence. The body, as such, knows only one time, the present, which is no time. Here again the theater positive shows its profound animosity toward society and tradition. It should not be concluded, however, that society has no need of an antisocial theater.

any such decision in itself. Its relation to "life" would therefore be dialectical rather than descriptive or prescriptive. It would aspire to the condition of music, and the norms that one would properly apply to it would have more to do with rhythm than with ideas or precepts.

This is surely, in fact, the case. The test of such works is not the validity of their ideas but the force and integrity of their psychic rhythm. Ionesco's superiority to Albee, for instance, lies in the fact that Ionesco is a master of rhythmic construction, to which he subordinates all thematic content, while Albee's rhythm is unstable and is frequently sacrificed for the sake of ideas, moral themes, symbolic portents, and funny lines.

The roots of modern tragicomedy lie in Chekhov, who was the first important modern playwright to make art out of the representation of the *qualities* of life rather than its actions. I have explained how he did this in an earlier chapter. His innovation made possible, though he did not know this, a purely theatrical theater, of which the modern epitome has been reached in the plays of Samuel Beckett.

En attendant Godot (1953; *Waiting for Godot*) is not only a masterpiece, but also the quintessence of modern tragicomedy, an achievement that contributed, no doubt, to Beckett's being awarded, in 1969, the Nobel Prize for Literature. The celebration this play received from the moment of its publication surprised no one more than Beckett himself, who did not at first think that it would interest anybody.

The number of Beckett's plays is small. In addition to *Godot*, the principal ones are *Endgame* (1957), *Krapp's Last Tape* (1958), *Happy Days* (1961), and *Play* (1963). It is a case of quality rather than quantity.

All of Beckett's plays are "games" for actors. In these games the audience also has a role to play, one that allows a certain freedom for improvisation of response, just as the technique required of the actors also includes a good bit of improvisatory invention. Long before he called one of his pieces *Play*, Beckett was writing playful pieces (nevertheless in great seriousness) in which the characters were clearly aware that they were participants in games. They engaged themselves in talk and went through numerous gestural routines in order to pass the time and give some structure, however fragile, to an otherwise empty existence. When Beckett implies that life is a game, he does not mean only that it is arbitrary and made up of (perhaps) enjoyable routines; he means also, and more importantly, that it is just something to do. As theater is for the passage of an evening, so life is for the passage of—life. We are all clowns (or servants, or entrepreneurs, or spouses—what is the difference?) wondering if our "bit" is sufficiently long and diverting to fill up the time allotted to us.

Thus, the "routine" supplants the plot. As in Chekhov, a minimal or "shadow" plot exists—namely, a waiting for what will never take place, though we should say *perhaps* never, for all Beckett's work is in the subjunctive—but this slender slip of a plot is mocked with fine irony by being used to structure each of the two acts almost identically. This means that the plot is insisted upon and made to cancel itself out at the same time. Plot is used to negate plot: it is made into a routine.

As a result the audience becomes aware, as it has hardly ever been aware before, that modern man tends to interpret experience as a plotless sequence of events. Beckett summed up in extraordinarily lucid form the pre-existent intuition that neither history nor the experience of an individual can be read as a "story" with a beginning, middle, and end. It was already known that the Christian plot for history, beginning at the creation of the world, undergoing a *peripeteia* at the Incarnation, and moving toward an eschatological fulfillment, had lost its authority for modern man. Beckett made many aware that it was not just this particular plot that was waning in power but also the very notion of *any* plot as a model for the interpretation of human existence.

If, as had been thought, the theater came about as a result of the combination of myth and ritual, Beckett seemed to show that the theater could still be the theater, and in a more fundamental way, if the myth component were taken away from it, leaving only the ritual element. But a ritual devoid of myth is indistinguishable from a game. It is purely a "routine," a positive datum of behavior having no other meaning than its own form.

In *Waiting for Godot*, nevertheless, mythical and symbolic fragments abound. Yet they are only fragments. As such they can tease interpreters of the play into Freudian, Jungian, Christian, Buddhist, and various philosophical readings of the work. None of these is conclusive because the fragments fit into no whole external to the play. Picked up from here and there, they are unified only within the structure of the play itself, which, being circular, can represent either all or nothing but cannot be pegged anywhere between.

This state of affairs accounts for the Beckett irony, which is so all-inclusive that it is difficult to think of any that might be greater, though more bitter kinds are easily possible. The control over form that Beckett exercises is exquisite and extends to every aspect of the theatrical medium, beginning with an extraordinary, evocative, and nuanced command of language. Seeing him so concerned with form, one is apt to suppose that he must be a modern exponent of classicism. Unlike the true classicist, however, he has not the slightest belief that the form of a work of art can bear an analogical relation to a reality outside itself. Thus when we say, as I did above, that *Waiting for Godot* summed up the audience's pre-existent intuition about experience, we must remember that that intuition denied form to everything outside of consciousness. "They give birth astride of a grave," says Pozzo in the play, "the light gleams an instant then it's night once more." [30]

"To find a form that accommodates the mess," Beckett has said, "that is the task of the artist now." [31] The stage is a model of consciousness, which, if it creates order, does so only to discover that order has no ontological ground.

Here we have the pure aesthetic manifestation of the modern quest turned into query. The search for reality has turned in upon itself, not now toward the interior subjectivity of the person (though that is still a corollary here) but inward to the form of the work of art, which is an island of structure in a sea of chaos.

The irony is that form *is* transparent to chaos, that its precision has nothing to mirror but confusion, that the nearer it approaches, through perfection of form, to an ideality of being, the more it declares its own emptiness. This is the ultimate statement of theat-

[30] *Waiting for Godot* (New York: Grove, 1954), p. 57.
[31] "Beckett by the Madeleine," by Tom F. Driver, in *Columbia University Forum* (Summer 1961) IV. 3., pp. 21–25. The quotation is from p. 23.

rical positivism, and it is not at all surprising that just on account of that ultimateness it touches upon a mystical intuition.

Upon this ultimate expression of pure theatricality in Beckett the Chekhovian element is impressed, and the two elements fuse with perfect accord. When the structuring element of consciousness is rendered completely autotelic it becomes empty. But it does not thereby cease to exist, although, as Beckett often indicates, it may long for its own demise. Nevertheless, existence remains, and in the mode of a suffering, an endurance, or, in the technical sense of the term discussed in the chapter on Chekhov, a passion. Like Chekhov, though in a highly simplified and economical way, Beckett is able to represent on the stage the verbal, physical, and psychic motions that belong to our endurance of time. Like Chekhov's plays, his are made up primarily of communications of the qualities of experience. What does it feel like to pass the time in the absence of action? Chekhov answers the question by description, we might say, while Beckett answers it more strongly with poetic understatement. Like Chekhov, he has reduced the moments of purpose and perception in the tragic rhythm to their barest minimum, and again like Chekhov he has found a way to show forth the soft rhythms that remain in the moment of passion, which is now extended to fill the whole play. But even more than with Chekhov, these rhythms are internal, for the social setting has entirely disappeared, and what remains is only a model of the consciousness of Western man, exhausted by history and longing for death, yet not able to imagine, even in death, the surcease of that which is his glory and his damnation—namely, his pellucid self-awareness.

With Beckett the development of modern theater, in reaching its epitome, seems also perhaps to have come to an end. The quest for reality, turned into a query, has no further to go. The theater now casts about for a new way to travel.

Between Beckett's pure theater positive and the Happening, which might seem to be its logical extension, there is a great break. The Happening is not pure theater but a rebellion against theater. Its patron saint, however, is Artaud. In this fact may be seen the ambiguity of the late modern theater. In fulfilling itself it exhausts itself and turns against itself. Artaud is the patron of "true" thea-

ter and of those who would abolish theater. Beckett is pure theater
and the beginning of anti-theater. And how could it be otherwise,
given that irony was the project to which the modern theater had
devoted itself?

15. LUIGI PIRANDELLO
(1867–1936)

LIKE SHAW, HOFMANNSTHAL, YEATS, and several other important figures of the modern theater, Pirandello's career bestrode
World War I. When his first novel was written in 1893, he had already published a small amount of verse. By the time the war began
he had published four novels and a considerable number of short
stories. Yet the Pirandello who concerns the historian of the modern theater did not exist, except in germination, until 1917, when
Cosi è, se vi pare (*Right You Are, If You Think You Are*) was
presented at the Virgilio Talli in Milan. Pirandello was then fifty
years old. He was to spend the next nineteen years, until his death
in 1936, becoming and being the great Italian "somebody" of the
modern theater. To one of his last plays he gave the name *Quando
si è qualcuno* (1933; *When Someone Is Somebody*).

If we speak of the theater theatrical, of the theater as imitation
of consciousness, and of theatrical positivism—terms employed in
the previous chapter to describe the recent drama of irony—
then it is surely Pirandello who will come most easily to mind.
More consistently and with greater sophistication than any other
playwright he employed the image of the theater as the image of
the human situation. What he drew from this image bore only a
slender resemblance to what Shakespeare, Calderón, and other
pre-moderns drew from it. In their works the image of the theater

had tended to bespeak the finitude of man and the world contrasted with the infinite reality of God and the eternality of the good, the true, and the beautiful. The idea of the mask and of theatrical "show" therefore bore a negative, though not necessarily an evil, connotation, pointing to the ephemeral in its contrast with the eternal. In Pirandello this negative connotation disappeared, or at least, if it in part remained, it was kept in dialectical and ironic relation with the notion of a naked, unmasked, and "real" truth. Although Pirandello, like many of his characters, cried to be released from his mask, to be rid of all imposture and fictive construction, he knew that this was impossible and that the wholehearted attempt to find such release is destructive. The theatrical is man's fate. He is condemned to it by consciousness. This ironic understanding of the human situation issues in tragicomedy, of which Pirandello was a master.

Like Chekhov's theater, Pirandello's is one of passion, although his colors are not muted like those of the gentle Russian but are strong and of bold contrasts, in keeping with their Mediterranean provenance. Thus, one does not say of Pirandello's plays, as he would of Chekhov's, that they subsist on a minimum of plot. On the contrary, they are richly plotted, and the plots are often melodramatic. Even so, the plot is not the "soul" of the Pirandellan play. The story, as such, carries neither the meaning nor the passion of the play. These belong to the situation, just as they do in Chekhov, and the "soul" of the play is to be found in the complexity of the qualities of the situation. If the "motion" of Chekhov's plays, like that of Beckett's, is minimal, that of Pirandello's is usually turbulent. It belongs, nonetheless, to the situation rather than the plot, and its end is the representation of the passion of human experience, the pathos of existence. Departing in modern fashion from Aristotle's canon, Pirandello in his mature plays presented no action that is "complete." He was much interested neither in the beginning of the story nor in its end but in the multifaceted and multileveled complexity of its middle part. The plot may help us to define the situation, but the plot does not imitate reality. The real is the situation, provided only that we grasp how consciousness robs every situation of simplicity and renders it ultimately unintelligible.

Pirandello, therefore, is an important forerunner of the avant-garde playwrights of the period after World War II. If the organization of this book were strictly chronological, he would have been considered before them. However, his stature is greater than most of theirs, greater even than Beckett's, although of none of his works can it be said, as it can of *Waiting for Godot,* that it epitomizes the modern development. Perhaps Pirandello is greater than most of his successors precisely because he does *not* carry the reconception of dramatic form as far as they.

Many of the greatest artists in history stand on the border between an earlier movement and the extreme forms of a new one—Michelangelo between the neoclassic and the baroque, Beethoven between classicism and romanticism, Strindberg between naturalism and expressionism. Pirandello stood, as it were, between realism, for which theater is imitation of life, and that later development for which theater is imitation of consciousness. In spirit he belongs mainly to the latter, but he retains something of the style of the former; and it is precisely the realism in his style, devoted to concerns that were later to shatter such style, that gives him a solidity and a depth most later work has not equalled.

With respect to his attitude toward consciousness, Pirandello also shows some difference from the later radicals of the theater. For him as for them, consciousness is a prison. One cannot escape from it, cannot be sure of any reality outside it, and cannot know by means of it the contours and substance of the "real" world. Yet for all this, Pirandello retains and emphasizes a deep compassion for the consciousness-imprisoned self. He is not content merely to show the limits of consciousness. Neither does he present the spectator with an existential choice that goes beyond what the play itself contains. In this sense, his theater is not as purely aesthetic as that of Ionesco and Beckett. Ionesco and Beckett imply, I believe, a human substance and freedom in the spectator that they do not represent upon the stage, for they believe that the theater cannot speak directly of freedom but can only, in the manner of art, suggest it by indirection. Pirandello is not that much interested in the spectator. His plays are not calculated to be one point of a triangle, of which the other two points would be the spectator and the author. He goes more along with the traditional convention, in which the audience is taken for granted, leaving the playwright free to concentrate on the relation between himself and his work. Therefore, he shows us, on the stage, selves imprisoned in their masks, which are the constructions of consciousness, and he makes us feel *their* plight. Our identification with them is more or less traditional.

This being the case, it is apparent that Pirandello assumes, and even dramatizes, a distinction between the self and its conscious-ousness. If consciousness is the prisoner, there is something impris-oned, and that is none other than the "person," whom Pirandello sometimes refuses even to give a name, calling him simply "the father," or "the mother," or "the neighbor," the better to preserve the difference between the appellation and the mystery behind it.

But how can the self be different from its consciousness? If not a consciousness, what else would it be? Pirandello does not know and does not try to say. He seems to refuse to think of it simply as the body, the way Beckett sometimes does, as if there were a Cartesian split between the physical and the mental worlds. Sometimes he refers to it as the "soul," though that word certainly does not sig-nify for him what it does for a Platonist or a Christian believer. In fact, Pirandello has pointed out that there is more than one soul in a man and that what unites them is inexplicable. "But what if we have within us," he asks, "four or five souls in conflict with one another—the instinctive soul, the moral soul, the emotional soul, the social soul?" Any one of these may be dominant at a given time, he notes, and may thus give rise to a "spurious interpretation of ourselves—of our inner being that we know nothing of, because it never reveals itself in its entirety, but sometimes in one way, sometimes in another, as life's events unfold." [1]

Pirandello rests content with an unexplained and perhaps ra-tionally unjustifiable view of the self as identical with neither the body nor the mind, nor with both taken together. This self suffers in its existence, is alone in its intuition of its reality and desire, is an object of faith to the "other," and is the ultimate locus of life. That this "nothingness" should, from within, judge consciousness

[1] From "L'Umorismo" (1908, revised 1920), a portion of which has been translated as "The Art of Humor" by John Patrick Pattinson in *The Massachusetts Review*, Vol. VI, No. 3 (Spring-Summer 1965), pp. 515–520. Quotation is from p. 518.

as unjust and untrue even while unable to escape from it is the ultimate Pirandellan irony—unless we are able to say that there is an even deeper one, namely that the prisoner obscured within the form of the character is the one whom Pirandello loves.

Pirandello knew himself to be a prisoner. Unfinished at his death was a book of reminiscences to which he had given the title "News of My Involuntary Journey on This Earth." He had not asked for life, and for most of his days it was not kind to him, yet he lived it with an ardor that provided inexhaustible springs of creativity. That he, like many another human being, should have loved life in spite of its cruelty to him may be regarded by the cynical as a sign of the perversity of human nature. With less prejudice we may say that it shows but another facet of the irony of existence, that man should cling to his own prisoner, to consciousness and to experience, knowing, like Virgil's Achilles in Hades, that he would rather be a slave among the living than a king among the dead.

Pirandello was born in Sicily of a well-to-do father, Stefano Pirandello, and a hard-working mother. The father's wealth, which came principally from sulfur mines, was subject to various ups and downs. Knowing that Luigi was not cut out for industry or business, Stefano sent him at the age of eighteen to the University of Rome to continue studies begun at the *lycée* in Palermo. After some time in Rome the young student moved on to the University of Bonn. He knew by now that he wished to become a writer. He was most excited by his reading of Schopenhauer and Nietzsche, but for his doctoral work he chose philology and prepared a thesis on the dialect of Sicilian Agrigento. This finished, he returned to Sicily and broke his engagement to the girl who was waiting for him there. Then he headed for Rome, his father providing a pension that would enable him to write in leisure.

Soon, however, Stefano Pirandello came up with a new idea: Luigi should marry the daughter of a business associate. The arrangement was more of a business deal than anything else, for there would be a considerable dowry, and it would represent a merger of capital between the two families. For some reason, Luigi Pirandello agreed to this, although he had seen the girl, Antonietta, only in chlidhood and although he knew the risk that such marriages entailed. In 1893 the couple came to their wedding night having never been alone before. Three children were born to them between 1895 and 1899.

Business turned out to be bad for the elder Pirandello and Antonietta's father. Their fortunes, now tied closely together, were swept away in a short time. This left Luigi with a wife, three children, and no money. He supported his family by teaching at the Normal College for Women in Rome.

Now the torments began in earnest. Antonietta did not recover from the shock occasioned by the loss of her dowry and from her difficult labor at the birth of her third child, troubles that came to her almost simultaneously. Physically weak and knowing that she had increased, rather than lightened, her husband's burdens, she took refuge in mental illness. Reading of her symptoms, one is inclined to think that she invented for her husband faults that would enable her to forget her own self-accusations. She decided that he was unfaithful. There was no evidence for this, since in fact it was not true, but that did not change her opinion. Her suspicions found "proof" in the circumstance of Pirandello's being a teacher of young women. When he denied her accusations she searched his pockets and notebooks and threw in his face every communication that he received from his pupils. Next she complained that he was spending money on clandestine loves. Vainly trying to silence her, Pirandello put her in charge of the family finances, such as they were. He received nothing but car fare to and from work. It made no difference, of course. In time she came to believe that he wanted to kill her. During the war, when Pirandello travelled to Bohemia to try, unsuccessfully, to arrange for the release of their son, who had been taken as a prisoner of war, Antonietta stayed at home with their daughter, Lietta, the other son being also in service. She thought that her husband had asked Lietta to poison her during his absence, and she forced the girl to taste first every dish that was set before her.

Had Pirandello been endowed with less sense of responsibility than he in fact possessed, his suffering might have been less intense. For a time, he arranged a separation by sending his wife home to Sicily, but since she did not improve there he allowed her to return. He then proposed to commit her to an asylum, but the family physician advised that she would be better off at home, and Pirandello accepted the consequences as his duty. Miserable in his own house, he nevertheless refused to take a mistress or in any way to be an unfaithful husband, not only from an innate sense of duty and family pride but also, perhaps, because he had once as a child discovered his own father keeping company with a "friend" and could remember the effect such revelations have upon a child.

He suffered thus until Antonietta died in 1918. So conscientious was he that sometimes it seemed to him there must be two Pirandellos—the one he knew from within and the one Antonietta ceaselessly described to him in vivid language. And if two, why not more? Circumstance forced him during these years to live a life outwardly without passion, consisting only of teaching, writing, and trying to please an ill wife. Inwardly, the passion burned intensely. The conflict not only provided the motivation for him to write a large number of novels and short stories, it also laid down in his mind the substance and manner of the theater that he would one day create. Like some deep process of crystallization, the theater of Pirandello took shape in his head before he came to the circumstances of life that would permit him to bring it to the stage.

Actually the forces at work in Pirandello were more complicated than they may appear from this sketch. What they were in their actuality it must be left to a biographer with psychological acumen to discover. Yet even in sketch the facts are such as to indicate how Pirandello's period of torment helped prepare him to express motifs that are of general import for the modern sensibility. What is important is the lack of congruence between different perspectives on the same reality. To live with one who is insane may seem an atypical and merely unfortunate experience, but it is paradigmatic of that modern epistemological quandary occasioned by the lack of ultimate confidence in any perceptions. "Insanity" thus becomes a very relative category, not clearly superior to sanity, perhaps not even very different from it. At any rate, no sure knowledge of the self can be derived from the "other," even if the "other" be sane.

Yet something of the same situation is present in self-knowledge. There, also, one has to reckon with a knower and a known. Solitude might help to simplify matters, though it could not, in the nature of the case, provide an ultimate solution. Moreover, what if solitude is a fiction? What if one knows that knowledge of the self is socially created, that it is produced by the interaction of many with each other through crossing lines of perception and reflection, and that even in solitude the "others" are present, if only in memory and imagination? In that case, my consciousness is not entirely my own, though it is nonetheless unique and indispensable to me. I am bound to the "others" by the very forms of my thought. Yet the more I know this, the more I know that there is something within me, an unfathomable interiority, that transcends and resists this situation. The real is therefore elusive, whether taken as objectivity, as subjectivity, or as both in interaction.

One is wrong to conclude that Pirandello was a nihilist who did not believe that anything is real. He simply knew that *human* reality is problematic:

> The sea is true, yes, and the mountain is true; the rock is true; the blade of grass is true; but man? . . . he cannot stop posing, even in front of himself, in some way, and he imagines so many things which he needs to believe true and take seriously.[2]

There was nothing in Pirandello of the perverse intention, seen, for instance, in Genet's early work, to exalt a sheer nothingness. But he knew that the real is forever elusive because of the nature of consciousness. Therefore, like Genet, though for somewhat different reasons, he was drawn ineluctably to the theater. His search for the real had to be expressed in theatrical terms—that is, through the drama of the interaction between selves, and through the modality of masks, personae, and theatrical artifice.

Had Pirandello been a Joyce or a Proust, he might have made the novel continue to serve his purpose. Yet he had, in reaction against Gabriele D'Annunzio and other Italian stylists whom he thought precious, rejected experimentation with purely verbal constructs. His attitude toward *words* was that they should be as direct as possible. Hence, it was not primarily through them that he would search for the means of expressing the elusiveness of reality but rather through the construction of a work as a whole, and this pointed to drama.

The intention that propelled Pirandello toward the theater was

2 *Ibid.*, p. 516.

in fact slow to work itself out. Between 1898 and 1916, the period of his great family suffering, he wrote seven plays: *La morsa (The Vise)*; *Lumie di Sicilia (Limes of Sicily)*; *Il dovero del medico (The Duty of a Physician)*; *Cece; Se non così; Pensaci, Giacomino! (Think, Giacomino!)*; and *Liola*. These are all closer to naturalism than to what we now think of as Pirandellan theater. Moreover, they did not inspire Pirandello to become a dramatist. They belonged to the period of gestation of the dramatist that was in him. In 1917 the waters broke.

Pirandello had had two plays presented in Rome in 1916, one in Milan in 1915, one in Rome in 1913, and two there in 1910. *Right You Are If You Think You Are* was written in six days and performed in Milan in June 1917. Its success was immediate. As a result, in the latter half of 1917 three other Pirandello plays were put on the stage. There were two more in 1918, including *Il giocco delle parti (Each in His Own Role)*, three in 1919, four in 1920. In 1921 there was *Sei personaggi in cerca d'autore (Six Characters in Search of an Author)*, which is by any standard one of the supreme dramatic creations of modern times. It was followed, in 1922, by a work that many admire even more, *Enrico IV (Henry IV)*, and in that same year three other Pirandello plays had their premières, including *Vestire gli inudi (To Clothe the Naked,* usually translated under the title *Naked)*. In 1923 the public saw *L'uomo dal fiore in bocca (The Man with a Flower in His Mouth)*, a short but extremely forceful play; *La vita che ti diedi (The Life I Gave You)*; and *L'altro figlio (The Other Son)*. And so it went until the year after Pirandello died, one to three new plays being seen almost every year, including *Lazzaro (Lazarus)* in 1929, *Come tu mi vuoi (As You Desire Me)* and *Questa sera si recita a soggetto (Tonight We Improvise)* in 1930, and *Quando si è qualcuno (When Someone Is Somebody)* in 1933. At his death Pirandello left unfinished a play called *I giganti della montagna (The Mountain Giants)*, which was performed in 1937. Altogether the theater of Pirandello consists of forty-four plays.[3]

The lonely suffering of Pirandello's married years gave way to international renown and honors as soon as he embarked in ear-

---

[3] For the dates of first performances, I have depended on the chronology given in Guy Dumur, *Luigi Pirandello, Dramaturge* (Paris: L'Arche, 1955), pp. 147–149.

nest upon his theatrical career. He was awarded the Legion of Honor by the French Government, the Commenda of the Crown of Italy, and in 1934 the Nobel Prize for Literature. In 1925 he founded, together with his son Stefano, the Theater of the Arts in Rome. With it, he made tours into many parts of Europe, the United States, and South America. This venture was artistically, though not financially, successful. The Theater of the Arts, which Pirandello saw as an Italian counterpart to the Théâtre du Vieux Colombier in Paris, was officially patronized by Benito Mussolini, who had come to power in 1922.

Pirandello belonged to the fascist party from its beginning. That his works are sympathetic to fascism would, however, be difficult if not impossible to show. As Guy Dumur has remarked, the works that Pirandello wrote "are not quite the sort to serve a 'new order.' " [4]

In his survey *The Drama of Luigi Pirandello*,[5] Domenico Vittorini has classified the plays in five groups: early naturalism, the drama of being and seeming, social plays, the drama of womanhood, and art and life. The classification is useful, perhaps, but it is by no means definitive, for there is much overlap, especially in the last four groups. Obviously the theatrical representation of confusions between appearance and reality is not a separate thing from the subject of art and life, and it cannot be said that Pirandello wrote social plays or dramas of womanhood that avoid the preoccupation with consciousness that characterizes the most famous of Pirandello's works. In fact, all Pirandello's plays after 1917 are variations on a single theme. They are saved from repetitiousness by the vigor with which the characters are drawn and the ingenuity with which new situations are conceived and analyzed. Hence, the flavor of each of the plays is distinct. One does not confuse *Right You Are* with *Each in His Own Role*, or the latter with *Each in His Own Way*, once one has responded to each play by reading it or seeing it performed. *Tonight We Improvise* is in no way a rehash of *Six Characters in Search of an Author*, although both plays explicitly use theatrical performance as their leitmotifs. Madness is a theme in *Right You Are*, *Henry IV*, and *Cap and Bells* (*Il beretto a*

---

[4] *Ibid.*, p. 38.
[5] New York: Dover, 1957.

sonagli, 1917), but there is no confusing one of these plays with another. Although Pirandello frequently writes about confusion, his mode of doing so is vivid, distinct, and specifically rooted in the characters drawn. He consistently shows that confusion arises from lucidity, not from the lack of it. His theater of the limits of consciousness is a theater of clear and distinct images.

The relation of mental images to reality is a philosophical problem. Pirandello, who was not a philosopher, was nevertheless at pains to show that the problem occurs in the life of every man. In his capacity as a playwright he wrestled with a question known to philosophy since the pre-Socratics and agonizingly acute in modern philosophy since the time of Hegel. The question is how thinking, which tends to employ "fixed" categories, can give knowledge of life, which is fluid, mobile, and ceaselessly changing from one state to another. For man, the desire to know and the urge to live are at odds.

This conflict is to be seen even in Pirandello's early naturalist plays, where its implications are not much drawn out. It is present, for instance, in *Limes of Sicily,* in which Pirandello contrasts the simplicity of his native land with the corrupt sophistication of the northern Italian cities. Micuccio Bonavion goes to a city in the north to visit the singer Teresina, his childhood sweetheart. By selling land his uncle had given him, Micuccio had paid Teresina's way to the conservatory at Naples. She has become successful, and Micuccio is going to be reunited with her after years of separation. Arriving at her house, he finds her about to entertain for the evening. Her dinner guests, we learn, are all male. Micuccio, who has come in his rude Sicilian dress and carries a small bag of limes, a valise, and a piccolo, is not invited to the party. He eats in a side room with Teresina's mother, who tries to tell him that Teresina is no longer worthy of his love. When Teresina comes in, he realizes how much she has changed. She quickly goes back to her friends, and Micuccio departs, leaving behind him the limes, symbol of the fragrance and simplicity of the land of the south. Teresina and her gay company devour the limes, filling the stage with coarse laughter as the curtain falls.

The play's contrast of innocence with corruption is simple enough. In the main, the work is nothing more than a naturalist description of the brief meeting of two worlds. Its interesting touch is the characterization of Micuccio, who is torn between the desire to know the ways of the sophisticates in Teresina's life and the urge to live, as he always has, according to the instinctive music of his heart. For a moment he sees the choice. Then he makes it in favor of his native self, and the play closes without having examined the choice in any detail.

In his later work Pirandello was to dwell upon characters who, unlike Micuccio, have stepped over the line dividing their innocence from sophistication. Civilization is a snare for the innocent heart. Delia Morello says in *Each in His Own Way*, "I, too, have learned to do my acrobatic stunts, by myself, coming from the country to the city—here—in all this falsity and unreality, which becomes more false and unreal from day to day." [6] But she knows that there is no way to go back to the simplicity from which one has come. "To try to recreate this simplicity in us and around us appears—is, indeed, false." Though Pirandello himself knew how great was the contrast between his native Sicily and the city life in which he suffered so much, he did not idealize the rural life. The civilization that ensnares his characters is metaphoric. It represents the growth of self-consciousness in the individual, the necessity of calculated adjustment to other persons. In *Limes of Sicily* such "civilization" is held up for scorn, but in later plays it is seen as the inevitable lot of man, his alienation from something within himself, to which he longs but is not able to return.

> At certain moments of inward silence, when our soul strips itself of all its habitual pretenses, and our eyes become more acute and discerning, we see ourselves in life, and life in itself, as in a kind of barren and troubling nakedness; . . . as if, in a flash, we became aware of a reality different from that which we normally perceive, a reality dwelling beyond human vision, outside the forms of human reason. . . . With a supreme effort, we seek to regain our normal consciousness of things, to reunite things with their habitual associations, to reconnect our ideas, to feel ourselves alive again as before, in the familiar way. But we can no longer have faith in this normal consciousness, these reconnected ideas,

6 Translated in Domenico Vittorini, *The Drama of Luigi Pirandello* (New York: Dover, 1957), p. 129.

because we know now that they are a trick of our own for living and that underneath there is something else, which man can face only at the price of death or madness.[7]

The prison of consciousness, once it has been formed in the individual by the necessities of social life, is not easily escaped. In fact, no escape is possible except by the annihilation of reason in death or its crucifixion in madness. Pirandello enunciated this idea in 1908 in his essay on humor, but he did not dramatize it until *Right You Are* in 1917. His supreme expression of it is *Henry IV,* the great work composed in 1921–2.

The play is set in a Tuscan villa decorated to resemble the palace of King Henry IV. The servants are in period costume. The opening scene, in which a new servant is being introduced to his duties, is expository. It informs us of the situation that obtains in the household. But we shall learn that the entire play is exposition, for with the exception of a single violent act at the end it is nothing but a series of repeated penetrations toward the heart of the situation. That the play is almost totally an attempt to understand and to *feel* the multiple dimensions of the situation points to Pirandello's modernity and the Chekhovian element in him.

Along with the new servant, the audience is informed that the master of the house is a madman who thinks that he is King Henry IV. We have first to get it straight that the Henry IV intended is not the former king of France nor he of England but the great emperor of Germany who was the sworn enemy of Pope Gregory VII and whom Gregory had once humiliated, making him stand barefoot in the snow at Canossa before the villa of the Marchioness Matilda of Tuscany, there to seek absolution from the pope, who was resident within. Inasmuch as Matilda was the ally of the pope, she was also Henry's enemy, but it was said that the emperor harbored a secret love for her.

The sequestration of our present Henry (we know no other name for him) in his imperially decorated villa and in his life of total fantasy has lasted for nearly twenty years. It began at a masquerade ball, to which the ill-fated man had gone in the costume of the emperor. Of this assumed identity he has been destined never

<hr />

7 "The Art of Humor," p. 515.

to be free. He had gone there in the company of a lady whom he loved, one Matilda Spinna, who had for the occasion presented herself as Matilda of Tuscany. There was also a rival, a Baron Belcredi, who had also taken part in the charade. At the ball there was an accident. The mock emperor was thrown from his horse and received a severe blow on his head. From that moment on he has been able to think of himself as none other than Henry IV. Finding him unable to be cured, his family and friends have sought to bring him a certain peace of mind by humoring his fancy. His sister (now deceased) established him in the palatial villa, and when visitors come they wear period costume and show themselves as contemporaries of the eleventh-century monarch.

The play describes a visit to the villa paid by Matilda Spinna, her companion, Baron Belcredi, her daughter Frida, and the latter's suitor, Charles Di Nolli, who is the nephew of the mad Henry. The presence of these visitors calls up memories of the fateful party many years ago. Henry IV is on his guard against these "friends," whom he suspects of plotting against him, particularly Belcredi. He indulges himself in tirades against them. It seems that Henry is still in love with Matilda, though he is also very bitter toward her because she has taken up with Belcredi, against whom his fury knows no bounds. He insists that Belcredi is Peter Damiani, the eleventh-century fanatical reformer, and blames him for all his troubles with the pope. Henry's early love for Matilda is presented by Pirandello in ironic reduplication by his showing the young Di Nolli in love with Frida, who looks exactly like the portrait of her mother that hangs in Henry's great hall.

Gradually, through the superb skill of Pirandello's dialogue, we become aware that Henry's madness is something less simple than hallucination. Like Hamlet's, there is method in it. When the visitors depart, Henry reveals himself to the servants. To their astonished ears he confides that he is not mad. With uncanny insight he describes to them the hypocritical motivations of those who visit him ostensibly out of pity but actually in order to make sure that he is still mad and thus safely out of their way. "And you," he turns on the servants, "are amazed that I tear off their ridiculous masks now, just as if it wasn't I who had made them mask themselves to satisfy this taste of mine for playing the madman!"

Yet the more he declares his sanity to them, and the reasons for his bitterness toward those who play roles in front of him, the more his sanity appears another kind of madness. It expresses itself in a torrential outpouring of dialectical thought, in which the exasperated man pretends at one moment to be playing with others, at the next derides the others for playing with him, and vaunts his disregard of logic. He plays logic for a mockery. What is strong and clear is the passion, the suffering of one shut up in his consciousness, so lucidly aware of himself that feeling exceeds action. At the end of Act II he pretends, in order to please one of his servants, to be Henry IV once more, and peace comes over him as the curtain falls.

In the play's final act Belcredi, Matilda, and the others learn that Henry IV is not mad. Coming out from behind his mask, he confronts them. In total command of the situation, he turns the tables on the others repeatedly. Matilda is not convinced that he is sane. Belcredi is sure of it. Henry IV recounts how he lived in oblivion for about twelve years, then gradually came to himself, only to realize that life had passed him by. There was a grayness inside him to match the gray of his hair, although in all those years he could not be said to have lived. Had he then come out from behind his mask, he would have had nowhere to go. Furthermore, he discerned something about his friends: although they had been living their lives, they were equally imprisoned in roles, in fictions of self-interpretation, of which the most galling was their belief that they had compassion for him. He suggests that Belcredi had purposely caused the fateful accident long ago. We begin to see that Henry IV has been biding his time, waiting for the moment of revenge.

Belcredi, who now sees what confronts him, declares: "You're no madman!" "I'm not mad, eh!" retorts Henry IV, "Take that, you! . . ." He quickly draws a sword from the scabbard of a servant and plunges it into Belcredi, sending him to his death. Then, "terrified by the life of his own masquerade which has driven him to crime," he gathers his servants around him and retreats into his shell of madness ". . . for ever!"

Insofar as *Henry IV* is a play of ideas, it dwells upon the dialectic of sanity and madness, reality and illusion. It is to this dialectic that the man called Henry IV continually refers in his speeches:

and the entire play, beginning with its setting, is arranged to make the dialectic, which is unresolved, a lively one for the audience. Nothing is as it seems. Behind every meaning there is another that contradicts it. The play moves restlessly between levels, presenting the situation always in the ironic mode.

That said, it must immediately be added that Pirandello seldom, perhaps never, sets up the dialectic of illusion and reality for its own sake. It is easy for a clever thinker to show that for every truth there is an opposite truth, for every interpretation a counterinterpretation. This Pirandello knew from his earliest readings in philosophy, and he wrote neither *Henry IV* nor his other major works to demonstrate it. Had he done so, he would have been merely flashy, and it is a bad production of his plays that leaves the audience admiring his ingenuity.

What interested Pirandello about the dialectical form of thought was what has interested other major thinkers—for instance, Hegel, Schelling, Kierkegaard, Nietzsche, Shaw, and Sartre —namely, the necessity to employ a dialectic in order to comprehend the developmental character of life. Formal logic, which has as its cardinal principle the law of noncontradiction, is a suitable control over language that describes fixed states of being. Such language must assume that an entity is purely itself and not also something other than itself. To describe the developmental character of life, however, such language is inadequate if not positively misleading. If the reality one wants to describe is living, which means that nothing stays the same, that the identities of living things are mutable, then it is necessary to employ a dialectical type of reason, in which the law of noncontradiction is no longer absolute and in which one will be constantly reminded of the inadequacy of form as a category unequivocally applicable to the metamorphoses of living things.

Translated into theatrical terms, dialectical reason means that every character is a mask. The character is the form of something other than itself—deeper, more mysterious, more mutable. If the playwright removes the character mask, revealing what it hides, he will move the dialectic to a new level, but he will not resolve it. The character newly exposed will prove to be another mask, negating and being negated by what it hides. And so on. A human being can be represented in the theater only as a set of masks, one inside another, all of them worn by an invisible presence. The character *as such* is only a stereotype (what else are the minor characters in most plays?). The *person* is revealed in the tension between the fixity of his character and the mobility of his inner life. This tension reappears on each successive level of analysis.

In a general sense the dialectic of character has always been known by playwrights. Pirandello's contribution was to bring the insight to a position of paramount importance in drama, giving it precedence over the plot. He also observed that in "real life" people tend to turn themselves into character stereotypes. They hope in this way to ensure their respectability, but the price they pay is self-alienation.

The layers of character masks that a person may be said to wear constitute an infinite series, in the sense that there are always more and more of them as long as life continues. Only of the dead person may it be said that he wears no mask. Of him it is all the same whether we say that he has become completely identified with his mask (the image of a death mask comes to mind) or whether we say that he is at last denuded of every mask. It is all the same because either proposition implies that the dialectic has ceased, the condition of those who are not living. This is the point of the ending of Pirandello's play *Naked*. The play's heroine, Ersilia Drei, has had to defend herself at every turn from various "benefactors" who have stripped from her, one by one, the masks with which she has tried to cover herself. She tries to protect herself from shame; they try to get to know her "as she is." Her basic motivation, however, is not to avoid shame but to preserve life. Even when, at the start of the play, she attempts suicide, her aim is to die as a living person, not as one already dead. It is this privilege that is taken away from her. "Go and tell," she says at the end of the play, "that this poor girl has died naked."

The deep agony of the man called Henry IV is the agony of one who knows that he cannot live without his mask but that, equally, he cannot live if he has no identity *but* the mask. If one were to give the play another title it might suitably be "The Man in the Mask." We never see this man. We do not even know his name. But from within the mask we hear his cries, the terrible sounds made by one who knows that he is not the madman they insist upon believing him to be, yet knows also that if he relinquishes his role he will have "nowhere to go." His desperate strategy is to use the mask in order to live, and this strategy fails. That is the tragedy of man, as Pirandello sees it. But this tragedy is also comic, in a bitter way, because its protagonist is not heroically engaged with titanic forces but is a ludicrous puppet whose rude gestures do not express by any suitable means the life of passion that he experiences within. Henry IV says:

> Do you know what it means to find yourselves face to face with a madman—with one who shakes the foundations of all you have built up in yourselves, your logic, the logic of all your constructions? Madmen, lucky folk! construct without logic, or rather with a logic that flies like a feather. Voluble! Voluble! Today like this and tomorrow—who knows? You say: "This cannot be"; but for them everything can be. You say: "This isn't true!" And why? Because it doesn't seem true to you, or you, or you . . . and to a hundred thousand others! One must see what seems true to these hundred thousand others who are not supposed to be mad! What a magnificent spectacle they afford, when they reason! What flowers of logic they scatter! I know that when I was a child, I thought the moon in the pond was real. How many things I thought real! I believed everything I was told—and I was happy! Because it's a terrible thing if you don't hold on to that which seems true to you today—to that which will seem true to you tomorrow, even if it is the opposite of that which seemed true to you yesterday. I would never wish you to think, as I have done, on this horrible thing which really drives one mad: that if you were beside another and looking into his eyes—as I one day looked into somebody's eyes— you might as well be a beggar before a door never to be opened to you; for he who does enter there will never be you, but someone unknown to you with his own different and impenetrable world.[8]

Later he insists:

> I would live it—this madness of mine—with the most lucid consciousness; . . . I am cured, gentlemen: because I can act the

[8] Act II. Translated by Edward Storer. In *Naked Masks: Five Plays*, by Luigi Pirandello, Eric Bentley, ed. (New York: Dutton, 1952), pp. 192–193.

madman to perfection, here; and I do it very quietly, I'm only sorry for you that have to live your madness so agitatedly, without knowing it or seeing it.[9]

The dialectical relation of person and mask obtains, for Pirandello, also with regard to situation. Every situation contains another. If you discover the inner situation, you are immediately either thrown back to the first or sent further inward to yet another. The only fixed situation, absolutely identical with itself, is, as Henry IV says, past history, "that cannot change" and is "fixed for ever." There every effect follows "obediently its cause with perfect logic." It is "beautiful, but it's finished!"

A living situation is never *a* situation but a complex of several, part of which denies or contradicts the rest, for thought cannot logically embrace the totality and the fluidity of life. In *Henry IV* the complexity of situations is dramatized by the superimposition of at least three "times"—that of the historical Henry IV at the end of the eleventh century, that of the present "Henry IV" being visited in his villa by his friends, and that of the masquerade ball eighteen or twenty years ago. Within each of these there is greater complexity, for the situation is different for each of the several participants.

The dialectic of situations belongs to almost all Pirandello's plays, but it is most famously represented in *Right You Are,* if only for the reason that it may be more easily grasped in that play than in some others. The townspeople who gather at Councillor Agazzi's apartment represent, as it were, the "normal" social situation. These people are, with one exception, well defined in each other's eyes, and they do not regard their own situation as problematic. They are simply respectable citizens who pride themselves on knowing what's what. Their situation would be unambiguous were it not for the presence among them of Agazzi's brother-in-law, Laudisi. He knows that any situation varies according to the perspective of the beholder and varies also from moment to moment as the beholder himself changes. Laudisi employs this knowledge in a goading and teasing way to cast an ironic light on the efforts of the others to discover the "truth," and because he does so he is al-

9 Act III. *Ibid.,* pp. 204, 205–206.

ienated from them, who find that they cannot be sure of themselves in his presence. That is as far as Pirandello goes in analyzing the dialectic of the situation that serves as the frame of the play.

Within the frame, however, three characters are introduced who represent the "core" situation of the play, and it is with the dialectic of this core that the play is primarily concerned, for it is there that genuine life is present. Signora Frola lives alone in an apartment next door to the Agazzis. Across town on the fifth floor of a tenement lives her son-in-law, Signor Ponza, with his wife. Signor Ponza keeps the two women apart. He does not allow his wife to go out and permits the women to communicate with each other only by letters exchanged in a basket that is lowered and raised when Signora Frola goes to the courtyard of the building where her daughter lives. Every day, sometimes more than once, Signor Ponza goes to visit his mother-in-law, whom he has established in comfort and to whose every need he attends; but he does not permit his wife to go there. What are the relationships that explain this bizarre situation?

Two contradictory explanations are given, one by Signora Frola, the other by Ponza. In the eyes of each, the other is deranged and lives under an ineradicable delusion. Signora Frola tells that her daughter once had to go to a sanitorium and that Ponza believed that she died. When she returned he would not accept her as his wife; but later he married her in a second ceremony and now believes that she is his second wife.

Ponza's version corresponds to this, but in reverse. According to him, Signora Frola's daughter did die, and the shock of it drove the mother mad. Later, when she saw Ponza with the second woman, she believed it was her own daughter returned to her. Out of regard for the old woman he has had to humor this illusion, but out of regard for his wife he has to keep them apart. The only way he can do the latter is to pretend to Signora Frola that he is mad.

The play moves by a series of interviews, in which we hear first one version and then the other, statement and counterstatement. In the second act Frola and Ponza are brought together on the stage, to face each other's stories. The results are inconclusive. In the third act Signora Ponza herself appears. Since she is veiled, it is impossible to see her features. In answer to questions, she declares that she is indeed the daughter of Signora Frola. She says also that she is the second wife of Signor Ponza. To herself, she adds, she is nobody. When it is objected that she must be either one or the other, she replies that she is whomever they believe her to be.

Such is the scheme of the play, but not the substance. The scheme is no more than a puzzle without a solution. If it were also the substance, as is sometimes supposed, *Right You Are* would be meretricious. The scheme is a kind of indirect communication, designed to point toward that which cannot be communicated directly—that is, the actual life that is going on in the Ponza-Frola family. It presents a logical contradiction precisely because it is life and not schema. The terms may be exaggerated (Pirandello calls his play a parable), but the reality is universal. Persons cannot be reduced to clear-cut identities without their being robbed of life, and their situation cannot be defined in unambiguous terms without its being destroyed.

Yet even this description of the matter may be misleading, for it employs the set terms of logical discourse. The better way to state the matter is the way of the dramatist. Pirandello's great achievement in *Right You Are* is to make his audience feel and intuit the actuality of the lives of his three ill-fated persons, even while those lives are shrouded in mystery. One sees the destructiveness of an insatiable desire for knowledge, he sees the anguish that it causes, for unknown reasons, in the lives of those being investigated, and he comes to recognize how incompatible are the desire to know and the desire to live.

Pirandello's attitude is therefore romantic and idealistic. He advises us not to trespass upon life, for which he has an almost sacred awe. Yet by the time he wrote *Right You Are* he had put behind him almost all signs of romantic nostalgia. He knew that the simple and innocent life is not a possibility for man. Therefore, like his character Laudisi, he regards the human lot with laughing irony. The unresolved dialectic of life is humorous to the intelligence and tragic to the feelings.

The lucid consciousness of which the mad Henry IV speaks and which Laudisi manifests is also, in Pirandello, a heightened consciousness of the theatrical mode of presentation. One stands outside himself, as Laudisi does in the famous speech of address to his image in the mirror, reminiscent of Gaev's address to the bookcase in *The Cherry Orchard*. Similarly, the audience is at once part of and mere witness to the dramatic event. Most of Pirandello's plays are written in a style that emerges from the proposition that the self-realization of life is analogous to the theatricalization of life. His play that emphasizes this most is *Six Characters in Search of an Author*.

In this play, as in *Right You Are*, there is a framing situation and a core, the latter played off against the former, while the genuine dialectic belongs only to the core. The six characters belong to a family in which a tragedy has occurred. The ironic idea of the play is that these characters are pure fictions until they can find an author who will fix their identities in the form of a play and show them forth upon the stage. At the same time Pirandello clearly shows that the reality of the characters and their story would disappear if this were to happen. He brings them onto the stage out of nowhere, mere phantoms searching for an incarnation. They ask the actors whom they find on stage to rehearse and perform their story. Unless they achieve theatrical representation they will not be sure of their own reality, for they seek a conscious and definitive knowledge of who they are and what has happened to them.

This desire, as it turns out, is frustrated; and it is precisely in the frustration that, paradoxically, the characters' reality is made undeniable for us. Each member of the family has a different memory of what has happened, a different perspective on the events and motivations that led up to that fatal gunshot that can be erased neither from their memories nor from ours. Therefore, each member of the family tries to take over the stage in order to use it for his own self-demonstration. These efforts make a definitive version impossible, and just for that reason they communicate to us the sense of a reality transcending art, existing by virtue of its inner contradictions. The dramatization of this dialectic is one of Pirandello's greatest achievements. So skillfully, so organically, so artfully is it handled that the play itself takes on "life," its own contradictions lending it strength at every turn.

Six Characters in Search of an Author has become a work emblematic of the modern theater in general. It is a play of which one feels that if Pirandello had not written it, it would have written itself. It embodies, in the deepest ironies of tragicomedy, the major premise of theatrical positivism, that the theater is the image of consciousness. The theater is not "all," just as consciousness is not "all." There is something "other," which may be called life and which resists the attempts of consciousness to know it fully. But consciousness is the "all" of knowledge, at once man's glory and his futility.

After Pirandello there would be more radical versions of theatrical positivism, from which the strands of realism that run through Pirandello's works would be removed one by one, leaving only, as it were, the theatrical web. But there would not be any, save perhaps only Beckett, who would show so clearly and so poignantly the tragicomic irony of the disjunction between passion and thought.

"Logic," Pirandello wrote, "abstracting ideas from feelings, tends precisely to fix what is mobile, mutable and fluid; tends to give an absolute value to something which is relative." [10] Out of this Pirandello saw the ills of human life proceeding. Yet he knew that the ills are not curable, that it is all one whether we say that they proceed from thought, which cannot accommodate feeling, or from feeling, which cannot conform itself to thought. To describe this condition, art has to find ways of speaking of both sides at once.

> Art, like all ideal or illusionary constructs, tends to fix life; it fixes it in a moment, or in various selected moments—the statue in a gesture, the landscape in a passing aspect—immutably. But what of the constant movement of successive aspects? And the perpetual state of fusion in which souls exist? [11]

There would have to be, as well as the art of the ideal, an art of humor. Pirandello called himself a "humorist." What he meant by humor corresponds exactly to what I have called irony in these pages. It has seldom been better described than by Pirandello, in these words:

> [T]he art of humor consists in the feeling for opposites, which is produced by the special activity of a reflective faculty that does not

[10] "The Art of Humor," p. 517.
[11] *Ibid.*

go into hiding, that does not become, as is usual in art, a form of feeling, but is feeling's opposite—though it follows the feeling step by step, as the shadow follows the body. The ordinary artist pays attention only to the body; the humorist pays attention to both body and shadow, and sometimes more to the shadow than to the body; he notes all the tricks of this shadow, the way it sometimes grows longer and sometimes grows squat, as though it were making faces at the body—which takes no notice of it, however, and is indifferent to it.[12]

Let us say then that the theatrical theater is a shadow theater. It is of puppets, masks, figments of imagination, the "reflective faculty." Yet it sometimes causes us to ask: what is the "body" that is casting these shadows? What is the living reality to which thought is mere shadow? At its finest, as in Pirandello, dialectical theater places us in Plato's cave. Just there and no further. We see the shadows. We hear the cries of the body. We cannot go outside.

12 *Ibid.*, p. 520.

16. BERTOLT BRECHT
(1898–1956)

> In the asphalt city I am at home.
> From the first
> Supplied with Extreme Unction in plenty:
> With papers. Tobacco. And brandy.
> Mistrustful and idle, and ultimately
> not discontented.
>
> —BERTOLT BRECHT [1]

BERTOLT BRECHT achieved his first stage success in 1922, when *Trommeln in der Nacht* ("Drums in the Night") was performed at the Kammerspiele in Munich. For the next decade, until Hitler took power, he was a major figure in that mélange of art and politics that distinguished Germany in the '20's. Born in Augsburg of middle-class parents, he had moved to Munich at the age of nineteen to study medicine and natural science. It was wartime, and he was called up as a medical orderly.

> I dressed wounds, applied iodine, gave enemas, performed blood transfusions. If the doctor ordered me: "Amputate a leg, Brecht!" I would answer: "Yes, Your Excellency!" and cut off the leg. If I was told: "Make a trepanning!" I opened the man's skull and tinkered with his brains.[2]

With such words as these, compounded of Charlie Chaplin, Georg Grosz, and Jaroslav Hašek, we enter the world of comic grotesque. Brecht was one of those who helped etch its features during the decade after the Great War. One of his first tasks when he

1 "Of Poor B.B." Translated in John Willett, *The Theatre of Bertolt Brecht* (New York: New Directions, 1959), p. 65.
2 Translated in Martin Esslin, *Brecht: The Man and His Work* (Garden City, N.Y.: Anchor Books, Doubleday, 1961), p. 7. The passage dates from 1935 and probably does not tell the truth. No operations were performed at the hospital where Brecht served. See Hugo Schmidt's notes in Brecht's *Manual of Piety*, translated and edited by Eric Bentley (Grove Press: New York, 1966), pp. 309f. I cite the statement for its savagely comic style.

moved to Berlin was to adapt Hašek's *Good Soldier Schweik* for the stage. It became (in 1928) one of the finest of Erwin Piscator's productions.

In Munich an unkempt, erratic young Brecht began to burrow his way into the artistic life of Germany at the same time that Hitler was burrowing into its political life. The fact is important, for one cannot understand Brecht without remembering that his rise to prominence paralleled Hitler's and that opposition to Nazism conditioned almost all his writing. Brecht lost his base of operations in Germany when Hitler took power, and from that time forward he had to survive by the use of craft and cunning.

Brecht dropped his medical studies in 1920 to become Dramaturg of the Munich Kammerspiele. During the next four years three of his plays were put on at Munich, including *Edward II,* which he and Leon Feuchtwanger adapted freely from Marlowe, debunking all the characters in turn and suggesting that all rulers are as arbitrary and jaded as the Nazis of Germany were already showing themselves to be. During these years one of Brecht's plays was also put on in Berlin and another at Leipzig. He wrote poetry, and in small cabarets he sang and played the guitar.

In 1924, the year after the beer-cellar *Putsch* in which the Nazis made a bid for power in Munich, Brecht moved to Berlin, where he worked for a time in Max Reinhardt's theater. By 1927 a new play, *Mann ist Mann,* had been put on in Darmstadt, a book of poems, *Hauspostille (Manual of Piety)*, had been published, and he had begun his collaboration with Kurt Weill. For the summer festival at Baden-Baden they created the first version of *Mahagonny,* by setting to music some of the poems from the *Manual of Piety.*

A second version of *Mahagonny* became the opera known as *Aufsteig und Fall der Stadt Mahagonny (Rise and Fall of the City of Mahagonny).* Produced at Leipzig in March 1930, it caused bedlam in the house. It is set in that mythical U.S.A. concocted by the imagination of the avant-garde of the time, but Mahagonny was Brecht's nickname for Berlin.

The annual festivals at Baden-Baden, which continued those begun in 1922 at Donaueschingen, brought together a number of musicians, writers, and painters who were interested in achieving a serious artistic critique of society through the use of not-so-serious forms. Paul Hindemith, Heinrich Burkard, Igor Stravinsky, Darius Milhaud, Ernst Křenek, Wilhelm Grosz, Ernst Toch, and Kurt Weill were among the musicians who took part in the festivals from time to time. They were interested in purging music of the rich, superfluous sound that Wagner and Strauss had heaped upon it. They were experimenting with various purposes to which jazz and the popular song might be put. Already, in France, Jean Cocteau had used a "pop" score for his play *Les Mariés de la Tour Eiffel* (1921) and had collaborated with Milhaud on a short popular opera, *Le Pauvre Matelot* (1926). *Rhapsody in Blue* had had its première in America in 1924, Stravinsky's *L'Histoire du soldat* in Lausanne in 1918, and his opera *Renard,* for "clowns, dancers, or acrobats," in 1915. *Renard* may be considered the beginning of the attempt in this century to join lowbrow with highbrow music. By 1927, when Brecht first worked at the Baden-Baden festival, the movement was in full swing, and he was a "natural" for it.

Behind this sort of experimentation lay a concern fundamental to Brecht's work from first to last—that the theater should employ those words and forms, and should address itself to those subjects, that the common people could be expected to understand and that affected their daily lives. His poetry, similar to that of Auden in the same period, was dry and pithy, and almost as direct in utterance as witty prose:

> The band in the van with rum-tum-tum
> Played him a rousing march.
> The soldier as he had been drilled
> Kicked his legs from his arse.[3]

These words are from *The Legend of the Dead Soldier,* which Brecht had written about 1918. For this unpatriotic, antiwar poem, his name was put high on the list of persons the Nazis planned to arrest when they took power.

The cartoon, the film, and the poster were the visual forms most apt for the sort of theater Brecht and his friends were after. Behind Brecht's work, says John Willett, "lies a whole Central European

[3] Esslin, *op. cit.,* p. 8.

movement of the 1920's which is far too little recognized: a movement for taking elements of popular and public and everyday art,
and using them to make something fresh." [4]

Art conceived in this way is didactic, for it causes the audience
to adopt a critical attitude toward materials and styles with which it
is already familiar. The attitude encouraged is ambivalent and
highly ironic. For instance, if a musician trained by Schönberg and
Webern spends his talent on a cabaret song, the song is bound to
be held somewhat at arm's length, perhaps even parodied. Yet at
the same time the song is affirmed by the same musician's fulfillment of heretofore unrealized musical potentialities within it. In
this way there emerges a kind of ironic musical idiom, which one
can recognize instantly in Kurt Weill's music of the 20's and in that
of many of his contemporaries.

Irony, if successful, is always instructive, but it is also enjoyable
for its own sake. One may relish the taste of it without being much
concerned with its moral effect. Brecht was different from most of
his colleagues at Baden-Baden in that he took the didactic force of
their ironic musical theater more seriously than they did. He set
out, he said, "more and more to emphasize the didactic at the expense of the culinary element." [5] A dispute over the "culinary
principle" led him to break with Hindemith after their collaboration on the *Badener Lehrstück* for the 1929 festival. "The
Lehrstück," said Brecht in a slap at Hindemith, "is designed to
clarify the ideas of its authors and of all those taking part, not to
provide anybody with an emotional experience." [6]

The *Badener Lehrstück* (a *Lehrstück* is a "teaching piece," or a
deliberately didactic play, usually short) was the sequel to *Lindberghflug*, performed the same year. Weill wrote most of the music
for *Lindberghflug*, though Hindemith contributed a few numbers.
The *Badener* had music by Hindemith alone. The piece about
Lindbergh, written for performance by boys and girls, praises
man's achievement in overcoming fear, the natural elements, and
what Brecht called the "Primitive." The *Badener* is more revolutionary. Its message is that acts of common charity are worthless

[4] *The Theatre of Bertolt Brecht*, p. 226.
[5] *Ibid.*, p. 134.
[6] *Ibid.*, p. 135.

until the world is changed. Until then, the only thing that matters is power.

The performance of the *Badener Lehrstück* is said to have caused a major scandal at Baden-Baden. Hindemith refused to cooperate with Brecht on additions to the text, so for the next festival (1930) Brecht turned to the composer Hanns Eisler, with whom he prepared a new *Lehrstück* called *Die Massnahme (The Measures Taken)*. It was Brecht's first explicitly communist work. In it four political agitators sent to China from Moscow describe how they had to shoot a fifth member of their party because of his "mistakes." He acquiesced in their decision, and the Chorus agrees it was the right thing to do. This clearly leftist revolutionary work was turned down by the festival leaders. It was performed instead by socialist-communist workers' choral societies in Berlin.

It was apparently in 1929 and 1930 that Brecht began to adopt communism as a body of doctrine. Since his student days he had been in deep sympathy with the lower classes. "I left my own class," he wrote in a poem, "and joined the common people." He had participated in the short proletarian uprising in Munich in 1918. After the première of *Mann ist Mann* (at Darmstadt, in 1926), he spent a vacation studying *Das Kapital.* He studied communist theory intensively at the Marxist Workers' College in Berlin in 1928 and 1929, and from then until his death in 1956, although he declined to live in the Soviet Union, he was pro-Russian in all kinds of political weather. Eisler, when Brecht began to work with him, was already well known as a composer of communist songs; and Eisler's brother Gerhard and their sister, Ruth Fischer, were prominent party officials. Ruth Fischer said that Brecht joined the party in 1930.[7] Brecht denied being a member when he testified before the House Un-American Activities Committee in Washington (1947). Whether he joined the party or not, his sympathies were with it.

We do not yet know enough about Brecht's personality or about his dealings with the party to describe the precise nature of communism's importance for him. It follows that we do not know what weight to give it in our assessment of his growth as a playwright.

[7] Esslin, *Brecht,* p. 149.

Should we say, for instance, that Marxist doctrine, as interpreted in Russia and Germany, aided him in his determination to be clear-headed, dispassionate, and "scientific"? Or should we say that these qualities were native to him and persisted *in spite of* his attraction to communist ideology? Was it communism that helped him rise above the other expressionists, or would he have done so anyway and perhaps even better without that commitment? Westerners are tempted to take the latter position, and it is not hard for them to point out a Brechtian individuality in his earliest works: *Baal* (1922), *Drums in the Night* (1922), and *Im Dickicht der Städte* (1923; *In the Jungle of Cities*).

It is probably best to interpret the contribution that communism made to Brecht's dramatic writing in the following general way. The penchant for dialectical thinking, not to mention sympathy for the lower classes, was his from the beginning. It is mentioned in the earliest descriptions of him. The dialectical ability to see the inherent contradictions in ideas and processes can of itself, however, lead to waywardness and even inertia: to remain useful it has to be systematized. Philosophers like Hegel and Marx create their own systems. Brecht, who was not a philosopher but merely a pragmatic dialectician, needed a system to operate within, and communism provided it. Socialism might also have provided this, but socialism in Germany in the '20's was pitifully weak. Furthermore, it smacked of compromise, and however much he may have accepted the necessity of all manner of tactical compromises, Brecht was never a compromiser in principle. He was never one to make peace with existence. That is why the spirit of classical tragedy is almost completely absent from his works, and the spirit of classical comedy, too.

Martin Esslin, in *Brecht: The Man and His Work,* speaks frequently of the tragic in Brecht.[8] The evidence he cites is important, but the word "tragic" is misleading. Irreconcilable conflict leading to human defeat is a necessary but not a sufficient cause of tragedy. A tragedian accepts such conflict as inherent in the structure of things and resigns himself to it. Brecht did not. Several of his characters—the victim in *Die Massnahme,* Shen Te, Mother Courage, even Galileo—might have become tragic heroes, but

8 See especially pp. 156, 235, 259.

Brecht did not allow it. Not even Baal, Brecht's earliest protagonist, is a tragic figure. He is, like the later protagonists, a romantic
seeker for "a better land," which has never been found.

By the same token, Brecht did not write comedy, which, even
more obviously, must be born of the spirit of compromise. The
material for comedy is there—the concern with making ends meet,
the necessity of getting along, and especially the wit. But Brecht's
eschatological hope (at first romantic and later communist) effectively prevented his striking a bargain with any cosmic order. Instead, it did away with cosmic order. Brecht allowed that science
discovers order in nature, but for him nature and history are radically split. There is no such thing as *human* nature. Hence, all
order that seems to define what man is—all political and historical
order—is malleable and can be changed. This attitude is present in
all Brecht's plays from *Baal* to *Die Tage der Kommune* (1948-9;
The Days of the Commune). It is a rejection of the tragic, and it
affects not only the themes of the works but also their tone and
style.

It is necessary to see in Brecht's adherence to communism the
manifestation of a quality that was basic to all he accomplished as a
playwright and man of the theater. That quality is determination.
A less resolute individual might have quit the cause. But Brecht
would see a thing through. Just as he would revise his plays continually, never thinking of them as finished, even after production
and publication, he wanted also to follow communism through. Its
truth was not, for him, a finished product. Rather, its dicta had
always to be questioned as soon as uttered. "My job," his Galileo
says, "is not to prove that I have been right so far, but to find out
if." Brecht told his students that this was the most important line
of the play for a Marxist. Although Brecht believed in an eventual
end to revolution, this belief was eschatological. He was never prepared to say that the dialectical process had anywhere reached its
end, not even in countries in which the proletarian revolution had
occurred. No wonder that communists found his plays useful in
pre-revolutionary conditions but embarrassing in post-revolution-
ary societies.

The determination to persevere in the dialectical search for
truth was as basic to Brecht's maturation as a playwright as to his

adherence to communism. There was something fanatical about it. Happily, it was a fanaticism about method far more than about specific contents and findings. Brecht had the fanaticism of the searcher, and it is this commitment to the search that placed him in the main stream of modern drama and enabled him to have such a profound effect upon it.

While Brecht's association with the Badener festivals was still going on, he and Kurt Weill created in Berlin their most famous work. The 200th anniversary of John Gay's *Beggar's Opera* was in 1928. This parody of eighteenth-century opera and satire of the aristocracy had much affinity with what the musical experimenters of the 1920's were doing. Brecht and Weill decided to use it as the basis for a new satire. They kept Gay's plot but changed the setting to a Victorian London of their own imagining and directed the satire at the bourgeoisie. Within the play, all values are upside down: crooks are heroes, and the audience cheers the underworld, despises the respectable, and applauds an ethic of survival by plunder. But the work is an indictment of the conditions that make its reversal of values necessary. It spreads a corrosive acid over the existing table of values.

The acid delighted the audience: *Die Dreigroschenoper (The Threepenny Opera)* opened at the Theater am Schiffbauerdamm, on August 31, 1928, and was an immediate hit. It made Brecht, Weill, and Lotte Lenya (who sang the part of Jenny) famous all over Germany and gave Brecht and Weill international reputations. The collaborators then tried to follow the success of *The Threepenny Opera* with another of the same type, but *Happy End* (1929) was a failure, and Brecht later disowned it. Its songs, however, were popular. They included the famous "Surabaya-Johnny." The musical also contained elements of situation, theme, and character that later appeared in *Die heilige Johanna der Schlachthöfe (Saint Joan of the Stockyards)*, one of Brecht's best works, written in 1929–30 but not performed until 1959 (at Hamburg).

At the same time as *Saint Joan*, Brecht wrote *Der Jasager* and *Der Neinsager (He Who Says Yes* and *He Who Says No)*, two *Lehrstücke* for school children. Here the theme—the individual's acquiescence in the social good—is the same as that which in-

formed *Die Massnahme* a few months later. The exploitation of
the weak by the powerful is the subject of the parable *Die
Ausnahme und die Regel* (*The Exception and the Rule*) written
in 1930.

Die Mutter (1930–1; *The Mother*), adopted from Gorki's
novel, is a propagandistic work that is exceptionally powerful.
Equally propagandistic was the film *Kuhle Wampe* (the name is
that of an impoverished working-class district of Berlin), which
Brecht wrote in 1932 with Ernst Ottwalt. Hanns Eisler wrote the
music, and Slatan Dudow directed. It was the second film Brecht
was involved with, the first having been an adaptation of *The
Threepenny Opera*, directed by G. W. Pabst. The film of *The
Threepenny Opera* was very successful, but in 1930 Brecht sued
the producers to protest their refusal to allow him to change the
outline, which he wanted to make more explicitly anti-capitalist.

Both *Die Mutter* and *Kuhle Wampe* encountered trouble with
the censors. The former was allowed only as a reading, which nevertheless worked quite well. The latter was nearly banned but was
finally let through with a few cuts. It was the only communist film
made in Germany under the Weimar Republic. For the left wing,
the political climate was more and more unfavorable. In January
1933, Hitler became chancellor. The Reichstag Fire occurred on
February 27, and the next day Brecht left Germany.

Exile took Brecht around the world. Looking for a haven in the
German-speaking world, he took his family first to Vienna, then to
Switzerland. Neither of these worked out, and they went to France.
At Paris in the spring of 1933 he and Kurt Weill wrote for Lotte
Lenya the ballet *Die sieben Todsünden der Kleinbürger* (*The
Seven Deadly Sins of the Petty Bourgeois,* also known as *Anna
Anna*), which George Balanchine staged at the Théâtre des
Champs-Élysées.

In Denmark Brecht found a place to settle. He lived in a farm-
house most of the time from the spring of 1933 to the summer of
1939. He wrote *Die Rundhöpfe und die Spitzhöpfe* (*The Round-
heads and the Peakheads*), *Furcht und Elend des Dritten Reich*
(*Fear and Misery in the Third Reich,* known in Eric Bentley's
version as *The Private Life of the Master Race*), *Die Gewehre der
Frau Carrar* (*Señora Carrar's Rifles,* partly based on Synge's *Riders*

to the Sea), and he elaborated his unused screen treatment of *The Threepenny Opera* into *The Threepenny Novel*. In Denmark he also wrote the first versions of *Galileo* and *Das Verhör des Lukullus* (*The Trial of Lucullus*). He began *Der gute Mensch von Sezuan* (*The Good Woman of Setzuan*) and *Mutter Courage und ihre Kinder* (*Mother Courage and Her Children*). He also was co-editor of a literary review, *Das Wort,* published in Moscow.

In the summer of 1939 Brecht moved to Sweden, in 1940 to Finland. There he wrote *Herr Puntila und sein Knecht Matti* (*Mr. Puntila and His Hired Man Matti*), also *Der Aufhaltsame des Arturo Ui* (*The Resistible Rise of Arturo Ui*). Then in June 1941 Brecht, with his family, traveled across the Soviet Union to Vladivostok and embarked on a Swedish ship bound for California. By the time they arrived, Hitler had invaded Russia. Brecht settled near Hollywood, where he lived rather quietly, his friends drawn from the German and Austrian refugees. He wrote a screenplay about Heinrich Heydrich, although the finished product, called *Hangmen Also Die,* did not include much of his work. The ubiquitous Hanns Eisler wrote the music. Brecht also wrote in California *Schweik im zweiten Weltkrieg* (*Schweik in the Second World War*), *Der kaukaische Kreidekreis* (*The Caucasian Chalk Circle*), and *Die Gesichte der Simone Machard* (*The Visions of Simone Machard,* in collaboration with Leon Feuchtwanger).

During these war years, three of his plays written in Denmark (*Courage, Setzuan,* and *Galileo*) were put on at Zurich. In 1945 *The Private Life of the Master Race* was produced in New York, with no success. After that, Brecht and Charles Laughton, in Hollywood, prepared an English version of *Galileo,* which was produced in Beverly Hills on July 30, 1947, by T. Edward Hambleton, later co-founder of the Phoenix Theater in New York. This production, starring Laughton, was moved to New York in December, but in neither place did it find an enthusiastic audience. (In the English-speaking world, *Galileo* did not succeed until the 1960 production by Bernard Miles at the Mermaid Theatre in London.)

Meanwhile, Brecht appeared (October 30, 1947) before the House Un-American Activities Committee in Washington, where he dissembled with such obsequiousness that the chairman of that committee, unaware of the irony with which Brecht had treated this inquest about communism in Hollywood, thanked him for his cooperation and let him go.[9] Brecht returned to New York and soon departed for Europe.

He had sat out most of the war in the country that was the bastion of capitalism, the land he had satirized, along with Germany, in many anti-fascist plays and poems. Congressmen had asked him if he was a communist or a writer of communist works, and he had said no. Peace had come. He had survived. He was 49 years old. He could go where he liked. It was time to start his theater career anew.

By January 1949 he had three live options before him. In East Berlin, where he produced *Mother Courage* that month, he was offered a company, a theater, and plenty of money to work with. In Zurich, where he had gone first from America (by way of Paris) and where *Courage, Puntila,* and his adaptation of *Antigone* (1948) had been recently done, he might make a base of operations. In addition, it was proposed in Salzburg that he take over the direction of drama at the Salzburg Festival, the post once held by Max Reinhardt.

We do not know how the various pros and cons weighed in Brecht's mind. He had not considered Russia a good place to live in 1941 (when he passed right through it on his way to America), and it was probably even less attractive in 1949. Berlin, on the border between East and West, might be another matter. This he chose, but before going there he made three precautionary moves. He acquired an Austrian passport, he established a bank account in Switzerland, and he put his literary copyrights in the hands of a West German publisher (Suhrkamp of Frankfurt). He then went to East Berlin to assume leadership of the Berliner Ensemble, the company established for him. Its director was his wife, the actress Helene Weigel, whom he had married in Berlin in 1928. He was the company's "artistic adviser."

From this point on, the career of Brecht as a playwright contains virtually nothing of note. He worked industriously on numerous projects, most of them adaptations—Molière's *Don Juan,* for instance—and he revised a number of earlier works. His last impor-

[9] See Esslin, *Brecht,* pp. 76–80.

tant completed play was *The Days of the Commune,* written just before he moved to East Berlin. The great achievement of the last years was the Berliner Ensemble, the superb company which Brecht fashioned into the perfect instrument to perform his plays and to vindicate his dramatic theories. He died of coronary thrombosis on August 14, 1956, and was buried in the Huguenot Cemetery opposite his apartment on Chauséestrasse.

Brechtian theory, as well as practice, may be described initially as anti-illusory. The root of this theory lies in the awareness that the art of theater is the art of pretending. Everyone knows this. There are, however, two resorts that may be taken on the basis of such knowledge. On the one hand, one may compound the pretense basic to all theater by pretending that the pretense is not going on, which leads to realism. On the other hand, one may decide that it is more honest, more interesting, and more effective to accept pretense as that beyond which theater cannot go. In that case, the strategy will be to make deliberate, unveiled use of specifically theatrical techniques. The audience will be faced with these openly. Its mode of response will therefore be something different from vicarious experience: it will be conscious experience of the actual dramatic event. By this means one arrives at "the theater positive," which we have encountered so often in the latter part of this study.

Brecht was not, of course, the first of the moderns to adopt the theater positive. Georg Büchner, who foreshadowed it, had a strong influence on Brecht. *Danton's Death* lies behind the structure and tone of *Baal,* Brecht's first play; and the principal forerunner of *The Good Soldier Schweik* is Büchner's *Woyzeck.* The French "renewal" of the stage, signalled by Jacques Copeau's open stage at the Théâtre du Vieux Colombier, had begun before World War I. German expressionism, French surrealism, and Russian constructivism were in full swing when Brecht joined the Kammerspiele at Munich. So there was nothing new in rejecting realistic theater; everyone who had any quarrel with the bourgeoisie despised the sort of theater that entertained them and eased their conscience by "taking them out of themselves." Brecht's distaste for this was the same as Ionesco's later: they both said it made them sick to see actors trying to convince audiences that they were not acting.

Brecht's distinctiveness lay in his insistence that the proper response of theater audience should be *intellection* rather than emotion. This did not necessarily flow logically from the anti-illusory position. It is quite possible to respond to anti-illusory theater in an emotional way or in a purely aesthetic way or with the spiritual intent that was Artaud's, letting the ideas and techniques serve primarily to create a non-intellectual response. Brecht thought this was what was happening with most expressionist drama, which he regarded as exalting instinct at the expense of reason. He thought it was what Hindemith and some others at the Baden-Baden festivals were willing to settle for—the "culinary principle," as he called it. Brecht believed that theatricalism should not even be employed to produce a socially useful state of emotion (here he was at odds with the Communist Party's desires) but should be employed to enable the audience to think. One of his pet ideas (it was not accepted) when he worked at Max Reinhardt's theater in the mid-'20's was to establish "smoking theaters," where the audience could light up and relax, eyeing the stage coolly, and thinking about what it saw. He desired, actually, an intellectuals' theater, and he believed that audiences made up of the common people also desired such a thing.

Concern for—insistence upon—the spectator's intellection accounts for the structuring of Brecht's plays. It is not surprising that audiences did not know what to make of *Baal*, to cite an early, precommunist work. It has almost no emotional "build." Its early scenes are as "strong" as the later ones, and as complicated. The major events are easily anticipated and are anticlimactic when they occur. Where, people asked (and still ask) is "the experience"? The answer is that there is not *an* experience but many, and they are produced, if at all, in one's head. If the play is to be enjoyed, the mind must pick up and analyze each particular scene, speech, and line as it comes, asking about its particular content and inner tension of ideas. Then one moves on to the next. The fitting of particulars into a whole is not the game to play.

One can see, then, the basis of Brecht's argument with Aristotle. Actually this argument has two bases, one a matter of dramatic theory, the other social. The social point is that Aristotle occupied a privileged position as the major philosophical authority behind

European culture from the thirteenth century until Nietzsche, at the end of the nineteenth. To rebel against the fundaments of that culture meant to rebel against Aristotle. This had been done in philosophy, but it had not been done explicitly in dramatic theory. That is the social impulse lying behind Brecht's own "Poetics," the *Little Organon for the Theatre,* which he wrote in 1948 but which had been growing in essays and notes long before.

The dramatic and theatrical point *contra* Aristotle centered in the idea of *catharsis.* This Aristotelian term has never been very clear, but at least it has meant that some operation of purging, cleansing, or "release" was to be performed upon the audience by the drama. Behind this lay the classical ideal of coming to terms with given reality. What one is purged of must be some element or quality within him that prevents his proper accommodation to things as they are. In Aristotle's view, drama gets rid of this, at least temporarily, and leads to an Apollonian balance or adjustment.

A revolutionary, be he political or any other sort, cannot accept the Aristotelian view. Brecht knew this. And he knew that if one rejected the cathartic effect of drama he rejected also the Aristotelian dramatic structure, its unity of action and its climax embedded in a "beginning, middle, and end."

Furthermore, that rejection also swept out the psychological description of character, at least the sort of psychology that had been growing in nineteenth-century literature and was being systematized by Freud. This for two reasons. First, the predicate of such psychology is that the "character" of an individual is more or less fixed and represents a sort of internal "fate." The drama of such a "character" will be primarily a revelation of what is "given" in the personality structure. Second, the aim of depth psychology is the adjustment of the person to reality. It is therefore of no direct use to a writer whose aim is to change reality.

Another kind of psychology was, however, available. J. B. Watson's "behaviorism" was fashionable in certain German circles of the '20's, and Brecht took up two of its main points: rejection of the conscious-unconscious dichotomy, and the insistence that the person is identical with his acts (behavior) in given situations.

The latter identification was, to Brecht's way of thinking, highly instructive for the playwright. The theater, after all, is a place where the acts of human beings are shown. The narrative sets up a situation, and the actor shows what the character *does* in it: to make love, to fight, to flee, to deceive, to take cover, to die, etc. Theater is a place where we observe the human gestures that result from existing situations and lead to new ones. "The truth is concrete," as Brecht's motto put it. The theater is the art of the concrete, and *the* concrete human reality is the act, or gesture.

Hence, Brecht's theory contains the important notion of a *Gestus.* This word, cognate with the English word *gesture,* is richer in German than in English, like the French word *geste.* Brecht says it means not only the specific gesture, as of a hand or a shoulder, but also all outward signs of social relations, "deportment, intonation, facial expression." [10] In fact, it means even more. It means the act or deed in its totality, *conceived as expressing a reaction to a situation.* The scene as a whole may therefore be envisioned as having a *basic Gestus (Grundgestus),* out of which many particular *Gestussen* grow. One may envision the stage design and the music also as expressive of the *Grundgestus.*

We have now identified the two ideas basic to Brecht's entire dramatic theory: the theater conceived as a place where *Gestussen* are shown, and the theater conceived as a house of intellection. From these two conceptions flow everything "Brechtian" in playwriting and directing, and from them flow the ideas of Epic Theater and alienation (*Verfremdung*).

Take music, for example. If it does not exist in the theater to provide or intensify emotion but rather to express a *Grundgestus,* then the music will be important not merely as *sound* but also as *act,* something *done* (performed). Therefore the musician will not be sequestered in the orchestra pit or the wings but will be on stage to be seen. And the composer will write music that is in closest possible rapport with the text, since the words and the music have the same function, which is to express the *Gestus* and nothing more. In short, neither the melody nor the musician has any function in the theater except to express *Gestus.* The actor has the same function, which he usually effects in a manner different from that of the musician; but if the actor turns singer, as he often does, this difference is overcome.

10 *Ibid.,* pp. 133–134.

Though Brecht was extremely anti-Wagnerian, his idea of musical theater is merely Wagner turned inside out. For both, there is no split in principle between drama, text, and music. The integration is complete. The difference is that in Wagner the integration is achieved under the rule of melody-*cum*-emotion, whereas with Brecht it is achieved under the rule of *Gestus-cum*-intellect.

What is true of theatrical music for Brecht is also true of every other theatrical resource. If the music can be put on stage to be seen as well as heard, so can the words. Hence, part of the text will appear on posters or on lantern-slide projections. Words chosen for this purpose are usually those that explain the situation and thus relieve the actors of some of their narrative function, but they can also sometimes describe the *Grundgestus* which the actors are to portray. In *Mother Courage* they do both:

> SPRING, 1624. IN DALARNA, SWEDEN, KING GUSTAVUS ADOLPHUS IS RECRUITING FOR THE CAMPAIGN IN POLAND. THE PROVISIONER ANNA FIERLING, KNOWN AS CANTEEN ANNA OR MOTHER COURAGE, LOSES A SON.[11]

"To lose a son"—and to lose him in the precise situation described —that is the *Grundgestus* of the scene which the audience is to watch.

Is light necessary to enable the audience to see the enactment? Then let there be not only light but *lights*, visible so we can see their function. Brecht wanted an utterly functionalist theater, born in the age of functionalist aesthetics, wherein both beauty and interest derive from appreciation of function.

What shall the light reveal? (In Brecht, light has *only* the function of revealing, never to set mood or to describe the time of day.) It shall reveal the actors in their setting. What sort of setting? The sort that helps describe the situation—not symbolically with abstract designs, and not slavishly realistic (the latter includes *unnecessary* detail and tends toward the establishment of mood), but such a set, made up of selected real objects and carefully executed design, as will *describe* the physical aspect of the situation as far as we need to know it in order to comprehend the *Gestus* that occurs

---

[11] Quoted from the English version by Eric Bentley. In Bentley, ed., *The Modern Theatre* (Garden City, N.Y.: Anchor Books, Doubleday, 1955), Vol. II, p. 238.

within it. The rule is: not illusion, but description. And this set, like everything else, will be shown *functioning*. If we see beyond the set into the wings, all right. No need for masking, as long as what we see is not overly distracting but reminds us that the set is there to function.

By the same token, a half-curtain is better than a whole curtain, since it speaks the more clearly of its function:

> . . . and make
> My curtain half-high, don't seal off the stage!
> Leaning back in his chair, let the spectator
> Be aware of busy preparations, made for him
> Cunningly . . .[12]

Brecht could have found all of these devices by looking back into the history of the stage (which he did), but they were also at his elbow in the expressionist theater, in the work of Russian directors who came to Berlin, in the French avant-garde, and—closest of all—in the productions of Erwin Piscator. From Piscator he picked up also the term "Epic Theater," which he used to describe not only the drama of episodic, non-Aristotelian structure that he advocated but also to refer to a theater employing techniques of the sort here mentioned.

There has been some discussion of how important Brecht's theory really is, it being suggested that it does not amount to much compared to his practical accomplishments as a writer and director. His theory is probably as important as other major dramatic theories, no less and no more. The theory was largely a rationalization of his own practice, an attempt to explain to himself and others the nature and purpose of what he was doing; but this is true of most theory. Even Aristotle, who never wrote or directed a play, did little but describe Sophocles' practice, linking it up with some of his own philosophical vocabulary. Brecht's theory, more than that of any other dramatist of this century, offers a rational structure which the director (or writer) of taste can use as a starting point. Its most useful part is its concept of *Verfremdungseffekt*.

This concept flows, like the rest of the theory, from the positing of *Gestus* and intellection as basic to the theatrical event. That is

---

12 Translated in Esslin, *Brecht,* p. 136.

not to say that Brecht deduced it *from* the postulates. He stumbled onto it in practice. But it has a logical relation to them, and this must be seen if it is rightly to be understood and appropriated.

Verfremdung is translated as "alienation." It literally means "making foreign." The *Verfremdungseffekt* is the result of making something to appear strange, odd, unfamiliar, remarkable, hence "distant." The French happily translate *Verfremdung* as *distançation*.

The Brechtian purpose in producing this effect is to cause the spectator to think. A good teacher, Brecht knew that thinking is not stimulated unless the familiar is made to appear odd. The mind is arrested and set to work only by the unexpected.

> The spectator of the *dramatic* theatre says: "Yes, I have felt the same.—I am just like this.—This is only natural.—It will always be like this.—This human being's suffering moves me, because there is no way out for him.—This is great art: it bears the mark of the inevitable.—I am weeping with those who weep on stage, laughing with those who laugh."
>
> The spectator of the *epic* theatre says: "I should never have thought so.—That is not the way to do it.—This is most surprising, hardly credible.—This will have to stop.—This human being's suffering moves me, because there would have been a way out for him. This is great art: nothing here seems inevitable.—I am laughing about those who weep on stage, weeping about those who laugh." [13]

The spectator is supposed *not* to identify with what he sees on stage. This nonidentification is what is meant by "alienation." But of course any play badly written or badly staged will result, by default, in nonidentification. Brecht is obviously after something different—namely, a nonidentification deliberately arranged in circumstances where identification would have been possible and does, in part, occur. The techniques for achieving this include not only those mentioned above but also a specific technique in acting and a technique in writing. In the former, the actor, in addition to portraying the character, also displays his attitude toward him. In

[13] From "Vergnügungstheater oder Lehrtheater" (1936). Translated in Esslin, *Brecht*. Quotation from pp. 129–130.

the latter, the narrative and *mimetic* line of the play is from time to time deliberately broken by interpolated comment or by a scene that shows the events from a different perspective. Songs and soliloquies are the most frequent means.

It is clear that a play cannot be made up entirely of alienation, for this is a negative concept and, as such, dependent upon a positive one. The absolutely alien is unintelligible. Brecht, like many another poet, wished to show the familiar in an unfamiliar aspect. It follows that in his theater identification (the feeling of rightness, verisimilitude, plausibility, inevitability) must alternate with nonidentification (an impression of wrongness, implausibility, impropriety). It is not the *state* of alienation or distance that is valuable but the *process* of its occurrence, for only the latter stimulates thought.

Brecht's theater, then, is rooted in a dialectic and is aimed at the production of a further dialectic—namely, that of the spectator's own thought, which must proceed by being aware of contradictions and tensions. I have already suggested that dialectical thinking was native to Brecht and antedated his adoption of Marxism. I am trying now to show that in his dramatic theory the dialectic is manifest primarily as *Verfremdungseffekt* and is rooted, so far as that theory is concerned, in a basic conflict between *Gestus* and intellection.

Neither behavior in itself nor the observation of behavior can be said to possess inherently any meaning or intellectual content. Watson's behaviorism was a radically positivistic psychology that cared not a whit for the subconscious and reduced consciousness to an epiphenomenon of physical behavior. Brecht, who was anti-religious and anti-metaphysical from an early age and who, as far as we know, was interested in no philosopher save Marx, had a strong streak of positivism in him. At the same time, however, he was an intellectual whose stock in trade was ideas. "Die Wahrheit ist konkret" (Truth is concrete) was his motto. The sentence is dialectical: its abstract form stands in ironic contradiction to its message.

This same contradiction, which happens to be of that fertile and useful kind we call dialectic, not of that sterile kind we call simply error, is carried over into the dramatic theory and practice, where it becomes *"Gestus* will produce intellection." The positive act in the positive situation is to be set forth objectively and incongruously in order to make one think about what it means.

That is the theory. In practice, Brecht went further and included songs and speeches that sometimes urged the intended message directly. What he never did, save perhaps in *Señora Carrar's Rifles,* was to write a *pièce à thèse,* in which the play's structure itself was so arranged as to lead necessarily to the desired conclusion.

And what if the spectator draws the "wrong" conclusions, or no conclusions at all? It was a risk the communist authorities were rarely willing to run, which accounted for the fact that Brecht's work was officially "forgotten" in the Soviet zone throughout the Stalinist period. Even to the present time he has not been much performed in communist lands except in East Berlin, where he provided window dressing for the Ulbricht government. Brecht has been more popular in the West, but probably for reasons he did not intend. He kept the dialectic so radically open that non-communists find little to stop them from thinking their own thoughts and reaching their own conclusions while watching works whose author hoped would propel them into creating the classless society.

Brecht rejected the *pièce à thèse* because he thought it a bourgeois construction. No doubt it was, but that did not prevent the Soviets from adopting it officially as "socialist realism." It was really Brecht's effective undercutting of the bourgeois mentality that made him unfit for communist consumption. He is admired, irrespective of geography, by those who do not feel obligated to maintain a bourgeois attitude to the *status quo* or who are in revolt against the classical ideal of making a bargain with reality. Brecht fosters, through the radical persistence of his dialectic, a spirit of intellectual and existential freedom.

Aside from *The Threepenny Opera,* Brecht is most widely admired for several long plays he wrote in exile: *Mother Courage, The Good Woman of Setzuan, Puntila, Galileo,* and *The Caucasian Chalk Circle.* These belong to what I may call (*pace,* Brecht) his opulent period. The adjective is suggested by several factors: the lavish productions of these plays put on by the Berliner En-

semble, the TNP (Théâtre National Populaire) in Paris, the Zurich
Schauspielhaus, and various other theaters; the expansiveness of
the plays themselves; their demonstration of the mastery of technique Brecht had achieved, as well as his wide range of reading in
literary and historical sources; and finally a certain relaxation in
them, which Brecht acknowledged and explained by saying that he
was no longer opposed to regarding the theater as a place of enjoyment, it was only a question of what we are to find enjoyable.

There is no doubt that these plays are superb. "Brecht's aim,"
John Willett writes, "was a many-sided, perfectly polished performance where the audience, by a simultaneous act of clearheaded
judgment, would wonder at the skill and beauty of the playing and
the sense of the play. . . . The means are often simple, familiar;
the subtlety lies in their combination and choice." [14] The second
sentence refers to the texts, but it also describes the ingredients of
good Brechtian acting and directing. One might also say that it
describes good theater in general. Brecht's plays happen to demand
that this ideal be closely approximated. In the long run it may be
that Brecht's greatest effect upon the theater will be his inspiration
to actors and directors to undertake a rigorous discipline for the
sake of their craft.

Brecht stands quite outside that strong tendency of modern theater I have formerly emphasized which makes theater an imitation
of the "prison of consciousness." For him, the subject-object relation was not a problem. Whereas a good bit of modern theater
(summed up in Beckett) locates itself at the end of action, where
all modes of action are exhausted and only the qualities of experience remain, Brecht's theater is rooted in action (*Gestus*) and
points explicitly toward its renewal.

What Brecht shares with other modern dramatists pre-eminently
is his profound sense of human self-alienation. But he does not as-
cribe this phenomenon to religious, existential, or psychological
causes. He ascribes it to contradictions in the structure of society,
and in man's failure to think his way out of these. This would be
an inadequate view, too unaware of evil, if it were not for Brecht's
anti-utopianism. It is true that he judged the present age in the
light of the age to come, but that age was not, for him, a state of

14 Willett, *op. cit.*, pp. 224–225.

perfection at which man might, in time, arrive and be content. It was a kind of hope transcending time, an eschatological promise. He had one eye on the present age and one eye on the age to come. In his plays the two visions have an ironic coexistence. Though this irony was often bitter, it was never desperate. It was "supplied with Extreme Unction in plenty."

17. JEAN GENET
(b. 1910)

IN JEAN GENET the modern theater has realized more fully than in any other dramatist the radical potentialities that belong to the theater when it is conceived as the imitation of consciousness. It is no accident that these potentialities have been fulfilled in a writer who spent his formative years as an outcast from society.

Genet was born in Paris in 1910. His father was unknown, and his mother put him into an asylum for orphans. A ward of the state, he was sent to foster parents who were Burgundian peasants. By the time he was fifteen he had been sentenced to a reformatory colony for stealing. There he became committed to an antisocial way of life, or rather to the antisociety of an underworld composed of thieves, murderers, pimps, and homosexuals. Subsequently he was in and out of prison repeatedly, in France and in other countries. While serving a sentence at the prison at Fresnes, he began to write, and there he completed his first book, *Notre-Dame-des-Fleurs,* in 1942.

By 1948 Genet was the author of three published novels (*Notre-Dame-des-Fleurs, Miracle de la rose,* and *Pompes funèbres*), two published plays (*Les Bonnes* and *Haute Surveillance*), and two long poems published together as *Chants secrets.* He was in prison, sentenced for life after his tenth conviction for theft. The most prominent literary figures of France petitioned for his release. Their number included Paul Claudel, François Mauriac, André

Gide, Jean-Paul Sartre, Jean Cocteau, and others. Pardon was granted by Vincent Auriol, then President of the French Republic.

The end of Genet's period of official condemnation plunged him into a crisis. He wrote no more for six years, while what he had already written was widely published. He became the subject of a mammoth work, *Saint Genet,* written by Jean-Paul Sartre.[1] The eminent publishing house Gallimard began to issue his *Oeuvres complètes,* of which the work by Sartre became, oddly, Volume I. Then in 1956 Genet published the first version of a new play, *Le Balcon* (*The Balcony*). His dramatic power continued to grow in *Les Nègres* (1958; *The Blacks*) and *Les Paravents* (1961; *The Screens*).

Having started as a writer of poems, novels, and autobiographical meditations, Genet was drawn ineluctably to the theater. What attracted him to it was not the gaining of an audience, although he got one, but rather that the theater is the one art which combines the two "unreal realities" upon which Genet's spiritual existence depends—the magic of words and the purity of ritual form. His instinctive feeling for theater is clear to anyone who reads the earlier works attentively. The books are made of a host of apperceptions that must be understood in theatrical terms: the tendency to regard character as the mask of hidden identity and essence; the subsequent doubt as to whether this essence is real or only an illusion produced by the mask—that is, by the very idea of mask; the emphasis upon the beauty of an act, any act, provided it is *complete,* which means when it is taken as ritual, since it is only in ritual and not in real life that an act may properly be said to be complete; the delight taken in transformations, whereby a straight or mundane reality is clothed in the majesty of a symbolic representation; the acute sensitivity to the gestural quality of words, whereby the word in itself is a kind of act performed by the hidden being of things, and the gestures of men are already words; the dialectic of presentation, whereby a work of art consists of a motion which is the search for the ideal or supremely "right" expression of its own inner potentialities.

Genet's theater would have to be a ritual theater. It could not,

---

[1] *Saint Genet: Comédien et martyr* (Paris: Gallimard, 1952). Translated by Bernard Frechtman as *Saint Genet: Actor and Martyr* (New York: Braziller, 1963).

like the theater of the boulevard, be the mere formalization of narrative into plot and intrigue. It would have to do with essences, fatalities, and magical transformations. His love of theater was, after all, born in him as he watched the liturgy of the Church.

> I would take communion at morning mass. The priest (a Spanish curé!) would take a host from the ciborium.
> "What sauce do they steep in?" I wondered. The sauce was the unction of the priest's pale fingers. In order to separate the hosts and take only one, he manipulated them with an unctuous gesture, as if he were stirring a thick liquid in a golden vase. Now, as I knew that they were flakes of dry white dough, I was astonished. . . . I felt God—or, rather than Him, a sickening impression of mystery—by means of a few evil and sordid details (arising from a childish imagination) of the Roman liturgy.[2]

The first play written by Genet was *Haute Surveillance (Deathwatch)*, performed February 24, 1949, at the Théâtre des Mathurins in Paris, directed by Genet himself. It is his only play set in prison. "The entire play," he advises, "unfolds as in a dream."

An overhead light in the prison cell where all the action takes place is harsh and direct. It falls upon the "violent" colors (white and black) of the prisoners' garb. Beneath its glare is played out an "ideal" fatality of criminals, in its effect so mesmerizing that it may be regarded as a kind of festival, or at any rate a ceremony, of that prison world which Genet's books had already described.

The principal character, Green Eyes, is a convicted murderer held in fearful esteem by his fellow prisoners. Two of these, Maurice and Lefranc, together with Green Eyes form a triangle, the inner dynamic of which provides the substance of the play. A fourth character, a Negro whose name is Snowball, affects the triangle but does not appear on stage.

Green Eyes stands at the apex. Both Maurice and Lefranc look up to him, defining themselves with reference to his being and his potency. By this, their relation to each other is also defined. These "definitions," however, are not abstract, though much idealization goes into them. They are worked out in a continual process of shifting alliances, influences, and compulsions. The process ulti-

---

2 *The Thief's Journal*, Bernard Frechtman, trans. (New York: Grove, 1964), p. 172.

mately reaches a climax in which Maurice is murdered by Lefranc.

Maurice, who at seventeen is the youngest of the three, conceives of Green Eyes as "the best of men," lordly in his independence, one to whom others are unnecessary, and therefore one who is to lesser men an absolute necessity, since slight creatures like Maurice can attain to glory only as they are the devotees of the truly great ones. Before Green Eyes, Maurice is spiritually prostrate. One of Genet's accomplishments is to make the audience feel this quality of spiritual devotion in Maurice at the same time that he is shown to be a mere sycophant and a queer.

Lefranc, twenty-three, the oldest of the trio, also looks up to Green Eyes, but with a different attitude. He would like to replace him in his pre-eminent position. Or, since that is for the present impossible, he would like to become like him, receiving a similar adulation and sharing his destiny as a murderer. This makes him, as it were, an angel in revolt. One might also say that it makes him a heterodox figure who introduces into the faith of Maurice an element of doubt and restiveness that Maurice's need of absolute devotion cannot accommodate. In particular, Lefranc tries to destroy Maurice's esteem for Green Eyes by telling him that Green Eyes has entered into some sort of alliance with Snowball, who dwells in another part of the prison. This suspicion not only renders Maurice jealous, it also makes him doubt the indifference and independence of Green Eyes, which he had thought to be two of the cardinal attributes of his "divinity." Upset by his doubt, Maurice begins to hate both the unseen Snowball and the "tempter" Lefranc. At the same time, he experiences a contrary emotion toward them, since if either of them should replace Green Eyes as the embodiment of power, Maurice would have to shift his allegiance, because he needs to adore power wherever it is most fully manifest. Caught between opposing desires, Maurice cannot function except by goading Lefranc to attack him. Thus he is murdered.

Green Eyes, a lordly criminal with his feet in chains, is untouched by the death of Maurice. However, he despises Lefranc, not because he thinks murder an act to be scorned but for quite the opposite reason: it is so holy an act (that is, so taboo) that it must come about purely because it is the murderer's destiny. Lefranc has tried to force the hand of destiny, to steal glory, as Prometheus stole the fire of heaven. His act of murder therefore lacks the ontological substance that belongs to Green Eyes', which was an *acte gratuit*. *Deathwatch* is Genet's dramatization of the apotheosis of the authentic murderer.

Genet's experience as a criminal and a prisoner gave him a strong sense of the limits of his world and thus prepared him to appreciate and exploit the finite space of the stage. It also taught him that the meanings and values of normal society may be turned wrong-side out. For psychological as well as sociological reasons, he has always been fascinated, even thrilled, by the capacities of imagination to transform anything into its opposite as by a magical operation.

In Genet the dramatist's adoption of a double perspective upon his material, which is the primary characteristic of romantic irony, is revealed to have ontological and moral importance. Especially in his earlier plays, Genet advocated the supremacy of Evil and the primacy of Nothingness. From the beginning he recognized that this was not only an offense to society but also a philosophical impossibility. He knew that his stance was perverse and that it was precisely the perversion that appealed to him. Thus, in him modern irony receives its deepest and most moral (that is, immoral) expression. The more Genet praises Evil and forces us to recognize it in ourselves, the more he makes us aware, by negative induction, of the validity of the Good. The more he exposes reality as the shell of Nothingness, the more he requires the real for the demonstration. This firm and inevitable interdependence of opposites accounts for the compulsive quality of the plays, which seem locked into their forms, or, to put it otherwise, seem as hard as erections. In the accuracy of his sense of proportion, Genet is like a classicist. In his exploitation of the dramatic possibilities of Evil mixed with illusion, he is reminiscent of the Jacobean dramatists, particularly John Webster, whom he read when he was in prison.

The Maids (*Les Bonnes*) was commissioned by Louis Jouvet, who produced and directed it at the Théâtre Athenée in Paris on April 17, 1947, with only moderate success. Although Genet said that it "was written out of vanity, but in boredom," it has proved to be one of his most often produced works, and justly so.

As in *Deathwatch,* the action of *The Maids* rises from the inner dynamic of a triangular relationship. At the apex is Madame, and at the other two points are her maids. As in *Deathwatch,* the figure at the apex is untouched by the jealousies of the other two characters, which in this play also lead to the murder of one by the other. Madame is on stage for only a brief time, but during the rest she is a vivid presence-in-absence. The symbol of an ideal reality, she is a stronger force when present to her servants' imaginations than when she appears in person.

When the play begins, the audience is unaware that Madame is absent. We see a lady at her toilet, dressed in her slip, choosing clothes for the evening. She gives abrupt, scornful orders to her maid, whom she calls Claire. Gradually we become aware that the relation between these two is not what we would expect of employer and servant. There are certain erotic overtones. Perhaps the maid adores her mistress and accepts her imperiousness because it stimulates a certain masochistic pleasure. Madame seems sadistically to enjoy being cruel to the maid. We also become aware that the relation of mistress to servant is exaggerated. Perhaps the two are playing roles. Is their relation so intimate that they sometimes change parts? Is the maid really the mistress? Has she perhaps fallen in love with her own maid, whom she then orders to wear her clothes, make herself beautiful, and give orders so that Madame may be abased before her? If so, we are witnessing the secret rituals that lie behind a *scandale.* We may have heard that Genet got the idea for the play from a newspaper story.

Suddenly the scene is shattered. An alarm clock rings. Thrown into panic, the two figures drop their roles. We learn, to our astonishment, that *neither* of them is Madame. They are both her maids. The ringing of the clock, which they have set, means that Madame is about to return. They begin to tidy up, to get rid of misplaced articles that might betray the game they play in her absence. They do this poorly, leaving certain telltale signs. We discover also that the stronger of the two, whose name is Solange, has been pretending to be the weaker. It was she who was called Claire. The real Claire had been playing Madame. The two maids are sisters.

Both Claire and Solange adore Madame. They also hate her,

partly because of her power over them and partly because each sister is jealous of the other. We are presented with a closed, dynamic system in which love, hatred, jealousy, desire for revenge, and desire for possession all feed upon each other. The stability of the system depends on its instability. It is doomed to self-destruction.

Madame has a male lover who is in jail. He was put there by Solange, who gave certain information anonymously to the police. He now telephones that he has been released on bail. Madame returns. She is as haughty, as overbearing, as in the performance of her given earlier by Claire, though in her own person this trait is not as "perfect" as in the imitation. The maids have planned to kill her by putting poison in her tea. The stated motive is revenge. It will be an act symbolizing the revolt of all maids, all servants and prisoners, against their superiors. The hidden motive, however, is to stabilize the relation between Claire and Solange by removing the one whom both desire. The plan is engineered by Solange, who persuades Claire to administer the poison. If the plan succeeds, Claire's guilt will place her forever in Solange's power.

All goes awry. Madame, excited by the prospect of seeing Monsieur again, refuses to drink her tea. She changes her clothes and departs. In her absence the maids return to their game. Claire will again pretend to be Madame. Solange will be Claire and will bring her the cup of poisoned tea. But the game has gone too far to remain pretense. It must reach a climax. At first the death of Madame is rehearsed as if it took place off-stage. It is not sufficient. Claire desires to give herself completely to Solange. "It would be too simple," she says, "to conspire with the wind, to make the night our accomplice. Solange, you will contain me within you." She reduces the scene to its essence: "We're alone in the world. Nothing exists but the altar where one of the two maids is about to immolate herself. . . . In prison no one will know that I'm with you, secretly."

Then occurs one of those magical transformations of which Genet is so fond. Claire, the weaker of the two, reveals herself as the stronger. She virtually mesmerizes Solange, feeding her the right lines to say and the right gestures to perform. Claire-Madame sits in her chair and orders her tea (in French, *tilleul,* or lime-blossom tea). Solange-Claire brings the fatal cup. Claire drinks it: "And you've poured it into the best, the finest tea set." Solange faces the audience without moving, "her hands crossed as if held by handcuffs," while the curtain descends.

In a foreword to an edition of *The Maids* in 1954, Genet complained that "even the finest Western plays" have "an air of masquerade and not of ceremony." By contrast, he declared, "the loftiest modern drama has been expressed daily for two thousand years in the sacrifice of the Mass." [3] *The Maids* is the best example of ritual theater known to modern drama. Its sense of form is acute, its writing lean, its series of agons forcefully built, its air of ceremonious fatality heavy. One is driven, for comparison, to speak of classical and neoclassical tragedy. Oreste F. Pucciani has analyzed it in terms of a five-movement structure analogous to the five acts of French tragedy. He calls it, correctly, "a nearly perfect tragedy in the French tradition." Genet inverts classical tragedy, he notes, by turning its kings and queens into housemaids; but he observes that Genet's wit transforms these lowly creatures "into queens of a sort." Genet, he says, "is Racine turned inside out." [4]

Genet's original plan was to have *The Maids* performed by male actors in women's clothing. This plan seems to have been carried out in only one production, that mounted by The Living Theater for touring performances in Europe in 1966 and 1967. Transvestism seems appropriate to the layers of perverse sexuality already contained in the script and to the sense of preposterous inevitability upon which it is built.

The Maids is a work in which the arbitrary and the necessary coalesce. It is arbitrary as all theater is, since in theater a performance is arranged by the will of the playwright. It is necessary in that it symbolizes a certain psychological compulsion in which desire and terror are inseparable. Both of these qualities, the theatrical and the psychological, have been grounded by Genet in an ontology of Evil, whereby the "lie" of theater and the destructive-

---

[3] The foreword has been translated by Bernard Frechtman as "A Note on Theatre" in the *Tulane Drama Review*, Vol. 7, No. 3 (Spring 1963), pp. 37–41. The quotations are from pp. 38 and 39.

[4] "Tragedy, Genet, and *The Maids*," in *Tulane Drama Review*, Vol. 7, No. 3 (Spring 1963), pp. 42–59.

ness of absolute desire receive their ultimate justification in an assertion of the primacy of Evil and Nonbeing over the Good and the True. On such a basis there may be wit but not comedy, immolation but not triumph. Those who are damned by society are, according to Genet, also damned by God. But in that very fact is to be seen their attraction and their glory. Genet sees it as a limitation of God that He cannot experience damnation.

The Balcony, written between 1954 and 1956, was the first work written by Genet after he had gained a wide audience and achieved a literary reputation. It demonstrated that, although he could hardly surpass the near-perfect formalism of *The Maids,* his theater was capable of a vast expansion in scope with no loss—and some would say with an increase—of power.

Like *The Maids,* the play opens with a "game." We see a bishop, in miter and gilded cope, sitting in his chair. On his feet are the cothurni of the Greek tragic actor. His shoulders are extraordinarily broad, his figure frighteningly large. He opens the play with these words:

> In truth, the mark of a prelate is not mildness or unction, but rather the most vigorous intelligence. Our heart is our undoing. We think we are master of our kindness; we are the slave of a serene laxity. In fact, it is something quite other than intelligence that is involved. . . . (*He hesitates.*) It may be cruelty. And beyond that cruelty—and through it—a skillful, vigorous heading towards absence. Towards Death. . . .[5]

To one side stands a woman. We learn that the bishop has heard her confess six deadly sins and has granted her absolution. In the doorway is Irma, a "madam." The scene is a studio in her brothel, the "bishop" a customer. The house has just provided the impostor with the make-believe he requires in order to satisfy his lust.

In the second scene we are in another studio. Like the first, it has a mirror which seems to reflect an unmade bed located, as it were, "in the first rows of the orchestra." A judge is punishing a thief who is a young girl. In the third scene we find a general putting his horse, who is a girl wearing a large tail, through its paces. In the

[5] Translated by Bernard Frechtman (New York: Grove, 1958), p. 1.

fourth a little old man in a dirty wig is whipped by a girl wearing leather boots and a corselet. In the fifth we come to the elegant room of Irma, and the plot begins.

Mme. Irma's brothel, a house of illusions, exists in the capital city of a regime beset by revolution. From outside the house, which is called The Balcony, one can hear occasional bursts of machine-gun fire. To the house come the mock bishop, general, and judge —that is, nobodies who here become august personages—and also a real official, though a petty one, the chief of police, who is a friend of Irma. He is the principal link between the house and the real world outside it. A girl named Chantal has deserted the house and joined the forces of the revolution. The insurgents are the enemy. They intend to destroy The Balcony along with the government, the queen, and the royal palace.

The sixth scene takes place outside the brothel. It is set in an old café held by the revolutionaries. Their campaign is faltering at the very moment it might succeed. In direct contrast to the house of illusions, the revolution has been conceived as a movement of reason and unadorned truth. It wants to destroy the symbols of royal authority, religion, and military power, which are the proto-types of Mme. Irma's shadow versions, in order to institute a rule of pure reason. But the revolutionaries are discovering that they cannot maintain the allegiance of their own followers on such a basis, for in the strain of battle the fighters lose heart without an emotional symbol around which they may rally. It is proposed to turn Chantal, the former whore of The Balcony into such a sym-bol. As one puts it, freedom is a fine thing, "but it would be even finer if freedom were a pretty girl with a warm voice." Roger, the leader of the revolution, eventually agrees, and Chantal sings. The revolution lives by adopting the "irrational" appeal of its opposi-tion.

Meanwhile the queen has perished, and her envoy comes to The Balcony to enlist the aid of Irma. Without *its* symbols, the government cannot live. Will Mme. Irma appear before the crowds as the queen, attended by her retinue including the "bishop," the "judge," and the "general"? She agrees, and a royal appearance is staged on The Balcony. Suddenly Chantal appears there also. A shot is fired, she falls, and the "general" and the "queen" carry her away dead. The "royal" party makes a procession through the city, and the revolution is over. The false figures have come to power.

The new regime is led by eminences who share a certain quality: all are figures of symbolic, rather than real, power. They have status without function, and they owe their position to this very fact. The sign of their symbolic status is that their images incite lust. That is the sign of their "reality." But there is one among them, the chief of police, of whom this is not true. He is merely a functionary and not a symbol of desire. Therefore he longs for someone to come to The Balcony desirous of "being" the chief of police. His other longing is to have a monument erected in his honor. It should be in the shape of an enormous phallus and should be located at the center of a mausoleum.

Now someone comes to The Balcony asking to play the role of the chief of police. It is Roger, the leader of the defeated revolution. In the studio he castrates himself. The chief of police is overjoyed. He descends into the new mausoleum studio saying he will stay two thousand years. He has been transformed into a symbol of sheer power, which is synonymous with death. Machine-gun fire starts up again in the streets. Irma sends everyone except the chief of police home by the door leading into the alley. She turns out the lights and covers the furniture as at the end of a working day. Tomorrow will be another. To the audience, her other customers, she says: "You must go home now, where everything—you can be quite sure—will be even falser than here."

The major theme of *The Balcony* may be stated as follows. The "real" world is saved by the illusory one. Deprived of its symbolic head, the queen, "real society" is forced to turn to Irma, whose business is the manufacture of illusions needed to satisfy the lusts of men. Since her pretended queenship and her false judge, general, and bishop serve as well as the "real" ones they succeed, we are to draw the implication that society's "real" symbols of authority are themselves only the manufactured products of a madame whom we may call Imagination. Like Irma, she is a mistress of lies. As such, she may be called Evil, yet society cannot exist without her. She stands, so to speak, between mankind and Nothingness, but whether as protectress or as betrayer it is impossible to say. Her opposite is not the "normal" world but pure rationality. The latter is not constructive. It can mount revolutions and fire machine guns but it cannot govern or inspire love. It is pure function devoid of status.

The corollary of these ideas is that the ultimate object of desire is death. All the performances in all the studios of The Balcony are modes of dying. The mausoleum studio is the epitome of the others. The destiny of all the characters is succinctly stated in one of the envoy's remarks about Irma: "The Queen attains her reality when she withdraws, absents herself, or dies." [6]

Irma is Genet. As playwright, he is the mistress of these illusions, the theater his bordello, we his paying customers. Presiding over all this, the author is like a dying queen—like Irma, who, in the last moments of the play, turns out the lights one by one. But this dying is perpetual. It will occur again tomorrow. Dying is only an act to be performed over and over again, always and always the same. Even death is not real. There is no reality. That is why the ending of The Balcony is pure contrivance. There is no logical end, and certainly none that is existential.

"One evening," writes Genet, "an actor asked me to write a play for an all-black cast. But what is a black? First of all, what's his color?" [7] From this request and this question emerged The Blacks: A Clown Show (Les Nègres, une clownerie). It was produced at the Théâtre de Lutèce in Paris in October 1959 to great acclaim. Roger Blin, who directed it, could not find thirteen professional Negro actors in Paris, and so he chose a cast of amateurs, whom he rehearsed for two years before the play's opening. This indicates that The Blacks was written during or before 1957, soon after Genet finished The Balcony.

To ask what is the color of a black is to ask two things: Is a black man always black? and What is blackness? Both of these questions are ontological in character. The Blacks is Genet's most ontological play, concerned even more than The Balcony with the question, What is real?

It is also the play that, among all of Genet's is most easily read as social commentary. Such a reading, however, may be erroneous, for

6 *Ibid.*, p. 106.
7 Preface to *The Blacks*, Bernard Frechtman, trans. (New York: Grove, 1960), p. 10.

the relation of the play to the subject of racial justice is at most indirect. One should say that racial conflict provides the occasion for the play, while its subject is something else.

The work is a (black) masque given for the entertainment of the (white) audience. It opens with eight Negroes, tackily dressed, dancing to strains of Mozart around a catafalque that contains, we are told, the body of a murdered white woman. There is to be a trial. The judges, who sit on an upper stage, are five white persons —that is, Negroes wearing white masks. They represent a queen, her governor, a missionary, a judge, and a valet.

In the first part of the play the "facts" of the murder are related piecemeal and with great imprecision. The victim seems to change from moment to moment, as does the motive. She was an old beggar woman, or a rich young woman, or a shy virgin, or some other kind of white woman. He (they) killed her for her money, or after a rape, or because he was spurned by a black woman, or because it was easy, or just because there has to be a new victim every night. The murder-rape is re-enacted. A Mr. Diouf, "a curate at St. Anne's" and an apologist for compromise, is made to play the victim. He dons the mask of a white girl. When he (she) is dead, he goes to heaven—that is, to the upper stage among the whites. From there he reports "that they lie or that they're mistaken. They're not white, but pink or yellowish." [8] He decides that he has become a pink woman and says that he moves about "in a light emitted by our faces which they reflect from one to another." [9]

The second part of the play is a contest of strength between black and white. Coming down from its upper level, the "white" court goes on a safari. In the African jungle, black and white meet on black territory. The white queen and a sixty-year-old Negro woman named Mrs. Felicity Trollop Pardon engage in a battle of words. Felicity envisions an all-black world: "Milk will be black, sugar, rice, the sky, doves, hope, will be black." Her long set-speech on this theme is of remarkable rhetoric and reminds one of Melville's chapter on whiteness in *Moby Dick*. The language of the play also calls to mind Renaissance extravagances and the verbal displays of the Jacobean dramatists.

[8] *Ibid.*, p. 93.
[9] *Ibid.*

The play ends as it began. The Negroes gather once more around the catafalque. They pull the sheet from it, revealing only a couple of the queen's chairs. They laugh wildly, then resume the Mozart dance. The show is over. Meanwhile, however, a real murder has been committed off-stage.

The play is a ritual with several meanings. On the surface of it, the blacks, who represent all classes of persons victimized by those in power, put on a "clown show" which, like a minstrel show, depicts the blacks as the white persons believe them to be—savage, stupid, erotic, given to aping white manners. Beneath the surface, however, there lies a ritual of revenge. If whites blame Negroes for murders they have not committed (the mock trial of the imaginary murderer of a nonexistent white woman), nevertheless Negroes are willing and able to revenge themselves by real murders, which they keep hidden (like the one off-stage). Furthermore, the ritual in which, for the benefit of the white audience, the Negroes mock themselves, contains also a bitter mockery of the whites. The very servility of the Negroes, since it is a pose, contains great scorn. An audience watching *The Blacks* finds itself drawn into the ritual only to be betrayed and ritually slain, as the "white court" is slain in the jungle.

The late Bernard Frechtman, Genet's able translator, has said that *The Blacks* is about power. That is true, but more fundamentally it is about energy, of which power is a principal manifestation. The play's obsession with energy means that Genet shifted ground considerably from *The Balony*. There the dialectic was between illusion and Nothingness, with the implication that at the bottom of all things there is nothing. In *The Blacks* the dialectic is between formless energy and its organization into forms of ritual and power. The play is continually dissolving, then coming again into shape. All its depictions are of epiphenomena. Yet when these disappear we are not plunged into Nothingness. Instead we descend into a primordial flux of energy out of which new rituals, oppressions, and revenges are born.

Perhaps Genet is suggesting that our conscious life, our political and social "realities," our exercise of power, our religions and systems of ideas, even our color and our sex, are all manifestations of a ceaseless energy that casts up in its irrational way the phenomena which we call, in the aggregate, life. Perhaps the vast quantities of psychic energy that *The Blacks* releases in its audience is the result not only of the audience's being attacked but also of Genet's having shattered the "atoms" of normal consciousness, letting loose the energies of which they are composed. One is fascinated by the power thus released even while he may be terrified by the prospect of its unpredictable fall-out.

However that may be, it is clear that the pertinence *The Blacks* has to "the racial problem" is not that of an advocate of the "cause" of Negroes, let alone that of one who pleads for justice. Genet's play has almost nothing in common with the angry outbursts of a James Baldwin or a LeRoi Jones and even less with liberal pleas such as were contained in the plays of the late Lorraine Hansberry. What he does show is that the relation of oppressor to oppressed is a relation containing enormous energies and that when this unstable relation is changed the energies pour out as violence directed not only against persons but against preconceived forms of consciousness. One could draw the conclusion that it would be safest to preserve the *status quo* in the hope of protecting society against the release of such energies, but Genet suggests that this is not possible.

In *The Blacks* Genet's narcissism, compulsive attraction to form, and ontological nihilism gave way to a kind of ontological affirmation. Outside the self's hall of mirrors he began to acknowledge the existence of "something." We may call it energy. However wild and terrifying, it is "there"; and it has power not only to destroy but also to create. *The Blacks* represented Genet's first step outside the prison of consciousness.

The first performance of *The Screens* took place in West Berlin in June, 1961. Roger Blin, who had spent a month helping Genet in Italy to polish the script, wanted to direct it in Paris. However, as he told Bettina Knapp in an interview published in 1963, "It cannot be produced in Paris. It's too dangerous since it deals with the Algerian War. The Arabs versus the French on stage. Why we would all be bombed!" [10]

The play was produced in 1962 in Vienna and in 1964 in Stockholm. A London production directed by Peter Brook in 1964 in-

10 *Tulane Drama Review*, number cited, p. 119.

cluded only the first half of the play and was shown only to invited audiences. The work at last reached Paris, without bombs, on April 21, 1966, when Jean-Louis Barrault presented it at the state-subsidized Théâtre de France. Roger Blin directed a cast of sixty that included Maria Casarés, Madeleine Renaud, and M. Barrault. *The New York Times* reported that, instead of causing the national scandal that some had predicted, the play emerged "as an unequivocal theatrical triumph, one of the major achievements of the French Theater since World War II." [11]

The Screens, which is the last work Genet has written, is of a larger scope than any of his earlier plays. It has over forty characters. The stage directions say that it should be put on in an open-air theater. It has seventeen scenes. The last scene employs nine screens, arranged on three separate levels, representing seven different localities, among them a prison, a village square, and a region of the dead. Large screens, "each about ten feet high," are used as the principal part of the set throughout the play, to which they have given their name. They are almost like part of the *dramatis personae.* Each is to be mounted on rubber-tired wheels so as to roll silently on a stage carpet when moved by a stagehand, whom the screen will hide. The screens are frequently used as canvases on which the characters draw objects to identify the locale of the action or to suggest important events that are taking place. The imaginative extravagance of this device as Genet employs it is unmatched in the modern theater. The whole work is lavish in conception. It is a spectacle, though quite unlike those usually found in the commercial theater.

In *The Screens* Genet has moved as far as possible from the prison world of his books and *Deathwatch. The Maids* had left the prison setting behind but had recreated the prison ethos among three members of a household. *The Balcony* had shown a great enlargement of scope but had insisted that men are confined within a system of illusions that reflect each other like so many mirrors. Its action had been placed in a brothel in a city. *The Blacks,* which seems to spread over an entire continent, had modified the psychology of the prison world, positing a genuine, nonillusory reality outside the confines of ritualized existence. Now in

11 April 22, 1966.

The Screens Genet made the action, while ostensibly occurring in war-torn Algeria, seem to take place in the vastness of the universe.

The subject of this remarkable play is the coincidence of absolute freedom with absolute dejection. Its villains are the French *colons* and the French military, who are the prisoners of narcissistic pride and have no existence save in their self-images. While they strut and murder and seek the "beauty" of privileged cruelty, the play's heart descends with the lowly Arabs into poverty, moral abjection, ugliness, and the end of all pretense. No doubt the Arabs are romanticized by being made, in their humiliation, greatly superior to their oppressors, but the play is not political. It is concerned with a moral reality, the name of which is *ascesis*.

The coincidence of freedom and dejection had been present in Genet's writing from the first, but it had always been presented as if Genet did not quite believe it, as if, seeing its irony, he loved it only as a beautiful fiction. In *The Screens* he presented it instead as a true paradox. The play, in spite of its massiveness, soars and glides like a giant bird. It is Genet's most sordid play, a work one has to say is conceived in filth, and at the same time it is exalted. It is a mystic vision of the spiritual triumph of the dispossessed. It is imbued with great love. It is Genet's *Inferno* and *Paradiso* in one, and if he has been silent since writing it perhaps the reason is that he knows himself already to have uttered his superlative song.

All the works of Genet until *The Blacks* are predicated upon a great, even a diabolic, falsehood. Genet, who had pledged himself as a child to the pursuit of Evil, created dazzling and sometimes beautiful works out of the insistence that Evil is superior to good because it is Nothingness expressed as pure form. Such a notion contains only the illusion of logic and can be maintained only by the sheer exercise of the will. Precisely this was its appeal to Genet. It contained superb possibilities for verbal and theatrical constructs. "My victory," said Genet in *The Thief's Journal,* "is verbal." The books and the early plays contained much genuine passion, which Genet betrayed, in both senses of the word: he revealed it and at the same time turned it into charade. This performance was capable of seducing some readers (so Genet seems to have hoped) into a love of Evil. Others it repulsed. Some, not seduced, were nevertheless thrilled by its diabolism. The most perceptive took it as an unparalleled expression of the philosophical, aesthetic, and moral perversity of which man is capable. Genet wrote in artistic form a phenomenology of sin. The miracle was that he was so acutely aware of what he was doing.

Then history seems to have intervened. The struggle of black men to free themselves from indignity and the struggle of North African Arabs to end colonial domination provided Genet in *The Blacks* and *The Screens* with material that not only appealed to his imagination but that seems also to have modified his moral and ontological understandings. In neither play did Genet espouse a social cause. In both the relation to political and historical matters was tangential. Yet tangents are not always to be despised, and Genet's brush with recent history seems to have occasioned in him a change. It seems to have enabled him to begin to conceive of a reality transcending human imagination, and to think of it not merely as the "God" whom Genet had met in ritual and whom he had had to oppose but as something that can be dimly sensed as authentic and true.

To read as few as two of Genet's works is to realize that they are interdependent. To read them all is to become aware that their unity, above and beyond matters of style, tone, and motif, is the unity of a moral—yes, a saintly—enterprise of extraordinary intensity. They record the pilgrimage of a criminal-saint who went out from his prison. At first he took its images and its rituals with him. Later he discarded them. They were too rich and too confining. He touched instead the real. He could not define it, but he could at last believe that it is there.

Genet has provided modern drama with its richest examples of what can be accomplished when the theater is employed as the imitation of consciousness. Yet, having done that, he went on to show more clearly than any other modern dramatist that the theater must eventually break out of that prison, even if all it can do is to grope toward what is outside, to which we give the loving name reality.

EPILOGUE

THIS HISTORY of the modern theater has not attempted to be complete. Not only does it lack the comprehensiveness of an encyclopedic treatment, but also it has been highly selective in the figures it has brought forward as representative of the several strands of development it has traced. The reader will no doubt think back upon certain omissions he would regard as glaring. There is one in particular that the author wishes to point out before turning, in the latter part of this conclusion, to more general and speculative matters.

The characterization of the "modern" which has been operative in the book from the start and which reached its climax in the chapter "Irony and the Destructive Fulfillment of Theater" has resulted in a neglect of the renewal of English playwriting that occurred in the 1950's. I have in mind the plays of John Osborne, Arnold Wesker, John Whiting, John Arden, Robert Bolt, and more recently Edward Bond. Harold Pinter was mentioned briefly in the aforesaid chapter.

I do not intend now to rehearse the accomplishments, quite varied in type and degree, of these distinguished writers and certain lesser ones who seem to have come in their wake. Important as they have been for the entertainment and instruction of their audiences, and for reclaiming a certain vigor for the British stage, their existence does not in any important way modify the main

455

features of the narrative I have been tracing. The early work of Osborne and most of that of Wesker was, it is fair to say, of more sociological importance than theatrical. It represented the initial entrance upon the British stage of scenes, characters, and outlooks characteristic of the British working class. It heralded a shift in English cultural life away from the hegemony of the "Oxbridge"-educated class, a shift made possible by the growing importance of the so-called red brick universities. Thus, not only new voices but also new *kinds* of voices began to be heard in the playhouses, pioneered in the courageous work of the English Stage Company at the Royal Court Theatre under the guidance of George Devine. This influence quickly spread and had a strong impact on the choice of plays and on directorial styles at the Royal Shakespeare Company and later at the National Theatre. But from a historical point of view, this phenomenon, which was absolutely necessary for the British theater, was strongly reminiscent of the socially conscious plays of the American theater in the 1930's. Perhaps because it was haunted by a sense of *déjà vu,* the British version did not last as long or contribute nearly as many plays as the American, and it soon began to feel exhausted. Wesker turned, in *The Kitchen* (1959) to the theatrical and symbolic, and so did Osborne in *The Entertainer* (1957). Recently Wesker has written less and less, while Osborne has cast about from one type of subject to another, all the while cultivating his principal strength, which is the composition of speeches of unusually powerful rhetoric.

Whiting, Arden, and Bolt are of very different types. All, however, are preoccupied with moral concerns, and in their several ways all seem bent upon recovering from the Western tradition certain values and modes of awareness that are in danger of being lost to modern society.

Recent British playwriting, then, while it has much intrinsic interest, does not seem to be of a type that can either negate or modify the general picture I have drawn of a modern theater that is increasingly ironic and increasingly confined in the "prison of consciousness." What recent British theater *has* done is to put itself firmly into that modern picture and thus to be in a position of readiness to take part in the "postmodern" developments that are at this moment making themselves felt in America and Europe.

It is now to our purpose to consider the crisis in which the theater finds itself at present. The "modern" theater described in this study is not identical with the "contemporary." A "postmodern" period has begun, and while it is too soon to determine what the lasting virtues and meanings of the new period will turn out to be, it is necessary to be clear about the fact that the theater of the future will certainly have a different relation to society from that which theater has traditionally enjoyed. Thus, although the future as such does not belong to our study, what does belong is the awareness that the "modern" theater has come to its achievements during a time when the theater as a social institution has moved toward the periphery of society. This change has come about for a variety of reasons. The purpose of the rest of this epilogue is to take note of these several factors with special reference to the decline of dramatic and histrionic sensibility in the modern audience.

Drama requires, for its maximum fulfillment, a high degree of social cohesion with regard to values, symbols, and myths. Drama must be predicated upon certain understandings of life and its processes held in common by the audience. Above all other arts, drama is the art of shared response. (At least, above all other arts of the spoken or written word, though perhaps not more than music or dance.) In a theater, one's feeling of solidarity with the audience is the prerequisite of his becoming involved with what happens on the stage. Without the former, the latter cannot be very great.

It does not follow that the main function of drama is to perpetuate or increase the cohesion of society. In fact, the history of drama shows the opposite to be true. Most major dramatists attack the solidarity of the audience, by attacking the values and received opinions the audience holds and which hold the audience together. It has been said, notably by Ferdinand Brunetière, that the "law of the theater" is conflict. The basic conflict is never the one on stage but rather the one between the playwright and the audience. The audience's shield of certainty is pelted by the playwright's arrows of doubt. For this reason it is the tragic destiny of drama to destroy the conditions necessary to its own greatness, to corrode its own foundations. After Sophocles, Euripides. After the conflict between certainty and doubt in the one the rabid bite of skepticism in the other. Then the history of Greek tragedy comes to a close. After Shakespeare, John Webster. After Ibsen, Alfred Jarry. After O'Neill and Williams, Edward Albee. Drama destroys, or at any rate helps to destroy, the sense of reality on which it feeds.

One way of describing the plight of drama today is to say that its own acids seem mild compared to other acids present in the culture. In 1611, at a time of cultural tension highly productive of drama, John Donne could write, "The new philosophy puts all in doubt." Were one to write such a line today, the response would be, "*Which* new philosophy puts all *what* in doubt?" The more open and "advanced" society becomes through industrialization and the growth of many political and intellectual opinions, the more the dramatist feels the uselessness of his task in the face of cultural fragmentation.

Brunetière was one of the critics who have drawn a sharp contrast between the drama and the novel. In his essay "The Law of the Theatre," written in 1894, he put it in the following way:

> The proper aim of the novel, as of the epic, of which it is only a secondary and derived form—what the naturalists call a sub-species or a variety—the aim of the *Odyssey* as of *Gil Blas,* of the *Knights of the Round Table* as of *Madame Bovary*—is to give us a picture of the influence that is exercised upon us by all that is outside of ourselves. The novel is therefore the contrary of the drama.

The opposition between the drama and the novel is a familiar one, and it is also familiar that the novel has come to occupy a place much closer to the concerns of modern man than the theater. "I should always," wrote Laurence Lerner, "suspect of mere nostalgia a critic who denied (even if he regretted) that [the novel] had become for us the central literary form." [1]

Mr. Lerner partly means that the novel has become the most popular form of literature, leaving aside for the moment the question of how popular literature itself may be, no matter of what

[1] *The Truest Poetry* (London, 1960), pp. 193–194.

kind. At the same time the novel has become the most relevant form of literature for modern man's self-understanding. Mr. Lerner means that for us the novel has assumed the place once held by the drama.

It is true that today certain types of literature are perhaps even more popular than the novel; and I shall not consider here the future of the novel itself, whose ills are being proclaimed and diagnosed on every hand. It may be that discursive prose is the most influential type of literature being written and published today. I am concerned with literature written to feed our imaginations, and especially to feed them by the telling of stories.

Unlike drama, the novel has a capacity to adapt itself kaleidoscopically to a multitude of shifting human perspectives. It is, as we know, closer akin to the motion picture than to the stage. In a novel, as in a film, the most important available technique is the close-up, a device invented not by D. W. Griffith but by Homer and resurrected in our time to revolutionize the art of narrative. (Film cutting, as an aesthetic technique, is an outgrowth of the close-up; not until the close-up became important did film cutting and the mobility of the camera become important or even much used.)

The novel and the motion picture share a penchant for detail. To be more accurate, I should say a penchant for the *casual* detail. When a playwright focuses upon a detail, he lifts it immediately, and sometimes in spite of himself, from the casual to the symbolic: Desdemona's handkerchief, the boots of Miss Julie's father, the electric light bulb in *A Streetcar Named Desire,* and so on. There are very few purely naturalistic plays because the stage has a tendency to turn *things* into symbols. Thus, the progenitor of symbolic drama in the modern theater was naturalism itself, a progression we have seen clearly in the career of Gerhart Hauptmann as well as in Strindberg and others. When the audience, being assembled in the theater, has its attention called to any detail, it asks, even if unconsciously, Why did you point us to that? What does that detail mean? This question does not arise nearly so fast or so insistently when one reads a novel. The reason is twofold.

First, one reads a novel by himself, wherever and whenever he pleases. Thus, he gives it a different sort of concentration from that which he gives a play, when he is a member of a particular audience at a particular place on a particular evening.

Second, the novel lives before one by virtue of the fact that it *flows*. A play does not flow, not even a play by Chekhov. It marches, or it dances. But a novel flows. Fast or slow, languid or turbulent, straight or meandering, it is a stream. Reading it, one moves along the stream of consciousness or the stream of life, and he is never unduly surprised nor automatically arrested by details encountered on the way. Any detail may be picked out by the novelist, examined, turned over, remarked upon, and then dropped back into the flux or left standing on the bank. To be sure, there are limits. The novel's unity and its theme do not allow for the appearance of details from life that are *utterly* irrelevant to the purpose in view, but the degree of that relevance may be very much lower in a novel than in a play, because we move on. The casual detail, interesting in its own right, is covered over in the succession of those that follow.

For this reason the question of symbolism appears to the novelist quite differently from the way it appears to the dramatist. A playwright discovers that in his first draft of the play, especially if he is just learning his craft, symbols grow up like weeds. This chair has suddenly turned into a throne. That bird the cat killed is proclaiming itself to be the human soul ravaged by time. And oh, how that potted plant in the window is carrying on! It is about to become Persephone. But suppose the playwright *wants* a symbol in his play. He had better watch out. That iguana under the porch will heave and throw the whole play out of balance.

The novelist has a different problem, provided he really is a novelist and not a playwright in disguise. His task is not to pull out unwanted symbols that grow of their own accord but rather to encourage them, lest they become lost in the flux. A symbolic play can be written by accident. A symbolic novel is an achievement.

This difference indicates the primary reason why the novel has become more directly relevant to modern experience than the drama. The basic temper of our age, philosophically speaking, is positivistic. This calls forth now and again countertendencies toward ethereal spirituality, a spirituality not oriented positively toward the public order or the order of human work but oriented toward fantasy and everything which at the moment goes under the name "expansion of consciousness." The culture seems to fluctuate between extremes of positivistic thought and mystical, otherworldly spirituality. This is hard on culture, certainly on drama, for the fluctuations do not much pause at the center to illuminate what may be called "the middle ground." On the middle ground the actual visible world of things and people is solid—just as solid as for positivism—but it is also capable of expressing that which is spiritual. In short, the world of the middle ground is charged with symbolic and analogical meaning. It is neither reduced to sheer "thingness" nor used as a mere point of departure for a spiritual "trip."

It is on the middle ground that drama has to stand. In the last analysis it may be that the novel does also, but the novel has consorted terribly well with the positivist drift in modern thinking because, as Laurence Lerner said, in the book already cited:

> The rise of the novel goes with and is a symptom of the concern for people as themselves, not for their symbolic significance, their supernatural backing, their patterning into types, but for their uniqueness.[2]

Thus, although it may be the case that in the long run the difficulties that have overcome the theater will also overcome the novel, the impact upon the novel is delayed.

It is well known that the theater is undergoing a crisis, and perhaps that it has lost a great degree of social importance. When we mention these things it is important to think not merely of the *symptoms* of the theatrical crisis. Such symptoms are the decline in the size of the theater audience, the inconvenience of going to the theater, the tone of gray disappointment that accompanies most of our visits there, the competition from movies and television, the high cost of tickets—in short, everything that seems to conspire to make theater going more of an ordeal than a joy. These are to be regarded as symptoms. They are the symptoms of a crisis in our *idea* of theater, our idea of what kind of place and what kind of activity the theater is, and what, if anything, is its function in our

2 *Ibid.,* p. 193.

lives. If one speaks of the death of theater, as some do, he refers to the fact that the theater has virtually ceased to serve as an aesthetic focus for contemporary experience.

What are the forces in modern society that have robbed the theater of its power to serve as a focus of common experience? To find them we should look not at certain obvious mistakes the modern age has made but rather at things the modern age has done well, things we can hardly imagine it as having done very differently or not having done at all.

One such factor, surely, is the development of technology, by which I mean not simply a certain form of knowledge and power but a scientific development that issues in a characteristic way of life, particularly urban life. I have in mind the phenomenon that Professor Harvey Cox and others have called *technopolis*.[3]

Modern urban life, characterized by increasing dependence on types of organization made possible by technology, has had a deleterious effect upon the theater. The irony of this is easy to see. For technological reasons, the theater today is concentrated in large cities. Theater work in all other communities is dependent on what is done in metropolitan centers. In the United States the life of the theater is almost completely determined by its fate in New York City, the recent development of residential theaters in various other places notwithstanding. At the same time, life in the technopolitan city is inimical to the aesthetics of theater. That is why great hopes come to be pinned on theaters outside New York; but these hopes are futile, because the same tendencies that make theatrical creativity so difficult in New York are present in other urban centers as well, though their rate of development may be a bit slower. In the long run, they will have, in Atlanta as in New York, the same discouraging effect upon histrionic sensibility.

There are many ways to describe why city life has this effect. The economist and the sociologist have much to say to the point; but with respect to aesthetic sensibility one may suggest that technopolis is anti-histrionic because technology *destroys space*. This dictum is not, of course, a literal statement. It carries a psychological and spiritual import. Technology renders all space the same,

[3] See *The Secular City*, by Harvey Cox. (New York: Macmillan, 1965).

tending to neutralize the meaning of space. It erodes the meaningfulness of particular places.

To be well adjusted to technopolis, to live the good life in a modern urban setting, one must be on the move. But this movement is not, strictly speaking, a movement to *places*. Instead, it is movement to where certain people happen to live, to where they gather, to certain equipment (people plus equipment equal "the office") or to where certain events are scheduled. The combination of people, equipment, and events may be called a *cluster*. In technopolis one goes to whatever cluster is important at the moment, and the cluster is far more important than the place.

It is not surprising, therefore, that the motion picture and television fare better in technopolis than does the theater. The motion-picture camera and the television camera, thanks to "cutting," move with a freedom so nearly absolute that change from place to place ceases to be important. This can be put inversely as well: with a camera, change of location and perspective is everything. It is so omnipresent, so much a part of the camera's innate potentiality, that it comes to be taken almost absolutely for granted. The movement that *is* important in film and television is a movement through time—the movement that is aesthetically arranged by cutting from one image to another regardless of space.

The theater, like dance and unlike cinema, is the art of the use of finite space. It requires a space that does not move, that is fixed and limited, that imposes restraints. The aesthetic of theater is in large part built upon the imaginative overcoming of fixed space, just as the aesthetic of painting is largely built upon the imaginative overcoming of a two-dimensional limitation. When the theater is at its height it binds infinite space into a nutshell, as Hamlet said.

> O God, I could be bounded in a nutshell and count myself a king of infinite space, were it not that I have bad dreams.
>
> (II.ii.260)

Hamlet was speaking, to be sure, of his mind, but the image was theatrical. His was a theatrical understanding of consciousness: an infinite abound concentrated into a finite arena.

In a society that, because of its technology, renders space per se of little account, the art of the theater must suffer. One reason that repertory theater is difficult is that the contemporary audience prefers to patronize *plays* rather than *theater*. This is particularly true in America and increasingly so on the Continent and in England. The patronage of individual plays, rather than of the theater as such, indicates a loss of histrionic sensibility.

The importance of space for histrionic sensiblity is to be discerned in every aspect of the several movements toward renewal which the modern theater has experienced—in the work of Appia and Craig, Copeau and Artaud, Robert Edmond Jones, Stanislavski, all the figures treated in the chapter on theater practice, and in the experiments with form that have occupied both major and minor playwrights. In retrospect we may notice that the modern theater's long and valiant attempt to make of the theater a unified and expressive instrument (see Chapter 5 especially) has been a poignant endeavor to assert the values of theatrical space against their erosion by the forces let loose by the industrial and technological revolutions. The most extreme statement of this intention is to be found in the theories of Artaud, but, as we have noted, Artaud's ideals are not realizable under the conditions of modern society. Technology is their enemy, and so is the subject-object split in modern thought, which was formalized by Descartes and intensified by Kant.

Utterly opposed to the histrionic sensibility and to the idea of theater is the Happening, in spite of what many of its enthusiasts have said. The Happening derives from painting and expresses nonhistrionic types of aesthetic response, for it ruthlessly subordinates space to *occurrence*. It is what I call a cluster. Therefore, the location of a Happening, in the sense of its being a finite space, is not important. In fact, Happenings usually avoid the theater. Important instead is the unforeseen, the unpredictable, the occurrence in time, which is the meaning I intend by the word "cluster." By contrast, that which is histrionic *fills space*. It fills it with event, to be sure, but it is a filling of space. We do not appreciate this partly because the technopolis does not prepare us to and partly because we so rarely see it. However, to cite a recent example, the excellence of the Royal Shakespeare Company's production of Harold Pinter's *The Homecoming* (1966) was largely due to the fact that the company found itself so well able to fill the total space occupied by the setting and the audience. Many spectators observed in *The Homecoming* an articulation of space comparable to the best that can be found in the art of dance. The most lively histrionic sensibility to be found in America is that of Martha Graham. Her work reveals the theatrical root from which have sprung the divergent stems known as drama and dance.

The theater is the marriage of time and space. It is the aesthetic of their fulfillment in purpose.

Still another cause of the loss of the histrionic is to be found in the modern search for meaning, particularly the quest for "authentic existence." There is felt to be an inherent antagonism between authenticity and form. Since the latter part of the eighteenth century our age has defined authenticity as that which proceeds from man himself and has rebelled against all that originates elsewhere. As if this were not enough, the idea of man himself has been taken to mean the individual. Beyond that, the individual has increasingly been taken to mean the individual in the present moment. Hence, the authentic is often associated with the spontaneous and the immediate. This leads to a revolt against all form that is *given,* a revolt against all received form. Classical form, of course, was attacked. August Wilhelm von Schlegel called classical form "mechanical" and by that word put it down. He preferred, he said, "organical" form. But the distinction between mechanical and organic form soon breaks down, for the simple reason that any form as such is enduring. Therefore, in the name of authenticity and spontaneity, frequently felt to be the same, the forms of one generation, by whatever adjective they be called, are rejected by the next. But it goes deeper than that.

The particular form created a moment ago is rejected now. Not only is the form of a previous generation rejected by this one, but also the form of one's creativity a while ago, yesterday or even this morning, which stands there more or less objectively opposed to the self comes to be rejected because it is already outside of consciousness. Existing by virtue of its perduring form, it seems to threaten the *now* of one's present authenticity. In certain historical moments this is liberating, but in our culture it has gone on for nearly two centuries and has come to be bad for most of the arts, worst of all for theater.

For some eighty years theater people have been babbling honorifically about new forms of theater, about experimental theater, about laboratory theater. They seem not to have noticed that it was the word "new" and not the word "forms" that carried their meaning and their intent. It goes almost without notice that the so-called experimentation is done without any controls and is therefore not experiment but sheer innovation. The postmodern mentality tries desperately to expunge from the theater its ritual quality, its formal rightness. The formal rightness of any play is such that we delight to see it done again and again, perhaps with some variations, but essentially the same. This establishes a kind of ritual character for the theater, and precisely this is today the theater's greatest embarrassment. There is an attempt radically to drive it out and replace it by that which is casual, unforeseen, impromptu—an attempt that consorts well with an aesthetic of what is frequently called "disposable art."

The theater is doing this just at the time when, because of the knowledge available through historical research, we have become acutely aware of the ritual quality of all theater. The ritual origin of theater and its latent ritualistic tendencies are common knowledge. But since postmoderns do not like ritual and certainly do not trust it, they tend to push that very quality to extremes in order to destroy it, by a strategy of turning form into formal*ism*. This is the tack taken by the so-called avant-garde theater from the 1950's onward, which is thus to be seen ambiguously either as the *terminus ad quem* of the development of the modern theater or as the formalistic decadence of that theater which creates the possibility of an anti-ritualistic (and anti-tragic) new departure.

The intensified formalism of Jean Genet results in very exciting theater. Genet is unique in having a very firm ritual instinct, and the effect in his particular case is not negative. In Beckett and Ionesco, however, it is; also in Pinter and Albee and by far the majority of the lesser playwrights of the moment. In historical perspective most drama since World War II must be seen as anti-ritual, an attempt to kill form with formalism.

In the modern world the notion of vicarious experience is very much in decline. Instead, there is a great longing for, and very much talk about, various types of immediate identification. The motion-picture screen and the television screen tend to present us with images and characters with whom we identify immediately, and this is a different thing from vicarious experience.

When the Elizabethans went to the theater, they did not see in Macbeth, Lear, Antony, or Coriolanus mirror images of themselves. Nor did they see characters with whom they might immediately identify. They saw heroic individuals in extraordinary stories, expressing themselves in extraordinary language. The audience brought to the theater a willingness to extend itself, to participate vicariously in an action that would never unfold the same way in real life.

The diminution of the capacity for vicarious experience began with the rise of the middle class. This class was the most self-occupied of any group in the history of the world. The reason was that the major hold it had on reality was money. Whoever owes his position in the world to money will tend to regard himself as a subject of unlimited interest. Money is not inherently interesting. The bourgeois, having only money to point to as his work, being therefore essentially uncreative, points to himself and his family as subjects that *are* interesting. He comes to see the world as an extension of himself. Uncreative in his work, he is actually afraid of vicarious experience, for he fears losing the only reality he knows—namely, himself. Hence, it is the bourgeoisie, more than the workers, who destroy the public and replace it by mass society. Perhaps the worker has been standardized by the conditions of his employment, but the bourgeois consciously *standardizes himself* in order that he may believe in himself by seeing how similar he is to his neighbor. It is the loss of capacity for vicarious experience—the ability to participate in the experience of another, who is unlike myself and whom I shall have to relate to myself by an act of imaginative correlation—it is this loss that is so terribly important in the loss of the histrionic and that accounts for the decreasing importance in drama of that element which Aristotle called the soul of tragedy—the plot, or the *mythos*.

Northrop Frye has called attention to the fact that periods of high tragedy (what he calls the "high mimetic") are periods in which the form of the aesthetic work is paramount and in which the relation of that form to life will have to be regarded as allegorical. I would prefer the term "analogical" to "allegorical." Nevertheless, the main point is clear: a passage has to be made from the formally mimetic to life by some kind of indirect interpretation in which an imaginative stretching is required. One has to see correspondences between things that are dissimilar but that share certain unstated yet fundamental properties. This has disappeared for most people, and with it has gone the great importance that used to be attached to plot. Not only plot, but also story. And as story and plot decline, so also does the importance of character.

In an article on character and theater in the *Tulane Drama Review* the psychiatrist Donald M. Kaplan called attention to problems that actors face when they are called upon to do something on stage other than to portray roles.[4] He quotes from a piece Michael Smith had written in *The Village Voice* describing his attempts to stage a one-act play by Sam Shepherd called *Icarus' Mother*. Smith had said:

> The actors had trouble. When, for example, two men were called upon to make smoke signals, they wanted to know exactly what they were doing and why they were doing it, and it was insufficient to tell them, although true, that all they were doing was making smoke signals, and the reason was Shepherd's and the play's rather than theirs. My first fault was failing to make this clear.[5]

Upon this Donald Kaplan comments:

> If that is *all* they want their actors to do, they must use children. Called upon to make smoke signals on stage, children would never ask exactly what they were doing. They would simply make smoke-signals. . . . But trained, adult actors just can't do this.[6]

The loss of vicarious experience, the loss of plot and story, the loss of character—these proceeding from the loss of the sense of finite space and of ritual form—all this is meant by the loss of the histrionic.

---

[4] "Character and Theatre: Psychoanalytic Notes on Modern Realism," in *Tulane Drama Review*, Vol. 10, No. 4 (Summer 1966).
[5] *Ibid.*, p. 96.
[6] *Ibid.*, pp. 96–97.

In the postmodern period, man seems, for better or worse, and whether consciously or unconsciously, to be attempting to find some mode of self-understanding that is different from the histrionic, to see himself as something other than an actor upon a world stage, to see himself as oriented in a way other than in space, and to see the patterns of his life in something other than ritual form. The question is whether that is possible, whether there are indeed nonhistrionic models for the growth and maturation of human being. Are there modes other than the dramatic for productively understanding what it is that occurs and should occur in the growth of the child from infancy to old age? If there are, then perhaps we shall be able to enter upon a new cultural period that can be no less exalted in its own way than have certain periods of the past.

I have tried to show that the development of the modern theater has been a paradigm of the development of modern consciousness. The theater's increasing alienation from society in the modern period only increases the aptness of the paradigm, since it has made the theater better able to exemplify the self-alienation of modern society. We stand now at a time when the modern period of the theater has ended, and this turns out also to be a time when modern society is in severe crisis. The new is upon us. It will require a new mode of consciousness. Whether and in what way the theater will participate in that remains to be seen.

SELECTED BIBLIOGRAPHY

NOT INCLUDED in this bibliography are (1) editions of the plays mentioned in the text, to say nothing of the hundreds not mentioned; (2) articles from magazines and journals, although the reader may wish to take note of the rich materials in *The Drama Review, Modern Drama,* and *Modern International Drama;* and (3) most of the works of modern cultural and intellectual history to which the author is indebted. Most of the secondary works cited in the text are here included, although some that are of minor importance have been omitted. It follows that this list embraces the major secondary sources used by the author during his researches, including a number not cited in the text. It is hoped that this material may assist those who wish to do further study.

ABEL, LIONEL, *Metatheatre*. New York: Hill and Wang, 1963.

ABRAMS, MEYER H., *The Mirror and the Lamp: Romantic Theory and the Critical Tradition*. New York: Oxford University Press, 1953.

AGATE, JAMES, ed., *The English Dramatic Critics: An Anthology, 1660–1932*. New York: Hill and Wang, 1958.

ALEXANDER, DORIS, *The Tempering of Eugene O'Neill*. New York: Harcourt, Brace & World, 1962.

APPIA, ADOLPHE, *The Work of Living Art*. The essay is translated by H. D. Albright, together with "Man Is the Measure of All Things." Translated and edited by Barnard Hewitt. Coral Gables, Fla.: University of Miami Press, 1960.

APPIA, ADOLPHE, *Music and the Art of the Theatre,* Robert W. Corrigan and Mary Douglas Dirks, trans. Coral Gables, Fla.: University of Miami Press, 1962.

ARCHER, WILLIAM, *The Old Drama and the New.* Boston: Small, Maynard, 1923.

ARTAUD, ANTONIN, *The Theater and Its Double,* Mary Caroline Richards, trans. New York: Grove, 1958.

ARTAUD, ANTONIN, *Antonin Artaud Anthology,* Jack Hirschman, ed. 2nd ed., rev. San Francisco: City Lights, 1965.

AUERBACH, ERICH, *Figura: Scenes from the Drama of European Literature.* New York: Meridian, 1959.

BARZUN, JACQUES, *Classic, Romantic and Modern.* Garden City, N.Y.: Anchor Books, Doubleday, 1961.

BENTLEY, ERIC, *In Search of Theater.* New York: Vintage, 1954.

BENTLEY, ERIC, *The Playwright as Thinker.* New York: Reynal & Hitchcock, 1946; 2nd ed., Meridian, 1955.

BENTLEY, ERIC, *Bernard Shaw, 1856–1950.* New York: New Directions, 1957.

BENTLEY, ERIC, ed., *Let's Get a Divorce! and Other Plays.* New York: Hill and Wang, 1958. Cited here for the essay by Bentley on the psychology of farce.

BINER, PIERRE, *Le Living Théâtre: Histoire sans Légende.* Lausanne: Éditions l'Age d'Homme, 1968.

BLAU, HERBERT, *The Impossible Theater.* New York: Macmillan, 1964.

BRADBROOK, M. C., *Ibsen, the Norwegian.* London: Chatto & Windus, 1948.

BRANDES, GEORG, *Henrik Ibsen,* authorized translation by Jesse Muir, revised by William Archer. New York: Benjamin Blom, 1964. Reprints part of a book published by Macmillan in 1899.

BRECHT, BERTOLT, *Brecht on Theatre,* John Willett, ed. New York: Hill and Wang, 1964.

BRUFORD, W. H., *Chekhov and His Russia.* New York: Oxford University Press, 1947.

BRUSTEIN, ROBERT, *The Theatre of Revolt.* Boston: Little, Brown, 1964.

CAMPBELL, G. A., *Strindberg.* London: Duckworth, 1933.

CARTER, LAWSON A., *Zola and the Theater.* New Haven and Paris: Yale University Press and Presses Universitaires de France, 1963.

CHARBONNIER, GEORGES, *Essai sur Antonin Artaud.* Paris: Éditions Pierre Seghers, 1959.

CHEKHOV, ANTON, *The Letters of Anton Pavlovitch Tchekhov to Olga*

Leonardovna Knipper, Constance Garnett, trans. New York: Doran, n.d.

CLARK, BARRETT H., *Eugene O'Neill.* New York: Dover, 1947.

CLARK, BARRETT H., ed., *European Theories of the Drama.* New York: Crown, 1947.

CLARK, BARRETT H., and FREEDLEY, GEORGE, eds., *A History of Modern Drama.* New York: Appleton-Century-Crofts, 1947.

CLAUDEL, PAUL, *Cahiers Paul Claudel: Correspondance avec Lugné-Poe, 1910–1918.* Paris: Gallimard, 1964.

CLURMAN, HAROLD, *The Fervent Years: The Story of the Group Theatre and the Thirties.* New York: Hill and Wang, 1957.

COE, RICHARD N., *Eugene Ionesco.* New York: Grove, 1961.

COLE, TOBY, ed., *Playwrights on Playmaking: The Meaning and Making of Modern Drama from Ibsen to Ionesco.* New York: Hill and Wang, 1961.

COPEAU, JACQUES, *Critiques d'un autre temps.* Paris: Éditions de la Nouvelle Revue Française, 1923.

CORRIGAN, ROBERT W., ed., *Theatre in the Twentieth Century.* New York: Grove, 1961.

DAHLSTRÖM, CARL ENOCH WILLIAM LEONARD, *Strindberg's Dramatic Expressionism.* New York: Benjamin Blom, 1965. First published, 1930.

D'HOMME, SYLVAIN, *La Mise en scène d'Antoine à Brecht.* Paris: Fernand Nathan, 1959.

DOWNER, ALAN S., *Fifty Years of American Theatre.* Chicago: Regnery, 1951.

DRIVER, TOM F., *The Sense of History in Greek and Shakespearean Drama.* New York and London: Columbia Press, 1960.

DRIVER, TOM F., *Jean Genet.* New York: Columbia University Press, 1966.

DUMUR, GUY, *Luigi Pirandello, Dramaturge.* Paris: L'Arche, 1955.

ELIOT, THOMAS STEARNS, *Poetry and Drama.* Cambridge, Mass.: Harvard University Press, 1951.

ELLMAN, RICHARD, *Yeats: The Man and the Masks.* New York: Dutton, 1948.

Encyclopédie du théâtre contemporain, Gilles Quéant, gen. ed. Paris: Les Publications de France; Vol. I, 1957; Vol. II, Olivier Perrin, ed., 1959.

ENGEL, EDWIN A., *The Haunted Heroes of Eugene O'Neill.* Cambridge, Mass.: Harvard University Press, 1953.

ESSLIN, MARTIN, *Brecht: The Man and His Work*. Garden City, N.Y.: Anchor Books, Doubleday, 1961.

ESSLIN, MARTIN, *The Theatre of the Absurd*. Garden City, N.Y.: Anchor Books, Doubleday, 1961.

ESSLIN, MARTIN, *Samuel Beckett: A Collection of Critical Essays*. Englewood Cliffs, N.J.: Prentice-Hall, 1965.

FERGUSSON, FRANCIS, *The Idea of a Theater*. Garden City, N.Y.: Anchor Books, Doubleday, 1953.

FERGUSSON, FRANCIS, *The Human Image in Dramatic Literature*. Garden City, N.Y.: Anchor Books, Doubleday, 1957.

FLEXNER, ELEANOR, *American Playwrights: 1918–1938*. New York: Simon and Schuster, 1938.

FOWLIE, WALLACE, *Dionysus in Paris: A Guide to Contemporary French Theater*. New York: Meridian, 1960.

FRANC, MIRIAM ALICE, *Ibsen in England*. Boston: Four Seas, 1919.

FRENZ, HORST, ed., *American Playwrights on Drama*. New York: Hill and Wang, 1965.

FREYTAG, GUSTAV, *Die Technik der Dramas. 1863. Freytag's Technique of the Drama*, Elias J. MacEwan, trans. Chicago: S. C. Griggs, 1895; reissued, New York: Benjamin Blom, 1968.

FRYE, NORTHROP, *Anatomy of Criticism*. Princeton: Princeton University Press, 1957.

FUCHS, GEORG, *Revolution in the Theatre*, Constance Connor Kuhn, trans. Ithaca, N.Y.: Cornell University Press, 1959.

GASSNER, JOHN, *Masters of the Drama*, 3rd ed. New York: Dover, 1954.

GASSNER, JOHN, *The Theatre in Our Times*. New York: Crown, 1954.

GASSNER, JOHN, *Form and Idea in Modern Theatre*. New York: Dryden, 1956.

GASSNER, JOHN, ed., *O'Neill, A Collection of Critical Essays*. Englewood Cliffs, N.J.: Prentice-Hall, 1964.

GELB, ARTHUR, and GELB, BARBARA, *O'Neill*. New York: Harper & Row, 1960.

GOSSE, EDMUND, *Henrik Ibsen*. New York: Scribner, 1908.

GROSSVOGEL, DAVID I., *The Self-conscious Stage in Modern French Drama*. New York: Columbia University Press, 1958.

GROTOWSKI, JERZY, *Towards a Poor Theatre*. Holstebro, Denmark: Odin Teatrets Forlag, 1968.

GUICHARNAUD, JACQUES, and BECKELMAN, JUNE, *Modern French Theatre from Giraudoux to Beckett*. New Haven: Yale University Press, 1961.

HEGEL, G. W. F., *Hegel on Tragedy*, Anne Paolucci and Henry Paolucci, eds. Garden City, N.Y.: Anchor Books, Doubleday, 1962.

HENDERSON, ARCHIBALD, *George Bernard Shaw: Man of the Century*. New York: Appleton-Century-Crofts, 1956.

HEWITT, BARNARD, *Theatre U.S.A., 1668–1957*. New York: McGraw-Hill, 1959.

HIMELSTEIN, MORGAN Y., *Drama Was a Weapon: The Left-Wing Theatre in New York, 1929–1941*. New Brunswick, N.J.: Rutgers University Press, 1963.

HINGLEY, RONALD, *Chekhov*. London: Allen & Unwin, 1950.

HUSSERL, EDMUND, *The Phenomenology of Internal Time-Consciousness*, James S. Churchill, trans. The Hague: Nijhoff, 1964.

IONESCO, EUGÈNE, *Notes and Counter Notes*, Donald Watson, trans. New York: Grove, 1964.

JACOBSEN, JOSEPHINE, and MUELLER, WILLIAM R., *The Testament of Samuel Beckett*. New York: Hill and Wang, 1964.

JAMES, HENRY, *The Scenic Art*. New York: Hill and Wang, 1957.

JOHNSON, WALTER, *Strindberg and the Historical Drama*. Seattle: University of Washington Press, 1963.

JONES, DAVID E., *The Plays of T. S. Eliot*. Toronto: University of Toronto Press, 1960.

JONES, ROBERT EDMOND, *The Dramatic Imagination*. New York: Theatre Arts Books, 1941.

JORGENSON, THEODORE, *Henrik Ibsen*. Northfield, Minn.: St. Olaf College Press, 1945.

KAYE, JULIAN B., *Bernard Shaw and the Nineteenth-Century Tradition*. Norman, Okla.: University of Oklahoma Press, 1958.

KENNER, HUGH, *Samuel Beckett*. New York: Grove, 1961.

KERNAN, ALVIN B., *The Modern American Theater: A Collection of Critical Essays*. Englewood Cliffs, N.J.: Prentice-Hall, 1967.

KIERKEGAARD, SØREN, *Either/Or*, 2 vols. Garden City, N.Y.: Anchor Books, Doubleday, 1959.

KIERKEGAARD, SØREN, *Crisis in the Life of an Actress, and other Essays on Drama*, Stephen Crites, trans. New York: Harper & Row, 1967.

KLAF, FRANKLIN S., *Strindberg: The Origin of Psychology in Modern Drama*. New York: Citadel, 1963.

KNIGHT, G. WILSON, *Henrik Ibsen*. New York: Grove, 1962.

KOHT, HALVDAN, *The Life of Ibsen*, 2 vols., Ruth L. McMahon and Hanna A. Larsen, trans. New York: Norton, 1931.

KOTELIANSKY, S. S., and TOMLINSON, PHILIP, trans. and eds., *The Life and Letters of Anton Tchekhov*. London: Cassel, 1925.

LALOU, RENÉ, *Le Théâtre en France depuis 1900.* Paris: Presses Universitaires de France, 1956.

LAMM, MARTIN, *Modern Drama,* Karin Elliott, trans. Oxford: Blackwell, 1952.

LEWES, GEORGE HENRY, *On Actors and the Art of Acting.* New York: Grove, 1957.

LEWIS, ALLAN, *The Contemporary Theatre.* New York: Crown, 1962.

LIND-AF-HAGEBY, L., *August Strindberg.* New York: Appleton, 1913.

MADSEN, BØRGE GEDSØ, *Strindberg's Naturalistic Theatre: Its Relation to French Naturalism.* Seattle: University of Washington Press, 1962.

MAGARSHACK, DAVID, *Chekhov the Dramatist.* New York: Hill and Wang, 1960.

MANDER, RAYMOND, and MITCHENSON, JOE, *Theatrical Companion to Shaw.* London: Rockliff, 1954.

MATTHEWS, BRANDER, ed., *Papers on Playmaking.* New York: Hill and Wang, 1957.

McGILL, V. J., *August Strindberg.* New York: Brentano's Publishers, 1930.

McMAHON, JOSEPH H., *The Imagination of Jean Genet.* New Haven and London: Yale University Press, 1963.

MEISEL, MARTIN, *Shaw and the Nineteenth-Century Theater.* Princeton: Princeton University Press, 1963.

MELCHINGER, SIEGFRIED, *The Concise Encyclopedia of Modern Drama.* George Wellwarth, trans.; Henry Popkin, ed. New York: Horizon, 1964.

MESERVE, WALTER J., ed., *Discussions of Modern American Drama.* Boston: Heath, 1965.

MORTENSEN, BRITA M. E., and Downs, Brian W., *Strindberg, An Introduction to His Life and Work.* Cambridge: Cambridge University Press, 1949.

NABOKOV, VLADIMIR, *Nikolai Gogol.* New York: New Directions, 1944.

NAGLER, A. M., *A Source Book in Theatrical History.* New York: Dover, 1959.

NATHAN, GEORGE JEAN, *Encyclopedia of the Theatre.* New York: Knopf, 1940.

NICOLL, ALLARDYCE, *The Development of the Theatre.* London: Harrap, 1927; 3rd ed., 1948.

NICOLL, ALLARDYCE, *World Drama from Aeschylus to Anouilh.* New York: Harcourt, Brace, n.d.

NIETZSCHE, FRIEDRICH, *The Birth of Tragedy and the Genealogy of*

Morals, Francis Golffing, trans. Garden City, N.Y.: Anchor Books, Doubleday, 1956.

PEACOCK, RONALD, *The Poet in the Theatre.* New York: Hill and Wang, 1960.

PRONKO, LEONARD CABELL, *Avant-Garde: The Experimental Theater in France.* Berkeley: University of California Press, 1963.

REQUE, A. DIKKA, *Ibsen, Björnson, Strindberg devant la critique Française, 1889–1901.* Paris: Librairie Ancienne Honoré Champion, 1930.

ROBERTS, R. ELLIS, *Henrik Ibsen.* London: Martin Secker, 1912.

ROUGEMONT, DENIS DE, *Love in the Western World,* Montgomery Belgion, trans. Garden City, N.Y.: Anchor Books, Doubleday, 1957.

SAINT-DENIS, MICHEL, *Theatre: The Rediscovery of Style.* London: Heinemann, 1960.

SARTRE, JEAN-PAUL, *Saint Genet: Comédien et martyr.* Paris: Gallimard, 1952. Translated by Bernard Frechtman as *Saint Genet: Actor and Martyr.* New York: Braziller, 1963.

SCOTT, NATHAN A., *Samuel Beckett.* London: Bowes and Bowes, 1965.

SHAW, BERNARD, *The Quintessence of Ibsenism.* New York: Hill and Wang, 1957.

SHAW, BERNARD, *Shaw on Theatre,* E. J. West, ed. London: MacGibbon & Kee, 1958.

SHAW, GEORGE BERNARD, *Shaw's Dramatic Criticism (1895–98).* Selected by John F. Matthews. New York: Hill and Wang, 1959.

SIMMONS, ERNEST J., *Chekhov: A Biography.* Boston: Little, Brown, 1962.

SLONIM, MARC, *From Chekhov to the Revolution: Russian Literature 1900–1917.* New York: Oxford University Press, 1962.

SLONIM, MARC, *The Russian Theater from the Empire to the Soviets.* New York: Collier Books, 1962.

SOKEL, WALTER H., ed., *Anthology of German Expressionist Drama.* Garden City, N.Y.: Anchor Books, Doubleday, 1963. See the introduction by Sokel.

SOUTHERN, RICHARD, *The Seven Ages of the Theatre.* New York: Hill and Wang, 1961.

SPANOS, WILLIAM V., *The Christian Tradition in Modern British Verse Drama.* New Brunswick, N.J.: Rutgers University Press, 1967.

SPENDER, STEPHEN, *The Struggle of the Modern.* Berkeley: University of California Press, 1963.

SPRIGGE, ELIZABETH, *The Strange Life of August Strindberg.* New York: Macmillan, 1949.

SPRINCHORN, EVERT, ed., *Ibsen: Letters and Speeches.* New York: Hill and Wang, 1964.

STANISLAVSKI, KONSTANTIN, *An Actor Prepares,* translated by Elizabeth Reynolds Hapgood. New York: Theatre Arts Books, 1936.

STANISLAVSKI, KONSTANTIN, *My Life in Art,* J. J. Robbins, trans. New York: Meridian, 1956.

STANISLAVSKI, KONSTANTIN, *Stanislavsky on the Art of the Stage,* translated with an introductory essay on Stanislavski's System by David Magarshack. New York: Hill and Wang, 1961.

STANTON, STEPHEN S., ed., *Camille and Other Plays.* New York: Hill and Wang, 1957. See the introduction, on the well-made play, by Stanton.

STARKIE, WALTER F., *Luigi Pirandello, 1867–1936.* Berkeley: University of California Press, 1965.

STENDHAL, *Racine et Shakespeare.* Paris: Jean-Jacques Pauvert, 1965.

STRINDBERG, AUGUST, *Letters of Strindberg to Harriet Bosse,* Arvid Paulson, ed. and trans. New York: Grosset & Dunlap, 1959.

STRINDBERG, AUGUST, *Open Letters to the Intimate Theater,* translated, with an introduction, by Walter Johnson. Seattle and London: University of Washington Press, 1966.

STUART, DONALD CLIVE, *The Development of Dramatic Art.* New York: Dover, 1960.

STYAN, J. L., *The Dark Comedy: The Development of Modern Comic Tragedy.* Cambridge: Cambridge University Press, 1962.

TILLICH, PAUL, *Die religiöse Lage der Gegenwart.* Berlin: Ulstein, 1926. Translated by H. Richard Niebuhr as *The Religious Situation,* New York: Holt, 1932; Meridian, 1956.

TINDALL, WILLIAM YORK, *Samuel Beckett.* New York: Columbia University Press, 1964.

TOULMIN, STEPHEN, and GOODFIELD, JUNE, *The Discovery of Time.* New York: Harper & Row, 1965.

TYNAN, KENNETH, *Curtains.* New York: Atheneum, 1961.

URE, PETER, *W. B. Yeats.* New York: Grove, 1964.

VALENCY, MAURICE, *The Flower and the Castle: An Introduction to Modern Drama.* New York: Macmillan, 1963.

VEINSTEIN, ANDRÉ, *Du Théâtre Libre au Théâtre Louis Jouvet.* Paris: Billaudot, 1955.

VITTORINI, DOMENICO, *The Drama of Luigi Pirandello.* New York: Dover, 1957.

WAGNER, RICHARD, *Wagner on Music and Drama,* Albert Goldman and

Evert Sprinchorn, eds.; H. Ashton Ellis, trans. New York: Dutton, 1964.

WEIGAND, HERMANN J., *The Modern Ibsen: A Reconsideration.* New York: Dutton, 1960.

WEIDELI, WALTER, The *Art of Bertolt Brecht,* Daniel Russell, trans. New York: New York University Press, 1963.

WELLWARTH, GEORGE, *The Theater of Protest and Paradox: Developments in The Avant-Garde Drama.* New York: New York University Press, 1964.

WILLETT, JOHN, *The Theatre of Bertolt Brecht.* New York: New Directions, 1959.

WILLIAMS, RAYMOND, *Drama from Ibsen to Eliot.* Harmondsworth, Eng.: Penguin, 1967.

YOUNG, STARK, *Immortal Shadows: A Book of Dramatic Criticism.* New York: Hill and Wang, 1958.

YOUNG, STARK, *The Theatre.* New York: Hill and Wang, 1958.

ZOLA, ÉMILE, *Le Roman expérimental,* 2nd ed. Paris: Charpentier, 1880. Cited for "Le Naturalisme au théâtre," pp. 109–156. The book is translated by B. M. Sherman as *The Experimental Novel, and Other Essays.* New York: Cassell, 1893.

ZUCKER, A. E., *Ibsen the Master Builder.* New York: Holt, 1929.

INDEX

PROPER NAMES AND TOPICS

PLAYS